ART, IDEOLOGY, AND THE CITY
OF TEOTIHUACAN

ART, IDEOLOGY, AND THE CITY OF TEOTIHUACAN

A Symposium at Dumbarton Oaks
8TH AND 9TH OCTOBER 1988

Janet Catherine Berlo, *Editor*

Dumbarton Oaks Research Library and Collection
Washington, D.C.

©1992, 2023 Dumbarton Oaks Research Library and Collection,
Trustees for Harvard University, Washington, D.C.
All rights reserved.

Manufactured in the United States of America by
Sheridan Books, Inc., 450 Fame Avenue, Hanover, PA 17331 | (717) 632-3535

Art, ideology, and the city of Teotihuacan : a symposium at Dumbarton Oaks,
8th and 9th October 1988 | Janet Catherine Berlo, editor. |
Washington, D.C. : Dumbarton Oaks Research Library and Collection,
Trustees for Harvard University, 1992.

Includes bibliographic references and index.

ISBN-10: 0-88402-205-6 [hardcover]
ISBN-13: 978-0-88402-205-3 [hardcover]
ISBN-13: 978-0-88402-515-3 [paperback]
LCCN permalink: https://lccn.loc.gov/92008244

1. Teotihuacán Site (San Juan Teotihuacán, Mexico)—Congresses.
2. Indian art—Mexico—San Juan Teotihuacán—Congresses.
3. Indians of Mexico—Mexico—San Juan Teotihuacán—Religion—Congresses.
4. San Juan Teotihuacán (Mexico)—Antiquities—Congresses.
5. Mexico—Antiquities—Congresses.
I. Berlo, Janet Catherine. II. Dumbarton Oaks.
F1219.1.T27 A73   1992
972'.52   92008244

EU GPSR Authorised Representative
LOGOS EUROPE, 9 rue Nicolas Poussin, 17000, La Rochelle, France
E-mail: Contact@logoseurope.eu

Contents

FOREWORD vii

PREFACE xi

SUSAN T. EVANS AND JANET CATHERINE BERLO
Teotihuacan: An Introduction — 1

MARTHA L. SEMPOWSKI
Economic and Social Implications of Variations in Mortuary Practices at Teotihuacan — 27

MICHAEL W. SPENCE
Tlailotlacan, a Zapotec Enclave in Teotihuacan — 59

MARGARET H. TURNER
Style in Lapidary Technology: Identifying the Teotihuacan Lapidary Industry — 89

RUBÉN CABRERA CASTRO
A Survey of Recently Excavated Murals at Teotihuacan — 113

JANET CATHERINE BERLO
Icons and Ideologies at Teotihuacan: The Great Goddess Reconsidered — 129

KARL A. TAUBE
The Iconography of Mirrors at Teotihuacan — 169

Contents

SABURO SUGIYAMA
Rulership, Warfare, and Human Sacrifice at the Ciudadela:
An Iconographic Study of Feathered Serpent Representations   205

GEORGE L. COWGILL
Teotihuacan Glyphs and Imagery in the Light of Some Early
Colonial Texts   231

JAMES C. LANGLEY
Teotihuacan Sign Clusters: Emblem or Articulation?   247

ESTHER PASZTORY
Abstraction and the Rise of a Utopian State at Teotihuacan   281

LINDA MANZANILLA
The Economic Organization of the Teotihuacan Priesthood:
Hypotheses and Considerations   321

RENÉ MILLON
Teotihuacan Studies: From 1950 to 1990 and Beyond   339

INDEX   431

Foreword

TEOTIHUACAN IS THE MOST SINGULAR SITE in Mesoamerican archaeology, effected in a mode not seen elsewhere. In size it stands apart from other urban areas, for by A.D. 500 it was the largest city the New World had ever produced. The statistics are overwhelming. According to René Millon and others, Teotihuacan concentrated 90 percent of the people living in the Basin of Mexico within its civic limits, achieving a population size of at least 125,000 within a city of about three square miles. The scale of its design and architecture was inordinately vast, too, for Teotihuacan's ceremonial precinct was a monumental stage for ritual and proclamation. Indeed Mesoamericanists are accustomed to superposed elevations and plans (drawn by Ignacio Marquina and others) that show the enormity of the Pyramid of the Sun at Teotihuacan in comparison to structures at Tikal, El Tajin, or Xochicalco, for example. Teotihuacan dwarfs the others by multiples. Then, extending beyond the great pyramids, courtyards, and avenues of the ritual center, the city was laid out according to an innovative grid plan that incorporated multi-family apartment units to concentrate the population.

A strong sense of hierarchical control is everywhere evident at Teotihuacan. Underlying the grandness of the city was an agricultural subsistence base, imperiled by its relatively high altitude and dry climate, that consequently demanded the strict control and management of water. The art and architecture is controlled in form, conventional, abstract, and patterned. Because Teotihuacan did not develop the Maya habit of naming and representing its elites on stone monuments and in other permanent forms, its rulers remain anonymous to us. Because its inhabitants chose not to develop a hieroglyphic writing system, we have little sense of personal history.

Teotihuacan is the only city in Mesoamerica that represents an entire culture, and in this respect the idea of Teotihuacan is very different from the idea of the Maya or the Aztecs. The difference in terminology and perception has come about partially because Teotihuacan *was* so different from the others, but it is also partially because of the limitations of our knowledge about the place. Teotihuacan seems not to have been a culture extending over an area of any great size, and the city itself was not, like Tikal or Palenque, one of several capitals or centers that shared an ideological and social system. Instead the Teotihuacan state, which was the most powerful force in Mesoamerica in the Early Classic Period, was composed of the city and its immediate hinterlands, and it appears elsewhere in Mesoamerica only in the form of distant Teotihuacan colonies situated within other cultural areas or in the indirect form of "influences" abroad. The perspective of Teotihuacan as an isolated monolith on the cultural landscape of Mesoamerica is further reinforced because we have not yet determined to everyone's satisfaction what language was principally spoken there. Thus it is impossible to refer to the people and culture of Teotihuacan in linguistic or ethnic terms as is the habit with the Zapotecs in Oaxaca or the Maya. Our referent has to remain the city itself—the people are described only as inhabitants of the city (Teotihuacanos). The scholarly focus is always drawn back to the singular city itself.

Another feature that sets Teotihuacan apart, as René Millon explains, is its old place in the history of Mexican consciousness. Teotihuacan has long been known as a ruined city. The Aztecs believed it to be the "abode of the gods," where the world was created, where time began, and they thus named it Teotihuacan. The city figures as a component of early Mexica history, and much later the culture hero Xolotl visited the ruins during the Alcohua migration into the Basin of Mexico and to Texcoco. After the Spanish invasion and conquest, Teotihuacan was visited, described, reconstructed, and partially excavated by travelers, archaeologists, and historians over several centuries. Its location near Mexico City makes it the one site almost all tourists to Central Mexico (as well as residents of the capital) have clamored around, and it is the one place visited by almost all Mesoamerican archaeologists. Thus, Teotihuacan has always been a part of the foundation for our understanding of Mesoamerican cultures.

In organizing this conference to focus on the city of Teotihuacan, Janet Berlo sought to explain the features that set Teotihuacan apart from other Mesoamerican places and cultural manifestations. As she and René Millon here indicate, specialist knowledge of Teotihuacan has changed dramatically in the past thirty to forty years, and a new synthesis was therefore needed. Together, the papers in this volume provide this appraisal, and, as Millon explains in greater detail in his essay, they reflect a new stage in Teotihuacan studies.

To me, one of the most exciting understandings to come out of the conference on which this volume is based was a revelation of the internal temporal dimension of Teotihuacan and the consequential hint of the city's political history. Previously, secure building sequences and distinct periods at Teotihuacan had not been much retrieved or integrated with other data outside of ceramic sequences. But archaeological and art historical work in the last decades has begun to pull apart the layers of time more widely. The distinct stages in the construction of the city are now much better under-

Foreword

stood, and, as Millon explains, they reveal at least one dramatic ideological shift that may have limited the personal power of the ruler in the late third century. This recent work has brought the leadership of Teotihuacan into much sharper focus. The rulers may still be anonymous because their names are unknown to us, but we have a much better sense of the nature of their rule. As these essays demonstrate, we are closer to understanding many more of the changing forces that guided Teotihuacan for more than half a millennium.

Elizabeth Hill Boone
Dumbarton Oaks

Preface

During 1986–87, while serving as Acting Director of Pre-Columbian Studies at Dumbarton Oaks, I undertook discussions with the Senior Fellows Committee concerning the feasibility of organizing a Dumbarton Oaks conference on the topic of Teotihuacan. We agreed that while the past three decades have witnessed tremendous advances in our understanding of Teotihuacan's art and archaeology, publication and dissemination of this data have not kept up with the explosion of knowledge. Indeed, no major international conference on Teotihuacan had been held since the 11th Mesa Redonda in Mexico in 1966.

As is customary in Dumbarton Oaks conferences, a balance was struck between art historical and archaeological research. We deliberately invited a number of younger scholars, whose work was not yet well known, to join their more distinguished elders. Moreover, we limited the topic to metropolitan Teotihuacan, agreeing that there had already been considerable attention paid in other symposia and publications to the topic of Teotihuacan "influence" elsewhere in Mesoamerica.

In October 1988 nearly two hundred scholars convened at Dumbarton Oaks for the conference, "Art, Polity, and the City of Teotihuacan," which I chaired. In addition to the contributions included here, at that conference Elizabeth Wolfe presented a paper on "Code and Meaning in the Art of Teotihuacan." Other commitments prevented her from publishing that essay here. Rubén Cabrera Castro, Saburo Sugiyama, and George Cowgill presented a timely paper on "Summer 1988 Discoveries at the Feathered Serpent Pyramid." That is replaced in this volume by Saburo Sugiyama's essay discussing the ongoing discoveries of those excavations. I am grateful to Susan Evans, who generously agreed to co-author the introduction with me, providing a balance of archaeological and art historical expertise.

As usual, Elizabeth Hill Boone has been a generous host and a valued advisor to both conference and publication. Our most sincere gratitude goes to her.

Janet Catherine Berlo
St. Louis
July 1991

Teotihuacan: An Introduction

SUSAN T. EVANS
PENNSYLVANIA STATE UNIVERSITY

JANET CATHERINE BERLO
UNIVERSITY OF MISSOURI AT ST. LOUIS

FIFTEEN HUNDRED YEARS AGO, the city of Teotihuacan in central Mexico was the largest settlement in the New World. In fact, with perhaps as many as 200,000 people (Millon 1981: 208) it was the sixth largest city in the world (Chandler and Fox 1974: 368). Teotihuacan's size and power declined drastically in the eighth century, and the ceremonial heart of the city shows evidence of destruction from that period, but Teotihuacan was never a "lost city": its massive monumental architecture—the Pyramids of the Sun and the Moon—have impressed observers since their construction 2,000 years ago, and its environs have been continuously occupied, even to the present day. In spite of these features, our knowledge of the place and how it functioned is limited, and only in the past thirty years have research efforts systematically addressed issues such as the extent of the city, its subsistence base, economic functions, sociopolitical organization, and belief system.[1] The papers presented in this volume focus on these last three topics, using recent studies of archaeological remains and artistic media to reconstruct these important areas of Teotihuacan's culture.

This introductory essay will provide a historical context for the papers, so that the particular research results and interpretations can be understood as they relate to the city's—and Mesoamerica's—setting, history, and cultural traditions.

---

[1] The Valley of Mexico Project, directed by Eric Wolf, had its inception in a conference in 1960. In his "Introduction" to *The Valley of Mexico*, Wolf (1976) describes "an agreement between René Millon and William T. Sanders to divide the work to be carried out in the Valley of Teotihuacan. Millon would focus on the study of the urban center, while Sanders would survey the rural portions of the Valley" (p. 5).

Susan T. Evans and Janet Catherine Berlo

THE ENVIRONMENTAL SETTING

Pre-Columbian Mesoamerica (Fig. 1) encompasses a geographically diverse area of generally shared cultural traits. Although there is tremendous linguistic variety within this area (languages in adjacent areas are as different as Chinese is from English), most basic features of culture were held in common. Over Mesoamerica's extent, people grew the same crops, used the same kinds of tools, reckoned social and political relations in the same general configurations, and revered the same features of their world. The coherence of these shared traits over such a broken and diverse environment may seem puzzling until we realize that it was the close juxtaposition of different climate zones (created by radical elevation differences at tropical latitudes) that set the stage for economic interdependence and general cultural interaction (Sanders and Price 1968).

Mesoamerica's geophysical spine is a set of mountain ranges that break up the area into coastal plains and higher altitude plateaux. At the highest elevation is a region called the central highlands, consisting of adjacent valleys of Morelos, Puebla, and Toluca, and the centrally located Basin of Mexico (Fig. 2). We refer to it as a *basin* because in Pre-Columbian times it had no outlet to the sea; all water draining from its surrounding mountains collected at the bottom, forming a system of connected lakes. The alluvial plain of the basin is the ring of virtually flat land surrounding these lakes, and above the plain a piedmont zone forms the sloping base of the mountains, the highest of which are the famous volcanoes Ixtaccihuatl and Popocatepetl.

The basin is subdivided into connected but distinct regions, valleys formed by low mountain chains. In the northeastern part of the basin, the Teotihuacan Valley (ca. 600 km^2) extends from the basin's eastern limits (the ridge of the Sierra de Nevada) down to the ancient bed of Lake Texcoco, bounded by the Patlachique and Malpais ranges on the south and by Cerro Gordo and adjacent hills on the north.

The climate of the Basin of Mexico is relatively mild and cool. The winter frost season runs from October to April; the rains usually begin in May, are heaviest in summer, and continue into fall. Over the area of the basin, the amount of rainfall varies along a continuous gradient from 1,100 mm/year (about 43 in.) in the south to less than 500 mm/year (ca. 20 in.) in the northeast, including the Teotihuacan Valley. These features of climate, conditioned by the high altitude of the basin, make the Teotihuacan Valley a high risk area for cultivation using traditional methods (Sanders, Parsons, and Santley 1979: 82–83).

This is important to our understanding of Teotihuacan's culture, because the limits on the subsistence base of this region show how the growth of

Teotihuacan: An Introduction

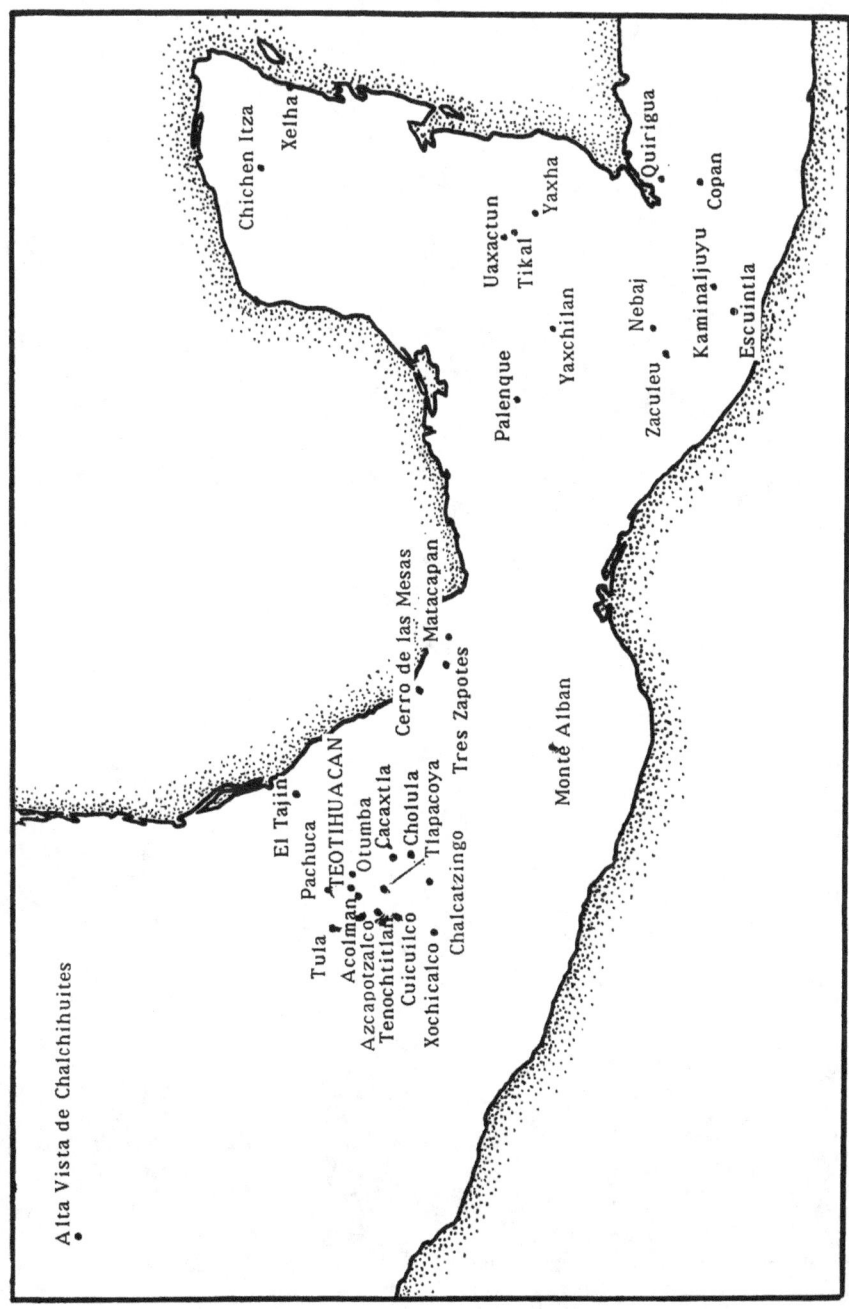

Fig. 1 Map of Mesoamerica showing sites named in this volume.

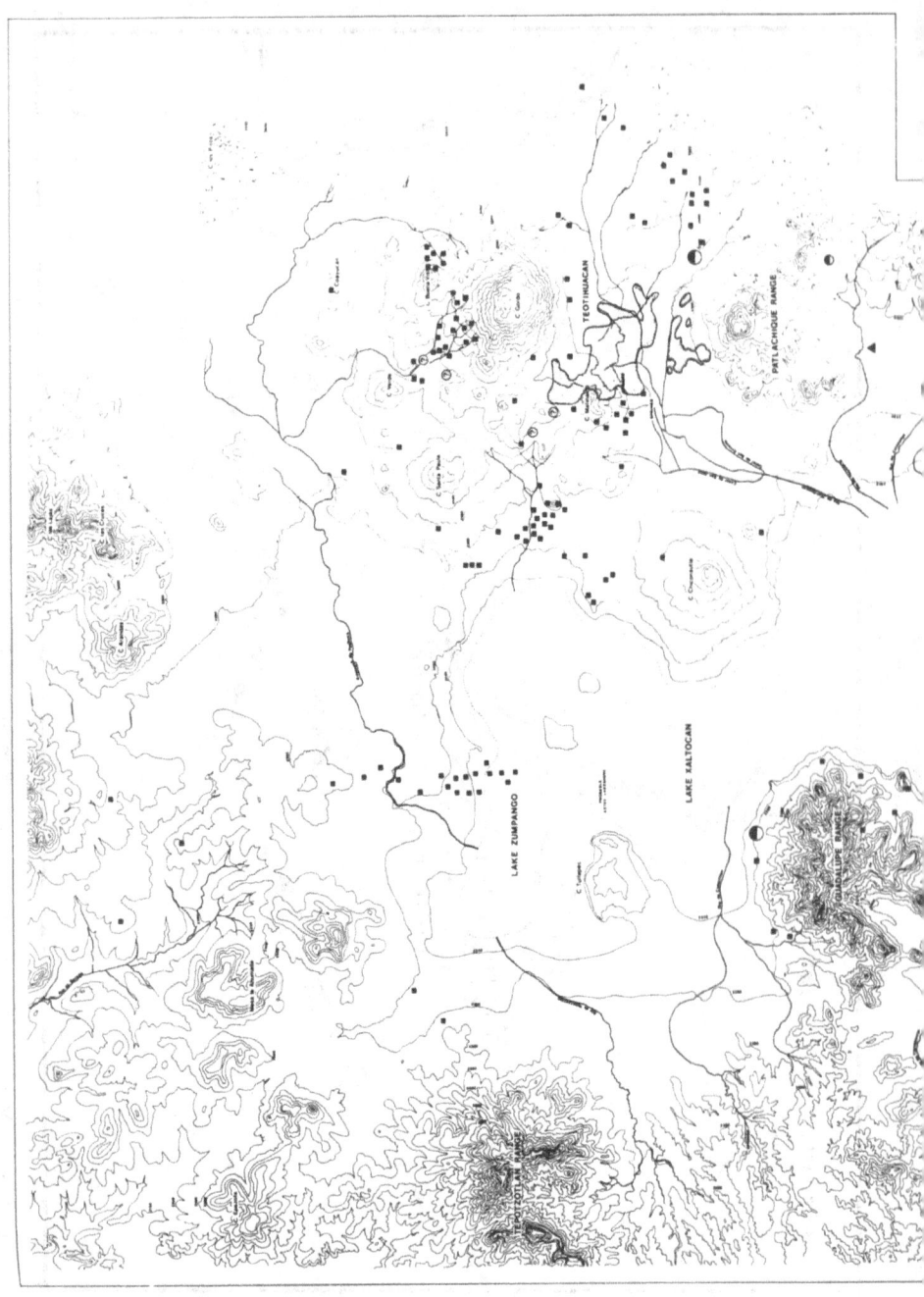

Teotihuacan: An Introduction

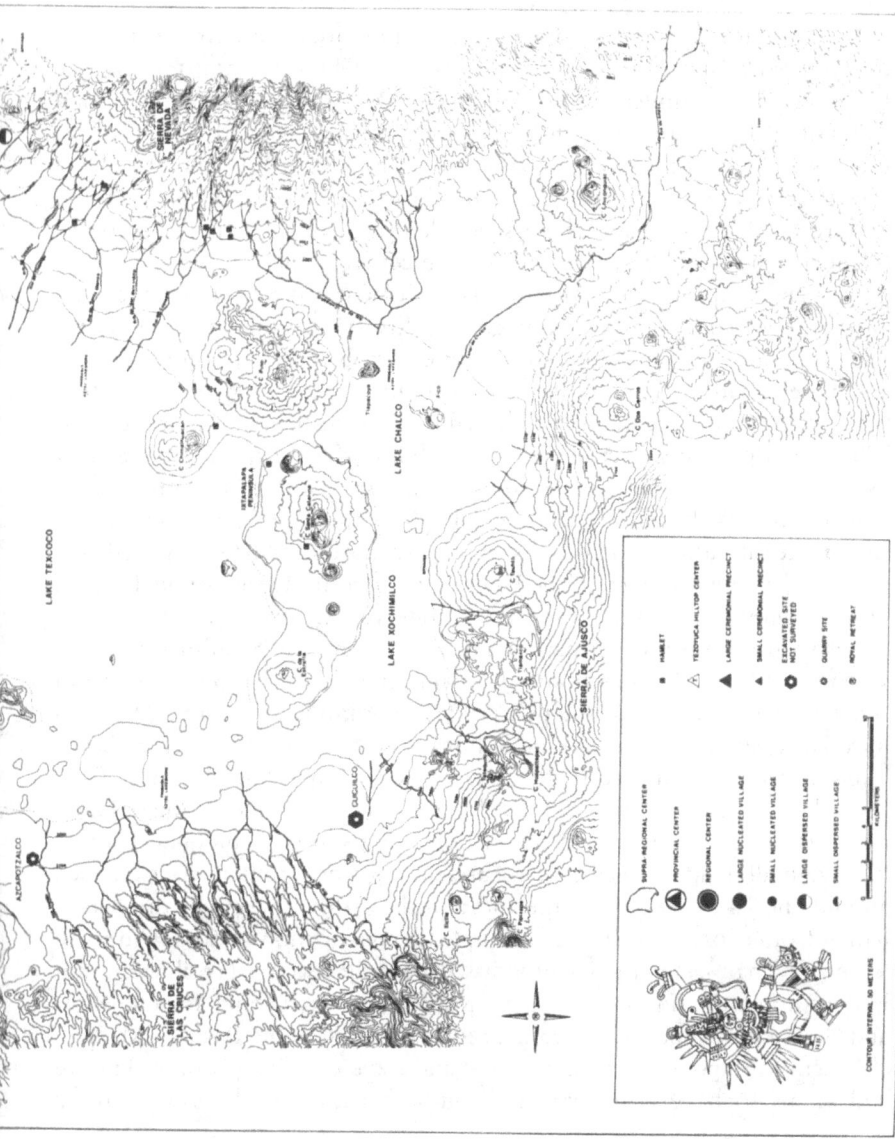

Fig. 2 Basin of Mexico ca. A.D. 100 (after Sanders, Parsons, and Santley 1979: map 13, used with permission of Academic Press).

Susan T. Evans and Janet Catherine Berlo

Teotihuacan depended on manipulation of water, a resource that had stringent spatial limits in the Teotihuacan Valley. In turn, the veneration of water as the source of life is an important component of Teotihuacan's belief system.

HISTORY OF THE BASIN AND THE TEOTIHUACAN VALLEY

A way of life centered on permanent communities and farming is a relatively recent innovation in the long history of human occupation of the New World. For millennia, people depended on foraged and hunted food and shifted their campsites throughout the year to take advantage of resources in various locations. In time, some foraged plants came to play a greater role in the diet, as people learned how to manipulate them to ensure a more reliable food supply and scheduled their yearly activities to do so (Flannery 1971). Increased dependence on certain plants led to increasingly permanent campsites, until year-round settlement was established in certain areas, supported by a mixed strategy of cultivation and foraging. As farming techniques became more sophisticated, crop repertoire more reliable, and material culture (e.g., stone tools, ceramics) more comprehensive, permanent settlements could be established in more challenging environments. The earliest permanent settlements in the Basin of Mexico date from at least 1500 B.C., and are found in the south, in the area of the Amecameca pass, which connects the basin with the Valley of Morelos.[2] From similarity of such material culture traits as ceramics, archaeologists have deduced that these settlements were established by migrants from Morelos or by denizens of the basin who adopted those traits (Sanders et al. 1979: 95).

Between the earliest permanent settlements and the Spanish Conquest, 3,000 years later, the sociopolitical organization of the basin evolved from small, socially egalitarian, and politically autonomous communities to complex, large, socially stratified, and politically centralized states such as that of Teotihuacan and (later still) the Aztec states in power at the time of the Spanish Conquest. The earliest villages' locations in the southern basin reflect their ability to farm in this region using simple techniques, because high rainfall made agriculture secure. Over time, settlement expanded around the lakes, except in the more arid northern basin. In the period dating from 650 to 300 B.C., for example, the only communities in the north were a few hamlets in the vicinity of what would become Teotihuacan, but in the southern basin the town of Cuicuilco numbered about 10,000 people and clearly functioned as a regional center, the first in the Basin of Mexico.

Cuicuilco's apogee was between 300 and 100 B.C., when it doubled in size and seems to have dominated the southern basin. At the same time, a

---

[2] Sanders (1981) and Sanders, Parsons, and Santley (1979) summarize and interpret the basin's culture history.

substantial community emerged at Teotihuacan. The Teotihuacan Valley had been settled relatively late because of natural constraints on agricultural productivity. We have already mentioned the aridity of this region; another, contrasting problem challenging the techniques of early agriculturalists would have been the swampy areas of the alluvial plain where water from the permanent springs accumulated. These problems required considerable intensive agricultural effort at canal building, both to facilitate draining boggy ground and to move water to irrigate dry land. Once manipulation of this water source for agricultural purposes was mastered, the alluvial plain of the Teotihuacan Valley became as productive as any other area in the basin, capable of supporting a large and dense population.

By about 100 B.C., Teotihuacan and Cuicuilco seem to have been balanced powers in the basin. They were roughly the same size and were the only two large centers. Then, fate took a hand. Sometime around 100 B.C. the volcano Xitle erupted, and its flow of lava began to cover Cuicuilco and the farm land that supported it. It should come as no surprise that, at the same time, Teotihuacan experienced prodigious growth; its population came to comprise 90% of that of the basin. It seems logical to assume that many Teotihuacanos at the turn of the millennium were descendants of refugees from Cuicuilco, and there may have been class distinctions benefiting the original Teotihuacanos. The Cuicuilcan's experience with natural disaster would have given them a predisposition toward respect for the Teotihuacan belief system.

HISTORY AND SETTING

Teotihuacan continued to grow in size and complexity, eventually (by about A.D. 500) numbering between 125,000 to 200,000 people. Most of the population living in the city worked part-time as farmers and part-time as craftspeople, cultivating the irrigated fields of the valley's alluvial plain and also making textiles, pottery, obsidian objects, and other goods. We do not know the language in use (see Cowgill and Millon, this volume, for brief explorations of this issue), but Totonac and Nahua (an early form of that spoken by the Aztecs) are principal candidates. Elements of the belief system can be discerned from their iconographic representations. These include objects of veneration familiar to us from other places in Mesoamerica as well as some that were apparently unique to Teotihuacan.

Although no one can deny that, in terms of human adaptation to any region, an adequate food supply has an ultimate primacy of importance, the landscape of the Teotihuacan Valley was much richer to the ancient Mesoamericans than its caloric potential. Mesoamerican belief systems stressed the spiritual power of all aspects of the physical world—features of the landscape, forces of nature—to such an extent that people saw the world around them as spiritually charged, and the personification of these forces as gods and goddesses was a secondary expression of them. This is in contrast to the religions of the West, where deities and their power are the principal focus. Space does not permit a detailed overview or analysis of Mesoamerican belief systems here,[3] but we make these points about the intrinsic spiritual value of the natural world in order to make Teotihuacan's physical context and its meaning understandable.

The city of Teotihuacan is located on the lower slope of Cerro Gordo, an eroded volcanic cone. This lower slope is a shelf of basalt, and under that shelf the springs have their origin. The springs turn this semi-desert region into a rich agricultural zone. The springs give life with their waters, and Cerro Gordo's Pre-Columbian name was Tenan, "Mother of Waters," far more revealing of the mountain's role in the life of the people than "Fat Mountain." As Berlo points out in her study (this volume), Great Goddess imagery at Teotihuacan combines attributes of earthly waters and the fertile mountain, among others.

Although the location of the city took advantage of the agricultural potential of the Teotihuacan Valley, the layout of the city reveals sensitivity to Teotihuacan's spiritual place in its setting. The map of the city (Fig. 3) reveals a sophisticated and grandiose overall plan, with civic-ceremonial architecture aligned along the major north-south causeway known as the Street of the Dead.[4] Temple complexes and palace buildings line this causeway, which is dominated by the Pyramid of the Sun on its east side (more than 200 m along the base, more than 60 m high) and the Pyramid of the Moon at its north end (smaller—only 35 m high—but its top is at the same level as the other pyramid, and they have the same general proportions; Fig. 4). The Ciudadela complex,[5] with the Temple of the Feathered Serpent, lies south of the Pyramid of the Sun. Across from the Ciudadela is a plaza area that may have been the city's market. In the rest of the city, which at its greatest extent covered more than 20 km^2, were walled apartment compounds, apparently the residences of groups of related families. Many of the compounds also functioned as craft production workshops (R. Millon 1981).

The Street of the Dead is not on a strict north-south axis, but is oriented 15°30' east of north. It is aligned with the summit of Cerro Gordo, where there was a temple (Heyden and Gendrop 1988: 26–29) and with the top of a

[3] Interested readers will find general overviews in D. Carrasco (1990) and Nicholson (1971); Townsend (1979) discusses the spiritual force of aspects of the environment. Ruiz de Alarcon's 1629 *Treatise* offers rare documentation of Contact period practices that no doubt had their antecedents in much earlier times.

[4] "Street of the Dead" is a name given to the thoroughfare in Aztec times. Its name in the Classic period is not known.

[5] Cowgill (1983) offers a comprehensive description and analysis of this complex and its possible uses. He points out that, while the whole Ciudadela is vast (covering 16 ha, nearly 40 acres), the actual usable interior space is quite small, only 11,000 to 15,000 m^2, making it unlikely that many ongoing administrative activities took place there.

hill in the Patlachique Range. There is tremendous visual power in this alignment and the positioning of Cerro Gordo and the two pyramids, from the perspective of anyone looking north along the Street of the Dead. Here the mastery of the integration of these built and natural landscape features is revealed. The proportional similarity of the two pyramids leads the eye to expect that the more distant one will be at least the same size (and its position at the end of the causeway may lead to the assumption that it is even the larger of the two). That it is, in fact, smaller, brings the massive mountain behind it telescoping forward, magnifying its visual impact. The relative size and placement of the pyramids is similar to a landscaping trick of giving depth to a small garden by using trees with leaves of similar shape but different size: place the small-leafed tree at the back of the garden and the eye, taking its cue from the large-leafed tree in the foreground, will perceive that the other tree is farther away than it actually is. At Teotihuacan the visual impact of this trick is then multiplied by the effect of the background mountain, whose proportions are not unlike those of the pyramids.

Another aspect of the psychological impact of the layout of the Street of the Dead is its partitioning: the pedestrian must surmount a set of bridge-like structures that interrupt the flat stretches. These may have served to control the flow of crowds (Wallrath 1966 [cited in Heyden and Gendrop 1988: 35]) but certainly have the effect of breaking up the experience of moving toward the pyramids into "a series of sequences, simple, yet rich in sensation, resulting from the changing view of the Pyramid of the Sun" (Hardoy 1964: 91, cited in Heyden and Gendrop 1988: 35).

The Pyramid of the Sun was the first of the monumental constructions to be built. It is located over a dry cave, where evidence suggests that ceremonies took place involving the veneration of fire and water (R. Millon 1981: 234). Caves are particularly sacred landscape elements in the Mesoamerican belief system, and their meaning is concatenated with the orifices of the living body: the earth as a living being, analogous to the human body with its orifices (López Austin 1984: 173). Chicomoztoc, the legendary set of sacred origin caves of people of the central highlands, has its counterpart in each of us. At Teotihuacan, the legendary place of the birth of the gods, the most impressive construction was placed over a cave (Heyden 1975).

No visitor to Teotihuacan will forget the sight of the pyramids, but few take notice of the Rio de San Juan, a stream whose channelized course crosses the Street of the Dead along an east-west axis between the Ciudadela and the Pyramid of the Sun. This river was the rippling, flowing source of life, fed by the springs of the sacred mountain, moving toward its use in the irrigation systems of the productive alluvial plain of the lower valley. The Rio de San Juan is now an unprepossessing streamlet; the flow from the springs today is only a fraction of what it once was, wells dug in the nineteenth century to supply the valley's haciendas punctured the aquifers,

Susan T. Evans and Janet Catherine Berlo

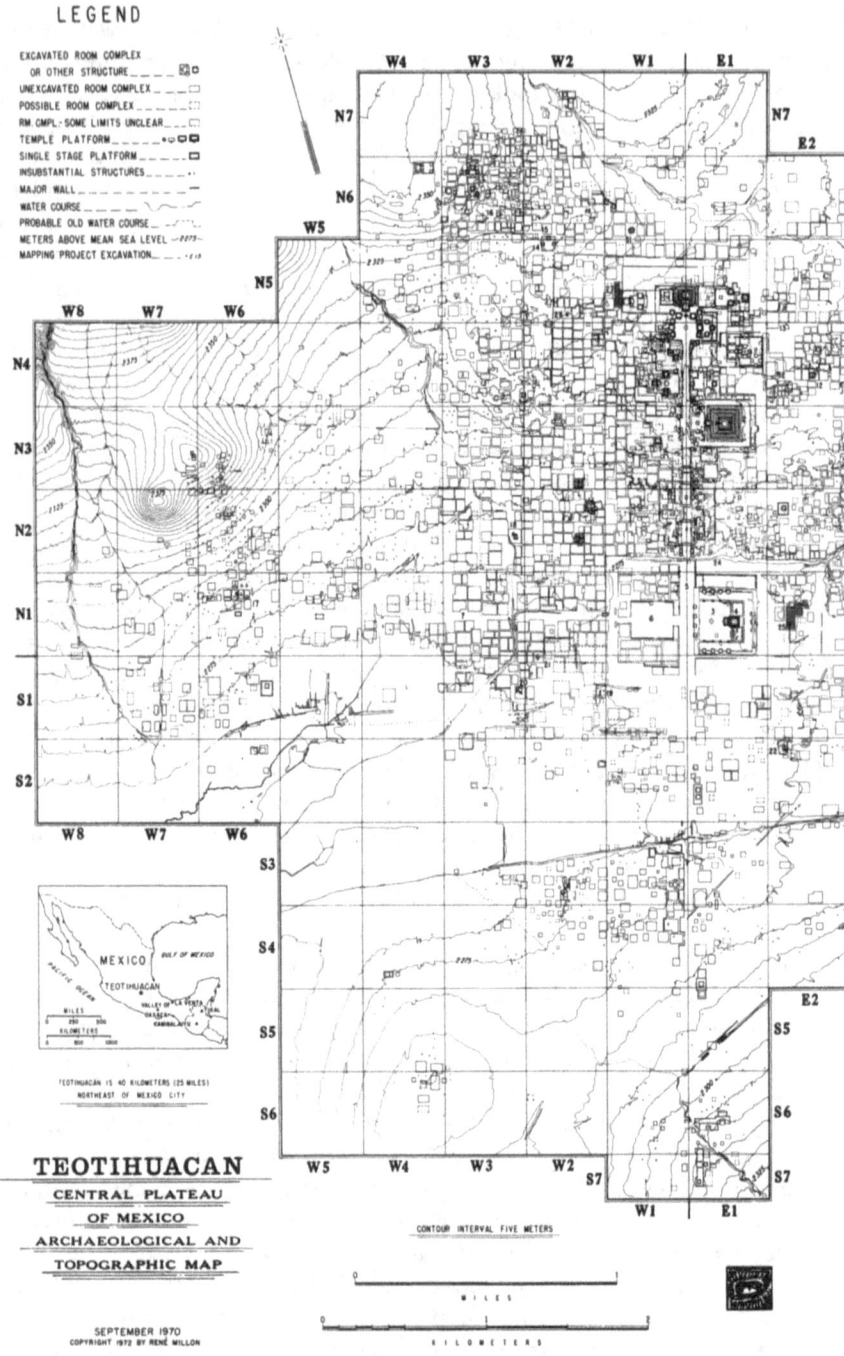

Teotihuacan: An Introduction

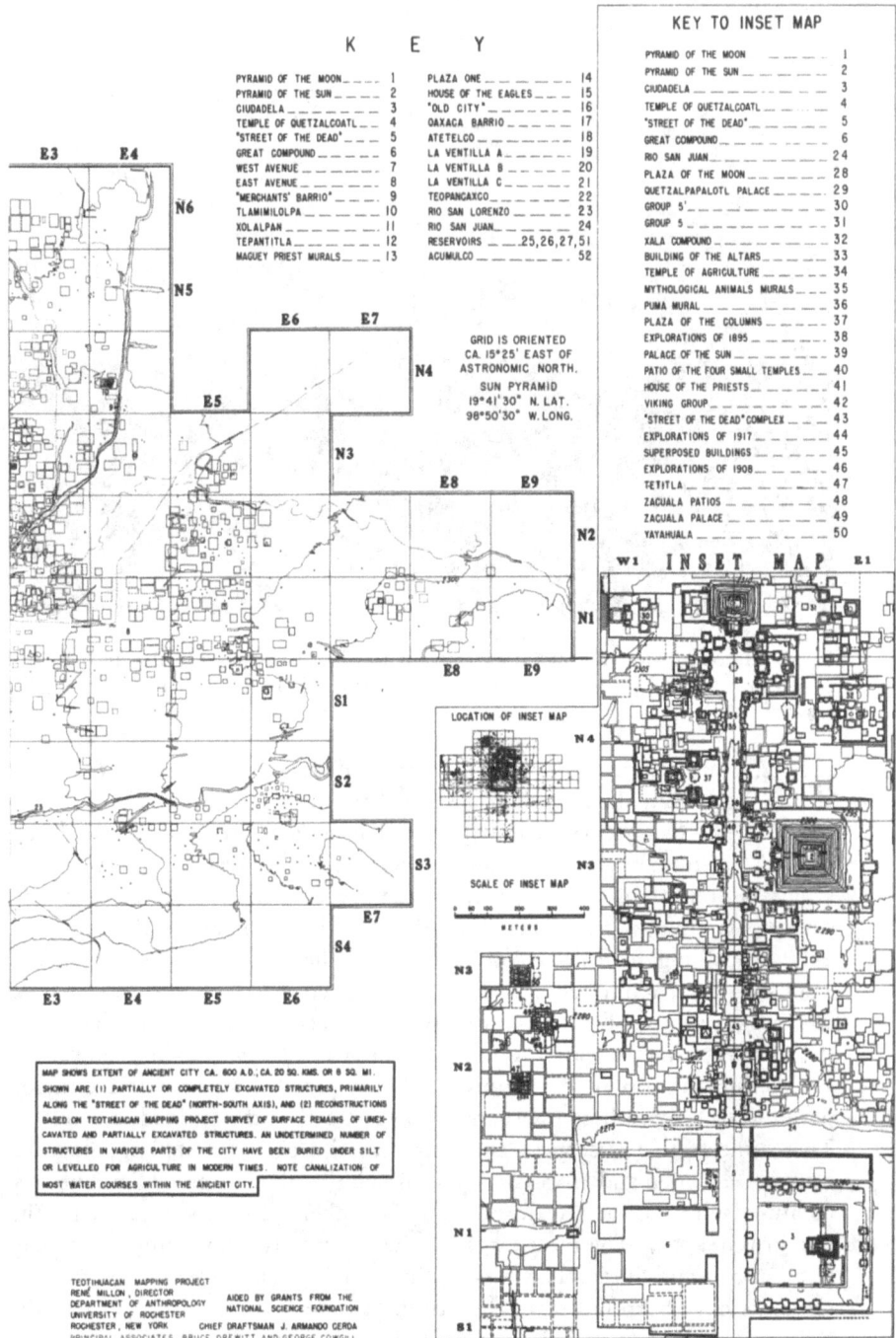

Fig. 3 Teotihuacan map including Street of the Dead detail (after Millon, Drewitt, and Cowgill 1973: fig. 7-3, courtesy of René Millon).

Susan T. Evans and Janet Catherine Berlo

Fig. 4 Looking north along the Street of the Dead toward the Pyramid of the Moon and Cerro Gordo, with the Pyramid of the Sun at right. Photo by S. T. Evans.

causing a diminution of the flow from natural springs (Sanders 1965). When Teotihuacan flourished, so did the river that ran through its heart.

Again, the Nahuatl language offers a clue to the spiritual meaning of this natural (yet human-shaped) landscape feature. In Nahuatl there is a strong affinity among things that flow: the water in rivers, the course of a road, the sinuous winding of a serpent, blood through the veins (López Austin 1967: 28), the ruffling of feathers on a banner in the breeze. If you travel, for example, you should begin your trip on the day named 1 Serpent, to take advantage of some of these affinities (Castillo Farreras 1969: 181). The affinities of things that flow are brought together iconographically in many ways at Teotihuacan, nowhere as impressively as in the bas reliefs on the temple-pyramid of the Feathered Serpent at the east end of the Ciudadela (Fig. 5). There, the feathered serpent conjoins several aspects of rippling, flowing imagery. Heyden and Horcasitas have noted that the Feathered Serpent was identified with flowing water long before other features such as wind (in Durán 1964: 325). The meaning of all these symbols is not completely clear (see Taube's and Sugiyama's essays, this volume), and indeed iconographic elements have been linked to the origin of time and calendrical succession (López Austin, López Luján, and Sugiyama 1991). The juxtaposition of serpents and water signs on the facade, however, is unmistakable. On level

Teotihuacan: An Introduction

Fig. 5 Detail of facade of the Temple of the Feathered Serpent. Photo by W. T. Sanders.

after level the imagery of things that flow is repeated, presenting the visual statement of the sacred value of the nearby river, multiplied in the seven levels of Teotihuacan's third-largest pyramid.

ART AND ICONOGRAPHY

Teotihuacan's politico-religious ideology was reinforced and promulgated through the arts. Civic architecture itself, as already mentioned, was laid out in a grand grid-plan superimposed on a landscape conjoining cave and mountain as the two fundamental aspects of sacred geography. Ambitious mural programs covered interior walls and exterior surfaces of many buildings, including residential structures of different social classes. Small-scale arts, mass-produced in large quantities, ranged from stone and obsidian items to ceramic figurines and incense burners to the cylindrical tripod vessel, ubiquitous at the city and widely traded and replicated throughout Mesoamerica.

Artistic workshops were among the many craft specialization complexes at the metropolis. Presumably these ranged from workshops that specialized in the mass-production of mold-made figurines to large-scale mural painting and architectural ateliers. Small, mold-made ceramic parts for incense burners were mass produced for quick assembly (Múnera n.d.; Berlo 1982).

Lapidary workshops refined jadeite, serpentine, *tecali,* and other materials for use in sumptuary arts (Turner, this volume).

Expert mural painters, like their counterparts in Renaissance Italy, exploited the durable properties of the true fresco technique in which pigments are applied to damp plaster, thus forming a long-lasting bond between pigment and ground. The careful and rapid preparation of the walls required for such a technique, as well as the deft handling of line and color, all point to the existence of highly specialized painting workshops. The artists used cartoons or stencil-patterns for repeating figures, then individualized some details, according to Arthur Miller's (1973: 32–33) painstaking analysis of painting technique. Miniature painting on lime-stuccoed vessels may have been a sub-specialty of these workshops.

In Teotihuacan art, the ideology of power is couched in religious terms—as it is throughout Mesoamerica—but the individual ruler is not emphasized as mediator between human and supernatural forces. Notably, nowhere in the city's public and monumental arts do we find explicit representations of rulers, yet we surmise from recent finds of high-status burials in the Temple of the Feathered Serpent that powerful individuals did rule. The avoidance of the "cult of the ruler" sets Teotihuacan apart from coeval Maya and Zapotec polities in which propagandistic imagery identifying the individual ruler with important supernaturals and deified ancestors and commemorating his military victories were primary concerns of public art. In comparison with other art styles in Mesoamerica, Teotihuacan's imagery is more metaphorical and its art style more abstract; it evinces less concern than Maya art, for example, with detailed naturalistic or veristic representations. As Arthur Miller observes:

> Teotihuacan painting is a presentation of images which have specific meaning in themselves apart from the visual world around the Teotihuacano. Teotihuacan painting does not refer to the real world as does representational painting employing the traditional Western artistic devices for rendering perspective. Teotihuacan painting refers to a symbolic concept. It is a presentation whose meaning is *in the image* and not anywhere else. (1973: 26)

The murals combine figural and emblematic forms, and their graphic clarity seems to have been a prime concern. Yet, paradoxically, the logographic clarity of the imagery is sometimes deliberately obscured by the artist's choice of colors of equal value or complementary colors to emphasize the flatness of the picture plane and to make it unreadable. Locked within this color field are glyphic emblems and figural forms. Images such as these might be characterized as "embedded texts," in which text and image fuse in one iconic presentation (Berlo 1983: 11–17). Such presentations focus on animals, plants, and abstract emblems as much as on semi-human representations.

Teotihuacan: An Introduction

The Teotihuacan art style is a sophisticated mix of representational and abstract forms. Processes of standardization and reduction are common throughout different media: the large-scale Sun and Moon Pyramids are miniatures of Cerro Gordo (see Fig. 4); the standard *talud-tablero* architectural profile repeats in variant forms from large-scale temple platforms to small-scale patio altars; complex iconographic programs are reduced and abstracted to symbolic notations, as in the various representations of the Great Goddess ranging from full-figure presentation to the notational "shorthand" of nosebar and earplugs (see Berlo, this volume, figs. 2, 15).

At one time, scholars characterized Teotihuacan's art as more "liturgical" in character (Kubler 1967) than the art of other Mesoamerican polities, but increasingly we are coming to see the distinctive Teotihuacan art style as a deliberate artistic strategy that fosters a corporate ideology. As Esther Pasztory has convincingly argued:

> Teotihuacan created a new artistic tradition to express the ways it was different from other Mesoamerican cultures. In many ways these conventions are the opposite or negate those of the contemporaries of Teotihuacan. This tradition had two aspects, content and form. In content, Teotihuacan rejected the politically instituted representations of rulers and captives. In form, Teotihuacan rejected the naturalistic, curvilinear styles of representation. The characteristic flatness, angularity, and abstraction of Teotihuacan art contrasts with the more realistic three-dimensional arts of the south. In the same way that Teotihuacan was built on a grid plan, its artistic conventions were created to express a socio-political reality that its people evidently felt differed from other Mesoamerican polities. (Pasztory 1988: 50)

This reality centered on group identity, deliberately fostered egalitarianism and veneration of natural forces without the intercession of the ruler-king (see Pasztory, this volume).

HISTORIOGRAPHY

Despite Désiré Charnay's claim more than a century ago that Teotihuacan had been so often described that there was little more to say (1887: 151), Charnay stood at the beginning of a sequence of explorers, archaeologists, and art historians who, in the past 100 years, have contributed to our understanding of Teotihuacan polity and world-view. Although we cannot recapitulate all the significant works here, we shall mention at least some highlights, giving special emphasis to those works that relate to the major themes of this volume: art, religion, and political organization. Millon (this volume) considers in greater detail some of the archaeological advances of the past forty-five years.

Susan T. Evans and Janet Catherine Berlo

Archaeological excavation began at Teotihuacan at the end of the nineteenth century, with the work of Batres (1889, 1906, 1912) and Peñafiel (1900). This was followed by Eduard Seler's systematic and ambitious study of Teotihuacan's artifacts, *Die Teotiuacan-Kultur des Hochlands von Mexiko* (1915). Seler's method included submitting the largest possible sample of material to analysis, describing forms carefully, and comparing objects for similarity of form and symbolic usage. These still comprise the basic steps of iconographic research. Seler is also well known for his use of ethnographic analogy, or the direct historic approach; his extensive study of late Mexican manuscripts provided Seler with a wealth of ethnographic data that proved useful in elucidating the meaning of earlier materials. This use of ethnographic analogy paved the way for subsequent generations of scholars to use this method as the predominant approach to the meaning of pre-Conquest Mesoamerican art. Yet Seler was much more cautious in the application of this method than many who followed him; he did not accept uncritically a direct line of continuity between Teotihuacan and Aztec cultures.[6]

After Seler's ground-breaking explication of art and symbolism, the next major achievement was the publication of Manuel Gamio's three-volume compendium *La población del Valle de Teotihuacan* (1922). Volume 1 presents all that was then known about Teotihuacan archaeology, including the results of Gamio's own extensive excavations at the Ciudadela begun in 1917. Whereas Seler had concentrated principally on the small-scale works of art and their iconography, Gamio delved into the entire range of works, providing site plans, building elevations, mural diagrams, and architectural reconstructions. Other volumes include ethnographic and environmental studies of the valley. For years his study remained the standard encyclopedic work on the site, and it still provides a wealth of information.[7]

The era from 1922 to 1950 was a period of constant activity and great strides in archaeology in Central Mexico, all of it building on the stratigraphic methodology introduced by Gamio.[8] George Vaillant (1938) was refining cultural sequences, while Eduardo Noguera (1935) and Pedro Armillas (1944, 1950) were excavating at Teotihuacan. The first comprehensive excavation reports were written by Sigvald Linné (1934, 1942), who published detailed documentation of stratigraphy, grave goods, ceramics, and architecture. Linné's thoroughly reported excavations provided much-needed information on the archaeological context of artifacts. Considering the amount of excavation conducted at Teotihuacan in the twentieth century, there is an unfortunate lack of well-published documentation of process and results.

[6] See, for examples, his comments on pages 419, 463, and 492 of the 1915 work.
[7] It has recently been reprinted in an inexpensive paperback edition in Mexico.
[8] For a summary of the important advances of this generation, see Armillas (1950).

Teotihuacan: An Introduction

By the 1940s, a large corpus of Teotihuacan materials was available for study. This decade witnessed a flowering of research by scholars interested in the meaning of these artifacts. In "Los dioses de Teotihuacan," Pedro Armillas (1945: 36) tried to establish a "stratigraphy of religious concepts in Mesoamerica" based on analysis of the archaeological record rather than ethnographic analogy. Although not entirely breaking free of the analogical tradition, Armillas did define the iconographic attributes of Teotihuacan's major deities. His concept of a stratigraphic approach to iconography was potentially of great methodological significance. This approach states in archaeological terms the same principles that art historian Erwin Panofsky set forth in *Studies in Iconology* (1939) and that underpin iconographic research in the history of art: one uncovers the meaning of a work of art primarily through the study of the art itself, as well as through inquiry into the historical character of a specific place and point in time. The stratigraphic approach to iconography advocated by Armillas did not appear to have much impact at the time. Only in the 1960s was a similar method proposed by George Kubler (1967, 1973), who rejected analogy in favor of direct analysis of objects within their own era.

In essays spanning nearly half a century, Hasso von Winning examined the meaning and usage of Teotihuacan symbols. His work (1987) is summarized in the two-volume study *La iconografía de Teotihuacan: Los dioses y los signos*. Since the time of Seler, most scholars have recognized the glyphic or emblematic quality of Teotihuacan art. Indeed, Seler (1915: 484) advised that "the development of the ornament had attained such a degree of conventionalism that instead of ornament we should talk of glyphs." Alfonso Caso concluded that the Teotihuacanos used the *tonalpohualli* or 260-day ritual calendar (1939), as well as other calendrical glyphs (1958–59). George Kubler (1967: 5) proposed a linguistic model for understanding the iconographic system, concluding that Teotihuacan art is logographic in character and combines "associative meanings in a quest for viable forms of writing." His method, involving configurational analysis, was built upon the work of Seler and von Winning yet went beyond them in his complete rejection of the use of Aztec sources.

Teotihuacan's glyphic system has been studied in detail by Langley (1986; this volume) and considered briefly by Berlo (1989). Although disagreement still exists about the language spoken at the metropolis, the structure of hieroglyphic notation at Teotihuacan seems to parallel that of the Aztecs, suggesting a Nahuatl affiliation (see Cowgill, this volume). Neither Teotihuacan writing nor iconography has received the kind of detailed attention that has been devoted to those of the Maya. Yet a small number of scholars have advanced our knowledge appreciably in the past few decades. Von Winning's work has already been mentioned; Clara Millon's studies (1973,

1988) have focused on the political dimension of Teotihuacan iconography. Esther Pasztory has provided penetrating analyses of numerous iconographic and iconological problems, ranging from specific deity images and iconographic programs (1972, 1974, 1976) to wide-ranging essays on the Teotihuacan artistic tradition (1988). Pasztory has also considered style as a carrier of meaning (n.d.; 1989; this volume). Janet Catherine Berlo has examined ceramic arts (1982), iconographic issues (1983; this volume), and Teotihuacan art outside the metropolitan boundaries (1984). Karl Taube's studies of the Teotihuacan Spider Woman and of the Cave of Origin (1983, 1986) have added appreciably to our knowledge of iconography, principally through a far-ranging comparative approach. Taube follows this method in his essay in this volume as well.

The acceleration of excavations at Teotihuacan starting in the 1940s and 1950s revealed a significant number of new mural paintings. The residential compounds of Tepantitla, Tetitla, Zacuala, and Atetelco were all excavated at that time. Documentation and publication of the murals afforded scholars a larger data base for interpretation of artistic style, iconography, and chronology (Villagra Caleti 1951, 1971; Séjourné 1959, 1966; Hall n.d.; Pasztory 1976). Arthur Miller's monograph, *The Mural Painting of Teotihuacan* (1973) set a rigorous standard for the study of ancient painting. His exhaustive documentation of the murals, many of them previously unpublished, and his discussion of style and technique remain unsurpassed. Interest in mural art continues (Berrin 1988; Cabrera Castro, this volume). In the early 1960s, excavations were conducted under the auspices of the Instituto Nacional de Antropología e Historia (INAH), principally along the Street of the Dead (Bernal 1963; Acosta 1964). This, too, led to further analyses of the city and its material culture (Sociedad Mexicana de Antropología 1966, 1972).

The Teotihuacan Mapping Project, under the direction of René Millon, commenced in 1962 with the ambitious agenda of providing a detailed surface survey and map of the entire metropolis (Millon 1967, 1970; Millon et al. 1973). Reports and dissertations completed under the purview of this project have refined our knowledge of craft production, residential organization, mortuary practices, rulership, social status, and regional relations (e.g., Cowgill 1983; Spence 1974, 1981, this volume; Sempowski n.d., this volume; Turner n.d., this volume; Barbour n.d.; for detailed examination of these topics and a thorough bibliography see Millon 1976, 1981, as well as McClung de Tapia and Rattray 1987).

Since 1980, the Proyecto Arqueológico Teotihuacán has brought to light even more data, principally in the Ciudadela (Cabrera Castro, Rodriguez, and Morelos 1982a, 1982b; Múnera n.d.). Most recently, the spectacular finds of offerings and burials under the Temple of the Feathered Serpent have caused a reassessment of our understanding of rulership, warfare, and sacrifice at the metropolis (Sugiyama 1989, this volume).

Teotihuacan: An Introduction

LATE CLASSIC DECLINE AND POSTCLASSIC HISTORY

What led to Teotihuacan's decline? This is another question without a clear and certain answer. We do know that there is evidence, dating from the eighth century, of destruction and vandalization of important monuments along the Street of the Dead. Millon (1981: 236) noted that "the evidence seems to show that the city was not destroyed in bitterly contested combat. In fact, it appears that most of the city was not destroyed at all. . . . The heart of the city was burned, but little else. The fire was very selective, confined largely to the monumental architecture on the 'Street of the Dead' and to temples and associated buildings in the rest of the city." Note that, in contrast to a scenario of utter desolation, Teotihuacan's demise as the premiere urban place of its time left a population numbering between 30,000 and 50,000 people, still one of the largest communities in the New World. Furthermore, the evidence of destruction of Teotihuacan's imperial administration accords with the conventions of conquest in the Basin of Mexico in later times; the Aztec glyph for conquest was a burning temple atop a pyramid.

No one city took over Teotihuacan's role. Three other cities in the central highlands—Tula, Cholula, and Xochicalco—became larger at this time, as did more distant places like El Tajin. Tula, in particular, seems to have directly benefitted from Teotihuacan's decline.[9] Although the Basin of Mexico experienced a population decline attendant upon the decline of Teotihuacan's power, when we consider the increase in population in the area of Tula, just to the north of the Basin, the total population of this larger area of the central highlands remains stable, suggesting that Tula accommodated the refugees.

The Basin of Mexico during the period from A.D. 800 to 1200 was something of a cultural backwater. The highly centralized settlement pattern of Teotihuacan in its prime evolved into a set of small, widely spaced towns with adjacent villages and hamlets. At around A.D. 1200, possibly due to a climate change increasing agricultural risk in the Tula area (Armillas 1969), another large population shift took place, this time involving wave upon wave of "Toltec" and other migrants moving south into the Basin of Mexico and its adjacent valleys (discussed in Calnek 1982; Carrasco 1971). These migrations are the seminal events of the native annals documented during the century after Spanish conquest, and the dates that they cite have been substantiated by archaeological evidence.[10] The migrants settled among the

---

[9] Diehl and Berlo (1989) present recent investigations of these topics.

[10] See Smith (1984) for a general discussion; Evans and Freter (n.d.) present confirmation from absolute dating. In the late sixteenth century Sahagun's informants recounted a sequence of events that has a rough correlation with actual fact: Teotihuacan had been founded by wandering peoples who built the pyramids and then left for Chicomoztoc, returning to the Basin of Mexico as migrating tribes (bk. 10, chap. 29, cited in Carrasco 1971: 459–460).

existing populations, and, in time, the set of city-states formed during this period became confederated, first by the Tepanecs, and then by the Aztecs of Tenochtitlan and their allies.

Teotihuacan as a community had shifted its locational focus away from the ruined ceremonial center, which continued to function as a magnet for pilgrimages. The new residential and administrative center for Teotihuacan was located in what is now San Juan Teotihuacan, about a kilometer west of the ceremonial center. Other, smaller communities were located on the periphery of the Street of the Dead complex, and no doubt many residents of these surrounding towns made a business out of serving the needs of visitors to the pyramids. Ethnohistoric evidence documents Teotihuacan's continuing status as a political center after its decline as a major capital (Nuttall 1926), and various annals refer to Teotihuacan as a *señorio* (regional capital with tributary villages) with its own ruling dynasty, paying tribute to Texcoco, then Azcapotzalco, then Texcoco again after the Tepanec Wars (ca. 1430). Tenochtitlan's rulers traveled to Teotihuacan for important ceremonies, including the interment of the dead, a practice that gave the ancient causeway its present name. The Aztecs believed that they lived in the fifth creation epoch of the world's history and that their world had been brought into being by the self-sacrifice of the gods at Teotihuacan.

Thus, in an important sense, Teotihuacan was the place where time began. This first great New World city emerged out of the interplay between the natural setting and human ingenuity and imagination. Although much of the culture of the ancient Teotihuacan is still difficult for us to understand, scholarly efforts such as those presented in this volume will elucidate the city's ways of life and system of beliefs.

BIBLIOGRAPHY

ACOSTA, JORGE
  1964 *El palacio del Quetzalpapalotl.* Instituto Nacional de Antropología e Historia, Mexico, D.F.

ARMILLAS, PEDRO
  1944 Exploraciones recientes en Teotihuacan, México. *Cuadernos Americanos* 16 (4): 121–136, Mexico.
  1945 Los dioses de Teotihuacan. *Anales del Instituto de Etnografía Americana* 6: 35–61. Universidad Nacionale de Cuyo, Mendoza.
  1950 Teotihuacan, Tula y los Toltecas. *Runa* 3: 37–70. Buenos Aires.
  1969 The Arid Frontier of Mexican Civilization. New York Academy of Sciences, *Transactions* (2nd ser.) 31: 697–704.

BARBOUR, WARREN
  n.d. The Figurines and Figurine Chronology of Ancient Teotihuacan, Mexico. Ph.D. dissertation, Dept. of Anthropology, University of Rochester, 1976.

BATRES, LEOPOLDO
  1889 *Teotihuacan or the Sacred City of the Toltecs.* Monographs of Mexican Archaeology, Mexico, D.F.
  1906 *Teotihuacan.* Fidencio S. Soria, Mexico, D.F.
  1912 Discubrimientos y consolidación de los monumentos arqueológicos de Teotihuacan. *Proceedings of the 18th International Congress of Americanists:* 188–193. London.

BERLO, JANET CATHERINE
  1982 Artistic Specialization at Teotihuacan: The Ceramic Incense Burner. In *Pre-Columbian Art History: Selected Readings* (Alana Cordy-Collins, ed.): 83–100. Peek Publications, Palo Alto.
  1983 The Warrior and the Butterfly: Central Mexican Ideologies of Sacred Warfare and Teotihuacan Iconography. In *Text and Image in Pre-Columbian Art* (J. C. Berlo, ed.): 79–117. BAR International Series 180, Oxford.
  1984 *Teotihuacan Art Abroad: A Study of Metropolitan Style and Provincial Transformation in Incensario Workshops.* BAR International Series 199, Oxford.
  1989 Early Writing in Central Mexico: *In Tlilli, In Tlapalli* before A.D. 1000. In *Mesoamerica after the Decline of Teotihuacan* (Richard A. Diehl and Janet Catherine Berlo, eds.): 19–47. Dumbarton Oaks, Washington, D.C.

BERNAL, IGNACIO (ED.)
  1963 *Teotihuacan: Descubrimientos, reconstrucciones.* Instituto Nacional de Antropología e Historia, Mexico, D.F.

BERRIN, KATHLEEN (ED.)
  1988 *Feathered Serpents and Flowering Trees: Reconstructing the Murals of Teotihuacan.* The Fine Arts Museums of San Francisco.

CABRERA CASTRO, RUBÉN, IGNACIO RODRIGUEZ, and NOEL MORELOS (EDS.)
  1982a Memoria del Proyecto Arqueológico Teotihuacan 80–82. *Colección Científica* 132. Instituto Nacional de Antropología e Historia, Mexico, D.F.
  1982b *Teotihuacan 80–82: Primeros resultados.* Instituto Nacional de Antropología e Historia, Mexico, D.F.

CALNEK, EDWARD
  1982 Patterns of Empire Formation in the Valley of Mexico, Late Postclassic Period, 1200–1521. In *The Inca and Aztec States 1400–1800* (G. A. Collier, R. I. Rosaldo, and J. D. Wirth, eds.): 43–62. Academic Press, New York.

CARRASCO, DAVID
  1990 *Religions of Mesoamerica.* Harper and Row, New York.

CARRASCO, PEDRO
  1971 The People of Central Mexico and Their Historical Traditions. In *The Handbook of Middle American Indians* 11 (R. Wauchope, G. F. Ekholm, and I. Bernal, eds.): 459–473. University of Texas Press, Austin.

CASO, ALFONSO
  1939 Tenían los Teotihuacanos conocimiento del Tonalpohualli? *El Mexico Antiguo* 4: 131–144.
  1958–59 Glifos teotihuacanos. *Revista Mexicana de Estudios Antropológicos* 15: 51–70.

CASTILLO, FARRERAS, VICTOR M.
  1969 Caminos del mundo Nahuatl. *Estudios de Cultura Nahuatl* 8: 175–187.

CHANDLER, TERTIUS, AND GERALD FOX
  1974 *3,000 Years of Urban Growth.* Academic Press, New York.

CHARNAY, DÉSIRÉ
  1887 *The Ancient Cities of the New World.* Chapman and Hall, London.

COWGILL, GEORGE
  1983 Rulership and the Ciudadela: Political Inferences from Teotihuacan Architecture. In *Civilization in the Ancient Americas* (R. M. Leventhal and A. L. Kolata, eds.): 313–343. University of New Mexico Press, Albuquerque.

DIEHL, RICHARD, AND JANET C. BERLO (EDS.)
  1989 *Mesoamerica after the Decline of Teotihuacan: A.D. 700–900.* Dumbarton Oaks, Washington, D.C.

DURÁN, FRAY DIEGO
  1964 *The Aztecs: The History of the Indies of New Spain* (D. Heyden and F. Horcasitas, trans. and annot.). Orion, New York.

EVANS, SUSAN T., AND ANNCORINNE FRETER
  n.d. Hydration Analysis of Obsidian from Cihuatecpan, an Aztec Period Village in Mexico. Paper presented at the meeting of the Society for American Archaeology, Atlanta, 1989.

Teotihuacan: An Introduction

FLANNERY, KENT V.
    1971   Archaeological Systems Theory and Early Mesoamerica. In *Prehistoric Agriculture* (S. Struever, ed.): 80–100. Natural History Press, Garden City, N.Y.

GAMIO, MANUEL
    1922   *La población del Valle de Teotihuacan*, 3 vols. Mexico (repr. 1979 with an intro. by Eduardo Matos Moctezuma, Instituto Nacional Indigenista, Mexico, D.F.).

HALL, CLARA, (cf. CLARA MILLON)
    n.d.   A Chronological Study of the Mural Art of Teotihuacan. Ph.D. dissertation, Dept. of Anthropology, University of California, Berkeley, 1962.

HARDOY, JORGE
    1964   *Ciudades Precolombinas*. Ediciones Infinito, Buenos Aires.
    1973   *Precolumbian Cities* (J. Thorne, trans.). Walker, New York.

HEYDEN, DORIS
    1975   An Interpretation of the Cave Underneath the Pyramid of the Sun in Teotihuacan, Mexico. *American Antiquity* 40: 131–147.

HEYDEN, DORIS, AND PAUL GENDROP
    1973   *Pre-Columbian Architecture of Mesoamerica*. Harry N. Abrams, New York.
    1988   *Pre-Columbian Architecture of Mesoamerica*. Electa/Rizzoli, New York.

KUBLER, GEORGE
    1967   *The Iconography of the Art of Teotihuacan*. Studies in Pre-Columbian Art and Archaeology 4, Dumbarton Oaks, Washington, D.C.
    1973   Science and Humanism Among Americanists. In *The Iconography of Middle American Sculpture*: 163–167. Metropolitan Museum of Art, New York.

LANGLEY, JAMES C.
    1986   *Symbolic Notation of Teotihuacan: Elements of Writing in a Mesoamerican Culture of the Classic Period*. BAR International Series 313, Oxford.

LINNÉ, SIGVALD
    1934   *Archaeological Researches at Teotihuacan, Mexico*. Ethnographic Museum of Sweden Pub. 1. Stockholm.
    1942   *Mexican Highland Cultures*. Ethnographic Museum of Sweden Pub. 7. Stockholm.

LÓPEZ AUSTIN, ALFREDO
    1967   Terminos de nahuallatolli. *Historia Mexicana* 17 (1): 1–36.
    1984   *Cuerpo Humano e Ideologia*, 2 vols. Instituto de Investigaciones Antropológicas, Universidad Nacional Autónoma de México, Mexico, D.F.

LÓPEZ AUSTIN, ALFREDO, LEONARDO LÓPEZ LUJÁN, AND SABURO SUGIYAMA
    1991   The Temple of Quetzalcoatl at Teotihuacan: Its Possible Ideological Significance. *Ancient Mesoamerica* 2: 93–105.

McClung de Tapia, Emily, and Evelyn C. Rattray (eds.)
    1987   *Teotihuacan: Nuevos datos, nuevas síntesis, nuevos problemas.* Universidad Nacional Autónoma de México, Mexico, D.F

Miller, Arthur G.
    1973   *The Mural Painting of Teotihuacan.* Dumbarton Oaks, Washington, D.C.

Millon, Clara
    1973   Painting, Writing, and Polity in Teotihuacan, Mexico. *American Antiquity* 38 (3): 294–314.
    1988   A Reexamination of the Teotihuacan Tassel Headdress Insignia. In *Feathered Serpents and Flowering Trees: Reconstructing the Murals of Teotihuacan* (Kathleen Berrin, ed.): 114–134. The Fine Arts Museums of San Francisco.

Millon, René
    1967   Teotihuacan. *Scientific American* 216 (6): 38–48.
    1970   Teotihuacan: Completion of Map of Giant Ancient City in the Valley of Mexico. *Science* 170: 1077–1082.
    1976   Social Relations in Ancient Teotihuacan. In *The Valley of Mexico* (Eric R. Wolf, ed.): 205–248. University of New Mexico Press, Albuquerque.
    1981   Teotihuacan: City, State, and Civilization. In *Handbook of Middle American Indians, Supplement 1: Archaeology* (Victoria R. Bricker and Jeremy A. Sabloff, eds.): 198–243. University of Texas Press, Austin.

Millon, René, Bruce Drewitt, and George Cowgill (eds.)
    1973   *Urbanization at Teotihuacan, Mexico. Vol. 1: The Teotihuacan Map.* University of Texas Press, Austin.

Múnera, Luis Carlos
    n.d.   Un taller de cerámica ritual en la Ciudadela, Teotihuacan. M.A. thesis, Escuela Nacional de Antropología e Historia, Instituto Nacional de Antropología e Historia, Mexico, D.F., 1985.

Nicholson, Henry B.
    1971   Religion in Pre-Hispanic Central Mexico. *Handbook of Middle American Indians* 10 (G. Ekholm and I. Bernal, eds.): 395–446.

Noguera, Eduardo
    1935   Antecedentes y relaciones de la cultura Teotihuacana. *El Mexico Antiguo* 3 (5–8): 3–95.

Nuttall, Zelia
    1926   Official Reports on the Towns of Tequizistlan, Tepechpan, Acolman, and San Juan Teotihuacan Sent by Francisco de Castaneda to His Majesty, Phillip II, and the Council of the Indies, in 1580. *Papers of the Peabody Museum* 11 (2): 45–86. Harvard University, Cambridge.

Panofsky, Erwin
    1939   *Studies in Iconology.* Oxford University Press, Oxford.

Pasztory, Esther
    1972   The Gods of Teotihuacan: A Synthetic Approach in Teotihuacan Ico-

nography. *Atti del XL Congresso Internazionale degli Americanisti* 1: 147–159. Rome.

1974   *The Iconography of the Teotihucan Tlaloc.* Studies in Pre-Columbian Art and Archaeology 15, Dumbarton Oaks, Washington, D.C.

1976   *The Murals of Tepantitla, Teotihuacan.* Garland Press, New York.

1988   A Reinterpretation of Teotihuacan and Its Mural Painting Tradition. In *Feathered Serpents and Flowering Trees: Reconstructing the Murals of Teotihuacan* (Kathleen Berrin, ed.): 45–77. The Fine Arts Museums of San Francisco.

1989   Identity and Difference: The Uses and Meanings of Ethnic Styles. In *Cultural Differentiation and Cultural Identity in the Visual Arts* (Susan J. Barnes and Walter Melion, eds.): 15–38. Studies in the History of Art 27, Center for Advanced Studies in the Visual Arts. National Gallery of Art, Washington, D.C.

n.d.   An Image is Worth a Thousand Words: Teotihuacan and the Meaning of Style in Classic Mesoamerica. In *Latin American Horizons* (Don Stephen Rice, ed.), Dumbarton Oaks, Washington, D.C. (in press).

PEÑAFIEL, ANTONIO

1900   *Teotihuacan: Estudio histórico y arqueológico.* Mexico, D.F.

RUIZ DE ALARCÓN, HERNANDO

1984   *Treatise on the Heathen Superstitions and Customs That Today Live among the Indians Native to This New Spain, 1629* (J. Richard Andrews and Ross Hassig, trans. and ed.). University of Oklahoma Press, Norman.

SANDERS, WILLIAM T.

1965   *The Cultural Ecology of the Teotihuacan Valley.* Mimeo distributed by the Department of Sociology and Anthropology, The Pennsylvania State University. University Park.

1981   Ecological Adaptation in the Basin of Mexico: 23,000 B.C. to the Present. In *Supplement to the Handbook of Middle American Indians* 1 (V. Bricker and J. Sabloff, eds.): 147–197. University of Texas Press, Austin.

SANDERS, WILLIAM T., JEFFREY R. PARSONS, AND ROBERT SANTLEY

1979   *The Basin of Mexico.* Academic Press, New York.

SANDERS, WILLIAM T., AND BARBARA PRICE

1968   *Mesoamerica.* Random House, New York.

SÉJOURNÉ, LAURETTE

1959   *Un palacio en la ciudad de los dioses.* Instituto Nacional de Antropología e Historia, Mexico, D.F.

1966   *Arquitectura y pintura en Teotihuacan.* Siglo XXI Editores, Mexico, D.F.

SELER, EDUARD

1915   Die Teotiuacan-Kultur des Hochlands von Mexiko. In *Gesammelte Abhandlungen zur Amerikanischen Sprach- und Altertumskunde* 5: 405–585. Behrend, Berlin.

SEMPOWSKI, MARTHA

n.d.   Mortuary Practices at Teotihuacan, Mexico: Their Implications for

Social Status. Ph.D. dissertation, Dept. of Anthropology, University of Rochester, 1983.

SOCIEDAD MEXICANA DE ANTROPOLOGÍA
1966, 1972   *Teotihuacan XI Mesa Redonda*, 2 vols., 1966, 1972. Mexico.

SMITH, MICHAEL E.
1984   The Aztlan Migrations of the Nahuatl Chronicles: Myth or History? *Ethnohistory* 31: 153–186.

SPENCE, MICHAEL W.
1974   Residential Practices and the Distribution of Skeletal Traits in Teotihuacan. *Man* n.s. 9 (3): 262–272.
1981   Obsidian Production and the State in Teotihuacan. *American Antiquity* 46 (4): 769–788.

SUGIYAMA, SABURO
1989   Burials Dedicated to the Old Temple of Quetzalcoatl at Teotihuacan, Mexico. *American Antiquity* 54 (1): 85–106.

TAUBE, KARL A.
1983   The Teotihuacan Spider Woman. *Journal of Latin American Lore* 9 (2): 107–189.
1986   The Teotihuacan Cave of Origin. *Res: Anthropology and Aesthetics* 12: 51–82.

TOWNSEND, RICHARD F.
1979   *State and Cosmos in the Art of Tenochtitlan*. Studies in Pre-Columbian Art and Archaeology 20. Dumbarton Oaks, Washington, D.C.

TURNER, MARGARET
n.d.   The Lapidary Industry of Teotihuacan, Mexico. Ph.D. dissertation, Dept. of Anthropology, University of Rochester, 1988.

VAILLANT, GEORGE C.
1938   A Correlation of Archaeological and Historical Sequences in the Valley of Mexico. *American Anthropologist* n.s. 40: 535–573.

VILLAGRA CALETI, AGUSTÍN
1951   Las pinturas de Atetelco en Teotihuacan. *Cuadernos Americanos* 55 (1): 153–162.
1971   Mural Painting in Central Mexico. In *Handbook of Middle American Indians* 10 (Robert Wauchope, ed.): 135–156. University of Texas Press, Austin.

VON WINNING, HASSO
1987   *La iconografía de Teotihuacan: Los dioses y los signos*, 2 vols. Universidad Nacional Autónoma de México, Mexico, D.F.

WALLRATH, MATTHEW
1966   The Calle de los Muertos Complex: A Possible Macrocomplex of Structures near the Center of Teotihuacan. In *Teotihuacan, Onceava Mesa Redonda* 1. Sociedad Mexicana de Antropología, Mexico, D.F.

WOLF, ERIC R.
1976   Introduction. In *The Valley of Mexico* (E. R. Wolf, ed.): 1–10. University of New Mexico Press, Albuquerque.

Economic and Social Implications of Variations in Mortuary Practices at Teotihuacan

MARTHA L. SEMPOWSKI

ROCHESTER MUSEUM AND SCIENCE CENTER

INTRODUCTION

AT ITS HEIGHT, TEOTIHUACAN was a powerful state with activities extending as far south as the Maya region in present-day Guatemala and north and west as far as the present state of Zacatecas. However, the specific character of those interactions—economic and/or political—in particular regions of Mesoamerica is not as clearly defined. Whatever the nature of Teotihuacan's external relations, they apparently provided a basis for the control of certain desired goods such as green obsidian and Thin Orange ware from relatively nearby, as well as for the acquisition of exotic items such as jade, marine shell, mica, rubber, cacao, copal, tropical skins and feathers, and cotton cloth from more distant sources. William Sanders and Robert Santley (1983) maintain that the latter represented "low consumption, limited use" goods that could be readily transported over long distances. They suggest that these goods constituted part of a long distance exchange network that was at least overseen if not controlled by the Teotihuacan state, and in which obsidian trade played a leading role (Sanders and Santley 1983: 266–267, 290). Within the city and its immediate hinterland, the state is thought to have exerted some measure of direct control over certain types of craft production such as obsidian, jade, and shell working (Spence 1981; Turner n.d.), and it seems likely that the production of some highly decorated ceramics may have been subject to a similar level of control.

There is a growing body of evidence pointing to deterioration in this complex system of external relations commencing as early as A.D. 500 and of problems in the domestic economy during the last century before the city's collapse (A.D. 650–750). To begin to understand the decline of Teotihuacan as a great economic power, we need to refine our understanding of the nature of the goods and materials involved in these processes of production and exchange, patterns of their use by Teotihuacanos, and the extent of their accessibility to various segments of the population at different times in the city's history.

Mortuary evidence is particularly relevant to these issues because many of the exotic goods acquired through Teotihuacan's international exchange network, as well as many locally produced "luxury goods," were destined for use as grave offerings and, unlike materials obtained through surface survey, often can be accurately dated through association with ceramics. Further, such goods can be evaluated as components of grave offerings of varying complexity and associated with individuals of identifiable age, sex, and group membership, thereby allowing inferences regarding their use by groups of varying status within the society.

The objective here is to examine the use and distribution of "luxury goods" in burial groupings during consecutive periods in the city's history and to present evidence for some apparent disjunctions in the pattern of artifact use, particularly of these "luxury goods," during the Metepec period (A.D. 650–750). The implications of these discontinuities are then reconsidered in light of other, independent information regarding Teotihuacan's economy during its final years.

What follows, then, is: (1) a brief overview of mortuary practices at Teotihuacan; (2) a discussion of the quantitative methods used in measuring the relative complexity of associated grave assemblages; (3) the identification of various types of grave inclusions as "luxury goods" during each period, on the basis of their consistent association with the most complex burial offerings; (4) a summary of evidence suggesting alterations in the use and distribution of these presumed "luxury goods" during the Metepec phase; and (5) a discussion of the import of these Metepec phase disjunctions in mortuary behavior in light of other findings regarding Teotihuacan's economy and polity.

MORTUARY PRACTICES AT TEOTIHUACAN

Overview

The summary of Teotihuacan burial practices that follows is drawn from a recent reanalysis for publication of a study of nearly 400 previously excavated burials from Teotihuacan, which provided the basis for a comprehensive survey of mortuary practices at Teotihuacan (Sempowski n.d.a, n.d.b). (Please consult the aforementioned sources for data on specific burial practices and methods of analysis.) The survey is based upon the widest body of data available at the time of the original study in 1978–82. However, a nearly equivalent number of burials have since been excavated from varying contexts in Teotihuacan, and it is hoped that information relating to these additional burials might eventually be incorporated into the existing database.[1]

The vast majority of the burials studied relate to the Middle Horizon, and all but a small number are considered to be interments of "intermediate status" individuals who were buried in apartment compounds located outside the city's center (cf. Evans and Berlo, this volume, fig. 3) (see discussion of status interpretations below). Exceptions include three burials from residential compounds located adjacent to the Street of the Dead, which are interpreted as the residences of individuals of somewhat higher social status, and twenty-seven burials located in public or non-residential structures, including the Pyramid of the Sun (1:N3E1) and the Temple of Quetzalcoatl (1:N1E1),[2] the two most important ceremonial structures in the city. Most of these pyramid burials are interpreted as dedicatory or sacrificial in nature, a conclusion supported by the recent discoveries of multiple primary interments of young adult males with tied hands, arranged in symmetrical fashion around and within the pyramid base of the Temple of Quetzalcoatl (see note 1) (Sugiyama 1989; Mercado Rojano 1987). Only five of the burials in this study seem to qualify, by virtue of their location and the elaborateness of the offerings with them, as possible interments of the truly elite at Teotihuacan. All five are associated with the Temple of Quetzalcoatl and its *adosada,* and each contains the secondarily deposited remains of one or two individuals.

For the majority of the burials studied, however, their context in apartment compounds away from the "Street of the Dead" suggests that they represent interments of "intermediate status" residents of the city, a broad classification divisible into at least three internal status levels, as defined by René Millon (1976: 227; 1981: 214). Within this intermediate level of society, it must be recognized that we are limited to an inherently biased sample of burials—those of individuals who were intentionally buried beneath the

---

[1] These additional excavations include 68 burials uncovered by Randolph Widmer and Rebecca Storey in a residential compound (33:S3W1) in the Tlajinga region of the city (Storey and Widmer 1982); 180 burials excavated in 1980 and 1981 by INAH personnel associated with the Proyecto Arquelógico Teotihuacano, from several locations close to the Street of the Dead (Gonzales Miranda and Gonzales 1982); at least 4 burials excavated in 1983 by Evelyn Rattray in the Tlamimilolpa compound (1:N4E4) (Rattray n.d.); an undetermined number of burials that Rattray excavated in 1984 in the Merchants' Barrio (Square N4E4) that are described by her as indicating atypical burial practices (Rattray n.d.: 75); and approximately 80 burials excavated by Saburo Sugiyama, Enrique Martinez, and George Cowgill on the north, south, and east sides and in a tunnel penetrating the south side of the Temple of Quetzalcoatl (Sugiyama 1989; Mercado Rojano 1987; Cowgill, personal communication to René Millon).

[2] These and subsequent references of this kind are to the locations of structures and other places on the Teotihuacan Map (see Evans and Berlo, this volume, fig. 3) (Millon, Drewitt, and Cowgill 1973).

floors of their homes, and whose interments, for whatever reasons, have been sufficiently well preserved to be discovered in excavation. This is based on the observation that the number of burials in excavated apartment compounds never approaches the total number of residents estimated to have occupied the building during its several centuries of use. It may be that specialized practices such as cremation and secondary deposition result in some interments being overlooked because their traces are more difficult to detect due to the fragmentary state of the remains or to partial or nearly complete removal. A second possibility is that residential interment may have been inappropriate for some members of an apartment compound group. Survey data gathered by the Teotihuacan Mapping Project indicate several special crematory or cemetery areas (24, 29, 31, 32:N4W3) that could account for the disposal of many of the city's deceased (Spence n.d.). Finally, Rebecca Storey (1987) has proposed another possible explanation based on the discovery of significant quantities of human skeletal material in redeposited fill in an apartment compound that she and Randolph Widmer excavated. She suggests that during the course of compound reconstruction or digging of burial pits, previous, long-forgotten burials may often have been encountered and the skeletal remains then discarded with refuse or used in building fill.

Therefore, unlike the situation in other parts of Mesoamerica, most burial data from Teotihuacan relate to persons of intermediate status, whose remains were interred in their houses and happen to have been well preserved. Nevertheless, it is possible to identify a considerable range of variation in the burial treatment afforded different individuals.

Age (adult versus sub-adult) appears to have been a significant factor in determining differential practices, especially regarding various aspects of body treatment. Newborns and fetuses, the age group receiving the most distinctive form of treatment, were often placed in ceramic vessels and buried in walls or altars; they rarely, if ever, were cremated, wrapped in textiles, or disinterred for reburial. Special offertory or dedicatory rites often appear to have accompanied such burials.

Residential group membership also seems to have been a critical differentiating factor, and it is clear that the ethnically and socially diverse populace of Teotihuacan was relatively free to maintain its own burial customs throughout centuries of residence in the city. This is best exemplified in the Oaxaca *barrio,* which exhibits a curious mixture of "Oaxacan-style" and Teotihuacan burial practices, involving multiple burials in stone-lined chambers, a high incidence of secondary skeletal manipulation and pigment usage, and the use of Oaxacan ceramics along with Teotihuacan wares in grave offerings (Spence, this volume). Such differentiation in group burial practices is indicated in other compounds throughout the city, albeit to a less obvious degree. Attempts to characterize Teotihuacan burial practices, therefore,

Variations in Mortuary Practices

necessitate some generalizations regarding the rich potpourri of mortuary treatment evident in the city.

The vast majority of Teotihuacan interments were in simple unlined pits under the concrete floors of the rooms and patios of residential structures. A few burials involved more elaborate construction of a grave chamber and, in some cases, appear to have accompanied the construction of the building itself, perhaps as "founders' burials." Approximately two-thirds of the burials studied were primary interments, while the remainder involved some form of post-burial treatment or redeposition. Frequently, but not always, secondary deposition of the remains was in double or multiple burial contexts. Skulls were occasionally removed for isolated burial or specialized treatment, but more frequently redeposition included an array of cranial and post-cranial remains. Skeletal remains were often painted with a reddish mineral pigment, such as cinnabar, as part of this post-burial procedure. A few undisturbed primary interments also show traces of pigment, suggesting that pigments were occasionally applied to body wrappings and were thus deposited on the bones as flesh and wrappings decayed. Overall, multiple interments account for just over one-third of the individuals under study, making single, primary, under-the-floor burial the most common mode of interment among undisturbed burials at Teotihuacan.

Flexed burials represent the norm at Teotihuacan (95.1% of all individuals) and include several variants: vertical flexed or seated, lateral flexed on either side, dorsal flexed, and ventral flexed (Figs. 1, 2). More than one-half of all adults were in a tightly flexed, upright or seated position, while the dorsal flexed arrangement seems to have been most common for immature individuals. Textiles were wrapped around the bodies of a number of adults (especially those buried during the Tlamimilolpa phase), perhaps to maintain the tightly flexed position. The predominant pattern of body orientation for vertical or lateral flexed burials was to the east and in a generally east-west direction for bodies in a dorsal or ventral position. For adults, the easterly orientation seems to have been followed with greatest regularity when the body was in the vertical flexed position, but it was also generally adhered to when the body was on either the left or right side. Sub-adults in the dorsal flexed position were most frequently headed to the east, although the orientation of sub-adult burials seems to have been subject to greater variability than it was for adults.

Slightly fewer than one-half of the 171 individuals actually examined showed evidence of some degree of exposure to fire. This ranges from complete cremation in which the bones are calcined and substantially reduced (Level I) to the barest traces of a blackened residue thought to result from moderate exposure to fire (Level IV). At all levels of exposure, it seems to have been a practice associated predominantly with adults, and it was more common in certain apartment compounds than in others. Cases of intense

Fig. 1 La Ventilla B Burial 66 (Index 228 LVB 66) showing skeleton in vertical flexed position, surrounded by associated grave goods. Late Tlamimilolpa phase. Photo by Juan Vidarte.

Fig. 2 La Ventilla B Burial XX (Index 297 LVB XX) showing skeleton in lateral flexed position, surrounded by associated grave goods. Late Tlamimilolpa phase. Photo by Juan Vidarte.

Variations in Mortuary Practices

Level I and Level II exposure indicated by charring and calcining are rare, involving only nine individuals. Most instances relate to Level III and Level IV exposure, which involves more equivocal evidence of burning. However, the consistency of the pattern of discoloration, particularly in terms of the affected areas of the skeleton, and the occasional association of these indicators with more direct evidence of burning (charcoal and charred textiles or artifacts) suggest that the custom of exposing the corpse to a small fire situated in front of the body may have been fairly typical at Teotihuacan.

No feature of Teotihuacan mortuary practice exhibits greater variability than the material offerings that accompanied the burials. Because of inconsistencies in excavation and reporting techniques, it is impossible to ascertain the exact proportion of burials associated with artifacts. However, in La Ventilla B, where excavation procedures were relatively uniform, approximately 70% of the burials were reported to have included artifacts. How accurately that figure reflects the frequency of this practice in other locations is, of course, uncertain.

Nevertheless, an analysis of the material goods associated with a total of 280 burials allows some generalizations regarding the nature of these assemblages and permits comparisons based on the relative complexity of individual grave offerings. Some of these offerings contained hundreds of objects of different types and materials, while others were extremely simple. Ceramic vessels, ranging from highly decorated cylindrical tripods to crude unfired miniatures, represent the most common category of grave inclusion, occurring in more than 80% of the burials. Obsidian artifacts, although far less prevalent than ceramics, occurred in more than 25% of the burials. Worked and unworked marine shell, including *Spondylus* and unidentified conchs from the Pacific, as well as a number of Atlantic varieties, was found in approximately 18% of the burials. As many as 15% of the burials included another exotic imported material—mica—while jadeite, the material so highly prized throughout Pre-Columbian Mesoamerica was reported in about 5% of the burials studied. Diatomaceous earth or ceramic figurines were found in about 15% of graves, and objects of slate, pyrite, and hematite in about the same number. Unmodified faunal remains occurred in approximately 10% of burials, and artifacts of worked bone and teeth in another 6%. Objects of ground and chipped stone, other than those mentioned above, were relatively rare in burials (less than 10%), but included artifacts of *tezontli,* alabaster, onyx, chert, sandstone, and other unidentified lithic materials.

Methods of Analysis

Further analysis beyond a general description of mortuary practices at Teotihuacan requires that comparisons be made between specific burials; the relative complexity of associated grave offerings was selected as the basis for such comparisons. Since the number of burials and the unwieldy variety in the size and contents of the offerings precluded impressionistic assessments of relative complexity, a standard quantitative method was adopted to provide a consistent basis for evaluation. It consisted of measuring the Quantity, the Diversity, and the Quality of the grave offering; standardizing the raw scores; and combining those scores into a standardized, composite *Offering Complexity* score.

Quantity was calculated on the basis of a raw count of 1 for each full-sized artifact in the grave and weighted partial counts for miniature vessels or other items (such as clay cylinders) that normally occur in very large quantities. The raw Diversity score was based on a count of 1 for each different type of object in the offering, while the Quality score again involved a weighted system based on the "exoticness" of the material used and/or degree of craftsmanship involved in the decoration or production of the item. These three raw scores were then standardized to allow their combination. The resulting composite score is considered to approximate more closely a conception of the overall complexity of an offering than would any one of the component scores individually.

Only those burials that could be assigned to one of the three broad periods of the Middle Horizon—the Tlamimilolpa, the Xolalpan, or the Metepec phase—were included in the quantitatively based comparisons. The result was a total of 162 residential burials that could be both quantified and assigned to a particular phase.[3] Sets of comparisons were then made between chronological periods and between burials of individuals of different age, sex, and residential location within each phase. It should be noted, however, that since the data employed in this study do not meet the most elementary requirements for the use of inferential statistics (i.e., randomly drawn and normally distributed samples), results are reported only descriptively, and no claims are made for their statistical significance.

Four offering categories (High, Intermediate, Low, and Very Low) were defined on the basis of Offering Complexity (all were within a general context of intermediate-status burials, see above). These categories, in turn, provided the structure for a qualitative analysis of the burial offerings from each phase. It is clear that no simple, direct inference can be drawn, regarding the relationship between grave offering complexity and social status. However, it would be equally unwise to deny the possibility that any such relationship exists. Therefore, it seems useful at this point to infer a tentative relationship between relative social status and relative grave offering complexity. It may be worth noting that such a relationship appears to be reflected qualitatively in the consistent occurrence of specific types of "luxury goods" in the relatively more complex offerings, as discussed below.

[3] Data on six additional Tlamimilolpa phase burials from ceremonial structures were also quantified, but were analyzed separately from the residential burials.

Variations in Mortuary Practices

Quantitative Differences between Phases and Residential Groups

Of particular relevance to this presentation are the quantitative comparisons between time periods and between residential groups. Table 1 shows mean and median composite Offering Complexity scores for each phase. It indicates a slight increase in complexity from the Tlamimilolpa phase to the Xolalpan phase and a subsequent decrease during the Metepec phase. The mean scores for burials from three apartment compounds (Tetitla 2:N3W2; Zacuala Patios 2:N2W2; and La Ventilla B 1:S1W3) are illustrated in Fig. 3. They suggest a rank ordering of the three compounds in terms of grave offering complexity and possible inferences regarding relative social status. Tetitla would be at the top of this relative order, Zacuala Patios in the middle, and La Ventilla B at the bottom.

TABLE 1. COMPOSITE OFFERING COMPLEXITY SCORES—STATISTICAL SUMMARY

Phase	n	Mean	Median
Tlamimilolpa (A.D. 200–450)	61	28.73	24.68
Xolalpan (A.D. 450–650)	72	32.82	26.84
Metepec (A.D. 650–750)	29	27.14	22.84

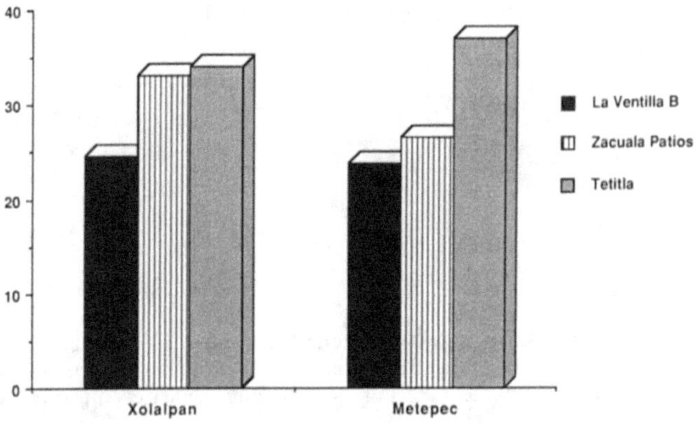

Fig. 3 Mean composite Offering Complexity scores in Xolalpan and Metepec phases for three residential compounds: La Ventilla B (1:S1W3), Zacuala Patios (2:N2W2), and Tetitla (1:N2W2).

Artifacts and Materials Associated with High Complexity Offerings

Also of interest for each phase is the identification of the goods and materials most frequently associated with the most complex offerings (i.e., the high end of the Complexity scale). Obviously, because the full range of grave offerings made at Teotihuacan has not survived, this list must be seen as representing only the first step in identifying what constituted "luxury goods" for this broad grouping of people of intermediate status.

Tlamimilolpa Phase. During the Tlamimilolpa phase, items of personal adornment were more frequently associated with offerings in the High Complexity category, but it was the material used in making these objects that was most critical. Jadeite was found only in burials designated as High Complexity; and although marine shell objects were found in much higher frequency in this group, they were not restricted to it. Large, direct-rim cylindrical tripods also showed exclusive association with the most complex group (e.g., see Linné 1942, figs. 198, 201; Noguera 1955, fig. 3). No "Tlaloc" vases were found in any of the residential burials studied from this phase.[4] *Copas,* amphoras, *floreros,* and small everted rim tripods (see Figs. 4, 5) seemed somewhat restricted in their association with High and Intermediate Complexity burials. Obsidian, painted slate, and diatomaceous earth figurines also occurred more frequently in graves of High and Intermediate Complexity. Mica and Thin Orange wares, however, occurred across the spectrum. The High Complexity category for the Tlamimilolpa phase includes burials from both Early and Late sub-phases and from compounds such as La Ventilla B (1:S1W3) and Tlamimilolpa (1:N4E4), which have been judged on architectural grounds and on later comparisons of burial offerings to be of relatively low intermediate status. Table 2 provides a tally of the goods and materials showing the most exclusive association with the High Complexity group of Tlamimilolpa phase burials. It should be noted that an Early and a Late sub-phase burial from La Ventilla B and a Late sub-phase burial from the Tlamimilolpa compound contained jade and shell (including *Spondylus* shell in one of them), as well as many of the more elaborate types of ceramic vessels described above.

---

[4] "Tlaloc" vases were found in some highly complex Tlamimilolpa phase burials in the Ciudadela, burials of individuals who would have been of high status in Teotihuacan society in contrast to the burials of the individuals under examination here.

Variations in Mortuary Practices

Fig. 4 (a) Dark brown polished *florero* from La Ventilla B Burial 110 (Index 272 LVB 110, Early Tlamimilolpa Phase; (b) polished black amphora from La Ventilla B Burial 100 (Index 262 LVB 100), Early Tlamimilolpa Phase; (c) polished yellow-brown spouted *copa* from Sitio 57, Burial 8 (Index 068 Sit 57-8), Late Tlamimilolpa phase. All vessels in Museo Nacional de Antropología. Photo courtesy of the Teotihuacan Mapping Project.

Fig. 5 Small everted rim tripod with incised decoration from La Ventilla B Burial III (Index 281 LVB IIIa-c), Early Tlamimilolpa phase. Museo Nacional de Antropología. Photo courtesy of the Teotihuacan Mapping Project.

TABLE 2. INCIDENCE OF SELECTED LUXURY GOODS IN HIGH COMPLEXITY BURIALS—TLAMIMILOLPA PHASE

	Jade	Shell	Mica	Large Cyl. Tripod	Small Ev. Rim Tripod	Copa, Amphora, or Florero	Ptd. Slate	Thin Orange	Diat. Earth	Obsidian
040 Tlam 1 (Late)	✓	✓	✓	✓	✓	✓	✓	—	✓	✓
063 Nog 1 (Late)	—	✓	—	✓	—	✓	—	—	—	—
165 LVB 3 (Late)	—	✓	—	✓	✓	✓	✓	✓	✓	✓
172 LVB 10 (Late)	—	—	—	—	—	✓	—	—	—	✓
183 LVB 21 (Early)	✓	✓	?	✓	✓	✓	—	—	—	✓
228 LVB 66 (Late)	✓	✓	✓	✓	✓	✓	—	—	—	✓
281 LVB IIIa–c (Early)	—	—	—	—	✓	✓	✓	✓	✓	—
295 LVB XVIII (Early)	—	—	—	—	—	✓	—	—	—	✓

Key to Burial Index Abbreviations
Tlam = Tlamimilolpa 1:N_4E_4
LVB = La Ventilla B 1:S_1W_3
Nog = Noguera excavation 1955 N_2E_1

Xolalpan Phase. During the Xolalpan phase, personal ornaments of jade continued to show exclusive association with the High Complexity group, and marine shell was also more common in that group. Three types of ceramics were uniquely associated with the most complex category—cylindrical tripods decorated by stucco-painting (Fig. 6), cylindrical tripods decorated by the plano-relief technique (Fig. 7), and "Tlaloc" vases (Fig. 8). *Floreros* were only slightly less exclusive to this group. Figurines of all types (ceramic, obsidian, and shell) were most commonly associated with more complex offerings. Interestingly, mica, which did not show any particular pattern of exclusivity in the preceding phase, seems to show it now. And although the frequency of Thin Orange vessels (Fig. 9) and obsidian artifacts is higher in offerings of greater complexity, it is important to note that they appear in offerings of all four categories. No differences could be detected between the Early and Late Xolalpan phases in terms of the overall distribution or frequency of these goods. Table 3 provides a summary of the occurrence of those artifacts most exclusively associated with High Complexity Xolalpan phase burials. Again, it should be noted that highly complex burial offerings that included jade, shell, mica, and the decorated ceramics described above occurred across a range of apartment compounds occupied by people of intermediate status—La Ventilla B, Tlamimilolpa, Yayahuala, Zacuala Patios, Zacuala Palace, and Tetitla.

Metepec Phase. During the Metepec phase, objects of personal ornamentation continued to be associated with the most complex offerings, but they were no longer of jade. Shell (including some identified as *Spondylus*) appears to have replaced it, and seems to have become even more exclusive in its association with High Complexity offerings than it had been earlier. Mica and obsidian also showed an increasing association with offerings of greater complexity, and overall, obsidian occurred much less frequently than during earlier periods. "Tlaloc" vases continued to be restricted to the High Complexity burials. No stucco-painted tripods were found in any Metepec burials, and tripods decorated by true and pseudo "plano-relief" (Fig. 10) are confined mainly to the most complex group, although a few crude examples are found in less complex offerings. Overall, the frequency and variety of Thin Orange ware declined, and while it occurred more commonly in the high group, it was found even in some Low Complexity offerings. Another noteworthy phenomenon is that the most typical, traditional Thin Orange ceramic form, the ring base hemispherical bowl, now also appears in a "local" clay (Fig. 11). Several new forms of ceramic objects (palettes, masks, and maskettes) occur in this phase and are associated with the more complex offerings. Table 4 tallies the occurrence of the Metepec phase artifacts showing the highest degree of exclusivity with the High Complexity grouping.

Fig. 6 Stucco-painted cylindrical tripod and lid, showing representation of the "Storm God." Provenance unknown. Photo courtesy of Dumbarton Oaks, Washington D.C.

Fig. 7 Plano-relief decorated cylindrical tripod with representation of "Storm God," wearing "tassel headdress." From Burial 2 at Zacuala Patios (Index 075 Zac 2), Late Xolalpan phase. Museo Nacional de Antropología. Photo courtesy of the Teotihuacan Mapping Project.

Fig. 8 "Tlaloc" vase from Tetitla Burial 9 (Index 114 Tet 9), Late Xolalpan phase. Museo Nacional de Antropología. Photo courtesy of the Teotihuacan Mapping Project.

Fig. 9 Thin Orange ring base hemispherical bowl with incised "S" and punctate design, from Palacio 3. Museo Nacional de Antropología. Photo courtesy of the Teotihuacan Mapping Project.

TABLE 3. INCIDENCE OF SELECTED LUXURY GOODS IN HIGH COMPLEXITY BURIALS—XOLALPAN PHASE

	Jade	Shell	Mica	"Tlaloc" Vase	Stucco-Ptd. Cyl. Tripod	Plano-Rel. Cyl. Tripod	Thin Orange	Copa, Florero	Obsidian	Figurine
041 Tlam 2 (Late)		✓					✓			✓
043 Tlam 4 (Late)		✓							✓	✓
052 Tlam 13 (?)	✓	✓			✓		✓			✓
053 Xol 1 (Early)						✓		✓	✓	✓
054 Xol 2 (Early)				✓		✓				✓
055 Xol 3 (Late)				✓	✓	✓	✓	✓		
056 Xol 4 (Late)			✓			✓	✓			
074 Zac 1 (Late)		✓				✓	✓			
075 Zac 2 (Late)		✓							✓	✓
076 Zac 3 (Late)		✓		✓					✓	✓
084 Zac 11 (Early?)	✓	✓		✓			✓		✓	✓
097 Zac 24 (Late)		✓		✓			✓		✓	
100 ZacPl 27 (Early)		✓	✓	✓			✓		✓	
114 Tet 9 (Late)			✓	✓			✓	✓	✓	
119 Tet 14 (Late)		✓				✓	✓	✓		
121 Tet 16ab (Early)		✓			✓		✓			✓
139 Tet M1 (Late)	✓	✓					✓	✓		✓
141 Yay 4ab (Late)							✓			
157 LVA III 3-5 (Early)		✓	✓							✓
181 LVB 19 (Late)	✓	✓						✓		
350 Oax 66 (Late)		✓							✓	

Key to Burial Index Abbreviations

Tlam = Tlamimilolpa 1:N4E4
Xol = Xolalpan 2:N4E2
Zac = Zacuala Patios 2:N2W2
ZacPl = Zacuala Palace 3:N2W2
Tet = Tetitla 1:N2W2
Yay = Yayahuala 1:N3W2
LVA = La Ventilla A 19:S1W2
LVB = LaVentilla B 1:S1W3
Oax = Oaxaca barrio 7:N1W6

Variations in Mortuary Practices

Fig. 10 Pseudo plano-relief decorated cylindrical tripod from Tetitla Burial 2 (Index 107 Tet 2), Metepec phase. Museo Nacional de Antropología. Photo courtesy of the Teotihuacan Mapping Project.

Fig. 11 Non-Thin Orange ring base hemispherical bowl from La Ventilla B Burial 65 (Index 227 LVB 65), Metepec phase. Museo Nacional de Antropología. Photo courtesy of the Teotihuacan Mapping Project.

TABLE 4. INCIDENCE OF SELECTED LUXURY GOODS IN HIGH COMPLEXITY BURIALS—METEPEC PHASE

	Jade	Shell	Mica	"Tlaloc" Vase	Ceramic Palette	Plano-Rel. Cyl. Tripod	Thin Orange	Obsidian
107 Tet 2	—	✓	✓	✓	✓	✓	—	—
115 Tet 10	—	✓	—	✓	✓	✓	✓	✓
116 Tet 11	—	✓	✓	✓	✓	✓	✓	—
186 LVB 24a–c	—	—	✓	—	—	—	—	—

Key to Burial Index Abbreviations
Tet = Tetitla 1:N2W2
LVB = La Ventilla B 1:S1W3

Variations in Mortuary Practices

Disjunctions Apparent in the Metepec Phase

Drawing together the evidence relating to these three broad chronological phases in Teotihuacan's history, it becomes apparent that crucial changes occurred in the use of "luxury goods" in burials during the Metepec phase, the final century before the demise of the city. Examining burial assemblages from all locations, we see a slight decline in the complexity of grave offerings from the Xolalpan to the Metepec phase; in fact, relatively few Metepec burials fall into the High Complexity category. However, as indicated in Fig. 3, this does not apply equally to each of the three residential groups that were compared. At Tetitla, Offering Complexity actually increased from the Xolalpan to the Metepec phase, while at La Ventilla B, it remained about the same. It is only at Zacuala Patios that a substantial decline is evident. The net effect is a widening gap between the complexity of grave offerings in Tetitla and those in the other two compounds.

In qualitative terms, Metepec phase grave offerings seem markedly impoverished by comparison to those of the preceding Xolalpan phase. Fig. 12 summarizes the frequency of various types of "luxury goods" in all burials

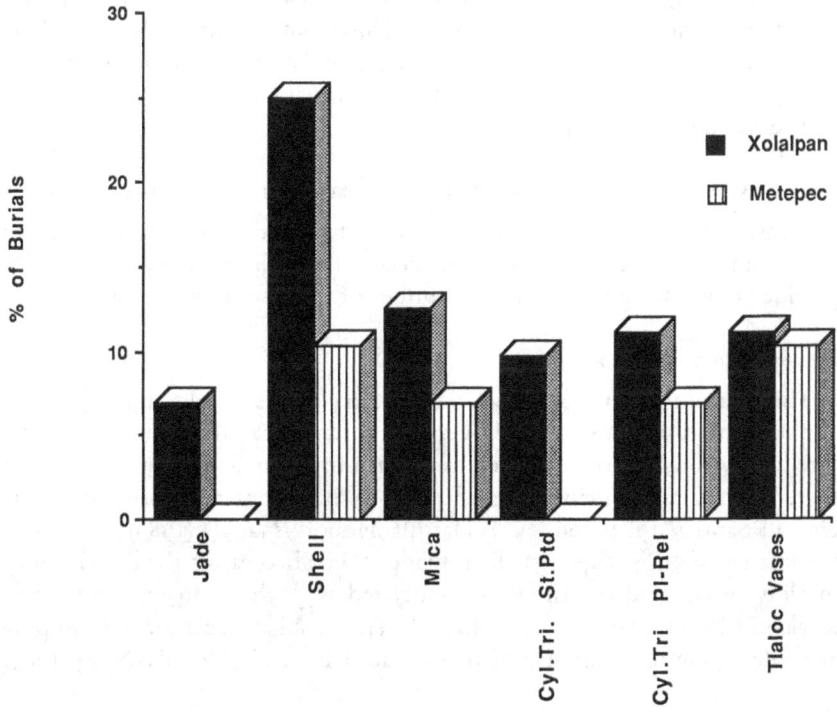

Fig. 12 Frequencies of specific classes of "luxury goods" in burials of the Xolalpan and Metepec phases.

relating to the Xolalpan and Metepec phases, regardless of the complexity grouping into which they fall. Jade, unquestionably the most exclusive of the "luxury goods," did not occur in any of the Metepec phase burials studied.[5] Shell seems to have become much more restricted in its use, occurring only in very simple forms and generally in only the most complex burials from Tetitla (one possible exception occurs in a burial from Zacuala Patios). Mica and obsidian also declined markedly in frequency. Stuccopainted cylindrical tripods did not appear in any of the Metepec phase burials studied. Cylindrical tripods decorated by the plano-relief technique and Tlaloc vases seem to have become not only rarer, but less well crafted. Furthermore, they were found only at Tetitla, not in any of the other compounds studied.

What seems most critical in characterizing the changes in Metepec burial practices in these three compounds is that there appears to be much greater disparity among them in the use of "luxury goods." For example, during earlier periods it was rare, but possible, for a particular individual in a compound occupied by people of relatively low status such as La Ventilla B to be buried with a grave assemblage that approximated the complexity of all but the largest offerings in Tetitla or Zacuala Patios—an offering that might have included even the most exclusive of "luxury goods" such as jade, shell, mica, and decorated ceramics (see Tables 2 and 3). During the Metepec period, that degree of overlap or comparability no longer seems to have existed (see Table 4).

POTENTIAL IMPLICATIONS OF TEMPORAL VARIATIONS IN MORTUARY PRACTICES

Consideration of these conclusions in light of a broader body of evidence concerning Teotihuacan's changing access to both imported and locally produced "luxury goods" raises a number of interesting questions.

Imported Luxury Goods

The assumption has been made that "luxury goods" (including jade, shell, and mica) that were exchanged over long distances in Mesoamerica, constituted "low consumption, limited use" items for a small number of elite, and therefore did not contribute significantly to the urbanization process (Sanders and Santley 1983: 266, 291). Hattula Moholy-Nagy's (1989) analysis of the incidence of *Spondylus* shell and jade at Tikal confirms their exclusivity in elite burials and the offerings associated with them, in that important lowland Maya center. She infers that, "there must have been strong sumptuary rules governing the use of these materials . . ." (Moholy-Nagy 1989:

---

[5] Recent discoveries in the North Palace of the Ciudadela indicate that jade continued to be used by high status residents of this important complex during the city's final days (Jarquin and Martinez 1982: 103, 107 foto 5; Gonzales Miranda and Gonzales 1982: plan ff. 426).

150). Perhaps, therefore, one of the most interesting observations that we can make about Teotihuacan burial practices is that they appear to reflect a quite different situation from that evident among the lowland Maya—one in which the populace at large had much freer access to exotic goods, at least prior to the Metepec phase (A.D. 650–750). Even for those persons of relatively lower intermediate status, such as the occupants of La Ventilla B, goods of imported materials such as jade, *Spondylus* shell, and mica were accessible for the provision of at least a few special burials.[6] One can speculate that a whole range of other types of more perishable "luxury goods" may also have been available to such people. Regardless of the position of these deceased individuals within their own group (and their number must have been considerable throughout the whole of the population), they surely could not have been considered the elite of Teotihuacan society.

This difference is believed to be significant enough to suggest some very fundamental differences between Teotihuacan and Maya societies. It is possible that a more broadly based demand for luxury goods was yet another of the factors that William Sanders (1978: 44) says gave Teotihuacan the "competitive advantage" in the interregional trade network. In any event, the burial data suggest that it was not until around A.D. 650 that accessibility to these goods became more limited, apparently placing them beyond the reach of ordinary Teotihuacanos. From the Early Tlamimilolpa through the Late Xolalpan phases, then, a broad cross-section of the Teotihuacan population seems to have had at least some access to a relatively steady supply of exotic "luxury" items imported through a complex and extensive international trade network.

The apparent continuity of this pattern of accessibility through the Late Xolalpan phase (A.D. 550–650) is also of great interest, in light of evidence that the Teotihuacan "presence" or role in several foreign areas, presumed to have been key nodes in this exchange network, peaked during the fifth century and was severely altered or diminished by A.D. 500–550. For example, it is now widely accepted that the period of most intense contacts between Teotihuacan and the lowland Maya (Tikal, Uaxacatun, and Yaxha) took place during the late fourth and early fifth centuries A.D. (Coggins n.d., 1979; Pasztory 1978; R. Millon 1988; Moholy-Nagy n.d.). Clemency Coggins' interpretation is particularly informative in its implications regarding the potential significance of Teotihuacan's role in that important Maya center during the reigns of Curl Nose and Stormy Sky (A.D. 380–457) (Coggins n.d.: 146–201, 250). Aside from the political and religious implications suggested by this close and apparently sustained relationship, it surely

---

[6] Evidence from Tlajinga 33 (33:S3W1), excavated by Storey and Widmer suggests the availability there of jade and shell (it is uncertain whether any of it is *Spondylus*) prior to the Late Xolalpan phase (Storey and Widmer 1982).

must have carried considerable economic advantages for both sides. To quote Coggins: "Feathers and shells were probably among the most important luxury imports to Teotihuacan from the south; and as was noted earlier, both were worn as personal regalia by Curl Nose and his associates" (Coggins n.d.: 155).

The nature and timing of the Teotihuacan presence in Kaminaljuyu, located in highland Guatemala, remains somewhat controversial, with hypotheses ranging from actual political takeover by representatives of the Teotihuacan state, to a militarily supported "port of trade," to an enclave of Teotihuacan merchants similar to the Aztec *pochteca* (Cheek 1977; Brown 1977; Sanders 1978). Margaret Turner maintains that, "known and proven sources of jadeite are almost exclusively in Guatemala . . . ," and that, "Kaminaljuyu is in close proximity to the Motagua River sources of jadeite and would have been in a perfect position to both exploit and control this valued material" (Turner n.d.: 235–236). She hypothesizes that Teotihuacan may have established a relationship with Kaminaljuyu in order to share in this control. Charles Cheek maintains that the period of most intensive Teotihuacan activities in Kaminaljuyu occurred between A.D. 500 and 550, after which Teotihuacan interests in the area were rather abruptly withdrawn (Cheek 1977: 443, 448–450). However, based on the intermediate role of Kaminaljuyu relative to the Teotihuacan/Tikal connection, René Millon argues that Teotihuacan's most intense contact with Kaminaljuyu must have been at least 100 years earlier than Cheek indicates, or about A.D. 400–450 (Millon 1988: 115).

Several other sites showing evidence of strong Teotihuacan influence lie within an environmental zone labeled the "peripheral coastal lowlands" by Parsons (1978: fig. 1). He maintains that any contacts between the Mexican and Maya areas would have necessitated transmission through this region, and in addition to providing easy access between the Gulf and Pacific coasts, these lowland areas would have offered a rich array of indigenous resources: cacao, cotton, shell, rubber, tropical bird feathers, and jaguar skins (Parsons 1978: 26). The Escuintla region located on the Pacific Guatemalan coast contains several such sites (see Parsons 1969; Berlo 1984), although again there is disagreement as to the timing of the Teotihuacan role there. Janet Berlo (1984: 201) suggests that it dates to A.D. 375–450, while René Millon (1988: 124) argues that it may have continued into the sixth century. Matacapan, on the Gulf coast of Veracruz, has been identified as an important Teotihuacan outpost thought to have served as a base of operations for support of activities in the Maya area (Parsons 1978: 29; R. Millon 1988: 125–126; Santley n.d.). Robert Santley (n.d.) reports that the Matacapan center was established as early as the fourth century, and Teotihuacan's role appears to have diminished in the sixth century (R. Millon 1988: 126).

Contacts between Teotihuacan and the Oaxaca area, with which Teotihuacan maintained a rather unique relationship, apparently took place over a long period of time (Spence, this volume), although Winter notes evidence of some decline in intensity about A.D. 500 (Winter 1979). Regarding Pacific coastal areas, Charles Kolb raises the possibility of several potential routes between Teotihuacan and source areas for Pacific varieties of marine shell found at Teotihuacan, including "Route E" to the coast of Guerrero, which he says represents "the shortest distance to any Pacific coast *Spondylus* source" (Kolb 1987: 119). Further, Florencia Müller (1979) specifically identifies Guerrero as the source of the Pacific marine shell so widely used in Teotihuacan. Although David Starbuck (n.d.: 144, app. V) maintains that "exchange networks" with these Pacific coastal sources of marine shell were disrupted after the "fall" of Teotihuacan (Starbuck n.d.: 144, App.V), the continuity of contact throughout the entire Middle Horizon has not been clarified.

Thus, it appears that the highly visible and influential role that Teotihuacan played throughout a wide area of Mesoamerica during the first part of the Middle Horizon had begun to decline as early as A.D. 450 to 500, and had been widely curtailed by A.D. 550. If the exchange of even some of the "luxury" materials mentioned above were in any way linked to or dependent on the "official" Teotihuacan connection in these regions, one might expect that a disjunction or alteration in the nature of that role would be reflected by at least temporary disruptions in the flow of goods. It seems interesting, then, that throughout the Late Xolalpan phase, 100 to 150 years after the retraction of the "official" Teotihuacan presence in these regions, we see no noticeable changes in the frequency or distribution of three nonperishable exotic materials (jade, shell, and mica) that are identifiable in Teotihuacan burials.

One possible explanation, of course, is that this represents no more than a lack of synchrony between the absolute chronologies of Teotihuacan and some of these other regions. Questions regarding the precision of the various regional chronologies have been raised by William Sanders (1977: 407; 1978: 43), John Paddock (1978: 47), and René Millon (1988: 115, 124).

Another rather obvious possibility is that the exotic materials specified here may have derived from regions other than those in question. Unfortunately, to date, the geographic source or sources of the jadeite used in Teotihuacan burials have not been identified, although the mountain slopes to the north of the Valley of Guatemala represent a distinct possibility (Turner n.d.: 236; Millon 1988: 122). Nevertheless, Margaret Turner (n.d.: 235) speculates that there may have been outcrops of jadeite in Puebla and Guerrero. Similarly, although we cannot presently identify the specific coastal areas from which the *Spondylus* and other species of Pacific shell used in Teotihuacan burials derived, Charles Kolb (1987: 116–121) has raised several possible source areas and routes to Teotihuacan, including Guerrero.

It is also conceivable that alternative sources of similar materials may have been sought, as a result of disruptions in traditional connections. It has been argued, for example, that around A.D. 500, a Teotihuacan center was constructed and mining operations undertaken at Alta Vista in the state of Zacatecas, far north of Teotihuacan (Aveni, Hartung, and Kelley 1982: 330–334). It has been suggested that this may have represented a new source for "blue-green" *chalchuiutl,* as well as many other types of precious minerals to supply the needs of Teotihuacan. Similarly, Atlantic species of marine shell may have been substituted for the more favored Pacific varieties, as we know they were after the fall of Teotihuacan (Starbuck n.d.: 112–159). Yet another possibility raised by Margaret Turner's (n.d.) analysis of jade working in Teotihuacan is that prized materials may have undergone extensive reworking (Turner n.d.). Thus, even if the supply of jade had slowed down, reworking of previously used objects might disguise the shortage, at least until new sources of raw materials could be exploited.

Another possibility that bears consideration is that the exchange of exotic goods had always been carried out on an informal private basis by professional merchants acting with relative autonomy from state control. Thus, even if the "official" role of Teotihuacan in these foreign places had declined, ordinary trade might have been relatively unaffected. Because of the perishable nature of so many of the goods involved, such informal processes would be unlikely to leave enduring traces in the archaeological record. Such a trading pattern has been suggested by René Millon (1988: 122) as preceding and perhaps precipitating the official Teotihuacan presence in Kaminaljuyu, and William Sanders suggests something similar in positing a second phase of contact at Kaminaljuyu, undertaken during the period of declining Teotihuacan power between A.D. 550 and 600. He interprets its nature as more of a private venture (Sanders 1977: 407; Santley 1983: 75–76). Similarly, at Tikal there is evidence of an attenuated and very different form of "Teotihuacan connection" until the end of the Middle Horizon (Moholy-Nagy, Asaro, and Stross 1984: 116; Millon 1988: 119).

All things considered, perhaps the most reasonable explanation is a relatively simple one—that following the retraction of Teotihuacan's sphere of power and influence sometime in the sixth century, trade was facilitated by intermediary groups advantageously situated in the coastal lowlands enroute between the Mexican and Maya regions (Parsons 1969, 1978; Millon 1988; Santley n.d.).[7] These centers, which had developed and expanded under Teotihuacan control, may have become increasingly autonomous in their activities, as René Millon (1988: 126) suggests for Matacapan in the

---

[7] Clara Millon called this possibility to my attention prior to the presentation of this paper at the Dumbarton Oaks conference in October 1988.

sixth century. Thus, the flow of exotic and other goods throughout the region might have continued without interruption. It may even be that the rising power of these intermediary trade centers served to hasten the decline of Teotihuacan's primacy in the interregional exchange network (see Diehl and Berlo 1989 for recent discussions of this issue).

We need finer control over the absolute chronologies of all of these regions, as well as good source analyses and intensive studies of reuse of jade, shell, and mica from reliably dated burial contexts to begin to distinguish among these various alternatives concerning the mechanisms involved in the procurement of exotic materials for Teotihuacan.

Equally important are the reasons underlying the apparent decline in the supply of those goods during the Metepec phase. Burial data indicate that by that time, jade, shell, and mica had become scarcer and more restricted in their use, suggesting possible cutbacks in supplies and/or a decline in the working of these materials in the city. Since these are phenomena unlikely to be detected in studies of surface materials because of problems of chronological control, these questions posed by the burial data should be seriously considered in designing future investigations of craft production in the city.

On the other hand, it is also possible that the data may not be reflecting a decline in supply, but simply a reduction in the availability of these goods to ordinary Teotihuacanos, created by increasing elite demand and/or newly enacted or more strictly enforced sumptuary laws regulating the use of these materials by people of lower status. Until recently, we have not had burial data from truly elite or high status residential contexts in Teotihuacan. As such data become available, comparisons of information from varying types of residential contexts should help in interpreting the nature of these apparent restrictions in the supply of "luxury goods" during the city's final century.

Locally Produced Luxury Goods

A number of researchers have pointed to evidence of internal problems in Teotihuacan during the Metepec phase (Litvak King 1970; Hirth and Swezey 1976; Garcia Cook and Trejo 1977; Millon 1981; Cowgill 1983; Storey 1985). They cite disruptions in the city's exchange system, problems in the food supply, malnutrition, high infant mortality, and declining population. On the other hand, countering the idea of obvious decline is the evidence for extensive construction activity along the Street of the Dead (R. Millon 1988), as well as for the production of some of the city's finest mural paintings (C. Millon 1972). Evelyn Rattray (1979) maintains that Thin Orange ware production was at its peak during the Metepec phase.

In the face of these conflicting indicators, the burial data can again be informative. They suggest a Metepec phase decline in the quantity and variety of obsidian objects available for use in burials, at least to the residents of these compounds. A slight decline is also apparent in the quantity and variety of Thin Orange ware in burials, suggesting that in spite of the high level of production cited by Rattray (1979), this ware may not have been as available to the general populace as it had been during the Xolalpan Phase. Similarly, the total absence of stucco-painted cylindrical tripods and the marked deterioration in the quantity and quality of other types of pottery may indicate that the production of certain types of luxury ceramics requiring a high level of craftsmanship may have been suffering, perhaps because of the loss of skilled craftsmen to emerging rival centers such as Xochicalco or El Tajin (Litvak King 1970: 140; Millon 1988: 131). Substitution of crude imitation "plano-relief" decorated tripods and non-Thin Orange ring base bowls in grave assemblages certainly seems to imply an attempt to maintain earlier burial customs in spite of declining access to the desired items. However, we must be cautious in that we are looking only at intermediate status burials; those from elite contexts might tell a far different story regarding the strength of various craft industries.

SUMMARY

A number of exotic and locally made items can be identified as "luxury goods" on the basis of the regularity of their association with relatively more complex grave offerings at Teotihuacan: jade, marine shell, mica, "Tlaloc" vases, and cylindrical tripods decorated either by stucco-painting or by the plano-relief technique. Accessibility to these goods does not seem to have been strictly controlled; rather the goods appear to have been available for use as potential grave offerings by groups of even quite average status at Teotihuacan. This relatively widespread accessibility appears to have continued unabated throughout most of the city's history—from at least the Early Tlamimilolpa phase (beginning about A.D. 200) through the Late Xolalpan phase (ending about A.D. 650). It is not until the final century prior to the city's demise that these goods seem to have become more restricted in their use.

Several dimensions of these conclusions seem noteworthy. First are the potential implications regarding the fundamental nature of Teotihuacan society, as one permitting broad, cross-societal accessibility to "luxury goods," particularly in contrast to contemporary Maya societies that may have been more restrictive. Second is the apparent continuity through the late sixth and early seventh centuries in the use and distribution of "luxury goods" imported from distant regions, in spite of major retractions in Teotihuacan's sphere of external relations from about A.D. 500–550. Last is the Metepec phase evidence for disjunctions in the use of both local and exotic goods in burial offerings, and its potential for specifying economic and social problems associated with this final period. Although this sample of burials is too small and the inferred social range too limited to allow complete answers to any of the issues raised here, the results suggest a number of hypotheses and

Variations in Mortuary Practices

some very specific strategies for testing with existing and new bodies of data. Such studies promise to enlarge our understanding of the changing nature of Teotihuacan's role in the complex arena of political and economic interaction in Mesoamerica during the Middle Horizon.

Acknowledgments The research on which this paper was based was partially supported by a grant from the National Science Foundation (BNS 10181). Dumbarton Oaks provided an exciting and stimulating forum for its original presentation. I would also like to express my sincere appreciation to Janet Berlo who, as editor of this volume, made many very valuable suggestions that contributed to the overall quality of the paper. Clara Millon, Lorraine Saunders, Margaret Turner, and my husband, John Sempowski, also commented on an earlier version of the paper and made observations that were extremely helpful. Finally, although I bear full responsibility for any errors in interpretation, I am indebted to René Millon for his thorough commentary and incisive suggestions, which added immeasurably to the fullness of the conclusions presented here.

BIBLIOGRAPHY

AVENI, ANTHONY F., HORST HARTUNG, AND J. CHARLES KELLEY
  1982 Alta Vista (Chalchihuites), Astronomical Implications of a Mesoamerican Ceremonial Outpost at the Tropic of Cancer. *American Antiquity* 47 (2): 316–335.

BERLO, JANET CATHERINE
  1984 *Teotihuacan Art Abroad: A Study of Metropolitan Style and Provincial Transformation in Incensario Workshops.* BAR International Series 199, Oxford.

BROWN, KENNETH L.
  1977 The Valley of Guatemala: A Highland Port of Trade. In *Teotihuacan and Kaminaljuyu,* (William T. Sanders and Joseph W. Michels, eds.): 205–395. Pennsylvania State University Press, University Park.

CHEEK, CHARLES D.
  1977 Teotihuacan influence at Kaminaljuyu. In *Teotihuacan and Kaminaljuyu.* (William T. Sanders and Joseph W. Michels, eds.): 441–452. Pennsylvania State University Press, University Park.

CLARK, JOHN E.
  1986 From Mountains to Molehills: A Critical Review of Teotihuacan's Obsidian Industry. In *Economic Aspects of Prehispanic Highland Mexico* (Barry L. Isaac, ed.): 23–74. Research in Economic Anthropology, Suppl. 2, JAI Press, Greenwich, Conn.

COGGINS, CLEMENCY
  1979 Teotihuacan at Tikal in the Early Classic Period. In *Actes du 42e Congrès International des Américanistes* 8: 251–269, Paris.
  1983 An Instrument of Expansion: Monte Alban, Teotihuacan and Tikal. In *Highland-Lowland Interaction in Mesoamerica: Interdisciplinary Approaches* (Arthur G. Miller, ed.): 49–68. Dumbarton Oaks, Washington, D.C.
  n.d. Painting and Drawing Styles at Tikal: An Historical and Iconographic Reconstruction. Ph.D. dissertation, Dept. of Fine Arts, Harvard University. University Microfilms, Ann Arbor, 1975.

COWGILL, GEORGE
  1983 Rulership and the Ciudadela: Political Inferences from Teotihuacan Architecture. In *Civilization in the Ancient Americas.* (R. M. Levanthal and A. L. Kolata, eds.): 313–343. University of New Mexico Press, Albuquerque.

DIEHL, RICHARD, AND JANET C. BERLO
  1989 *Mesoamerica after the Decline of Teotihuacan: A.D. 700–900.* Dumbarton Oaks, Washington, D.C.

GARCIA COOK, ANGEL
  1981 The Historical Importance of Tlaxcala in the Cultural Development of the Central Highlands. In *Supplement to the Handbook of Middle American Indians, Vol. 1: Archaeology* (Victoria R. Bricker and Jeremy A. Sabloff, eds.): 244–276. University of Texas Press, Austin.

GARCIA COOK, ANGEL, AND ELIA DEL CARMEN TREJO
    1977 Lo teotihuacano en Tlaxcala. *Comunicaciones* 14: 57–70 (Puebla: Fundación Alemana para la Investigación Científica).

GONZALES MIRANDA, LUIS ALFONSO, AND DAVID FUENTES GONZALES
    1982 Informe de labores realizados por la sección de antropología física en el proyecto arqueológico Teotihuacan. In *Memoria del Proyecto arqueológico Teotihuacán* 1 (Rubén Cabrera Castro, Ignacio Rodriguez, and Noel Morelos, eds.): 421–449. Instituto Nacional de Antropología e Historia, Mexico, D.F.

HIRTH, KENNETH G.
    1978 Teotihuacan Regional Population Administration in Eastern Morelos. *World Archaeology* 9: 320–333.

HIRTH, KENNETH G., AND WILLIAM SWEZEY
    1976 The Changing Nature of the Teotihuacan Classic: A Regional Perspective from Manzanilla, Puebla. *Las fronteras de Mesoamérica, XIV Mesa Redonda* 2: 11–23. Sociedad Mexicana de Antropología, Mexico, D.F.

JARQUIN ANA MARÍA, AND ENRIQUE MARTÍNEZ
    1982 Exploración en el lado este de la Ciudadela. In *Memoria del Proyecto Arqueológico Teotihuacán 80–82,* 1 (Rubén Cabrera C., Ignacio Rodríguez, and Noel Morelos, eds.): 19–47. Instituto Nacional de Antropología e Historia, Mexico, D.F.

KELLEY, J. CHARLES
    1985 The Chronology of the Chalchihuites Culture. In *The Archaeology of West and Northwest Mesoamerica* (Michael S. Foster and Phil C. Weigand, eds.): 269–287. Westview Press, Boulder, Colo.

KOLB, CHARLES C.
    1987 *Marine Shell Trade and Classic Teotihuacan, Mexico.* BAR International Series 364 (A. R. Hands and D. R. Walker, gen. eds.). Oxford.

LITVAK KING, JAIME
    1970 Xochicalco en la caída del clásico: Una hipótesis. *Anales de Antropología* 7: 131–144. Universidad Nacional Autónoma de México, Mexico, D.F.

LINNÉ, SIGVALD
    1942 *Mexican Highland Cultures: Archaeological Researchers at Teotihuacan, Calpulalpan and Chalchicomula in 1934–35.* Ethnographic Museum of Sweden, n.s. Pub. 7. Stockholm.

MERCADO ROJANO, ANTONIO
    1987 ¿Una sacerdotisa en Teotihuacan? *México Desconocido* 121: 6–9. Mexico, D.F.

MILLON, CLARA
    1972 The History of Mural Art at Teotihuacan. In *Teotihuacán, XI Mesa Redonda* 2: 1–16. Sociedad Mexicana de Antropología, Mexico, D.F.

MILLON, RENÉ
　1970　Teotihuacan: Completion of Map of Giant Ancient City in the Valley of Mexico. *Science* 170: 1077–1082.
　1976　Social Relations in Ancient Teotihuacan. In *The Valley of Mexico* (Eric R. Wolf, ed.): 205–248. University of New Mexico Press, Albuquerque.
　1981　Teotihuacan: City, State, and Civilization. In *Supplement to the Handbook of Middle American Indians, Vol. 1: Archaeology* (Victoria R. Bricker and Jeremy A. Sabloff, eds.): 198–243. University of Texas Press, Austin.
　1988　The Last Years of Teotihuacan Dominance. In *The Collapse of Ancient States and Civilizations* (Norman Yoffee and George L. Cowgill, eds.): 102–164. The University of Arizona Press, Tucson.

MILLON, RENÉ, BRUCE DREWITT, AND GEORGE L. COWGILL
　1973　*Urbanization at Teotihuacan, Mexico, Vol. 1: The Teotihuacan Map.* University of Texas Press, Austin.

MOHOLY-NAGY, HATTULA
　1989　Formed Shell Beads From Tikal, Guatemala. In *Proceedings of the 1986 Shell Bead Conference.* Research Records no. 20 (Charles F. Hayes III, ed.): 139–156. Rochester Museum and Science Center, Rochester, N.Y.
　n.d.　Late Early Classic Problematical Deposits: A Preliminary Report on Teotihuacan-Style Burials at Tikal, Guatemala. Paper presented at 52nd annual meeting of the Society for American Archaeology, Toronto, 1987.

MOHOLY-NAGY, HATTULA, FRANK ASARO, AND FRED H. STROSS
　1984　Tikal Obsidian: Sources and Typology. *American Antiquity* 49 (1): 104–117.

MÜLLER, FLORENCIA
　1979　¿Que significado tiene la distibución de los elementos teotihuacanos en Guerrero? In *Los procesos de cambio, XV Mesa Redonda* 2: 343–350. Sociedad Mexicana de Antropología, Mexico, D.F.

NOGUERA, EDUARDO
　1955　Extraordinario Hallazago en Teotihuacan. *El México Antiguo* 8: 43–56. Sociedad Alemana Mexicanista, Mexico, D.F.

PADDOCK, JOHN
　1978　The Middle Classic Period in Oaxaca. In *Middle Classic Mesoamerica: A.D. 400–700* (Esther Pasztory, ed.): 45–62. Columbia University Press, New York.

PARSONS, LEE A.
　1969　Bilbao, Guatemala: An Archaeological Study of the Pacific Coast Cotzumalhuapa Region. *Publications in Anthropology* 12. Milwaukee Public Museum.
　1978　Artistic Traditions of the Middle Classic Period. In *Middle Classic Meso-*

america: A.D. 400–700 (Esther Pasztory, ed.): 108–142. Columbia University Press, New York.

PASZTORY, ESTHER
1978 Historical Synthesis of the Middle Classic Period. In *Middle Classic Mesoamerica: A.D. 400–700* (Esther Pasztory, ed.): 3–22. Columbia University Press, New York.

RATTRAY, EVELYN C.
1979 La cerámica de Teotihuacan: Relaciones externas y cronología. *Anales de Antropología* 16: 51–70. Universidad Nacional Autónoma de México, Mexico, D.F.
n.d. The Merchants' Barrio Teotihuacan Mexico. Preliminary Report Submitted to the Instituto Nacional de Antropología e Historia and the Instituto de Investigaciones Antropologicas, Universidad Nacional Autónoma de México, 1987.

SANDERS, WILLIAM T.
1977 Ethnographic Analogy and the Teotihuacan Horizon Style. In *Teotihuacan and Kaminaljuyu* (W. T. Sanders and Joseph W. Michels, eds.): 397–410. Pennsylvania State University Press, University Park.
1978 Ethnographic Analogy and the Teotihuacan Horizon Style. In *Middle Classic Mesoamerica: A.D. 400–700* (Esther Pasztory, ed.): 35–44. Columbia University Press, New York.

SANDERS, WILLIAM T., AND ROBERT S. SANTLEY
1983 A Tale of Three Cities: Energetics and Urbanization in Pre-hispanic Central Mexico. In *Prehistoric Settlement Patterns* (E. Z. Vogt and Richard M. Leventhal, eds.): 243–291. University of New Mexico Press, Albuquerque.

SANTLEY, ROBERT S.
1983 Obsidian Trade and Teotihuacan Influence in Mesoamerica. In *Highland-Lowland Interaction in Mesoamerica: Interdisciplinary Approaches* (Arthur G. Miller, ed.): 69–124. Dumbarton Oaks, Washington, D.C.
n.d. Teotihuacan Influence at Matacapan: Alternative Models and Explanatory Frameworks. Paper Presented at the 52nd annual meeting of the Society for American Archaeology, Toronto, 1987.

SEMPOWSKI, MARTHA L.
n.d.a Mortuary Practices at Teotihuacan, Mexico: Their Implications for Social Status. Ph.D. dissertation, Dept. of Anthropology, University of Rochester, 1982. University Microfilms, Ann Arbor.
n.d.b Mortuary Practices at Teotihuacan, Mexico: Their Implications for Social Status. In *Urbanization at Teotihuacan, Mexico, Vol. III: Mortuary Practices and Skeletal Remains at Teotihuacan: Analyses and Observations*, by Martha L. Sempowski and Michael W. Spence (René Millon, ed.). University of Utah Press, Salt Lake City.

SPENCE, MICHAEL W.
1981 Obsidian Production and the State in Teotihuacán. *American Antiquity* 46 (4): 769–788.

n.d. Skeletal Morphology and Social Organization in Teotihuacan, Mexico. In *Urbanization at Teotihuacan, Mexico, Vol. III, Mortuary Practices and Skeletal Remains at Teotihuacan: Analyses and Observations*, by Martha L. Sempowski and Michael W. Spence (René Millon, ed.). University of Utah Press, Salt Lake City.

STARBUCK, DAVID R.
n.d. Man-Animal Relationships in Pre-Columbian Central Mexico. Ph.D. dissertation, Dept. of Anthropology, Yale University, 1975. University Microfilms, Ann Arbor.

STOREY, REBECCA
1985 An Estimate of Mortality in a Pre-Columbian Urban Population. *American Anthropologist* 87 (3): 519–535.
1987 A First Look at the Paleodemography of the Ancient City of Teotihuacan. In *Teotihuacan: Nuevos datos, nuevos síntesis, nuevos problemas* (Emily McClung de Tapia and Evelyn C. Rattray, eds.): 91–114. Instituto de Investigaciones Antropológicas, Serie Antropológica 72. Universidad Nacional Autónoma de México, Mexico, D.F.

STOREY, REBECCA, AND RANDOLPH J. WIDMER
1982 Excavations at Tlajinga 33. In *A Reconstruction of a Classic Period Landscape in the Teotihuacan Valley*, by William T. Sanders, Deborah Nichols, Rebecca Storey and Randolph Widmer. Final Report to the National Science Foundation (Grant BNS 8005754).

SUGIYAMA, SABURO
1989 Burials Dedicated to the Old Temple of Quetzalcoatl at Teotihuacan, Mexico. *American Antiquity* 54: 85–106.

TURNER, MARGARET H.
n.d. The Lapidary Industry of Teotihuacan, Mexico. Ph.D. dissertation, University of Rochester, 1988. University Microfilms, Ann Arbor.

WEIGAND, PHIL C.
1982 Mining and Mineral Trade in Prehispanic Zacatecas. In *Mining and Mining Techniques in Ancient Mesoamerica* (P. C. Wiegand and G. Gwynne, eds.). *Anthropology* 6 (1–2): 175–188.

WINTER, MARCUS C.
1979 El impacto Teotihuacano y procesos de cambio en Oaxaca. In *Los procesos de cambio, XV Mesa Redonda* 2: 359–367. Sociedad Mexicana de Antropología, Mexico, D.F.

Tlailotlacan, a Zapotec Enclave in Teotihuacan

MICHAEL W. SPENCE
UNIVERSITY OF WESTERN ONTARIO

INTRODUCTION

IN THE TEOTIHUACAN MAPPING PROJECT'S SURVEY high levels of foreign-appearing ceramics were noted in the surface collections from a cluster of sites near the western edge of the city, in an area now called Tlailotlacan (Millon 1973: 41–42; Paddock 1983; Rattray 1987). Their identification as Oaxacan types led to excavations in 1966–67 in one of the apartment compounds, TL7. Twenty years later, in the summers of 1987 and 1989, I excavated part of an adjacent structure, TL6. The results of the two excavations indicate that the Middle Horizon occupants of Tlailotlacan were indeed Zapotecs, or at least had a number of practices and material items that have their closest parallels in the Valley of Oaxaca, some 400 km to the southeast.

The extent of the area is not entirely clear. Using surface collections Evelyn Rattray (1987: 253, fig. 4) includes sites in the north half of N1W6, the south half of N2W6, and the north part of N2W5, with perhaps some spillover into N1W5 and the south half of N1W6. Test excavations by Consuelo Quintana (1987) to the south and west of our excavations suggest a more restricted area, one perhaps limited to ten or eleven apartment compounds around TL6 and TL7 (with a total population of some 600 to 700 individuals) and one apartment compound (18:N2W5) with a few adjacent open sites well to the northeast.

The results of the more recent work in TL6 are presented below. Emphasis is placed on the variety of ways in which the inhabitants of Tlailotlacan expressed and maintained their distinctive ethnic identity over some centuries of residence in one of the largest urban centers of the world. Tlailotlacan, in fact, offers us a rare opportunity to study ethnic pluralism over a span of time well beyond the few years or decades generally accessible to ethnologists.

Michael W. Spence

THE TL7 EXCAVATION

Work in 1966 and 1967 was largely confined to TL7, site 7:N1W6 of the Teotihuacan map (Millon, Drewitt, and Cowgill 1973). The excavation was initially conducted by the University of the Americas, under the direction of John Paddock and Evelyn Rattray. Later, Juan Vidarte extended the excavation for the Teotihuacan Mapping Project. In most respects, TL7 is similar to Teotihuacan residential structures. Nevertheless, Zapotec features appeared in a variety of contexts (Millon 1973: 41–42; Rattray 1987).

The most spectacular find was a Zapotec-style tomb with an antechamber. A large upright stone of local material, carved with a Zapotec glyph and the number nine in bar and dot numerals, formed the doorjamb on one side of the entrance to the main chamber (Millon 1973: 41–42, fig. 60a–b). The stone had apparently been taken from the facade of the Old Temple of Quetzalcoatl (Sugiyama 1989: 104). Despite at least two pre-Hispanic disturbances, it could be determined that the tomb had held the remains of six individuals and a dog (Spence 1976, n.d.). Two of the individuals were subadults: a fetus or infant represented only by part of the right temporal bone and a child of five to seven years represented by several cranial and mandibular fragments. The absence of other sub-adult bones suggests that these two individuals may have been placed in the tomb as secondary burials or, in the case of the infant, perhaps even by accident. Offering material had apparently included both Teotihuacan and Zapotec style ceramics, though most had been removed or destroyed in the previous entries (Rattray n.d.).

Elsewhere in TL7 plowing had disturbed a Late Xolalpan burial with three adult skeletons and an offering (Paddock 1983: 171; Rattray 1987: 244–245). Two of the adults were extended burials, a position virtually absent in Teotihuacan but standard in the Valley of Oaxaca. The offering, though badly disturbed, apparently included several Teotihuacan vessels, red ochre, a miniature roller stamp, and other items of bone, obsidian, pyrite, and shell. Definitely associated with the burials were elements of an urn of Monte Alban II–III A Transition style made from local Teotihuacan clay (Rattray 1987: 245, 249, fig. 1). A hand from a second urn, probably of Oaxacan clay, was in the layer immediately beneath the burial (Rattray 1987: 245, fig. 2K).

An Early Xolalpan adult secondary burial was accompanied by a variety of Teotihuacan vessels, nine Thin Orange bowls, a Zapotec bowl, an obsidian blade, a jadeite bead, a figurine, and parts of a Zapotec urn made of Teotihuacan clay (Evelyn Rattray, personal communication, 1981; Sayre and Harbottle n.d.). A nearby Late Xolalpan offering, perhaps redeposited from elsewhere in the structure, consisted of four Thin Orange bowls, several Teotihuacan vessels, and a matte miniature, but included no Zapotec items or human bone. At other points in the structure there were found a fetal skeleton with no offering, the cranium and mandible of an adult female with a Xolalpan period Teotihuacan censer, and a complete Zapotec urn that had been ritually smashed in a small room immediately south of the principal temple. This urn, of Oaxacan clay, was of early Monte Alban III A style (Millon 1967; 1973: 41, figs. 58–59).

The ethnic identity of the TL7 occupants was also expressed in a variety of Zapotec ceramic types, described elsewhere by Evelyn Rattray (1987, n.d.). There is evidence, in the form of unfired and rejected Zapotec ceramics from both TL6 and TL7, for the presence of a workshop somewhere in the near vicinity (Krotser 1987: 426). The ceramics recovered from TL6 are much the same as those described by Rattray (1987) for TL7. The TL6 material is discussed in more detail in the following section.

THE TL6 ARCHITECTURAL SEQUENCE

The 1987 and 1989 excavations were conducted in site 6:N1W6, the structure immediately to the east of 7:N1W6 (Millon et al. 1973). Work focused on the northeast part of the building in 1987, where we excavated 130 m^2 to subsoil. A patio-platform complex, two tombs, and a number of burials and offerings were found. In 1989 the scope of the excavation was doubled, extending farther to the west and south. A second patio-platform complex, two more tombs, and several additional offerings and burials were revealed (Spence 1990). However, because the 1989 data have not yet been fully analyzed, the following account is based primarily on the findings of the 1987 season. It is thus restricted to the northeastern part of the structure, where a complex construction sequence of seven stages has been defined.

Initially the area served as an agricultural field. Although the ceramics suggest the presence of occupation in the immediate vicinity, the only structural evidence consists of three small postholes in the original ground surface. A network of small (25–30 cm wide) canals, probably for irrigation, crossed the area. The fill in the channels consisted of water-sorted sand and pebbles, with water-rolled sherds of the Tzacualli and Miccaotli phases, suggesting that the system may have been in use until some point late in the Miccaotli phase (ca. A.D. 150–200).

In Stage 2 the area was covered with layers of fill, the first stage in the construction of the TL6 structure. A stone-faced altar complex was built on the fill and was soon covered by a small adobe platform. There was a large room to the east of the platform. Associated ceramics suggest an Early Tlamimilolpa (ca. A.D. 200–300) date for this activity.

Two consecutive cobble floors were laid over much of the area in the third stage, covering the adobe platform and abutting the newly erected first stage of the East Platform (Fig. 1). Eight offerings are associated with the two floors. Most of the offerings consist of two vessels, one placed upside-down over the other, in a small pit under the associated floor. The offering ceramics suggest a Late Tlamimilolpa phase date. They include three-

Michael W. Spence

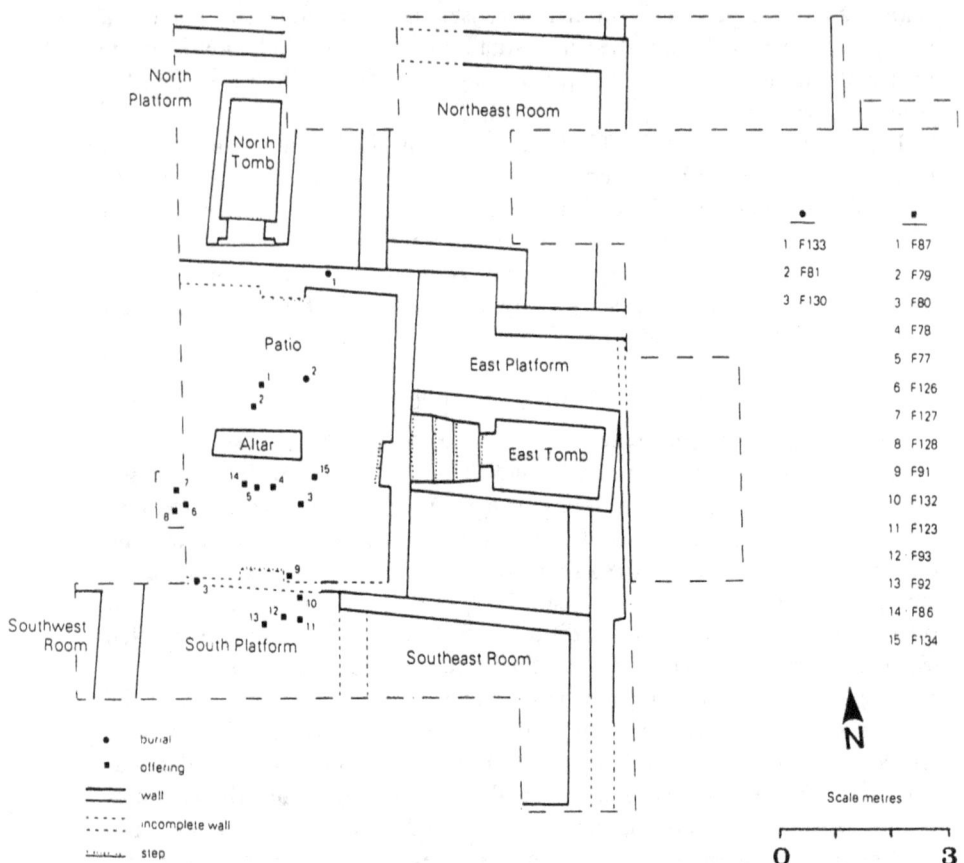

Fig. 1 TL6 excavation (architecture shown at Stage 6)—direction arrow to 9° 25′ east of true, or astronomic, north. The site grid is oriented to 13° 09′ east of astronomic north. Drawing by Mindy Gordon.

handled covers, Thin Orange ring base bowls, a polished black bowl with an incised "cloud" motif (cf. Séjourné 1966: fig. 77), and two vessels of Zapotec style. One of these is a deep conical bowl with a burnished interior and a diagonally scraped exterior (Fig. 2). The other, from a different offering, is a low, wide bowl with a flat base, three small conical nubbin supports, and a slightly convex wall (Fig. 3). The red-on-brown decoration consists of a red rim, groups of vertical stripes around the exterior, groups of vertical stripes and broader panels on the interior wall, and peripheral tabs and a central five-point star on the interior base. Although apparently a local product, the vessel bears its closest resemblance to the A9 type of Monte Alban II (Caso, Bernal, and Acosta 1967: 70, figs. 48–50, 194).

Tlailotlacan, a Zapotec Enclave

Fig. 2 Conical bowl from offering. Photo by Saburo Sugiyama.

Fig. 3 Bichrome bowl from offering. Photo by Saburo Sugiyama.

Stage 4, dated by fill ceramics to the Early Xolalpan phase (ca. A.D. 450–550), saw the construction of a new stone floor over the Stage 3 floors, the addition of rooms at the northeast and southwest corners of the patio, the burial of an infant without an offering in the patio, the expansion of the East Platform, and the construction of the East Tomb.

The tomb was cut into the East Platform from its surface. Its long axis is oriented east-west (to be more precise, 99° east of magnetic north), with the antechamber on the west. The main chamber (195 cm long × 125 cm wide, and more than 1 m deep), has walls of cut stone set in mud mortar (Fig. 4). The chamber floor is of dirt, cut into a hard layer of sterile soil (the B horizon) with no further preparation. The ceiling, of large concrete and

Michael W. Spence

Fig. 4 East Tomb, looking west to antechamber.

stone slabs, had collapsed into the tomb at some time after its abandonment. The antechamber, 105 cm wide, has three stone steps leading from the surface of the East Platform to the doorway into the main chamber. The doorway has been created by two salients of cut stone extending from the north and south walls of the tomb, forming the west wall of the main chamber with a gap in the center for the door. Although the walls of the tomb and antechamber have been made of stones cut only on their inner, or visible, faces, the antechamber steps and the doorjambs are more carefully constructed of stones cut on all faces.

The contents of the tomb had been largely removed at some later stage. However, enough scattered material remained to show that two adults, one probably a male, had been present. The right tibia of one adult has four deliberate transverse cuts across its medial surface, perhaps the result of some ritual. Of the offering only two jadeite beads, a small piece of turquoise inlay, an obsidian blade fragment, several small pieces of mica and shell, and part of a poorly finished bowl remain.

In Stage 5, later in the Early Xolalpan phase, the patio received a concrete floor and three more offerings of paired vessels. These included Thin Orange bowls (one with incised and punctated decoration) and an everted rim bowl with the cloud motif. An infant burial was placed in the patio and covered with a large *olla* sherd and a complete grooved rim bowl of Monte

Alban type G12 (see Fig. 9; Caso et al. 1967: 25–26). The shallow, smooth form of the grooves and the absence of incising on the interior base are characteristic of the Monte Alban II–IIIA Transition variant of this type (Marc Winter, personal communication).

A platform may have been created in Stage 5 at the south side of the patio, over the location of the earlier adobe platform (see Fig. 1). The North Platform was raised over an adult burial that had been placed in a slight hollow cut into the original ground surface. The body had been placed on its right side in a loosely flexed position, oriented north-south with the head to the south. The only definite grave offering was a bifacially worked obsidian artifact with the base missing, though a number of ceramic items (to be discussed later) may also have been part of the original offering.

When the patio was surfaced in concrete, a rectangular, stone-lined burial cist was prepared in its center. Although much of the bone and offering material was removed in a later stage, enough remained to show that the skeleton of a young adult of indeterminate sex had rested in extended position in the cist, with the head to the east. Associated items had included at least four small pendants of marine shell, a bone needle, cut mica, and a Teotihuacan censer bowl of the Early Xolalpan phase. A small altar with a concrete *talud* facing was then erected over the cist, sealing it.

At some point in the sequence, probably in Stage 5 or 6, much of the skeletal and offering material was removed from the East Tomb chamber, and a jumble of ceramics and human bone was deposited in the antechamber. This deposit rested in a layer of soil and rubble on the steps, indicating that the tomb had already begun to deteriorate. The large slabs of roofing material that fell in the final collapse, however, overlay the offering. Material in the deposit included the mouth part of a broken Teotihuacan-style censer mask, more of the small bowl that was found on the main chamber floor, some mica fragments, and ten paired miniatures (four matte globular *ollas;* two vases and two *copas* of copoid ware; and two crude tripod jars with burnished bodies, one with stick-burnished triangles on the neck). Also in the antechamber, but somewhat separated spatially from this cluster, were a small pendant of cut marine shell and an Early Xolalpan vase of *copa* ware with tripod hollow cylindrical feet (cf. Séjourné 1966: pl. 58). The latter rested upside-down on the lowest step, near the doorjamb of the main chamber.

The presence of parts of the bowl in both the main chamber and the antechamber deposit suggests that at least some of the antechamber material had originally been part of the main chamber offering. The human skeletal material in the antechamber deposit, however, is definitely from an individual not represented in the main chamber. It is the very incomplete and totally disarticulated skeleton of an elderly male. The bone produced a radiocarbon date of A.D. 250 ±60 years (TO-882), suggesting that it may be from an earlier burial that had been exhumed and transferred in part to the antechamber.

In Stage 6, which may be Late Xolalpan or Metepec phase (ca. A.D. 550–700), three more offerings were placed around the altar in the patio. The North Tomb was created in the North Platform, with its long axis oriented 13° 02′ east of magnetic north (20° 09′ east of astronomic north). The antechamber is to the south. The tomb reached and disturbed the earlier burial at the base of the platform, and in fact may have been intended to locate and incorporate that individual. Four additional adults, including both males and females, were later deposited in the main chamber, though this apparently occurred over some period of time. Most of the bones were bunched along the side and end walls, with some elements closest to the walls standing on edge—the pattern that would be expected to develop if the bones had been pushed aside to make room for later interments. The few articulated elements left show that at least one of these individuals had been extended with the head to the south.

Grave goods occurred at two levels in the North Tomb. The lower material rested in a thin layer of soil that covered the dirt floor of the tomb. A number of rather scattered items were included, some disturbed but others apparently still in their original positions: the handle of a Zapotec style ladle censer (*sahumador*); the head and foot of a Teotihuacan style figurine; three figures (one humanoid) of cut mica; a piece of cut marine shell; a polished black *florero* of the Miccaotli phase (ca. A.D. 150–200); a Metepec phase (ca. A.D. 650–750) tripod vase with hollow, grooved feet and cross-hatched stick polishing on the exterior walls (Fig. 5), identical to one from Tetitla burial 30 (Rattray n.d.); a small, everted bowl with a polished interior and wiped exterior; a crudely modeled tripod jar with an irregularly smoothed, unburnished exterior; and ten miniature vessels of Thin Orange. The latter include *ollas,* amphoras, jars, bowls (one with incised and punctated decoration), and a tripod cylindrical vase with an encircling band of stamped decoration near the base. The mixture of period styles and the evidence of disturbance suggest that these offerings represent more than one episode. Some, particularly the censer handle and the Thin Orange miniatures, may have accompanied the original burial, while others, for example the Metepec tripod vase, had probably been deposited at the time of tomb construction or in later entries.

In a slightly higher layer of soil were found a greenstone figurine, a circular ornament of marine shell, a jadeite bead, and a polished globular, corrugated jar, probably of Tlamimilolpa date. The jar had been smashed and somewhat scattered.

Stage 7, of the Metepec phase (ca. A.D. 650–750), saw the destruction of the central altar and the removal of the contents of the sub-altar cist. A thumb-decorated Metepec phase *candelero* was deposited in the cist fill. The

Fig. 5 Stick-polished tripod vase, North Tomb. Photo by Saburo Sugiyama.

patio was then covered with a floor of flat stones and a pair of Metepec three-handled covers were placed near where the altar had been. The entrance to the North Tomb was sealed about this time.

This lengthy sequence shows the development of a patio-platform complex over some 550 years, from the Early Tlamimilolpa to the Metepec phase. The architecture could be considered standard Teotihuacan: platforms around a sunken patio with a central altar, floors of stone (cf. Storey and Widmer n.d.) and plastered concrete, *talud* platform faces, etc. In TL7 the Teotihuacan orientations of the walls, including those of the tomb, and the *talud-tablero* architecture of the principal temple support this (Millon 1973: 41–42).

Nevertheless, very similar patio-platform complexes characterize Oaxacan architecture (Winter 1974, 1986). The TL6 complex would fit comfortably into the more elaborate levels of Winter's type 2 compound in Monte Alban (Winter 1986: 357–360). Although some major wall orientations in TL6 correspond well with the "cardinal directions" of Teotihuacan (see Fig. 1), the tomb walls and the north wall of the southeast room follow a quite different orientation. The North Tomb's long axis is 4° 44' east of the Teotihuacan north-south axis, to fall at 13° 02' east of magnetic north. This orientation, though not Teotihuacan, was apparently not a Monte Alban one either (Blanton 1978: 45; Aveni 1980: 249, 313).

The general architectural features, then, cannot be assigned unequivocally to one or the other culture. Although they may be of Teotihuacan derivation, they would certainly not have seemed alien to a middle or high status Zapotec family. The two tombs and the stone-lined cist, on the other hand, are clearly Zapotec. They represent a complex mortuary program that does not seem at all Teotihuacan, where the majority of interments follow a

Michael W. Spence

fairly straightforward pattern of primary burial in simple pit graves (Serrano and Lagunas 1975; Spence n.d.; Storey n.d.—but note Storey and Widmer n.d.: 47–48). The TL6 system does fit well with the complex patterns observed in the Valley of Oaxaca, where tombs were entered repeatedly for the deposition of new interments and the bones of earlier burials were pushed to the sides (Séjourné 1960; Romano 1974; Winter 1986: 360; Flannery 1983: 135). Because mortuary programs generally reflect the social and political complexities of the societies that produce them (Binford 1971), the TL6 tombs may well indicate the transplanting of Zapotec patterns of kin group organization and hierarchy to Tlailotlacan and their survival there to some point in the Metepec phase, at or near the end of Teotihuacan's existence.

THE ZAPOTEC CERAMICS OF TL6

Most of the ceramics recovered from TL6 are standard Teotihuacan vessels manufactured in the various workshops around the city. A wide range of forms are present: *ollas,* bowls, *comals,* censers, burners, figurines, and so on. These predominate not only in fill contexts, where their significance is somewhat uncertain, but also in the offerings and burials. However, a minority of the ceramic material (some 2,400 sherds, or about 3.3% of the total) was produced in the local workshop, most of it in Zapotec styles (Krotser 1987: 426). Only a very small amount of the TL6 ceramics may actually have been imported from Oaxaca (cf. Rattray 1987; Abascal, Harbottle, and Sayre 1974; Sayre and Harbottle n.d.).

The Zapotec types from the 1987 excavation in TL6 are described herein. Counts are generally based only on rims, but at times also include sherds from the main body. They are vessel counts, in the sense that sherds believed to be from the same vessel were counted as one. Data on the very similar TL7 ceramics have been presented by Rattray (1987, n.d.). Although reference will be made to the Monte Alban categories of Caso, Bernal, and Acosta (1967), these cannot be applied directly to the Tlailotlacan material. The Monte Alban categories are based on paste color and composition. The Tlailotlacan ceramics, produced from Valley of Teotihuacan clays, have a distinctive set of paste characteristics. One striking commonality between the Tlailotlacan and Zapotec ceramics, though, is the high frequency of medium and dark grey surfaces, indicating their manufacture in a reducing atmosphere. Reduction firing in kilns was a standard method in Monte Alban and apparently in Tlailotlacan, but most Teotihuacan vessels were fired in the open air and so are of lighter colors (Krotser 1987).

Coarse Domestic Wares

Conical Bowls (413 rim sherds). The conical bowl is the most common Zapotec domestic type recovered at TL6. Further analysis may yield subtypes, but at present only a single, rather variable category can be described. The vessels are flat-bottomed, relatively deep, with outleaning walls that are either direct or slightly flaring (Figs. 2, 6a–m, 7). Lips (Fig. 6a–m) are flat, convex, or bolstered by a fillet of clay added to the exterior and well blended with the rim (cf. Fig. 6f, h, j, m). Diameters at the lip range from 130 to 530 mm. Base-wall angles are generally in the 115°–140° range. Monte Alban forms included in this category are deep conical bowls, *apaxtles*, and *macetas* (cf. Caso et al. 1967: figs. 175, 223).

Interior bases are wiped but unburnished, while the interior walls are burnished, usually on the original surface but occasionally on a slip, to the middle or anterior part of the lip. The rest of the lip is wiped. In some

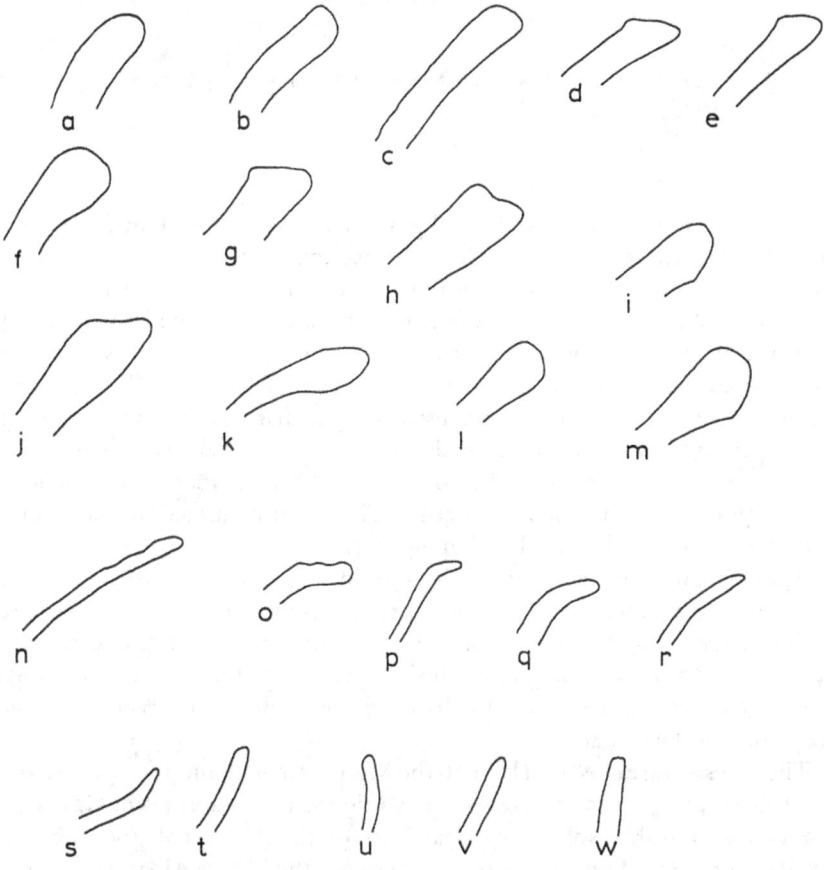

Fig. 6 Rim profiles (vessel body to left): a–m conical bowls; n–o grooved rim fine ware; p–r everted rim fine ware; s–v convex rim fine ware; w direct rim fine ware. Drawing by Mindy Gordon.

Michael W. Spence

Fig. 7 Conical bowl, exterior surface. Photo by Saburo Sugiyama.

vessels there is a "thumb band," a slightly depressed strip about 1 cm wide encircling the exterior rim just below the lip, apparently created by drawing the thumb or finger around the rim. The exterior wall, from the rim down at least to the mid-point and often to the base, is finished by scraping perpendicular or diagonal to the rim, done with a hard-edged, somewhat irregular tool when the clay was wet or drying (Figs. 2, 7). This process leaves a rough, irregular surface, usually with diagonal or slightly arcing coarse striations. The scraping tends to be more marked towards the rim, sometimes removing up to 3 mm of the vessel surface there. The intent of the scraping was apparently decorative. The exterior surfaces of the vessels had been smoothed before the scraping started.

Approximately 60 percent of the interior bases have incised patterns. They generally extend a very short distance up the interior wall, to where the burnishing starts. Most consist of a series of irregular, rather carelessly applied arcs, often overlapping with short lines and other elements (Fig. 8). To judge by the thicknesses of the bases, this incising occurs over the whole size range of the category.

These vessels are closely related to the Monte Alban domestic types G1 and G2 (Caso et al. 1967: 23–24, figs. 1–2). The incised bases are of type G21, a G1 variant distinguished solely by its basal decoration (Caso et al. 1967: 67, fig. 43; Rattray 1987). The only difference between the Monte Alban vessels and their Tlailotlacan counterparts is the greater frequency of interior burnishing in the latter. Though variants of G1 and G2 persist through much of the Monte Alban sequence, the decorated G21 bases seem to be well represented

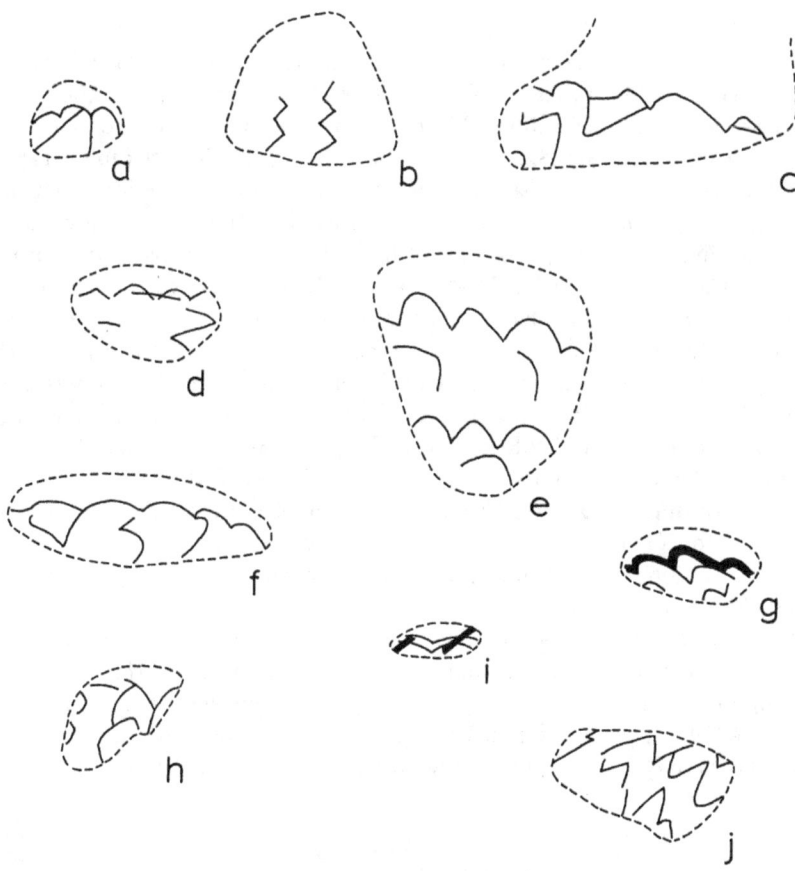

Fig. 8 Incised designs, interior bases of conical bowls. Drawing by Mindy Gordon.

in Period II and persist into the II–IIIA Transition (Caso et al. 1967: 293, 347–348; Kowalewski, Spencer, and Redmond 1978: 179, no. 1194; Bernal and Oliveros 1988: 44; Marc Winter, personal communication).

Other Forms. Ollas, jars, and very shallow bowls or plates were also produced in the Tlailotlacan workshop but are much less common. Though typologically distinguishable from their Teotihuacan counterparts, they may not be as thoroughly Zapotec in style as the conical bowls. A large *olla* from beneath the adobe platform, for example, has a wedge rim vaguely like early Teotihuacan rims but quite unlike those of Monte Alban. *Comales* are relatively common and are similar in form to those of Monte Alban II (Marc Winter, personal communication).

Michael W. Spence

Fine Wares

Grooved Rim Bowls (46 rim sherds). These are the Tlailotlacan versions of the G12 type of Monte Alban (Caso et al. 1967: 25–26, figs. 4, 130–131). Related types also appear in the Mixteca and Cañada areas (cf. Fowler and Paddock 1975; Spencer 1982: fig. A20; Spores 1983). In Tlailotlacan the type is characterized by two broad, pre-firing grooves around the interior rim (Figs. 6n–o, 9). The TL6 vessels are low and flat-bottomed, with outleaning walls and direct to flaring rims. Three have the more sharply everted rims characteristic of Monte Alban Ib–II (Fig. 6o; Kowalewski et al. 1978: 179, no. 1227). However, none has the elaborately decorated bases that appear in Period I at Monte Alban (Kowalewski et al. 181, no. 1297; Caso et al. 1967: figs. 130–131). Both interior and exterior surfaces of the TL6 bowls are generally well burnished, though a few have matte exteriors. Diameters at lip are 210–330 mms, and colors are usually grey or medium to dark brown. In Monte Alban the type dates to Periods I, II, and II–IIIA Transition; it may not continue into Period IIIA (Fowler and Paddock 1975: 167–168). Those like the Tlailotlacan variant, with shallow grooves along the interior rim but without basal incising, are particularly common in the Transition period (Marc Winter, personal communication).

Other Rim Forms (73 rim sherds). There are also a variety of ungrooved fine vessel rims, including everted, direct and convex forms (Fig. 6p–w). Although most are bowls, a few vases and jars are represented too. Surfaces are grey or black, generally polished on both interior and exterior. Many of these vessels may be related to the Monte Alban G3 type (Caso et al. 1967:

Fig. 9 *(above)* Grooved rim fine ware bowl, patio burial of infant. Photo by Saburo Sugiyama.

Fig. 10 *(opposite)* Zoomorphic bowl fragments and a figurine headdress (upper row, center). Photo by Saburo Sugiyama.

Tlailotlacan, a Zapotec Enclave

24–25; see also Rattray n.d.).

Zoomorphic bowls (45 rim sherds). A number of shallow bowls have tails and wings or fins modeled on the rims, with further details added by incising and occasionally excising (Fig. 10; Rattray 1987: fig. 2i–j). Very similar specimens in Monte Alban are dated to Periods I and II (Caso et al. 1967: 218–219, fig. 183; Kowalewski et al. 1978: 177, no. 1111). However, the same modeling and incising techniques were also used in other types. Figurine headdresses occasionally have incised or punctated decoration that, in small fragments, is difficult to distinguish from the zoomorphic bowls (cf. Fig. 10, upper row, center). Also, some large Monte Alban effigy whistles have similar appendages (Caso et al. 1967: fig. 240f). Nevertheless, most such pieces in TL6 seem to be from the small zoomorphic bowls.

Micaceous Ware (14 rim sherds). Several rims and bodysherds, approximately 9 percent of the fine ware sherds, were made of mica-rich pastes that produced glittering surfaces. Sherds of this ware proved to be of Oaxacan clay (Sayre and Harbottle n.d.; Rattray n.d.; Garman Harbottle, personal communication). Surface colors range from grey and black to salmon, probably representing variation in the firing conditions. Several bowl rims of the ware have already been enumerated in the preceding categories: one grooved, six everted, two direct, two slightly convex, and three zoomorphic bowl rims (cf. Fig. 10, lower row, left). One vase fragment has a short, hollow support.

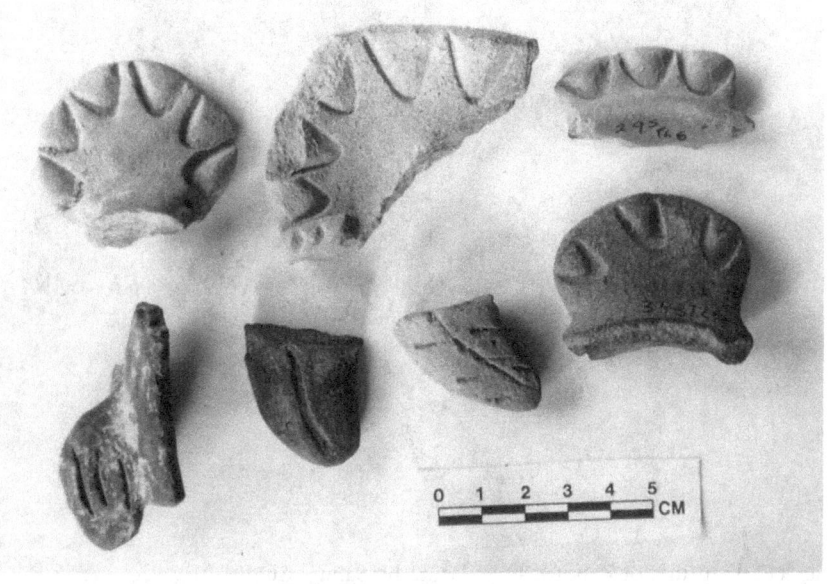

Michael W. Spence

Ritual Artifacts

Censers (sahumadores—26 rim, body, and handle sherds). The bowls are hemispherical with unburnished surfaces, the exteriors usually rougher. The interiors often show burning, and occasionally have an adhering red pigment. Only 36 percent of the bowl bodysherds are perforated. Most of the rims have finger impressions spaced along the lip. Fragments of two strap handles and five ladle handles were recovered. One of the ladle handles is an open variant, like a Monte Alban II specimen (Caso et al. 1967: fig. 227d). Ladle censers with perforated hemispherical bowls are also present in TL7 (Rattray 1987: fig. 2d–g), and in Monte Alban in Periods II and IIIA (Caso et al. 1967: 249, 358, figs. 227, 293b–c).

Figurines (160 fragments). Generally grey to black in color, these figurines are crudely hand modeled with limbs that taper to bluntly pointed extremities (Fig. 11). There is no attempt to depict hands or feet by modeling or incising. However, about 30 percent of the limbs are decorated with one or more lines crudely incised along the length of the limb or, rarely, with punctates (Fig. 11, bottom row). Bodies include both human and animal forms, two of the former with appliquéd breasts (Fig. 11).

Both human and animal heads were found (cf. Rattray 1987: 249; n.d.). The animal heads are crudely modeled, with appliqué eyes (the pupils gener-

Fig. 11 Figurines of Zapotec style. Photo by Saburo Sugiyama.

Tlailotlacan, a Zapotec Enclave

ally made with punctates) and often appliqué noses and ears. Frogs are frequently portrayed, bats more rarely.

Although more carefully formed, the human heads are still crude (Fig. 11, top row). Eyebrows and the oval, slightly diagonal outlines of the eyes are created by incision, with pupils represented by punctates in only a minority of cases. Mouths are protruding, usually modeled from the clay of the head rather than appliquéd. Most of the human heads correspond well to Type 1 of Monte Alban I and II (Caso et al. 1967: 269–270, figs. 238b, 239a, 240a–b,e, 241a–c). Carl Kuttruff (1978: 380, 382, fig. A VIII-1 P–S) assigns this type to Period II. No examples of Types 2, 3, or 4 were found. The TL6 animal heads are similar to those described by Kuttruff, and may be primarily of the II–IIIA Transition or Period IIIA (Kuttruff 1978: 387, 389, fig. A VIII-4; Caso et al. 1967: 360).

Urns (10 fragments). Fragments of forearms, feet, and headdresses were recovered (Fig. 12), clearly from anthropomorphic urns like those of TL7 (Millon 1967; Rattray 1987, n.d.) and Monte Alban (Caso and Bernal 1952; Kuttruff 1978). Unfortunately, none is complete enough to provide a date or any clues to the person or deity represented. All are fill inclusions, rather than offering material.

Tubes (6 specimens). These are large tubular pieces, scraped along the

Fig. 12 Urn fragments. Photo by Saburo Sugiyama.

exterior surfaces, like those of Monte Alban II through IIIA (Caso et al. 1967: 251, 304, 358, fig. 230). Although here classified with the ritual materials, it is possible that they may also have had a utilitarian function (Caso et al. 1967: 251).

Although some of the Tlailotlacan workshop products approximate Teotihuacan types, most are clearly local variants of Oaxacan types. In fact, the similarities between the Tlailotlacan vessels and their Oaxacan counterparts are often strong enough to require paste analysis to distinguish them. The Tlailotlacan Zapotec types include both domestic and ritual forms. Most were apparently intended to function in the daily life of the people, but a few, in particular the urns, must have been used only in very restricted and special contexts.

As John Paddock (1983) has pointed out, the vast majority of the Tlailotlacan Zapotec types fit well in the Monte Alban II–IIIA Transition. The one major exception to this, the early period IIIA urn from TL7, is actually an import from the Valley of Oaxaca (Millon 1967; Rattray 1987: 249). Robert Drennan (1983: 369) places the end of Period II at about A.D. 200, with IIIA dating A.D. 200–450, equivalent to the Tlamimilolpa Period of Teotihuacan. The II–IIIA Transition period, then, probably dated about A.D. 150–250.

The presence of these early styles in Xolalpan and even Metepec phase levels at Tlailotlacan is puzzling. John Paddock (1983; Fowler and Paddock 1975) has suggested that they represent only a brief, early occupation by immigrants from the Valley of Oaxaca. Within one or two generations these immigrants had become acculturated, but their earlier debris was incorporated into the fill of later architectural levels. This, however, seems unlikely. It requires the assumption that virtually all of the Zapotec types appearing in offering contexts in TL6 and TL7 were heirlooms. An alternative explanation for this phenomenon will be offered in the following section.

ETHNIC EXPRESSION IN TLAILOTLACAN

The archaeological evidence indicates that the people of Tlailotlacan were Zapotecs who came to Teotihuacan from the Valley of Oaxaca during the Monte Alban II–IIIA Transition period (Millon 1973: 41–42). However, ethnic identity is not simply a historically derived fact. It is a construct, responsive in some degree to the wider socioeconomic environment of the group (Hodder 1978; Higgins 1986: 405). The Tlailotlacanos, then, cannot be expected to simply reproduce the Zapotec culture from which they originated (Cohen 1969: 9, 47–50; Santley, Yarborough, and Hall 1987: 88; Schildkrout 1974: 216–217). For one thing, a certain amount of acculturation to the larger Teotihuacan community would have been inescapable. Many of the material necessities of life were made in specialized workshops beyond the enclave (Spence 1981; Krotser 1987). The Tlailotlacanos' use of these items, though it cannot be considered evidence for the deliberate acceptance of Teotihuacan ways, would nevertheless have placed some severe constraints on the expression of their own ethnic identity. In statistical analyses the surface collections of Tlailotlacan cluster with a variety of other sites beyond the enclave, suggesting that the Tlailotlacanos used the Teotihuacan ceramic complex in much the same way as the rest of the city's inhabitants (Altschul n.d.: 167–178; 1987: 209–214). Beyond this, however, the presence of Teotihuacan items like censers in Tlailotlacan ritual contexts indicates some deeper degree of acculturation to the larger society (Millon 1973: 42).

Only some Zapotec practices would have been retained. There was inevitably some selection, though the factors encouraging the retention of particular traits and the lapse of others are not yet very clear (Barth 1969: 14; Buchignani 1987: 21; McLaughlin 1987: 57). Those persisting in Tlailotlacan touched on a wide range of situations, including elite and non-elite contexts, daily domestic activities and household ritual, and occasional, more elaborate public rituals. Not all of these were necessarily intended to express the ethnicity of the Tlailotlacanos. The practice of tomb burial certainly carried that message, but may have been retained primarily to express and reinforce the local sociopolitical hierarchy.

The wide variety of contexts in which ethnicity was expressed probably reflects the range of functions that it performed, impinging on virtually every aspect of community life: maintenance of a distinction from the larger Teotihuacan society, the demonstration of adherence to the community's values and beliefs, enculturation of the young, presentation of the local political hierarchy to significant outsiders, and the support of important social and economic ties with related groups beyond Teotihuacan (Cohen 1969; Wobst 1977; Hodder 1978). Some of these functions are best handled by occasional public rituals, others by daily household practices. Some, like enculturation, are largely female tasks, while others, for example the validation of political authority, fall more in the male domain.

Ian Hodder (1978, 1979, 1981, 1982) has explored the functions and correlates of ethnicity among several East African tribes. He found that the public expression of ethnic identity intensified in situations of intergroup hostility and competition over resources, despite frequent exchange and even intermarriage across tribal boundaries. Ethnic affiliation served essentially to ensure protection and support by fellow tribesmen and to justify the exploitation of outsiders (Hodder 1978: 51). Martin Wobst (1977) examined ethnic groups in Yugoslavia, with similar results. Expressions of ethnic identity were oriented primarily toward competing groups or toward members of the local society beyond the household. Identity was displayed in those items of dress and adornment most easily visible to others.

The emphasis in Tlailotlacan on artifacts used in household activities, then, was somewhat unexpected. Anthropologists have generally considered the audience for ethnic expression to be either outsiders or those other members of the local social unit, beyond the household, who assess the individual's conformity to the group's norms and values (Barth 1969: 36–37; Wobst 1977: 327–328; Hodder 1978: 49, 50). Behavior and artifacts that function within the context of the immediate family would not normally be exposed to this sort of inspection and so would not be expected to play a significant role in the expression of ethnic identity (Wobst 1977: 323–324).

Santley et al. (1987: 87) have pointed out that food preparation and consumption, together with the associated technology, may be used as vehicles for ethnic expression because meals are occasions for family gathering and communication and, at times, for hospitality to visitors. Probably more important, though, is the role of these household items in enculturation. In situations like that in Tlailotlacan, where most adults of both sexes were part of the enclave culture and where occupation was expected to continue for generations, the enclave could only survive through a persistent and intensive program of enculturation of the young, their immersion from birth in the ways and symbols of the community. The household environment, with its constant presentation of Zapotec symbols and practices, would have been of fundamental importance in this effort. The various artifacts involved in it (conical bowls, fine wares, figurines, etc.) should thus be viewed as the instruments as well as the products of enculturation.

A variety of other practices would also have supported the enclave, insulating it to some degree from the larger society of Teotihuacan. Religion is often a major factor in such situations (cf. Cohen 1969: 149–160; Berlo 1984: 133, 137). The Tlailotlacanos had a number of distinctive rituals on both the household and public levels, involving the use of Zapotec style figurines, urns, and *sahumadores,* and the common practice of extended burial. Their supernatural figures were also different. Frogs and bats were commonly featured in the TL6 figurines, and two of the TL7 urns depict the Deity with Serpent Mouth Mask (Rattray 1987).

The Zapotec glyphs on the locally made doorjamb stone of the TL7 tomb and in the headdress of one of the TL7 urns suggest the continued use of the Zapotec language. Joyce Marcus (personal communication) has pointed out that the use of Zapotec glyphs would have been necessary in mortuary contexts, if the information was to reach the Zapotec ancestors. However, it is not clear how glyphs are related to the spoken language (Marcus 1980: 64). Thus, their presence does not necessarily prove the survival or widespread use of the Zapotec language in Tlailotlacan, though it seems probable. It would have been facilitated by the practice of ethnic endogamy, with enclave occupants drawing on their own or related communities for marriage partners. The osteological evidence from TL7 suggests some degree of endogamy (Spence 1976, n.d.).

As mentioned earlier, the apparent persistence of Monte Alban II and II–IIIA Transition forms for some centuries in Tlailotlacan requires some explanation. William Fowler and John Paddock (1975) believe that this persistence is illusory, and that these Zapotec features actually survived for only one or two generations. There is, however, another explanation. The new symbolic load assigned to these ceramics in the maintenance of a beleaguered ethnic identity would have had the effect of freezing their forms, protecting them from the normal processes of change over time. They had become instruments of enculturation and visible expressions of conformity, so change in them would have been perceived as a rejection of the community's values and ways (Barth 1969: 36–37; Wobst 1977: 327–328; Hodder 1978: 49–50). Also, contacts between the inhabitants of Tlailotlacan and the people of the Valley of Oaxaca seem to have been intermittent and restricted after the founding of the enclave. Monte Alban IIIA imports are very rare in Tlailotlacan, although they and even some Monte Alban IIIB items appear elsewhere in Teotihuacan (Rattray 1987: 256). There would thus have been little direct stimulus for the people of Tlailotlacan to "update" their ceramic assemblage.

THE ECONOMIC ROLE OF THE ENCLAVE

Ethnic boundaries in pluralistic contexts tend to persist when they are instrumental in securing access to some vital resource (Despres 1975: 199–200, 204; Hodder 1979, 1981). Presumably, then, there is an important economic factor in the survival of Tlailotlacan. However, the excavations have uncovered no evidence of specialized production in the area other than the manufacture of Zapotec-style ceramics. Data from the city at large indicate that these rarely left the enclave (Rattray 1987: 253). There are a few sites (16–18:N2W5) some 540 m northeast of Tlailotlacan that also have a high proportion of Zapotec sherds, but these are not identical to those of Tlailotlacan (Rattray 1987: 253). The assemblage is dominated by conical bowls, called *apaxtles,* at the larger end of the Tlailotlacan size range, and by large, thick, flat-faced plates or lids totally absent in Tlailotlacan. These may well reflect the practice of some specialized activities in the N2W5 sites, but without excavation they cannot be identified or related to Tlailotlacan.

In the absence of evidence for specialized production in Tlailotlacan itself, the economic role of the inhabitants may have been that of middlemen in the trade of items produced elsewhere. The Hausa of Sabo offer a very instructive analogy (Cohen 1969). Sabo was a Hausa enclave in the Yoruba city of Ibadan. The Hausa inhabitants of Sabo used their ethnic identity to secure control over the trade of a variety of products, particularly kola nuts and cattle, among the Hausa in their homeland to the north, the Yoruba of Ibadan, and the Hausa of similar enclaves in other southern cities. This situation continued for more than half a century, a culture developing within Sabo which, although Hausa, was different in several important respects from that of the homeland.

Tlailotlacan may have followed a very similar course. There are sites elsewhere in central Mexico with a mixture of Teotihuacan- and Oaxacan-related materials (Díaz 1980; Crespo and Mastache 1981). It is possible that these, together with others still unidentified, were linked in a trade network protected from competitive intrusions by their common language and culture and by the social ties created by frequent intermarriage. The ceramics of El Tesoro and Acoculco in the Tula region are virtually identical to those of Tlailotlacan, and suggest that these sites may have been settled from Tlailotlacan (Crespo and Mastache 1981).

There is no direct evidence yet in the form of debris or storage accumulations in Tlailotlacan for any particular commodity in this network. Probably more than one item, from more than one source, was involved. Evelyn Rattray (n.d.) has suggested that the Tlailotlacanos might have controlled the flow of Thin Orange pottery into Teotihuacan. Thin Orange sherds are common in the site fill. In fact, one of the characteristics of sites in the area is a high proportion of Thin Orange (Altschul 1987: 212–213, tables 5–6; Cowgill, Altschul, and Sload 1984: 160–165). Thin Orange bowls make up 27% of the patio offering vessels, and there is the remarkable offering of Thin Orange miniatures in the North Tomb. Thomas Charlton (n.d.: 29) has noted the association of Thin Orange and Oaxacan grey wares on trade routes into the Valley of Teotihuacan.

Lime from the Tula region, exploited by communities like El Tesoro and transported to Teotihuacan for the preparation of plaster, may have been another commodity (Sanders, Parsons, and Santley 1979: 126–127; Díaz 1980; Crespo and Mastache 1981). One of the burials found in the 1989 excavation was an extended adult male with a miniature *olla,* a shell bead, a stone plaster smoother, and two flat-faced polishing stones, perhaps the tool kit of a mason. The fine green obsidian of Pachuca may also have been distributed in part through Tlailotlacan. Blades, cores, and some points of this material were reaching Oaxaca in the Middle Horizon (Finsten n.d.: 204–206, table 35; Winter 1989). There is no evidence of obsidian working in Tlailotlacan, but the enclave inhabitants might still have been obtaining and passing on refined cores and blades. Virtually all of the Tlailotlacan-produced conical bowls found outside Tlailotlacan come from five sites in map square N1W2 (Rattray 1987: 253). Four of these sites are obsidian workshops of the Great Compound regional workshop area, where quantities of green obsidian blades and cores were produced (Spence 1981; Altschul n.d.: 144–146).

Tlailotlacan, a Zapotec Enclave

THE COMPARATIVE ANALYSIS OF ENCLAVES

Tlailotlacan is not the only ethnic enclave to have been examined archaeologically (cf. Willey 1953). Other analyses have focused on an Assyrian merchant enclave in Anatolia (Ozguç 1963), the Teotihuacan presence in highland Guatemala (Sanders and Michels 1977; Berlo 1984) and in Veracruz (Santley et al. 1987), and a Gulf Coast enclave in Teotihuacan (Rattray 1987). As such studies accumulate, a set of appropriate questions is developing. These include the function of the enclave and its relationship, if any, to the homeland. Some may be political extensions of the homeland: embassies, garrisons, the quarters of royal agents involved in elite trade, and so on. In situations like Tlailotlacan and Sabo, on the other hand, the enclave is quite independent of the homeland. Indeed, the homeland may be represented by no more than one terminal in a widespread trade network. This will have a profound effect not only on the role of the enclave and its articulation with the host society, but also on the ways in which ethnicity is expressed and the audience toward which such expressions are directed. A political outpost, for example, may be more apt to celebrate its relationship to the homeland in major elite ceremonies like the burial of its leaders (if they are buried locally) and to ensure that the audience for these expressions includes some members of the host elite. Mounds A and B in Kaminaljuyu may be a case in point (Kidder et al. 1946).

An enclave of Assyrian merchants from Assur has been identified in Kanesh, an Anatolian city (Ozguç 1963). They controlled the trade of gold, silver, copper, and precious stones from Anatolia to Assur and the return flow of tin and textiles, as well as the local distribution of a variety of other items. The enclave was probably an Assyrian colony, the resident merchants under the political domination of Assur (but note Adams 1974: 246). The domestic artifacts are all of local Hatti types, reflecting the paucity of Assyrian women in the colony. In contrast, the Tlailotlacanos evidently had little or no formal political relationship with Monte Alban. The location of the enclave near the edge of the city and its low to medium status suggest that it was not involved in mediating the apparently amicable relationship that prevailed between the ruling elites of the two cities (Millon n.d.; Marcus 1980: 56–59; 1983).

Also of importance is the composition and turnover of the enclave personnel. An enclave of foreign men taking their spouses from the host society will quickly become acculturated, their distinct identity manifested only in certain male-oriented aspects of culture like weaponry and some rituals (cf. Berlo 1984: 129, 137, 193–194). In situations where ethnic endogamy is practiced, however, there will be a more pervasive and durable expression of ethnicity (Sanders 1977; Santley et al. 1987: 86). This was apparently the case in Tlailotlacan and at Matacapan, a site in the Gulf Coast region with a major zone of Teotihuacan-style public and residential

Michael W. Spence

structures and quantities of locally made versions of Teotihuacan cylindrical tripods, hemispherical ring base bowls, *candeleros,* and figurines (Santley et al. 1987: 89–97). The Matacapan enclave may have been linked to the "Merchants' Barrio," an area near the east edge of Teotihuacan with high proportions of pottery imported from Tajin, the Gulf Coast, and various places in the Maya region (Rattray 1987).

Finally, if the enclave personnel make frequent and prolonged visits to the homeland, are replaced often by new agents, or make it a point to take their spouses from the homeland, the enclave will present a more comprehensive and up-to-date version of the homeland culture. On the other hand, when contact with the homeland is brief, rare, or restricted to only a small proportion of the enclave occupants, the enclave will have a more fragmented and anachronistic version. This was clearly the case with Tlailotlacan, and it underscores the fact that the enclave was not simply a political or economic outpost of Monte Alban. Although the elites of Teotihuacan and Monte Alban interacted well into, and perhaps through, the Monte Alban III A period (Millon 1973: 41; Marcus 1983), any significant cultural interchange between the Tlailotlacan enclave and the Valley of Oaxaca had apparently withered by the end of the II–III A Transition. Contacts after that were probably limited largely to merchants, and may have been somewhat sporadic.

Acknowledgments The TL6 excavation was supported by a grant from the Social Sciences and Humanities Research Council of Canada. I am very grateful to Rubén Cabrera Castro and Evelyn Rattray for their support and assistance. My thanks to Saburo Sugiyama and Laura Finsten for their help, to Mark Borland for his supervisory skills, and to René Millon, Joyce Marcus, Steve Kowalewski, and Marc Winter for their comments on a previous draft of this paper.

BIBLIOGRAPHY

ABASCAL, RAFAEL, GARMAN HARBOTTLE, AND EDWARD SAYRE
    1974   Correlation between Terra Cotta Figurines and Pottery from the Valley of Mexico and Source Clays by Activation Analysis. In *Archaeological Chemistry* (C. W. Beck, ed.): 81–99. Chemical Society, Washington, D.C.

ADAMS, ROBERT MCCORMICK
    1974   Anthropological Perspectives on Ancient Trade. *Current Anthropology* 15: 239–258.

ALTSCHUL, JEFFREY H.
    1987   Social Districts of Teotihuacan. In *Teotihuacan: Nuevos datos, nuevas síntesis, nuevos problemas* (Emily McClung de Tapia and Evelyn C. Rattray, eds.): 191–217. Instituto de Investigaciones Antropológicas, Serie Antropológica 72. Universidad Nacional Autónoma de México, Mexico, D.F.
    n.d.   Spatial and Statistical Evidence for Social Groupings at Teotihuacan, Mexico. Ph.D. dissertation, Brandeis University, 1981.

AVENI, ANTHONY F.
    1980   *Skywatchers of Ancient Mexico*. University of Texas Press, Austin.

BARTH, FREDRIK
    1969   Introduction. In *Ethnic Groups and Boundaries* (F. Barth, ed.): 9–38. Little, Brown, Boston.

BERLO, JANET CATHERINE
    1984   *Teotihuacan Art Abroad: A Study of Metropolitan Style and Provincial Transformation in Incensario Workshops*. BAR International Series 199, Oxford.

BERNAL, IGNACIO, AND ARTURO OLIVEROS
    1984   *Exploraciones arqueológicas en Dainzú, Oaxaca*. Instituto Nacional de Antropología e Historia, Colección Científica Arqueología 167. Mexico, D.F.

BINFORD, LEWIS
    1971   Mortuary Practices: Their Study and Their Potential. In *Approaches to the Social Dimensions of Mortuary Practices* (James A. Brown, ed.): 6–29. Society for American Archaeology Memoir 25. Washington, D.C.

BLANTON, RICHARD
    1978   *Monte Alban: Settlement Patterns at the Ancient Zapotec Capital*. Academic Press, New York.

BUCHIGNANI, NORMAN
    1987   Ethnic Phenomena and Contemporary Social Theory: Their Implications for Archaeology. In *Ethnicity and Culture* (Réginald Auger, Margaret Glass, Scott MacEachern, and Peter McCartney, eds.): 15–24. University of Calgary, Calgary.

CASO, ALFONSO, AND IGNACIO BERNAL
    1952   *Urnas de Oaxaca*. Instituto Nacional de Antropología e Historia Memorias 2. Mexico, D.F.

Caso, Alfonso, Ignacio Bernal, and Jorge R. Acosta
  1967   La Cerámica de Monte Albán. Instituto Nacional de Antropología e Historia Memorias 13. Mexico, D.F.

Charlton, Thomas H.
  n.d.   Final Report of a Surface Survey of Preconquest Trade Networks in Mesoamerica. Unpublished manuscript, 1977.

Cohen, Abner
  1969   Custom and Politics in Urban Africa: A Study of Hausa Migrants in Yoruba Towns. University of California Press, Berkeley.

Cowgill, George L., Jeffrey Altschul, and Rebecca Sload
  1984   Spatial Analysis of Teotihuacan: A Mesoamerican Metropolis. In *Intrasite Spatial Analysis in Archaeology* (Harold J. Hietala, ed.): 154–195. Cambridge University Press, Cambridge.

Crespo Oviedo, Ana María, and Alba Guadalupe Mastache de E.
  1981   La presencia en el área de Tula, Hidalgo, de grupos relacionados con el barrio de Oaxaca en Teotihuacan. In *Interacción cultural en México central* (Evelyn Rattray, Jaime Litvak King, and Clara Díaz O., eds.): 99–106. Universidad Nacional Autónoma de México, Mexico, D.F.

Despres, Leo
  1975   Toward a Theory of Ethnic Phenomena. In *Ethnicity and Resource Competition in Plural Societies* (L. Despres, ed.): 187–207. Mouton, The Hague.

Díaz, Clara Luz
  1980   *Chingú, un sitio clásico del área de Tula, Hgo.* Instituto Nacional de Antropología e Historia, Colección Científica Arqueología 90. Mexico, D.F.

Drennan, Robert D.
  1983   Appendix: Radiocarbon Dates for the Oaxaca Region. In *The Cloud People: Divergent Evolution of the Zapotec and Mixtec Civilizations* (Kent V. Flannery and Joyce Marcus, eds.): 363–370. Academic Press, New York.

Finsten, Laura
  n.d.   The Classic-Postclassic Transition in the Valley of Oaxaca, Mexico: A Regional Analysis of the Process of Political Decentralisation in a Prehistoric Complex Society. Ph.D. dissertation, Purdue University, 1983.

Flannery, Kent V.
  1983   The Legacy of the Early Urban Period: An Ethnohistoric Approach to Monte Alban's Temples, Residences, and Royal Tombs. In *The Cloud People: Divergent Evolution of the Zapotec and Mixtec Civilizations* (Kent V. Flannery and Joyce Marcus, eds.): 132–163. Academic Press, New York.

FOWLER, WILLIAM A., AND JOHN PADDOCK
1975 Nexos Teotihuacan—Monte Albán vistos en la cerámica. *XIII Mesa Redonda de la Sociedad Mexicana de Antropología, Arqueología II*: 163–177. Sociedad Mexicana de Antropología, Mexico, D.F.

HIGGINS, MICHAEL J.
1986 ¿Quiénes son los migrantes étnicos al teatro urbano del valle de Oaxaca? In *Etnicidad y pluralismo cultural; la dinámica étnica en Oaxaca* (Alicia M. Barabas and Miguel A. Bartolomé, eds.): 401–421. Instituto Nacional de Antropología e Historia, Mexico, D.F.

HODDER, IAN
1978 The Maintenance of Group Identities in the Baringo District, W. Kenya. In *Social Organization and Settlement: Contributions from Anthropology, Archaeology and Geography, Part 1* (David Green, Colin Haselgrove, and Matthew Spriggs, eds.): 47–73. BAR International Series 47, Oxford.
1979 Economic and Social Stress and Material Culture Patterning. *American Antiquity* 44: 446–454.
1981 Society, Economy, and Culture: An Ethnographic Case Study Amongst the Lozi. In *Pattern of the Past: Studies in Honour of David Clarke* (Ian Hodder, G. Isaac, and N. Hammond, eds.): 67–95. Cambridge University Press, Cambridge.
1982 *Symbols in Action*. Cambridge University Press, Cambridge.

KIDDER, ALFRED, JESSE JENNINGS, AND EDWIN SHOOK
1946 *Excavations at Kaminaljuyu, Guatemala*. Carnegie Institution of Washington Pub. 561. Washington, D.C.

KOWALEWSKI, STEPHEN A., CHARLES SPENCER, AND ELSA REDMOND
1978 Appendix II: Description of Ceramic Categories. In *Monte Alban: Settlement Patterns at the Ancient Zapotec Capital* (Richard Blanton): 167–193. Academic Press, New York.

KROTSER, PAULA H.
1987 Levels of Specialization Among Potters of Teotihuacan. In *Teotihuacan: Nuevos datos, nuevas síntesis, nuevos problemas* (Emily McClung de Tapia and Evelyn Rattray, eds.): 417–427. Instituto de Investigaciones Antropológicas, Serie Antropológica 72. Universidad Nacional Autónoma de México, Mexico, D.F.

KUTTRUFF, CARL
1978 Appendix VIII: Figurines and Urn Fragments from the Monte Alban Survey. In *Monte Alban: Settlement Patterns at the Ancient Zapotec Capital* (Richard Blanton): 379–402. Academic Press, New York.

MCLAUGHLIN, CASTLE
1987 Style as a Social Boundary Marker: A Plains Indian Example. In *Ethnicity and Culture* (Réginald Auger, Margaret Glass, Scott MacEachern, and Peter McCartney, eds.): 55–66. University of Calgary, Calgary.

Michael W. Spence

MARCUS, JOYCE
    1980   Zapotec Writing. *Scientific American* 242 (2): 50–64.
    1983   Teotihuacan Visitors on Monte Alban Monuments and Murals. In *The Cloud People: Divergent Evolution of the Zapotec and Mixtec Civilizations* (Kent V. Flannery and Joyce Marcus, eds.): 175–181. Academic Press, New York.

MILLON, RENÉ
    1967   Urna de Monte Albán IIIA encontrada en Teotihuacán. *Instituto Nacional de Antropología e Historia Boletín* 29: 42–44.
    1973   The Teotihuacan Map, Part 1, Text. In *Urbanization at Teotihuacan, Mexico, Vol. 1: The Teotihuacan Map* (René Millon, ed.). University of Texas Press, Austin.
    n.d.   Progress Report No. 9. Unpublished manuscript, 1967.

MILLON, RENÉ, BRUCE DREWITT, AND GEORGE L. COWGILL
    1973   The Teotihuacan Map, Part 2, Maps. In *Urbanization at Teotihuacan, Mexico, Vol. 1: The Teotihuacan Map* (René Millon, ed.). University of Texas Press, Austin.

OZGUÇ, TAHSIN
    1963   An Assyrian Trading Outpost. *Scientific American* 208 (2): 96–106.

PADDOCK, JOHN
    1983   The Oaxaca Barrio at Teotihuacan. In *The Cloud People: Divergent Evolution of the Zapotec and Mixtec Civilizations* (Kent V. Flannery and Joyce Marcus, eds.): 170–175. Academic Press, New York.

QUINTANA, CONSUELO
    1987   Excavaciones al SE del denominado "Barrio Oaxaqueño" de Teotihuacan. Paper presented to the XX Mesa Redonda, Sociedad Mexicana de Antropología. Mexico, D.F.

RATTRAY, EVELYN C.
    1987   Los barrios foráneos de Teotihuacan. In *Teotihuacan: Nuevos datos, nuevas síntesis, nuevos problemas* (Emily McClung de Tapia and Evelyn Rattray, eds.): 243–273. Instituto de Investigaciones Antropológicas, Serie Antropológica 72. Universidad Nacional Autónoma de México, Mexico, D.F.
    n.d.   The Teotihuacan Ceramic Chronology. Unpublished manuscript, 1979.

ROMANO, ARTURO
    1974   Sistema de enterramientos. In *Antropología física: Época Prehispánica* (Javier Romero M., ed.): 83–112. Instituto Nacional de Antropología e Historia, Mexico, D.F.

SANDERS, WILLIAM T.
    1977   Ethnographic Analogy and the Teotihuacan Horizon Style. In *Teotihuacan and Kaminaljuyu* (William T. Sanders and Joseph Michels, eds.): 397–410. Pennsylvania State University Press, University Park.

SANDERS, WILLIAM T., AND JOSEPH MICHELS (EDS.)
  1977   *Teotihuacan and Kaminaljuyu.* Pennsylvania State University Press, University Park.

SANDERS, WILLIAM T., JEFFREY R. PARSONS, AND ROBERT SANTLEY
  1979   *The Basin of Mexico: Ecological Processes in the Evolution of a Civilization.* Academic Press, New York.

SANTLEY, ROBERT, CLARE YARBOROUGH, AND BARBARA HALL
  1987   Enclaves, Ethnicity, and the Archaeological Record at Matacapan. In *Ethnicity and Culture* (Réginald Auger, Margaret Glass, Scott MacEachern, and Peter McCartney, eds.): 85–100. University of Calgary, Calgary.

SAYRE, EDWARD, AND GARMAN HARBOTTLE
  n.d.   The Analysis by Neutron Activation of Archaeological Ceramics Related to Teotihuacan: Local Wares and Trade Sherds. Unpublished manuscript, 1979.

SCHILDKROUT, ENID
  1974   Ethnicity and Generational Differences among Urban Immigrants in Ghana. In *Urban Ethnicity* (Abner Cohen, ed.): 187–222. Tavistock Publications, London.

SÉJOURNÉ, LAURETTE
  1960   El simbolismo de los rituales funerarios en Monte Albán. *Revista Mexicana de Estudios Antropológicos* 16: 77–90.
  1966   *Arqueología de Teotihuacan: La cerámica.* Fondo de Cultura Económica, Mexico, D.F.

SERRANO, CARLOS, AND ZAID LAGUNAS
  1975   Sistema de enterramiento y notas sobre el material osteológico de La Ventilla, Teotihuacán, México. *Instituto Nacional de Antropología e Historia Anales* IV: 105–144.

SPENCE, MICHAEL W.
  1976   Human Skeletal Material from the Oaxaca Barrio in Teotihuacan, Mexico. In *Archaeological Frontiers: Papers on New World High Cultures in Honor of J. Charles Kelley* (Robert Pickering, ed.): 129–148. Southern Illinois University, Carbondale.
  1981   Obsidian Production and the State in Teotihuacan. *American Antiquity* 46: 769–788.
  1990   Excavaciones en Tlailotlacan, Teotihuacan. Segunda temporada. *Consejo de Arqueología Boletín, 1989:* 128–130.
  n.d.   Human Skeletal Material from Teotihuacan. Unpublished manuscript, 1990.

SPENCER, CHARLES
  1982   *The Cuicatlán Cañada and Monte Albán: A Study of Primary State Formation.* Academic Press, New York.

Spores, Ronald
 1983 Ramos Phase Urbanization in the Mixteca Alta. In *The Cloud People: Divergent Evolution of the Zapotec and Mixtec Civilizations* (Kent V. Flannery and Joyce Marcus, eds.): 120–123. Academic Press, New York.

Storey, Rebecca
 n.d. The Paleodemography of Tlajinga 33: An Apartment Compound of the Pre-Columbian City of Teotihuacan. Ph.D. dissertation, Pennsylvania State University, 1983.

Storey, Rebecca, and Randolph Widmer
 n.d. Excavations at Tlajinga 33. In *A Reconstruction of a Classic Period Landscape in the Teotihuacan Valley* (William T. Sanders, Deborah Nichols, Rebecca Storey, and Randolph Widner). Unpublished report, National Science Foundation, Washington, D.C., 1982.

Sugiyama, Saburo
 1989 Burials Dedicated to the Old Temple of Quetzalcoatl at Teotihuacan, Mexico. *American Antiquity* 54: 85–106.

Willey, Gordon R.
 1953 A Pattern of Diffusion-Acculturation. *Southwestern Journal of Anthropology* 9: 369–383.

Winter, Marcus C.
 1974 Residential Patterns at Monte Alban, Oaxaca, Mexico. *Science* 186: 981–987.
 1986 Unidades habitacionales prehispánicas en Oaxaca. In *Unidades habitacionales mesoaméricanas y sus áreas de actividad* (Linda Manzanilla, ed.): 325–374. Universidad Nacional Autónoma de México, Mexico, D.F.
 1989 La obsidiana en Oaxaca prehispánica. In *La obsidiana en Mesoamérica* (Margarita Gaxiola G. and John E. Clark, eds.): 345–362. Instituto Nacional de Antropología e Historia, *Colección Científica Arqueología* 176.

Wobst, Martin
 1977 Stylistic Behavior and Information Exchange. In *For the Director: Research Essays in Honor of James B. Griffin* (C. Cleland, ed.): 317–342. University of Michigan Museum of Anthropology Anthropological Papers 61.

Style in Lapidary Technology: Identifying the Teotihuacan Lapidary Industry

MARGARET H. TURNER
MASSACHUSETTS COLLEGE OF ART

ALTHOUGH THEY ARE HALLMARKS of two distinctive and very different Mesoamerican lapidary traditions, the serpentine Teotihuacan-style mask and the jadeite Olmec-style mask in the Robert Woods Bliss Collection at Dumbarton Oaks (Fig. 1a–b) are alike in two important ways. Both were carved from the green stone that was so highly prized by most Mesoamerican societies, and both were carved with the same basic repertoire of stone-working techniques, a repertoire that remained fundamentally unchanged from the Preclassic through the Post-Conquest periods throughout the region. In these two respects, Olmec and Teotihuacan lapidary styles are linked. Yet the modeling of the form, the mode of representation, and the basic visual possibilities seen in the material by Teotihuacan and Olmec lapidaries are quite distinct. Some of these differences in style, as well as some similarities, can be attributed to what has been called the *technological style* used to create the lapidary object.

Technological style is a term first used by Heather Lechtman (1977) in her analysis of Andean metals and metal-working techniques. As a concept, technological style can encompass information on the way in which specific raw materials are chosen, obtained, and processed; the techniques used to achieve certain design features; and the ways in which artists and craftspeople are both socially and economically organized to produce the desired objects. The extent to which these factors are controlled by the artists themselves or by an outside authority can also be an aspect of technological style. The concept of technological style asserts that the very activities that produce the artifact are themselves stylistic (Lechtman 1977: 5).

I have investigated the technological style of lapidary production at Teotihuacan (Turner n.d.) using lapidary materials—fine stone and shell—obtained through intensive surface collection of the entire city and through a series of twenty-eight test excavations conducted by the personnel of the Teotihuacan Mapping Project (Millon 1973). These lapidary materials afforded

Fig. 1a Teotihuacan-style mask. Serpentine. Robert Woods Bliss Collection, Dumbarton Oaks, Washington, D.C.

an excellent opportunity to study the range of fine stones and shells chosen by Teotihuacan's residents as well as the techniques used to carve them. The unique nature of the Teotihuacan Mapping Project data means that lapidary usage in a large number of social environments within the city is represented. These areas include the Pyramids of the Sun and Moon and the residential and ritual complexes around them, the temples, apartment compounds and other structures lining the Street of the Dead and East and West Avenues, and

Style in Lapidary Technology

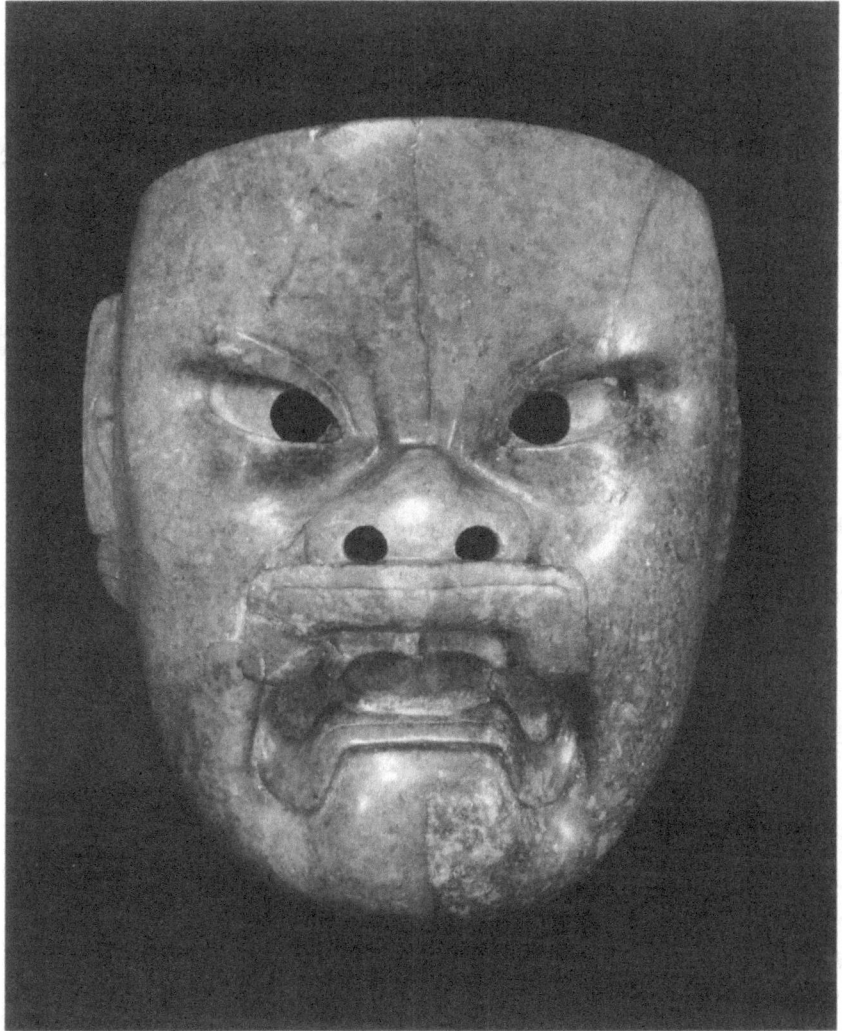

Fig. 1b Olmec-style mask. Jadeite. Robert Woods Bliss Collection, Dumbarton Oaks, Washington, D.C.

apartment compounds and other structures in all quadrants of the city (Millon, Drewitt, and Cowgill 1973). The results of this analysis identify Teotihuacan lapidary production as an industry with two kinds of workshops and two levels of production. One level of production is best exemplified by the data recovered through excavation in an area of the city known as the lapidary *barrio*.

Margaret H. Turner

THE TEOTIHUACAN LAPIDARY *BARRIO*

The most important collection of lapidary materials made in the Teotihuacan Mapping Project survey comes from an area on the northeast margin of the city. A *barrio* of several apartment compounds in square N3E5 (Millon, Drewitt, and Cowgill 1973: 49) was first thought to have been an area where lapidaries worked when surface collection revealed quantities of fine stone and shell debris far in excess of that collected at the other apartment compounds surveyed. Following this discovery, test excavation 18 was conducted at site 8 in square N3E5 in 1968. Again, the quality and quantity of fine stones and shells found through excavation contributed to the identification of this *barrio* as an area of lapidary workshops. In what follows I will describe what has been learned of the materials, techniques, and organization of Teotihuacan's lapidaries through analysis of the Teotihuacan Mapping Project data. What begins to emerge from this analysis is an identifiable lapidary industry with a distinctive technological style.

I have classified five kinds of stone as "fine stone" with the belief that they were also classified as such by the Teotihuacanos (Turner 1987: 466). These are jadeite, serpentine, onyx or *tecali,* slate, and mica. Related lapidary-quality materials in use in the city included various species of marine shell of both Atlantic and Pacific origin, freshwater shell, quartz, chert, chalcedony, and other minerals such as pyrite, malachite, cinnabar, and hematite. These materials occur in the Teotihuacan Mapping Project collections in the form of small objects intended for personal adornment or ritual use in both complete and broken states. Some of these objects include beads and small plaques or pendants in jadeite, serpentine, quartz, steatite, and shell; the distinctive *tau*- or T-form found in the Teotihuacan Mapping Project collections in serpentine, slate, and nacreous shell (Fig. 2) (see also Séjourné 1966: lám. 31); and the slate or shale figurine form also illustrated by Manuel Gamio (1922, 1: lám. 100i–n), which has come to be called the Tzacualli figurine after its discovery in Tzacualli phase contexts during the 1959 exploration of the tunnels in the Pyramid of the Sun (Millon, Drewitt, and Bennyhoff 1965: 24–25).[1]

These kinds of objects were the majority of items made by lapidaries at Teotihuacan. They are found in almost every context in the city from the Pyramid of the Sun and surrounding residential and ritual complexes to the apartment compounds lining East and West Avenues and to the outlying apartment compounds relatively far from the city's center. The ubiquitous occurrence of these forms suggests that they constitute an assemblage of lapidary items commonly used by Teotihuacanos in many levels of that society. These items are not of the rarity or quality of the Teotihuacan-style

---

[1] The objects illustrated in Figs. 2–12 were photographed by Robert R. Turner and are in the collections of the Teotihuacan Mapping Project, San Juan Teotihuacan, Mexico.

Style in Lapidary Technology

Fig. 2 Serpentine *tau*. TE 18 8:N3E5.

mask, nor of the ritual importance of the pyrite-backed slate mirrors to be discussed below, but they can be said to have played an important role in personal adornment and ritual for many Teotihuacan residents.

The test excavation and surface collection in the lapidary *barrio* area (TE 18; 8:N3E5) provided important data for the identification of fine stone and shell workshop sites (Krotser n.d.) The test pit was placed in site 8 of square N3E5 within the walls of an apartment compound and along the southern edge of a modern road. A series of earth, rather than concrete, floors encountered during the excavation led the investigators to suggest that lapidaries had worked in an interior open-air patio with packed-earth floors. The data recovered from this single 2 × 2 m test pit include many hundreds of fragments of serpentine and slate debris; some broken ornaments of jadeite, serpentine, and slate; and shell debris and broken ornaments from a few species of shell, but especially from tree oyster (*Isognomon alatus*), an Atlantic species. In addition, waste fragments discarded when these same fine stones and shells were worked were recovered from collections made on the surface of the apartment compounds represented as sites 1, 2, 3, 5, and 7 in square N3E5 of the Teotihuacan Map.

MINUTE DEBITAGE

The most conclusive evidence that the group of apartment compounds in square N3E5 was indeed a *barrio* of lapidary workshops comes from minute debitage (fragments 1 mm or less in greatest length) (Fig. 3) recovered through flotation of soils from all layers of TE 18. All of the fine stone and shell types present in larger fragments of debitage or broken ornaments were present in the minute debitage from flotation. Even jadeite, which was not heavily represented in debris or broken ornaments, was present in the minute debitage.

Fig. 3 Minute debitage from flotation. TE 18 8:N3E5.

Minute debitage is important to the identification of workshop sites because it allows the investigator to differentiate actual workshop sites from waste dumps or storage areas. Minute debitage represents waste material small enough to be left *in situ* even if workshop floors were periodically swept clean of larger waste fragments (Fladmark 1982; Vance 1987: 58–59). These larger fragments could have been treated in one of three ways: left on workshop floors, discarded entirely in waste dumps, or stored for eventual re-use. Data from TE 18 suggest that certain stones and shells were more valued than others and that waste from these different categories of materi-

Style in Lapidary Technology

als was treated differently. For example, serpentine and slate waste and fragments of shell of the tree oyster species were left on the earth floors of the workshop. Although they may have been periodically gathered and discarded, waste fragments from these lapidary materials are found in great abundance both on the surface of the lapidary *barrio* and on all floors uncovered in TE 18. In contrast to this, waste from the more valued jadeite and shell species such as *Spondylus* sp. was almost non-existent in both surface collection and excavation. The small amounts of jadeite available to the lapidaries of these workshops were likely to have been worked and reworked down to the smallest possible fragments. Large waste fragments of jadeite and other more valued stones and shells would not have been left on workshop floors but may have been stored for re-use. The importance of identifying minute debitage from this site was emphasized when jadeite, very sparsely represented in TE 18 in larger waste fragments as discussed earlier, appeared in the minute debitage from flotation. The identification of minute debitage at this site, therefore, is a clear identification that the apartment compound designated as 8:N3E5 on the Teotihuacan Map was an actual lapidary workshop site and not simply a waste dump or storage area.

Minute debitage from TE 18 is also indicative of lapidary techniques. Traces of these techniques such as drill scars, fine lines caused by grinding, and marks caused by percussion and pressure flaking all can be seen even on these very small fragments with, and on some pieces without, microscopic enlargement.

LAPIDARY TECHNIQUES

For more detailed information on the technical processes used by the lapidaries of this *barrio* of workshops, analysis of the larger fragments of debris and broken ornaments was necessary. These items showed that Teotihuacan lapidaries used much the same repertoire of techniques identified by Tatiana Proskouriakoff (1974) in her analysis of the Sacred Cenote collection from Chichen Itza. These techniques included fracturing, grinding, sawing, grooving, incising, drilling, and polishing. Such techniques also were used by lapidaries in many other areas of Mesoamerica (Covarrubias 1946; Johnson 1976).

Fracturing

The surface of the lapidary *barrio* is littered with serpentine, shell (Fig. 4), and slate waste—the products of the fracturing process. Much of this waste material bears the scars of this fracturing in the form of long striations or grooves made by thin pointed instruments. Serpentine is especially vulnerable to showing these marks by virtue of its fibrous cleavage and relative softness (2–5 on the Mohs scale). A serpentine core with these long,

Fig. 4   Shell waste. TE 18 8:N3E5.

grooved striations was found on the surface of site 1 in the lapidary *barrio*. Slate, in contrast, breaks with a splintery fracture at right angles to the direction of the pressure resulting in platey fragments with splintered sides or ends. The tools used in this pressure fracturing technique are also found in the *barrio*. These are usually *lajas* or building stones reused and formed into pointed instruments capable of providing both the weight and the sharp edge necessary to fracture serpentine. Obsidian tools are also a possible candidate for pressure fracture of finer or more easily fractured stones such as mica or slate, and would have worked on shell as well.

Sawing

Sawing is one of the most essential lapidary operations. It could be used both in the preliminary layout of the piece to be carved and as a more precise way to achieve certain design features. In the lapidary *barrio* sawing is evident on many discarded fragments of slate, serpentine, jadeite, and shell, as well as on pieces broken in the manufacturing process. Traces of sawing include septums left in the center of flat surfaces when sawing proceeded from either side to meet in the middle (Fig. 5). The rough edge, or septum, may have been given a cursory grinding or polishing, but more often it was

Style in Lapidary Technology

Fig. 5 Sawn jadeite with septum. TE 18 8:N3E5.

left untreated. The side with the septum might then become the back of the object. The saw ridges left on waste products are frequently visible without microscopic examination. With the microscope, however, these ridges are more sharply defined and show the characteristic wedge-shaped, flat-bottomed scar left by a rigid saw.

In the lapidary *barrio*, the only candidates for sawing implements actually found are obsidian and some quartz and chert blades. It is highly probable that Teotihuacan lapidaries also used the more efficient method provided by hardwood blades used in conjunction with an abrasive material.

String or cord sawing is often suggested as a common Mesoamerican lapidary technique (Lothrop 1955). The Maya used this technique with great expertise (Proskouriakoff 1974). However, at Teotihuacan, lapidary styles do not appear to have called for frequent use of the string saw. In the lapidary *barrio*, one piece of square-cut *tecali* (Fig. 6) shows evidence of cord sawing on two sides in the form of cuts with very narrow, rounded troughs. However, this technique was best adapted for making interior, curvilinear cuts in designs, something not found in the more angular Teotihuacan lapidary work.

Margaret H. Turner

Fig. 6 Cut and sawn *tecali*. TE 18 8:N3E5.

Grooving and Incising: The Teotihuacan Mask and the Mezcala Lapidary

The lapidary *barrio* materials are primarily waste and broken, discarded objects and therefore do not have many traces of grooving or incising techniques. However, grooving and incising were techniques known to the lapidaries who carved the Teotihuacan-style masks and figurines. In these masks, stone bowls, and figurative sculpture, grooving is used to carve and delineate features. Both grooving and incising are used to provide design elements. Comparison of techniques used in Teotihuacan lapidary work with those used by Mezcala sculptors shows very similar use of grooving to delineate some facial features in masks, as well as arms and legs in figurines.

Louise Paradis has suggested that Mezcala lapidaries may have carved the famous Teotihuacan masks (Millon 1988: 132; Paradis n.d.). There is no direct evidence at this time to confirm that Mezcala lapidaries worked at Teotihuacan itself, although Paradis has suggested this as a possibility (n.d.: 15). Moreover, she has suggested that patterns in the distribution of the ceramic type called Granular Ware may provide at least a partial link between the Mezcala lapidaries of Guerrero and Teotihuacan.[2] While Granular

[2] Granular Ware has a wide distribution in the same north-central region of Guerrero where the Mezcala lapidary tradition is believed to have originated and flourished (Paradis n.d.). At Teotihuacan, Granular Ware was "in wide use . . . for hundreds of years" (Millon 1988: 132).

Style in Lapidary Technology

Ware has a wide distribution in Teotihuacan, there is as yet no direct correlation between the distribution of this ceramic type and the possibility of Mezcala lapidaries living and working in Teotihuacan itself. It is obvious, however, that the creators of the Teotihuacan masks used some of the same technical devices, including grooving, found on Mezcala sculptures. One possibility is that some Teotihuacan-style masks actually were made in Guerrero by Mezcala lapidaries and exported to Teotihuacan. Further testing in Guerrero and Teotihuacan might clarify the degree to which Mezcala lapidaries contributed to the Teotihuacan lapidary tradition.

The often-illustrated Teotihuacan-style mask with turquoise, serpentine, and shell mosaic overlay in the National Museum of Anthropology in Mexico City, for example, was recovered from a tomb in Tlapa, Guerrero (Westheim 1965: 97). The turquoise overlay and design in *Spondylus* shell may be Postclassic in date (Esther Pasztory, personal communication, 1985); there was no turquoise recovered from Teotihuacan Mapping Project (TMP) surface collection or excavation, suggesting that turquoise was not among the fine stones used regularly in Teotihuacan lapidary work (Turner n.d.: 54–55).[3] The mask itself is carved in unmistakable Teotihuacan style.

Drilling

Conical, biconical, and tubular methods of drilling were known and used at Teotihuacan. Evidence of these drilling techniques occurs in beads broken in the process of manufacture. In examples of biconical drilling, the drill scar shows succeedingly smaller levels of rings within the drill hole until the mid-point is reached. The bead is then inverted and the drilling process commences again from the other side (Fig. 7). Conical drilling does not

---

Surface distributions of Granular Ware at Teotihuacan were plotted on ceramic distribution maps prepared by George Cowgill using the Teotihuacan Mapping Project Computer Data File. Cowgill (personal communication, 1989) found a minor concentration of Granular Ware in square N3E5, the location of the lapidary *barrio*. High concentrations of Granular Ware relative to other wares were found in squares N5W2 (west of the Pyramid of the Moon) and N6W2 (the Old City). High absolute concentrations of Granular Ware occurred in squares N6W2, N6W3 (the Old City), and N4W2 (one square west of the square where the Street of the Dead includes the Moon Plaza and the Plaza of the Columns).

In his study of Teotihuacan Granular Wares, Charles Kolb (1988) does not include Guerrero among the potential locations for the manufacture of Granular Ware ceramics. However, he does discuss evidence of ceramics with granular paste from Xochipala and Cacahuamilpa in Guerrero but considers these examples to be distinct from "Classic" Granular Ware (Kolb 1988: 239). Kolb's report focuses on southern portions of the Basin of Mexico, sites in the State of Morelos, and on the possibility of undiscovered ceramic workshops in both the Old City and southern sections of Teotihuacan itself as likely areas to investigate for Granular Ware manufacturing sites.

[3] Michael Spence (this volume) reports that a small piece of turquoise inlay was recovered from the floor of a tomb during his recent excavation in the Oaxaca Barrio.

appear to have been as frequent in beads made at Teotihuacan, although some examples are known. Conical drilling techniques were sometimes used to perforate thin pendants.

Tubular drills were used to create small elongated beads. To date, no long tubes like those found in the Cenote at Chichen Itza (Proskouriakoff 1974) or the 14-inch-long examples from Costa Rica (Lothrop 1955) have been found at Teotihuacan. One fragment of a tubular, or bar, bead appeared in the surface survey of Oztoyahualco (1:N5W2) conducted by René Millon and others in 1959. This fragment has a groove around one end and may have been several inches in length when complete. A tubular drill was also used to drill the small slate pendant illustrated in Fig. 8. The lapidary who attempted to drill this piece abandoned it, thus leaving the characteristic tubular drill scar.

Excavators recovered one small, broken chalcedony drill in the lapidary *barrio*. This is the only known example of a drill from TMP collections. It is likely that hollow bone or cane drills were also used at Teotihuacan. Characteristic drill scars occur on several Teotihuacan-style masks, on incomplete earspools, and on other ornaments in the TMP collections. This scar consists of a round "core" left within the larger, surrounding drill hole. This interior core is the characteristic remnant of a hollow drill and was usually removed, perhaps with a string or cord saw. Evidence for hollow drills comes from *tecali* cores, one of which was found in the lapidary *barrio* (Fig. 9). These drill cores are the remains of hollow drilling of a block of *tecali* in the preparation of the interior of a *tecali* bowl. This process was identified at Tula (Diehl and Stroh 1978) after the production technique was initially identified by Noemi Tejera (1970). The *tecali* drill cores and the broken sherds of *tecali* bowls found in the lapidary *barrio* and in other locations in the city proved that Teotihuacan lapidaries used this process as well.

Beveling

Beveling is one technique used by Teotihuacan lapidaries that was not mentioned by Proskouriakoff (1974) in her study of Maya jades. Lapidaries planed the edges of selected pieces of jadeite, serpentine, slate, and shell downward, thereby creating a three-dimensional effect. The *tau*- or T-shape (see Fig. 2) is an example of this technique.

Polishing

The final finishing technique used by Teotihuacan lapidaries was polishing. Although some fragments and broken objects in the lapidary *barrio* are polished, there is very limited evidence to suggest how this polishing was accomplished. Polishing stones of quartz and *tezontle* (volcanic tuff) could have provided the preliminary abrasion, but they could not have achieved the high burnish found on completed objects. Various authors have speculated

Style in Lapidary Technology

Fig. 7 Broken quartz bead with biconical drill scar. 11:N1W2.

Fig. 8 Drilled slate pendant with tubular drill scar. 2:N1W2.

Margaret H. Turner

Fig. 9 *Tecali* drill core. TE 18 8:N3E5.

that polishing was done with the use of abrasives in conjunction with leather hides, cane, and gourds. None of these materials has survived in the archaeological record of the lapidary *barrio*. Therefore conclusions regarding the polishing methods of Teotihuacan lapidaries must await evidence from future excavation.

The lapidary techniques just described were used on all of the materials found in the *barrio* workshops, including the small amount of jadeite found there. Jadeite and *Spondylus* shell are usually associated with high status contexts throughout Mesoamerica, including those at Teotihuacan. As stated above, jadeite was worked in the lapidary *barrio,* but apparently only in limited quantities. It is possible that the only jadeite worked by the lapidaries there was actually being re-worked from broken or discarded ornaments. *Spondylus* shell is almost totally absent in the lapidary *barrio*. Only a very few fragments of any shell species other than the tree oyster (*Isognomon alatus*) were recovered in excavation or survey there. Therefore, the small amount of "high status" fine stones and shells found in the lapidary *barrio* excavation suggests that the products of these workshops were destined for use in the middle ranges of Teotihuacan society (see Sempowski n.d.) rather than for those in the highest social strata. The objects created in the lapidary *barrio* were used for adornment and ritual of a personal nature rather than for insignia of rank or office or for state ritual. Many objects found in very high

Style in Lapidary Technology

status contexts—including jadeite and serpentine figurines, pyrite-backed slate mirrors, and the famous Teotihuacan-style masks—may have been made in other lapidary workshops either in the city or perhaps beyond its boundaries. In Teotihuacan itself, evidence for the production of one of these items comes from an area that may represent a second kind of workshop and another level of lapidary production.

SPECIALIZED LAPIDARY WORKSHOPS

Evidence from Teotihuacan Mapping Project Test Excavation 5 (TE 5; 6G:N5W1) in the precinct to the west of the Pyramid of the Moon (Millon, Drewitt, and Cowgill 1973: 18) provides data on one possible workshop location where the distinctive pyrite-backed slate mirrors may have been produced. The collection from this small test excavation included a very large number of slate waste fragments as well as broken slate mirrors (Fig. 10) and other slate ornaments with pyrite backing (Figs. 11, 12). Some of these objects have the distinctive red-orange stain that appears when pyrite is chemically altered over time.

This precinct has also been identified as an area of highly specialized obsidian working, perhaps under the control of the officials associated with the Moon Pyramid (Spence 1981). I have suggested that this area may also have functioned as a workshop whose lapidaries were specialized in the art of creating these slate mirrors (Turner n.d.: 126–127). This is subject to confirmation through additional excavation and material analysis. Meanwhile, a convincing argument can be made for a level of lapidary production in the city that was more specialized and perhaps more controlled than that which took place in the lapidary *barrio*.

Production in this workshop would have been under the jurisdiction of precinct officials, as would distribution of the finished items. Whether the lapidaries who created these fine slate mirrors were full-time workers or were recruited from other lapidary workshops to donate part of their labor to the service of the temple is a question that will demand development of new research designs. What does emerge from the Moon Precinct data and from the lapidary *barrio* excavation is the outline of a lapidary industry with at least two levels of production and two kinds of workshops.

ADMINISTRATION AND CONTROL IN THE TEOTIHUACAN LAPIDARY INDUSTRY

The identification of at least two levels of lapidary production at Teotihuacan raises several important questions concerning the role of the state in the city's lapidary industry. What was the extent of state involvement in procurement of precious materials? Did the state control ultimate access to sources of fine stone and shell? How was distribution of these precious raw materials administered? To what degree did state involvement in production and

Margaret H. Turner

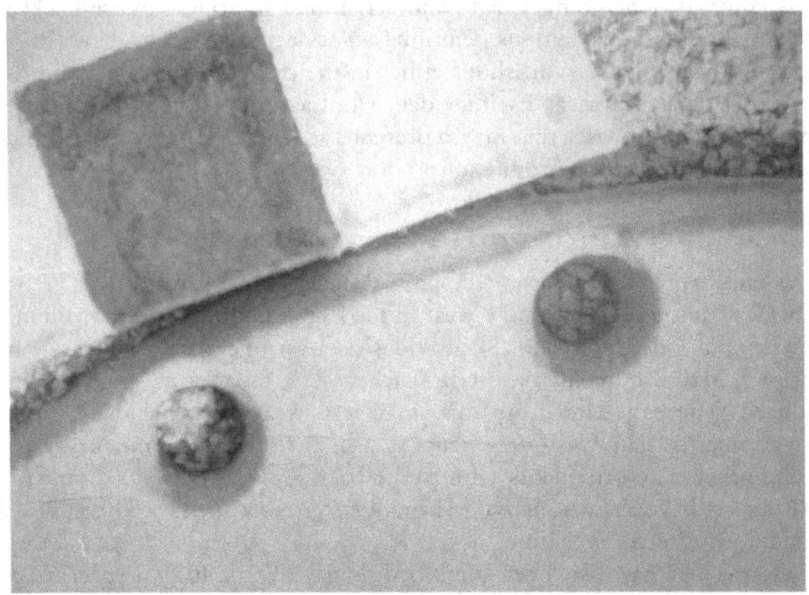

Fig. 10 Slate mirror with double drilled holes. TE 5 6G:N5W1.

Fig. 11 Small slate plaque, beveled. Front face. TE 5 6G:N5W1.

Style in Lapidary Technology

Fig. 12 Small slate plaque with pyrite encrustations. Obverse. TE 5 6G:N5W1.

distribution of finished items differ in lapidary workshops of the two types discussed here?

In order to begin to answer some of these questions we can look to the enormous amount of recent evidence that has been collected in other areas beyond the Teotihuacan region. Phil Weigand's research (1982) in the mineral-rich Chalchihuites district of Zacatecas has suggested that Teotihuacan was heavily involved in the exploitation of mines rich in hematite, malachite, limonite, cinnabar, pyrite and chalcopyrite, chert, and other stones including blue-green stones such as chrysocolla. Weigand (1982: 90) has suggested that expansion and economic exploitation in a region so distant from the metropolis must have required a sustained effort on the part of a state apparatus with vast resources in time and manpower. Teotihuacan is identified as the most likely source of this effort.[4]

All of the minerals that could have been obtained from the Chalchihuites mines are represented in the TMP collections. Although some of these minerals, such as cinnabar, could have been obtained from areas closer to Teotihuacan, others, such as malachite, could not. Trace analysis of some of

---

[4] René Millon (1988: 132–134) discusses in detail the evidence for Teotihuacan's relationship with Northern and Western Mexico.

these minerals might clarify their origin and the extent of Teotihuacan involvement in the Chalchihuites mines.

The Teotihuacan-Tikal-Kaminaljuyu connection has been discussed in great detail by many investigators (Brown 1977; Cheek 1977; Coe 1972; Coggins 1979; Millon 1981, 1988; Sanders 1977). One motivating factor often cited for Teotihuacan dominance of Kaminaljuyu is the control of sources of precious materials including jadeite and Pacific shell, especially *Spondylus*. Trace element analysis of jadeite and other green stone from Teotihuacan could be compared to mineral profiles established by Foshag (1955) for the Kaminaljuyu jades excavated by Kidder, Jennings, and Shook (1946). This comparison should tell us whether the Motagua River Valley was also the source of the jadeite and serpentine worked by Teotihuacan lapidaries. Marine shell, especially *Spondylus*, was highly prized at both Teotihuacan and Kaminaljuyu. Certainly control of areas close to the marine environments rich in this shell species could have been sought by Teotihuacan through its relations with Kaminaljuyu.

There is abundant evidence of the use of *Spondylus* shell at Teotihuacan. Some of this evidence comes from the 1959 surface collection and series of test excavations in Oztoyohualco (the "Old City") by René Millon and a team of investigators prior to inception of the Teotihuacan Mapping Project. In this collection *Spondylus* (species *princeps* and *calcifer*) is found in quantities larger than in any other surface collections made later by the TMP. Some of this shell is worked, usually by the addition of a simple drill hole through the beak. Others are waste material discarded when a shell was sawn to separate the reddish-orange outer layer from the white interior. Some are unaltered valves. Many of the specimens have either been burned or exposed to fire. This finding is consistent with other data that suggest that this area was the location of a cemetery where cremation was practiced. Other data from locations in the "Old City" or adjacent to it have contributed to identification of one site (4:N6W4) (Millon, Drewitt, and Cowgill 1973: 6) as a possible shell workshop specializing almost entirely in *Spondylus* (Turner n.d.: 145).

The frequent use of *Spondylus* shell in ritual at Teotihuacan suggests that sources of shell and perhaps fine stones exploited by the state might have included areas closer to the immediate Teotihuacan region. Likely sources would have been marine shell from Guerrero, jadeite and serpentine from Puebla and Guerrero, and *tecali* and mica from sources in Puebla and Oaxaca. In the immediate Teotihuacan region, there are chert sources to the northwest and quartzite in the Guadaloupe range to the southwest. Slate is also available in the Teotihuacan Valley area.

The Teotihuacan state did maintain economic and political ties with many polities in regions both near to and far from the Teotihuacan Valley. In some instances these ties may have involved actual control over important economic resources on the part of the state. Fine stones and shells were of great importance to the prestige of many institutions and individuals throughout Teotihuacan society. The pursuit of these precious materials affected the economic policy of the Teotihuacan state. At Kaminaljuyu, this policy appears to have been aggressively pursued until the highland Maya center was under Teotihuacan political as well as economic dominance (Millon 1988: 121–123). Further research may prove that this situation prevailed in the mineral-rich area of Zacatecas as well. Closer to home, the Teotihuacan state also seems to have had control over many mineral sources. Evidence from the Teotihuacan Sphere and the Teotihuacan Corridor (Garcia Cook 1981; Millon 1981, 1988) suggests that resources may have been exploited with different degrees of administrative domination flowing from the city itself or from out-lying secondary centers.

Within the city itself, city or state officials may have been responsible for channeling most of the fine stone and shell into the workshops. The Teotihuacan Mapping Project evidence does show, however, that this process was selective. The lapidary *barrio* received most of the more common and easily obtainable fine stones—slate, serpentine, some mica, and primarily one species of shell (*Isognomon alatus;* tree oyster) from the Atlantic. In more specialized workshops such as the possible slate mirror workshop in the Moon Precinct area, only the materials necessary to produce the desired item were provided or allowed, and nothing more. Production and distribution of the finished product may have followed this model as well, with minimal state or city control in the lapidary *barrio,* and almost total control in the precinct and specialized workshops.

The location of the different categories of workshops also speaks to the issue of state control. The lapidary workshop in N3E5 is located on the outskirts of the city. Yet, it is also on the terminus of the northeast route from Otumba, Tlaxcala and Veracruz, and the Gulf Coast beyond. An entrepreneurial group of traders or lapidaries may have been instrumental in the decision to place the lapidary *barrio* at the end of this route for convenient access to the goods coming into the city by way of it. However, given the propensity of the Teotihuacan state for consolidating people and resources, it is also plausible that the state had, at the very least, some influence in deciding the placement of the *barrio,* perhaps as part of its urban plan. The potential interaction between artisan and state in decision making at this level is an intriguing aspect of craft production at Teotihuacan with ramifications for the technological style of lapidary production. In the lapidary *barrio,* production itself might have been almost entirely independent of state interference given that only certain types, quantities, or quality of stones and shells may have been permitted to be received and worked. The state also might have played a less manipulative role in the final distribution of the lapidary *barrio*'s products, as these items are found in almost every social context within the city. Some evidence from apartment compounds along East Avenue and the small north-south street in square N1E4 also suggests that lapidary items were among the goods being transported to the Great Compound for distribution or exchange (Turner n.d.: 161, 162).

There is less doubt that the locations of the Moon Precinct slate mirror workshop and the *Spondylus* shell workshop in the Old City were quite purposeful. Both were located where their products would be used by the appropriate people and in the appropriate circumstances. Every phase of production in the Moon Precinct lapidary workshop could have been easily managed by temple officials and distribution tightly controlled. The products of the *Spondylus* shell workshop in the Old City were destined for use in mortuary rituals and cremation. Although the use of *Spondylus* shell does not appear to have been restricted to mortuary practices at Teotihuacan, its distribution may have been more controlled than other shell species and its use limited to certain categories of persons.

CONCLUSION: TECHNOLOGICAL STYLE OF THE TEOTIHUACAN LAPIDARY INDUSTRY

The technological style of Teotihuacan's lapidary industry is characterized by various degrees or kinds of control: control of resources and distribution of raw materials; control in the use of an established repertoire of techniques; control of locations considered suitable for production; control of the distribution of certain categories of objects to the proper recipients. As discussed earlier, in certain circumstances control in these matters seems to have been exercised by the state, although in other circumstances the state appears to have left a significant degree of control in the hands of *barrio* or local authority.

This controlled technological style is represented on the ground by the two kinds of lapidary workshops and the two levels of lapidary production identified above as constituting the Teotihuacan lapidary industry. The lapidary *barrio* on the northeastern margin of the city is an example of a local workshop with a range of products destined for general market distribution and consumption. Control over workshop organization and the ultimate disposition of goods at this level of production was most likely vested in the office of *barrio* leaders. State control at the local level would have been exercised in the form of restricted access to the quantities and types of raw materials permitted in this type of workshop.

The second level of lapidary production at Teotihuacan is represented by workshops such as the one dedicated to the production of pyrite-backed slate mirrors adjacent to the west side of the Pyramid of the Moon. Lapidaries in this workshop and others like it specialized in the creation of a single category of object. State control over specialized production may have been

Style in Lapidary Technology

total—from the purposeful location of workshops in temple precincts and other highly regulated areas, to the selection and organization of workers, to the determination of what would be produced and from which raw materials, and finally, to the distribution of the finished product to a restricted category of persons.

The identification of a Teotihuacan lapidary industry with two kinds of workshops, two levels of production, and a controlled technological style strongly warrants a consideration of the way in which this technological style influenced the appearance of the objects produced.

I suggest that this controlled technological style had a direct impact on the visual possibilities Teotihuacan's lapidaries saw in their materials. The same forms were repeated over and over, sometimes in different types of stone or shell, but with very little latitude for variation. Individual technique was suppressed to the point that it is possible to speak of standardization— perhaps one of the hallmarks of a true industry.

Even the Teotihuacan mask (see Fig. 1a), frequently seen as the masterpiece of the Teotihuacan style of lapidary art, was highly standardized. It was not a portrait mask. Paul Westheim (1965: 142) wrote that the human element in Teotihuacan masks was "refined and reduced to a minimum by means of form"—a form I have theorized was dictated and controlled, whether consciously or unconsciously, by technological style. Westheim's description of Teotihuacan masks was focused on his finding the Teotihuacan mask distinct from other types of Mesoamerican masks in two ways.

> First is the tendency to widen the head. . . . the verticality is totally eliminated. The height and the width of the mass of the head are approximately equal, but the surfaces of the ears transform it into a horizontally stretched rectangle. . . . The second tendency is to flatten the cubic mass, giving it almost a bidimensional effect, but not to the extent that it resembles a sculpture in relief. There is cubic development but the cubic is repressed and modified toward the plane. The artist aspires both to plasticity and the plane, and with an unparalled sensibility that is revealed in each of these masks and in each of them astounds us anew, he achieves the exact point where the two opposing tendencies seem reconciled in a happy balance. (Westheim 1965: 142)

The same two tendencies that Westheim saw in the creation of the Teotihuacan mask apply as well to the small *tau*- or T-forms (see Fig. 2) found so often and in so many contexts in the city. The controlled technological style of the Teotihuacan lapidary industry dictated that the same visual possibilities be seen in the material during the creation of lapidary objects as monumental as the mask and as exquisitely simple as the *tau*.

BIBLIOGRAPHY

BROWN, KENNETH L.
    1977   The Valley of Guatemala: A Highland Port of Trade. In *Teotihuacan and Kaminaljuyu*. (William T. Sanders and Joseph W. Michels, eds.): 205–395. Pennsylvania State University Press, University Park.

CHEEK, CHARLES D.
    1977   Teotihuacan Influence at Kaminaljuyu. In *Teotihuacan and Kaminaljuyu*. (William T. Sanders and Joseph W. Michels, eds.): 441–452. Pennsylvania State University Press, University Park.

COE, WILLIAM R.
    1972   Cultural Contact between the Lowland Maya and Teotihuacan as Seen from Tikal. In *Teotihuacan, XI Mesa Redonda* 2: 257–271. Sociedad Mexicana de Antropología, Mexico, D.F.

COGGINS, CLEMENCY
    1979   Teotihuacan at Tikal in the Early Classic Period. In *Actes du 42e Congrès International des Américanistes* 8: 252–269. Paris.

COVARRUBIAS, MIGUEL
    1946   El arte "Olmeca" o de La Venta. *Cuadernos Americanos* 28 (4): 153–179.

DIEHL, RICHARD A., AND EDWARD G. STROH, JR.
    1978   Tecali Vessel Manufacturing Debris at Tollan, Mexico. *American Antiquity* 43: 73–79.

FLADMARK, K. R.
    1982   Microdebitage Analysis: Initial Considerations. *Journal of Archaeological Science* 9: 205–220.

FOSHAG, WILLIAM F.
    1955   Chalchihuitl—A Study in Jade. *American Mineralogist* 40: 1062–1070.

GAMIO, MANUEL
    1922   *La población del valle de Teotihuacan*, 3 vols. Secretaria de Agricultura y Fomento, Instituto Nacional Indigenista, Mexico, D.F.

GARCIA COOK, ANGEL
    1981   The Historical Importance of Tlaxcala in the Cultural Development of the Central Highlands. In *Supplement to the Handbook of Middle American Indians, Vol: 1 Archaeology* (Victoria R. Bricker and Jeremy A. Sabloff, eds.): 244–276. University of Texas Press, Austin.

HANDBOOK OF THE ROBERT WOODS BLISS COLLECTION
    1963   *Handbook of the Robert Woods Bliss Collection of Pre-Columbian Art*. Dumbarton Oaks, Washington, D.C.

JOHNSON, MARY LOU
    1976   Identificación de jade y técnicas para trabajarlo en Mesoamerica. In *Las Fronteras de Mesoamerica, XIV Mesa Redonda* 2: 125–130. Sociedad Mexicana de Antropología, Mexico, D.F.

KIDDER, ALFRED V., JESSE JENNINGS, AND EDWIN M. SHOOK
    1946   *Excavations At Kaminaljuyu, Guatemala*. Carnegie Institution of Washington Pub. 561. Washington, D.C.

KOLB, CHARLES
  1988 Classic Teotihuacan Granular Wares: Ceramic Ecological Interpretations. In *Ceramic Ecology Revisited 1987: The Technology and Socioeconomics of Pottery, Part II* (Charles C. Kolb, ed.): 227–344. BAR International Series 436, Oxford.

KROTSER, PAULA H.
  n.d. TE 18: Test Excavation in the Lapidary Barrio (8:N3E5). Manuscript on file, Department of Anthropology, University of Rochester, 1968.

LECHTMAN, HEATHER
  1977 Style in Technology—Some Early Thoughts. In *Material Culture: Styles, Organization and Dynamics of Technology*. (Heather Lechtman and Robert Merrill, eds.): 3–20. West Co., St. Paul.

LOTHROP, SAMUEL K.
  1955 Jade and String-Sawing in Northeastern Costa Rica. *American Antiquity* 21: 43–51.

MILLON, RENÉ
  1973 *Urbanization at Teotihuacan, Mexico, Vol. 1: The Teotihuacan Map.* University of Texas Press, Austin.
  1981 Teotihuacan: City, State, and Civilization. In *Supplement to the Handbook of Middle American Indians, Vol. 1: Archaeology.* (Victoria R. Bricker and Jeremy A. Sabloff, eds): 198–243. University of Texas Press, Austin.
  1988 The Last Years of Teotihuacan Dominance. In *The Collapse of Ancient States and Civilizations.* (Norman Yoffee and George L. Cowgill, eds.): 102–164. University of Arizona Press, Tucson.

MILLON, RENÉ, BRUCE DREWITT, AND JAMES A. BENNYHOFF
  1965 The Pyramid of the Sun at Teotihuacan: 1959 Investigations. *Transactions of the American Philosophical Society*, n.s. 55 (6). Philadelphia.

MILLON, RENÉ, BRUCE DREWITT, AND GEORGE L. COWGILL
  1973 *Urbanization at Teotihuacan, Mexico, Vol. 1: The Teotihuacan Map.* University of Texas Press, Austin.

PARADIS, LOUISE I.
  n.d. Teotihuacan and Precolumbian Guerrero. Unpublished manuscript, 1987.

PROSKOURIAKOFF, TATIANA
  1974 *Jades from the Cenote of Sacrifice, Chichen Itza, Yucatan.* Memoirs of the Peabody Museum of Archaeology and Ethnology 10 (1). Harvard University, Cambridge.

SANDERS, WILLIAM T.
  1977 Ethnographic Analogy and the Teotihuacan Horizon Style. In *Teotihuacan and Kaminaljuyu* (William T. Sanders and Joseph W. Michels, eds.): 397–410. Pennsylvania State University Press, University Park.

SÉJOURNÉ, LAURETTE
  1966 *El lenguaje de las formas en Teotihuacán.* INAH, Gabriel Mancera 65, Mexico, D.F.

SEMPOWSKI, MARTHA
    n.d. Mortuary Practices at Teotihuacan, Mexico: Their Implications for Social Status. Ph.D. dissertation, University of Rochester, 1983.

SPENCE, MICHAEL W.
    1981 Obsidian Production and the State in Teotihuacan. *American Antiquity* 46 (4): 769–788.

TEJERA, NOEMI CASTILLO
    1970 Tecnología de una vasija en travertino. *Boletín del Instituto Nacional de Antropología e Historia* 41: 48–52.

TURNER, MARGARET H.
    1987 The Lapidaries of Teotihuacan, Mexico: A Preliminary Study of Fine Stone Working in the Ancient Mesoamerican City. In *Teotihuacan. Nuevos datos, nuevas síntesis, nuevos problemas* (Emily McClung de Tapia and Evelyn C. Rattray, eds.): 465–471. Instituto de Investigaciones Antropológicas, Serie Antropológica 72. Universidad Nacional Autónoma de Mexico, Mexico, D.F.
    n.d. The Lapidary Industry of Teotihuacan, Mexico. Ph.D. dissertation, University of Rochester, 1988.

VANCE, ELIZABETH D.
    1987 Microdebitage and Archaeological Activity Analysis. *Archaeology* 40 (4): 58–59.

WEIGAND, PHIL C.
    1982 Mining and Mineral Trade in Prehispanic Zacatecas. In *Mining and Mining Techniques in Ancient Mesoamerica* (P. C. Weigand and G. Gwynne, eds.) *Anthropology* 6 (1–2): 175–188 (special issue).

WESTHEIM, PAUL
    1965 *The Art of Ancient Mexico* (Ursula Bernard, trans.). Anchor, New York.

A Survey of Recently Excavated Murals at Teotihuacan

RUBÉN CABRERA CASTRO

TEOTIHUACAN ARCHAEOLOGICAL ZONE

D URING ARCHAEOLOGICAL EXCAVATIONS at Teotihuacan from 1980[1] through 1982, new mural paintings were discovered (see Fig. 1). Although few in number, these paintings contain new symbolic elements whose iconographic significance should be interpreted by specialists. The information that I present concerning mural painting is confined to a general description of the new findings. I do not venture into the realm of symbolic interpretation or a discussion of technical considerations. I make reference to the stratigraphic and architectural context of each mural. Only in a few cases are comments made about the motifs, comparing them to other known murals. I hope that the data presented in this way are useful to specialists in Teotihuacan iconography and mural painting, so that more research into the interpretation of the new murals can be carried out. The mural paintings presented here come from the ceremonial center, residential, and palace zones. One should take into consideration that the majority of these buildings still do not have a precise date, for they are still in the process of study.

PAINTED FLOOR, SUBSTRUCTURE 1B' OF THE CIUDADELA

The building named 1B' (Millon, Drewitt, and Cowgill 1973) was explored during Manuel Gamio's excavations from 1919 through 1922, but did not reveal information regarding its chronology or function. During the work of the Teotihuacan Archaeological Project 1980–82, some stratigraphic pits were dug to obtain materials that could clear up the problem of the structure's age. Ultimately, seven architectural superpositions were detected, two of which show the remains of mural painting: substructures 4 and 5 (Cabrera Castro 1982: 75–87) (See Fig. 1, no. 1).

The level of construction that we have named substructure 4 (Cabrera

[1] This article was translated by Lorraine A. Williams-Beck.

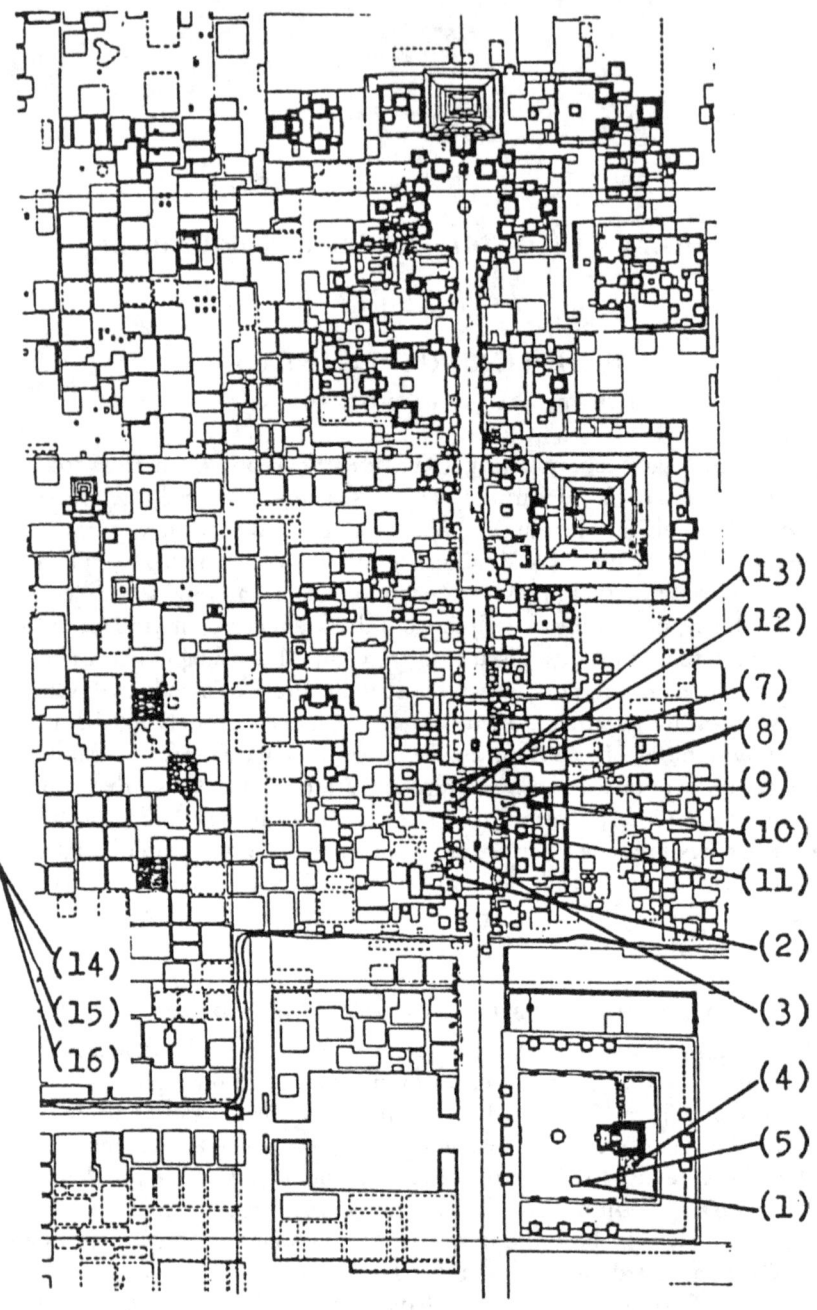

Recently Excavated Murals

Fig. 1 (*opposite*) Map showing the location of mural paintings 1980–82: 1. Painted floor, Sub-4 of building 1B', Ciudadela; 2. Painted Adoratory, Sub-3 of the Superposed Altars; 3. Detail of mural in the substructure of the Group of the Superposed Buildings; 4. Portico mural, Substructure of the Red Palace, Ciudadela; 5. Painted basal portion, Sub-2 of building 1B', Ciudadela; 6. Not on this map; 7. Feline, Sub-1 of building 40F, West Plaza Group; 8. Geometric design, Substructure in the plaza of the Superposed Stairways, East Plaza Group; 9. Thin-lined Scrolls or Volutes, West Plaza Group; 10. Thin-lined Scrolls or Volutes, West Plaza Group; 11. Thin-lined Scrolls or Volutes with a red disk, southwest section of the Group of the Superposed Buildings; 12. Shields or *chimallis*, West Plaza Group; 13. Swords or *macuahuitls*, West Plaza Group; 14. Level 3 of Atetelco, north section; 15. Level 3 of Atetelco, north section; 16. Level 3 of Atetelco, north section.

Castro 1982: 81) consists of a painted floor badly destroyed by looters' pits that penetrate through to the bottom of the structure. Floor fragments left intact are painted in two tones: pale brown (10YR7/3 and 10YR6/3), which acts as a background for strong red (10R5/8 to 10R6/8 according to the Munsell Soil Chart [1974]). The motifs represented in this floor painting are geometric scrolls or volutes (Fig. 2) similar in style to the ballcourt reliefs at El Tajin, Veracruz. Similar motifs occur elsewhere at Teotihuacan; for example, the basal portion of the Superposed Buildings (Fig. 3, 4). This building is decorated with circles and hooks or volutes, stylized designs in Tajin style (Marquina 1981: 97). Chronologically, Clara Millon (1972: 5) includes this within the style group that pertains to Period 2. Representations of volutes also appear in Teotihuacan Ballcourt markers (Aveleyra 1963: 235–237).

The painting in Fig. 2 is noteworthy for several reasons. It is only the second example that we have in Teotihuacan of floor painting, the other example being on the floor of portico 24 of Tetitla, found and reported by Séjourné (1966: 285, fig. 166), which Arthur Miller groups in category VI of natural motifs (Miller 1973: 22, 128, figs. 255–257). The mural painting under consideration, together with examples from another shrine also discovered in 1980–82, suggests that Teotihuacan in its early years had strong cultural relations with the Veracruz coast, particularly with El Tajin.

PAINTED ADORATORY, PLAZA OF THE SUPERPOSED ALTARS

The Plaza of the Superposed Altars is formed by structures 52, 52A, and 54 of the quadrant N2W1 (Millon, Drewitt, and Cowgill 1973) (see Fig. 1, no. 2). It is part of the group of the Superposed Buildings whose exploration was first begun with Leopoldo Batres. The new section where this plaza is located was excavated in 1980–82 (Sanchez 1982: 249–270).

The Plaza of the Superposed Altars is delimited by three pyramidal bases, with an adoratory in the center. It has three levels of construction distributed in the same form, one on top of the other. The adoratory of the lowest

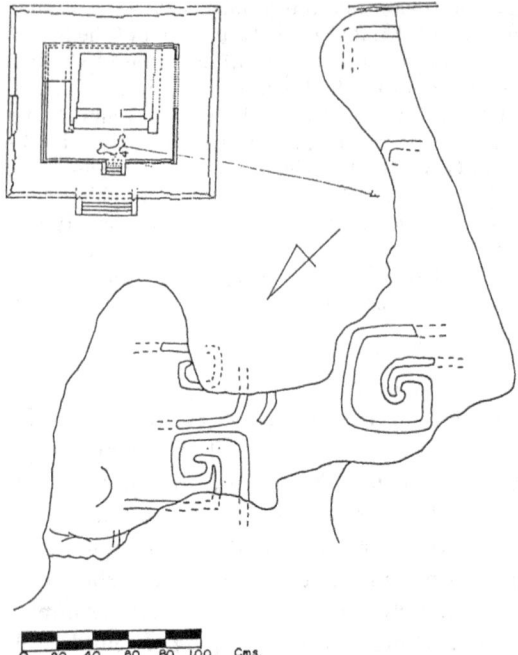

Fig. 2 Substructure 4 of Building 1B', Ciudadela. Fragment of a mural painting on the red painted, plastered floor.

Fig. 3 Altar of the adoratory in the Plaza of the Superposed Altars.

Recently Excavated Murals

Fig. 4 Altar, north side of the adoratory in the Plaza of the Superposed Altars.

level (corresponding to the oldest era there) is painted on four sides in green, white, and red not only in the *taluds* but also the *tableros* and moldings. The design of the *taluds* and lower moldings is based on volutes formed with continuous lines (Figs. 3 and 4). These symbols are very similar to the example mentioned from the basal portion of the Group of the Superposed Buildings. Because of its stratigraphic location, it should correspond to the same construction level, and to the same epoch.

PORTICO MURAL, SECTION E OF GROUP 1E IN THE CIUDADELA

A fragment of mural painting located in group 1E habitation area, south of the Temple of Quetzalcoatl (See Fig. 1, no. 4), also has designs of red volutes (Fig. 5). This fragment occurs in a substructure under the last construction level of this complex, on top of the *talud* of the north portico of section E. This was destroyed in part by the subterranean excavations carried out in 1939 (José Perez 1939).

Saburo Sugiyama, who was part of the Archaeological Project team in 1980–82, carried out excavations here in order to verify the stratigraphic relationship with the Temple of Quetzalcoatl. It was then that this mural fragment was found. Because of its style and stratigraphic location, it relates to the prior two examples. Although a small fragment, it is important nonetheless. It is represented on a *talud* wall of white plaster that forms part of a portico leading to the interior of a room. The red designs are delimited with a scribed line, and the floor of the portico is also painted with a thin red band.

Remnants of mural painting that had been applied directly to mud-plaster were found here, according to Sugiyama. This technique was also used on

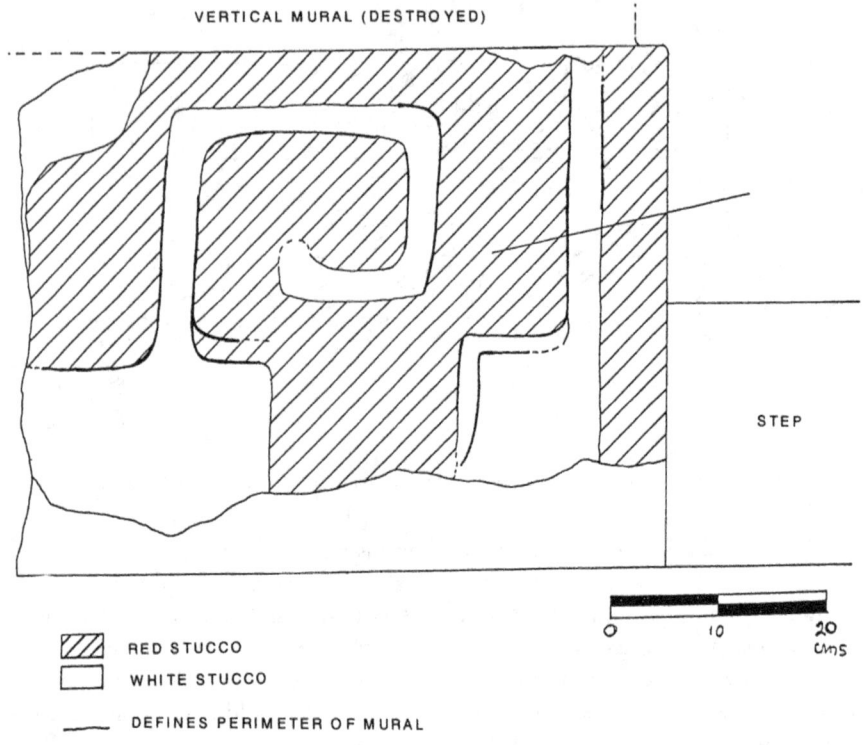

Fig. 5 Portico of Substructure of Group 1E in the Ciudadela.

the north side of the Temple of Quetzalcoatl, in a substructure of group 1D. Because of their fragmentary nature, these elements are not presented here.

SUBSTRUCTURE 2 OF BUILDING 1B' OF THE CIUDADELA

In the sequence of seven superpositions of Building 1B' of the Ciudadela (where the painted floor of Fig. 2 occurs; see Fig. 1, no. 5), there is another substructure that was completely painted when in use. It has a pyramidal base, an almost square floor plan, and a surface area of 12 × 13 m per side. A stairway attached to the west side is delimited by *alfardas*.

The *taluds* of this building were decorated in their entire extension, but due to the poor state of conservation of the areas unearthed, it is difficult to decipher the motifs represented. On parts of the north wall there is fragmentary evidence of rhomboid figures in red with green bands, outlined in black (Fig. 6a). The stairway of the building and the *alfardas* were painted with black and green circles on a red background and outlined in black. Because of the bad state of preservation, the total number of these motifs has not been calculated.

Recently Excavated Murals

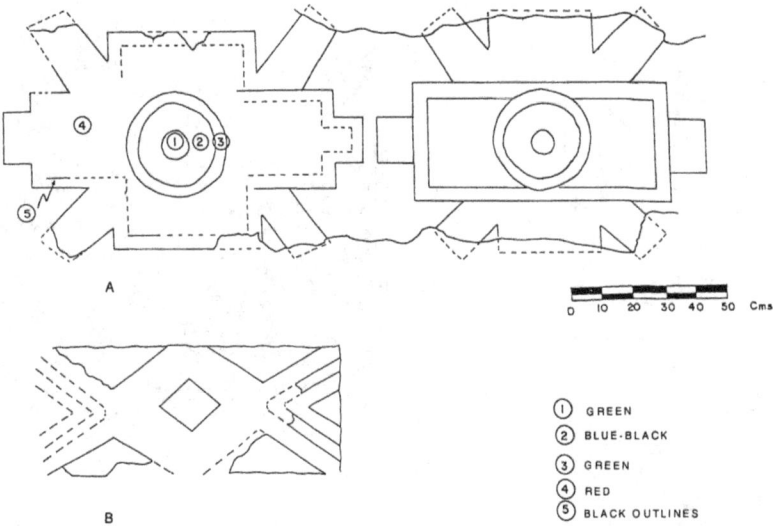

Fig. 6 Painted designs on Substructure 2, Building 1B' of the Ciudadela: (a) rhomboid on north wall, in red with green bands; (b) *tablero* designs.

The best preserved mural painting in this building occurs as the principal theme in the *tableros:* red geometrical figures on a green background, well defined due to their good state of preservation (Fig. 6b). They are composed of two rectangles overlain at right angles and sharing the same center, which itself is marked by three concentric circles painted green and black; four thinner bands radiate from the corners at 45° angles from the principal lines. This entire design is outlined in black. The length of these figures varies; the longest measures 1.21 m, and the shortest is 1.04 m. They are placed one after the other covering the entire width of the *tablero* along each of the four sides of the building. Based upon these measurements, and considering the dimensions of the *tableros,* there should have been a total of thirty-one figures. Six appear, three on each side of the stairway of the main facade. On the north *tablero,* eight figures are placed one after the other within a distance of 12 m. Presumably the south side would have had eight figures as well, and the back side of the building (13 m long) would have had nine, making a grand total of thirty-one repeated figures. Their red color varies from 10R3/6 to 10R1/8 according to the Munsell Chart (1974).

This motif may have a calendrical or astronomical meaning. It is reminiscent of page 1 of the Codex Féyérváry-Mayer, in which the five regions of the universe are represented according to indigenous concepts (Gendrop 1979: 41, Fig. 47). The central space is where humankind lives, flanked by the four cardinal directions, each with its ritual meaning, gods, and animal (Fig. 7).

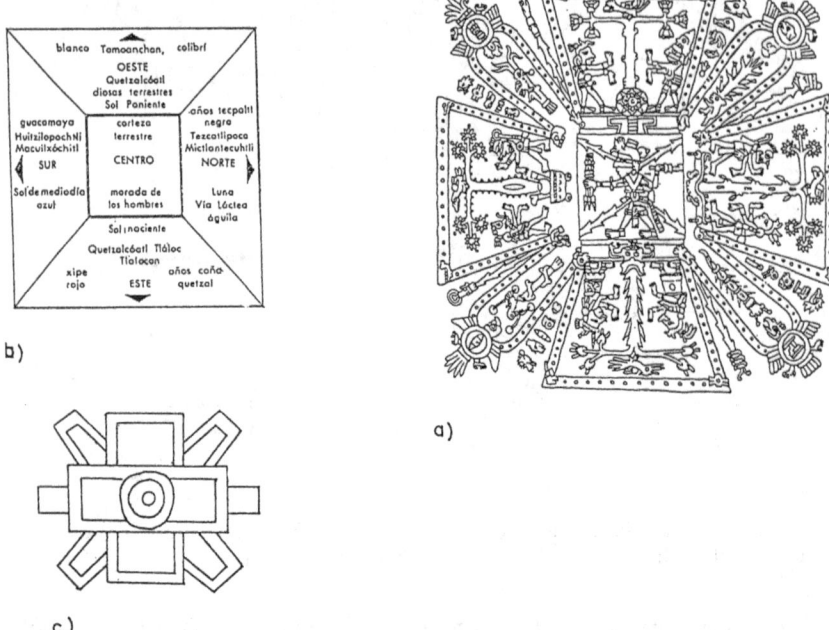

Fig. 7 Comparison with the cosmogram in the Codex Féjérváry-Mayer: (a) Féjérváry-Mayer page 1; (b) diagram of the associations for the world directions; (c) design from Substructure 2, Building 1B' of the Ciudadela, Teotihuacan.

This geometric figure has also been identified elsewhere at Teotihuacan. For example, it occurs in the floor plan of the structure in front of the Pyramid of the Moon (Schondube 1975: 242). A similar motif occurs in a mural fragment from the south portico of the west group of Tetitla. Séjourné defines it as the glyph for movement (Séjourné 1966: 249). Similar motifs occur on some ceramic decorations found during 1980–82 in the north quadrangle of the Ciudadela (Munera and Sugiyama n.d.).

GEOMETRIC DESIGN IN THE FORM OF SQUARES

Two mural painting fragments were found east of the Street of the Dead facing the recently explored West Plaza Group (see Fig. 1, no. 8). These fragments are part of the interior molding of the *tablero* from the substructure pertaining to the next to last level of occupation (Fig. 8). They have been removed for treatment and protection with the intention of returning them to their original place later. The larger fragment measures a bit more than 1 m × 32 cm. Geometric motifs based on small alternating squares painted in white and red give the sense of reticulated space. This space is

Recently Excavated Murals

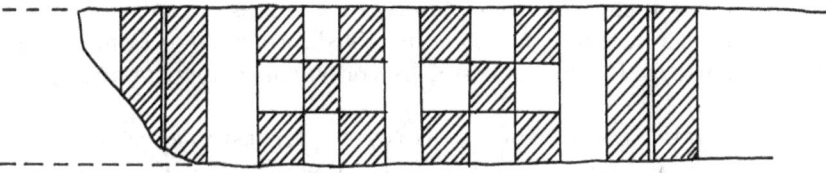

Fig. 8   Geometric design of squares, facing the West Plaza Group.

bordered by two red lines. The motif repeats along the *tablero* molding as do other motifs in Teotihuacan.[2]

FELINE MURAL, WEST PLAZA GROUP

The West Plaza Group forms part of the Street of the Dead complex. During its exploration by the Teotihuacan Archaeological Project 1980–82, various mural painting fragments were discovered in substructures as well as in the last level of occupation. The example presented here occurs in the northwest corner of building 40F (in N2W1 quadrant), on the *tablero* that forms part of the substructure (see Fig. 1, no. 7). (That is to say, the first level of the structure where mural painting is found was covered by the construction of various rooms that pertain to the next level of construction in this place. See Morelos 1982: 311–315.)

The principal figure of this mural (Fig. 9) is a stylized frontal feline, painted light red (10R5/6). The feline's feet rest on two scrolls that appear to be adorned with feathers. The eyes of the animal are circular with concentric lines in black, yellow, and red. The feathers that adorn it appear white, but surely they were painted green as seen in other parts of the mural. The lateral parts are repeated toward the outer extremes of the *tablero*. Between the central figure and the drawings on either side, clusters of white feathers are outlined, as all the design is, by a thin line in soft red.

Fig. 9   Feline mural, West Plaza Group.

---

[2] My description of these murals is based on photographs, because the original fragments are still covered with plaster left by the restorers. Study of the actual fragments will surely augment the present information.

The murals discussed so far are associated with substructures from different epochs. Those that remain to be described correspond to a late architectural context, the Period 4 discussed by von Winning (1987, 1: table 3).

THIN-LINED SCROLLS OR VOLUTES, WEST PLAZA GROUP

In some of the main rooms that surround the principal plaza of the West Plaza Group, various mural fragments with volutes of an intense red color occur (see Fig. 1, nos. 9 and 10). A continuous band of volutes or water signs frame the *taluds* in the same monochrome red as the porticos. This is also the case in the two rooms or temples located on either side of the main entrance of the West Plaza Group (Figs. 10, 11).

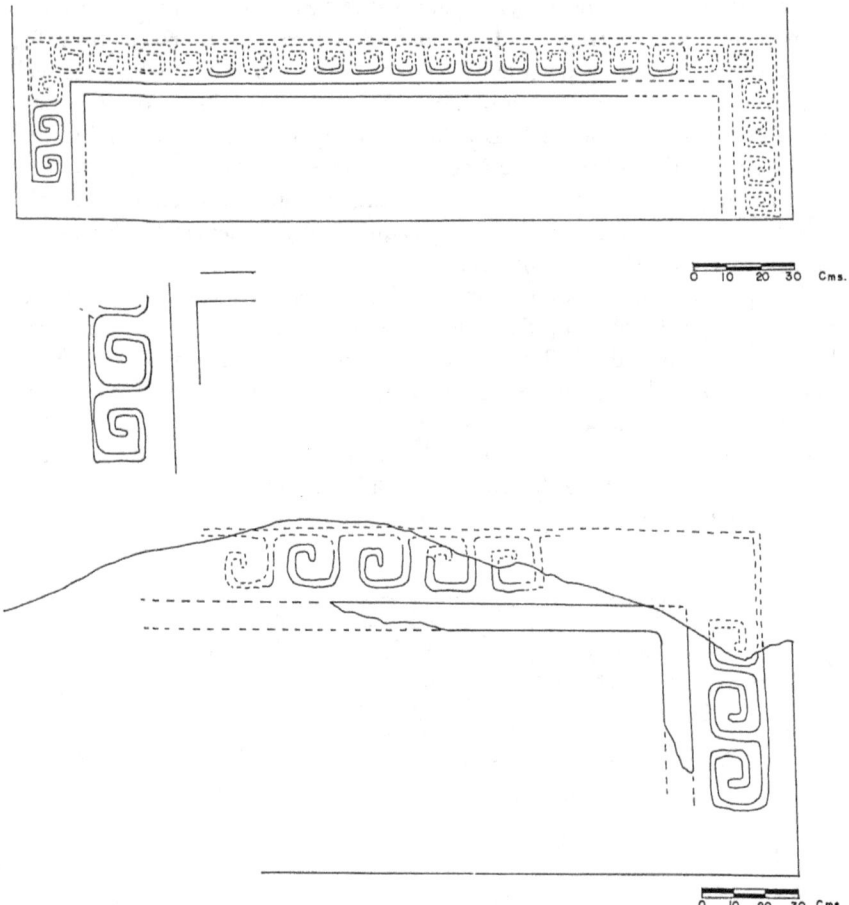

Figs. 10, 11   Scrolls or volutes, West Plaza Group.

Recently Excavated Murals

Similar motifs were also found in the group of the Superposed Buildings (see Fig. 1, no. 11). They occurred on the portico *talud* of several entry ways. Each portico mural depicts a great disk painted light red (Munsell [1974] 7.5 R5) over a background of a stronger red (Munsell [1974] 7.5R4/6). This design is framed by a strip of double volutes on the upper edge of the walls that border the portico of the rooms. The colors in the volutes are the same light red on a background of stronger red (Fig. 12). These are not new motifs; they appear repeatedly in the extensive corpus of Teotihuacan mural painting, generally in secondary positions framing motifs or central themes. They also occur on the moldings of the *tableros,* as in the case just presented from the adoratory of the Superposed Altars (see Fig. 2).

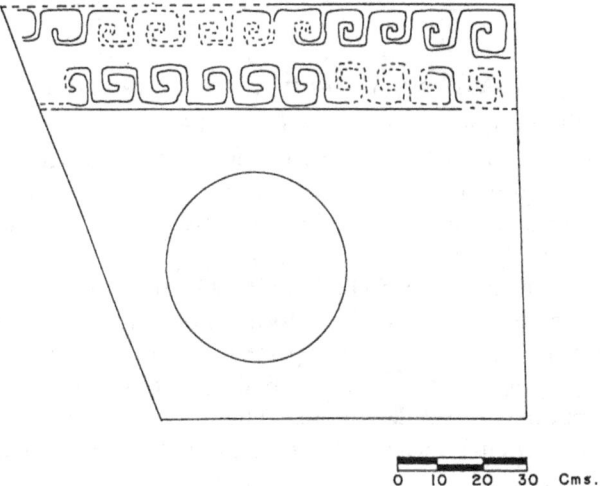

Fig. 12 Scrolls or volutes with a red disk, southwest section, Group of the Superposed Buildings.

CHIMALLIS OR SHIELDS, WEST PLAZA GROUP

In one of the un-named shrines in the West Plaza Group (see Fig. 1, no. 12), other pictorial examples that seem to be shields were found (Fig. 13). These circular figures measure 52 cm in diameter and have two diagonal stripes in their center. They are painted intense red (Munsell [1974] 7.5R4/6) on a background of a lighter red (Munsell [1974] 7.5R6/4). From these circles emit a series of twenty-two tassels or bunches of feathers whose tips are inclined toward the same direction, as if in motion. These motifs are repeated on the walls of the portico. The entire group is bordered by a red strip with small semicircles painted in the same tone of red.

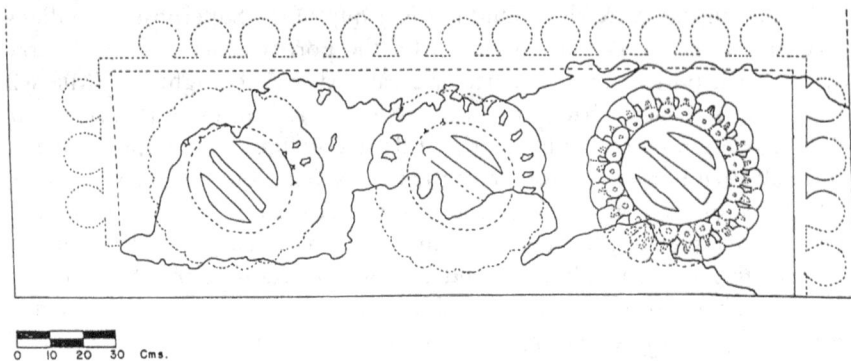

Fig. 13 Shields or *chimallis*, West Plaza Group.

SWORDS OR *MACUAHUITLS*, WEST PLAZA GROUP

In a southeast room of the West Plaza Group, very close to the Street of the Dead (see Fig. 1, no. 13), another mural painting fragment was found (Fig. 14). The figures on this fragment are formed by a succession of points or acute triangles that emerge lined up along two central bars drawn in the same tone of red (Munsell [1974] 7.5T4/6) applied on the white plaster wall. These suggest obsidian-edged clubs, or Pre-Hispanic swords. Four of these are joined in pairs at the base. They form an open angle uprooted close to the floor, where a horizontal strip is painted in the same red color.

In the lower corners of the wall, on both sides of the central motif, other drawings appear with similar figures. The upper part of the mural is destroyed. The room in which this painting is found does not occupy a promi-

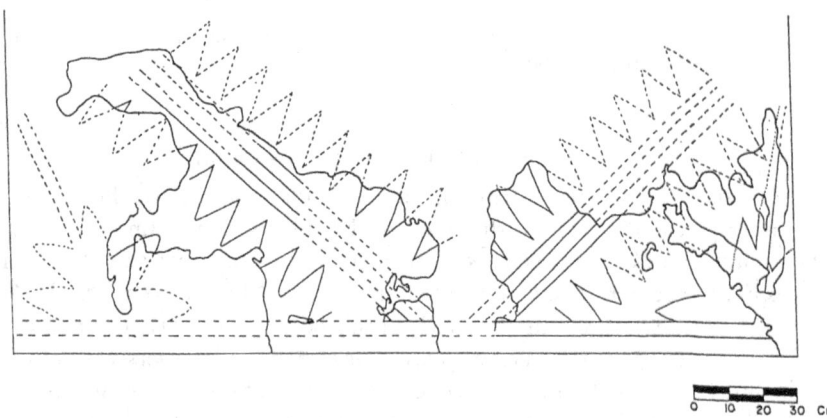

Fig. 14 Swords or *macuahuitls*, West Plaza Group.

Recently Excavated Murals

nent place within the architectural group; it is a small room added on to a room aligned toward the Street of the Dead.

The examples of mural painting presented here all come from the center of the city. Smaller murals, or ones that have become indistinct because of accumulations of salts on their surface, have not been included here. Eventually these fragments will be cleaned and analyzed more thoroughly. We also did not include new murals found at Atetelco (see Fig. 1, nos. 14, 15, 16), a site also explored in part during the work of the Teotihuacan Archaeological Project 1980–82. The excavation in the northern portion of this group, under the direction of archaeologist Laurette Séjourné, revealed some animal representations, including coyotes and birds from whose jaws emerge elaborate speech scrolls containing, among other elements, water, conch shells, and marine shells, as well as cacti and obsidian knives. The study of these materials is at present in preparation. The arduous work of reconstruction has not yet been concluded. Figs. 15 and 16 depict several of the new murals from Atetelco. These correspond to familiar themes found in mural painting throughout the city of Teotihuacan. Further analysis of the murals presented here, as well as other newly excavated murals (Millon 1988), should eventually add more to our knowledge of Teotihuacan and its pictorial traditions.

Fig. 15   Zoomorphic figure, Atetelco.

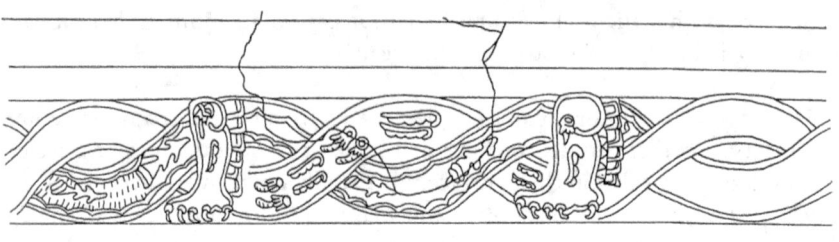

Fig. 16   Border framing a zoomorph, Atetelco.

BIBLIOGRAPHY

AVELEYRA ARROYO DE ANDA, LUIS
    1963   La estela teotihuacana de La Ventilla, *Cuadernos* 1. Museo Nacional de Antropología, INAH, México.

CABRERA CASTRO, RUBÉN
    1982   La excavación de la Estructura 1B en el interior de la Ciudadela. In *Memoria del Proyecto Arqueológico Teotihuacán 80–82* (Rubén Cabrera Castro, Ignacio Rodriguez, and Noel Morelos, eds.): 75–87 *Colección Científica* 132. INAH, Mexico, D.F.

GAMIO, MANUEL
    1979   *La población del Valle de Teotihuacan*, 2. Ed. Facsimilar, Instituto Nacional Indigenista, Mexico, D.F.

GENDROP, PAUL
    1979   *Arte prehispánico en Mesoamérica*. Centro de Investigaciones arquitectonicas Escuela Nacional de Arquitectura UNAM. Editorial Trillas. Mexico, D.F.

MARQUINA, IGNACIO
    1981   *Arquitectura prehispánica Vol. I*, 2nd ed. Memorias del INAH, Mexico, D.F.

MILLER, ARTHUR G.
    1973   *The Mural Painting of Teotihuacan*. Dumbarton Oaks, Washington, D.C.

MILLON, CLARA
    1972   The History of Mural Art at Teotihuacan. In *Teotihuacan: XI Mesa Redonda*. Sociedad Mexicana de Antropología: 1–16, Mexico, D.F.

MILLON, RENÉ, BRUCE DREWITT, AND GEORGE COWGILL (EDS.)
    1973   *Urbanization at Teotihuacan, Mexico, Vol. 1: The Teotihuacan Map*. University of Texas Press, Austin.

MORELOS, NOEL
    1982   Exploraciones en el area central de la Calzada de los Muertos, al norte del rio San Juan, dentro del llamado Complejo—Calle de los Muertos. In *Memoria del Proyecto Arqueológico Teotihuacán 80–82*. (Rubén Cabrera Castro, Ignacio Rodriguez, and Noel Morelos, eds.): 271–317. *Colección Científica* 132. INAH, Mexico, D.F.

MUNERA CARLOS, AND SABURO SUGIYAMA
    n.d.   El catálogo de moldes y reproducciones en cerámica del Cuadrángulo Norte de La Ciudadela, Teotihuacán (in preparation).

MUNSELL
    1974   *Munsell Soil Color Charts*. Baltimore, Md.

PEREZ, JOSÉ
    n.d.   Informe general del proceso de excavaciones practicadas en sistemas de pozos y tuneles en diversos sitios de mayor in terés del interior de monumentos de La Ciudadela en la zona arqueológica de San Juan

Teotihuacán, estado de México. Unpublished manuscript on file, Dirección de Monumentos Prehispánicos, Instituto Nacional de Antropología e Historia, Mexico, 1939.

SANCHEZ, JESUS
1982 Exploraciones en el area SW del Complejo Calle de los Muertos. In *Memoria del Proyecto Arqueológico Teotihuacán 80–82* (Rubén Cabrera Castro, Ignacio Rodriguez, and Noel Morelos eds.): 249–270. *Colleción Científica* 132. INAH, Mexico, D.F.

SCHONDUBE, OTTO
1975 Interpretación de la estructura ubicada al pie de la Pirámide de la Luna, Teotihuacán. In *XIII Mesa Redonda: Balance y perspectiva de la antropología mesoaméricana y del norte de México* 2: 239–246. Sociedad Mexicana de Antropología. Mexico, D.F.

SÉJOURNÉ, LAURETTE
1966 *Arquitectura y pintura en Teotihuacán*. Siglo XXI Ediciones. Mexico, D.F.

VON WINNING, HASSO
1987 *La iconografía de Teotihuacan: Los dioses y los signos*, 2 vols. Universidad Nacional Autónoma de México. Mexico, D.F.

Icons and Ideologies at Teotihuacan: The Great Goddess Reconsidered

JANET CATHERINE BERLO
UNIVERSITY OF MISSOURI AT ST. LOUIS

INTRODUCTION

For more than a century, Teotihuacan's images and icons have been the object of scholarly scrutiny. Yet major questions about the nature of the image system, the divinities portrayed, and the uses of art at this great metropolis remain unanswered. Until recently, the primary method for deducing meaning in the art of Teotihuacan has been analogy with the much better known Aztec system. This method had its genesis in the early investigations by Eduard Seler (1915) and others, conducted at a time when scholars had no idea of the vast temporal gap between the civilizations of Teotihuacan and the Aztec. It was followed as a matter of course by most scholars of the twentieth century, until critique of such methods by George Kubler caused some researchers to reflect upon the pitfalls of the "direct historical approach."[1]

Currently, some investigators, such as Esther Pasztory (1988a: 49, 50; this volume) and René Millon (this volume) stress the fundamental difference between Teotihuacan and its successors and contemporaries. Others stress the fundamental unity in Mesoamerican ideologies (Taube 1983, 1986). My own work (1983b; 1989a) and that of others (Cowgill, this volume; Heyden 1975, 1981; von Winning 1968, 1987) suggests that many religious, iconographic, and ideological threads bind Teotihuacan, the Toltecs, and the Aztecs into the fabric of one civilization with numerous historical permutations. Yet, we must always be cautious in using Aztec data to shed light on Teotihuacan, for in the past, this approach has obscured just as much as it

---

I would like to acknowledge the great intellectual generosity of Clara Millon during the preparation of this study. I benefitted greatly from our conversations and her rigorous criticism.

[1] For examples of its use, see Willey (1973) and Furst (1968, 1974). For Kubler's critique of this method, see his various works (1967, 1970a, 1970b, 1972, 1973a, 1973b).

has revealed, as I shall discuss below. It is incumbent upon us to explore the meaning of differences as well as similarities, in using Aztec sources.

Until recently, a *reductive* rather than a *deductive* method has been used when applying Aztec sources to the study of Teotihuacan divinities. In a great deal of the literature on Teotihuacan, just one Aztec god, Tlaloc, has been given preeminence. Indeed, the label *Tlaloc* has been given indiscriminately to most of the major icons there since E. T. Hamy (1882) first proposed that the Aztec rain god Tlaloc was depicted in the art and signs of Teotihuacan. In 1915, Seler suggested that Tlaloc was the only god who could be identified with any certainty there (1915: 194).[2] Alfonso Caso's influential article (1942) that interpreted the newly discovered Tepantitla mural as Tlaloc's earthly paradise (Fig. 1) set the stage for a host of further

Fig. 1 Great Goddess mural, Tepantitla Patio 2.

---

[2] Despite this pronouncement, later in the same article Seler suggests that the Teopancaxco priests (see Seler 1915: pls. 10–12 for illustration) are followers of the goddess of the moon and the earth and that the netted disk icon is a symbol of this moon goddess (1915: 200).

Icons and Ideologies at Teotihuacan

identifications focusing solely on Tlaloc.[3] So, for example, in subsequent literature we find diverse images labeled as Tlalocs. The frontal deities of Tetitla Portico 11 (Fig. 2) customarily are nicknamed "jade Tlalocs," despite the fact that they do not wear the rain god's characteristic eye goggles. Mural 1 in Zone 3 (Fig. 3) is reconstructed with the ringed eyes of Tlaloc, despite the fact that only the bottom tips of a three pronged nosebar are extant on the face, a nose bar that is just as often worn by another deity.[4] Most recently, the 1982 INAH publication of excavations at Teotihuacan interprets as Tlaloc a major new architectural sculpture unearthed in a plaza flanking the Street of the Dead (see Pasztory, fig. 1, this volume; Cabrera Castro, Rodriguez, and Morelos 1982: 312). This is not Tlaloc at all, as Pasztory has pointed out (1988a: 70), and as I shall reiterate below.

Fig. 2   Frontal deity, Tetitla Portico 11.

---

[3] See, for example, Pijoan (1969: 45, 55) and Covarrubias (1957: 141); Kubler is an exception, avoiding the issue of sex by describing the "water image" at Tepantitla (1975: 39).
[4] This reconstruction was based on the border imagery of frontal ringed-eye Tlaloc icons. Today, scholars recognize the fact that border imagery does not necessarily restate the central iconographic message. The border Tlalocs occur in a band of circular and tubular jade beads, a motif recalling the abstract goddess icon at Techinantitla, discussed below.

Fig. 3 Frontal figure with morning glories, Mural 1, Zone 3. Drawing by Felipe Dávalos (after Miller 1973: fig. 85).

Much of the generalist literature on Mesoamerica continues to stress Tlaloc's preeminence at Teotihuacan. For example, Michael Coe (1977: 91) calls the Tepantitla figure a rain god, as does Nigel Davies (1983: 79). Johanna Broda (1987: 71) says "In Classic period Teotihuacan, Tlaloc seems to have been the main deity of the official state cult depicted on murals and sculptures." Yet increasing evidence suggests that the Rain God was not, in fact, the main deity there. Until the 1970s, Tlaloc's eye rings imposed a kind of tunnel vision on the study of Teotihuacan iconography. It was not until Peter Furst and Esther Pasztory independently arrived at interpretations of the central figure of the Tepantitla mural as a goddess that Tlaloc's hegemony at Teotihuacan began to wane (Furst 1974; Pasztory 1973, 1976a).[5] Over the past few years, some of us who study Teotihuacan art have taken for granted certain features of "the Great Goddess" of Teotihuacan, yet her range of attributes has not been fully discussed in one place. In this essay, I shall synthesize what a number of scholars have written about her and point out some further attributes. Then I shall offer some additional ideas about the image of the Great Goddess at Teotihuacan, and suggest that if we understand her, we can better understand the shifts in religious ideology that took place during the 700 years between Teotihuacan's waning and Aztec ascendancy in the Valley of Mexico. In order to better elucidate these ideological shifts, I shall close with some ethnographic analogies drawn from other New World and Old World cultures.

---

[5] Before Furst and Pasztory's analyses, Kubler (1967: fig. 5, caption) had called the figure female without explaining his reasons.

Icons and Ideologies at Teotihuacan

IDENTIFICATION OF THE GODDESS

Over the years, there had been a few isolated identifications of a female deity in Teotihuacan's murals. Laurette Séjourné (1966: 252) called the yellow frontal face on Tetitla Portico 1 (Fig. 4) the only female representation in Teotihuacan painting. She identified it with the Aztec goddess Chantico, principally because of the yellow face, one of Chantico's attributes. In 1972, Peter Furst took the bold step of suggesting that "perhaps the ... fundamental deity of Teotihuacan was the Mother Goddess" (1974: 198).[6] He identified the central, frontal figure in the Tepantitla "Tlalocan" mural as a goddess (see Fig. 1), flanked by priestesses or priestess-impersonators wearing female garb. The vine-like plant that flowers behind her he identified as the psychotropic morning glory, *Rivea corymbosa,* known to the Aztecs as *ololiuqui*.

Fig. 4 Yellow frontal face, Mural 2, Portico 1, Tetitla (after Miller 1973: fig. 234).

Esther Pasztory, in her 1972 dissertation, more cautiously identified the Tepantitla image as possibly "a female earth deity who lives in Tamoanchan, the paradise of the west" (1976a: 175). The major breakthrough in our understanding of the imagery of the Great Goddess occurred with Pasztory's 1973 article "The Gods of Teotihuacan," where she identified the goddess as a predecessor to the Aztec Xochiquetzal and extended this identification to a number of other mural images as well. In the Temple of Agriculture mural, the goddess is depicted in monumental mountain-like form in relationship to her worshipers (Fig. 5). In the previously mentioned "jade Tlalocs" of Tetitla Portico 11 (see Fig. 2), she wears the nosebar and has the cascading watery bands known from the Tepantitla mural (see Fig.

---

[6] According to Furst, he first proposed this in an unpublished paper in 1970 (1974: 193). His 1974 publication was based on a lecture given in 1972 in Cambridge, England.

Fig. 5 Offering Scene Mural (since destroyed), Temple of Agriculture. Drawing by L. Batres (after Gamio 1922, 1: lám. 33).

1). In the Palace of the Jaguars mural (Zone 2, Patio 20) (Fig. 6), a similar headdress, hair, and face occur, but the mouth is revealed, showing fierce bared teeth. The body is replaced by a shield-like form with aquatic motifs. In the Divine Hands mural of Tetitla (Fig. 7), the Goddess is represented by several of her most significant attributes: the bountiful hands, the mirror, and the headdress. Pasztory (1973: 154–155) noted that the Goddess had both a creative and a destructive aspect and was linked to death as well as to fertility and plenty.

We see in these examples that representations of the goddess range from the highly descriptive version at Tepantitla to the highly reductive divine hands and headgear at Tetitla, where key symbolic attributes stand in for the more fully realized anthropomorphic form. We now recognize this metonymic impulse as a central feature of Teotihuacan iconography, as well as Mesoamerican iconography as a whole.[7] This makes iconographic identification difficult at times, for a shifting constellation of attributes are recombined into different guises for different purposes.

Karl Taube (1983) enriched the identification of the Tepantitla goddess in a provocative essay on the "Teotihuacan Spider Woman" in which he

[7] See, for example, Pasztory 1973; Langley 1986; and Berlo 1983a, 1989a.

Icons and Ideologies at Teotihuacan

Fig. 6 Rendering of frontal icon in the Palace of the Jaguars mural, Patio 20. Drawing by Felipe Dávalos (after Miller 1973: fig. 47).

Fig. 7 Divine Hands mural. Room 11, Mural 1, Tetitla (after Villagra Caleti 1971: fig. 15).

charted the various insignia associated with this deity, including spiders, mirrors, feathered headgear with bird heads, and netted shields. Taube convincingly argued that divination (both through mirrors and through casting) was one of the goddess' primary traits.[8] This interpretation elucidates the meaning of the gesture (hands scattering beans) in the Tetitla Portico 1 mural (Miller 1973: fig. 231), as well as the ubiquity of the circular mirror element (see, e.g., fig. 7).

I have suggested that a Teotihuacan goddess with attributes that prefigure the Aztec goddesses Xochiquetzal and Itzpapalotl appears as a militaristic butterfly deity both at the metropolitan center and in the Pacific slopes and highlands of Guatemala (Berlo 1983b). This deity occurs both in human form and in shorthand symbolic form on pottery vessels and *incensarios*. Her principal diagnostic features are butterfly wings (sometimes represented in *quechquemitl*-like form), and a headdress with the curled proboscis and antennae of a butterfly. On a cylindrical tripod vessel from Tomb B-II at Kaminaljuyu (Fig. 8), the Goddess wears the butterfly wing garb and butterfly headgear.

Fig. 8 Butterfly Goddess painted on cylindrical tripod vessel. Burial II, Mound B, Kaminaljuyu, Guatemala (after Kidder, Jennings, and Shook 1946: fig. 207h).

[8] Taube also convincingly argued for a historical relationship between the Teotihuacan divinity and Spider Grandmother of the American Southwest: "Both are associated with the earth, caves, water, precious stones, war, clairvoyance, and powerful shamanic creatures. Moreover, both appear to have figured prominently in myths concerning creation and the emergence" (1983: 140).

Icons and Ideologies at Teotihuacan

At Xelha, on the Caribbean coast of Quintana Roo, a Teotihuacan-style mural may depict a martial version of this goddess (Fig. 9).[9]

Hasso von Winning (1987) includes goddess imagery in his study of Teotihuacan iconography. He distinguishes the Great Goddess as she occurs in the Tepantitla mural and several monumental sculptures from other female deities (1987: 135–140). He finds images of Xochiquetzal and Goddess 7 Reptile Eye limited mainly to minor arts (1987: 155–160).

Most recently, Clara Millon (1988) has discussed Great Goddess iconography, principally as it occurs in mural fragments from the Techinantitla apartment compound. She has identified a series of unusual semi-abstract mural fragments in diverse museum collections as depictions of the Great Goddess in her ferocious aspect, with bared teeth and claws (see Pasztory, this volume, fig. 24). Jade beads, flowers, and a red and yellow saw-tooth border design are prominent in this representation of the goddess. Excavations by René Millon suggest that these murals adorned an inner room at Techinantitla. Its anteroom featured profile Storm Gods in procession toward the Goddess' inner room (R. Millon 1988: 96–108).

It is curious that scholarly attention was drawn to the Great Goddess principally through mural imagery, for images of her on stone monuments

Fig. 9   Teotihuacan Butterfly Goddess in mural painting at Xelha, Quintana Roo. Drawing by Karl Taube.

[9] I am grateful to Karl Taube for first informing me of this image and for allowing me to publish his drawing of it. To my knowledge, it is the only instance of a mural in full Teotihuacan style outside of Central Mexico.

have been known since the nineteenth century. Indeed, the only two really monumental sculptures known from Teotihuacan both depict her: the giant, twenty-two-ton volcanic stone water goddess brought to Mexico City by Leopoldo Batres in 1889,[10] (see Pasztory, fig. 5, this volume) and the so-called "Coatlinchan Idol" found unfinished at the quarry site southwest of Texcoco (Fig. 10). The former monument has long been recognized as a goddess, based upon her female garb. She wears a skirt and a *quechquemitl* with water design borders. The Coatlinchan monument, in contrast, is sketchier in its conception and lacks detail, yet its proportion and outline suggest that it was meant to represent the same figure. Its arms extend outward, and its hands (which are lacking) would have been prominently featured. At more than 7m in height and 180 tons, it is considerably larger than the other monumental Goddess statue.

To my knowledge, only von Winning (1987: 135–140) has drawn attention to the fact that these two sculptures relate to the murals under discussion:

> La "Gran Diosa de Teotihuacan" es un numen que se representa en dimensiones extraordinarias lo que puede haber sido inspirado por la monumentalidad de las dos grandes pirámides para cuyos recintos fueron destinadas. Se reúnen en las estatuas los conceptos primordiales de los dioses de la tierra, de la vegetacion y del agua, y probablemente también los del Dios Viejo del Fuego, deidades que en el transcurso del tiempo se evolucionaron hasta constituir configuraciones con rasgos determinados propios. En ambas esculturas se exalta la figura humana en forma estática e imponente, con un mínimo de atributos que caracterizan a las demás deidades del panteón teotihuacano. (1987:139–140)

There exists a smaller version of these mountains of stone (Fig. 11). This three-foot-tall sculpture is monumental in its conception. Its exaggerated hands recall the hands on a stone Old God brazier in the Teotihuacan site museum, as well as the Great Goddess murals at Tepantitla and Tetitla that focus on the hands of the deity (see Figs. 1, 2).

At Teotihuacan, the Great Goddess is often depicted in emblematic fashion, with iconic parts standing in for the anthropomorphic whole, as Pasztory first demonstrated in 1973 in terms of the divine hands, headdress, nosebar, and mouth with teeth. Esther Pasztory, Clara Millon, Karl Taube, and I all believe that various frontal icons in Teotihuacan murals may also refer to the Goddess. The circular, netted icons of Zones 3 and 5a may depict her in emblematic form (Figs. 3 and 12). The morning glory vine and pendant nosebar of the Zone 3 mural (see Fig. 3) are prominent in her anthropomorphic representations at Tetitla and Tepantitla, as are the headdress and

---

[10] Hermann Beyer (1965: 419–423) reported in 1920 that the side of this monument was known since 1840, but not until 1864 was it unearthed in its entirety.

Icons and Ideologies at Teotihuacan

Fig. 10 "Coatlinchan figure" of water goddess; Museo Nacional de Antropología, Mexico.

Fig. 11 Miniature stone goddess, Philadelphia Museum of Art 50. 134. 282.

Janet Catherine Berlo

cascade of emblems from the hands that are depicted in the Zone 5a mural, though in this case the cascades flow from animal claws (Fig. 12). These claws occur in a number of other murals that show the open mouth first conjoined with the jade beads and sawtooth headdress decoration known from her other representations (see Pasztory, this volume, fig. 24).

A version of the goddess in flight appears in a Zone 5a mural (Fig. 13), where she descends from intertwined vines reminiscent of those at Tepantitla (cf. Fig. 1). Pasztory (1973: 93) recognized that this mural related to goddess imagery, but because most Mesoamerican "diving gods" are masculine, she said it might be a masculine variant. I think that all current evidence supports the view that this figure is the Great Goddess herself. As in her Escuintla and Kaminaljuyu manifestations (see Fig. 8; Berlo 1989b: fig. 8.2), she has *quechquemitl*-like wings. Bird heads are prominent, occurring on her wings, as her headgear, on her legs, and on her tail feathers. From her outstretched hands cascade small glyphic emblems such as hands, masks, jade beads, and nose plugs. Her face is painted red, with blue and white stepped lines and a yellow band around the mouth.[11] Her teeth are bared.

In addition to the murals and large-scale monuments just discussed, the Teotihuacan Goddess appears in a variety of stone, ceramic, and slate objects

Fig. 12   Circular netted deity image, Mural 2, Portico 18, Zone 5a (after Miller 1973: fig. 124).

[11] As in many of her other portraits at Teotihuacan, here her primary color is red. Yellow is also prominent in her representations.

Icons and Ideologies at Teotihuacan

as well. A magnificent stuccoed and painted bowl in the Dumbarton Oaks Collection depicts both anthropomorphic and emblematic versions of the goddess (Fig. 14). The frontal anthropomorphic icon has a red face and butterfly proboscis headgear. The figure's arms are extended, and the hands grasp scepters from which cascades of water flow. Within the water are glyphic symbols familiar from many of her other manifestations. Large wing-like elements form her body. This image alternates with a short-hand emblematic

Fig. 13 Winged goddess descending from vines. Mural 3, Room 12, Zone 5a (after Gendrop 1971: 96).

Fig. 14 Thin-Orange ware frescoed bowl depicting the goddess; Dumbarton Oaks B.64 TP.

Janet Catherine Berlo

version in which wings, butterfly eyes, antennae, and proboscis are carefully rendered. Above the emblem, a variant of the 7 Reptile Eye glyph appears. This glyph is often found in association with the goddess; indeed, von Winning (1987: 155–160) believes that 7 RE is one goddess variant.

An impressive stone relief excavated by Rubén Cabrera Castro depicts the deity in characteristic frontal pose (see Pasztory, this volume, fig. 1). She wears the pronged nose piece and the bird-and-feather headdress familiar from the murals. In her outstretched hands, she carries emblems that seem to link fire and water (see Langley, this volume). This eloquent image makes a vivid contrast with a minimalist stone sculpture that may represent the goddess at her most abstract: rectangular headpiece, earplugs, and nosebar (Fig. 15). A miniature stela (also excavated by Cabrera) portrays the goddess, as does a related stela that appeared in a recent American auction catalogue (Figs. 16, 17; Harmer Rooke Galleries 1987: fig. 37). In both instances, her sex is indicated by the *quechquemitl*. The Harmer Rooke catalogue (1987: 10) erroneously describes this as a "rare Toltec stele" depicting on one side a chief and on the other side "Choc [sic], the rain God." Whether this small (15″) stone slab comes from Teotihuacan itself or another site, it clearly represents a version of the goddess in human form on one side, and in her fierce, fanged, open-mouthed and taloned aspect on the other.

Fig. 15   Abstract stone sculpture of headdress, nosebar, and earspools; Teotihuacan.

Icons and Ideologies at Teotihuacan

Fig. 16 (*left*) Miniature stela of the goddess, excavated by the Proyecto Arqueológico Teotihuacan. Photo courtesy of Rubén Cabrera Castro.

Fig. 17 (*right*) Teotihuacan-style stela (after Harmer Rooke Galleries 1987: fig. 37).

A number of stone cult icons are known that depict the goddess. Some of these were excavated by the Proyecto Arquelógico under the direction of Rubén Cabrera Castro (Fig. 18); others have long been known, such as the female figure in Vienna's Museum für Völkerkunde (see Pasztory, this volume, fig. 23).

Two slate mirror backs of uncertain provenience depict the goddess in her characteristic frontal pose (Figs. 19, 20). In the Cleveland Museum mirror back (Fig. 19), she wears butterfly headgear and presides over a watery place. Profile humans approach her, just as they do in the Tepantitla mural (see Fig. 1). In Fig. 20, she wears a mirror in her headgear. The flaming emblems that she carries recall those on the monumental block-relief illustrated in Pasztory's Fig. 1 (this volume). A Teotihuacan-style stucco painted mirror back excavated at Kaminaljuyu, Guatemala, depicts a Tlaloc-Goddess conflation (Kidder, Jennings, and Shook 1946: Fig. 175a). Except for the goggled eyes, this is a typical representation of the goddess. Even the *u*-shaped container in

Fig. 18 Small-scale stone female figure, excavated by the Proyecto Arqueológico Teotihuacan. Photo courtesy of Rubén Cabrera Castro.

front of the figure with a mirror on it is common in the goddess' other depictions (see Figs. 1, 2; Taube 1983: fig. 5; Berlo 1989b: pl. 8.3, fig. 8.2).

Although certainly not every female figure that appears at Teotihuacan is necessarily an incarnation of this goddess, some small-scale ceramic objects show aspects of her headgear that are recognizable from her large-scale icons. Some figurines and cylindrical tripods show her with the mirror diadem headdress and profile bird (Figs. 21, 22). Some of the Teotihuacan host figurines may well represent the goddess in her aspect of protectress of warriors—as the Great Mother with her warrior subjects carried safely inside her (Fig. 23).[12] Such objects were found not only at metropolitan Teotihuacan, but in southern Guatemala, where Teotihuacano militaristic imagery is common (Berlo 1984).

[12] Warren Barbour suggests that the host figurines with legs to the side are female, while those with crossed legs are male (lecture, Columbia University, fall 1986). I believe that all may represent the goddess and that overt signs of sex and rank were carried by the perishable clothing and insignia worn by such figures.

Icons and Ideologies at Teotihuacan

Fig. 19 Slate mirror back of unknown provenience; Cleveland Museum of Art 89.65, James Albert and Mary Gardner Ford Memorial Fund.

Fig. 20 Slate mirror back. Photo courtesy of Nicholas Hellmuth, Foundation for Latin American Anthropological Research.

Fig. 21 Cylindrical tripod vessel with female imagery; Diego Rivera Museum, Mexico.

Fig. 22 (*left*) Female figurine from Teotihuacan; Museo Nacional de Antropología, Mexico.

Fig. 23 (*right*) Teotihuacan-style hollow torso figurine from Escuintla, Guatemala. Photo courtesy of Nicholas Hellmuth, Foundation for Latin American Anthropological Research.

GODDESS OR GODDESSES?

When confronted with so many varied images in a number of different media, of course the obvious question is whether we are faced with one goddess or a number of different goddesses. Scholarly literature amply documents the iconography and roles of various Aztec goddesses.[13] Yet scholars from Arild Hvidtfeldt (1958) to Richard Townsend (1979: 29) have observed that the Aztec "pantheon" may not really be a list of individual divinities but rather a metaphoric panoply of names that describe diverse attributes. So, for example, many of the goddesses seem to be variant aspects of one earth goddess (Broda 1987: 102–104). Her range of attributes is quite broad, extending from fertility and childbirth to death and destruction. Indeed, H. B. Nicholson (1971: table 3) groups most of the Aztec goddesses as part of a Teteoinnan complex.[14]

Increasingly, scholars are loathe to pin Aztec names onto Teotihuacan deities. Although Kubler has followed this approach for many years, more recently, the Millons have advocated the use of descriptive names rather than Nahuatl ones (for example, the Storm God rather than Tlaloc, and the Feathered Serpent rather than Quetzalcoatl). We should be wary of assigning the name of any one Aztec goddess onto the Teotihuacan deity, though in the past a number of us have used the names Xochiquetzal (Pasztory 1972), Itzpapalotl (Berlo 1983b), and Toci (Taube 1983: 128–129) in our definitions of her. Esther Pasztory has nicknamed her "the Ambivalent Goddess" in order to encompass her life-giving and death-dealing aspects. Clara Millon (1988: 228) suggests that it would be most accurate to speak of a "Great Goddess Complex," since we are unsure of the degree to which "her different personalities may have been rendered as distinct entities." I concur with this assessment, for it stresses her all-pervasive role at Teotihuacan without limiting her to one Aztec incarnation.

Like Chalchihuitlicue, the Teotihuacan deity is goddess of earthly waters that gush forth from the mountain over which she presides in the Tepantitla mural (see Fig. 1). Like Itzpapalotl, the Great Goddess is a patroness of warfare; she assumes a butterfly guise and demands sacrifices, both locally and in distant lands (Berlo 1983b). Like Teteoinnan, she is "mother of the gods, heart of the earth" (Anderson and Dibble 1970: 15). Finally, she is the fertile mountain itself from which all things come. Tenan, "mother of stone," is the indigenous name for the volcano behind the Pyramid of the Moon (Tobriner 1972; Nuttall 1926: 47). The monumental stone block images (see Fig. 10), the Temple of Agriculture mural (see Fig. 5), and the great Tepantitla mural (see Fig. 1) all eloquently express this aspect of the goddess, as perhaps do the Sun and Moon Pyramids themselves (Fig. 24).[15]

---

[13] See Heyden (1974), Sullivan (1982), Klein (1988), and McCafferty and McCafferty (n.d.).
[14] See also Pasztory's remarks (1987: 454).
[15] Cecelia Klein has pointed out that in the Selden Roll, Xochiquetzal is portrayed in the form

Fig. 24 Sun and Moon Pyramids and Cerro Gordo behind; Teotihuacan, Mexico.

TRANSFORMATIONS OF THE GREAT GODDESS IN CENTRAL MEXICO:
A DIACHRONIC PERSPECTIVE

Teotihuacan's emphasis on a female deity is unusual in Mesoamerica. Although Taube (1983) has insightfully compared Teotihuacan's Great Goddess with Spider Grandmother of the Pueblo peoples of the American southwest, the most striking New World ethnographic parallel seems to be with the Kogi, a mostly unacculturated group of Chibcha speakers in northern Colombia. The Kogi religious system is a rich and complex one, and at its heart is the Great Mother, sometimes called Spider Woman (Reichel-Dolmatoff 1987). She is the mother of creation who formed the nine layers of the Kogi universe and introduced hallucinogens to humans. This feature is reminiscent of the linkage of the Teotihuacan Great Goddess with the psychotropic morning glory in the Tepantitla mural (see Fig. 1). In the offspring of the Kogi Mother Goddess, jaguar and serpent symbolism abounds. Her four sons are the lords of the four directions; each has fire

---

of a frontal, anthropomorphic mountain. Klein (1976: 69) suggests that the Temple of Agriculture murals at Teotihuacan (see Fig. 5) may represent this same sort of conceptualization.

sticks and either a mirror or an axe as his emblem (Reichel-Dolmatoff 1987: 95–100). In all of these features, the Kogi Mother Goddess provides a remarkable comparison to Teotihuacan's Great Goddess, in whose myriad representations we find many similar references.

In looking for Mesoamerican parallels to the Teotihuacan deity, Classic Maya iconography provides nothing even remotely equivalent. In the underworld scenes on Maya vase painting, for example, the actors are overwhelmingly male. The Hero Twins belong to a kind of men's club, where the only females in attendance are literally just that: in attendance. Except for the moon goddess, most are minor figures. Despite the paucity of female deities in Classic Maya visual imagery, one inscription at Palenque suggests that the Maya, at least at Palenque, traced their lineage back thousands of years into mythic time, to an ancestral female deity who was, literally, the mother of the gods. At age 780 years she gave birth to the Palenque triad (Lounsbury 1976: 217–221). The ruler Pacal claimed legitimacy for his rule from his identification with her power.

Andrea Stone has suggested that Maya elite men appropriated the traditional fertility role of women. In bloodletting and other rituals they transferred women's inherent powers of fertility and fructification to themselves, so that *they* became the progenitors of life.[16] In Central Mexico, in contrast, fertility seems to be firmly within the hands of the Great Goddess. From the artistic evidence it is clear that we have no cult of the individual ruler (male or female) as the conduit for such forces. The goddess works without human intermediary.

The Great Goddess of Central Mexico may not have had her genesis at Teotihuacan. The association of goddesses, earthly waters, caves, and the fruits of the earth may well be an ancient idea in Mesoamerica. Although the figure at Chalcatzingo nicknamed "El Rey" is commonly described as male,[17] the figure does wear a skirt, and the garment that is typically called a cape could just as well be a *quechquemitl* (Fig. 25). Could the jade beads on the skirt and the quetzal feathers in the headgear be naming elements (Chalchihuitlicue? Xochiquetzal?)? Is this a Formative era representation of the land of mist, water, and verdant plant growth pictured so vividly at Tepantitla? Perhaps it is significant that this unusual rock-face carving occurs not in the Olmec heartland but closer to Central Mexico where such ideas reach their fullest form in the Classic Period. The relief is cut high up on one of the twin hills of Chalcatzingo, along the natural watercourse that rains run down (Grove 1987: 431). Doris Heyden (1981: 20) calls the

---

[16] See Andrea Stone (1988, n.d.). See also J. E. S. Thompson (1939) for the role of the Maya moon goddess.

[17] See, for example, David Grove (1987: 110) and Jorge Angulo (1987: 140). Carlo Gay (1972: 38–45) describes it in gender-neutral terms. Peter Joralemon (1981: 163), however, identifies it as an important female.

Janet Catherine Berlo

Fig. 25 Monument 1, Chalcatzingo, Morelos.

Chalcatzingo figure an oracle, though she does not suggest its sex, and compares it to the Cave under the Sun Pyramid. Interestingly, Teotihuacan-style paintings have been found on the wall of Cave 19 at Chalcatzingo (Grove 1987: fig. 12.45), suggesting that this place of two hills and many caves may have had sacred significance to the Teotihuacanos.

At Teotihuacan, the Great Goddess may well have been the preeminent deity, as Esther Pasztory suggests (this volume). Or she may have been half of an essential male-female duality of which the Storm God (usually referred to as "Tlaloc") was the other half. Donald McVicker (n.d.: 175, 181) suggests that the Storm God had greater preeminence in residential compounds, while the Great Goddess predominated in the more public domains along the Street of the Dead, where Tlaloc imagery is notably absent. Although it may be true that Tlaloc imagery is absent along the Street of the Dead, the number of images of the Goddess at Tepantitla, Tetitla,

Icons and Ideologies at Teotihuacan

Techinantitla, and elsewhere does not support McVicker's thesis that Tlaloc is preeminent in the residential compounds.[18]

Even if the Great Goddess and Storm God are the fundamental mythic pair at Teotihuacan,[19] the goddess is decidedly more prevalent in public monumental sculpture and slightly more prevalent in mural programs, especially in the case of frontal cult icons. Both Clara Millon and Esther Pasztory have observed that most frontal icons at Teotihuacan seem to depict the Great Goddess. Moreover, René Millon (1988: 103, 111, n. 25) notes that in the murals excavated in 1984 in Techinantitla, processional Storm Gods ring an anteroom leading to an inner room where the main icon is the Great Goddess in her destructive guise.

Notably, both the Great Goddess and the Storm God have roles to play in the city's external affairs. It is unclear, however, why the Storm God seems preeminent in Teotihuacan-related arts among the Peten Maya, whereas the Great Goddess predominates in the piedmont and highlands (Coggins n.d; Berlo 1984). Both at home and abroad, each has aspects relating variously to fertility, water, militarism, and sacrifice (Berlo 1983b; C. Millon 1988; Pasztory 1974).

An instructive contrast can be drawn between Teotihuacan's male-female divine duo and the preeminent dual gods of the Aztec state. Such a comparison demonstrates a remarkable shift across time in state-sponsored religion in Central Mexico. Although the Aztecs had a panoply of gods, the essential dual gods in terms of public religious practice were Tlaloc and Huitzilopochtli, two male gods whose twin temples at Tenochtitlan were the heart of the Aztec world (just as the Pyramids of the Sun and Moon were the heart of the Teotihuacan world). Much has been written on Tlaloc as the link with the ancestral Mexican past and Huitzilopochtli as the tribal god of the wandering Mexica, who was transformed into one of the great gods of the Aztecs.[20]

Myth tells of Huitzilopochtli's conquest over his elder sister Coyolxauhqui. While Huitzilopochtli was in the womb of their mother Coatlicue,

---

[18] R. Millon (1988: 105) says that the city's three principal deities are the Great Goddess, the Storm God, and the Feathered Serpent. I agree with McVicker (n.d.: 184) that, after the era of the Pyramid of the Feathered Serpent, feathered serpent imagery fades in prominence, being more of an enframing image than a central deity icon. One important exception to this, however, is the prominent place given to four serpents in the "Feathered Serpents and Flowering Trees" mural from Techinantitla. Esther Pasztory suggests that this late example may be a deliberate reference to the ancient imagery of the Temple of the Feathered Serpent (in Berrin 1988: 158). The preponderance of three-temple complexes early in Teotihuacan's history suggests a triadic division that could, in fact, correspond to R. Millon's three deities. It may be significant that shortly after Teotihuacan's decline, a Teotihuacan-related deity triad is featured at Xochicalco (see Pasztory 1976b).

[19] For notions of pairing, duality, and moieties at Teotihuacan, see Becker (1975) and McVicker (n.d.).

[20] See, for example, Brotherston (1974); Klein (1980); Pasztory (1987, 1988b); Broda (1987); Matos Moctezuma (1987); Carrasco (1987); Boone (1989).

Janet Catherine Berlo

Coyolxauhqui and her 400 siblings plotted to kill their mother and unborn brother. Yet Huitzilopochtli was alerted to this plot, and his first act, directly after his birth, was the slaughter of Coyolxauhqui:

> Then he pierced Coyolxuahqui, and then quickly struck off her head. It stopped there at the edge of Coatepetl. And her body came falling below; it fell breaking to pieces; in various places her arms, her legs, her body each fell. (Anderson and Dibble 1978: 4)

Memorialized in stone, her dismembered body lies at the base of Huitzilopochtli's pyramid at Tenochtitlan (Fig. 26).

There are many ways of reading this image. It has been suggested by Eduardo Matos Moctezuma that the placement of this sculpture at the base of Huitzilopochtli's temple is part of a living myth in which the temple *is* the mountain of Coatepec where Huitzilopochtli slew his sister, and that this

Fig. 26   Relief of dismembered Coyolxauhqui; Templo Mayor, Mexico.

Icons and Ideologies at Teotihuacan

myth is periodically reenacted through the beheading of female sacrificial victims (Matos Moctezuma 1987: 198–201). Pedro Carrasco suggests that in this myth Huitzilopochtli takes over the actions of the female warrior Coyolxauhqui:

> Before, it was Coyolxauhqui who generated the ferocity of battle and transmitted it to her siblings. Now it is Huitzilopochtli who embodies enormous aggression and attacks. We are told again and again about his aggression, but most importantly that he attacks and sacrifices all the other deities in the drama. It is a myth not just about one sacrifice but about a sudden increment in human sacrifices to include all warriors who come to the Templo Mayor-Coatepec. (Carrasco 1987: 135)

Read in this way, the myth is the underpinning of the Aztec ideology of large-scale sacrifice.

To these readings of this important myth, I would add another, for such myths are multivocal. Interpreted structurally and metaphorically, it can be seen as the domination of the Mexica male war god over the Great Goddess of the Central Mexican past.[21] In the myth, Huitzilopochtli's actions are ostensibly to protect his mother Coatlicue. Coyolxauhqui and the 400 plot to kill their mother Coatlicue in their anger over her unusual pregnancy. Huitzilopochtli "protects" his mother by killing all of the other children. The Florentine Codex then relates:

> When he had slain them, when he had taken his pleasure, he took from them their goods, their adornment, the paper crowns. He took them as his own goods, he took them as his own property, he assumed them as his due, as if taking the insignia to himself. (Anderson and Dibble 1978: 5)

By his actions, Huitzilopochtli becomes not just the only child but the only warrior. Moreover, he successfully tames the multiple powers of the Goddess. After Huitzilopochtli kills the goddess and appropriates her warrior aspect, subsequent festival practice depicts the proper relationship of females to this male authority figure: goddess impersonators sweep his temple, and other females are sacrificial victims.

I do not mean to suggest that the roles of the goddesses were completely overshadowed in Aztec times. Indeed, they were not, as numerous monumental cult images demonstrate. But one of the central myths of the Aztec empire *is* this struggle between the newly born male warrior god and the warrior goddess who preceded him. I believe that this myth structurally embodies the ideological struggle between the Great Goddess of the Central

---

[21] See Broda (1987: 78–80) for a brief discussion of the identification of Coyolxauhqui and the ancient earth goddess Cihuacoatl-Coatlicue.

Mexican past and the new Aztec order in which the significant ties of mythic kinship are redrawn to emphasize the male lines of Huitzilopochtli and Tlaloc. In this fraternal kinship network, the northern invaders and their ancestral god Huitzilopochtli are firmly linked with the Central Mexican past, embodied by Tlaloc.

I have outlined the pivotal role of the Great Goddess in Classic period Central Mexico and her literal vanquishment by Huitzilopochtli in Aztec times. But the role of the goddess in religion and ideology in the intervening centuries between the fall of Teotihuacan and the rise of the Aztec remains problematic. The relatively small corpus of art at Tula contains few images that suggest the continuation of a monumental iconic tradition of goddess veneration. One unusual stone monument depicts a figure wearing a *quechquemitl* and a trapeze-and-ray headdress (Fig. 27). Its original location and function are unknown. Although the goddess herself is not predominant in Tula's monumental arts, some of her martial emblems, such as butterfly pectoral ornaments and headgear, are worn by Toltec warriors (Diehl 1983: figs. 21–23).

Monumental images as well as emblems of the goddess occur at Xochicalco. Esther Pasztory (1973) has identified the image on Stela 1 of the Xochicalco stela triad as an earth goddess (Fig. 28). The 7 Reptile Eye glyph appears above her head, an association carried over Teotihuacan. Below her bust are emblems familiar from Teotihuacan: fierce teeth and outspread hands (see Figs. 1, 2, 4, 6, 13).[22]

Discovery in 1987 of more Maya-style murals at Cacaxtla, Tlaxcala, gives another hint of some continuation of the Central Mexican tradition of goddesses of water and fertility, even after the decline of Teotihuacan. At Cacaxtla, a life-sized pair of winged, blue, male and female deities are painted in Maya style, bordered by Teotihuacan-style star bands. They hold stars in their hands. John Carlson (n.d.) has identified these as rain deities linked with a pan-Mesoamerican cult of Venus-regulated ritual warfare.

Numerous female figurines in epigonal Teotihuacan style have been excavated elsewhere in Tlaxcala. Many of them wear rosette headdresses, have large powerful hands, or carry tiny figures inside them (Spranz, Dumond, and Hilbert 1978: pls. 21–26; Spranz 1982). They demonstrate that veneration of the goddess did flourish during the centuries intervening between the decline of Teotihuacan and the rise of the Aztecs. During the Postclassic period, the fragmentation of the Great Goddess into numerous goddesses for different purposes may have been achieved. By the sixteenth century,

---

[22] In the Cortez Palace in Cuernavaca is an unusual monument from Xochicalco nicknamed "La Malinche." It may depict a female figure wearing a *quechquemitl* and seated within a niche. This identification is equivocal, however, and the placement of this monument within the Xochicalco sequence is unclear.

Icons and Ideologies at Teotihuacan

Fig. 27 Sculpture of female figure from Tula; Museo Nacional de Antropología, Mexico.

when the Hispanic friars wrote about Aztec religion, a number of regional and specialized variants were in evidence.

GENDER STUDIES AND ETHNOGRAPHIC ANALOGIES IN THE ANALYSIS OF PRE-COLUMBIAN RELIGIOUS SYSTEMS

During the past twenty-five years, feminist scholarship has transformed and revitalized many disciplines, including art history, literary studies, and anthropology. Although feminist scholarship is protean and too wide in its scope to be easily characterized, two main thrusts have been evident: the inclusion of new data on women, often by women scholars, and the reanalysis of long-existing data according to new paradigms in order to yield fresh interpretations.[23] These approaches have invigorated numerous disciplines within the humanities and social sciences. Surprisingly, few scholars have applied these recent advances in gender studies to the analysis of Pre-Columbian societies. Virginia Miller (1988: vii–xviii) briefly surveys the literature on women in Pre-Columbian art and archaeology. Few of the studies she cites take an overtly feminist stance or provide new paradigms for the understanding of gender dynamics.

[23] For the presentation of new data, see Bell (1983), Weiner (1976), Harris and Nochlin (1976); for the application of new paradigms to pre-existing data, see Leacock (1981) and Berlo (1991).

Fig. 28 Line drawing of Stela 1, Xochicalco (after Saenz 1961, pl. 2).

Icons and Ideologies at Teotihuacan

Among the exceptions are a number of ethnohistoric studies. The colonial Aztec era is rich in documentary evidence, which has only just begun to be reanalyzed. Anthropologist June Nash has commented on the position of women in Aztec and colonial Aztec society (1978, 1980; Leacock and Nash 1981).[24] Betty Ann Brown (1983) has demonstrated that an art historical analysis that gives as much credence to visual imagery and its female protagonists as it does to texts and their male authors reveals that Sahagún's *Primeros Memoriales* is a rich source of information about the sacerdotal roles of Aztec women. Her analysis suggests that although Sahagún's research questionnaire (and the text that resulted from it) did not pursue information on women's religious roles, native artists depicted with accuracy women's ceremonial roles.

McCafferty and McCafferty (1988; n.d.), too, subject Colonial documents to reanalysis, finding that Colonial sources distort the role of both Aztec women and Aztec goddesses, viewing them through a European, androcentric lens. The McCaffertys (n.d.: 8) submit that the roles of Aztec goddesses provide alternatives to the dominant male ideology. They argue that a view of Aztec society focusing on gender complementarity reveals that Aztec women had access to power in diverse economic, political, ritual, and social arenas (1988).

The most recent and most sophisticated reappraisal of the role of women (both mythic and historic) in ancient Mesoamerica is Susan Gillespie's *The Aztec Kings* (1989). The first half of the book (pp. 3-120) is a brilliant structural analysis of women's key roles in the royal Aztec dynasties. Royal women from successive historical eras are shown to be permutating manifestations of one another, all recalling aspects of the Aztec mother earth goddess. Gillespie discusses the "ennobling power of women," pointing out that royal women lend legitimacy to rulership, even though pictorial king lists show only males as rulers (pp. 20-21). Royal women (and the goddesses who preceded them in mythic time) cause new historical cycles to commence and keep the wheels of kinship and kingship turning. This is a dynamic reanalysis of women's role in Aztec royal lineage, one that draws its insights both from structuralist analysis and gender analysis.

Though all of the examples just cited draw from Colonial accounts, it is possible to hypothesize about gender shifts in eras predating the ethnohistoric record, as I have done in this essay. While such efforts can never be more than well-supported hypotheses, they at least ask new questions and reexamine material from a fresh perspective.

The rise of the so-called "New Archaeology" predates the rise of feminist scholarship by at least a decade. Proponents of New Archaeology

---

[24]For an insightful critique of her work, see McCafferty and McCafferty (1988: 46-48).

recommend the use of ethnographic analogies to understand the underlying social processes in Mesoamerica.[25] Such analogies are useful, not only in the economic and political spheres (where they are most often invoked), but also in the ideational realm. The history of religion has much to say about the processes by which deities are conflated and transformed—how old icons are cut to fit new ideologies.

I have suggested that by the late Postclassic era, Teotihuacan's Great Goddess was fragmented into various roles. Different names were applied to her various aspects, and these may have been treated as different goddesses. Scholars have documented a similar process in the ancient Mediterranean world, and examples from this region may profitably be compared with the Mesoamerican situation.

Gaia was the Great Mother Goddess of Bronze Age mythology. In the Orphic hymns, she is invoked as: "Divine Earth, mother of men and of the blessed gods, you nourish all, you give all, you bring all to fruition, and you destroy all" (Athanassakis 1977: 37). She is celebrated as: "The oldest of all, hard, splendid as rock. Whatever there is that is of the land, it is she who nourishes it" (Boer 1970: 5). Such paeans indicate that this deity had apparently a great deal in common with her Teotihuacan counterpart. Moreover, Gaia was the original Oracle of Delphi, called "Primeval Prophetess" (Farnell 1907: 8; Harrison 1927: 68).

By the time that Hesiod interpreted the myths of Greek and pre-Greek peoples (ca. 700 B.C.), Gaia had been fragmented into the familiar Olympian goddesses, among them Demeter, Artemis, Aphrodite, and Athena. As Demeter, she emerges as the central figure in the Eleusinian Mysteries, with their emphasis on pilgrimage, transformation, the underworld, and agricultural fertility (Harrison 1903: 120). The Great Goddess at Teotihuacan may have functioned in a similar manner.

More than twenty years ago, Stephen Borhegyi first suggested that Teotihuacan was a place of pilgrimage. In a posthumous article (1972), he provided a provocative reconstruction of Teotihuacan religious practice, based on a Mediterranean analogy. He believed that Teotihuacan's power derived not from its economic base or its obsidian industry, as subsequent archaeologists have proposed, but from its religion, which he believed held sway in a manner similar to ancient Greek mystery religions. Doris Heyden (1975) also proposed Teotihuacan as a great pilgrimage center, with the subterranean cave beneath the Sun Pyramid as an oracular shrine. Mirror fragments, often used in Mesoamerican divinatory practice, were found there, and the *Relación Geográfica* of 1580 refers to an oracle at Teotihuacan, suggesting the remembrance of an ancient and powerful tradition (Heyden 1975: 142). In this volume, René Millon makes a case for Teotihuacan's

---

[25] See, for example, Ascher (1961), Charlton (1981), Sanders (1981), and Marcus (1989).

profoundly attractive ideology being based on its preeminence as the place where time began, with the cave under the Sun Pyramid being the point of origin.

In the Mediterranean, as the ancient Greek Mother Goddess was fragmented into various roles, Zeus, the reigning warrior patriarch of the Olympian pantheon, appropriated some of the Goddess's powers, even going so far as to produce offspring through parthenogenesis: the goddess Athena sprang from his head. Zeus' various exploits, which tame and domesticate the goddesses, can be seen as equivalent to Huitzilopochtli's vanquishing of Coyolxauhqui and taking over her powers.

Both in Classical Greece and Postclassic Central Mexico, these gods usher in a new age, with new heroes whose exploits become the legitimating myths of the state. In time, of course, the rule of the Olympian gods gave way to Christianity, as did Huitzilopochtli's reign. Huitzilopochtli, however, did not have deep roots in the Valley of Mexico, so he was successfully eradicated by the Spaniards.[26] Tlaloc was not eradicated, and neither was the Great Goddess whose power Huitzilopochtli had usurped. The cult of the Virgin of Guadalupe, prompted by the visions of a Nahuatl peasant, Juan Diego in 1531, may be viewed as just another stage in the reign of the Great Goddess of Central Mexico. Just as the ancient agricultural goddesses of Europe were conflated with some early medieval saints, and ultimately with the Virgin Mary (Berger 1985), the cult of the Virgin in Mexico today carries foward some traits of Teotihuacan's Great Goddess. Veneration of a female divinity who is the focus of pilgrimage and who is associated with mountains and sacred waters is a pervasive and long-lasting mythologem in Mesoamerica.[27]

In conclusion, artistic evidence suggests that the Great Goddess of Teotihuacan was a divinity of polyvalent roles, whose far-reaching presence was commemorated in monumental and small-scale arts in diverse media. In examining the diachronic changes in religious iconography in Central Mexico, I have put forward the hypothesis that one of the most significant changes in religious ideology focuses on successive gender shifts in the most powerful deities. The ancestral Great Goddess of Central Mexico, whose strongest manifestations were at the metropolis of Teotihuacan, diminished in importance during the Postclassic era and was firmly deposed by Huitzilopochtli's rise to power. The subsequent imposition of Christianity in the sixteenth century, in turn, eclipsed Huitzilopochtli. Syncretistic trends in Mexican Christianity gave rise to the re-emergence of a goddess-

---

[26] On the local eradication of Huitzilopochtli and his transformations in European pictorial imagery, see E. H. Boone (1989).

[27] For a review of the literature on this topic, see Berlo (1984: 173–189).

like religious figure who has been the central focus of devotion for more than four centuries.

Historian Linda Gordon (1986: 20) has observed that "most historiographic progress—perhaps most intellectual progress—proceeds by rearranging relationships within old stories, not by writing new stories." The Aztecs rearranged the relationships of mythic figures within the old stories, so that the power of the ancestral Central Mexican goddess was neutralized, and the power of the young male war god prevailed. Colonial missionaries rearranged the stories so that a Mediterranean-based mother-son dyad took root in Central Mexican soil. The missionaries may have intended the son to be the dominant figure, but native peoples, in turn, rearranged the story yet again, so that over the past 450 years the mother has eclipsed her son. These events can be analyzed as part of the processual pattern in the history of religion in which new ideologies are formed and ancient icons are recut to fit them.

As we continue to write the history of ancient Mesoamerican art, modern scholars continue the practice of rearranging the relationships within the old stories. Earlier generations wrote the story of Teotihuacan with the central place given to the Storm God. In the past twenty years, we have reconsidered the relationships, and the Great Goddess has come to the forefront of the story at Teotihuacan once again.

BIBLIOGRAPHY

ANDERSON, A. J. O., AND CHARLES DIBBLE (EDS.)
    1970   *Florentine Codex, Book One.* School of American Research and the University of Utah Press, Provo.
    1978   *Florentine Codex, Book Three.* School of American Research and the University of Utah Press, Provo.

ANGULO VILLASEÑOR, JORGE
    1987   The Chalcatzingo Reliefs: An Iconographic Analysis. In *Ancient Chalcatzingo* (David Grove, ed.): 132–160. University of Texas Press, Austin.

ASCHER, ROBERT
    1961   Analogy in Archaeological Interpretation. *Southwest Journal of Anthropology* 17: 317–325.

ATHANASSAKIS, A. N. (TRANS.)
    1977   *The Orphic Hymns.* Scholars Press, Missoula, Mont.

BECKER, MARSHALL
    1975   Moieties in Ancient Mesoamerica: Inferences on Teotihuacan Social Structure. *American Indian Quarterly* 2 (3): 217–236, 315–330.

BELL, DIANE
    1983   *Daughters of the Dreaming.* McPhee Gribble, Melbourne.

BERGER, PAMELA
    1985   *The Goddess Obscured: Transformations of the Grain Protectress from Goddess to Saint.* Beacon Press, Boston.

BERLO, JANET CATHERINE
    1983a   Conceptual Categories for the Study of Texts and Images in Mesoamerica. In *Text and Image in Pre-Columbian Art* (Janet Catherine Berlo, ed.): 1–39. BAR International Series 180, Oxford.
    1983b   The Warrior and the Butterfly: Central Mexican Ideologies of Sacred Warfare and Teotihuacan Iconography. In *Text and Image in Pre-Columbian Art* (Janet Catherine Berlo, ed.): 79–117. BAR International Series 180, Oxford.
    1984   *Teotihuacan Art Abroad: A Study of Metropolitan Style and Provincial Transformation in Incensario Workshops.* BAR International Series 199, Oxford.
    1989a   Early Writing in Central Mexico: *In Tlilli, in Tlapalli* Before 1000 A.D. In *Mesoamerica After the Decline of Teotihuacan* (Richard A. Diehl and Janet Catherine Berlo, eds): 19–47. Dumbarton Oaks, Washington, D.C.
    1989b   Art Historical Approaches to the Study of Teotihuacan-Related Ceramics in Escuintla, Guatemala. In *New Frontiers in the Archaeology of the Pacific Coast of Southern Mesoamerica* (F. Bové and L. Heller, eds.): 147–165. Arizona State University Anthropological Research Papers 39, Tempe.
    1991   Beyond *Bricolage:* Women and Aesthetic Strategies in Latin American Textiles. In *Textile Traditions in Mesoamerica and the Andes* (M. B.

Schevill, J. C. Berlo, and E. Dwyer, eds): 437–479. Garland Press, New York.

BERRIN, KATHLEEN (ED.)
    1988 *Feathered Serpents and Flowering Trees: Reconstructing the Murals of Teotihuacan.* The Fine Arts Museums of San Francisco.

BEYER, HERMANN
    1965 La gigantesca diosa de Teotihuacan. *El Mexico Antiguo* 10: 419–423.

BOER, CHARLES (TRANS.)
    1970 *The Homeric Hymns.* Swallow Press, Chicago.

BOONE, ELIZABETH HILL
    1989 Incarnations of the Aztec Supernatural: Images of Huitzilopochtli in Mexico and Europe. *Transactions of the American Philosophical Society* 79 (2). Philadelphia.

BORHEGYI, STEPHEN F.
    1972 Pre-Columbian Contacts—the Dryland Approach: The Impact and Influence of Teotihuacan Culture on the Pre-Columbian Civilizations of Mesoamerica. In *Man Across the Sea* (C. Reilly et al., eds.): 79–105. University of Texas Press, Austin.

BRODA, JOHANNA
    1987 Templo Mayor as Ritual Space. In *The Great Temple of Tenochtitlan* (J. Broda, D. Carrasco, and E. Matos Moctezuma, eds.): 61–123. University of California Press, Berkeley.

BROTHERSTON, GORDON
    1974 Huitzilopochtli and What Was Made of Him. In *Mesoamerican Archaeology: New Approaches* (Norman Hammond, ed.): 155–166. University of Texas Press, Austin.

BROWN, BETTY ANN
    1983 Seen but Not Heard: Women in Aztec Ritual—the Sahagun Texts. In *Text and Image in Pre-Columbian Art* (Janet Catherine Berlo, ed.): 119–153. BAR International Series 180, Oxford.

CABRERA CASTRO, RUBÉN, IGNACIO RODRÍGUEZ, AND NOEL MORELOS (EDS.)
    1982 Memoria del Arqueológico Teotihuacan 80–82. *Colleción Científica* 132. Instituto Nacional de Antropología e Historia, Mexico, D.F.

CARLSON, JOHN
    n.d. Star Wars and Maya Merchants at Cacaxtla. Unpublished manuscript, 1990.

CARRASCO, PEDRO
    1987 Myth, Cosmic Terror, and the Templo Mayor. In *The Great Temple of Tenochtitlan* (J. Broda, D. Carrasco, and E. Matos Moctezuma, eds.): 124–162. University of California Press, Berkeley.

CASO, ALFONSO
    1942 El paraíso terrenal en Teotihuacan. *Cuadernos Americanos* 6 (6): 127–136.

CHARLTON, THOMAS H.
 1981   Archaeology, Ethnohistory, and Ethnology: Interpretive Interfaces. In *Advances in Archaeological Method and Theory* 4: 129–176. Academic Press, New York.

COE, MICHAEL
 1977   *Mexico,* 2nd ed. Praeger, New York.

COGGINS, CLEMENCY
 n.d.   Painting and Drawing Styles at Tikal: An Historical and Iconographic Reconstruction. Ph.D. dissertation, Dept. of Fine Arts, Harvard University, 1975.

COVARRUBIAS, MIGUEL
 1957   *Indian Art of Mexico and Central America.* Alfred A. Knopf, New York.

DAVIES, NIGEL
 1983   *The Ancient Kingdoms of Mexico.* Penguin Books, London.

DIEHL, RICHARD A.
 1983   *Tula: The Toltec Capital of Ancient Mexico.* Thames and Hudson, London.

FARNELL, L. R.
 1907   *The Cults of the Greek States* 3. Oxford University Press, Oxford.

FURST, PETER T.
 1968   The Olmec Were-Jaguar Motif in the Light of Ethnographic Reality. In *Dumbarton Oaks Conference on the Olmec* (E. Benson, ed.): 147–174. Dumbarton Oaks, Washington, D.C.
 1974   Morning Glory and Mother Goddess at Tepantitla, Teotihuacan: Iconography and Analogy in Pre-Columbian Art. In *Mesoamerican Archaeology: New Approaches* (Norman Hammond, ed.): 187–215. University of Texas Press, Austin.

GAMIO, MANUEL
 1922   *La población del Valle de Teotihuacan,* 3 vols. Secretaría de Agricultura y Fomento, Mexico, D.F.

GAY, CARLO T.
 1972   *Chalcacingo.* Akademische Druck- u. Verlangsanstalt, Graz.

GENDROP, PAUL
 1971   Murales prehispánicos. *Artes de México* 144. Mexico, D.F.

GILLESPIE, SUSAN
 1989   *The Aztec Kings: The Construction of Rulership in Mexica History.* University of Arizona Press, Tucson.

GORDON, LINDA
 1986   What's New in Women's History. In *Feminist Studies, Critical Studies* (Teresa de Laurentis, ed.): 20–30. Indiana University Press, Bloomington.

GROVE, DAVID (ED.)
 1987   *Ancient Chalcatzingo.* University of Texas Press, Austin.

GUZMÁN EULALIA
    1972   Disquisiciones acerca de Teotihuacan. In *Teotihuacan, Onceava Mesa Redonda* 2: 125–139. Sociedad Mexicana de Antropología, Mexico, D.F.

HAMY, E. T.
    1882   La croix de Teotihuacan au musee du Trocadero. *Revue d'Ethnographie* 1: 410–428. Paris.

HARMER ROOKE GALLERIES
    1987   *Auction Catalog* XXVII. New York.

HARRIS, ANN SUTHERLAND, AND LINDA NOCHLIN
    1976   *Women Artists: 1550–1950*. Alfred Knopf, New York.

HARRISON, JANE E.
    1903   *Prolegomena to the Study of Greek Religion*. Cambridge University Press, Cambridge.
    1927   *Myths of Greece and Rome*. Ernest Benn, London.

HEYDEN, DORIS
    1974   La diosa madre: Itzpapalotl. *Boletin* 2: 3–14. Instituto Nacional de Antropología e Historia, Mexico, D.F.
    1975   An Interpretation of the Cave Underneath the Pyramid of the Sun in Teotihuacan, Mexico. *American Antiquity* 40: 131–147.
    1981   Caves, Gods, and Myths: World-View and Planning in Teotihuacan. In *Mesoamerican Sites and World Views* (E. P. Benson, ed): 1–35. Dumbarton Oaks, Washington, D.C.

HVIDTFELDT, ARILD
    1958   *Teotl and Ixiptlatli: Some Central Conceptions in Ancient Mexican Religion, with a General Introduction to Cult and Myth*. Munksgaard, Copenhagen.

JORALEMON, PETER DAVID
    1981   The Old Woman and the Child: Themes in the Iconography of Pre-Classic Mesoamerica. In *The Olmec and Their Neighbors* (Elizabeth Benson, ed.): 163–180. Dumbarton Oaks, Washington, D.C.

KIDDER, A. V., J. JENNINGS, AND E. SHOOK
    1946   *Excavations at Kaminaljuyu, Guatemala*. Carnegie Institution of Washington Pub. 561. Washington, D.C.

KLEIN, CECELIA F.
    1976   *The Face of the Earth: Frontality in Two-Dimensional Mesoamerican Art*. Garland Press, New York.
    1980   Who Was Tlaloc? *Journal of Latin American Lore* 6 (2): 155–204.
    1988   Rethinking Cihuacoatl: Aztec Political Imagery of the Conquered Woman. In *Smoke and Mist: Mesoamerican Studies in Memory of Thelma O. Sullivan* (J. Kathryn Josserand and Karin Dakin, eds.): 237–277. BAR International Series 420, Oxford.

KUBLER, GEORGE
    1967   *The Iconography of the Art of Teotihuacan*. Studies in Pre-Columbian Art and Archaeology 4, Dumbarton Oaks, Washington, D.C.

1970a Period, Style, and Meaning in Ancient American Art. *New Literary History* 1 (2): 127–144, Charlottesville.
1970b Jaguars in the Valley of Mexico. In *The Cult of the Feline* (E. P. Benson, ed): 19–44. Dumbarton Oaks, Washington, D.C.
1972 La evidencia intrinseca y la analogia etnologica en el estudio de las religiones mesoamericanas. *Religion en Mesoamerica: XII Mesa Redonda:* 1–24. Sociedad Mexicana de Antropologia.
1973a Iconographic Aspects of Architectural Profiles at Teotihuacan and in Mesoamerica. In *The Iconography of Middle American Sculpture:* 24–39. Metropolitan Museum of Art, New York.
1973b Science and Humanism Among Americanists. In *The Iconography of Middle American Sculpture:* 163–167. Metropolitan Museum of Art, New York.
1975 *The Art and Architecture of Ancient America,* 2nd ed. Penguin Books, London.

LANGLEY, JAMES C.
1986 *Symbolic Notation of Teotihuacan.* BAR International Series 313, Oxford.

LEACOCK, ELEANOR
1981 *Myths of Male Dominance: Collected Articles on Women Cross-Culturally.* Monthly Review Press, New York.

LEACOCK, ELEANOR, AND JUNE NASH
1981 Ideologies of Sex: Archetypes and Stereotypes. In *Myths of Male Dominance* (Eleanor Leacock, ed.): 242–263. Monthly Review Press, New York.

LOUNSBURY, FLOYD
1976 A Rationale for the Initial Date of the Temple of the Cross at Palenque. In *Segunda Mesa Redonda de Palenque* (M. G. Robertson, ed.): 211–224. Robert Lewis Stevenson School, Pebble Beach, Calif.

MARCUS, JOYCE
1989 From Centralized Systems to City-States: Possible Models for the Epiclassic. In *Mesoamerica After the Decline of Teotihuacan: A.D. 700–900* (Richard A. Diehl and Janet Catherine Berlo, eds): 201–208. Dumbarton Oaks, Washington, D.C.

MATOS MOCTEZUMA, EDUARDO
1987 Symbolism of the Templo Mayor. In *The Aztec Templo Mayor* (Elizabeth Boone, ed.): 185–209. Dumbarton Oaks, Washington, D.C.

MCCAFFERTY, SHARISSE, AND GEOFFREY MCCAFFERTY
1988 Powerful Women and the Myth of Male Dominance in Aztec Society. *Archaeological Review of Cambridge* 7 (1): 45–59.
n.d. Xochiquetzal: Images of the Goddess in Aztec Society. Unpublished manuscript. SUNY, Binghamton.

MCVICKER, DONALD
n.d. Approaches to the Mural Art of Teotihuacan. Unpublished manuscript.

MILLER, ARTHUR G.
  1973 *The Mural Painting of Teotihuacan.* Dumbarton Oaks, Washington, D.C.

MILLER, VIRGINIA (ED.)
  1988 *The Role of Gender in Precolumbian Art and Architecture.* University Press of America, Lanham, Md.

MILLON, CLARA
  1988 Great Goddess Fragment. In *Feathered Serpents and Flowering Trees: Reconstructing the Murals of Teotihuacan* (Kathleen Berrin, ed.): 226–228. The Fine Arts Museums of San Francisco.

MILLON, RENÉ
  1988 Where Do They All Come From? The Provenance of the Wagner Murals from Teotihuacan. In *Feathered Serpents and Flowering Trees: Reconstructing the Murals of Teotihuacan* (Kathleen Berrin, ed.): 78–113. The Fine Arts Museums of San Francisco.

NASH, JUNE
  1978 The Aztecs and the Ideology of Male Dominance. *Signs: Journal of Women in Culture and Society* 4 (2): 349–362.
  1980 Aztec Women: The Transition from Status to Class in Empire and Colony. In *Women and Colonization: Anthropological Perspectives* (Mona Etienne and Eleanor Leacock, eds.): 134–148.

NICHOLSON, H. B.
  1971 Religion in Pre-Hispanic Central Mexico. In *Handbook of Middle American Indians* 10 (Robert Wauchope, ed.): 395–446. University of Texas Press, Austin.

NUTTALL, ZELIA (ED.)
  1926 Official Reports on the Towns of Tequizistlan, Tepechpan, Acolman, and San Juan Teotihuacan. *Papers of the Peabody Museum* 11 (2): 45–86. Harvard University, Cambridge.

PASZTORY, ESTHER
  1972 The Gods of Teotihuacan: A Synthetic Approach in Teotihuacan Iconography. *Atti del XL Congresso Internazionale degli Americanisti* 1: 147–159. Rome.
  1974 *The Iconography of the Teotihuacan Tlaloc.* Studies in Pre-Columbian Art and Archaeology 15. Dumbarton Oaks, Washington, D.C.
  1976a *The Murals of Tepantitla, Teotihuacan.* Garland Press, New York.
  1976b The Xochicalco Stelae and a Middle Classic Deity Triad in Mesoamerica. *Proceedings of the 23rd International Congress of the History of Art* 1: 185–215. Granada.
  1987 Texts, Archaeology, Art, and History in the Templo Mayor: Reflections. In *The Aztec Templo Mayor* (Elizabeth Boone, ed.): 451–462. Dumbarton Oaks, Washington, D.C.
  1988a A Reinterpretation of Teotihuacan and Its Mural Painting Tradition. In *Feathered Serpents and Flowering Trees: Reconstructing the Murals of*

Teotihuacan (Kathleen Berrin, ed.): 45–77. Fine Arts Museums of San Francisco.

1988b The Aztec Tlaloc: God of Antiquity. In *Smoke and Mist: Mesoamerican Studies in Memory of Thelma Sullivan* (J. K. Josserand and Karin Dakin, eds.): 289–327. BAR International Series 402, Oxford.

PIJOAN, JOSE
1969 *Summa Artis X: Arte Precolumbiano, Mexicano y Maya*, 5th ed. Espasa-Calpe, Madrid.

REICHEL-DOLMATOFF, GERARDO
1987 The Great Mother and the Kogi Universe: A Concise Overview. *Journal of Latin American Lore* 13 (1): 73–113.

SAENZ, CESAR
1961 Tres estelas en Xochicalco. *Revista Mexicana de Estudios Antropológicos* 17: 39–65.

SANDERS, WILLIAM T.
1981 Classic Maya Settlement Patterns and Ethnographic Analogy. In *Lowland Maya Settlement Patterns* (Wendy Ashmore, ed.): 351–369. University of New Mexico Press, Albuquerque.

SÉJOURNÉ, LAURETTE
1966 *Arquitectura y pintura en Teotihuacan*. Siglo XXI Editores, Mexico, D.F.

SELER, EDUARD
1915 Similarity of Design of Some Teotihuacan Frescoes and Certain Mexican Pottery Objects. In *Proceedings of the 18th International Congress of Americanists*: 194–202.

SPRANZ, BODO
1982 Archaeology and the Art of Mexican Picture Writing. In *The Art and Iconography of Late Post-Classic Central Mexico* (Elizabeth Boone, ed.): 159–173. Dumbarton Oaks, Washington, D.C.

SPRANZ, BODO, E. DUMOND, AND P. P. HILBERT
1978 *Die Pyramiden vom Cerro Xochitecatl, Tlaxcala (Mexico)*. Franz Steiner Verlag GMBH, Wiesbaden.

STONE, ANDREA
1988 Sacrifice and Sexuality: Some Structural Relationships in Classic Maya Art. In *The Role of Gender in Pre-Columbian Art and Architecture* (Virginia Miller, ed.): 75–103. University Press of America, Lanham, Md.
n.d.   Aspects of Impersonation in Classic Maya Art. In *Sixth Palenque Round Table, 1986* (M. G. Robertson, ed.). University of Oklahoma Press, Norman.

SULLIVAN, THELMA
1982 Tlazolteotl-Ixcuina: The Great Spinner and Weaver. In *The Art and Iconography of Late Post-Classic Central Mexico* (Elizabeth Boone, ed.): 7–35. Dumbarton Oaks, Washington, D.C.

TAUBE, KARL
    1983   The Teotihuacan Spider Woman. *Journal of Latin American Lore* 9 (2): 107–189.
    1986   The Teotihuacan Cave of Origin. *Res: Anthropology and Aesthetics* 12: 51–82.

THOMPSON, J. ERIC S.
    1939   The Moon Goddess in Middle America. *Contributions to Anthropology and History* 5 (29): 121–73. Carnegie Institution of Washington, Washington, D.C.

TOBRINER, STEPHEN
    1972   The Fertile Mountain: An Investigation of Cerro Gordo's Importance to the Town Plan and Iconography of Teotihuacan. In *Teotihuacan, Onceava Mesa Redonda* 2: 103–115. Sociedad Mexicana de Antropología, Mexico, D.F.

TOWNSEND, RICHARD
    1979   State and Cosmos in the Art of Tenochtitlan. *Studies in Pre-Columbian Art and Archaeology* 20. Dumbarton Oaks, Washington, D.C.

VILLAGRA CALETI, AGUSTÍN
    1971   Mural Painting in Central Mexico. *Handbook of Middle American Indians* 10 (Robert Wauchope, ed.): 135–156. University of Texas Press, Austin.

VON WINNING, HASSO
    1968   Der Netzjaguar in Teotihuacan, Mexico: Eine Ikonographische Untersuchung. *Baessler-Archiv* N.F. XVI: 31–46.
    1987   *La iconografía de Teotihuacan: Los dioses y los signos*, 2 vols. Universidad Nacional Autónoma de México, Mexico, D.F.

WEINER, ANNETTE
    1976   *Women of Value, Men of Renown: New Perspectives in Trobriand Exchange.* University of Texas Press, Austin.

WILLEY, GORDON
    1973   Mesoamerican Art and Iconography and the Integrity of the Mesoamerican Ideological System. In *The Iconography of Middle American Sculpture:* 153–162. Metropolitan Museum, New York.

The Iconography of Mirrors at Teotihuacan

KARL A. TAUBE
UNIVERSITY OF CALIFORNIA AT RIVERSIDE

INTRODUCTION

FROM OLMEC TIMES to the period of Spanish contact, polished stone mirrors were an important component of Mesoamerican costume, ritual, and iconography. Although mirrors of the Formative and Postclassic periods are well known, there has been little interest in the intervening Classic Period of highland Mexico. In two previous studies, I noted that representations of mirrors are extremely common in the iconography of Teotihuacan (Taube 1983, 1986). However, until now, there has been no detailed discussion of mirrors at Classic Teotihuacan.[1] In this essay, I will describe particular forms and types of Teotihuacan-style mirrors, both actual examples in the archaeological record, and their representation in Teotihuacan art. I shall demonstrate that at Teotihuacan mirrors were more than simple ornaments of dress. These ancient mirrors expressed a rich body of esoteric lore, much of it also present among Postclassic and even contemporary peoples of Mesoamerica. The varied meanings and uses of mirrors at Teotihuacan will be elucidated by their form and contexts in Teotihuacan iconography, by data from archaeological excavations, and finally, by mirror symbolism known from other cultures of ancient Mesoamerica.

FORMAL IDENTIFICATION OF TEOTIHUACAN MIRRORS

Actual Mirrors in Archaeological Contexts

Three types of mirror stone were used at Teotihuacan: mica, obsidian, and iron pyrite.[2] This study will focus upon the most elaborate mirror type,

---

[1] Following the 1988 presentation of this paper at Dumbarton Oaks, Margaret Young-Sánchez (1990) published a study on Teotihuacan mirrors. Young-Sánchez has arrived at many of the same conclusions concerning the identification of mirrors at Teotihuacan.

[2] Rather than being formed of carefully cut mosaic, obsidian mirrors were of single slabs of fractured stone. Linné (1934: figs. 320, 321, 323, 324) illustrates several examples from his Xolalpan excavations. Kidder, Jennings, and Shook (1946: fig. 56) illustrate an ovoid piece of flaked obsidian excavated at Kaminaljuyu. Although they tentatively identify it as a scraper,

the circular mirror of pyrite mosaic. Circular mirrors of iron pyrite mosaic are fairly common in the archaeological remains of Teotihuacan. They are composed of iron pyrite tesserae glued upon a thin stone disk, usually of slate. Two pairs of holes for suspension are usually carved on opposite edges of the backing stone. At times, the exterior of the backing disk is richly carved or painted. The opposing side, the polished pyrite mosaic, originally would have provided a brilliant golden surface. However, because iron pyrite is not a stable mineral, at the time of discovery the mirror surface is heavily corroded, often no more than a yellowish or rusty red stain. Thus pyrite mirrors have been frequently misidentified as paint palettes, pot lid covers, or simply resin-painted disks.

Unfortunately, although mirrors are relatively common at Teotihuacan (cf. Seler 1902–23, 5: 431; Linné 1934: 154; 1942: 136; Rubín de la Borbolla 1947: fig. 14; Séjourné 1959: 65; Heyden 1975: 131, fig. 2), there is relatively little information describing their precise archaeological context. However, this is not true for the great site of Kaminaljuyu, which had intense and profound contact with Teotihuacan during the Early Classic period. Excavations by the Carnegie Institution of Washington uncovered a great many pyrite mirrors in Early Classic Esperanza phase burials at Mounds A and B of Kaminaljuyu (Kidder, Jennings, and Shook 1946). Several of the mirror backs contained scenes rendered in pure Teotihuacan style (Fig. 1).

The Kaminaljuyu excavators, Kidder, Jennings, and Shook (1946: 130) did not consider the pyrite mosaic disks to be mirrors, because they lacked a smoothly reflective surface. However, although a single reflective surface is important for cosmetic use, this is by no means the only function of mirrors. It is clear that in ancient Mesoamerica, mirrors were also important in costume and divinatory scrying. Rather than being devices for personal cosmetic use, the circular pyrite mirrors functioned primarily in dress and divination.

Rimmed disks encircled by plumes are extremely common in the art of Teotihuacan (Fig. 2). They are represented in polychrome murals, painted and carved vessels, ceramic *incensarios*, figurines, and monumental stone sculpture. Although these disks may differ in detail, they tend to have a rim that, when rendered in sculpture, is found to be raised slightly above the central disk. Plumes, rendered in a variety of ways, commonly radiate from the raised rim. Quite frequently, these feathered disks are depicted upon

---

one side of the item is formed by a single smooth flake; more likely, it is an obsidian mirror. Similar crude mirrors are embedded in the walls of Kaminaljuyu Structure D-III-1 (Rivera and Schavelson 1984: fig. 1).

The Iconography of Mirrors

Fig. 1 Kaminaljuyu mirror back depicting Teotihuacan Spider Woman; note mirror in bowl near base (after Kidder, Jennings, and Shook 1946: fig. 175a).

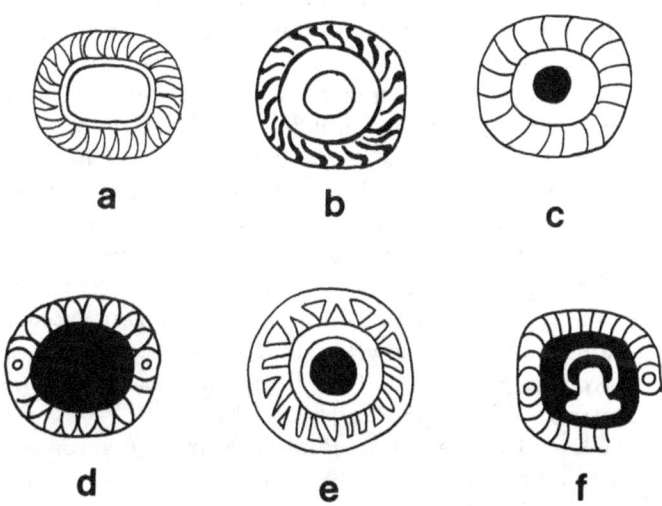

Fig. 2 Examples of mirrors in Teotihuacan art. (a–b) Mirrors with feathered rims (after Langley 1986:318); (c) Mirror with feathered rim (after Miller 1973: fig. 191); (d) Back mirror with opposing flares on rim (after Miller 1973: figs. 199–200); (e) Headdress mirror (after Miller 1973: fig. 210); (f) Back mirror with central and flanking spools (after Miller 1973: fig. 149).

costumes, where they appear as medallions worn on the brow, chest, or the small of the back. Smaller ceramic versions, evidently copies of the actual items found on Teotihuacan costume, appear as *adornos* on Teotihuacan *incensarios*. It is most telling that the better preserved of these circular *adornos* contain a central face of reflective mica (Berlo 1984: 48), clearly to depict the shining surface of a mirror. In other words, the small, circular mica-encrusted *adorno* medallions are copies of actual round mirrors.[3]

Mirrors Worn at the Small of the Back

In costume, the largest and most complex of the circular medallions tends to be the back mirror. It occurs as a part of belt assemblages and frequently has a pendant tassel of cloth, feathers, or tails (Fig. 3). It is quite clear that this device is an Early Classic form of the Postclassic *tezcacuitlapilli*, a mirror worn at the small of the back. In the art of Postclassic highland Mexico there are innumerable examples of back mirrors. Some of the finest examples appear with Early Postclassic Toltec figures. Long ago, Seler (1902–23, 5: 275) interpreted these back elements as mirrors at Chichen Itza. Later excavations at Tula and Chichen Itza provided striking confirmation of his early identification. The large Atlantean warrior columns unearthed by Jorge Acosta at Tula each wear the back device, here rendered with smoking serpents within the four radiating quadrants (see Fig. 12c). Actual mirrors of this design have been excavated at Chichen Itza. Here four Xixiuhcoa—turquoise or fire serpents—appear in the turquoise rim encircling the central pyrite mosaic (see Fig. 19d).

Numerous depictions of back mirrors occur in Classic Maya art, often on pieces exhibiting strong Teotihuacan influence.[4] The Teotihuacan warrior figures on the sides of Tikal Stela 31 provide two views of an Early Classic back mirror (Fig. 4a). Whereas the left figure displays the mirror face within its encircling rim, the opposing figure provides a view of the mirror back. The pair of short vertical lines near the edge of the disk probably depicts the holes drilled for suspension, now held by lashes of cord. Yet another Early Classic Tikal piece, a two-part effigy *incensario*, contains an excellent representation of a back mirror, complete with a pendant tassel (Fig. 4b). The four Late Classic sculptures from Tikal Burial 195 each depict God K presenting a similar back mirror (Fig. 4c).

The Early Classic Esperanza phase tombs at Kaminaljuyu contain graphic information regarding the use and form of Early Classic pyrite mirrors.

---

[3] A circular device virtually identical to Teotihuacan mirror medallions appears on a series of stone beads reportedly from the Rio Balsas region of Guerrero. In the center of the disk, corresponding to the pyrite mirror face, there is a small inlay of iron pyrite (see von Winning and Stendahl 1968: pl. 46).

[4] It is widely recognized that the stucco facade at Acanceh, Yucatan, is rendered in strong Teotihuacan style. No less than five of the stucco figures wear back mirrors (see Seler 1902–1923, vol. 5).

The Iconography of Mirrors

. 3 Representations of Teotihuacan-style back mirrors in Classic Mesoamerica. Back mirror worn by figure in Teotihuacan mural (from Miller 1973: fig. 149, ail); (b) Back mirror worn by blow gunner, detail of incised Teotihuacan vase er Linné 1942: fig. 175).

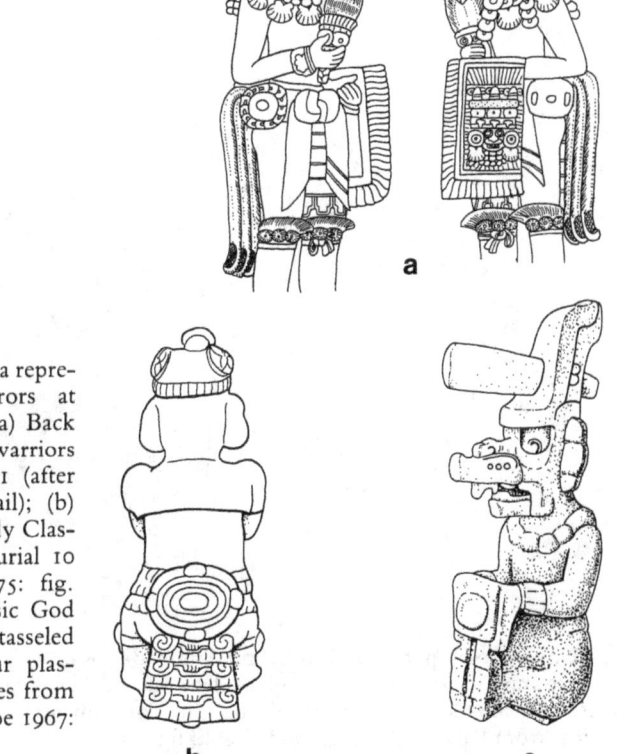

. 4 Classic Maya repre-
tations of mirrors at
:al, Guatemala. (a) Back
·rors worn by warriors
sides of Stela 31 (after
e 1967: 49, detail); (b)
:k mirror on Early Clas-
effigy vessel, Burial 10
>m Coggins 1975: fig.
)); (c) Late Classic God
figure holding tasseled
·ror, one of four plas-
·d wooden effigies from
rial 195 (from Coe 1967:

Two of the individuals in Tomb B-I were found with pyrite mirrors placed at the small of the back (Fig. 5a). One of the mirrors, that found on Skeleton 2, had a backing richly ornamented in Classic Veracruz style (Fig. 5b). The carved surface was placed face up, against the back of the body. This indicates that even with finely carved mirror backs, the pyrite facing, not the backing, was the displayed surface of Classic period back mirrors.

The archaeological occurrence of back mirrors in burials is not restricted to Kaminaljuyu. In the recently discovered burials at the Temple of Quetzalcoatl at Teotihuacan, mirrors are similarly placed in the small of the back. In Burial 190, no fewer than fifteen individuals were interred with back mirrors (Sugiyama 1989: 97).

In a great many Teotihuacan representations of mirrors, the edges of the disks are separated into a series of petal-like curving bands (Figs. 2, 6a–b). Although these bands often appear to represent feathers, in other instances, they may actually refer to a solid portion of the mirror. At Kaminaljuyu, the pyrite face of one Early Classic mirror was found to be composed of a central disk surrounded by six curving pieces (Fig. 6a). A fragmentary Early Classic mirror excavated at Zaculeu bears a similar pattern, although here

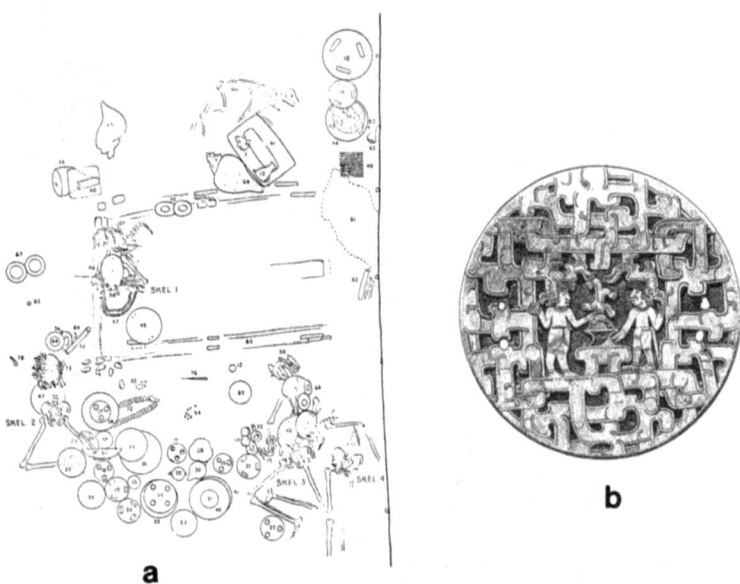

Fig. 5 Early Classic pyrite back mirrors, Tomb B-I, Kaminaljuyu. (a) Detail of tomb, note mirrors at lower backs of Skeleton 2 and Skeleton 3 (from Kidder, Jennings, and Shook 1946: fig. 31, detail); (b) Back mirror in association with Skeleton 2 (from Kidder, Jennings, and Shook: fig. 156).

The Iconography of Mirrors

the curving petals appear to have been fashioned from single plates of iron pyrite (Woodbury and Trik 1953: 233). The overall pattern of the Zaculeu piece is strikingly similar to mirrors represented in Teotihuacan art (Fig. 6b).

Kidder, Jennings, and Shook (1946: 127) note that during their excavation of the Kaminaljuyu Esperanza tombs, jade was found with most mirrors, usually in close association with the reflective pyrite surface. Due to the corrosion of the pyrite, it was frequently difficult to determine the original orientation of the jade. Nonetheless, they were able to reconstruct some of the original assemblages. The face of one pyrite mirror was flanked by jade flares, giving the overall impression of a pair of earspools (Fig. 6c). This

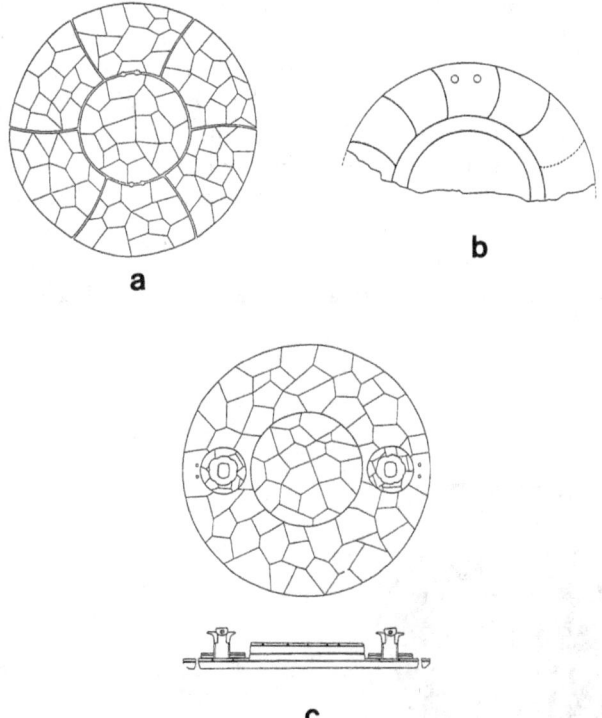

Fig. 6 Examples of Teotihuacan-style mirrors from the Maya region. (a) Mosaic pyrite mirror face, Tomb A-VI, Kaminaljuyu (from Kidder, Jennings, and Shook 1946: fig. 53d); (b) Mosaic pyrite mirror face, Early Classic tomb in Structure 1, Zaculeu (from Woodbury and Trik 1953: fig. 130); (c) Pyrite mirror ear flares on rim, Tomb A-III Kaminaljuyu (from Kidder, Jennings, and Shook 1946: fig. 53c).

same assemblage appears with Teotihuacan-style representations of mirrors. On one *incensario,* the mirror and flares are modeled three dimensionally, with mica occupying the central mirror space (Berjonneau, Deletaille, and Sonnery 1985: pl. 172). Mirrors with identical pairs of earflares often occur as back mirrors in Teotihuacan murals (see Figs. 2c, 2e). Here the stone spools are rendered as two concentric circles on the mirror rim.

In a great many representations of mirrors at Teotihuacan, a spool appears in the center of the mirror face (see Fig. 2e). In this case, it is usually rendered in profile, with the bell-shaped outline clearly visible. At first sight, this could serve to discount a mirror identification; such an element would clearly inhibit the reflective quality of the mirror. Nonetheless, virtually identical jade spools have been found on actual excavated Early Classic pyrite mirrors at Kaminaljuyu. In Tomb A-IV, a jade spool with a central carved disk was found on a pyrite mirror (Kidder, Jennings, and Shook 1946: figs. 26, 143b). Although making no mention of similar mirrors in Teotihuacan art, Kidder, Jennings, and Shook (1946: 127) suggest that both this flare and another example were originally placed in the center of iron pyrite mirrors. On Yaxchilan Stela 11, there is a Late Classic Maya representation of an elaborate back mirror with the central spool or flare (see Fig. 19c). In this case, a pendant tassel is pulled through the center of the flare.

A Teotihuacan mural currently on display in the De Young Museum of Art, San Francisco, displays an interesting version of the back mirror (Fig. 7). Here the central mirror surface contains a glyph-like element probably representing a jade face pendant. In Teotihuacan murals, similar pendants are frequently found falling in streams. The placement of jade upon mirror

Fig. 7 Detail of Teotihuacan back mirror with probable jade head in center, from a mural on display in the M. H. de Young Memorial Museum, San Francisco.

The Iconography of Mirrors

faces appears to have a relatively common practice in the Maya region. In the Esperanza phase burials at Kaminaljuyu, jade beads were found placed with pyrite mirrors (Kidder, Jennings, and Shook 1946: 127). A cache from Early Classic Quirigua was formed of three bowls with matching lids containing a vast amount of worked jade (Ashmore 1980: 38, 39). Wendy Ashmore (personal communication, 1988) notes that at least two of the bowls appear to have contained the remains of pyrite mirrors. In one Late Classic Maya cache at San Jose, Belize, a single large jade bead was placed against a pyrite mirror (Thompson 1939: 184).

The practice of placing carved beads and pendants on pyrite mirrors continued into the Early Postclassic period at Chichen Itza. A pyrite and turquoise mirror—of the type commonly worn as *tezcacuitlapilli* at Chichen and Tula—was discovered on the jade inlaid jaguar in the inner Castillo at Chichen Itza. A finely carved human-head pendant and other jades were placed on the central mirror face (Eroza Peniche 1947: 248, fig. 15). A cache in the Temple of the Chac Mool contained another pyrite and turquoise mirror; here a large jade sphere, a human-face jade pendant, and beads of jade and shell lay on the pyrite center (Morris, Charlot, and Morris 1931: 186–188, fig. 120). The reason for the placement of pendants and other jade objects on pyrite mirrors may be partly due to the value of the pyrite mirrors.[5] According to Kidder, Jennings, and Shook (1946: 131), "nothing produced in aboriginal America seems to rival these plaques in the matter of skilled and meticulous workmanship." In burials or dedicatory offerings, precious jade would be an especially appropriate item to accompany the obviously esteemed mirrors.

Mirrors Worn upon the Chest

Along with serving as back devices, circular mirrors are frequently worn on the chest of Teotihuacan figures. At times, they are supplied with the flanking pair of spools observed on many Teotihuacan back mirrors, thereby firmly identifying them as such (Fig. 8). Breast mirrors with two rim flares are extremely common on Teotihuacan figurines; in a recent publication, von Winning (1987, 2: 57) considers this device, "el pectoral con dos bolitos de barro," to be a specific trait of one figurine type. Kidder,

---

[5] However, this may not be the only reason worked jade items were placed on mirrors; certain pieces of jade may have been prized for their divinatory powers. Thus the jade sphere found in the Temple of the Chac Mool cache was immediately identified by Yucatec Maya as a divinatory *sastun*. According to Diego de Landa, the Contact Period Yucatec had small divinatory stones termed *am*, meaning "spider" in Yucatec (Tozzer 1941: 154, see n. 608, 775). Old jades or heirlooms may have been especially prized for scrying or sortilage. In many regions of Mesoamerica, beads and other items found in the fields are believed to have supernatural powers to be used for divination (e.g., Ramirez Castañeda 1912: 354; B. Tedlock 1982: 81).

Karl A. Taube

Fig. 8 Breast mirror appearing on Teotihuacan figurine, note pair of flanking spools (from Séjourné 1966b: fig. 96).

Jennings, and Shook (1946: 126) note that in the Early Classic tombs at Kaminaljuyu, large mirrors were often placed on the breast of the deceased. In the region of Escuintla, Guatemala, mirrors of similar scale often appear on the chest of *incensario* figures. Here they also occur with the flanking spools on the mirror rim (e.g., Hellmuth 1975: pl. 23c). In a great many examples at Escuintla and Teotihuacan, the mirror face is occupied by forms of the Reptile Eye glyph, a sign that is still not fully understood (e.g., Hellmuth 1975: pls. 26, 27).

Mirrors Worn in Headdresses

In Teotihuacan costume, mirrors are quite frequently placed in the center of headdresses worn by women, men, and gods (Fig. 9). When worn by figures, these mirrors occur in a broad variety of headdress types. However, Teotihuacan headdresses also appear as isolated iconographic motifs. In this context, the headdress is of a very specific form (Fig. 9d-e). This device, termed the Feather Headdress Symbol by James Langley (1986: 114), is a broad headdress with feather crest emanating from the top and frequently the sides. In the center of the Feather Headdress Symbol, circular mirrors may be prominently displayed.

The Iconography of Mirrors

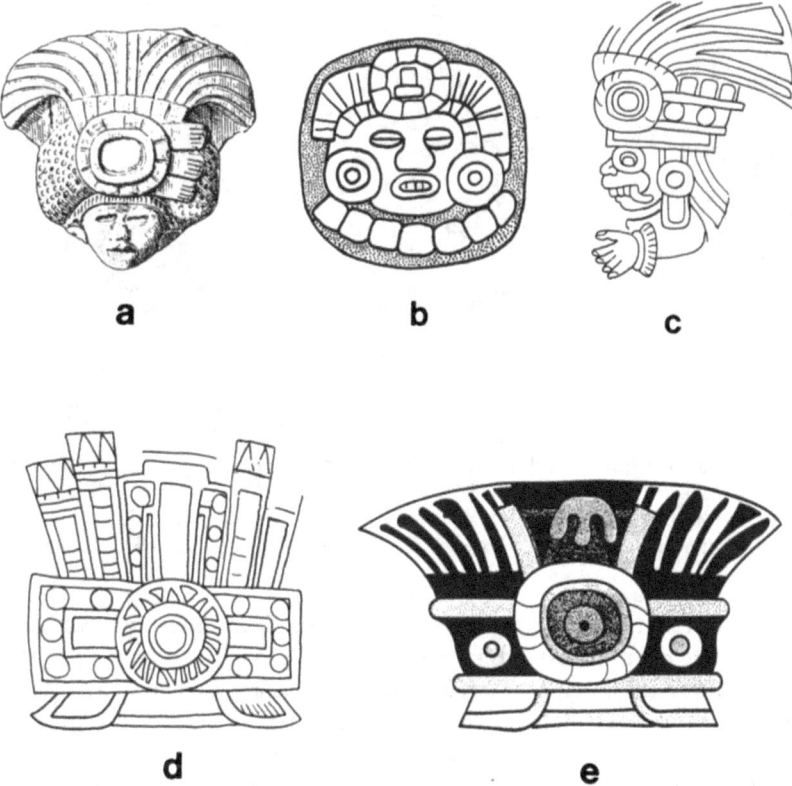

Fig. 9 Mirrors appearing in center of Teotihuacan-style headdresses. (a) Figurine head with mirror in headdress (from Seler 1902–23, 5: 463, fig. 54a); (b) Teotihuacan-style figure with headdress mirror; note flare in center of mirror. Stela 23, Kaminaljuyu (after Parsons 1986: fig. 190); (c) Teotihuacan Tlaloc with headdress mirror (after Miller 1973: fig. 202); (d) Headdress occurring in Teotihuacan mural (after Miller 1973: figs. 210-211); (e) Headdress occurring in Teotihuacan mural (from Langley 1986: fig. 32).

Large Mirrors Not Worn in Costume

Unlike mirrors made from a single stone, there is virtually no limit to the potential diameter of pyrite mosaic mirrors. Larger mirrors simply require a broader backing and more pyrite tesserae. Certain Teotihuacan mirrors were probably too large for personal adornment. Instead, they seem to have been placed on altars or held in the arms during particular rites. Three of the Teotihuacan figurines contained within the hollow figure from Becan, Campeche, hold very large mirrors to their chests (Fig. 10a). A remarkable

Karl A. Taube

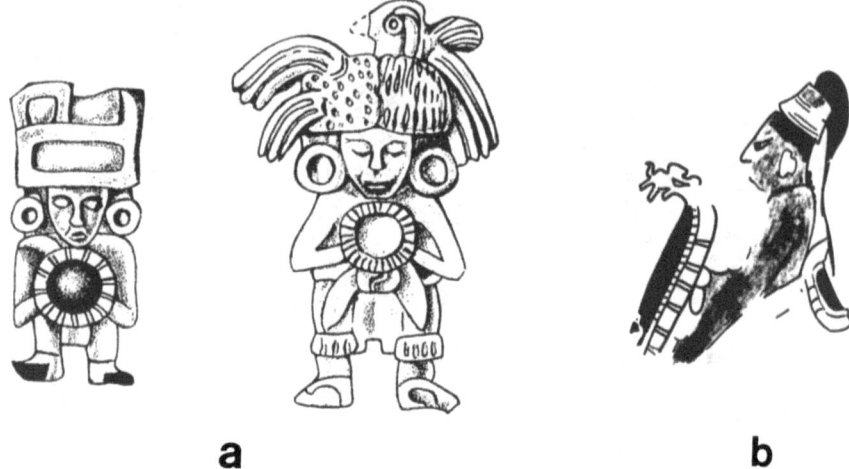

a **b**

Fig. 10 Classic figures holding out large circular mirrors. (a) Teotihuacan-style figurines with mirrors, Becan (from Ball 1974: 8); (b) Detail of Late Classic vase painted in "pink glyph style." Male holds large mirror with petalled edges and skeletal serpent head at top; note mirror worn at small of back (after Kerr 1989: 89).

Late Classic cache excavated at Monte Alban contained sixteen figures, three holding large rimmed disks. Elizabeth Easby and John Scott (1970: fig. 163) have identified these Zapotec circular devices as mirrors. The Classic Maya also seem to have fashioned extremely large circular mirrors. In one Late Classic scene, a man holds a great rimmed mirror that dwarfs the mirror worn upon his back (Fig. 10b). Unfortunately, the lower portion of the mirror is effaced, but given the present appearance, the diameter was perhaps half a meter. Although the scale should not be taken too literally, it is entirely possible that pyrite mirrors of this size were fashioned in ancient Mesoamerica.

THE SYMBOLIC SIGNIFICANCE OF TEOTIHUACAN MIRRORS

The varied forms of Teotihuacan mirrors are interesting in their own right, but clearly they were more than articles of beauty and adornment. In many scenes, they appear in strange and still poorly known contexts, curiously combined with seemingly disparate elements. Given our limited understanding of the iconography, a symbolic interpretation of Teotihuacan mirrors is no easy task. However, there are constructive avenues of approach. For one, there is the complex iconography frequently appearing on actual Teotihuacan mirror backs. In addition, the form and archaeological context of excavated mirrors can provide valuable clues to their use and significance.

The Iconography of Mirrors

Aside from actual mirrors and their archaeological associations, Teotihuacan representations of mirrors also present detailed symbolic information. In the art, mirrors could be readily depicted not only as they appear but also as they were symbolically perceived, frequently by the substitution or juxtaposition of other distinct elements. Although extremely important, direct substitutions frequently alter the form of the mirror. It is thus useful to have a firm context in which the varied forms interrelate. Costume serves this purpose very well, because the forms can be readily translated to the human plane. Thus, for example, circular pools or giant eyeballs can be readily identified as mirrors when they appear on Teotihuacan dress. I have noted three areas where mirrors commonly appear in Teotihuacan costumes: against the lower back, on the chest, and in the center of the headdress. In the context of these specific regions, many varied motifs substitute for the mirror face. Those to be discussed are mirrors as human eyes or faces, flowers, fiery hearths, pools, webs, shields, the world or the sun, and caves or passageways.

The Mirror as an Eye

Cecelia Klein (1976: 208–213) has suggested that at Teotihuacan and in the later iconography of Central Mexico, the ringed eyes found on Tlaloc and other deities may refer to mirrors. In support, Klein (1976) cites abundant evidence that the Aztec identified mirrors with eyes. Thus, in Book 10 of the Florentine Codex, both the eye and pupil are described as *tezcactl*, or mirror. The association of mirrors with eyes is widespread in Mesoamerica. In contemporary Tzotzil Maya, one word for pupil or eye is *nen sat*, *nen* meaning "mirror" and *sat*, "eye" or "face" (Laughlin 1975: 251).[6] Nicholas Saunders (1988: 14–19) notes that reflective mirror stones were used to represent eyes in Olmec, Maya, Teotihuacan, and Aztec sculpture. According to Saunders (1988), the Mesoamerican identification of mirrors with eyes may derive from the strongly reflective quality of jaguar eyes.

At Teotihuacan, mirrors were strongly identified with eyes. Along with the Teotihuacan use of pyrite, mica and obsidian are frequently used in Teotihuacan sculpture to represent the shining pupil. George Kubler (1967: 9) notes that eyes in Teotihuacan iconography represent shining brilliance; thus they are commonly found in streams and other bodies of water. On one Teotihuacan-style mirror back excavated at Kaminaljuyu, a series of eyes encircles the rim (see Fig. 1). Human eyes are also used to represent the

---

[6] In the creation account of Quichean *Popol Vuh*, the omniscient people of maize had their sight damaged by the creators. This adjustment of human eyes to their present limited state was compared to misting the surface of a mirror: "They were blinded as the face of a mirror is breathed upon" (D. Tedlock 1985: 167). The Quichean phrase for "the face of the mirror," *u vach lemo*, can refer simultaneously to both the face and eye; in Quiche, *vach* signifies "eye" as well as "face" (Edmonson 1965: 139).

gleaming mirror face. Thus, the shining center of both the headdress and breast mirrors can be replaced with a single large eye (Fig. 11b–c). The Teotihuacan identification of mirrors with eyes is so widespread that they may be even rendered in the form of an eye, lenticular but with the raised rim and radiating feathers found with mirrors (Fig. 11a).

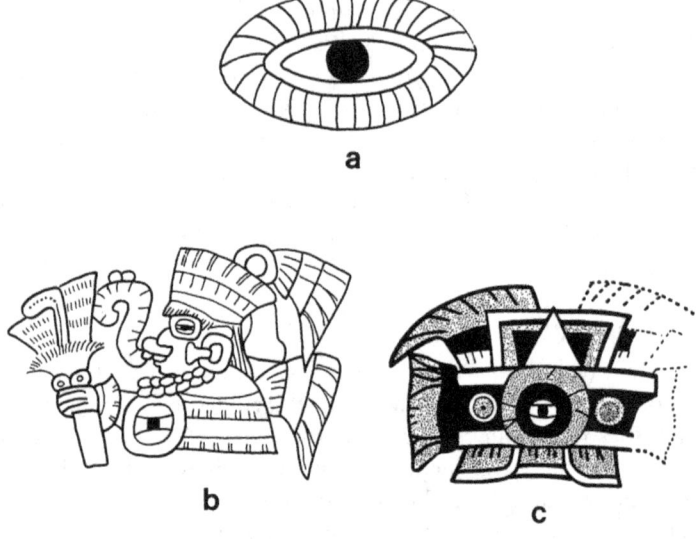

Fig. 11 Teotihuacan substitutions between mirrors and eyes. (a) Teotihuacan *incensario adorno* in the form of an eye with a mirror edging, from item on display in the Museo Nacional de Antropología e Historia, Mexico City (for photo, cf. Berlo 1984: pl. 26); (b) Warrior figure with eye replacing mirror of breast piece (after von Winning 1987, 1: fig. 1j); (c) Eye replacing mirror in center of headdress motif (from Langley 1986: fig. 33).

The Mirror as a Face

Like the Tzotzil and other Maya groups, the Aztec words for eye and face are semantically related. Thus the Nahuatl word for eye, *ixtelolotli*, derives from a word for face, *ixtli* (see Sahagún 1950–1971, bk. 10: 112). Similarly, Teotihuacan mirrors were identified not only with eyes but also with the entire face. It has been noted that mirrors are frequently flanked by a pair of flares resembling earspools (Fig. 12a). I suspect that these spools serve to convert the mirror into an animate being or face. The use of earflares to create a face may also be seen on Teotihuacan style braziers, where a prominent pair of spools converts the vessel into a human head (Fig. 12b); at times, even a nosepiece and jade necklace are added (e.g., Berlo 1984: pls.

The Iconography of Mirrors

35, 42). In one Teotihuacan mural, a netted, feather-rimmed mirror replaces the face of the Netted Jaguar (see Berlo, this volume, fig. 12). At Early Postclassic Tula, all of the Atlantean column *tezcacuitlapilli* have faces corresponding to the region of the pyrite mirror (Fig. 12c). Although it is conceivable that this face is a reflection of an individual bending over or kneeling behind the Atlantean warrior, it is far more likely a deified personification of the mirror. Among the Huichol, who have perhaps the most complex mirror lore known for contemporary Mesoamerica, circular glass mirrors used in divination are referred to as *nealika,* a term meaning "face," as well as the round mirror (Lumholtz 1900: 108; Seler 1902–23, 3: 363; Negrín 1975: 18–19).

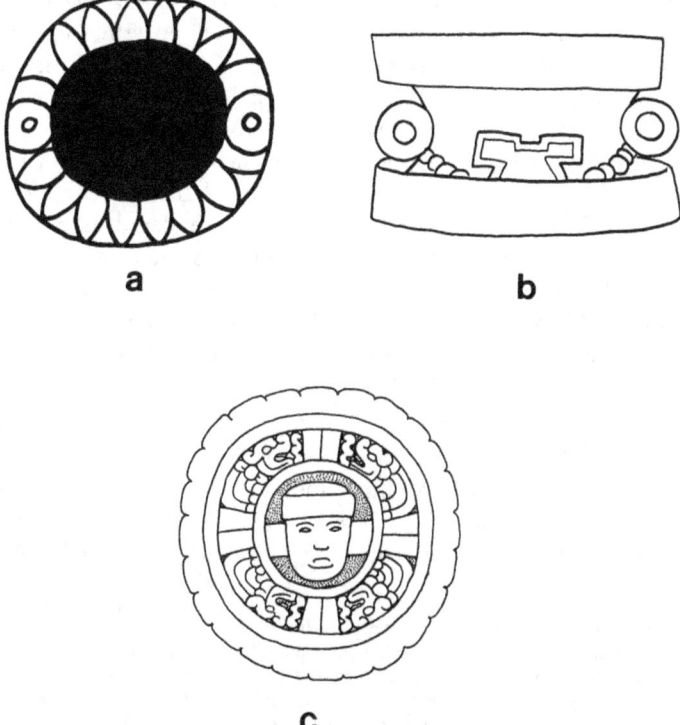

Fig. 12 The identification of mirrors with faces. (a) Teotihuacan representation of back mirror with flanking flares resembling earspools (after Miller 1973: figs. 199-200); (b) Teotihuacan-style *incensario* base with earspools, necklace, and nosepiece. Lake Amatitlan, Guatemala (after Berlo 1984: pl. 232); (c) Early Postclassic depiction of *tezcacuitlapilli* with face corresponding to area of pyrite mirror (from Tozzer 1957).

Karl A. Taube

The Mirror as a Flower

Teotihuacan mirrors were also compared to flowers.[7] Two of the Esperanza phase mirrors excavated at Kaminaljuyu bear representations of flowers. On one example, flowers are painted near the rim of the mirror back (Kidder, Jennings, and Shook 1946: fig. 205b). The other mirror depicts both frontal and profile views of flowers, here surrounding the mirror face (Kidder, Jennings, and Shook 1946: fig. 53e). On one Early Classic Maya vessel, the center of a tasseled back mirror contains two outcurving bands (Fig. 13c). This same pair of curving bands frequently extrude from the corolla of Teotihuacan style flowers (e.g., Linné 1934: fig. 25).[8] The earflare occurring in the center of many Teotihuacan mirrors refers not to a face but to another natural form, a flower (Fig. 13a). At times, this central device is notched, much like the funnel-shaped profile representations of flowers in Teotihuacan iconography (Fig. 13b).

An *incensario* excavated in the Tetitla compound bears *adorno* butterflies upon mica-encrusted mirror medallions, as if the buttterflies were gathering nectar off the mirror face (Berlo 1984: pl. 19). Another Tetitla *incensario* depicts butterflies upon similar mirror medallions, although here the inner rim is composed of a four-petaled flower (Berlo 1984: pl. 23).[9] It has been noted that there is a great deal of variety in the form of Teotihuacan mirror rims; a great many petaled rims do closely resemble flowers (Fig. 13d). At times, the mirror rim appears to be simply rendered as a four-petaled flower, with the pyrite surface corresponding to the center of the flower. Mirrors of this type are found as breast ornaments, on the waist, and in the center of headdresses (Fig. 13f–g). However, it is unlikely that all these four-petaled devices appearing on costumes are mirrors; smaller examples could easily refer to actual flowers.

The Mirror as Fire

The common presence of butterflies and mirrors upon Teotihuacan *incensarios* is not coincidental; both relate to fire. In the iconography of Postclassic Central Mexico, butterflies are frequently identified with flames.

---

[7] Although it may seem a great jump—from faces to flowers—it is not, because in Teotihuacan iconography even the human face may be rendered as a flower. One Escuintla *incensario* depicts a human face with pyrite eyes in the center of a great petaled flower; a butterfly is at the lower edge, as if to suck its nectar (see Hellmuth 1975: cover). In another scene, the flower replaces a face placed in the center of a headdress (Linné 1934: fig. 25).

[8] At the Postclassic site of Tulum, Quintana Roo, petaled disks with two volutes rising out of the center alternate with similar disks containing eyes (see Miller 1982: pls. 25, 28). It is probable that both petaled disks refer to mirrors, here metaphorically represented as both eyes and flowers.

[9] A large Postclassic obsidian mirror in the American Museum of Natural History, New York, still retains its original gilt wooden rim. Both sides of the rim are carved with a repetitive series of four-lobed elements closely resembling flowers (see Saville 1925: pl. LI).

The Iconography of Mirrors

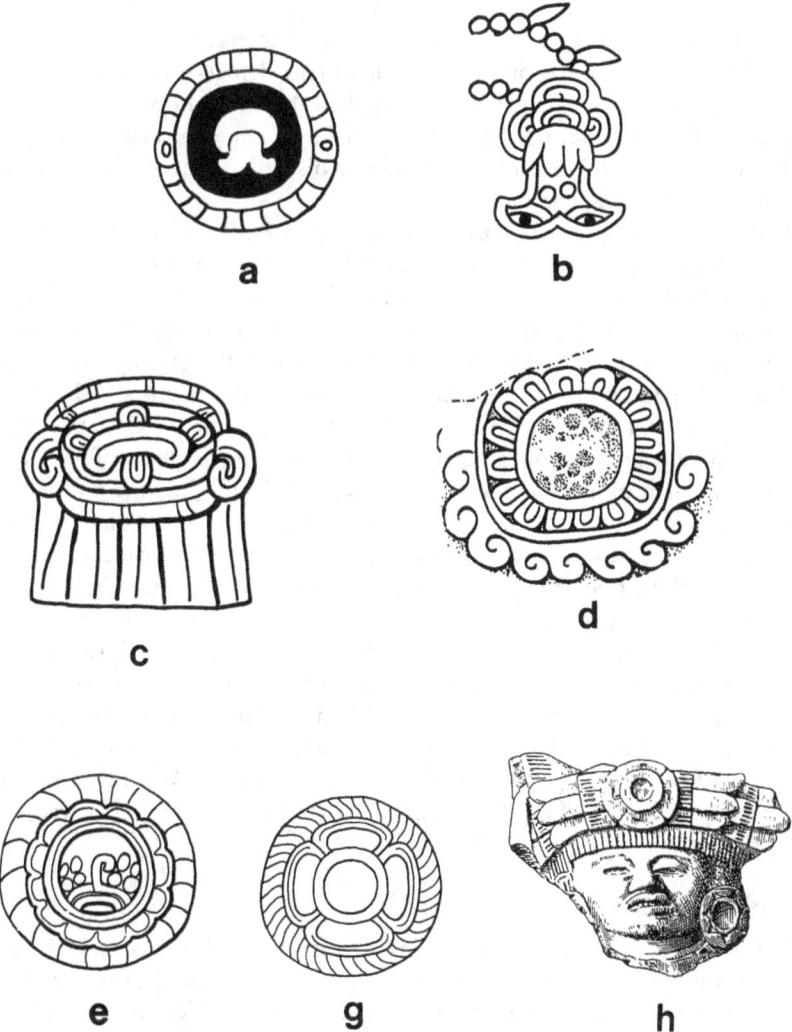

Fig. 13 Early Classic representations of mirrors and flowers. (a) Teotihuacan back mirror with central flare resembling flower (after Miller 1973: fig. 366); (b) Profile rendering of flower, Tepantitla (after Miller 1973: fig. 158); (c) Detail of back mirror from Early Classic Maya vessel; note pair of elements curling out from center of mirror face (after Hellmuth 1987: fig. 495); (d) Mirror with petaled rim; detail of bas-relief from Tepecuacuilco, Guerrero (after Diaz 1987: 10); (e) Mirror flower with Reptile Eye sign on mirror face (after Hellmuth 1975: pl. 33); (f) Four-petaled mirror flower with feather rim (after Caso 1966: fig. 19c); (g) Rimmed four-petaled flower worn in the headdress of a female figure (from Seler 1902–23, 5: 463).

Karl A. Taube

Since the work of Seler (1902–23, 4: 722), it has been generally recognized that butterflies were identified with flames at Classic Teotihuacan as well. At Teotihuacan, the bright, shining surface of mirrors was compared to fire.[10] The back of one Teotihuacan-style mirror depicts a goddess covered with fire signs; pairs of burning torches flank her headdress and her body (see Berlo, this volume, fig. 20). Trapezoidal eyes conventionally associated with the rims of Huehueteotl censers can be discerned both on her costume and the large flanking torches.

In ancient Mesoamerica, mirrors widely appear with burning hearths or censers. At the Maya sites of Zaculeu and Nebaj, actual pyrite mirrors were placed in Early Classic ceramic censers (Woodbury and Trik 1953: 233; Smith and Kidder 1951: 69, fig. 36, no. 21; fig. 42, nos. 47, 48). Similarly, burning mirrors are placed within censers on Codex Borgia page 63 and on Vaticanus B page 66 (Fig. 14a). In both instances, the mirrors and censers serve as hearths for Chantico, the Postclassic fire goddess. Codex Borgia page 49 depicts another burning mirror, here serving as hearth for a large *olla* (Fig. 14b). With its blue segmented and petaled rim, the mirror is clearly derived from the Toltec pyrite *tezcacuitlapilli* (Figs. 14c, 19d). Like the four smoking Xiuhcoatl serpents surrounding the Early Postclassic *tezcacuitlapilli* mirror face, the Codex Borgia mirror is framed by four burning Xixiuhcoa. On Codex Borgia page 2, Xiuhtecuhtli creates fire in a mirror placed on the back of a Xiuhcoatl (Fig. 14c). This serpent recalls an Aztec sculpture representing a Xiuhcoatl with burning mirrors on its back (Fig. 14d). In the iconography of Late Postclassic Central Mexico, burning mirrors served as an emblem of Tezcatlipoca, whose name means "smoking mirror." The contemporary Huichol also identify mirrors with fire. According to one Huichol myth recorded by R. M. Zingg (1938: 702), fire first appeared as a mirror.

The Mirror as Water

Although the glint of the mirror was identified with fire in ancient Mesoamerica, the reflective surface was often compared to a pool of water. This may be seen on Codex Borgia page 17, where a water-filled mirror replaces the conventional smoking mirror worn at the back of Tezcatlipoca's head; the day sign *Atl,* or water, is placed upon the mirror sign (Fig. 15a). The early Aztec greenstone goddess recently discovered at the Templo Mayor is another example (Fig. 15b). Although the large rimmed disk upon her abdomen contains a clear water sign, López Austin (1979: 145) identifies it

---

[10] In a recent study, Coggins (1987) stresses the association of pyrite mirrors with fire in ancient Mesoamerica and suggests that they were an important component of calendrical new fire ceremonies.

The Iconography of Mirrors

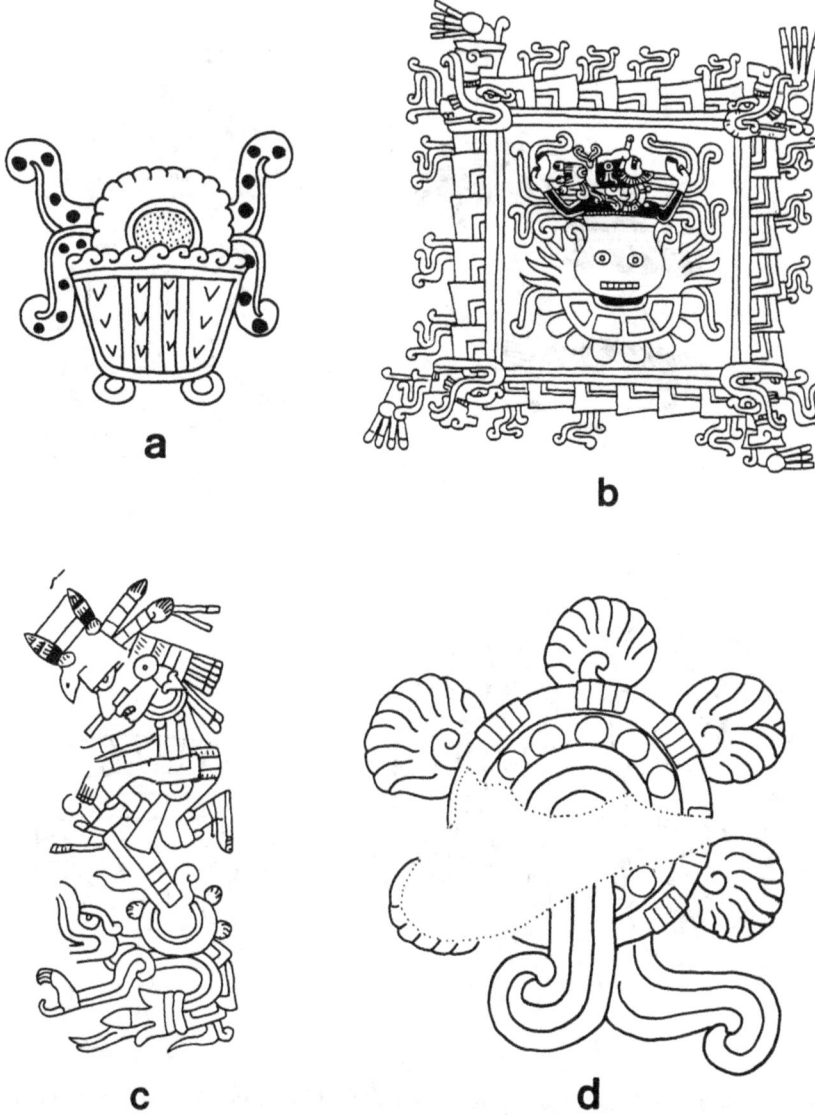

Fig. 14 The identification of mirrors with fire in Postclassic Central Mexican iconography. (a) Burning mirror in spiked brazier. Codex Borgia page 63; (b) Turquoise back mirror forming hearth; note four fire serpents framing mirror. Codex Borgia page 46; (c) Xiuhtecuhtli making fire on mirror placed on back of Xiuhcoatl. Codex Borgia page 2; (d) Smoking mirror on Xiuhcoatl stone sculpture, from a piece in the Museo Nacional de Antropología e Historia, Mexico City.

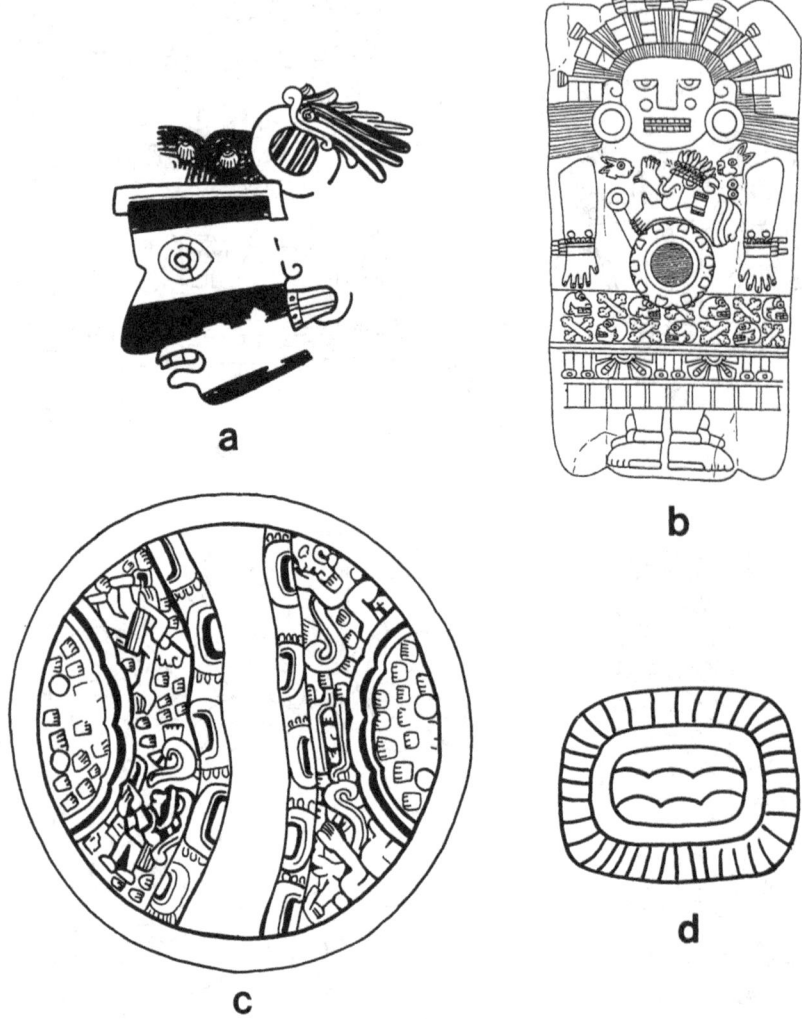

Fig. 15 The identification of mirrors with water in Central Mexican iconography. (a) Detail of Tezcatlipoca with water mirror at back of head; note day sign *Atl* on mirror. Codex Borgia page 17; (b) Early Aztec greenstone figure of skirted female with water mirror on abdomen (from López Austin 1979: fig. 4); (c) Teotihuacan-style mirror back from Guacimo, Costa Rica; note scalloping, a Teotihuacan convention for bodies of water (after Stone and Balser 1965: fig. 22); (d) Teotihuacan ceramic molded design of scalloped water sign within petaled ring, probably a mirror rim (from Séjourné 1966a: fig. 29).

as a mirror.[11] An Early Classic Teotihuacan-style mirror excavated at Guacimo, Costa Rica, depicts a series of footprints and four individuals next to scalloped chevron bands, a Teotihuacan convention for bodies of water (Fig. 15c). This same water sign appears on an impressed stamp design from Teotihuacan, here within a petaled feather rim (Fig. 15d). Like the cited Postclassic examples, this device seems to represent the mirror as a pool of water.

In Mesoamerica and the American Southwest, the reflective surface of water-filled bowls is frequently used for divinatory scrying. In the Colonial Yucatec *Motul Dictionary*, *nenba* is glossed as "mirarse el espejo, o en agua" (Barrera Vásquez 1980: 565). At Teotihuacan and among the Classic Maya, mirrors were actually placed in bowls, as if they were shining pools of water. At the Maya site of Nebaj, mirrors were discovered within ceramic bowls (Smith and Kidder 1951: 69). Similar mirror-bowls are found in Late Classic Maya polychrome palace scenes (Fig. 16a). In Teotihuacan iconography, mirror-bowls are relatively common, with the mirror placed upright in a bowl rendered in profile. On one of the mirror backs from Kaminaljuyu, this composition appears beneath a frontally facing Teotihuacan goddess (see Fig. 1). An Early Classic Escuintla style *incensario* contains an elaborate form of mirror bowl. Here a mirror with flanking ear flares serves as the body of a butterfly rising or perhaps shining out of a water-filled bowl (Fig. 16b).

The Mirror as a Web

The circular pyrite mirror also appears to have been compared to a woven disk or spider web. The netted disks appearing in Teotihuacan iconography constitute a form of mirror, here depicted with a loosely woven surface.[12] In one scene, a netted mirror with a central reflective eye is flanked by two types of plants (Fig. 17a). One form is the waterlily, evidently to denote the disk as a pool of water. The other plant, flanking both sides of the disk, is probably cotton and may refer to the woven nature of the disk. The bolls appear in the form of notched circles in the center of florate forms. The same notched circle—Circle I of James Langley (1986: 304)—commonly appears near the butts and tips of Teotihuacan darts, areas entirely appropriate for bolls of cotton.

Along with the netted disks, Teotihuacan mirrors are also identified with realistically depicted spider webs. In part, this may be due to the linear patterns created by the mosaic surface, which bear resemblance to cobwebs.

---

[11] Fray Bernardino Sahagún (1950–71, bk. 2: 183) describes an Aztec spring used for penitential bathing. This spring was termed *tezcaapan*, which Cecilio Robelo (1980: 551) glosses as "en el agua de espejo o como espejo."

[12] At El Tajin, male figures wear back mirrors having a simple form of the netted disk, here formed by two twisted cords (see Kampen 1972: figs. 22, 23).

Karl A. Taube

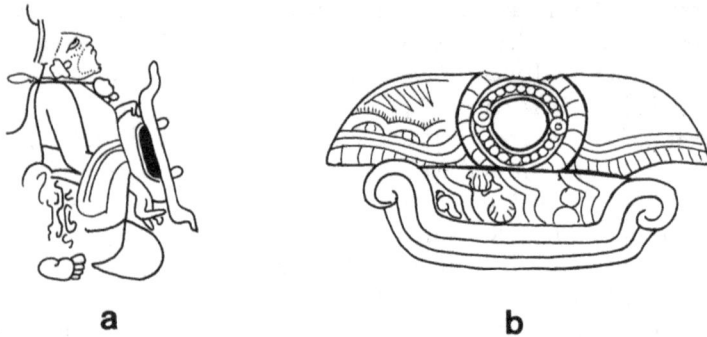

Fig. 16 Representations of mirror-bowls in Maya and Teotihuacan art. (a) Detail of Maya polychrome depicting individual holding mirror placed in bowl (after M. Coe 1975: no. 12); (b) Detail of Escuintla *incensario* representing mirror with butterfly wings in water-filled bowl (after Hellmuth 1975: pl. 32).

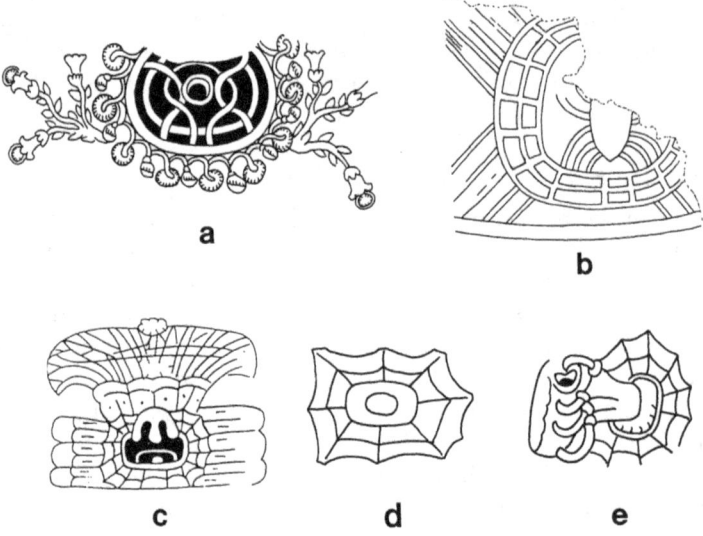

Fig. 17 Woven disks, webs, and mirrors in Teotihuacan iconography. (a) Netted disk with central eye and surrounding waterlily and probable cotton plants (after Miller 1973: fig. 85); (b) Spider in center of web (drawn after photo courtesy of James Langley); (c) Headdress with spider web and heart substituting for central mirror (after Seler 1902–23, 5: 513); (d) Spider web with central rimmed disk (after Séjourné 1966a: fig. 86); (e) Bird foot clutching heart in center of rimmed web; note probable cotton sign inside ring (after Cisneros Gallery 1969: pl. 11).

The Iconography of Mirrors

In a number of instances, Teotihuacan representations of spider webs do closely resemble circular mirrors. James Langley (personal communication, 1988) has called my attention to an interesting example appearing on a painted stucco vessel in the Musee de L'Homme, Paris. In the partly effaced scene, a spider occurs in the center of a web rendered in the form of a segmented rim with diagonal stays (Fig. 17b). The web closely resembles a mirror placed on a crossroads, a convention found at Teotihuacan. On one incised Teotihuacan vessel, a realistic spider web substitutes for the mirror in the center of a headdress, the usual location of the pyrite mirror (Fig. 17c). The web center contains a heart surrounded by a circular rim. A good many realistic spider webs contain this central rim, which may refer to a mirror (Fig. 17d–e).[13] A fragmentary mural depicts the the central rim with interior notching to denote cotton; a taloned foot clutching a heart emerges from the center of the device (Fig. 17e).

The identification of mirrors with spider webs continued after Classic Teotihuacan and appears to have been present among the Postclassic Mixtec. Among the contents of Tomb 7 at Monte Alban was a gold mirror back representing a spider (Caso 1965: 927, fig. 57). A mosaic cache, reportedly from a Mixtec area of Puebla, contained a series of turquoise mosaic mirrors (Saville 1922). In the center of several examples, there is a device composed of radiating lines and concentric circles, a form closely resembling a spider web (Saville 1922: pl. 23). John Pohl (personal communication, 1988) has pointed out to me an interesting series of entires in the sixteenth century Pedro de Alvarado Dictionary. Whereas the Mixtec term for a bright or clean mirror is glossed as *yuudoo,* or "stone *ndoo,"* the word for spider web is "animal *ndoo,*" *ndoo* being a Mixtec term for clean or brilliant. In modern Huichol lore, mirrors and other *nealika* are identified with spider webs. According to one contemporary Huichol account, the first *nealika,* or "instrument for seeing," was a spider web woven over a gourd bowl (Negrín 1975). One type of Huichol *nealika,* the "front shield," closely resembles the centrally rimmed spider web of Teotihuacan iconography. Formed of thread woven upon radiating splints, the front shield contains a central rim, often with a mirror at its center (Zingg 1938: 620; Furst 1978: 32).

The Mirror as a Woven Shield

The Tetitla compound at Teotihuacan contains a series of murals representing an entity that has been identified as a spider goddess (Taube 1983). She stands within a U-shaped foaming bowl identical to the mirror bowls found in Teotihuacan iconography (see Berlo, this volume, fig. 2). Indeed,

---

[13] A unprovenanced silhouette monument, possibly from Kaminaljuyu, depicts an interesting form of the centrally rimmed web, here containing a crouching and possibly aged male (Parsons 1986: fig. 151).

her outstretched upper garment suggests a mirror placed edgewise in the bowl (see Taube 1983: fig. 5). However, her garment also refers to another circular item, a woven war shield with a pendant tassel. The tassel, appearing as the rhomboid forming her skirt, is frequently found on Teotihuacan shields (Fig. 18e). At Teotihuacan, mirrors were identified with war shields to such a degree that frequently it is difficult to tell them apart. Like the mirror, Teotihuacan shields are frequently round with a raised rim surrounded by feathers (Fig. 18). Circular Teotihuacan-style shields often have central tassels that not only resemble flowers but also the single spool often placed in the center of Teotihuacan mirrors (Fig. 18b–c).[14]

The back mirrors commonly worn by Teotihuacan warriors do closely resemble tasseled shields. John Carlson and Linda Landis (1985: 124) note that in the context of Classic Maya skybands, mirrors are frequently infixed in the center of shields. In terms of war, mirrors placed on the chest and lower back of Teotihuacan figures could have had a protective function, to guard either against supernatural powers or the blows of actual weapons. However, the inherent qualities of the mirror itself may have also alluded to war. The Postclassic Tezcatlipoca, the god of the smoking mirror, was considered a warrior. Possessing both attributes of fire and water, the Teotihuacan mirrors recall the Aztec concept of *atl-tlachinolli,* or "water-fire," the Aztec phrase for war.[15]

The Mirror as the Sun

Given their association with a broad spectrum of disk-shaped objects found in the natural and cultural worlds, the round mirrors of Teotihuacan could well have expressed larger cosmological concepts, such as the world, the sun, or the moon. There are strong indications that among the inhabitants of Postclassic Central Mexico, the earth was perceived metaphorically as a great round mirror (López Austin 1979: 145; Taube 1983: 122–127). However, due to our limited understanding of Teotihuacan signs, it is difficult to make an explicit case for a similar concept among the ancient Teotihuacanos. John Carlson (1981: 125) has suggested that concave Olmec mirrors represented the sun and, in support, notes that the contemporary Huichol identify mirrors with the sun. A similar belief is found among the

---

[14] The Aztec compared shields to flowers. In the *Cantares Mexicanos,* shields are described as blooming flowers: "Las flores del escudo abren sus corolas, se extiende la gloria, se enlaza en la tierra" (León-Portilla 1984: 130). Then there is the Nahuatl *chimalxochitl,* or "shield flower," the term for the giant sunflower (*Helianthus annuus*). With its large, central face and encircling petal rim, the sunflower is strikingly similar to Teotihuacan mirrors, all the more so when one compares the tightly packed, mosaic-like seed corolla to the pyrite mirror surface.

[15] In the description of the *veintena* festival of Pachtontli on Aztec Telleriano-Remensis page 6, there is an illustration of Tezcatlipoca with his smoking mirror foot. It is composed of a circular mirror with a burning serpent and water. The accompanying Spanish gloss describes the mirror as *agua y abrasamiento,* or water and fire, i.e., war.

Fig. 18 Depictions of shields in Classic Mesoamerica. (a) Detail of shield on Classic Maya stela (after von Winning and Stendahl 1968: pl. 468); (b) Teotihuacan shield with central tassel resembling flower (after Lothrop et al. 1957: pl. xxv–xxvi); (c) Spear with shield bearing traits of mirror, web, and flower; detail of unprovenanced Early Classic mural (after Miller 1973: fig. 359); (d) Teotihuacan round shield with dart (after Lothrop et al. 1957: pl. xxxiii); (e) Tasseled and feather-fringed Teotihuacan shield (after Séjourné 1966a: fig. 165).

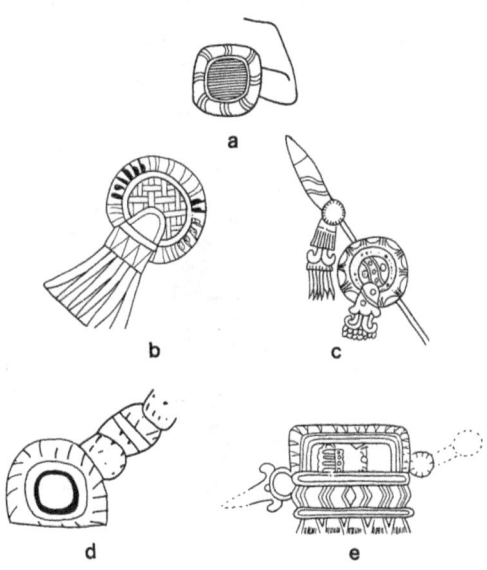

modern Sierra Totonac, who refer to the sun as *Espejo Sol,* or "sun mirror" (Ichon 1973: 107). Among the Classic Maya, mirrors were also identified with the sun. Solar mirror cartouches surrounded by four serpent heads occur in both Early and Late Classic Maya iconography (Fig. 19a–b).[16] On Yaxchilan Stela 11, Bird Jaguar wears such a cartouche as a back mirror (Fig. 19c). This back device is clearly related to the Toltec-style turquoise and pyrite *tezcacuitlapilli,* with its four radiating Xiuhcoatl serpents at the rim (see Figs. 12c, 19d).

The Early Postclassic Toltec turquoise mirrors seem to represent the sun, and this is also true for certain Aztec mirrors of the Late Postclassic. Fray Diego Durán (1964: 140) mentions a mirror that was to be fashioned for the Templo Mayor, "the shining mirror that was to represent the sun." One Aztec sculpture depicts a seated figure wearing a smoking representation of the fifth sun as a mirror upon his back (Fig. 20a). Long ago, Herbert Spinden (cited in Saville 1922: 75) compared the Aztec Calendar Stone to a great turquoise mosaic disk, noting that the sculpture contains a band of

---

[16] The solar *kin* sign with the notched mirror rim also appears in the Initial Series introductory glyph for the month variant of Yaxkin (Thompson 1950: fig. 22, nos. 31–32). The solar *kin* sign is generally considered to be a stylized representation of a flower (Thompson 1950: 142). Thus the Classic Maya *kin* sign mirrors combine the concepts of mirror, sun, and flower.

Karl A. Taube

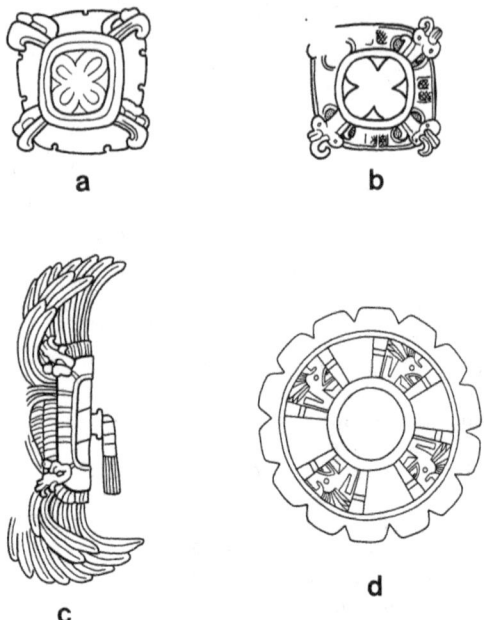

Fig. 19 Representations of serpents surrounding solar mirrors in the Maya region. (a) Early Classic Maya solar *kin* sign with four hook-snouted serpents, Tikal Stela 1; (b) Late Classic Maya *kin* sign with four skeletal serpent snouts, Piedras Negras Stela 10; (c) Late Classic Maya back mirror with four skeletal serpent heads at corners, Yaxchilan Stela 11; (d) Schematic rendering of actual turquoise and pyrite mirror from the Temple of the Chac Mool, Chichen Itza; note four Xiuhcoatl serpents surrounding mirror face (after Morris, Charlot, and Morris 1931: frontispiece).

quincunxes, the Aztec sign of turquoise (Fig. 20b). Had Spinden been aware of the still undiscovered Early Postclassic turquoise back mirrors, he surely would have noted the shared presence of burning Xiuhcoatl serpents on both the Calendar Stone and turquoise-encrusted mirrors. The format of the Aztec Calendar Stone appears to be primarily based on the Toltec style turquoise-rimmed pyrite mirror.

The Mirror as a Cave

The Aztec Calendar Stone represents the face of the fifth sun, Nahui Ollin, passing up through the surface of a turquoise-rimmed mirror. In Mesoamerica, mirrors are widely considered to be supernatural caves or passageways. The mirror presents a world to be looked into, but also one that living beings cannot pass. Thus the Huichol believe that mirrors serve

The Iconography of Mirrors

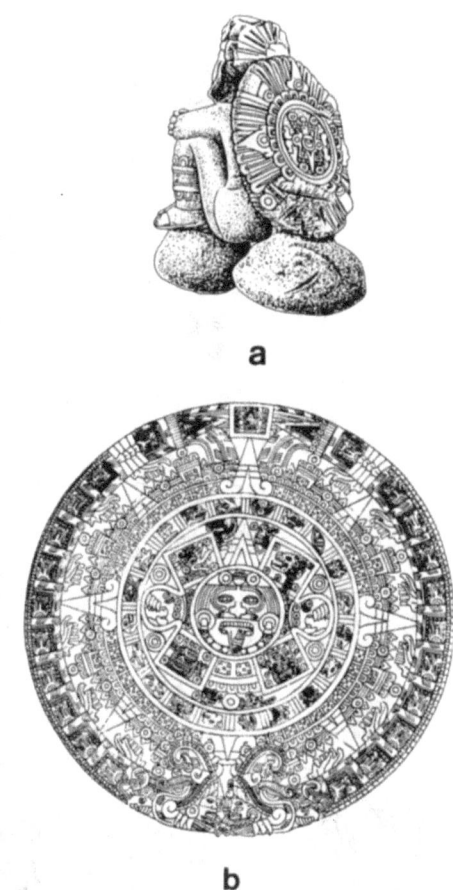

Fig. 20 Aztec representation of solar mirrors. (a) Figure wearing back mirror containing smoking fifth sun (from Taube 1983: 36a); (b) Calendar Stone with segmented rim containing day signs and encircling ring of turquoise quincunxes; two burning Xiuhcoatl serpents lie at edge of disk.

as caves for the gods and ancestors to enter into the human world. On *nealika* disks, the Huichol can represent this passageway with a mirror or simply a hole placed in the center of the device (Negrín 1975: 19; Furst 1978: 32). Similarly, the Aztec Anahuatl chestpiece can be either a white-rimmed mirror or only a white ring (Nicholson and Berger 1968: 20). In Classic Maya art, not only faces but entire bodies can be found in the center of mirrors. An example is Caracol Stela 5, where figures emerge out of burning petaled mirrors ornamented with hook-nosed serpents (Fig. 21a).[17] In Maya art, serpents are commonly found emerging through the face of mirrors (Fig. 21b–d). Examples appear at Protoclassic Kaminaljuyu, Late

[17] At Yaxchilan, figures impersonating the sun and moon sit within mirrors placed near the top of the monument. Tate (n.d.: 63–67) terms the devices "ancestor cartouches," noting that on Yaxchilan Stela 11, the figures are clearly ancestors of Shield Jaguar.

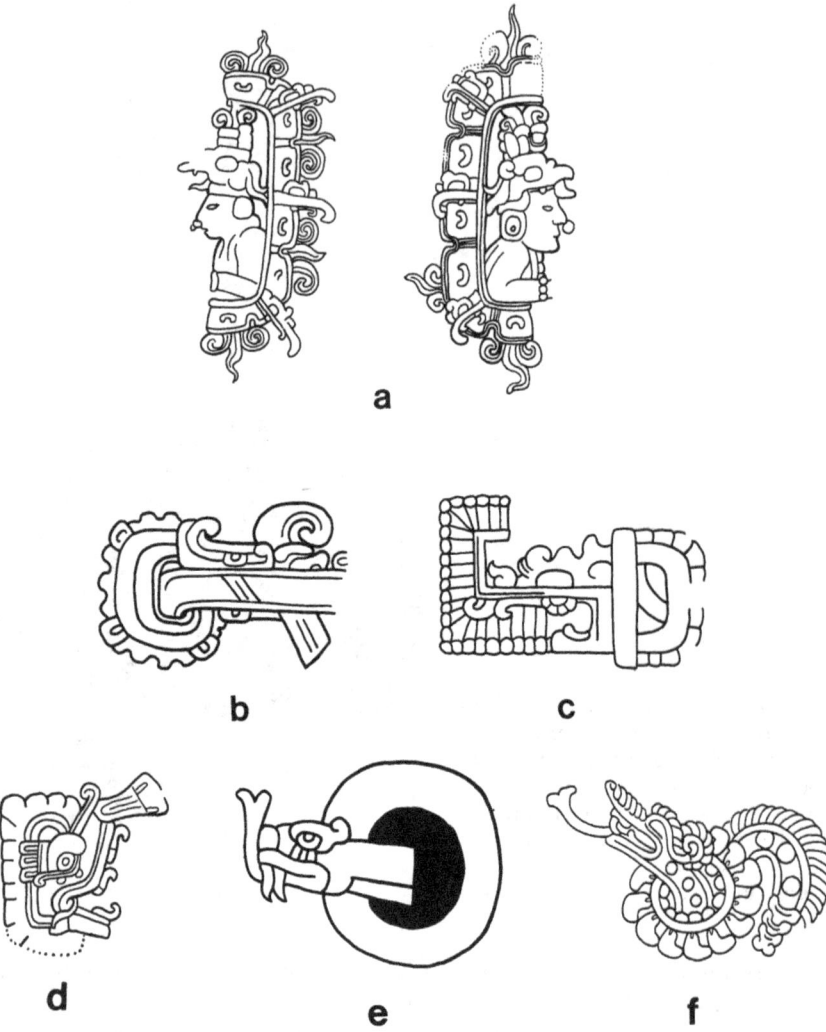

Fig. 21 Pre-Hispanic representations of mirrors as passageways. (a) Classic Maya depiction of burning, petaled mirrors containing human figures; note hook-snouted serpents. Detail of Caracol Stela 5 (after Beetz 1981: fig. 6); (b) Protoclassic serpent emerging out of notched mirror; detail of Altar 14, Kaminaljuyu; (c) Serpent emerging out of mirror with *nen* reflection sign; detail of Sarcophagus Lid, Palenque; (d) Serpent head emerging from mirror worn at back of head, Mound 1, Santa Rita (after Gann 1900: pl. XXIX); (e) Serpent emerging out of surface of blue-rimmed mirror; detail of Codex Cospi page 24; (f) Detail of ceramic bowl from Las Colinas; feather serpent passes through mirror rim (from Taube 1986: fig. 8b).

The Iconography of Mirrors

Fig. 22 Feathered serpent passing through feathered mirror rim, Temple of Quetzalcoatl, Teotihuacan.

Classic Palenque, and in the Postclassic murals of Santa Rita and Tulum.[18] This concept was also present in Central Mexico. On page 24 of the Late Postclassic Codex Cospi, a serpent emerges through the face of a blue-rimmed mirror (Fig. 21b).

At Teotihuacan, serpents were also identified with mirror caves. In one Teotihuacan headdress, a pair of plumed serpents flank a shining quatrefoil cave device substituting for the central headdress mirror (Taube 1986: fig. 9). The Las Colinas Bowl depicts the Teotihuacan feathered serpent passing through a mirror rim (Fig. 21f). This motif is repeated on a monumental scale at the Temple of Quetzalcoatl, where two forms of serpents, Quetzalcoatl and an early form of the Xiuhcoatl appear on a great facade of feathered mirrors. Like the Las Colinas scene, the body of the feathered serpent is depicted passing through the feathered mirror rim (Fig. 22). Far from being inert slabs of stone, Teotihuacan mirrors were vital passageways from which gods and ancestors communicated with the world of the living.

CONCLUSIONS

In this study, I have argued that pyrite mirrors are extremely common in the costume and iconography of Teotihuacan. The majority of feathered medallions found in Teotihuacan iconography are representations of mirrors.

[18] The examples from Santa Rita and Tulum are mirrors worn at the back of the head. Although this is not a Teotihuacan or Classic Maya convention, it is commonly found in Postclassic Central Mexican codices (e.g., Codex Fejérváry-Mayer page 1, Codex Laud page 13).

Karl A. Taube

At Teotihuacan, pyrite mirrors were an important component of both ritual and dress. The wearing of circular mirrors on the chest and brow can be easily traced to the Early and Middle Formative Olmec period, although here the devices were usually fashioned of grey iron oxide ores, such as magnetite and hematite, not golden pyrite (Carlson 1981: 123, 124; Heizer and Gullberg 1981: 112). However, the use of large mirrors on the back seems to have been an Early Classic innovation. This may have been partly due to the increased use of pyrite mosaic, which allowed for larger mirrors to be fashioned. During the Classic period, pyrite back mirrors were widespread in Mesoamerica; they were especially popular at Teotihuacan and serve almost as a hallmark of Teotihuacan costume and influence.

In consideration of the Kaminaljuyu tombs and representations in Classic Maya art, it is clear that pyrite mirror plaques were an important cult object shared between the Teotihuacanos and the Classic Maya. Many of the same forms and attributes found with mirrors at Teotihuacan were also present among the Classic Maya. Unfortunately, Classic Maya pyrite mirrors have received little recent attention. Although it is beyond the scope of this study, an iconographic analysis of Classic Maya pyrite mirrors could shed much light not only on Maya mirror use but also on that of Classic Teotihuacan.

It has been noted that Teotihuacan mirrors did not simply symbolize one object but were identified with a wide range of things, such as eyes, faces, flowers, butterflies, hearths, pools of water, webs, woven shields, and caves. At first sight, this may appear strange, but it is clear that among later peoples of Mesoamerica, mirrors were also thought of in a variety of ways. Thus, among the modern Huichol, mirrors are considered to be faces, fire, the sun, and caves, and they are linked to a wide variety of other objects having similar circular forms.[19] Thus, like the Asian mandala, the mirrors are imbued with meaning and are causally linked to basic objects and even organizational principles of the world. With their identification with eyes, faces, and passageways, it is fairly clear that Teotihuacan mirrors were used in divination, a means of seeing into the supernatural world. The association of the diurnal flowers and butterflies with mirrors suggests that the golden pyrite disks were closely identified with the sun, an association found with the contemporaneous Classic Maya and later peoples of Mesoamerica. Although the mirrors of Teotihuacan display much that is innovative and unique, they also demonstrate the direct participation of this great center in the broader cultural sphere of Mesoamerica.

[19] Seler (1902–23, 5: 368–369) describes some of the overlapping meanings of the mirror and other circular forms among the Huichol: "Sun-disk, face, eye, mirror, full blown flower, are all cognate ideas. The sun's disk rising above the horizon is to the Huichol Indian, a nealika 'face,' and he also calls the round mirror which he buys of the Mexican dealer, a nealika. The moon, as Lumholtz heard, is a sikuli 'eye,' and this word *sikuli* is equivalent to "mirror" as the same Indian told the traveller" (English trans. in Bowditch 1939, vol. 3, pt. 3: 11).

BIBLIOGRAPHY

ASHMORE, WENDY
    1980   Discovering Early Classic Quirigua. *Expedition* 23 (1): 35–44.

BALL, JOSEPH
    1974   A Teotihuacan-Style Cache from the Maya Lowlands. *Archaeology* 27 (1): 2–9.

BARRERA VÁSQUEZ, ALFREDO (ED.)
    1980   *Diccionario Maya Cordemex: Maya-Español, Español-Maya*. Ediciones Cordemex, Mérida.

BEETZ, CARL P.
    1981   *The Monuments and Inscriptions of Caracol, Belize*. University Museum Monograph 45. The University Museum, University of Pennsylvania, Philadelphia.

BERJONNEAU, GERALD, EMILE DELETAILLE, AND JEAN-LOUIS SONNERY
    1985   *Rediscovered Masterpieces of Mesoamerica: Mexico-Guatemala-Honduras*. Editions Arts, Bologne.

BERLO, JANET CATHERINE
    1984   *Teotihuacan Art Abroad: A Study of Metropolitan Style and Provincial Transformation in Incensario Workshops*, BAR International Series 199, Oxford.

BOWDITCH, CHARLES P. (SUPERVISOR)
    1939   *Gesammelte Abhandlungen zur Amerikanischen Sprach- und Alterthumskunde, Vols. I–V by Eduard Seler* (Engl. trans). Carnegie Institution of Washington, Cambridge, Mass.

CARLSON, JOHN B.
    1981   Olmec Concave Iron-Ore Mirrors: The Aesthetics of a Lithic Technology and the Lord of the Mirror. In *The Olmec and their Neighbors: Essays in Memory of Matthew W. Stirling* (Elizabeth P. Benson, ed.): 117–147. Dumbarton Oaks, Washington, D.C..

CARLSON, JOHN B., AND LINDA C. LANDIS
    1985   Bands, Bicephalic Dragons, and other Beasts: The Skyband in Maya Art and Iconography. *Fourth Palenque Round Table, 1980* (Merle Greene Robertson, gen. ed.): 115–140. Pre-Columbian Art Research Institute, San Francisco.

CASO, ALFONSO
    1938   *Exploraciones en Oaxaca, quinta y sexta temporadas, 1936–1937*. Instituto Panamericano de Geografía e Historia, Pub. 34. Mexico, D.F.
    1965   Lapidary Work, Goldwork, and Copperwork from Oaxaca. In *Handbook of Middle American Indians* (Robert Wauchope gen. ed.) 2 (2): 896–930. University of Texas Press, Austin.
    1966   Dioses y signos Teotihuacanos. In *Teotihuacan: Onceava Mesa Redonda*: 249–279. Sociedad Mexicana de Antropología, Mexico, D.F.

CISNEROS GALLERY
 1969 *Surrealism in Pre-Columbian Art.* Cisneros Gallery, New York.

COE, MICHAEL D.
 1975 *Classic Maya Pottery at Dumbarton Oaks.* Dumbarton Oaks, Washington, D.C.

COE, WILLIAM R.
 1967 *Tikal: A Handbook of the Ancient Maya Ruins.* The University Museum, University of Pennsylvania, Philadelphia.

COGGINS, CLEMENCY
 1975 Painting and Drawing Styles at Tikal: An Historical and Iconographic Reconstruction. Ph.D. dissertation, Harvard University. University Microfilms, Ann Arbor.
 1987 New Fire at Chichen Itza. *Memorias del Primer Coloquio Internacional de Mayistas:* 427–484. Universidad Autónoma de México, Mexico, D.F.

DIAZ, CLARA LUZ
 1987 *El occidente de Mexico.* García Valadés Editores, Mexico, D.F.

DURÁN, FRAY DIEGO
 1964 *The Aztecs: The History of the Indies of New Spain.* (D. Heyden and F. Horcasitas, trans. and annot.). Orion, New York.

EASBY, ELIZABETH K., AND JOHN F. SCOTT
 1970 *Before Cortez: Sculpture of Middle America.* The Metropolitan Museum of Art, New York.

EDMONSON, MUNRO S.
 1965 *Quiche-English Dictionary.* Middle American Research Institute, Pub. 30. New Orleans.

EROZA PENICHE, JOSÉ A.
 1947 Descrubimiento y exploración arqueológica de la subestructura del Castillo en Chichen-Itzá. *Vigesimoséptimo Congreso Internacional de Americanistas* 2: 229–248. Instituto Nacional de Antropología e Historia, Mexico, D.F.

FURST, PETER T.
 1978 The Art of Being Huichol. In *Art of the Huichol Indians* (Kathleen Berrin, ed.): 18–34. Harry N. Abrams, New York.

GANN, THOMAS
 1900 Mounds in Northern Honduras. *Nineteenth Annual Report of the Bureau of American Ethnology, 1897–1898,* Part 2: 655–692. Washington, D.C.

HEIZER, ROBERT F., AND JONAS E. GULLBERG
 1981 Concave Mirrors from the Site of La Venta, Tabasco: Their Occurrence, Mineralogy, Optical Description, and Function. In *The Olmec and Their Neighbors: Essays in Memory of Matthew W. Stirling* (Elizabeth P. Benson, ed.): 109–116. Dumbarton Oaks, Washington, D.C.

HELLMUTH, NICHOLAS M.
 1975 *The Escuintla Hoards: Teotihuacan Art in Guatemala.* Foundation for Latin American Research Progress Reports 1 (2). Foundation for Latin American Research, Guatemala City, Guatemala.

1987 *Monster und Menschen in der Maya-Kunst.* Akademische Druck- u. Verlagsanstalt, Graz.

HEYDEN, DORIS
1975 An Interpretation of the Cave Underneath the Pyramid of the Sun in Teotihuacan, Mexico. *American Antiquity* 40: 131–147.

ICHON, ALAIN
1973 *La religión de los Totonacos de la sierra.* Instituto Nacional Indigenista, Mexico, D.F.

KAMPEN, MICHAEL E.
1972 *The Sculptures of El Tajín, Veracruz, Mexico.* University of Florida Press, Gainesville.

KERR, JUSTIN
1989 *The Maya Vase Book: A Corpus of Rollout Photographs of Maya Vases* 1. Kerr Associates, New York.

KIDDER, ALFRED V., JESSE D. JENNINGS, AND EDWIN M. SHOOK
1946 *Excavations at Kaminaljuyu, Guatemala.* Carnegie Institution of Washington Pub. 561. Washington, D.C.

KLEIN, CECELIA F.
1976 *The Face of the Earth: Frontality in Two-Dimensional Mesoamerican Art.* Garland, New York.

KUBLER, GEORGE
1967 *The Iconography of the Art of Teotihuacan.* Studies in Pre-Columbian Art and Archaeology 4. Dumbarton Oaks, Washington, D.C.

LANGLEY, JAMES C.
1986 *Symbolic Notation of Teotihuacan: Elements of Writing in a Mesoamerican Culture of the Classic Period.* BAR International Series 313, Oxford.

LAUGHLIN, ROBERT M.
1975 *The Great Tzotzil Dictionary of San Lorenzo Zinacantan.* Smithsonian Institution Contributions to Anthropology 19. Washington, D.C.

LEÓN-PORTILLA, MIGUEL
1984 *Literaturas de Mesoamérica.* Secretaría de Educación Pública, Mexico, D.F.

LINNÉ, SIGVALD
1934 *Archaeological Researches at Teotihuacan, Mexico.* Ethnographical Museum of Sweden Pub. 1, Stockholm.
1942 *Mexican Highland Cultures.* Ethnographical Museum of Sweden, n.s. Pub. 7. Stockholm.

LÓPEZ AUSTIN, ALFREDO
1979 Iconografía Mexica. El monolito verde del Templo Mayor. *Anales de Antropología* 16: 133–153.

LOTHROP, S. K., W. F. FOSHAG, AND JOY MAHLER
1957 *Robert Woods Bliss Collection: Pre-Columbian Art.* Phaidon, London.

Karl A. Taube

LUMHOLTZ, CARL
 1900 *Symbolism of the Huichol Indians.* Memoirs of the American Museum of Natural History 1. American Museum of Natural History, New York.

MALER, TEOBERT
 1901 *Researches in the Central Portion of the Usumatsintla Valley.* Memoirs of the Peabody Museum of American Archaeology and Ethnology, Harvard University 2 (1). Peabody Museum, Harvard University, Cambridge, Mass.

MILLER, ARTHUR G.
 1973 *The Mural Painting of Teotihuacan.* Dumbarton Oaks, Washington, D.C.
 1982 *On the Edge of the Sea: Mural Painting at Tancah-Tulum, Quintana Roo, Mexico.* Dumbarton Oaks, Washington, D.C.

MORRIS, EARL H., JEAN CHARLOT, AND ANN AXTEL MORRIS
 1931 *The Temple of the Warriors at Chichen Itza.* Carnegie Institution of Washington Pub. 406, Washington, D.C.

NEGRÍN, JUAN
 1975 *The Huichol Creation of the World.* E. B. Crocker Art Gallery, Sacramento.

NICHOLSON, H. B., AND RAINER BERGER
 1968 *Two Aztec Wood Idols: Iconographic and Chronologic Analysis.* Studies in Pre-Columbian Art and Archaeology 5. Dumbarton Oaks, Washington, D.C.

PARSONS, LEE ALLEN
 1986 *The Origins of Maya Art: Monumental Stone Sculpture of Kaminaljuyu, Guatemala, and the Southern Pacific Coast.* Studies in Pre-Columbian Art and Archaeology 28. Dumbarton Oaks, Washington, D.C.

PIÑA-CHAN, ROMAN
 1960 Algunos Sitios Arqueológicos de Oaxaca y Guerrero. *Revista Mexicana de Estudios Antropológicos* 16: 65–76.

RAMIREZ CASTAÑEDA, ISABEL
 1912 El Folklore de Milpa Alta, D.F., Mexico. *18th International Congress of Americanists:* 352–361, London.

RIVERA, VICTOR, AND DANIEL SCHAVELZON
 1984 Los tableros de Kaminaljuyu. *Cuadernos de arquitectura mesoamericana* 2: 51–56.

ROBELO, CECILIO A.
 1980 *Diccionario de Mitologia Nahuatl*, 2 vols. Editorial Innovación, Mexico, D.F.

RUBÍN DE LA BORBOLLA, DANIEL F.
 1947 Teotihuacan: Ofrendas de los templos de Quetzalcóatl. *Anales del Instituto Nacional de Antropología e Historia* 2: 61–72. Mexico, D.F.

SAHAGÚN, FRAY BERNARDINO
 1950–71 *Florentine Codex: General History of the Things of New Spain* (A. J. O. Anderson and C. E. Dibble, trans.). School of American Research, Santa Fe.

SAUNDERS, NICHOLAS J.
1988 "Chatoyer," Anthropological Reflections on Archaeological Mirrors. In *Recent Studies in Pre-Columbian Archaeology* 1 (Nicholas J. Saunders and Olivier de Montmollin, eds.): 1–39. BAR International Series 313, Oxford.

SAVILLE, MASHALL H.
1922 *Turquoise Mosaic Art in Ancient Mexico*. Contributions of the Museum of the American Indian, Heye Foundation 6. Heye Foundation, New York.
1925 *The Wood-carver's Art in Ancient Mexico*. Contributions of the Museum of the American Indian, Heye Foundation 9. Heye Foundation, New York.

SÉJOURNÉ, LAURETTE
1959 *Un palacio en la ciudad de los dioses: Exploraciones en 1955–1958*. Instituto Nacional de Antropología e Historia, Mexico, D.F.
1966a *Arqueología de Teotihuacan: La ceramica*. Fondo de Cultura Económica, Mexico, D.F.
1966b *El lenguaje de las formas en Teotihuacan*. Instituto Nacional de Antropología e Historia, Gabriel Mancera 65, Mexico D.F.

SELER, EDUARD E.
1902–23 *Gesammelte Abhandlungen zur Amerikanischen Sprach- und Altertumskunde*, 5 vols. Ascher, Berlin.

SMITH, A. LEDYARD, AND ALFRED KIDDER
1951 *Excavations at Nebaj, Guatemala*. Carnegie Institution of Washington Pub. 594. Washington, D.C.

STONE, DORIS, AND CARLOS BALSER
1965 Incised Slate Disks from the Atlantic Watershed of Costa Rica. *American Antiquity* 30 (3): 310–329.

SUGIYAMA, SABURO
1989 Burials Dedicated to the Old Temple of Quetzalcoatl at Teotihuacan, Mexico. *American Antiquity* 54 (1): 85–106.

TATE, CAROLYN
n.d. The Language of Symbols in the Ritual Environment of Yaxchilan, Chiapas. Ph.D. dissertation, Dept. of Art History, University of Texas at Austin, 1986.

TAUBE, KARL A.
1983 The Teotihuacan Spider Woman. *Journal of Latin American Lore* 9 (2): 107–189.
1986 The Teotihuacan Cave of Origin. *Res: Anthropology and Aesthetics* 12: 51–82.

TEDLOCK, BARBARA
1982 *Time and the Highland Maya*. University of New Mexico Press, Albuquerque.

TEDLOCK, DENNIS
    1985   *Popol Vuh: The Definitive Edition of the Mayan Book of the Dawn of Life and the Glories of Gods and Kings.* Simon and Schuster, New York.

THOMPSON, J. ERIC S.
    1939   *Excavations at San Jose, British Honduras.* Carnegie Institution of Washington Pub. 506. Washington, D.C.
    1950   *Maya Hieroglyphic Writing: An Introduction.* Carnegie Institution of Washington Pub. 589. Washington, D.C.

TOZZER, ALFRED M.
    1941   *Landa's Relacion de las Cosas de Yucatan.* Papers of the Peabody Museum of American Archaeology and Ethnology 18. Harvard University, Cambridge.
    1957   *Chichen Itza and its Cenote of Sacrifice: A Comparative Study of Contemporaneous Maya and Toltec.* Memoirs of the Peabody Museum of American Archaeology and Ethnology 11–12. Harvard University, Cambridge.

VON WINNING, HASSO
    1987   *La iconografía de Teotihuacan: Los dioses y los signos,* 2 vols. Universidad Nacional Autónoma de México, Mexico, D.F.

VON WINNING, HASSO, AND ALFRED STENDAHL
    1968   *Pre-Columbian Art of Mexico and Central America.* Harry N. Abrams, New York.

WOODBURY, R. B., AND A. S. TRIK
    1953   *The Ruins of Zaculeu, Guatemala.* William Bird Press, Richmond, Va.

YOUNG-SÁNCHEZ, MARGARET
    1990   Veneration of the Dead: Religious Ritual on a Pre-Columbian Mirror-Back. *The Bulletin of the Cleveland Museum of Art* 77(9): 326–351.

ZINGG, R. M.
    1938   *The Huichols: Primitive Artists.* G. E. Stechert, New York.

Rulership, Warfare, and Human Sacrifice at the Ciudadela: An Iconographic Study of Feathered Serpent Representations

SABURO SUGIYAMA
ARIZONA STATE UNIVERSITY

THE PYRAMID OF THE FEATHERED SERPENT at Teotihuacan has remained a puzzle despite considerable study (e.g., Gamio 1922; Reygadas Vértiz 1930; Rubín de la Borbolla 1947; Armillas 1947; Drucker n.d.; Cabrera et al. 1982a, 1982b; Cowgill 1983; Sugiyama 1989a, 1989b; Taube n.d.; R. Millon 1988a). This *talud* and *tablero* pyramid is located within the Ciudadela, a major architectural complex at Teotihuacan that is also not well understood. The interpretation I propose both makes sense of the pyramid iconography and relates the iconography to recently discovered archaeological evidence. This specific, historical reading of the iconography can aid in future attempts to reconstruct the specific events that took place in Teotihuacan.

Any iconographic interpretation must take into account both the context in which the work was created and the particular way the symbols are combined. There are general meanings to the various elements in any composition; there are meanings of components that can be established with reference to other works of art. However, the process of interpretation is not simply one of attempting to establish meanings of individual components and then combining them for an overall meaning. Just as a single set of words could be combined to form many different messages, a single set of iconographic elements can express many different meanings. Although I use general meanings drawn from other art works and general associations, I will try to make a close, contextual reading of the particular iconography to arrive at an interpretation that is specific and historical and represents the circumstances in which it was created.

Saburo Sugiyama

IDENTIFICATION OF THE PYRAMID OF THE FEATHERED SERPENT RELIEFS

The pyramid is covered with a repeated motif of carved stone figures (Fig. 1). The main image consists of an undulating feathered serpent body with snake rattles at the tail end. This low-relief profile form is punctuated by alternating frontal head-like images in high relief. These massive carved stones are tenoned into the pyramid facade. Of these images, one is readily recognizable as the head of a feathered serpent, a familiar figure in Mesoamerican iconography. The other image is less clear. It has always been interpreted as a head, and various deity names have been associated with it: Tlaloc (Gamio 1922: LXVI; Reygadas 1930: 166; Armillas 1945: 24–26), Youalcoatl, a form of Quetzalcoatl (Armillas 1945: 24), Itzpapalotl, the obsidian butterfly (Linné 1934: 30), a terrestrial crocodilian tail-head (Coggins n.d.), *cipactli*, an alligator-like creature known from Aztec codices (Drucker n.d.: 13), and Xiuhcoatl or the Fire Serpent (Caso and Bernal 1952: 113–116). Whatever the specific identity assigned to the head, several analysts (e.g., R. Millon 1976: 237, 238; M. Coe 1981: 168; Drucker n.d.: 16; Coggins n.d.) have suggested that the two alternating images on the pyramid symbolize duality.

Recently both Karl Taube and I independently concluded that the unidentified head is actually a representation of a headdress (Sugiyama 1989b; Taube n.d). The creature represented in the form of the headdress is the serpent. Thus the temple iconography depicts fairly naturalistic feathered serpents that have serpent headdresses superimposed on their bodies.

The interpretation of the unidentified head as a headdress representation is supported by a close analysis of its compositional elements and by a variety of similar depictions in Teotihuacan art. The main part of the unidentified figure (Fig. 2) is rectangular and has two sets of circular elements. The higher pair of circles are unadorned; the second set of circles are farther apart and ringed by two scalloped borders. The outer of these borders continues from the front of the figure to the sides, where it curls in a circle. The sides of the figures are bordered by feather-like carvings. Jutting out beneath this main section, in even higher relief, is a narrow rectangular section; suspended from this are curved, teeth-like elements. Above the main part is a section that terminates in a tassel on the side.

The lower circles are the feathered eyes of the creature. They are typical "bird's eyes" shared by several different beings in Teotihuacan art, but the curling terminal form is characteristic of the feathered serpent. The head has only an upper jaw, below and inside of which a nose pendant (the lower rectangular section; Fig. 2a) is depicted; such nose pendants sometimes appear immediately below a complex headdress (e.g., Caso 1966: fig. 2b; Gamio 1922: lám. 33) but are never depicted below an animal's upper jaw in Teotihuacan iconography. On the other hand, representations of humans wearing headdresses in the form of animal heads with only upper jaws are quite common in Teotihuacan iconography (e.g., Fig. 3). A series of in-

Rulership, Warfare, and Human Sacrifice at the Ciudadela

Fig. 1 Section of the facade of the Pyramid of the Feathered Serpent (after Séjourné 1966a: fig. 32).

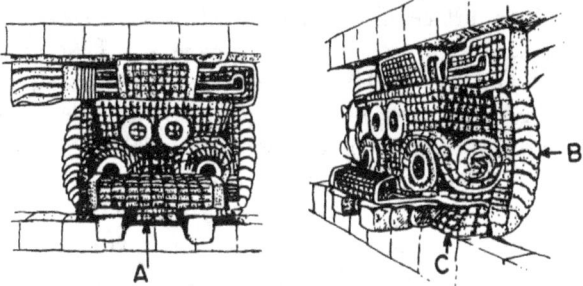

Fig. 2 Detail of headdress representation (after Caso and Bernal 1952). (a) Nose pendant which is depicted below and inside an upper jaw; (b) Lateral cluster of feathers, which may be part of the headdress, or the fringe of a large disk on which the headdress is attached; (c) Trapezoidal beaded part adjacent to fangs (see text for detailed interpretation).

Fig. 3 Detail of a Tepantitla mural. A feathered serpent on which a headdress representation is superimposed can be seen in the border. The figure wears an animal headdress with no lower jaw (after Miller 1973: 100).

wardly curved fangs attached to the upper jaw is also a characteristic of the feathered serpent. Two lateral clusters of feathers are typical of headdress representations (Fig. 2b). The element at the top of the head has been identified as a knot (Caso and Bernal 1952: 113) and is similar to a knot depicted on the headdresses of the first person in four figures on a Monte Alban stela (Estela Lisa of the South Platform), who have been identified as Teotihuacan emissaries (Fig. 4b). The trapezoid, beaded part (Fig. 2c) adjacent to the fangs at the lower corners of the headdress is similar to the interior veil-like element that usually occurs on typical feathered headdresses. The pair of circles above the creature's eyes are goggles, also commonly depicted on Teotihuacan style headdresses. The corn-like or beaded texture that covers most of the surface of the head could be a representation of plaques similar to those used for the surface of headdresses in Teotihuacan. These are often of worked shell and appear both at Teotihuacan and elsewhere, such as in the Maya zone (von Winning 1981; Berlo n.d.). At any rate, somewhat similar representations of headdresses suggest that the texture refers to the material of which the headdress is composed (Séjourné 1966b: 105, fig. 61; 1966c: 97, 98, fig. 43; Hellmuth 1975: 14, 64).

Representations of headdresses not attached to heads are quite common at Teotihuacan. There are several examples of such independent representations in which the headdresses overlap the curving body of a feathered serpent. In the border of the mural paintings of a "procession of priests" at Tepantitla (see Fig. 3), headdress representations with feathered eyes are depicted independently on the feathered serpents' bodies. The fragmented

A **B**

Fig. 4 Monte Alban representations of visitors from Teotihuacan (after Marcus 1983: fig. 6-5). (a) A figure wearing a headdress with a serpent head representation, from Stela 7 of the South Platform at Monte Alban; (b) Two figures wearing different types of headdress from the Estela Lisa of the South Platform at Monte Alban. The second figure has a name glyph that includes a possible serpent representation and a treble-scroll compound.

Rulership, Warfare, and Human Sacrifice at the Ciudadela

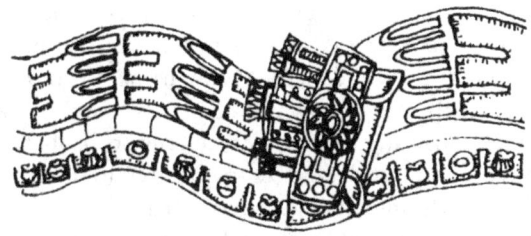

Fig. 5 Detail of a Zacuala mural showing part of a feathered serpent's body with an overlapping headdress representation (after Séjourné 1966a: fig. 9 and Miller 1973:112–113).

mural from the principal patio of Zacuala (Fig. 5) also shows the headdress superimposed on the body of the feathered serpent.

Elsewhere I have suggested (Sugiyama 1989b) that the pyramid iconography does not symbolize dualism. The principal motif is a feathered serpent swimming in water. Only the feathered serpent in naturalistic form is represented on the staircase at the entry of the temple. There is thus no "dual" representation on the most prominent part of the pyramid. This supports my contention that the rest of the facade also does not symbolize dualism. The lack of dualism is also evidenced by the architectual data. Twin temples, an architectural type widely diffused in Mesoamerica in Postclassic religious centers, normally have rectangular platforms. That of the Feathered Serpent Pyramid is square (Cabrera and Sugiyama 1982). In fact, there is no architectural evidence of twin temples on a pyramid-platform at any place in the city.[1]

RECENT EXCAVATIONS AT THE PYRAMID OF THE FEATHERED SERPENT

Excavations carried out recently at the pyramid have provided a great deal of new information on the chronology and function of this structure and also shed light on the meaning of the structure's iconographic program. Excavations were conducted by the Instituto Nacional de Antropología e Historia (INAH) of Mexico in 1980–82 and 1983–84 under the direction of Rubén Cabrera Castro (Cabrera et al. 1982a, 1982b). Five important burial pits were encountered, on the north and south sides of the Pyramid of the Feathered Serpent, including two multiple burials with lithic, shell, and bone offerings (Sugiyama 1989a). The discovery of thirty-nine individuals,

---

[1] René Millon (1976: 238) argues that the excavation in the floor of the upper tunnel in the Pyramid of the Sun revealed a small part of a *talud*, which might have been a part of a twin temple.

which stratigraphically correspond to the time of the construction of the temple around A.D. 150 or a little later, some with their hands joined behind their backs as if they had been tied, seems to indicate that human sacrifice was being carried out at the Ciudadela. My own analysis of the excavation reports concerning the former discoveries of burials found around the pyramid and at its top demonstrates that all these burials probably formed part of a great ritual grave complex dedicated to the Pyramid of the Feathered Serpent. In total, the offerings included more than 835 obsidian projectile points, blades, knives, human or serpent figurines; more than 550 greenstone objects, including beads and earplugs; more than 150 shells; more than 4,600 carved shell beads or pendants, including imitations of human teeth. There are also fourteen human maxillae and four human mandibles, and more than thirty-four slate or pyrite disks, among others. The evidence from Burial 190, a multiple interment on the south side of the pyramid, in which eighteen individuals were found, suggests that the individuals were military persons or individuals attired as soldiers. Elements considered diagnostic of this military identity include 169 obsidian points and 16 slate disks. The Aztecs called these *tezcacuitlapilli*. Such disks, worn at the small of the back, frequently appear in representations of men bearing arms in Teotihuacan murals. There were also four human mandibles and fourteen human maxillae, in addition to a great quantity of shell material worked into human tooth form and imitation maxillae, all suggestive of some kind of military trophy. In addition, all the individuals were males between the ages of 18 and 55 years, making their identity as soldiers more likely.

Further excavations were conducted in 1988 in a joint project of INAH and Brandeis University organized by Rubén Cabrera Castro, George Cowgill, and myself. This project is ongoing, and I will only report on its findings briefly (for more detail, see Cabrera, Cowgill, Sugiyama, and Serrano 1989; Cabrera, Cowgill, and Sugiyama 1990, n.d.; Cabrera, Sugiyama, and Cowgill 1991). The new work revealed a more complicated and extensive burial system than had been expected. More multiple burials were discovered on the east side of the temple, and a tunnel into the interior revealed mass burials similar to Burial 190 inside the structure. The location of the burials found so far is shown in Fig. 6. The burials uncovered in 1988 had offerings similar to those of Burial 190: obsidian points, slate disks known among the later Aztecs as *tezcacuitlapilli* (see Taube, this volume, for a discussion of these as mirrors), human maxillae (Fig. 7), and shell imitations of human teeth and jaws. The individuals were again male and of military age; the evidence that the hands of the majority of the skeletons had been tied (Fig. 8) and that many were interred facing outward, as if guarding the interior, was very clear. Also discovered were canid maxillae, possibly of dogs or coyotes. Clara Millon (1973, 1988) has pointed out the military associations of coyote representations in Teotihuacan iconography.

Rulership, Warfare, and Human Sacrifice at the Ciudadela

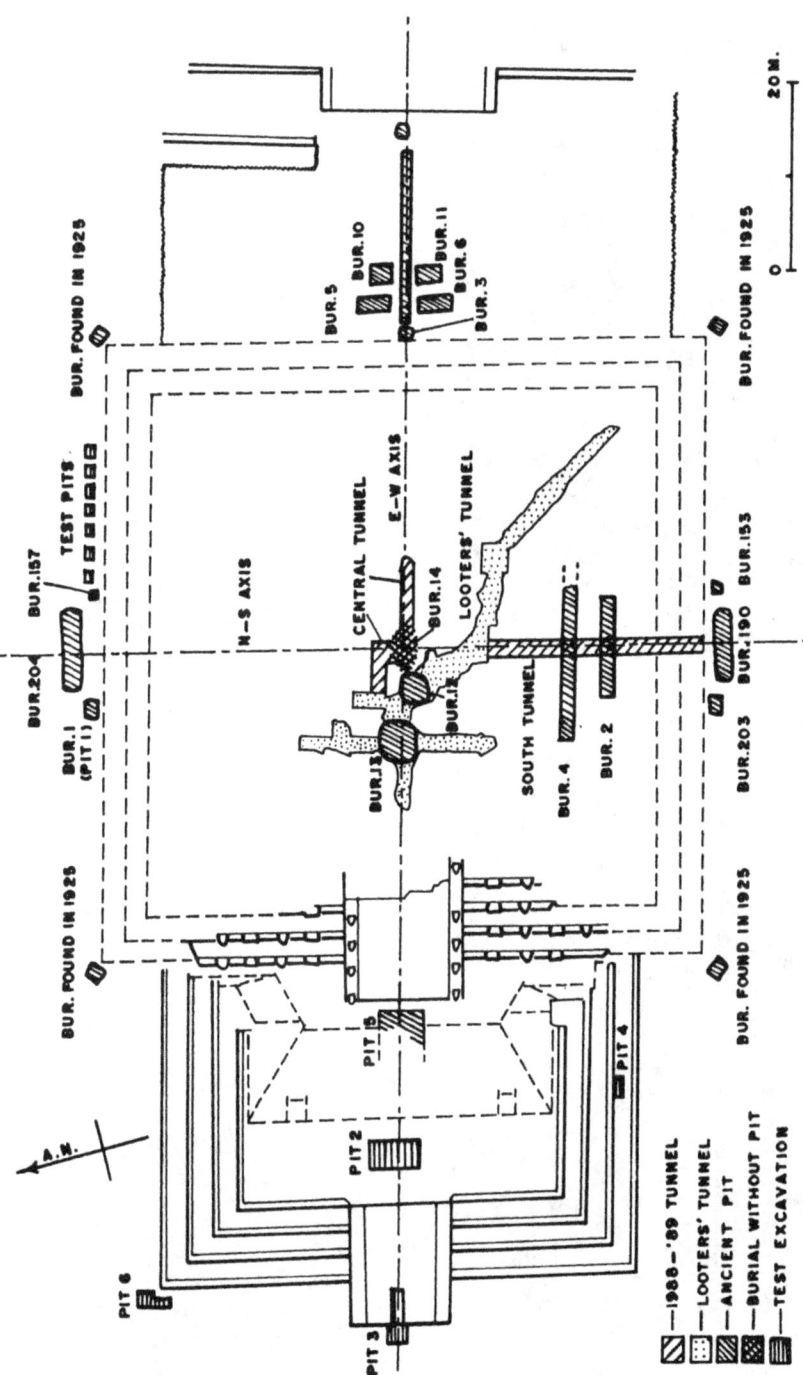

Fig. 6 General plan of the Feathered Serpent Pyramid, showing areas excavated, locations of the burials found to date, and looters tunnel (after Cabrera, Sugiyama, and Cowgill 1991).

Fig. 7 Detail of an individual from Burial 5. A necklace made of nine human maxillae, shell beads, five obsidian projectile points, and dental inlays in upper frontal incisors can be observed.

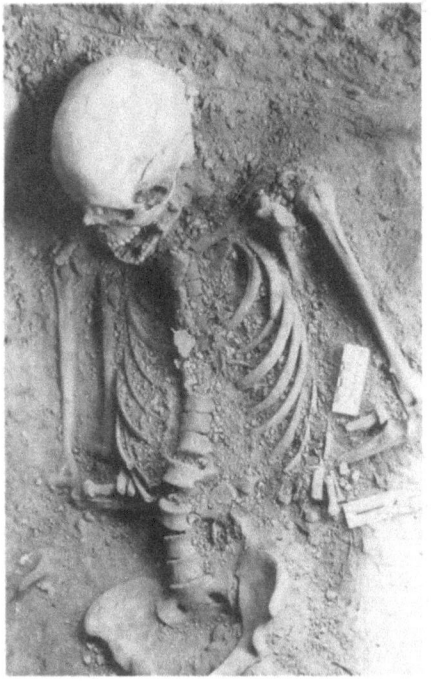

Fig. 8 Detail of an individual from Burial 6. The forearms were found under the body, crossed at the wrists, as if the hands had been tied behind the back.

Rulership, Warfare, and Human Sacrifice at the Ciudadela

There are now more than eighty individuals, and if the patterns that have emerged continue, there will be well over a hundred individuals in total (see Addendum below). On the basis of the evidence, I believe that a massive sacrifice of principally military personages was made at the dedication of the Pyramid of the Feathered Serpent.[2]

SERPENTS WITH THE SYMBOLS OF MILITARISM, SACRIFICE, AND AUTHORITY

How are the images of a feathered serpent swimming in water, its body sometimes punctuated by a headdress representation of itself, related to a structure that was apparently dedicated by the sacrifice of dozens of soldiers? In order to understand a specific historical event, we need a contextual reading of iconography. I will begin with the central image, that of the feathered serpent. Its general meaning is that of a deity or perhaps a representation of the entire sacred realm. However, there are certain aspects, or attributes, of this deity that are being stressed on the pyramid facade.

Many different entities have military associations at Teotihuacan, including the coyote (C. Millon 1973, 1988), the jaguar (Kubler 1972), and the bird (von Winning 1948). The feathered serpent also has military aspects. Fig. 9 depicts an individual wearing both a feathered serpent headdress and a feathered serpent representation at his waist. He carries a shield and a spear, establishing his military identity. Another example is a relief incised on a Teotihuacan vessel (Fig. 10), in which a figure bearing arms wears a large feathered serpent headdress. One of the figures in the procession that Clara Millon (1988) and René Millon (1988b: 113) have interpreted as generals has a sign cluster that consists of a feathered serpent head resting on a mat and an independent headdress (C. Millon 1988: fig. V.5). This sign cluster may represent the name of this military individual or the name of a group with which he was affiliated.

The feathered serpent was also associated with sacrifice. In Fig. 11, a figure kneels on one knee, wielding a knife in his left hand. A feathered serpent emblem is at his belt, and a feathered serpent head is depicted next to his knee with an unidentified element below the jaw. Beneath his left arm is

---

[2] Although the majority of the individuals discovered in and around the Feathered Serpent Pyramid seem to be males adorned with militaristic ornaments, there are also a few females interred without any martial offerings. One individual (Burial 153) discovered in a small pit near the multiple burial has been identified as a young adult female (21–35 yrs.) by physical anthropologists Carlos Serrano and Emma Flores (Sugiyama 1989a: 88). The only associated materials were 1,606 small worked spiral shells, probably beads on a necklace. Another individual discovered in a pit on the north side, which corresponds to Burial 153 with respect to the west-east axis, had similar offerings and may contain a female. However, data on individuals discovered on the north side are limited (Mercado 1987). It seems likely that the burial complex dedicated to the Temple of the Feathered Serpent does not consist simply of warriors but probably also includes people of different social status, although only these individuals have been discovered to date. Such differences may be reflected in the quality of the offerings associated with the burials.

Fig. 9 Plaque relief from the ceramic workshop discovered in the compound on the north side of the Ciudadela. The figure wearing the feathered serpent headdress has martial elements (after Múnera, n.d.).

Fig. 10 Relief motifs on a Teotihuacan vessel. The headdress that the figure wears appears to be a serpent representation because of the form of the fangs and the curled attachment next to the large eye (after Séjourné 1964: fig. 8).

Fig. 11 A scene demonstrating the association of the feathered serpent with human sacrifice depicted on a tripod vessel. A figure, probably a ballgame player, has a knife in his left hand, below which a human head is shown, and two feathered serpent images at the belt and next to the right knee, below which an abstract representation of an upper jaw is shown horizontally (after Berlo 1984: pl. 181).

a human head. In a design on a ceramic vessel, a feathered serpent head is shown in association with a triple-drop sign, which may represent the heart or blood, next to the upper jaw (Fig. 12). Fig. 13 also shows the association of the feathered serpent with a heart. In two Monte Alban representations of Teotihuacanos (see Fig. 4a,b), human figures are associated with feathered serpent signs and heart signs. In another representation (Fig. 14), a frontal feathered serpent head appears beneath the head of a figure associated with a depiction of droplets that may be water and/or blood.

Finally, the feathered serpent is associated with authority. One way in which this is expressed is through association with a mat. In many depictions of the feathered serpent (e.g., Fig. 14; C. Millon 1988: fig.V.5; Séjourné 1966b: 18–19; von Winning 1987: 130–131, fig. 3a, d–m) the serpent is shown resting on a mat, a symbol of authority and rulership well known throughout Mesoamerica (e.g., C. Millon 1988: 119).

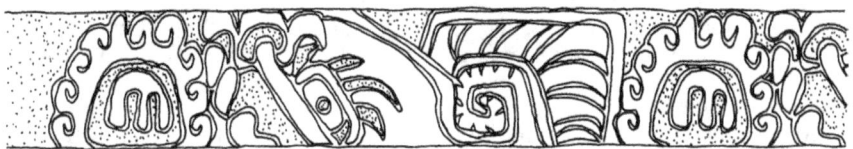

Fig. 12 Stylized serpent representation with a triple-drop sign, which may symbolize the heart or blood, in front of the upper jaw (after Séjourné 1966b: fig. 112).

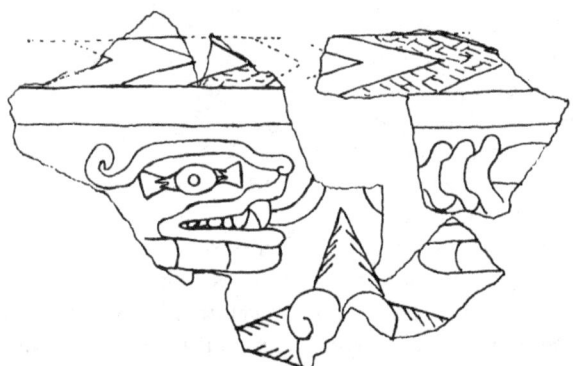

Fig. 13 Incised motif on a Teotihuacan vessel discovered in the North Palace of the Ciudadela, from the collection of the Proyecto Arqueológico Teotihuacan 1980–82 of the INAH. A serpent's head and rattle with trilobal sign surrounded by possible representations of knives are represented below the geometric motif, the chevron chain, which has specific sacrificial, military, and cult associations (Berrin 1988: 196–197).

Saburo Sugiyama

Fig. 14 Motif on a Thin Orange ceramic fragment, from the collection of the Proyecto Arqueológico Teotihuacan 1980–82 of the INAH (after Sugiyama 1989b).

Most crucial for understanding the iconography of the Pyramid of the Feathered Serpent, however, is the association of the serpent with a headdress that symbolizes authority of a very significant nature. I have already noted that the depiction of an independent headdress is common in Teotihuacan. Clara Millon's studies (1973, 1988) have made a persuasive case for the tassel headdress as a symbol of authority that appears to be linked to the military, and also as a symbol for Teotihuacan outside of the city. What, then, is the significance of the headdress in association with the feathered serpent on the pyramid and elsewhere?

On a tablet from Palenque (Fig. 15), the figure on the left presents a beaded headdress to the other figure. Linda Schele and Mary Ellen Miller (1986: 112, 114) interpret this as the critical scene of an accession in which the king, Pacal, sitting on a double-headed jaguar bench, is receiving from his mother a "drum-major headdress," the crown used by Palenque kings.[3] It seems that the presentation of a headdress representing authority is also depicted in Teotihuacan iconography. A ceramic fragment of a Teotihuacan type has representations of three shells and a hand on which a beaded headdress is placed, as if authority is being conferred (Fig. 16).

In two Teotihuacan murals (Fig. 17a), the Storm God is depicted carrying a symbolic lightning bolt in his left hand and something that René Millon

---

[3] Hasso von Winning (1981) identifies this as an elaborate form of a Teotihuacan headdress. He considers that perhaps the scene depicts a gift from Teotihuacan, or that the headdress may signify authority being conferred.

Fig. 15 King Pacal's accession depicted in low-relief on the Oval Palace Tablet at Palenque (after Schele and Miller 1986: fig. II, 5). His mother "extends a Drum-major headdress, the crown used by Palenque kings, toward her son, giving him the first part of the regalia that will transform him into the king" (Schele and Miller 1986:114).

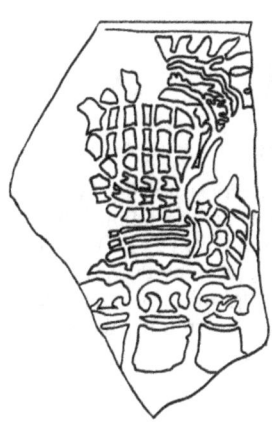

Fig. 16 Representation of the presentation of a beaded headdress, which rests on a hand with three shells below it (after von Winning 1981: fig. 5).

has termed a "bundle, box, or container" in his right hand (Millon 1988b: 100). This object is, in fact, a headdress. Comparison with the headdress of the Storm God in Fig. 17b or Fig. 18 reveals that the object has the plumed feathers that crown the headdress, the two rectangular strips that fall from the rear of the headdress, the two sections that emerge from the headdress at oblique angles, and the same type of decoration. Absent is the disk (thus we see the interior of the lower section of the headdress), which was perhaps removable. This Storm God in Fig. 17a carries a headdress that seems to be

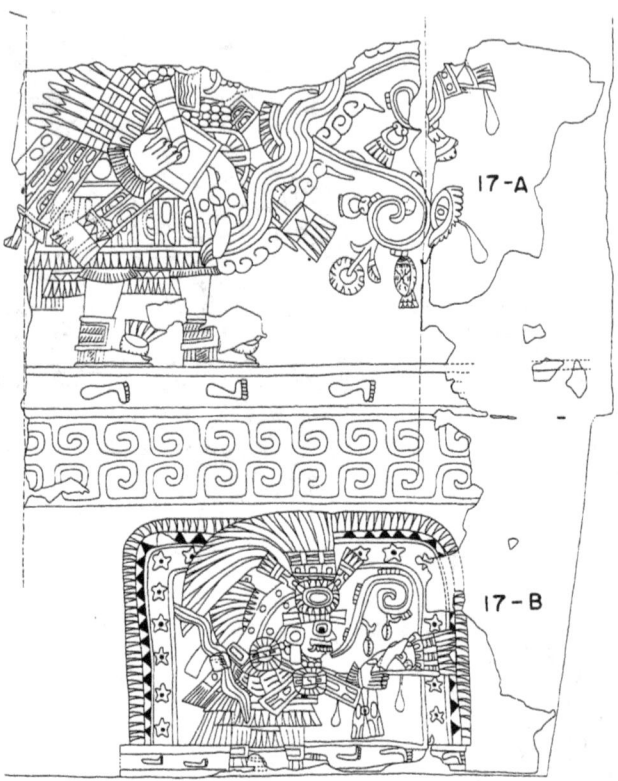

Fig. 17 Mural discovered at Techinantitla in 1984 (after Berrin 1988: fig. IV, 21b). (a) A figure that can be identified as the Storm God by the fang descending from the upper jaw and the edge of a goggle on his eye (Berrin 1988: fig. IV, 21c) carries a lightning bolt in his left hand and a headdress similar to that worn by the Storm God in (b) and Fig. 18; (b) This Storm God representation has a lightning bolt in his right hand and in the other, a headdress resting on a flat object, a duplicate of his own.

a duplicate of the one worn by the other Storm Gods in Figs. 17b and 18. (Note that the proportions are correct. The object on his arm would be the right size for his own headdress.) The reason for this is revealed in Fig. 17b. Here the Storm God is presenting an object on some sort of platter. This object, too, seems to be a headdress. The top plumes are on the right; the back strips hang off the platter on the left.

A very similar Storm God (Fig. 18) discovered in the same anteroom has identical component elements except for the object grasped in his right hand. Here, he has a tasseled ear of maize and a squash plant (R. Millon 1988b: 100). Therefore, it seems logical to assume that, just as the Storm

Fig. 18 Mural discovered at Techinantitla in 1984. This Storm God representation consists of the same components as that in Figure 17b, except that the headdress in his left hand has been replaced by maize and squash (after Berrin 1988: fig. IV, 21a).

God has been shown bringing substantial food to humankind, here the same god delivers a headdress, the symbol of divine authority or rulership. The implication here may be that the Storm God gives to humans not just what they need to feed themselves but what they need to govern themselves as well.

We do not know to whom the headdress is being presented, of course. Is this a generalized depiction of the gift of divine authority to humans? Or is this a depiction of the divine sanction of an individual ruler or dynasty, used to justify that dynasty's rule? At any rate, the connection between the deity and the headdress seems clearer: the headdress is a representation of the power or authority of that deity and is apparently some sort of earthly manifestation of that authority. It is a gift from the god. It symbolizes the power and attributes of the deity.

Saburo Sugiyama

I propose that the Feathered Serpent Pyramid facade can thus be "read" as a message about some sort of earthly manifestation of the feathered serpent deity. The builders of the temple or those buried within it, or both of these, may be the bearers of the headdress, symbolizing the incarnation of the feathered serpent's divinity and power. Both the archaeological and the artistic evidence indicate that the deity's associations with the military and with sacrifice were paramount in this structure. Karl Taube (n.d.) has pointed out that there is a similar pair of serpents in Classic Maya iconography, a "platelet mosaic" form and a more naturalistic creature. "In Classic Maya iconography, the two forms of the serpent differ slightly in context. The mosaic version appears primarily as an object to be worn in the context of rulership and impersonation, whereas the other, more animate form can occur in isolation, as if it were a living mythical entity" (Taube n.d.: 12). I believe that the Teotihuacan feathered serpent and the headdress carry similar meanings.[4]

The archaeological evidence uncovered in the 1980s brought out an unexpected possibility with regard to the interpretation of the pyramid's function: it may be a ruler's tomb. A despotic ruler may have ordered the building of the monumental structure and the sacrifice of dozens of Teotihuacan warriors upon or before his death to guard his resting place. It may be that, even if this were a ruler's tomb, the tunnel now being dug into the pyramid will not reveal an important burial at the center of the structure. There is evidence that rulers were not necessarily entombed in the center of the pyramids at structures A and B in Kaminaljuyu, which seem to have been modeled closely on the Pyramid of the Feathered Serpent (Kidder, Jennings, and Shook 1946). Actually a series of structures built one within another, these pyramids contain several burial complexes. In most cases, the principal burials are located in front of the staircase at the entrance of the pyramid. One of the earliest structures (Structure A-2-b) at Kaminaljuyu, however, has a burial (Tomb A-I) in its center.

It is possible that an important burial was located beneath the staircase of the Pyramid of the Feathered Serpent. Excavation carried out there by José Pérez in 1939 and a re-excavation conducted by Cowgill in 1988 revealed a large pit, rich offerings, and evidence that the pit had very probably been looted in Teotihuacan times (Cabrera, Cowgill, and Sugiyama 1990, n.d.;

---

[4] Extending the meaning of the two serpent forms, Taube supports the interpretation of dualism at the Pyramid of the Feathered Serpent in Teotihuacan. He proposes that there are two different deities; the Feathered Serpent and "War Serpent," the ancestor of Xiuhcoatl, suggesting the association of the former with fertility and the interior affairs of the state and the latter with military conquest and empire. Although the functional difference between the representation of the entire Feathered Serpent and its symbolic expression in the form of a headdress, a symbol composed of the head and a curled extension, is conceivable, as I have discussed in this paper, I cannot "read" the explicit expression of dualism in the iconography of the Feathered Serpent Pyramid.

Rulership, Warfare, and Human Sacrifice at the Ciudadela

Cabrera, Cowgill, Sugiyama, and Serrano 1989; Cabrera, Sugiyama, and Cowgill 1991). However, the fact that many of the sacrificial victims were placed facing outward in a sitting position, as if guarding something in the center, leaves open the distinct possibility that an important burial is located there. If this is a tomb, then the pyramid iconography may be an assertion of the divine authority of the person buried there, an expression of the ruler's link with the feathered serpent god, and his identification with the military and sacrificial aspects of the deity.

There are still certain problems to be resolved in conjunction with this interpretation. The pyramid was most likely constructed about A.D. 150 (Sugiyama 1989a, n.d.); yet much of the mural and other artistic evidence we have cited comes from several centuries later. Ascribing meaning to an earlier period on the basis of later evidence is always risky.

The issue is complicated in this case in particular by the fact that we know that only a few decades after the completion of the Pyramid of the Feathered Serpent, some intentional destruction and possible looting of the pyramid took place, and that a new platform was built obscuring much of the front facade of the pyramid.[5] René Millon (1988b: 113) suggests that the later structure was dedicated to the Great Goddess and was intended "symbolically to moderate the earlier celebration of the military exploits of the now-dead leader." The pyramid may have been built just before a turning point in the city's history and, indeed, may have helped to cause a major shift, in which despotic rulership was overturned or constrained and replaced by collective rulership. "Whatever form a limitation on the exercise of power may have taken, it seems likely to have been institutionalized as a reaction to the rule of a despot" (R. Millon 1988b: 112).

If the system represented by the Pyramid of the Feathered Serpent was overturned or sharply changed, later evidence might be particularly inappropriate. However, as we know from a great deal of other evidence throughout Mesoamerican history, there are always elements of continuity even in the midst of great change. If the pyramid represents a ruler as well as the feathered serpent deity, the family of that ruler may well have survived. The dynasty celebrated on the pyramid facade could be ancestral to the family or individual represented by the feathered serpent/headdress glyph in the procession of generals (e.g., Séjourné 1966b: fig. 117; C. Millon 1988: fig. V.5).

---

[5] I have discussed in earlier articles (Sugiyama 1989a, n.d.) the fact that the Feathered Serpent Pyramid seems to have been destroyed intentionally, referring to the archaeological evidence. The excavation conducted by George Cowgill in 1988 at the top of the New Platform at the Ciudadela uncovered many fragments of burned clay with a variety of motifs in low relief. These seem to have been originally part of the walls of a building atop the Feathered Serpent Pyramid before the walls were fragmented and dumped in the fill of the construction of the New Platform. This suggests that the original temple atop the Feathered Serpent Pyramid was modified, destroyed, or looted.

Saburo Sugiyama

There is no reason to think that, even if autocratic rule had been replaced by collective leadership, the royal family would not have remained an important political force in Teotihuacan.[6]

Ongoing work at the Pyramid of the Feathered Serpent will help us both to make direct, archaeologically based observations about Teotihuacan society and to gain a better understanding of this society's artistic self-representation.

ADDENDUM

This manuscript was completed in early 1989. Since that time, further excavations were carried out by the same project (now officially of INAH) in the second half of 1989. The project was headed by Rubén Cabrera Castro, with the participation of George Cowgill and myself, then of Brandeis University and now of Arizona State University, and Carlos Serrano and Emily McClung de Tapia of the Universidad Nacional Autónoma de México, Mexico City, with funding from the National Geographic Society. These subsequent excavations uncovered more and more complex data, but I have not modified my original text to reflect new ideas that have evolved as a result of these newer discoveries, except to add Fig. 6, which shows the burial complex as revealed at the termination of our fieldwork, and some up-to-date bibliographic citations. Nonetheless, I feel a brief review of the more recent excavation results is appropriate. The more recent references, especially Cabrera, Sugiyama, and Cowgill (1991) provide more detailed information on this work.

To the east of the temple platform four multiple burials (Burials 5, 6, 10, and 11) were found, as well as four disturbed or incomplete individual burials. The offerings associated with them again suggest a militaristic aspect. The offerings include: obsidian projectile points, shell beads and pendants (some of which are in the form of human teeth arranged to imitate human maxillae), slate disks (usually found in the pelvic area), and real human maxillae used as adornments (usually found in the region of the thorax).

As mentioned in the text, a tunnel dug into the pyramid interior from the south face in 1988 revealed two multiple burials (Burials 2 and 4). Further excavation of the tunnel toward the center of the pyramid took place in 1989, during which a looters' tunnel was encountered. The looters' tunnel

---

[6] It seems that Feathered Serpent symbols may have been used to identify members of a "royal family" and to emphasize their sacred lineage and power. A possible example may be found in the representations of Teotihuacanos at Monte Alban: one figure wears a feathered serpent headdress and has a name glyph with a heart symbol in it (Fig. 4a); another has a name glyph composed of a feathered serpent symbol and a heart symbol (Fig. 4b). Perhaps these elements were reminiscent of an event that had taken place at the Pyramid of the Feathered Serpent.

Rulership, Warfare, and Human Sacrifice at the Ciudadela

apparently had its entrance at the southeast corner of the pyramid and from there ran diagonally toward the center. According to results of test excavations made in the tunnel floor, the excavators of the ancient tunnel reached two multiple burials located near the center and looted them so that the original stratigraphy of the burial pits was very disturbed. However, the looters never arrived at the true center of the structure, where we were able to recover a great quantity of information through the intensive excavation of an intact multiple burial located there.

This burial contained twenty individuals and the richest offerings known to date from Teotihuacan. It includes more than 400 greenstone objects worked in the form of cones, earspools, nose pendants, figurines, beads, and *resplandores;* more than 800 obsidian objects in the form of projectile points, prismatic blades (many more than 20 cm long), perforators, bifacial knives, and anthropomorphic and zoomorphic eccentrics; over 3,400 shell objects, both natural and worked in the form of beads, pendants, and earspools; one fragmentary ceramic Tlaloc vessel; slate disks; a few animal bones; and organic remains, such as plants, textiles, fibers, and wood.

On the basis of current knowledge, no one individual in the burial appears to have been treated with special care so as to be readily distinguished from the other individuals; more valuable or numerous offerings do not appear to be associated with any particular individual. As a general rule, objects were found near the central part of the burial in greater concentrations than in peripheral areas and seem to have been placed over the buried individuals as general offerings. Moreover, unlike Burials 2 and 4 discovered earlier, the central burial did not consist of an excavated pit surrounded by masonry walls. Instead, the individuals were laid directly on the natural *tepetate* subsoil and covered by the mud and stones that comprise the fill of the pyramid without any protective structure. The twenty skeletons, probably all males, were discovered in various positions, and some of them evidently had their hands tied behind their backs. These facts suggest that the individuals buried at the center in anonymous fashion were sacrifical victims whose arrangement in the burial had highly symbolic meaning.

The interpretation of the two looted burials encountered by the ancient tunnel (Burials 12 and 13) will be difficult and controversial, because the amount of information lost on account of the looting is serious and unrecoverable. However, looters usually leave something for archaeologists to think about. Human bones in anatomical relation were found in the original fill that the looters left undisturbed near the northeast corner of the Burial 12 pit. More human bones, together with fragments of offerings, including greenstone, obsidian, and shell objects, were recovered in the secondary fill, or disturbed layers, of the pit, as well as on the tunnel floors that correspond to the level of the looting episode at Burial 12. The remaining individual's forearms were discovered in a crossed position below the hip bones, as if this individual also had been buried with hands tied behind the back. The field data suggest that, at one time, Burial 12 had consisted of several sacrificed people with rich offerings, probably including several fine ceramic vessels, in contrast to the central burial. Furthermore, the stratigraphy of the pit, along with the fact that the pit was not symmetrically located in relation to other burials, suggests that Burial 12 originally may have corresponded to an earlier structure and been reused as a burial pit at the onset of the construction of the Feathered Serpent Pyramid. Some stratigraphic information about this earlier structure was recovered from an area close to Burials 12 and 13.

The Burial 13 pit (Fosa 4), located on the central east-west axis of the pyramid, was 4.3 m east-west, 3.9 m north-south, and 1.5 m deep. Here the looters also left intact a small portion of the original fill, in which we discovered one complete skeleton of a robust adult male. This individual was located very near the west wall of the pit on the same central east-west axis. Stones covering the skeleton were placed there apparently to protect him. He was found in a flexed ventral position with his hands unbound. The accompanying greenstone ornaments are unusually large and include beads, earspools, and a nose pendant of rectangular form combined with a bifid tongue-like part extending below it. The objects not taken by looters, but left in disturbed layers of the pit, include human bones corresponding to several individuals, greenstone, shell, and obsidian offerings, some of which were quite different from those found in the central burial.

The field data fitted in with the interpretation that the person discovered in Burial 13 was one of the principal occupants of the whole burial complex associated with the Feathered Serpent Temple. However, the fact that this individual was not centrally located in the pit, and the fact that the high-quality offerings discovered in the secondary fill evidently do not pertain directly to him, may be taken to imply that there was a more important person or persons interred along with him. One possible interpretation of the evidence at hand is that there had been a ruler, or king, who was buried at the time of the temple's construction, and the "soldiers" interred in and around the temple represent the sacrifice of "royal retainers" (as suggested by George Cowgill, personal communication). However, we must also consider the workforce required to build the temple and the person or group that directed the construction after the supposed king was already deceased. Alternatively, if a living ruler had personally overseen the construction and mass-sacrifice ritual expecting his or her body to be buried in the temple when he died, the large pit found in front of the staircase, or a pit (yet undiscovered and intact) between the staircase and Burial 13 on the temple's central east-west axis, would have been more likely places for the interment. The former possibility remains an undetermined question, since the pit in front of the temple staircase, which was discovered in 1939 (Rubín de la

Rulership, Warfare, and Human Sacrifice at the Ciudadela

Borbolla 1947) and re-excavated by Cowgill and Oralia Cabrera during this project, had been looted apparently at the time of the construction of the New Platform. The latter possibility, which remains to be tested in the future, may be supported by a piece of evidence related to a construction event on the facade of the temple.

There is clear evidence, still visible today, that the staircase of the temple had suffered an intentional destruction at some time before the facade was covered by the building of the New Platform (Sugiyama n.d.). Many large stone blocks, originally used to form the staircase, had been removed. Repairs were made on this section using smaller, unworked stones, and the reconstructed parts were then covered with typical Teotihuacan concrete. I am not sure what this means. If we look, however, for a reason for the intentional destruction, taking into account the chronological order of construction episodes and burial episodes, it might be explained as related to the burial of a ruler who died after the completion of the temple and before the covering of the facade by the New Platform and was placed under the staircase which was eventually repaired. In this case, the temple must still have been in use after his or her death, because it would not have been necessary to repair the staircase if plans to cover the facade with a new construction were already being made.

I am convinced that any attempt to elucidate the relation of rulership to the construction and/or function of the temple necessarily must include an interpretation of the symbolic meaning involved in the sacrificial burials. What should be closely investigated is the degree to which the expression of ritual through mass sacrifice reflects the actual social organization. The involvement of persons of apparently different social ranks or classes, such as soldiers and priests, may have been part of a collective performance dramatizing religious beliefs or a mythical worldview, rather than a direct reflection of the real hierarchical order operating in Teotihuacan society. The main question is how the ruler was involved in such ritual performance.

Regardless of these theories, the existence of a ruler's tomb was not definitely proved by our excavations. Instead of answering the questions raised in this paper, the new data obtained in late 1989 demand a more thorough analysis of recovered materials and a more specific and historical interpretation of them, including a contextual analysis of the symbolism involved in the burial complex, architecture, and iconography of the Feathered Serpent Pyramid.

Acknowledgments This iconographic study integrates a brief description of the results of the excavations carried out at the Pyramid of the Feathered Serpent in 1988 and 1989 by the INAH in Mexico and Brandeis University, thanks to the generosity of Rubén Cabrera Castro and George Cowgill, co-coordinators of the project. Cabrera also gave permission to use drawings of

Saburo Sugiyama

materials from Proyecto Arqueológico Teotihuacán 1980–82, and Cowgill read an earlier draft of this paper and provided valuable comments on it. I am very grateful to both. I owe my special gratitude to Janet Catherine Berlo, who gave me an opportunity to discuss the significance of our excavation project and commented very carefully on my draft. I would like to express my appreciation to Lillian Thomas, a member of our excavation project, with whom I discussed ideas related to the paper and from whom I received valuable corrections of my English. I also owe thanks to Kitsie Henchman-Sallet, who carefully reviewed the final version. Finally, I must mention my debt to my wife, Kumiko, for her drawings for this paper and for her support in my career as an archaeologist.

BIBLIOGRAPHY

ARMILLAS, PEDRO
1945 Los dioses de Teotihuacan. *Anales del Instituto de Etnografía Americana* 6: 35–61. Universidad Nacional de Cuyo, Mendoza.
1947 La serpiente emplumada, Quetzalcóatl, y Tláloc. *Cuadernos Americanos* 31 (1): 161–178. Mexico, D.F.

BERLO, JANET CATHERINE
1984 *Teotihuacan Art Abroad: A Study of Metropolitan Style and Provincial Transformation in Incensario Workshops.* BAR International Series 199, Oxford.
n.d. The Teotihuacan Trapeze and Ray Sign: A Study of the Diffusion of Symbols. M.A. thesis, Dept. of the History of Art, Yale University, New Haven, 1976.

BERRIN, KATHLEEN (ED.)
1988 *Feathered Serpents and Flowering Trees: Reconstructing the Murals of Teotihuacan.* The Fine Arts Museums of San Francisco.

CABRERA CASTRO, RUBÉN, IGNACIO RODRIGUEZ, AND NOEL MORELOS (EDS.)
1982a *Teotihuacan 80–82: Primeros resultados.* Instituto Nacional de Antropología e Historia, Mexico, D.F.
1982b *Memoria del Proyecto Arqueológico Teotihuacán 80–82*, vol. 1. *Colección Científica 132.* Instituto Nacional de Antropología e Historia, Mexico, D.F.

CABRERA CASTRO, R., G. L. COWGILL, AND S. SUGIYAMA
1990 El Proyecto Templo de Quetzalcoatl y la practica a gran escala del sacrificio humano. In *La Época Clásica: Nuevos hallazgos, Nuevas ideas.* Instituto Nacional de Antropología e Historia, Mexico, D.F.
n.d. Informe para el Consejo de Arqueología: Proyecto Templo de Quetzalcóatl, primera temporada de campo. Manuscript on file, Departamento de Monumentos Prehispánicos of the Instituto Nacional de Antropología e Historia, Mexico, D.F.

CABRERA CASTRO, R., G. L. COWGILL, S. SUGIYAMA, AND C. SERRANO
1989 El Proyecto Templo de Quetzalcóatl. *Arqueología* 5: 51–79. Instituto Nacional de Antropología e Historia, Mexico, D.F.

CABRERA CASTRO, R., AND S. SUGIYAMA
1982 La reexploración y restauración del Templo Viejo de Quetzalcóatl. In *Memoria del Proyecto Arqueológico Teotihuacán 80–82* (R. Cabrera et al., eds.): 163–183. Instituto Nacional de Antropología e Historia, Mexico, D.F.

CABRERA CASTRO, R., S. SUGIYAMA, AND G. L. COWGILL
1991 The "Templo de Quetzalcóatl" Project at Teotihuacan: A Preliminary Report. *Ancient Mesoamerica* 2 (1): 77–92.

CASO, ALFONSO
1966 Dioses y signos teotihuacanos. *Teotihuacan: Onceava Mesa Redonda:* 249–275. Sociedad Mexicana de Antropología, Mexico, D.F.

Caso, A., and Ignacio Bernal
1952 Urnas de Oaxaca. Instituto Nacional de Antropología e Historia, Memorias 2. Mexico, D.F.

Coe, Michael D.
1981 Religion and the Rise of Mesoamerican States. In *The Transition to Statehood in the New World* (Grant D. Jones and Robert R. Kautz, eds.): 157–171. Cambridge University Press, Cambridge.

Coggins, Clemency
n.d. Reflections on Teotihuacan. Paper presented at the 51st annual meeting of the Society of American Archaeology, New Orleans, 1986.

Cowgill, George L.
1983 Rulership and the Ciudadela: Political Inferences from Teotihuacan Architecture. In *Civilization in the Ancient Americas* (R. M. Leventhal and A. L. Kolata, eds.): 313–343. University of New Mexico Press, Albuquerque, and Peabody Museum, Harvard University, Cambridge.

Drucker, R. David
n.d. Renovating a Reconstruction: The Ciudadela at Teotihuacan, Mexico: Construction Sequence, Layout, and Possible Uses of the Structure. Ph.D. dissertation. The University of Rochester, 1974.

Gamio, Manuel
1922 *La población del Valle de Teotihuacan*. Secretaría de Agricultura y Fomento, Dirección de Antropología, Mexico, D.F.

Hellmuth, Nicholas M.
1975 *The Escuintla Hoards: Teotihuacan Art in Guatemala*. Foundation for Latin American Anthropological Research Progress Report 1 (2). Guatemala City, Guatemala.
1978 Teotihuacan Art in the Escuintla, Guatemala Region. In *Middle Classic Mesoamerica: A.D. 400–700* (Esther Pasztory, ed.): 71–85. Columbia University Press, New York.

Kidder, A. V., J. Jennings, and E. Shook
1946 *Excavations at Kaminaljuyu. Guatemala*. Carnegie Institution of Washington Pub. 561. Washington, D.C.

Kubler, George
1972 Jaguars in the Valley of Mexico. In *The Cult of the Feline* (Elizabeth P. Benson, ed.): 19–50. Dumbarton Oaks, Washington, D.C.

Linné, Sigvald
1934 *Archaeological Researches at Teotihuacán, México*. Ethnographic Museum of Sweden Pub. 7, Stockholm.

Marcus, Joyce
1983 Teotihuacan Visitors on Monte Alban Monuments and Murals. In *The Cloud People: Divergent Evolution of the Zapotec and Mixtec Civilizations* (Kent V. Flannery and Joyce Marcus, eds.): 175–181. Academic Press, New York.

MERCADO ROJANO, ANTONIO
   1987   ¿Una sacerdotisa en Teotihuacán? *México Desconocido* 121: 6–9. Mexico, D.F.
MILLER, ARTHUR G.
   1973   *The Mural Painting of Teotihuacan.* Dumbarton Oaks, Washington, D.C.
MILLON, CLARA
   1973   Painting, Writing, and Polity in Teotihuacan, Mexico. *American Antiquity* 38 (3): 294–314.
   1988   A Reexamination of the Teotihuacan Tassel Headdress Insignia. *Feathered Serpents and Flowering Trees: Reconstructing the Murals of Teotihuacan* (Kathleen Berrin, ed.): 114–134. Fine Arts Museums of San Francisco.
MILLON, RENÉ
   1976   Social Relations in Ancient Teotihuacan. In *The Valley of Mexico: Studies in Pre-Hispanic Ecology and Society* (Eric R. Wolf, ed.): 205–248. University of New Mexico Press, Albuquerque.
   1988a The Last Years of Teotihuacan Dominance. In *The Collapse of Ancient States and Civilizations* (Norman Yoffee and George L. Cowgill, eds.): 102–164. University of Arizona Press, Tucson.
   1988b Where Do They All Come From? The Provenance of the Wagner Murals from Teotihuacan. In *Feathered Serpents and Flowering Trees: Reconstructing the Murals of Teotihuacan* (Kathleen Berrin, ed.): 78–113. Fine Arts Museums of San Francisco.
MÚNERA, LUIS CARLOS
   n.d.   Un taller de cerámica ritual en la Ciudadela, Teotihuacán. M.A. thesis, Escuela Nacional de Antropología e Historia, Mexico, D.F., 1985.
REYGADAS VÉRTIZ, JOSÉ
   1930   Las últimas excavaciones en la Zona Arqueológica de Teotihuacán. *Anales del XX Congresso Internacional de Americanistas* 2 (1): 161–167. Impresa Nacional, Rio de Janeiro.
RUBÍN DE LA BORBOLLA, DANIEL F.
   1947   Teotihuacan: Ofrendas de los templos de Quetzalcóatl. *Anales del Instituto Nacional de Antropología e Historia* 2: 61–72. Mexico, D.F.
SCHELE, LINDA, AND MARY ELLEN MILLER
   1986   *The Blood of Kings: Dynasty and Ritual in Maya Art.* George Braziller Inc., New York.
SÉJOURNÉ, LAURETTE
   1957   *Pensamiento y religión en el México antiguo.* Fondo de Cultura Económica, Mexico, D.F.
   1964   La simbología del fuego. *Cuadernos Americanos* 135 (4): 149–178.
   1966a *Arquitectura y pintura en Teotihuacán.* Siglo XXI Editores, Mexico, D.F.
   1966b *Arqueología de Teotihuacan: La cerámica.* Fondo de Cultura Económica, Mexico, D.F.
   1966c *El lenguaje de las formas en Teotihuacán.* Gabriel Mancera 65, Mexico, D.F.

SUGIYAMA, SABURO
    1989a Burials Dedicated to the Old Temple of Quetzalcoatl at Teotihuacan, Mexico. *American Antiquity* 54 (1): 85–106.
    1989b Iconographic Interpretation of the Temple of Quetzalcoatl at Teotihuacan. *Mexicon* 11 (4): 68–74.
    n.d. Nuevos datos arqueológicos sobre el Templo de Quetzalcóatl en la Ciudadela de Teotihuacán y algunas consideraciones hipotéticas. Paper presented at the XLVth International Congress of Americanists, Bogotá, Colombia, 1985.

TAUBE, KARL A.
    n.d. The Temple of Quetzalcóatl and the Cult of Sacred War at Teotihuacan. *Res: Anthropology and Aesthetics* (in press).

VON WINNING, HASSO
    1948 The Teotihuacan Owl-land Weapon Symbol and its Association with "Serpent Head X" at Kaminaljuyú. *American Antiquity* 14 (2): 129–132.
    1981 An Iconographic Link between Teotihuacan and Palenque. *Indiana* 5: 15–32. Berlin.
    1987 *La iconografía de Teotihuacan: Los dioses y los signos*, 2 vols. Universidad Nacional Autónoma de México, Mexico, D.F.

Teotihuacan Glyphs and Imagery in the Light of Some Early Colonial Texts

GEORGE L. COWGILL

ARIZONA STATE UNIVERSITY

INTRODUCTION

SOME AUTHORITIES, notably George Kubler (1972), have warned us against uncritically using knowledge about the Aztecs to interpret earlier Mesoamerican societies. Assuredly, many centuries separate the Aztecs from Teotihuacan, and sometimes they clearly misunderstood or reinterpreted aspects of Teotihuacan symbolism. An example is an Aztec stone brazier, superficially similar to a Teotihuacan "Old Fire God," but with Storm God symbols and other features that never occur on Teotihuacan examples (Pasztory 1983: 176, pl. 141). Moreover, Aztec society was very different from that of Teotihuacan in many respects. Nevertheless, it is increasingly clear that there were many broad continuities (as noted, for example, by Berlo 1989). Obviously we must be careful, look for specifics more than generalities, and be sensitive to differences as well as resemblances.

In this paper, I add some points of resemblance not previously observed. A number of terms that occur in sixteenth century Nahuatl texts, the *Cantares mexicanos* and the *Psalmodía christiana,* are highly apposite to some signs and images in Teotihuacan mural paintings. Most specifically, one of the plant names that occurs in these texts, "red bone-flower," is a highly plausible reading of one of the compound glyphs associated with flowering trees or plants in recently discovered murals. Another name, "red basket-flower," is perhaps related to another of these glyphs. These observations, as well as other features of the *Cantares* and the *Psalmodía,* add to evidence for continuities in ritual themes, concepts, and imagery between Teotihuacan and Aztec society.

The fact that a few terms current in sixteenth-century Nahuatl are obvious readings for certain Teotihuacan glyphs might seem to strengthen somewhat the case that an early form of Nahuatl was an important language at Teotihuacan. However, semantically similar terms may well exist in other Mesoamerican languages. There is still no consensus about the dominant language of Teotihuacan (surely to some extent a polyglot city) and the evidence presented here does not resolve this question. Further study of Teotihuacan signs and glyphs may well shed much light on the language of Teotihuacan. However, the data to be discussed here provide evidence for continuities in concepts rather than in language.

TEOTIHUACAN WRITING

I should emphasize that when I speak of glyphs I am not just talking about standardized signs. The use of standardized signs at Teotihuacan is well known, even though the meanings of most are still uncertain. George Kubler (1967) tabulated fifty-two, and James Langley (1986) has greatly refined and expanded this list. They and other scholars, notably Clara Millon (1973) and Hasso von Winning (1987), have offered interpretations of specific signs and groups of related signs.

Others, including Alfonso Caso (1967) and Thomas Barthel (1982) have argued that, in addition to calendrical glyphs, these standardized signs constitute "true writing." In fact, while agreeing that the signs carry extremely important information, I (and most other scholars, I believe) consider them at most a borderline form of writing. It is likely that they stood for general concepts rather than specific words, and it is not clear that their sequence is important—a group of signs perhaps stands for a juxtaposition of concepts rather than for a specific utterance with a syntactic structure. Perhaps the closest analogy in our own culture is such standardized signs as one sees at turnpike exits: the "pump" sign, the "plate and cutlery" sign, or the "hand and dripping faucet" sign.

In 1952, Agustín Villagra discovered numerous mural fragments at the Tetitla apartment compound that bore figures he immediately recognized as glyph-like (Villagra 1954). These include compound glyphs (see especially Foncerrada de Molina 1980) and fragments with sequences of at least two compound glyphs. It seems likely that the original panel contained either extended texts, several small figures each associated with one or more glyphs, or both. Clara Millon (1973) called attention to these Tetitla inscriptions and illustrated some. However, they have attracted little attention, perhaps because the remains are fragmentary and come from a single room of a single apartment compound. Also, Millon (1973: 299–300) and others (e.g., Karl Taube, personal communication, November 1988) see Maya aspects in the associated pictorial context and think the glyphs may not be a native Teotihuacan text.

In addition, by 1973 two figures wearing the tassel headdress and accompanied by glyphs were known from looted murals (C. Millon 1973). These strengthen the case that the Tetitla inscriptions were a native production. Thanks to the diligence and perceptiveness of the Millons, we now know that the tassel headdress paintings and many other looted murals come from

Teotihuacan Glyphs and Imagery

a small neighborhood or *barrio,* called Amanalco, about 600 m east of the Moon Pyramid, and a high proportion are from a single, exceptionally large compound called Techinantitla (Berrin 1988; R. Millon and Sugiyama n.d.). Among other things, the paintings greatly enlarge the corpus of Teotihuacan glyphic inscriptions. It is still very small, but it significantly improves our opportunities for decipherment. It seems likely that more texts can be found in future excavations in the Amanalco *barrio* and perhaps elsewhere in Teotihuacan.

THE GLYPHS IN THE FLOWERING TREES MURALS

Included in the Techinantitla paintings are panels framed by feathered serpents, showing a number of plants or flowering trees (Figs. 1–3; see also Pasztory 1988: 136–161, pls. 1, 3–13; figs. VI.3–VI.8). Compound glyphs are superposed on the plants. Nine different glyphs occur in several sets (Pasztory 1988: 137, 144–146). Their meanings are unknown. Trees are associated with genealogies in some Postclassic documents, and the glyphs might be the names of lineages (Pasztory 1988: 161). Alternatively, they might be place names, as suggested by Janet Berlo (1983) for other plants with glyphs in the Tepantitla apartment compound, or they may be the names of the plants themselves (Pasztory 1988: 159, 161). Esther Pasztory (1988: 161) notes that these last possibilities are not mutually exclusive; names of plants might also be the names of places. In the sixteenth-century texts plants or flowers are themselves often metaphors for people (Burkhart n.d.; Bierhorst 1985a), and thus named plants might also represent persons, lineages, or other groups.

It is not likely that the panels represent some sort of botanical text, but they may be connected with a ritual invocation of the names of plants or flowers, perhaps especially flowers of medicinal or ritual significance. The frequent occurrence of passages naming flowers in certain sixteenth-century texts offers support for this interpretation. Furthermore, as Pasztory (1988) notes, flowers or plants comprise elements of some of the compound glyphs, while flowers are not yet known in any other Teotihuacan glyphs. Also, few if any of the glyphs associated with these plants are known in other contexts, such as in association with figures wearing the tassel headdress, where meanings such as names of individuals, lineages, groups, titles of office, or possibly places are most likely. Altogether, then, it is most probable that the glyphs associated with the plants name or at least refer directly to the plants. The flowers growing from the plants are themselves differentiated. It may be, however, that the Teotihuacanos found it hard to show nine kinds of flowers in ways that would be easily and reliably distinguished, and felt it desirable to supplement differences in how the flowers were drawn by adding glyphs. Pasztory (1988: 159) points out that at Tepantitla some plants are shown realistically and are identifiable without

Fig. 1 Feathered serpent and flowering trees mural, general view. The Fine Arts Museums of San Francisco, Bequest of Harold J. Wagner.

Fig. 2 Flowering tree mural fragment: red bone-flower (right). INAH, Mexico. Photo courtesy of the Fine Arts Museums of San Francisco.

Fig. 3 Flowering tree mural fragment: red pack-basket flower (center). INAH, Mexico. Photo courtesy of the Fine Arts Museums of San Francisco.

George L. Cowgill

glyphs, while others are shown as generic flowering trees and have associated glyphs.

Two papers on the tree murals by Sally Shore (n.d.a.,b) offer very useful discussions of the tree paintings and their associated glyphs. However, it is precisely the glyph that Shore (n.d.a: 35) terms "most problematic" that I find most interesting. It is a compound composed of a pink or red bone and a flower of the same color (Fig. 2).

THE RED BONE-FLOWER IN SIXTEENTH CENTURY TEXTS

The *Psalmodía christiana* is a collection of songs or chants for church festivals composed in Nahuatl between 1558 and 1560 by Fray Bernardino de Sahagún and his Nahuatl-speaking assistants (Burkhart n.d.). Although these texts are obviously Christian and most follow Old World models, some contain a great deal that is indigenous, although not obviously idolatrous, and in these parts many flowers are named. A passage in a recent translation by Louise Burkhart (n.d.) says:

> There our lord's flowery mountain lies visible, lies giving off warmth, lies dawning. Its fragrance, its emanation, its scent lies reaching far, lies spreading over all the land.
>
> The red bone flowers, the jade tobacco flowers, the red roses, the red jar flowers lie bursting into precious bloom, lie flaming, lie waving, lie dripping with golden dew.
>
> The roses, dark red ones, pale ones, the red feather flowers, the golden flowers lie there waving like precious bracelets, lie bending with quetzal feather dew. They spread about giving off warmth. They lie extended over all the land, scented and fragrant.
>
> Quite high above the spring dwells the precious heavenly flower, the completely good maiden, Saint Clare. She stands as the very tassel, the very cusp of God's mountain!

The scene invoked is reminiscent of the Tepantitla mural of the Great Goddess (see Berlo, this volume, Fig. 1; see also discussions by Pasztory and Berlo, this volume). This is but one of the passages in sixteenth-century texts that seem to connect with Teotihuacan images. There is danger of reading too much into isolated examples, but the cumulative weight of this and other passages certainly justifies a more systematic comparison of Teotihuacan and sixteenth-century imagery than is possible here. For the present I will only emphasize occurrence of the "red bone-flower."

A second excerpt is from a song for Christmas celebrations:

> Various flowers lie giving off fragrance. The red bone flowers lie gathered together. They lie blooming, they lie dripping with

golden quetzal feather dew. May the golden flowers spread scattering, spread sprinkling! Alleluia!

The cacao flowers, the popcorn flowers, the red basket flowers lie waving with quetzal feather dew, lie shimmering like gold, spread giving off jade warmth. Various precious stones lie collected there, there in Bethlehem. Alleluia!

The heart flowers, the quetzal feather bell flowers, the red jar flowers stand giving off fragrance, lie dawning, spread giving off golden warmth. Alleluia!

The roses, the crow flowers lie dawning. Alleluia! Alleluia!

The jade flowers spread sparking, the red bone flowers lie gathered together. Alleluia! Alleluia! (Burkhart n.d.)

The term translated as "red bone-flower" is *tlapalomisuchitl* in the Nahuatl text. This is an orthographic variant whose more standard spelling would be *tlapalomixochitl*. It can be analyzed linguistically as a compound of *tlapalli* (which seems to convey the general idea of "colorful," but is often translated "red"), *omitl* (bone or awl), and *xochitl* (flower). The Nahuatl dictionary of Molina (1970 [1571]) does not list *tlapalomisuchitl* but gives "*Omixuchitl*. açucena" (1970: 76, verso). A modern Spanish dictionary gives, for *azucena*, "white or madonna lily." Sahagún's Florentine Codex, Book 11 (Dibble and Anderson 1963: 210) gives for *omixochitl* "It has slender stalks; it has foliage, blossoms. Its blossom is white. [It is like] a small spindle whorl on top; the base is slender, a little long; therefore it is named *omixochitl*. It is of pleasing odor, fragrant, sweet; a precious thing, useful." This is followed by his entry for *tlapalomixochitl*, "It is the same. However, it is chili-red, dark colored, striped with color, color-striped. It becomes dark colored." Charles Dibble and Arthur Anderson identify *omixochitl* as *Polianthes tuberosa*, or *Polianthes mexicana*. Dibble and Anderson (1963: figs. 666, 715, following p. 220) show the *omixochitl* and the *tlapalomixochitl* (fig. 716). John Bierhorst (1985b: 346) says that *tlapalomixochitl* is the "colorada" form (or stage?) of the tuberose, the tuberose flower in the purplish-orange stage(?), more likely a red or crimson flower that in some respect resembles the tuberose(?) [his question marks]. For *omixochitl* Bierhorst (1985b: 250) has "tuberose, *Polianthes*." Bierhorst (personal communication, October 1988) notes that the *omixochitl* is also described and illustrated by Francisco Hernández (1959: 79–80), as well as two kinds of plant called *tlalomixochitl*, yet another related plant name. Shore (n.d.a: 12, 35) says that in an unpublished paper Tracy Bechtholdt identified the plant in the murals associated with the bone-flower glyph as *Contuna bixafolia*. However, this proposed identification must have been based only on the appearance of the flowers in the murals.

The *Cantares mexicanos* are other Nahuatl texts assembled in connection with the work of Fray Bernardino de Sahagún. John Bierhorst has recently provided an English translation, with introduction and commentary, and an accompanying Nahuatl-English dictionary and concordance (Bierhorst 1985a,b). Although the copy we have is later, Bierhorst (1985a: 4) concludes that most texts were taken from the lips of informants in the third quarter of the sixteenth century. He thinks that a few were possibly composed before the Conquest, and one or two may be as late as the 1580s (Bierhorst 1985a: 9). Most of these texts are not directly related to church rituals but to song and dance performances that the Indians were permitted to engage in. Under the circumstances, they could hardly be expected to contain anything openly heathen or otherwise subversive, and it is clear that many of the texts as we have them are stongly influenced by the Conquest, and none can be considered a trustworthy copy of a pre-Conquest version. Nevertheless, it is equally clear that a very large number of pre-Conquest elements are preserved in the *Cantares*.

Not surprisingly, because probably many of the same people contributed to both the *Cantares* and the *Psalmodía,* they show many resemblances in style and imagery. *Tlapalomixochitl* occurs once, in line 29 of folio 46v, song 61 (Bierhorst 1985a: 290–291). John Bierhorst translates the term as "crimson lily," a term that is reasonable and more euphonious than the literal "red bone-flower," although it would never have suggested any connection with a Teotihuacan glyph to a non-Nahuatlist.

THE RED PACK-BASKET FLOWER

Another of the tree murals' glyphs, referred to by Janet Berlo (1989) as a "netted ovoid," and called "net cartouche" by Sally Shore (n.d.a,b) may represent a basket, although the evidence is less strong than for the red bone-flower (Fig. 3; see also Pasztory 1988: 138–157; pls. 1d, 8, 12; figs. VI.3e, 6a, 6e, 7). The *Psalmodía* refers to *tlapaloacalsuchitl,* which Louise Burkhart (n.d.: 8, 12) translates as "red basket flowers." In the more elaborate Jesuit orthography used by John Bierhorst in his dictionary-concordance, this is *tlapalhuahcalxochitl,* literally red pack-basket flower, the name of a highly prized red flower (Bierhorst 1985b: 346). It occurs twice in the *Cantares,* on line 19 of folio 59, song 63E (Bierhorst 1985a: 306–307) and on line 1 of folio 79v, song 89A (Bierhorst 1985a: 410–411). In the Florentine Codex Sahagún says of *tlapaluacalxochitl:* "It is chili-red, of average size. A precious thing, it is one which can be claimed as what one merits. I claim it as merited. I appropriate it. I take it to myself" (Dibble and Anderson 1963: 209).

Fray Bernardino de Sahagún describes the *uacalxochitl* as a creeping and climbing vine (Dibble and Anderson 1963: 209). Bierhorst (1985b: 346) says that because the *uacalxochitl* of the Florentine Codex is almost certainly an aroid, the *tlapaluacalxochitl* is perhaps an aroid as well. It is illustrated by Dibble and Anderson (1963: fig. 711 [b], following p. 220). Pasztory (1988: 161) says the associated flower in the Techinantitla murals "may represent a datura."

Teotihuacan Glyphs and Imagery

The Teotihuacan glyph is not necessarily a pack-basket, but this is a plausible interpretation of it. One might compare it with what are clearly pack-baskets carried by figures in murals from the Zacuala Palace (Séjourné 1959: 31, fig. 12, and 33, lám. 29; and Miller 1973: 112, figs. 206, 208). The Techinantitla glyph has a much looser weave and no opening on top is shown. It is more like a bag than a basket or a "cage of boards or slats" (Bierhorst 1985b: 127, for *huahcalli*), but I do not think this rules out "pack-basket" as a possible reading. Lyle Campbell (personal communication, May 1989) notes that, while the *huahcal* in Mexico means a "carrying crate made of sticks/small limbs," in some other varieties of Nahua it means a "gourd."

In the first of my proposed readings a flower is actually part of the compound glyph, but it is lacking in this case. This inconsistency is bothersome, but does not rule out a reading along the suggested lines.

I have not yet seen connections between any of the other flowers named in the *Cantares* and the *Psalmodía* and Teotihuacan glyphs, but others may find such connections in these or other sixteenth-century texts. Janet Berlo (1983: 15–17; 1989: 20–23) notes a quite different connection. Another of the glyphs associated with flowering trees or plants at Techinantitla is a tripartite sign consisting of a severed human arm surmounted by a bivalve shell attached to a sheaf-like object (Pasztory 1988: pls. 1b, f, 3c, 7, 13; figs. VI.3b, 3g, 4b, 5c, 6f, 8a). Berlo points out that a severed human arm occurs as the main sign for Acolhuacan, Coliman, and several other place names in the Codex Mendoza. It also occurs in the sign for Acolman, which is particularly close to Teotihuacan. In all these cases the connection rests on the fact that the Nahuatl word for arm is *acolli*. However, this is not an example of the rebus principle, because, as pointed out to me by Henry Nicholson (personal communication, October 1988) and Louise Burkhart (personal communication, October 1988), Acolhuacan means "place of those who have arms." Thus, it does not depend on a pun that would only work in Nahuatl, and the Teotihuacan glyph can only be taken as evidence suggesting a continuity in concept, but not necessarily in language. It does, however, support Berlo's view that the trees and their glyphs may represent, at least in part, place names. Limited searching has not revealed any plant name beginning with *acol* or *aco*. I suspect that the puzzles presented by this Teotihuacan glyph will not be resolved until we have readings for the bivalve shell and the sheaf-life object as well as the severed arm.

Janet Berlo (1983: 16) also notes that another of the nine Techinantitla glyphs associated with the flowering trees, a group of three maguey spines (Pasztory 1988: pls. 1b, 9; figs. VI.3c, 6b, 8b) is similar to Aztec glyphs for places whose names included the element *huitz,* referring to magueys. Again, no rebus principle is implied.

George L. Cowgill

BROADER RESEMBLANCES BETWEEN TEOTIHUACAN MURALS AND AZTEC IMAGERY

It is highly unlikely that the *Cantares mexicanos* preserve any substantially unchanged pre-Conquest performances and also unlikely, given the lapse of time, that any Aztec performance was really close to any Teotihuacan performance. Nevertheless, there are many elements in the *Cantares* that seem highly applicable to aspects of Teotihuacan murals. For example, passages such as "I offer good songs as jades . . ." (Bierhorst 1985a: 147) or "I'm carving our good songs as jades" (Bierhorst 1985a: 177) call to mind the roundels often infixed in Teotihuacan sound scrolls, which are interpreted as perforated jade disks (Langley 1986: 125–133, 282, sign 171). Another passage links javelins and birds (Bierhorst 1985a: 185). Some of the birds in Techinantitla murals carry javelins, and the bird/javelin combination occurs elsewhere in images with Teotihuacan connections, as on Stela 31 at Tikal (C. Millon 1988: 129, fig. V.18). Many general themes in the *Cantares*, such as ritual song and dance intended to evoke the presence of dead heroes and/or kings, may be highly applicable to certain Teotihuacan murals, including some of those at Techinantitla and Atetelco discussed by Clara Millon (1988). This is a topic that deserves more attention than I can give it here.

THE LANGUAGE OF TEOTIHUACAN

The Techinantitla glyphs I have discussed do not seem to be of the rebus type. That is, they do not depend on using a picture of one thing to stand for a word or syllable that has a similar sound but a meaning not easily depicted, as we might use a picture of a tin can and a tied cord to stand for *cannot*. Many Aztec glyphs are pictographic or ideographic, using literal renderings of objects or actions or depictions of objects linked to particular concepts by convention (e.g., reed mat for rulership), but others employ the rebus principle, as in using teeth and gums (*tlantli*) for the locative suffix *-tlan* (Berlo 1989: 20). If the Teotihuacan glyphs in question are not of the rebus type, the semantic correspondences have no phonetic implications and do not imply that Nahuatl was necessarily an important language at Teotihuacan. Plant names translatable as "red bone-flower" and "red basket-flower" may occur in other Mesoamerican languages.

A number of linguists doubt that any languages of the Nahua group were important in central Mexico until post-Teotihuacan times (e.g., Kaufman n.d.; Knab n.d.; Justeson et al. 1985; Campbell 1988: 19). One reason is that some loan words in Lowland Maya languages from other Mesoamerican sources, especially Totonac, show sound shifts that suggest that they were adopted by the Maya during, roughly, the time when Teotihuacan flourished, while loans into Mayan from Nahua languages appear to be later. On the other hand, Alvin Luckenbach and Richard Levy (1980), on lexicostatistical grounds, argue for Nahua languages in central Mesoamerica as

Teotihuacan Glyphs and Imagery

early as the sixth century A.D.; that is, if our current beliefs about chronology are correct, a century or two before the end of Teotihuacan's dominance. I am far more skeptical of the accuracy of glottochronology than are Luckenbach and Levy. Their estimate may well be correct, but it does not eliminate the possibility that Nahua speakers were unimportant in central Mexico before the decline of Teotihuacan. On the other hand, it adds to the difficulty of thinking that Nahua speakers played a major role in the rise of Teotihuacan in the last century B.C. and first century A.D.

Nevertheless, although Lyle Campbell (1988) favors Totonac as a most likely language for Teotihuacan, he does not feel that Nahua can be completely ruled out, and he says there are "some suggestive tidbits that might lead us to suspect that it's been around longer than we think" (Campbell, personal communication, May 1989). He also notes that the Papantla Totonac dictionary of Hermann Aschmann (1973) gives *lúcut* for "bone" and *acalúcut, calúcut* for "flor de isote o de pito." This lead needs further investigation, but it distinctly suggests that *bone-flower* could be a Totonac term as well as a Nahuatl term. Unfortunately, I have not yet seriously searched dictionaries of other Mesoamerican languages. In 1580 it was said that there were a few speakers of Otomí and Popolocan, as well as Nahuatl, in the Teotihuacan Valley (Nuttall 1926: 55, 56, 61), but this need not mean that those languages have a long history in the area.

The ceramic evidence is also open to various interpretations. The people who occupied Teotihuacan soon after the destruction of its principal temples and palaces (at the end of the Metepec phase) made pottery related to the broad complex called Coyotlatelco. Admittedly there are some continuities with Metepec ceramics, but I am more impressed by resemblances to ceramics from as far northwest as the states of Durango and Zacatecas (for a similar view see Mastache and Cobean 1989). It is tempting to equate rapid change in central Mexican ceramics after the end of Teotihuacan dominance with the arrival of Nahua speakers from the northwest. Guadalupe Mastache and Robert Cobean (1989: 55–56) argue that in the Tula area, makers of Coyotlatelco-like pottery—who had various cultural affinities with the northern periphery of Mesoamerica—occupied hilltop sites that overlap chronologically with Teotihuacan-related settlements in the same area. This argument is urgently in need of testing through better chronological control, as the authors recognize, but, at any rate, it is consistent with linguistic hints that Nahua-speakers may have first entered central Mexico in significant numbers long after Teotihuacan was founded but somewhat before its decline. However, there are alternative explanations for the contrast between Coyotlatelco and Teotihuacan ceramics. William Sanders (1989) thinks that Coyotlatelco developed locally, and his viewpoint cannot be ruled out. The collapse of the dominant ideology of Teotihuacan and its loss of strongly centralized political control might themselves have been enough to encourage rapid change in ceramics as well as other aspects of culture.

Thus, it is still not clear what language or languages were dominant at Teotihuacan. The linguistic evidence is extremely important, but not as yet conclusive, and we can only talk of the betting odds in favor of various alternatives. In view of the existence of foreign enclaves, such as the Oaxaca *barrio,* there is no doubt that the city was polyglot, but presumably one dominant language was associated with the Teotihuacan state. At the moment the evidence leans a little in favor of Totonac, but Nahuatl and other languages should not be ruled out.

Knowledge of the languages of Teotihuacan bears on problems about the downfall of the city discussed by René Millon (1988: 156–158). It is too simple to say that linguistic continuity implies that inhabitants of the city were the direct agents of destruction, while late arrival of Nahua-speakers implies destruction by foreigners. Even if Teotihuacan was Nahua-speaking, the city might have been destroyed by outsiders, and even if some other language was dominant at Teotihuacan, Nahua speakers may have arrived in central Mexico only after the city's destruction by insiders. And, of course, the destruction may have been due to some combination of forces from within and outside the city. Surely the events leading to the decline and fall of the city were complex. Among other things, it is conceivable that in early Teotihuacan the dominant language was Totonac (or possibly something else) and that late in the city's history Nahua speakers infiltrated, perhaps rather peaceably, and made their language important within the city some time before its destruction. In spite of the many possibilities, however, knowledge of the language (or languages) of Teotihuacan will have an effect on how we view the decline of the Teotihuacan state, the purposeful demolition of critical structures and monuments in the city, and the transition to post-Teotihuacan society.

CONCLUSION

At least one, and perhaps two, of the glyphs in the flowering trees murals at Techinantitla can be read as plant names that were current among the sixteenth-century Aztecs. Semantically similar names may occur in Totonac and perhaps other Mesoamerican languages. Thus, these particular glyphs probably will not provide much evidence about the dominant language of Teotihuacan, although further study of all known Teotihuacan glyphs is likely to provide data highly relevant to this question. Most important, for the moment, is evidence for continuity in concepts. It is not simply that the terms in question, *red bone-flower* and *red basket-flower,* can be found in Nahuatl dictionaries or that they are included among the large number of plants named and described in encyclopedic sources such as the Florentine Codex and the Badianus Herbal. The words occur in those sources, but they

Teotihuacan Glyphs and Imagery

also occur among the much more limited number of plant names in the *Cantares mexicanos* and the *Psalmodía christiana*. Both of these, although subject to strong Spanish Christian influence, are ritual texts. This suggests that these plants were among those of decided ritual significance to the Aztecs. It is very likely that more than simple continuity in plant names is involved; that there is also continuity in significant ritual symbolism. This supposition is further supported by additional similarities between these sixteenth-century texts and some of the themes, scenes, and specific elements in a number of Teotihuacan murals.

Acknowledgments I thank Kathleen Berrin, who very promptly and generously provided slides of the flowering trees murals that were used to illustrate the oral presentation of this paper and gave permission to publish Figs. 1–3, which are also published with the permission of the Instituto Nacional de Antropología e Historia. Several persons have commented on earlier versions; especially useful were comments and information provided by Janet Catherine Berlo, John Bierhorst, Louise Burkhart, Lyle Campbell, and Karl Taube. Among other things, they have saved me from some embarrassing errors. Responsibility for any remaining defects is solely my own. An anonymous reviewer reminded me of the information on languages in the 1580 *relaciones* published by Zelia Nuttall (1926).

BIBLIOGRAPHY

ASCHMANN, HERMANN P.
    1973   *Diccionario Totonaco de Papantla.* Summer Institute of Linguistics, Mexico, D.F.

BARTHEL, THOMAS S.
    1982   Veritable "Texts" in Teotihuacan Art? *The Masterkey* 56 (1): 4–12.

BERLO, JANET CATHERINE
    1983   Conceptual Categories for the Study of Texts and Images in Pre-Columbian Art. In *Text and Image in Pre-Columbian Art* (J. Berlo, ed.): 1–39. BAR International Series 180, Oxford.
    1989   Early Writing in Central Mexico: *In Tlilli, In Tlapalli* before A.D. 1000. In *Mesoamerica After the Decline of Teotihuacan* (Richard Diehl and Janet Berlo, eds.): 19–47. Dumbarton Oaks, Washington, D.C.

BERRIN, KATHLEEN (ED.)
    1988   *Feathered Serpents and Flowering Trees: Reconstructing the Murals of Teotihuacan.* The Fine Arts Museums of San Francisco.

BIERHORST, JOHN
    1985a   *Cantares Mexicanos: Songs of the Aztecs.* Stanford University Press, Stanford.
    1985b   *A Nahuatl-English Dictionary and Concordance to the Cantares Mexicanos.* Stanford University Press, Stanford.

BURKHART, LOUISE M.
    n.d.   Nahuas in God's Garden: Nature and the Sacred in Sahagun's Psalmodia Christiana. Paper presented at the Annual Meeting of the American Anthropological Association, Chicago, 1987.

CAMPBELL, LYLE
    1988   *The Linguistics of Southeast Chiapas, Mexico.* Papers of the New World Archaeological Foundation 50. Brigham Young University, Provo, Utah.

CANGER, UNA
    1988   Nahuatl Dialectology: A Survey and Some Suggestions. *International Journal of American Linguistics* 54: 28–72.

CASO, ALFONSO
    1966   Dioses y signos Teotihuacanos. In *Teotihuacan: Onceava Mesa Redonda:* 249–279. Sociedad Mexicana de Antropología, Mexico, D.F.

DIBBLE, CHARLES E., AND ARTHUR J. O. ANDERSON
    1963   *Florentine Codex: General History of the Things of New Spain. Book 11—Earthly Things.* The University of Utah, Salt Lake City.

FONCERRADA DE MOLINA, MARTA
    1980   Mural Painting in Cacaxtla and Teotihuacan Cosmopolitism. In *Third Palenque Round Table, 1978, Part 2* (Merle Greene Robertson, ed.): 183–198. University of Texas Press, Austin.

HERNÁNDEZ, FRANCISCO
    1959   *Historia Natural de Nueva Espana* 2. Universidad Nacional Autónoma de México, Mexico, D.F.

JUSTESON, JOHN, LYLE CAMPBELL, WILLIAM NORMAN, AND TERRENCE KAUFMAN
    1985   *The Foreign Impact on Lowland Maya Language and Script.* Middle American Research Institute Pub. 53. Tulane University, New Orleans.

KAUFMAN, TERRENCE
    n.d.   The Geographical Spread and Linguistic Diversification of Nahua: Foreign Contacts. Paper presented at the annual meeting of the American Anthropological Association, Washington, D.C., 1989.

KNAB, TIM
    n.d.   Teotihuacan, Toltecs, and Aztecs: A Linguistic View. Manuscript, 1984.

KUBLER, GEORGE
    1967   *The Iconography of the Art of Teotihuacan.* Studies in Pre-Columbian Art and Archaeology 4. Dumbarton Oaks, Washington, D.C.
    1972   La iconografía del arte de Teotihuacan. In *Teotihuacan: XI Mesa Redonda:* 69–85. Sociedad Mexicana de Antropología, Mexico, D.F.

LANGLEY, JAMES C.
    1986   *Symbolic Notation of Teotihuacan.* BAR International Series 313, Oxford.

LUCKENBACH, ALVIN H., AND RICHARD S. LEVY
    1980   The Implication of Nahua (Aztecan) Lexical Diversity for Mesoamerican Culture-History. *American Antiquity* 45: 455–461.

MASTACHE, ALBA GUADALUPE, AND ROBERT H. COBEAN
    1989   The Coyotlatelco Culture and the Origins of the Toltec State. In *Mesoamerica after the Decline of Teotihuacan: A.D. 700–900* (Richard Diehl and Janet Berlo, eds.): 49–67. Dumbarton Oaks, Washington, D.C.

MILLER, ARTHUR G.
    1973   *The Mural Painting of Teotihuacan.* Dumbarton Oaks, Washington, D.C.

MILLON, CLARA
    1973   Painting, Writing, and Polity in Teotihuacan, Mexico. *American Antiquity* 38 (3): 294–314.
    1988   A Reexamination of the Teotihuacan Tassel Headdress Insignia. In *Feathered Serpents and Flowering Trees: Reconstructing the Murals of Teotihuacan* (Kathleen Berrin, ed.): 114–134. The Fine Arts Museums of San Francisco.

MILLON, RENÉ
    1988   The Last Years of Teotihuacan Dominance. In *The Collapse of Ancient States and Civilizations* (N. Yoffee and G. Cowgill, eds.): 102–164. University of Arizona Press, Tucson.

MILLON, RENÉ, AND SABURO SUGIYAMA
    n.d.   Concentración de pinturas murales en un gran conjunto arquitectónico al este de la Plaza de la Luna en Teotihuacan. Instituto Nacional de Antropología e Historia, Mexico, D.F. (in press).

MOLINA, FRAY ALONSO DE
    1970   *Vocabulario en Lengua Castellana y Mexicana y Mexicana y Castellana.* Editorial Porrua, Mexico, D.F. (first pub. 1571, Mexico City).

NUTTALL, ZELIA
    1926   Official Reports on the Towns of Tequizistlan, Tepechpan, Acolman, and San Juan Teotihuacan sent by Francisco de Castañeda to His Majesty, Philip II, and the Council of the Indies, in 1580. *Papers of the Peabody Museum* 11 (2): 45–86. Harvard University, Cambridge.

PASZTORY, ESTHER
    1983   *Aztec Art.* Harry N. Abrams, New York.
    1988   Feathered Serpents and Flowering Trees with Glyphs. In *Feathered Serpents and Flowering Trees: Reconstructing the Murals of Teotihuacan* (Kathleen Berrin, ed.): 137–161. The Fine Arts Museums of San Francisco.

SANDERS, WILLIAM T.
    1989   The Epiclassic as a Stage in Mesoamerican Prehistory: An Evaluation. In *Mesoamerica after the Decline of Teotihuacan: A.D. 700–900* (Richard Diehl and Janet Berlo, eds.): 211–218. Dumbarton Oaks, Washington, D.C.

SÉJOURNÉ, LAURETTE
    1959   *Un palacio en la ciudad de los dioses: Exploraciones en Teotihuacan 1955–58.* Instituto Nacional de Antropología e Historia, Mexico, D.F.

SHORE, SALLY T.
    n.d.a.   A Discussion of the Glyphs on the Tree Murals at the De Young Museum. Unpublished manuscript, 1983.
    n.d.b   Observations on the Flowers and Glyphs of the Flowering Tree Murals, De Young Museum, San Francisco. Unpublished manuscript, 1984.

VILLAGRA, AGUSTÍN
    1954   Trabajos realizados en Teotihuacan: 1952. *Anales del Instituto Nacional de Antropología e Historia* 6: 69–78.

VON WINNING, HASSO
    1987   *La iconografía de Teotihuacan: Los dioses y los signos,* 2 vols. Universidad Nacional Autónoma de México, Mexico, D.F.

Teotihuacan Sign Clusters: Emblem or Articulation?

JAMES C. LANGLEY

INSTITUTE OF ARCHAEOLOGY, LONDON UNIVERSITY

INTRODUCTION

THE STUDY OF THE NOTATIONAL USE of symbols of Teotihuacan has followed a very different course from the epigraphy of other Mesoamerican cultures. Although Seler (1915: 428–429) asserted seventy-five years ago that the Teotihuacanos were well on their way to developing hieroglyphic writing, several compelling reasons have directed scholarly enquiry towards the general meaning of their signs rather than the search for precise logographic or phonetic readings and the syntactic rules that govern their use. Among the reasons have been our ignorance of the language or languages spoken at Teotihuacan, the scanty evidence for the use of the calendar (and even of numbers), the fact that nothing that we can recognize as a document has come to light, and that there are, in the culture's artistic output, few sign clusters of the sequential pattern that texts most commonly take.

The consequence is that our knowledge of Teotihuacan signs has been a by-product of iconographic analysis. This has yielded a good deal of information about the Teotihuacan culture, including the notational signs and the complexes into which they appear to fall (e.g., C. Millon 1973; von Winning 1987). However, because the meanings derived by this type of analysis are generic, the aim of interpretation might be described as "comprehension" of sign clusters rather than the literal readings that are the objective of epigraphy. A large class of sign clusters in any culture, for example heraldic devices, are understood in this way, and the word *emblem* in my title is intended to express this mode of interpretation.

The term *articulation* is used to describe the way in which words or sounds correspond with signs in a writing system, as in Mesoamerican scripts as diverse as those of the Maya and Aztecs. Over the years some efforts have been made to extract such explicit readings from Teotihuacan signs, as in the work of Alfonso Caso and others on calendrical data, toponyms, and personal names. Unfortunately, the results have been meager, but this may be due to the limited data available rather than the intrinsic nature of the sign system. The question how far the Teotihuacanos had progressed towards a writing system in the traditional sense remains open.

My own interest has lain in exploring the extent of the sign repertoire and the ways in which signs cluster, on the hypothesis that patterned clusters of signs imply meaning and that the structure of the clusters may provide clues to sign usage. It is this last aspect of clustering that is examined herein. It falls far short in objective of the recently proposed readings of Teotihuacan signs in the Nahuatl and Maya languages (Barthel 1982, 1986, and Brown n.d., respectively) but in view of the small data sample and large speculative element involved in such endeavors, it has seemed preferable to explore the facts of sign clustering before approaching the larger task of linguistic interpretation. It is true that persuasive visual analogies exist between Teotihuacan sign clusters and those of several other Mesoamerican cultures, but, since there is no necessary connection between sign and sound in these cultures, I suspect that a large body of evidence and collaboration with linguists and ethnohistorians will be required if we are to address the language issue effectively.

This paper is part of a larger study the aim of which is to record and analyze all linear sign clusters that can be identified on Teotihuacan artifacts. Many of the data are newly acquired and await fuller examination. However, the issues are clear, and the following examination of four sets of sign clusters will, I hope, yield evidence of meaning and of the ways in which signs may have been used to express it. The time depth of these usages is uncertain. The artifacts on which the sign clusters appear are dated to the latter part of the site's history; that is, from the late Tlamimilolpa to Metepec phases (A.D. 350–750). There is thus no direct evidence of continuity from earlier times, although this would seem a reasonable assumption pending the availability of further data.

STORM GOD INSIGNIA

The first sign cluster to be examined, the familiar Storm God insignia, was widely used at Teotihuacan in pottery decoration, stone sculpture, and, more rarely, mural painting. The way in which it is derived from the features of the Storm God is illustrated by a somewhat abstract representation of the deity (Fig. 1) that includes four roundels representing earplugs and eyes; a headband with triple knot; Fangs A (the curved upper canines of the jaguar) and the Bigotera (as Mexican scholars have called the moustache-like motif). In addition, there is a truncated headdress that may represent half a quincunx or *Kan* Cross sign.[1] Characteristics of what have been interpreted by Esther Pasztory (1974) as two deities, Tlaloc A and B, are here combined (as is not uncommon), which is one of the reasons for

---

[1] For an explanation of the Storm God designation and for the nomenclature and illustration of signs see Langley (1986: 175, note 5, and appendix 7 respectively).

Teotihuacan Sign Clusters

Fig. 1   Stylized head of the Storm God on a fragmentary champleve cylinder tripod vessel in the Ethnografiska Museet, Stockholm.

thinking that the Storm God is in fact a single deity, the variations in whose depiction merely emphasize different aspects of his persona or vocation. This versatility has familiar parallels in Christian iconography and is important in its implications for the interpretation of the insignia.

The insignia take a variety of forms, including naturalistic representation of the deity or of his facial features, depictions of his headdress, and abstract compositions consisting of permutations of several signs either diagnostic of or closely associated with him. To focus the discussion, we will examine this last type, first published by E. T. Hamy in 1882, when he christened a stone sculpture from the Superposed Buildings at Teotihuacan, "The Cross of Tlaloc" (Fig. 2). It is composed of the Bigotera, Fangs B (straight fangs of the serpent) and a bifurcated tongue. Examples of this specific image are rare but it is combined with a triplet of circles on an *adorno* (a small decorative ornament affixed to pottery vessels) in the Diego Rivera Museum (Fig. 3). In other variants, the Storm God may be denoted by the Circle Triplet and a pair of circles or roundels, representing his goggled eyes (Fig. 4) or Fangs A (Fig. 5). However, the most common form of insignia is undoubtedly that in which the Bigotera and Circle Triplet appear alone (Fig. 6) or with other signs (but without either type of fanged mouth). Most characteristic is the combination with a *Kan* Cross (Fig. 7), but Hasso von Winning illustrates an example in which the *Kan* Cross is replaced by a half-star (1987, 2: fig. 3f, following p. 66) and there is a rather more complex insignia including both *Kan* Cross and paired circles (Fig. 8).

In analyzing these insignia, a distinction must be made between those signs diagnostic of the Storm God and others which, while associated with

249

James C. Langley

Fig. 2 "The Cross of Tlaloc" (after Seler 1915: pl. XIII-2, following p. 585).

Fig. 3 Storm God insignia. A pottery *adorno* in the Diego Rivera Museum, Mexico.

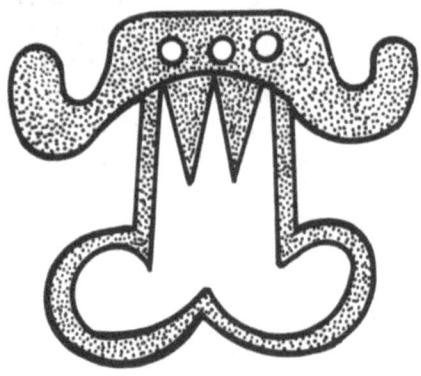

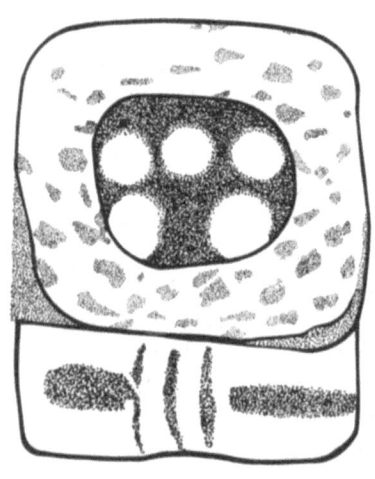

Fig. 4 Storm God insignia. A small pottery fragment, probably part of a double shield carried by a figurine. Peabody Museum of Archaeology and Ethnology, Harvard University.

Teotihuacan Sign Clusters

Fig. 5 Storm God insignia. A shield held by a fragmentary pottery figurine. Musée de l'Homme, Paris.

Fig. 6 Storm God insignia. A small pottery stamp in a private collection.

Fig. 7 Storm God insignia on shields held by pottery figurines in private collections. Drawings by author and H. von Winning.

James C. Langley

Fig. 8 Storm God insignia. A stone *almena* in a private collection.

him, also appear in many different contexts. A reasonable hypothesis is that the former provide a summary representation of the deity and invoke his patronage and protection or express some form of allegiance to him. The significance of the latter is more problematical, but they may provide a supplementary gloss to the insignia's meanings as well as reinforcing their deity identity. The *Kan* Cross and star have close associations with water and the Rain God in several Mesoamerican cultures. The Circle Triplet is somewhat more enigmatic: it does appear in the Storm God's headdress (Fig. 9), but occasionally the number of circles is four or five. It is, therefore, possible that it has some numerical significance, though this seems unlikely in the context. Eduard Seler (1915: 428) makes a connection with the three pads on the paws of jaguar sculptures (Fig. 10), but the reasons for its frequency in the symbolism of Teotihuacan are probably more comprehensive: a recognition of the prevalence of the motif in nature and the ancient usage of the roundel and circle in Mesoamerica as symbols for *precious* and *liquid*. It is not uncommon, for example, in depictions of conch shells (Fig. 11) and butterflies (Fig. 12), both of which have a close relationship to water. Roundels also appear in the Tassel Headdress (Fig. 13) of which Clara Millon has made a profound study (1973, 1988). As in the case of the Storm God's own headdress, the number of roundels in the Tassel Headdress is usually three, but four and five also occur. Whether these roundels and Circle Triplet signify the same thing is a moot point, but the association of both with Storm God imagery suggests this possibility. The martial characteristics of many of the figures wearing the Tassel Headdress

Teotihuacan Sign Clusters

Fig. 9 (*right*) Head of the Storm God. A fragmentary pottery figurine from the Metepec Pyramid excavations, 1979. Photo by Sue Scott.

Fig. 10 (*below*) Onyx jaguar in the Museum of Mankind, London (after Seler 1915: fig. 15).

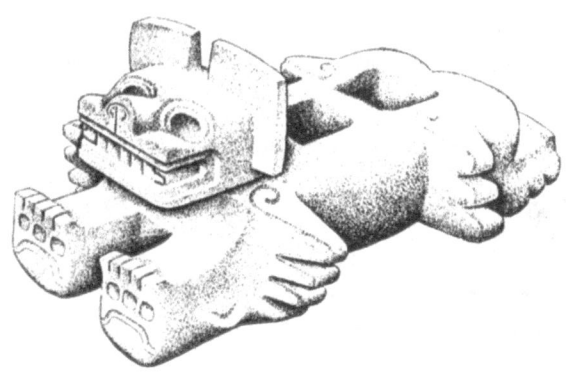

(both in the metropolis and as far afield as the Peten; Fig. 14) accords well with the artifact on which the insignia most frequently appear: the shield. The evidence, therefore, points to a clear identification of the Circle Triplet with liquid, the Storm God, and martial activity.

The case for the martial connotation of the Storm God insignia is strengthened by analogy with other Mesoamerican cultures as brief examples from the Maya area, Cacaxtla, and the Aztec period will demonstrate. Although the processes by which they were diffused are uncertain and regional stylistic differences are apparent, the essence of the insignia remains the same over a thousand years or so, and their military character is even more explicitly expressed than at Teotihuacan.

Fig. 11 Feathered conch shell. Bas-relief stone sculpture in Substructure 2 under the Quetzalpapalotl Palace (after Bernal 1963: fig. 16).

Fig. 12 Butterfly wing. Pottery *adorno*. Published with the permission of the Director of the Peabody Museum of Archaeology and Ethnology, Harvard University.

Fig. 13 Tassel Headdress. Detail of a mural painting in the M. H. de Young Memorial Museum, San Francisco.

Teotihuacan Sign Clusters

Fig. 14 Stela 11, Yaxha, Guatemala.

In the Maya area a striking early example of the insignia was discovered on a columnar sculpture at Tikal during the 1982–84 excavation of Group 6C-XVI.[2] It was associated with *talud-tablero* architecture and is, in general configuration, similar to the "ballcourt marker" from La Ventilla. The top of the column takes the form of a feathered disk on one side of which appears a quintessential Storm God insignia, consisting of Circle Triplet and Bigotera, while on the other there is a close approximation to the Teotihuacan "Bird and Weapon" symbol (von Winning 1987, 1: 85–90), a martial device consisting of a profile bird and hand-held *atl-atl*. These clusters are repeated in the Maya text on the shaft of the column, which records the victory of Tikal over Uaxactun in A.D. 378. Later in the Classic period Maya depictions of the insignia departed significantly from the Teotihuacan model in style and content, but their general sense remained the same. (In

---

[2] This significant find was described by John Carlson during the symposium and cited as a rare example of a text relating to Teotihuacan written by a contemporaneous literate society. See also Fialko 1986.

James C. Langley

Fig. 15 the deity's knotted headband, goggle eye, Fangs A, and *Kan* Cross are associated with typically Maya motifs such as the blood symbol below the fangs.) Of these insignia, Linda Schele (n.d.: 9) has written: "the Tlaloc complex . . . is consistently associated with bloodletting rituals and with war to take captives for sacrificial rites."

Outside the Maya area, a similar significance is evident at Cacaxtla where the ninth-century battle murals associate the insignia directly with soldiers wearing the regalia of leadership (Fig. 16). However, the closest visual

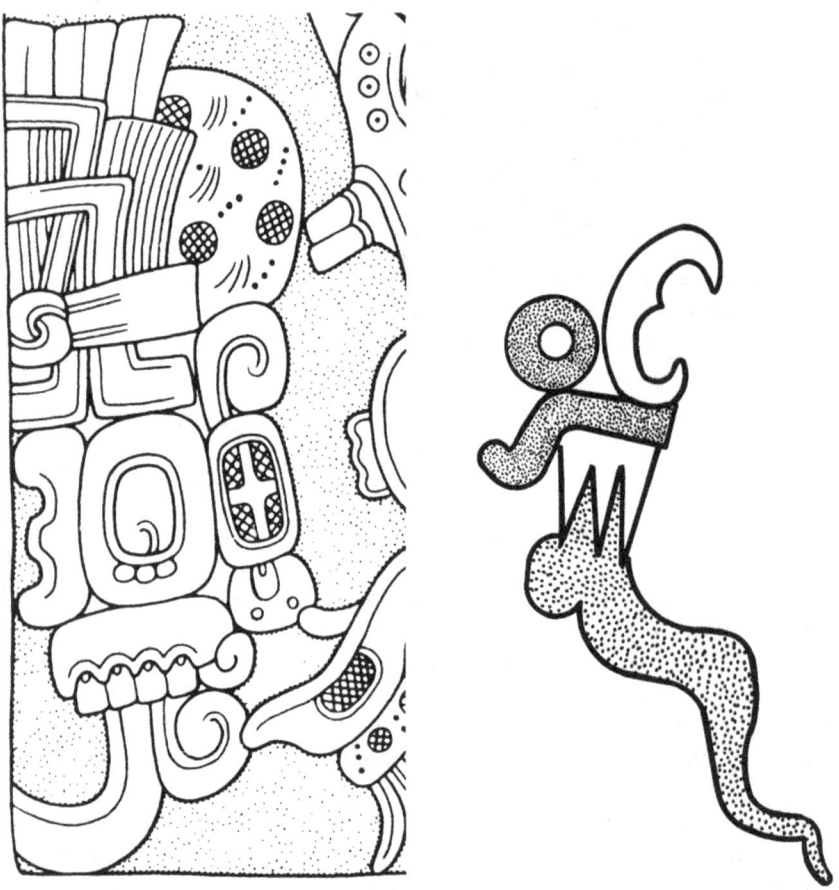

Fig. 15 (*left*) Storm God insignia. Detail of lintel 25, Yaxchilan (after Graham and von Euw 1977: fig. 3: 55).

Fig. 16 (*right*) Storm God insignia. Detail of a mural painting in Edificio B, Cacaxtla, Mexico.

Teotihuacan Sign Clusters

parallels, apart from the early Tikal example, are to be found in the Central Highlands during the Aztec period. Many Aztec and Tlaxcalan shields bear motifs with a striking resemblance to those of Teotihuacan. The class of shields relevant for present purposes is that called Texaxacalo Chimalli in Fray Bernardino de Sahagún's *Primeros Memoriales* (Fig. 17; Seler 1960–61a: 579). Antonio Peñafiel (1903) illustrates several variants that he calls by this name, those reproduced in Figs. 18 and 19 being the closest to Teotihuacan imagery. The second of these motifs is given the alternative name Tlahuiztli Chimalli which, according to Rémi Siméon's dictionary (1981), might be translated as "insignia shield." Seler (1960–61a: 583, fig. 158) reproduces an illustration from Sahagún of a shield by this name, saying that it was borne by military commanders of lesser rank (Fig. 20).

In considering all the analogies cited and the imagery of the Teotihuacan insignia there seems no doubt that they may be comprehended as emblems of military leadership related to the Storm God, implying that this deity was, inter alia, the patron of the warriors who fought under his insignia, much as the Crusaders a few centuries later sailed for the Holy Land under the banners of Christ.

Fig. 17   Texaxacalo Chimalli. Detail of an illustration in Sahagún's *Primeros Memoriales* (after Seler 1960–61a: 576, fig. 114).

Fig. 18 (*left*) Texaxacalo Chimalli. Detail of an illustration in the Lienzo de Tlaxcala (after Peñafiel 1903: pl. 70 B).

Fig. 19 (*below left*) Texaxacalo Chimalli. Detail of a painting (after Peñafiel 1903: pl. 15 D).

Fig. 20 (*below right*) Chimallauiztli. Detail of an illustration from Sahagún's *Primeros Memoriales* (after Seler 1960–61a: 593, fig. 158).

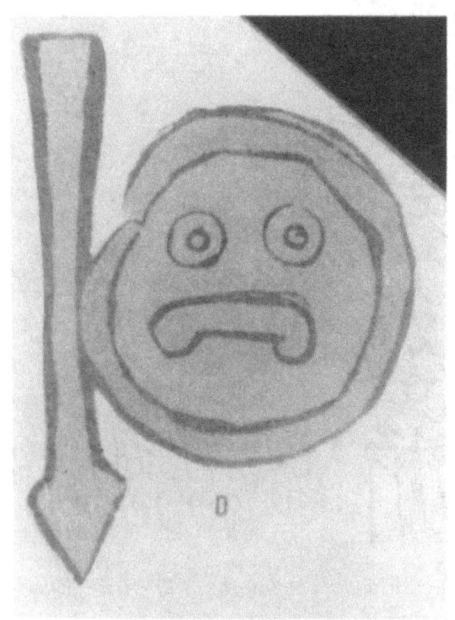

Teotihuacan Sign Clusters

We may never know how the Teotihuacanos referred to their insignia, but the Aztec analogy suggests several possibilities. The Aztec term *insignia shield* may have carried over from Teotihuacan. Alternatively, shields may, as in Tenochtitlan, have been named after their principal motif or by reference to the constituents of that motif or the materials of which they were made. For example, Eduard Seler (1960–61a: 553) cites the Tozmiquizyo Chimalli, the yellow skull shield, noting that the expression *tozmiquizyo* is derived from *toztli,* a yellow parrot of whose feathers the shield is made, and *miquiztli,* meaning death, the main motif on the shield being a skull. Finally, the vertical arrangement of the signs of the Storm God insignia suggests the possibility, admittedly remote, of a phonetic element in the nomenclature of Teotihuacan shields.

SIGN CLUSTERS ASSOCIATED WITH *INCENSARIOS*

Storm God insignia are fairly simple and homogeneous, but there are other sign clusters of much greater complexity and variability. The three selected for examination are found on a type of *incensario* characterized by a human-head mask in a recess within a border of *adornos* (Fig. 21). This type of artifact has been extensively studied, notably by Janet Berlo (1982, 1983, 1984), but relatively little attention has been paid to the details of its sign clustering. It is widely diffused geographically, and its symbolism is rich and varied. It is therefore necessary to limit the enquiry to a few examples from the metropolitan area in the hope of discerning sign patterns from which more general inferences about meaning and phraseology may be drawn.

The factual information available to us about *incensarios* is relatively limited. Those of known provenance have been recovered from palaces and residential compounds (not the major religious structures of the site). They are usually found in caches that appear to be dedicatory or, rarely, in burials. George Kubler has suggested their use in funerary rites (Kubler 1967: 9), while Janet Berlo has discussed the importance of incense burning in the ritual of pre-Hispanic Mesoamerica and the compositional diversity of the *incensario,* suggesting that they may have been made "to the particular ritual requirements of a specific occasion" (Berlo 1982: 93). The prominence of butterfly imagery in their composition has long been recognized (Séjourné 1959b) and Berlo has stressed the martial aspects of their iconography. One major uncertainty has been the level at which the ritual in which they were involved was performed, the possibilities ranging from elite ceremonies to family or personal religious observances.

Very interesting light is cast on this question by the excavation by Carlos Múnera (n.d.), during the Proyecto Arqueológico Teotihuacan 1980–82, of an *incensario* workshop in a walled compound close to the Ciudadela's northwest corner. This is the first such workshop to come to light in

James C. Langley

Fig. 21 An *incensario* of the "recessed head" type in a private collection.

Teotihuacan, and its excavation proved remarkably productive, yielding more than 3,000 molds and 15,500 mold-made artifacts, the great majority being components of *incensarios*. The workshop is thought to have functioned from the late Tlamimilolpa phase (A.D. 350–400) to the last days of the city, but the deposits were shallow and most of the recovered material dates to the terminal period. Múnera reports that there were only two narrow exits to the exterior in the substantial wall that surrounded the workshop. To Múnera and Rubén Cabrera Castro (personal communication, 1988) this deliberate isolation and the location of the workshop immediately adjacent to the Ciudadela suggest that it and its output were closely controlled by the residents of the Ciudadela, thought to have been the power center of Teotihuacan, the implication being that *incensarios* played an important role in the religious and political life of the city, whose rulers regulated their use and distribution.

If this is correct, *incensarios* were not part of a popular or family cult, a conclusion that tends to be confirmed by excavations at other Teotihuacan sites in the past few decades. For example, very few *adornos* were encountered in the surface collections and excavations of the Teotihuacan Mapping Project (as compared to the much greater frequency of figurines and *candeleros,* which are thought to have served in popular ritual). In addition, while fragments of *incensarios* were found in household refuse during the Maquixco Bajo excavations of 1961–62, William Sanders, Jeffrey Parsons, and Robert Santley (1979: 352) comment that, like stone censers of the Huehueteotl type, they were probably used in courtyard rather than personal ritual. One would therefore expect the symbolism of the *incensario* to reflect the preoccupations of the elite and the dominant ideology of the Teotihuacan state. It is within this perspective that three sets of sign clusters found on components of the *incensario* will be considered: those associated with headdresses, those on lateral tablets, and the "Manta Compound."

Incensarios and the Headdress Complex

The importance of the headdress as an indicator of status, rank, and occupation at Teotihuacan has long been recognized, but its symbolism has not been analyzed comprehensively and its appearance on *incensarios* and in abstract compositions has been relatively neglected. This is hardly surprising in the case of *incensarios* of the "recessed head" type, because those from Teotihuacan itself rarely include a headdress. The human mask is usually disembodied and clearly dissociated from any headdress elements, such as the array of feathers at the top of the *incensario* (Fig. 21). The headdress is, however, an integral part of the depiction of the recessed head on many *incensarios* from the Escuintla department of coastal Guatemala and from Xico, Mexico (Berlo 1984: pt. 2, plates); there are also a few examples from the metropolitan area, of which Fig. 22 is representative. This is one of a relatively small group of *incensarios* that were preassembled and fired as complete units rather than the more usual practice of piecemeal assembly after firing of the separate elements (Berlo 1982: 92). In this case, the human head wears a headdress the upper part of which consists of a wide feather array to which are affixed an indeterminate number of dartbutts. Below this is a motif consisting of two feathered eyes joined by a cylindrical bridge and, beneath that, three quatrefoil *adornos*.

Headdresses incorporating elements with a probable symbolic connotation are common at Teotihuacan and appear to serve a variety of purposes. They may identify classes of the civil authority, as has been decisively demonstrated by Clara Millon (1973); Esther Pasztory (1976: 121) has suggested a similar role in respect to deities. Much the same configuration of headdress and signs also occurs in the abstract compositions on pottery and in mural paintings, which I have called the "Feather Headdress Symbol" (Langley 1986: 107–121), of which Fig. 23 is illustrative. There is thus a fairly wide range of artifacts and representational modes in which the headdress complex

James C. Langley

Fig. 22 An *incensario* of the "recessed head" type, assembled before firing. Courtesy of the Museo Nacional de Antropología, INAH, Mexico (Inventory #9-4256).

appears. It is easily recognized, thanks to the conventionalized depiction of the headdress, but is extremely variable in its associated sign clusters.

This is not the occasion to attempt a detailed enumeration, but it appears that each of the main usages of the headdress is associated with a characteristic group of signs. Thus, in the Tassel Headdress analyzed by C. Millon (1973), tassels of a specific kind combine with dartpoints and roundels in a number of different ways. Another group of signs, including the half-star, feathered disk, and obsidian knife, appears on zoomorphic headdresses, in which the main element is likely to be a feline, avian, crocodilian, or butterfly head. The Feather Headdress Symbol appears with clusters that include the Trapeze and Ray (TR), Reptile's Eye (RE), and Comb and Bar (C&B) signs, various forms of the Trilobe, feathered eyes, the fanged mouth, and so forth. Although there is some overlap, this correlation between distinctive groups of signs and different headdress usages is also seen in the *incensario* headdress cluster. Its signs are those most frequently found as *incensario adornos* and include, notably, the dartbutt, quatrefoil, and paired feathered eyes. In dis-

Teotihuacan Sign Clusters

Fig. 23   The Feather Headdress Symbol (after Caso 1967: 159, fig. 11 L).

cussing the Teotihuacan-derived *incensarios* of Escuintla, Janet Berlo (1983: 83) has written that "their symbols refer almost exclusively to motifs of warfare and a martial butterfly." This appears equally applicable to the headdress symbolism of the Teotihuacan *incensario* in Fig. 22. There seems little doubt, in terms of both context and configuration, that the feathered-eye motif depicts that of the butterfly, while the dartbutts have a clear martial connotation. The quatrefoil is less easy to interpret, but a number of possible meanings are suggested by the rich floral metaphors of the Postclassic period among which are the association of flowers with blood, warfare, and death.

The evidence of the *incensario,* and more generally of the other usages of headdress symbolism, is that the signs that cluster in the headdress context convey information that bears directly on some aspect—such as rank, function, or name—of the personage involved. Articulation of this headdress information, in the sense described earlier, is also possible, but, in view of the relatively unstructured arrangement of the signs, it seems more likely that their usage is emblematic. This is less certain of other clusters on *incensarios* some of whose signs may be aligned in linear sequences.

Sign Clusters on the Lateral Tablets of Incensarios

The recess within which the human-head mask is placed on Teotihuacan *incensarios* is usually framed on either side by a rectangular lateral tablet of irregular shape. Occasionally the tablets, which are mold-made, are plain, but more often they bear motifs whose symbolism is directly relevant to the interpretation of the third set of sign clusters in this study, those that sometimes appear on the two lateral tablets. For this reason, the tablets and motifs will be examined before proceeding to an analysis of the sign clusters.

Laurette Séjourné (1959a: 117–121), noting the predominance of butterfly and avian elements in the symbolism of *incensarios,* has written that their lateral tablets invariably take the form of butterfly wings. Thanks to data that have since become available, it is now apparent that they may instead represent a shield or a sheaf of darts. Even in the case of the right lateral tablet of the type illustrated in Fig. 28, a more accurate description would be a bisected butterfly that can be resuscitated by combination with its mirror-image (Fig. 24). This composite image has an interesting counterpart in a vessel lid in the Diego Rivera Museum (Fig. 25). The left lateral tablet may be intended to represent a bisected bird (Fig. 26) rather than a butterfly. The sharper wing projection and typically pleated tail section are avian traits, but the evidence is not decisive.

Fig. 24 Butterfly formed by the right lateral tablet of an *incensario* in a private collection and its mirror image.

Teotihuacan Sign Clusters

Fig. 25 Butterfly appliqué on the lid of a pottery vessel in the Diego Rivera Museum, Mexico.

Fig. 26 The left lateral tablet of an *incensario*. Courtesy of the Museo Nacional de Antropología, INAH, Mexico (Inventory #3374).

Butterflies and birds are closely associated with martial imagery at Teotihuacan, and it is not surprising to find this same association on the two lateral tablets. However, their symbolism is subtly differentiated, and the left tablet evokes war much more directly than does that on the right side. Typically there is a row of from three to five dartbutts affixed along the top of the left tablet. Below there is often a mold-impressed butterfly (see Figs. 26 and 27). The tablet in Fig. 27 also includes a sign cluster along its lower edge. It consists of a central C&B sign, while in the two left-hand pleats of the tail section, there are vertical bands containing the Rhomboid Eye and Elongated Eye, respectively. Hasso von Winning (1987, 2: 79) and others have interpreted these as signs for fire and water, and I have argued that in this particular cluster they anticipate the Aztec *atl-tlachinolli* and carry the same general sense of warfare (Langley 1986: 102–103).

This striking parallel between imagery and linguistic metaphor is encouragement to look for other motifs on the tablet that might have idiomatic equivalents. If the tablet represents a bird, its association with darts recalls the "owl and weapon" symbol that is common on pottery artifacts and in mural paintings (von Winning 1987, 1: 85). (For a series of naturalistic representations of this martial bird, see Berrin 1988: 168–176.) The expressions *war-bird* or *spear-bird* suggest themselves as descriptive terms for such representations. Alternatively, if the tablet represents a butterfly, the association between butterfly and war or butterfly and obsidian dart spring naturally to mind.

Fig. 27 Fragmentary left lateral tablet of an *incensario*. Photograph by Saburo Sugiyama, courtesy of the Proyecto Arqueológico Teotihuacan 80–82, INAH, Mexico.

Teotihuacan Sign Clusters

The right lateral tablet is no less complex. The example (Fig. 28) contains a rare, but not atypical, combination of signs and imagery. The symbolism of war is notably absent. In its place we have what von Winning (1977b) has convincingly shown to be fire signs and elements of what I have called the core cluster because of the frequency with which a small group of signs permutates in the imagery of Teotihuacan (Langley 1986: 103–107). On the main body are the Interlocking Scrolls (a variant of the Fire Bundle sign), here associated with black-painted asterisks. In the four corners there are two core cluster signs: Interlaced Bands and what appears to be a nose pendant.

The semicircular motif at the top of the tablet is, I suggest, not a sign but the stylized eye of the butterfly here combined with the serrated C&B fire sign. There is a remarkable similiarity between this combination and the so-called RE glyph at Xochicalco (Fig. 29). This suggests that a reconsideration of Laurette Séjourné's (1962) case for the equation of the glyph with the butterfly rather than the reptile may be in order. On the band along the right

Fig. 28   (*left*) The right lateral tablet of an *incensario* in a private collection.

Fig. 29   (*right*) So-called Reptile Eye glyph on Stela 1, Xochicalco (after Caso 1962: fig. 4b).

side of the tablet (the butterfly's antenna) there is a sequence of four signs from the core cluster terminating in another variant of the C&B sign (Fig. 30). The four signs are a quatrefoil frontal flower, Trefoil E and Nose Pendant E (as I have called them for want of better identification), and Interlaced Bands. Only the C&B sign is common to the two lateral tablets, implying that the two variants of this third sign cluster differ significantly in meaning.

The first and fourth signs are familiar and have their counterparts in both the Aztec and Maya glyphic systems. The second and third signs are unique to Teotihuacan. Trefoil E is very common and appears in contexts that suggest its importance. For example, it occurs as the principal motif on several pottery vessels (e.g., Linné 1934: fig. 17). It has been called a snail shell, a heart, and, more plausibly, a cotton boll.[3] There is no doubt that it bears a resemblance to the Aztec sign for cotton (Fig. 31), but its occurrences at Teotihuacan suggest the need for a more symbolically charged interpretation. Two possible lines of enquiry lead in rather different directions. The first approach would seek a metaphorical meaning such as the association of cotton and clouds recorded by J. Eric S. Thompson in the Maya area (Dienhart 1986: 55). Both Seler and Séjourné illustrate pottery vessels that appear to make the same association at Teotihuacan (Seler 1915: 526, fig. 179; Séjourné 1966a: fig. 121). A second approach is to explore the variations in the depiction of the sign, particularly noticeable in the length and shape of the projecting stem, which can be elongated and approach the form of a dart point (Fig. 32). The existing evidence is inconclusive, but the Aztec association of unspun cotton with certain death rituals is suggestive (Seler 1960–61c: 245–246).

Although specimens of the third sign from the Múnera excavation give a zoomorphic impression (Fig. 33), I am inclined to stick to my earlier identification of it as a nose pendant, with the upper element as a knot or fastening. However, with all the uncertainties, an interpretation of the whole sign cluster cannot yet be offered. Its structure implies the encoding of a sequential message, while the context suggests that it may refer to fire, death, and the hereafter. The fact that there are five examples of the cluster in the data sample leads to the conclusion that the message is formulary or generic in character. The tablet as a whole reflects a concept such as that of "fire-butterfly."

Whether the two variants of the sign cluster just discussed appear together on the same *incensario* is at present uncertain. Two tablets bearing these

---

[3] The proposed identifications of Trefoil E are due, respectively, to Eduard Seler (1915: 526), Laurette Séjourné (1959a: 121), and C. Millon (personal communication, 1985). Luis Múnera (n.d.: 122, lám. 35, caption) tentatively concurs with this last identification. Since then, my attention has been drawn to the similarity of the punctate variant of the sign to the Maya depiction of copal.

Teotihuacan Sign Clusters

Fig. 30 (*left*) The "Core cluster" on the right lateral tablet in Fig. 28.

Fig. 31 (*above*) The Aztec sign for cotton (after Seler 1960–61c: 242, fig. 30).

Fig. 32 (*below*) Trefoil E on a fragment of stuccoed and painted pottery (after Séjourné 1966a: fig. 66).

James C. Langley

Fig. 33 Pendant Nose E on a pottery *adorno* and its mold. Photograph by Saburo Sugiyama, courtesy of the Proyecto Arqueológico Teotihuacan 80–82, INAH, Mexico.

variants were found in a rescue excavation at San Sebastian Xolalpan, a Teotihuacan *barrio,* but there was no evidence of the rest of the *incensario* apart from several detached *mantas*. It may, however, be said that all the complete specimens of the "recessed head" type of *incensario* in the data sample have two lateral tablets and that their symbolism usually includes a clear allusion to war and a fire-butterfly.

The Manta Compound

The fourth and last set of sign clusters to be discussed appears on small rectangular *incensario adornos* called *mantas* that are affixed along the lower edge of the recess flanked by the two lateral tablets (see Fig. 21). There are usually four such *adornos* (identical except for color) on each *incensario,* but the number may vary. Without exception they bear elaborate symbolic compositions, the central sign cluster of which I have called the Manta Compound (Langley 1986: 153–167). It is formed from a repertoire of about a dozen signs. Although the number of possible combinations is enormous, the signs cluster in fairly well-defined ways in vertical strata to form a limited, though still large, number of compounds (Fig. 35). In addition, there is almost always a superfixed motif, usually some form of feather fringe, and often a subfix such as an RE or its variant, the RM sign.

It has been useful for analytical purposes to consider each stratum of the compound separately, but it is now clear that the *manta* constitutes a symbolic whole. This is signified (see e.g., Fig. 34) by the band that binds its various elements into a single bundle. These elements can be summarized as

Teotihuacan Sign Clusters

Fig. 34 The Manta Compound with RE 3 sign on a pottery *adorno*. Courtesy of the Proyecto Arqueológico Teotihuacan 80–82, INAH, Mexico.

Rectangle - Triangle

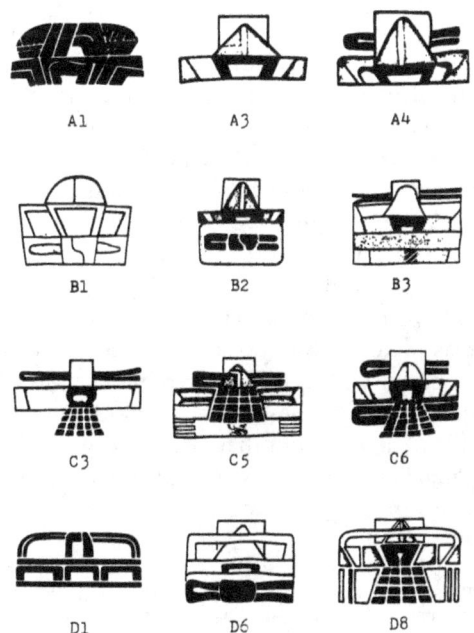

Fig. 35 Some examples of the Manta Compound.

follows. Along the top is a feather fringe that may represent fire or the concepts of high rank and divinity. Below is a triangle resting on or behind a trapezoidal form, enclosed in some kind of folded material and superimposed on a bow and rectangle. Below this is a short section of twisted cord and the RE 3 sign. The rectangle probably represents a wooden rod. Perhaps, in the context of this compound, it is a fire drill. I have previously called the triangle a knot but now think it is better described as the loop of a band whose ends are intertwined to create a bond around, say, a bundle of sticks (Figs. 36, 37). Alfonso Caso (1967: 178 and Fig. 15m–o) suggests the possible derivation of the triangular element of the year sign from just such a motif in the headband of the God Cocijo. The trapezoidal element has been the subject of much speculation, but there is a remarkable pottery mold from Múnera's excavation that proves it to be the loop of a twisted cord (Fig. 38), which, in the case of the *manta* under discussion, appears below. Finally, the *manta* includes the RE sign whose interpretation remains controversial despite several scholarly analyses.[4]

It is perhaps significant that the *manta* compound is composed of signs with a calendrical connotation in the Postclassic period. It combines a familiar abbreviated form of the Mesoamerican year sign, the looped twisted cord (Nicholson 1966), with an alternative form of the Aztec Xiuhmolpilli, a knotted cord (Saenz 1967: 24). Other signs, such as the triangle and RE, also lend themselves to the calendrical hypothesis. However, this kind of analogical evidence cannot be conclusive, and the precise significance of the cluster at Teotihuacan is uncertain. First, if the usage of the *manta* is calendrical, what type of information is encoded? Some *manta* compounds are so abbreviated that only a general reference to the cycles or passage of time seems likely. Others (see the *manta* in Fig. 34) seem to incorporate more precise calendrical information in their sign clusters. For example, there is some correlation between variations in *manta* imagery and the number of dots within the RE and RM signs, suggestive of numerical coefficients (Langley 1986: 145–148, 167–170). A much broader question is raised by the appearance of this same symbolism in more narrowly martial contexts, for example, the use of the TR year sign in military headdresses and of the Manta Compound as the breastplate of the Storm God and warriors (Fig. 39). Issues of this kind cannot be convincingly answered on the basis of our present data, and it seems prudent to limit oneself to the hypothesis that *manta* imagery embodies a calendrical element and that *incensarios* were the focus of a state ritual, with strong martial overtones, whose purpose appears to have been commemorative, dedicatory, or testimonial.

---

[4] Among those who have written about the RE sign have been Eduard Seler (1915: 482–486), Hermann Beyer (1922), Hasso von Winning (1961), Alfonso Caso (1967: 164–165), and Laurette Séjourné (1962).

Teotihuacan Sign Clusters

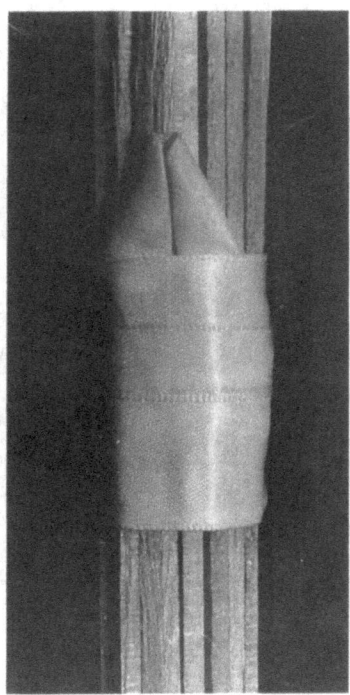

Fig. 36 (*left*) The Firewood Bundle on a pottery *adorno*. Courtesy of the Teotihuacan Mapping Project.

Fig. 37 (*right*) Simulation of the triangular looped cord.

Fig. 38 Trapezoidal loop and twisted cord on a pottery *adorno*. Photograph by Saburo Sugiyama, courtesy of the Proyecto Arqueológico Teotihuacan 80–82, INAH, Mexico.

James C. Langley

Fig. 39 Pottery figurine depicting the Storm God with the Manta Compound as a breastplate. Published with the permission of the Director of the Peabody Museum of Archaeology and Ethnology, Harvard University.

CONCLUSION

This study has been based on the examination of one type of Storm God insignia and of three sets of sign clusters on one type of *incensario*. Even such limited data do, however, suggest a number of conclusions. In the first place, both the iconographic imagery and the sign clusters cited in this paper have a larger content of martial symbolism than has been suspected, reinforcing the conclusion of my study (Langley 1986) that military power and sacrifice were the principal subjects of the Teotihuacan notational system. This is at variance with the traditional view of Teotihuacan as a theocratic society whose art and symbolism were primarily religious, but it is compatible with the archaeological evidence of militarism emerging in the excavations conducted by INAH in the Ciudadela since 1980 (Sugiyama 1989).

Second, the data provide some grounds for thinking that Teotihuacan sign usage involved both emblem and articulation. The artifacts on which the Storm God insignia most often appear, the shield and the *almena* (a merlon affixed to the edge of a roof), lend themselves to the emblematic use of signs, and the configuration of the clusters suggests the same conclusion. Although a logographic usage is certainly not excluded, it seems more likely that the clusters express the general concept of patronage by, or allegiance to, the Storm God. The variety of ways in which the signs of the cluster combine would otherwise imply an equally large number of verbal expressions to describe nuances of that affiliation.

Their somewhat different configuration is part of the reason for thinking that articulation is involved in some of the *incensario* sign clusters. Close juxtaposition and linear arrangement are typical of the logographic or phonetic use of signs. Moreover, several of the signs in the clusters are used glyphically in other Mesoamerican writing systems. I have also suggested that there are broader analogies between some Teotihuacan sign clusters and idiomatic expressions in other cultures of the Central Highlands.[5] These parallels are certainly not conclusive, but, faced as we are with the unknown linguistic affiliations of Teotihuacan, the exploration of possible equivalencies in languages such as Nahuatl offers one possible route towards the interpretation of its sign clusters. In doing so one must bear in mind both the well-known objections to the notion of linguistic continuity between the two cultures and the fact that the Teotihuacan sign system is different from and less rigorously pictographic than that of the Aztecs.

It is impossible to assert with any degree of confidence that sign usage at Teotihuacan was the equivalent of writing in the traditional sense, and I have therefore preferred to refer to it as notation, meaning an autonomous form of graphic communication distinct from any pictorial imagery with which it might be associated. From the data presented here we can be confident that emblems of various kinds were widely used in the culture, that sign usage included the arrangement of signs in linear sequences characteristic of verbal texts, and that the sign system was capable of signifying concepts such as war, sacrifice, and, probably, ritual events (see Cowgill, this volume). The rarity of linear sequences is a serious impediment to the study of the system, but it is reasonable to hope that future research will yield the additional data that will aid in the solution of the linguistic and interpretative challenges posed at this stage of our studies.

Acknowledgments I am profoundly grateful to Dr. García Moll, Director General of the INAH, for permission to examine the Teotihuacan *incensarios* in the Museo Nacional de Antropología in Mexico City; to Professor Rubén Cabrera Castro for providing material for study from his extensive excavations in the context of the Proyecto Teotihuacan 80–82; and to Dr. Rosemary Joyce for access at short notice to the Teotihuacan collection of the Peabody Museum, Cambridge, Mass. I also owe a debt of gratitude to many others: to Dr. George Cowgill, who guided my footsteps through the

---

[5] During the symposium H. B. Nicholson made the point that the *atl-tlachinolli* metaphor occurred not only in Nahuatl but in Mixtec and Otomi, and possibly other Mesoamerican languages. For further discussion of analogies between Teotihuacan sign usage and Aztec verbal expressions see Janet Berlo (1989: 47–48) and George Cowgill (this volume).

James C. Langley

collections of the Teotihuacan Mapping Project, and to Saburo Sugiyama for other original material. Maestra Clara Diaz facilitated my work in the Museo Nacional de Antropología, was invariably supportive, and made a valuable contribution to the artifactual analysis. Finally, Drs. Clara and René Millon and Dr. Janet Berlo read and commented on an earlier draft of this paper.

BIBLIOGRAPHY

BARTHEL, THOMAS S.
  1982   Veritable "Texts" in Teotihuacan Art? *The Masterkey* 56 (1): 4–12.
  1986   Deciphering Teotihuacan Writing. *Indiana* 11: 9–18.

BERLO, JANET CATHERINE
  1982   Artistic Specialization at Teotihuacan: The Ceramic Incense Burner. In *Pre-Columbian Art History: Selected Readings*, 2nd ed. (A. Cordy-Collins, ed.): 83–100. Peek Publications, Palo Alto.
  1983   The Warrior and the Butterfly: Central Mexican Ideologies of Sacred Warfare and Teotihuacan Iconography. In *Text and Image in Pre-Columbian Art* (Janet C. Berlo, ed.): 79–117. BAR International Series 180, Oxford.
  1984   *Teotihuacan Art Abroad: A Study of Metropolitan Style and Provincial Transformation in Incensario Workshops*. BAR International Series 199, Oxford.
  1989   Early Writing in Central Mexico: *In Tlilli, In Tlapali* before A.D. 1000. In *Mesoamerica after the Decline of Teotihuacan, A.D. 700–900* (Richard A. Diehl and Janet C. Berlo, eds.). Dumbarton Oaks, Washington, D.C.

BERNAL, IGNACIO (ED.)
  1963   *Teotihuacan: Descubrimientos, reconstrucciones*. Instituto Nacional de Antropología e Historia, Mexico, D.F.

BERRIN, KATHLEEN (ED.)
  1988   *Feathered Serpents and Flowering Trees: Reconstructing the Murals of Teotihuacan*. The Fine Arts Museums of San Francisco.

BROWN, DAVID
  n.d.   The Linguistic Affiliation and Phoneticism of Teotihuacan Iconography. Ph.D. dissertation, University of New Mexico, Albuquerque, 1988.

BEYER, HERMANN
  1922   Sobre una plaqueta con una deidad Teotihuacana. *Memorias y Revistas de la Sociedad Científica "Antonio Alzate"* 40: 549–558.

CABRERA CASTRO, RUBÉN, IGNACIO RODRIGUEZ, AND NOEL MORELOS (EDS.)
  1982   Memoria del Proyecto Arqueológico Teotihuacan 80–82. *Colección Científica* 132. Instituto Nacional de Antropología e Historia, Mexico, D.F.

CASO, ALFONSO
  1962   Calendario y escritura en Xochicalco. *Revista Mexicana de Estudios Antropológicos* 18: 47–79.
  1966   Dioses y signos Teotihuacanos. In *Teotihuacan: Onceava Mesa Redonda*: 249–279. Sociedad Mexicana de Antropología, Mexico, D.F.
  1967   *Los calendarios prehispánicos*. Universidad Nacional Autónoma de México, Instituto de Investigaciones Históricas, Serie de Cultura Náhuatl, Monografía 6. Mexico, D.F.

DIENHART, JOHN M.
   1986   The Mayan Glyph for Cotton. *Mexicon* 8 (3): 52–56.
FIALKO, VILMA
   1986   El Marcador de juego de pelota de Tikal. In *Primer Simposio Mundial sobre Epigrafía Maya:* 61–80. Asociación Tikal, Guatemala.
GRAHAM, IAN, AND ERIC VON EUW
   1977   *Corpus of Maya Hieroglyphic Inscriptions 3 (1), Yaxchilan*. Peabody Museum of Archaeology and Ethnology, Harvard University, Cambridge.
HAMY, E. T.
   1882   La Croix de Teotihuacan au Musée du Trocadero. *Revue d'Ethnographie* 1: 410–428. Paris.
KUBLER, GEORGE
   1967   *The Iconography of the Art of Teotihuacan*. Studies in Pre-Columbian Art and Archaeology 4. Dumbarton Oaks, Washington, D.C.
LANGLEY, JAMES C.
   1986   *Symbolic Notation of Teotihuacan: Elements of Writing in a Mesoamerican Culture of the Classic Period*. BAR International Series 313, Oxford.
LINNÉ, SIGVALD
   1934   *Archaeological Researches at Teotihuacan, Mexico*. N. S. Publication 1. The Ethnographical Museum of Sweden, Stockholm.
MILLON, CLARA
   1973   Painting, Writing, and Polity in Teotihuacan, Mexico. *American Antiquity* 38 (3): 294–314.
   1988   A Reexamination of the Teotihuacan Tassel Headdress Insignia. In *Feathered Serpents and Flowering Trees: Reconstructing the Murals of Teotihuacan* (Kathleen Berrin, ed.): 114–134. The Fine Arts Museums of San Francisco.
MILLON, RENÉ
   1973   *Urbanization at Teotihuacan, Mexico, Vol. I: The Teotihuacan Map*. University of Texas Press, Austin.
   1987   The Last Years of Teotihuacan Dominance. In *The Collapse of Ancient States and Civilizations* (Norman Yoffee and George L. Cowgill, eds.): 102–164. University of Arizona Press, Tucson.
MÚNERA, LUIS CARLOS
   n.d.   Un taller de cerámica ritual en la Ciudadela, Teotihuacan. M.A. thesis, Escuela Nacional de Antropología e Historia, Mexico, D.F., 1985.
NICHOLSON, H. B.
   1966   The Significance of the "Looped Cord" Year Symbol in pre-Hispanic Mexico: An Hypothesis. *Estudios de Cultura Nahuatl* 6: 135–147.
PASZTORY, ESTHER
   1974   *The Iconography of the Teotihuacan Tlaloc*. Studies in Pre-Columbian Art and Archaeology 15. Dumbarton Oaks, Washington, D.C.

1976 The Murals of Tepantitla, Teotihuacan. Garland Publishing Inc., New York.

PEÑAFIEL, ANTONIO
1903 Indumentaria antigua: Armas, vestidos guerreros y civiles de los antiguos Mexicanos. Mexico, D.F.

SAENZ, CESAR
1967 El fuego nuevo. Serie Historia XVIII. INAH, Mexico, D.F.

SANDERS, WILLIAM T., JEFFREY R. PARSONS, AND ROBERT S. SANTLEY
1979 The Basin of Mexico. Academic Press, New York.

SCHELE, LINDA
n.d. The Tlaloc Complex in the Classic Period: War and the Interaction between the Lowland Maya and Teotihuacan. Paper presented at the symposium "The New Dynamics," Kimbell Art Museum, Fort Worth, 1986.

SÉJOURNÉ, LAURETTE
1959a Un palacio en la Ciudad de los dioses (Teotihuacan). Instituto Nacional de Antropología e Historia, Mexico, D.F.
1959b El culto de Xochipilli y los braseros teotihuacanos. El Mexico Antiguo 9: 111–124.
1962 Interpretacíon de un jeroglífico teotihuacano. Cuadernos Americanos 124 (5): 137–158.
1966a Arqueología de Teotihuacan: La cerámica. Fondo de Cultura Economica, Mexico, D.F.
1966b El lenguaje de las formas en Teotihuacan. Gabriel Mancero 65, Mexico, D.F.

SELER, EDUARD
1915 Die Teotiuacan-Kultur des Hochlandes von Mexico. In Gesammelte Abhandlungen zur amerikanischen Sprach- und Altertumskunde 5: 405–585. Behrend, Berlin.
1960–61a Altmexikanischer Schmuck und soziale und militarische Rangabzeichen. In Gesammelte Abhandlungen zur amerikanischen Sprach- und Altertumskunde 2: 509–619. Akademische Druck- und Verlagsanstalt, Graz. Reprinted from Zeitschrift für Ethnologie 21: 69–85, 23: 114–144 (1889–91).
1960–61b Altmexikanische Schilde. In Gesammelte Abhandlungen zur amerikanischen Sprach- und Altertumskunde 2: 664–668. Akademische Druck- und Verlagsanstalt, Graz. Reprinted from Internationales Archiv für Ethnographie 5: 168–172 (1892).
1960–61c Die Pauke von Malinalco und das Zeichen atl-tlachinolli. In Gesammelte Abhandlungen zur amerikanischen Sprach- und Altertumskunde 3: 221–304. Akademische Druck- und Verlagsanstalt, Graz. Reprinted from Mittheilungen der Anthropologischen Gesellschaft in Wien 34: 222–274 (1904).

SIMÉON, RÉMI
1981 Diccionario de la lengua náhuatl o mexicana (J. Oliva de Coll, trans.), 2nd ed. Siglo Veintiuno, Mexico, D.F.

SUGIYAMA, SABURO
    1989   Burials Dedicated to the Old Temple of Quetzalcoatl at Teotihuacan, Mexico. *American Antiquity* 54 (1): 85–106.

VON WINNING, HASSO
    1961   Teotihuacan Symbols: The Reptile's Eye Glyph. *Ethnos* 26 (3): 121–166.
    1977a   Los incensarios teotihuacanos y los del litoral pacífico de Guatemala: Su iconografía y funcíon ritual. *Sociedad Mexicana de Antropología, XV Mesa Redonda* 2: 327–334. Mexico, D.F.
    1977b   The Old Fire God and His Symbolism at Teotihuacan. *Indiana* 4: 7–61.
    1987   *La iconografía de Teotihuacan: Los dioses y los signos*, 2 vols. Universidad Nacional Autónoma de México, Mexico, D.F.

Abstraction and the Rise of a Utopian State at Teotihuacan

ESTHER PASZTORY

COLUMBIA UNIVERSITY

THE AZTEC-TEOTIHUACAN CONNECTION

IN 1967 GEORGE KUBLER WROTE a brief analysis of Teotihuacan iconography in which he suggested that the images did not represent gods, but signs that functioned as nouns, adjectives, and verbs do in language. With the brashness of the new Ph.D., I questioned this approach on the basis that all known pre-Hispanic religious systems had some form of deities with cults and priests, and I could not imagine how a system such as the one he proposed could have worked in practice (Pasztory 1972). I was convinced that Teotihuacan must have had some type of deities on some basic level. Moreover, I argued that, if used carefully, sixteenth-century sources about Aztec culture and religion could be used to reconstruct some aspects of life at Teotihuacan. I then proceeded to identify several images, which had been called Tlaloc before but had features different from Tlaloc, as a goddess whose distinctive features were a nosebar and a bird in the headdress. Because her usual associations are water and vegetation, I felt that she was a nature goddess and called her the Teotihuacan equivalent of the Aztec Xochiquetzal, or Flower Quetzal, on the basis of what I took to be a quetzal bird in her headdress. Since then, Janet Berlo (1983a), Clara Millon (1988), Karl Taube (1983), and Hasso von Winning (1987) have worked on the iconography of one or more Teotihuacan goddesses, and the current consensus is that there is, in fact, one goddess with several aspects, including a military persona whom Berlo once compared to the Aztec goddess Itzpapalotl, or Obsidian Butterfly. From about A.D. 200 in the Tlamimilolpa period, the image of this goddess is progressively more frequent in art, and, especially in the mural art of the last two centuries of the life of the city, she is shown as superior to Tlaloc, the Storm God, and was apparently the major deity of Teotihuacan. The recent find of a large sculpture representing her in the Calle de los Muertos Complex, which George Cowgill (1983) believes may have been the administrative and palatial center for the city, reinforces her centrality and importance (Fig. 1). Our Xochiquetzal-Itzpapalotl has now come to be called the Great Goddess (see Berlo, this volume).

This is the gratifying part of that early work. Much of the rest I will have to recant: George Kubler was closer to the truth than I. Indeed, I now believe that Teotihuacan had a flexible symbol system that was compounded to fit various situations. I was also misguided in using Aztec parallels and texts. Beyond a very general identification of deities, which would have worked just as well without Aztec names, the Aztec texts did not help to carry the analysis very far. After nearly a decade of work on Aztec art, I became convinced that the Aztec-Teotihuacan connection is as minimal as George Kubler said it was. The Aztec sojourn has made it possible for me to see Teotihuacan from an Aztec perspective, and it looks almost entirely alien. Montezuma II would have understood Pacal and his court at Palenque more easily than seventh-century Teotihuacan.

Teotihuacan is the most nebulous of the great cultures of Mesoamerica because it has had the misfortune to be seen through Aztec glasses. Whenever television has a program on the Aztecs, Montezuma's soldiers are seen scrambling over the pyramids of Teotihuacan. To explain Teotihuacan religion, guides at the site retell Aztec myths. Well-read intellectuals on both

Fig. 1 Stone carving of a goddess(?) with nosebar and birds in her headdress. Found in the Calle de los Muertos Complex excavations under the direction of Rubén Cabrera Castro in 1982 (after Berrin 1988: 71, fig. III 25b).

Abstraction and the Rise of a Utopian State

sides of the Atlantic routinely refer to "Teotihuacan of the Aztecs" (Baudrillard 1988: 51). This view is not limited to laymen, but its reverberations still occur among scholars specializing in Mesoamerica. It goes back to the early interpretive work of Eduard Seler (1915), who was a great Aztec scholar and saw Teotihuacan as merely early Aztec. It has been continued in the influential work of Alfonso Caso (1966). My early work on iconography was firmly in that tradition (Pasztory 1974, 1976).

The arguments for Aztec-Teotihuacan continuity are present, but very limited. Tenochtitlan and Teotihuacan were both great cities in the same ecological area, dealing with some similar practical problems of agriculture and daily life. They were both planned on a grid and similarly oriented. Both of these features, however, could be the result of the Aztec copying of Teotihuacan and not necessarily the survival of a tradition. Moreover, the political situation, demographic pattern, and land use were vastly different. Although some deities, most prominently Tlaloc, are found in both cultures, most of the Postclassic pantheon is missing at Teotihuacan, and most Teotihuacan beings, such as the net jaguar, are missing in the Aztec sacred image system. There is a similarity in the picture writing systems, but it is no more specifically Aztec rather than Mixtec, and it may be no more than a shared Central Mexican system (see Berlo 1989). The Aztecs are known to have adopted many of the customs of the settled peoples they conquered, which may have included elements ultimately of Teotihuacan derivation, but at present it is nearly impossible to determine what these are.

Recent research has continued to erode the specificity of the connections between Teotihuacan and the Aztecs (Pasztory 1988a; Umberger 1987). Evidently, the Aztecs were very much interested in the ruins and monuments of Teotihuacan, which they imitated in works of their own. Their fascination, however, does not display inside knowledge. It seems that Teotihuacan was something of a mystery to the Aztecs, and they made up their own legends to explain its presence and what its connection might be to them. These legends therefore tell us a great deal about the Aztecs, but very little about Teotihuacan.

SEMIOTIC ANALYSIS

Rather than following the path of elusive continuities with the Aztecs, I have decided to focus on what was unique about Teotihuacan, what did not outlast its fall and collapse, and what made Teotihuacan different both from the Aztecs and from their contemporary neighbors. I am not the first to note many of these features, but I bring them together in a new general interpretation. In the absence of texts I have chosen to interpret the material remains semiotically, much as Roland Barthes (1982) interprets chopsticks as representatives of Oriental ethos and practice. He does not do it by analyzing the

Esther Pasztory

Oriental literature or oral commentary on the subject, trying to look at the material from the inside, but as a Frenchman looking at it from the outside. His analysis is based on the overall structure of the activity of eating, on the level that is usually taken for granted and accepted unconsciously in society. In this passage he compares Oriental and Occidental approaches:

> At the Floating Market in Bangkok, each vendor sits in a tiny motionless canoe, selling minuscule quantities of food. . . . From himself to his merchandise, including his vessel, everything is *small*. Occidental food, heaped up, dignified, swollen to the majestic, linked to a certain operation of prestige, always tends towards the heavy, the grand, the abundant, the copious; the Oriental follows the converse movement, and tends toward the infinitesimal. . . . The harmony between Oriental food and chopsticks cannot be merely functional, instrumental. The foodstuffs are cut up so they can be grasped by the sticks, but also the chopsticks exist because the foodstuffs are cut into small pieces; one and the same movement, one and the same form transcends the substance and its utensil: division . . . [the chopsticks] . . . in order to divide, must separate, part, peck, instead of cutting, and piercing, in the manner of our implements; they never violate the foodstuff: either they gradually unravel it . . . or else prod it into separate pieces . . . thereby rediscovering the natural fissures of the substance . . . by chopsticks food becomes no longer prey to which one does violence . . . but a substance harmoniously transferred." (Barthes 1982: 15–18)

Semiotic analysis reveals unconscious patterns of cultural structuring that are usually not the subject of discourse within the culture. Therefore the lack of verbal or textual information is not an insurmountable obstacle, as it is for the recovery of myths and legends. We may discuss whether we want to serve Beef Wellington or a leg of lamb for a dinner party, but we are unlikely to discuss the fact that our culture has selected large roasts as appropriate for such occasions, since that is a cultural fact that has been internalized and "naturalized." We assume that it is normal. Semiotic analysis is potentially of great value for the reconstruction of the lifeways of archaeological cultures where no texts or language remain.

My aim is to reconstruct Teotihuacan from the point of view of an outsider. I shall do this on the basis of the structuring principles, selections, omissions, forms, and signs chosen in their works of art and architecture. My assumption is that built into all objects is an implicit and perhaps largely unconscious expression of beliefs about the nature of the world, society, and man's place in it. This can be reconstructed without ever knowing the actual

Abstraction and the Rise of a Utopian State

names of deities, cult practices, or myths, the specificity of which may be forever lost to us.

Semiotic analysis is usually used to tear apart works of Western art and literature in order to reveal a vast ocean of underlying meanings beneath the apparent conventional meanings. Lacking conventional meanings, I am going to use semiotic analysis to *create* underlying meanings for the culture of Teotihuacan. The surprise in this analysis is that underlying meanings may be more detailed and specific than one would think and can suggest very specific historical and descriptive possibilities. As a result of this analysis, Teotihuacan emerged for me with a new and in some ways unexpected character profile. Some of these characteristics contradict what we know about Teotihuacan from other sources such as archaeology. Rather than smoothing these over and trying to make them fit, I prefer to allow the contradictions to exist. Contradictions reveal areas of great interest, still little understood.

I am aware of the dangers of this approach, for there is no outside body of material to turn to for support or proof. After all, even Roland Barthes often turns to the medium of *haiku* poetry, to corroborate his perceptions of the Orient. Data from archaeological excavations can sometimes be used to confirm or deny propositions derived from works of art, but there is no foolproof way to circumvent circular reasoning. The only tests that I can see for this kind of interpretation are internal coherence, parsimoniousness of explanation of the existing facts, and predictive value. If new and very different works fit into the paradigm, this may be a "proof" that it works. For example, the discovery of the Calle de los Muertos Complex sculpture, the iconography of which is close to that of the Goddesses defined before, confirms the validity of that classification (Fig. 1). It does not, however, confirm the interpretation of that class of images as "the Goddess." Interpretation is still a matter of judicious judgment forged out of intangibles such as one's basic concepts of how art and society operate, how one draws connections between facts and insights, or a subjective "feel" for the material.

SALIENT AND UNIQUE ASPECTS OF TEOTIHUACAN

The most striking aspect of Teotihuacan that did not outlast the fall of the city is that nearly everyone in the Valley of Mexico resided in the great city. People were not distributed in hierarchically related hamlets, villages, small towns, major towns, and a capital city, as in Aztec times (Sanders, Parsons, and Santley 1979). Teotihuacan was one huge city with the hinterland only sparsely populated. After A.D. 200, this concentration of population lived in masonry apartment compounds (R. Millon 1973, 1981). About 2,000 apartment compounds have been mapped by René Millon's project (Cowgill, personal communication, 1987). Evidently they varied in size and layout, but certain patterns suggest that a norm or ideal type was in the mind of the original planners (Figs. 2, 3). More than half of the apartments are roughly 60 m². Although fewer than a dozen have been partly or fully excavated, certain features are common. They had walled exteriors with few entrances and central patios with a shrine or a temple (Fig. 4). Each of the family apartments consisted of rooms arranged around an atrium. The foundations reveal that early in the life of the compound someone usually received an impressive burial, and this individual may have been of high status at the

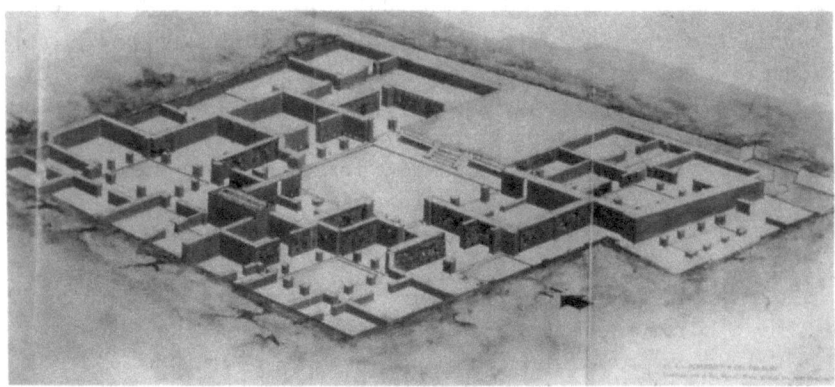

Fig. 2 Zacuala apartment compound plan and isometric rendering (after Séjourné 1959: fig. 8).

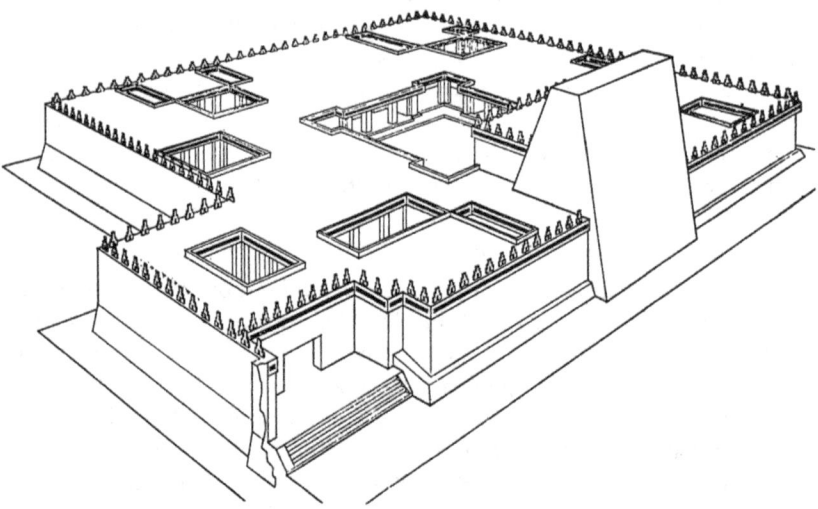

Fig. 3 Zacuala apartment compound, elevation drawing showing entrance and street (after Séjourné 1959: fig. 8).

Abstraction and the Rise of a Utopian State

time of the building of the compound. Otherwise, the subfloor burials indicate that the inhabitants of a compound had varying status from great to quite humble (Sempowski n.d.). Status differences were also great between some compounds in different parts of the city. In their structure the compounds exhibit a uniformity of a basic apartment compound concept and a variety that suggests the importance of adapting the overall concept to a given family situation or other practical matters.

Most remarkable about the apartment compounds is the fact that solidly built masonry structures were erected for the large majority of the city dwellers. These compounds were first thought to be "palaces" because their spacious patios and rooms seemed good enough for any Mesoamerican elite (Séjourné 1959). No other common people in Mesoamerican history lived in such houses. Until about A.D. 200, the population of Teotihuacan lived in more modest semi-perishable dwellings that were presumably razed when the decision to build the apartment compounds was made. Such housing is unique to Teotihuacan and indicates something about its social and political structure: most of the population of the city lived in nearly "palatial" dwellings.

A second, highly significant aspect of the apartment compounds is that these dwellings housed multi-family groups of sixty to a hundred individuals. Both before and after Teotihuacan, the population of the Valley of Mexico preferred to live in more dispersed, smaller family groups. The large number of people within a single dwelling and the permanent architectural

Fig. 4 Yayahuala apartment compound, central patio and shrine.

form of the compound suggest that the material remains may reflect a highly organized social unit. It is my hypothesis that these apartment/compound social units may have had political rights and obligations of significance in the overall structure of Teotihuacan. Besides the apartment compound, its associated sociopolitical system also disappeared after its collapse. Teotihuacan must have provided economic and political incentive for people to live crowded in one large city, and, within the city, in highly structured multi-family dwellings. These features lead me to believe that Teotihuacan might have been a very organized and integrated city in which the apartment compounds played a crucial role. By contrast, Aztec cities were much more loosely structured, with what seems to be more room for mobility and competition within and between cities. In fact, as I will suggest, internal organization was one of the major preoccupations of the city of Teotihuacan and one of the purposes of the symbolic communication coded in its works of art.

I am going to suggest that Teotihuacan was a culture with a utopian view of the world, in which the individual was de-emphasized for the sake of the group, but in which the citizen members enjoyed high status and material benefits as a part of the group. Teotihuacan, in my view, was a Mesoamerican social and religious experiment in the creation of a society that did not glorify a divine king and warrior aristocracy above a farming people. The Teotihuacan concept of the utopian city included the entire population living in the same type of dwellings all within view of the great pyramids. I shall present some aspects of this hypothesis on the basis of some features of Teotihuacan art and by a re-examination of the nature of its religion.

ABSTRACTION IN ART AND UTOPIAN VISION

The art style of Teotihuacan is as unique as the apartment compounds. Teotihuacan had the most abstract style in all of Mesoamerican history (Fig. 5). I shall define *abstraction* as the tendency to reduce forms to geometric simplicity, such as the circle or the square, and to render the physical world flat and two-dimensional rather than to create the illusion of three-dimensionality and naturalistic appearance. Abstraction does not mean the lack of identifiable figures or a subject; it is a way of rendering images. Abstraction at Teotihuacan results in an art that is ornamental and symbolic and in which the aim of the artist is not to recreate a perceptual equivalent of the natural world. These features have long been noted, but their significance has not been analyzed in relation to the city. I have suggested previously that this abstract style was on some level an intentional cultural choice by Teotihuacan (Pasztory n.d.). It was a way in which they expressed their rejection of the naturalistic, more organically structured traditions of the Olmec, Izapan, Maya, and Monte Alban cultures. These southern traditions were familiar not just through the many

Abstraction and the Rise of a Utopian State

Fig. 5 Colossal stone carving of a goddess, possibly that of Water. Ht. 3.90 m, wt. 22 tons. National Museum of Anthropology, Mexico City. Photo courtesy of Instituto Nacional de Antropología e Historia, reg. no. 6-0168.

well-documented "visits" to other cities, but very likely through monuments not far from the Valley of Mexico such as Chalcatzingo in Morelos, where Olmec monumental sculpture could be seen in three dimensions as well as in relief (Fig. 6). Someone in Teotihuacan times visited the caves of Chalcatzingo and left Teotihuacan style paintings on its walls (Apostolides 1987: 193) (Fig. 7). Teotihuacan clearly differentiated itself from its neighbors by negating their naturalistic artistic canons. They could have tried to relate themselves to some great earlier culture or people, such as the Olmec, but did not do so, unlike the Maya who made much of their Olmec connection in reworking heirloom jades, or the Aztecs who imitated both Toltec and Teotihuacan sculpture and architecture in order to link themselves with the cultures of the past.

Although we cannot know exactly why the people of Teotihuacan chose to turn toward abstraction in art, similar situations elsewhere may supply a clue. Whenever a form of abstraction in art supplants a naturalistic tradition, some of the arguments for it have been the same. In Western art history there have been two such times, once when Early Christian art supplanted the Classical tradition in the first centuries of the Christian era, and the other when the Modernist movement began at the end of the nineteenth century and may be currently ending in Postmodernism (Figs. 8, 9). In both of these highly dissimilar situations, abstraction was a conscious and emphatic negation of naturalism that was seen as somehow being "degenerate" or empty and inappropriate to a new social or religious situation. Abstraction was presented by its spokesmen as a style of greater purity, spirituality, almost a kind of Platonic ideal being. Plato himself criticized the naturalistic Greek art of his own time as representing false values in its emphasis on reality and transience. He much preferred Egyptian art for being closer to unchanging ideals (Gombrich 1960: 126).

Fig. 6 Olmec-style carved seated figure, excavated at Chalcatzingo, Monument 16. National Museum of Anthropology, Mexico City (after Grove 1987: figs. 9, 18).

Fig. 7 Teotihuacan-style paintings found in Cave 19 at Chalcatzingo (after Grove 1987: figs. 12, 45).

Abstraction and the Rise of a Utopian State

Fig. 8 (*left*) Mosaic of Empress Theodora, San Vitale, Ravenna, A.D. ca. 540–547.

Fig. 9 (*right*) Woman with Statuette. Fernand Leger, 1925, oil on canvas, 62 × 50 cm. Collection of Yvonne Zervos (after Zervos 1952: 23).

In medieval European art, excessive realism in depiction had to be avoided because it was an affront to God to rival his act of creation in images. This idea was expressed by Augustine in *De doctrina christiana*, A.D. 426 (Shaw 1983: 592). The Modernist drive to abstraction is still being debated, but its fundamental aim is seen by some as a reaction against an earlier aristocratic tradition and a degenerate classicizing style inappropriate to the vision of a capitalist, industrial, and democratic culture. The art associated with the Russian revolution, for example, was abstract in its initial phases in order to express the concepts of a communist utopia to come (Barron 1980: 15). Besides the presentation of abstraction as a purity that is something of a moral force, it was also presented by its spokesmen as a form of rational and intellectual order that was contrasted to the disorder of naturalism. Medieval art focused on the spirituality of Christianity and life after death rather than this life, while Modernist art focused on a utopian vision of progress, technological modernization, egalitarianism, and democracy. For inspiration, Modernist art sought to go back even to primitive roots. Although the Modernist aesthetic and ethic was held at first with nearly religious fervor only by an avant garde, subsequently it became the style of the elite and of official culture in the capitalist West (Foster 1985: 157–210).

Because the art of Teotihuacan is predominantly religious, I will suggest that abstraction at Teotihuacan was first and foremost a negation of other Mesoamerican traditions and that Teotihuacan once had a powerful religion with a message in which the ideas of some kind of higher purity was combined with concepts of rational order and organization. Teotihuacan may have been built as a utopian city putting into practice a cosmic vision of the world that was entirely new in the history of Mesoamerica and that did not outlast its collapse.

I am using the word *utopian* in a literal sense. The concept of a Utopia, or of a perfectly ordered social world built all at once from a conceptual plan, is, in European thought, first given expression in Thomas More's book, *Utopia,* published in 1516, which is based in part on the exciting discovery of the New World by Columbus, and also on Plato's *Republic.* More and Plato contrast their rational, centrally organized, and partially egalitarian states with the aristocratic and unjust states of their day. Because of the discovery of the New World and the chance for Europeans to build a more perfect high civilization on virgin territory, utopian ideas were very popular in the sixteenth century. Both the settlers in the United States and the countries of Latin America were at one time or another inspired by Utopian principles. Jean Baudrillard (1988) sees the United States as the practical fulfillment of European economic and political utopian dreams on American soil. In Latin America, though the dreams were not necessarily democratic, they were still utopian in the sense of a more rational government. Thus, many colonial cities were built on a grid plan to avoid the haphazard plan of the irregularly developed cities of Europe, and to create an appropriate physical context for what might be a better life in the New World. I am suggesting that the grid layout and plan of the city of Teotihuacan is a material representation of some kind of rational social planning that may be characterized as utopian—by which I mean something that was thought to be better, more organized, or more appropriate than what had existed before. Obviously, Teotihuacan's vision was not secular humanist, but the vision of a perfectly ordered world couched in religious terms consistent with the development of early states throughout the world (Wheatley 1971).

THE IDEAL: DEPERSONALIZATION AND STANDARDIZATION

The second remarkable feature of Teotihuacan representation in art is that more than half of the imagery deals with signs and animals rather than humans and, when humans are present, they are entirely depersonalized. Most striking is the absence of a public dynastic art, like the Olmec heads, Maya stelae, or the Monte Alban conquest reliefs. In Aztec art, too, Tizoc, Ahuitzotl, and Montezuma II were frequently represented on public monu-

Abstraction and the Rise of a Utopian State

ments either as persons or by their glyphs. At Teotihuacan, both portraiture and named individuals are lacking, except in rare instances towards the end of Teotihuacan when its communal structure may have begun to break down. Clara Millon (1988) discusses several figures from Techinantitla with tassel headdresses that suggest their elite status and the glyphs, that may be their names in front of them (Fig. 10). So far, these are still the exception rather than the rule. Moreover, despite the glyphs, the profile figures themselves are identical, just like all the other so-called priest figures in Teotihuacan representation.

Fig. 10 Figures wearing tassel headdresses with emblems or glyphs in front of them, from the Techinantitla apartment compound (after Berrin 1988: 116, figs. V3, V4).

As individualism and portraiture are lacking in representation, so is narrative. Figures do not interact as they do in Olmec and Maya art. Representations do not tell a story either of the human or the divine realm. Evidently the idea that is being negated at Teotihuacan with such vigor is the institution of the semi-divine dynastic ruler. The animus toward a personality cult is so great, that, in fact, the human element itself is played down. It is metaphorically represented by symbols and animals or by a limited repertory of human types. With a couple of minor exceptions, Teotihuacan human figures in two-dimensional art never look out and engage the viewer, but are always in profile. The frontal position is reserved for deities. Whenever humans and deities are shown together, the humans are always second in importance. Teotihuacan depersonalization in art has two aspects; one is the avoidance of the powerful individual ruler, and the other is the general de-emphasis on the human in favor of symbolic expression or the divine.

I have begun with what Teotihuacan art is not, because I believe that a major aspect of this tradition *was* a negation of the traditions of others. Teotihuacan art also represents a positive ideal of the universe and man's role in it. Rather than focusing on a unique and individual dynastic ruler or on other human individuals, Teotihuacan develops the concept of the "collective persona" in a variety of new types of objects. The famous Teotihuacan mask is a prime object of this collective persona (Fig. 11). These masks would have looked less blank with their inlaid eyes and teeth that are now generally gone, but the horizontal eyes, flat cheeks, and abruptly cut off foreheads represent a remote and stylized being. The open mouths and projecting lips are the most dramatic features of the faces and indicate, as I will discuss later, the importance of oral expression. There are more masks from Teotihuacan than from any other Mesoamerican culture,

Fig. 11 Green serpentine mask. Ht. 21.6 cm, w. 20.5 cm. B-54.TS Dumbarton Oaks, Washington, D.C.

Abstraction and the Rise of a Utopian State

and I think that is no accident. The mask is Teotihuacan's ideal form, in that it is something that hides the individuality of the wearer by an outward facade of impersonal uniformity. The emotional effect that masks suggest, which may be the ideal of the Teotihuacan collective persona, is calm and withdrawn. Paul Westheim's (1965: 142, 143) prescient analysis of the masks of Teotihuacan prefigures these conclusions, although he wrote at a time when too little was known about Teotihuacan to anchor his visual interpretation. These masks are not worn over the face, they are substitutes for the face. It is frustrating that we do not know more about the archaeological contexts of masks. They are generally believed to be funerary, yet of the three found by archaeologists, none were in burials. The large ones excavated by Rubén Cabrera Castro come from corridors within palace administrative temple areas, such as the Ciudadela (Cabrera, Rodriguez, and Morelos 1982a, 1982b). With the exception of the small mask fragment excavated by Sigvald Linné at Xolalpan (Linné 1934: fig. 275), they are not found in apartment compounds. I have suggested elsewhere that the masks were a part of composite deity images dressed in cloth and feathers and perhaps associated with the temples (Pasztory 1988b). Because so many of them were found by looters at the end of the nineteenth and the beginning of the twentieth centuries, I suggest that they come from the temple structures lining the Avenue and from other highly visible buildings.

Besides their impersonality, Teotihuacan masks are known for their standardized and repeated forms. Such standardization in art is an expression of what, for Teotihuacan, appears to have been an ideal of collective uniformity. This is evident also in the misnamed "portrait" figurines that consist of identical mold-made heads set up on individual handmade bodies (Barbour n.d.) (Fig. 12). There is something quite strange in the combination of the dancing or otherwise contorted figures and these uniform, mask-like faces. Although we have no clear idea of what people did with these figures—possibly they dressed them up and put something in their curved hands—their structure is eloquent. They express visually something that may have been very important at Teotihuacan: a recognition of human vitality and variability on which a social mask of uniformity is superposed.

THE REAL: INDIVIDUAL VARIATION AND ETHNIC HETEROGENEITY

The structure of the portrait figurines suggests that the masks of uniformity are an ideal and not necessarily a reality. This can be related to what we know of the population of the city. All lines of inquiry suggest a heterogeneous center. This heterogeneity goes back to its early growth and is a feature of its later history. The explosive growth of the city in the Patlachique and Tzacualli periods is coeval with the general depopulation of other centers in the Valley and suggests the immigration of large groups of people to Teotihuacan (Cowgill n.d.). René Millon (1981: 235) suggests that they

Fig. 12 "Portrait" figurine. Head mold-made, body handmade, clay. Museum of the American Indian, New York.

went there in part on a religious mission to build the great pyramids. The point that I wish to make here is that these people need not all have been ethnically or even linguistically the same, and some of this variability may have been accepted so long as they fitted into the evolving religious and political system of Teotihuacan.

The Pyramids of the Sun and Moon are actually three temple complexes, with two small pyramids enclosing a plaza in front of the major structure. More than twenty-three temple complexes have been mapped, and many of them go back to the Tzacualli period. They vary in size and perhaps were arranged hierarchically in terms of importance, beginning with the Pyramid of the Sun. Elsewhere, I have suggested the possibility that these three temple complexes might correspond to some kind of city division of the population, perhaps even going back to the founding of the city and the different groups that came together to build it (Pasztory 1988b). They might reflect the presence of a variety of different social groups at Teotihuacan of

Abstraction and the Rise of a Utopian State

possibly different origins who were not necessarily blended into a "melting pot" but whose differences may have been maintained and perhaps even built into the political structure of the city. Even if these groups were not ethnically different, the presence of three temple complexes suggests a decentralized pattern of ritual organization. It has been suggested that in later times the population of Teotihuacan may have remained high only with the help of immigration from the outside. Because of the presence of high infant mortality found in some excavations, it has been argued that immigration may have been essential for the life of the city (Storey 1985). Therefore, some of those "family" members in the multi-family apartment compounds need not have been blood relations. Excavations have shown districts of Oaxaca individuals in the west (see Spence, this volume) and possibly Maya or Veracruz traders in the east. Teotihuacan was, then, at all times a diverse and heterogeneous city, and the vision of collective uniformity suggested by the masks and the art style is apparently an ideal. The structure of the portrait figurines indicates further that Teotihuacan was aware of and gave expression to the interplay of variability and uniformity in its own makeup.

THE CONTINUITY OF PRECLASSIC POPULAR RITUAL

The portrait figurine is remarkable for another reason: at the time that it was made, in the Xolalpan period, A.D. 400–600, few people in Mesoamerica were making small clay figurines. In many areas, such as the Maya region and Oaxaca, figurine manufacture was common in the Preclassic period and related to popular cult activity. By the Classic period, however, they stopped being made in some areas, such as Lowland Maya, and although we do not know what exactly happened, their absence coincides with the development of the elite and dynastic ruler cult. Although Teotihuacan avoids dynastic imagery, it continues a tradition of popular origin embodied in the figurine cult. Although we do not know exactly what was done with the figurines, they are usually found in household contexts that suggest family altars or curing rituals, after which the objects were discarded. Figurines continued to be made in the millions for apparently similar purposes throughout the life of the city.

Besides the figurines, two other ritual objects at Teotihuacan derive from the traditions of the earlier centers in the Valley of Mexico: Storm God vessels and Old Man braziers (Figs. 13, 14). The braziers are associated later with the central altars of the apartment compounds. The Storm God vessels are often modest objects frequent in burials. Neither of these objects is aristocratic or visually refined. Although Teotihuacan does not seek to associate itself with any great earlier dynasties and their arts, it preserves a very clear link with the popular, non-elite traditions of the Valley of Mexico.

Fig. 13 Storm God Vessel, terracotta. Museum für Völkerkunde, Vienna, reg. no. 4829.

Fig. 14 Brazier supported on the head of an "Old God," stone. Teotihuacan Regional Museum (after *Masterworks of Mexican Art*, 1963).

Abstraction and the Rise of a Utopian State

DIAGRAMS: A PREOCCUPATION WITH STRUCTURAL RELATIONS

Maya art at its height in the eighth and ninth centuries developed narrative representations in murals, reliefs, and vase painting. At Teotihuacan the cultural and artistic emphasis was usually not on narrative, but rather on the representation of structural relations. The Teotihuacan form is something like a diagram that can express visually both social and cosmic relationships. The plan of the city is, of course, the basic Teotihuacan diagram in which the relationship of the individual to apartment compound, neighborhood, and local and central temples is clearly marked. This plan was probably created as an image of cosmic order, and its geometric rigidity expresses its diagrammatic purpose. To put it another way, the people of Teotihuacan were living in a huge diagram, and in the first two centuries of the existence of the city there was little in the way of visual arts besides architecture and the modest figurines, braziers, and vessels, which continued the forms of pre-Teotihuacan prototypes at least in permanent media.

The wealth and flourishing of the city in the Tlamimilolpa and Xolalpan periods were not manifested in great religious building programs, but in the building of apartment compounds. These are visually and architecturally codifications of the relationships of the inhabitants to one another and to the center. Coeval with the apartment compounds is the invention of the ceramic incense burner, often found associated with the central altars or courtyards of apartment compounds and perhaps replacing, duplicating, or elaborating on the function and meaning of the Old God censers (Fig. 15). These ceramic censers are unlike the Old Man censers and the Storm God vessels in being complex and sophisticated creations. Their sophistication, however, is entirely in the realm of structural relations. On the first, cursory glimpse, the censer seems to represent a person peering out of the temple doorway, which, if it was like the temple represented in the murals of Tetitla (A. Miller 1973: fig. 317) we can reconstruct in general form. Reading the censer thus is to interpret it naturalistically and anthropomorphically. A second glance, however, denies this reading. The "face" turns out to be a separate mask, clearly attached to the chimney in the back (Fig. 16). There is no way to know how this was seen by the people of Teotihuacan. My argument is that an ambiguity between a naturalistic and a diagrammatic representation is built into the visual structure of the censers. This approach is the opposite of that of the urns of Monte Alban in which the effigy is so anthropomorphized that we are hardly aware it is an urn and not a sculpture. (When these censers were recreated in Escuintla for a population that had some link with Teotihuacan culture but was not basically Teotihuacan in character, the masks had a tendency to become more like the face of a person, and some censers became more like effigy urns [Berlo 1984].) The insistence on the use of the disembodied mask is therefore thoroughly Teotihuacan and unique to it (Fig. 17).

Fig. 15 Composite ceramic censer, front view. Teotihuacan Regional Museum. Photo courtesy of INAH.

Fig. 16 Composite ceramic censer, back view. Teotihuacan Regional Museum, storeroom.

Abstraction and the Rise of a Utopian State

Fig. 17 Clay mask originally from a composite ceramic censer. National Museum of Anthropology, Mexico City.

The signs surrounding the mask on the frame were individually made in molds in great quantities and a large variety. They were either glued on separately, or once a selection was made, they were fired with the censer. (The *adornos* and the censer are often made from different clays, which is proof that even in their manufacture, they were treated as assembled objects. The clay of the censers often is more solid, while the *adornos* may be made of lesser quality [Berlo 1982].) The purpose of making the censer and *adornos* separately can only have been to provide variety within a standardized structural format. Which masks and symbols were selected and how they were put together may have expressed the nature of the being represented, as suggested by Janet Berlo (1983a, 1982), or it may have expressed the aspect of the being important for the group, such as the members of the apartment compound. Most censers seem to represent the Goddess or animal impersonations such as birds and butterflies. This suggests that the worship of the Great Goddess may have been universal, but that her relation to each compound was different. The censer is an object in which many small pieces are brought together to create a whole—like the many apartment compounds that make up the city. The vision of the inner sanctum is a mask, which may stand for the image of the gods in the great temples of the center of the city. On a structural level the censer may represent the relationship of one segment of the community to the whole. Teotihuacan may have had only few deities worshiped by all, but in ways appropriate and different in each group. The emphasis seems to have been as much on the groups worshiping them as on the deities. In terms of relationships presented, the censers suggest an ideal harmony that is based on three important Teotihuacan values: hierarchy (the placement of the large mask in the center); individual variety (the selection of *adornos*); and order (the placement of the *adornos* in various sets in horizontal and vertical relationships). The image created is a three dimensional diagram. The metaphor for harmony is not the organic integration of the biological body, as in naturalistic representation, but the geometric relationships discovered between things as in abstraction.

HIDING MEANINGS: WRITING VS. SPEECH

The face of the being within the censer is hard to see. The mask is placed deep inside, overshadowed by the frame, and the mouth of the mask is further hidden by a large nosebar (see Fig. 15). We know that this is a mask, and that there is nothing behind it other than the chimney. The nosebar is worn in Teotihuacan art by a wide variety of humans and deities, and it is one of its most distinctive items of costume and insignia. The nosebar comes in a variety of angular shapes, and its effect is to blot out the mouths of figures, much as the black bars cut out the features of criminals in newspapers. On a structural level the hiding of the mouth suggests a cutting off of speech and communication. The conclusion I have finally come to is that one of the reasons that we have had so much trouble reconstructing the nature of life and thought at Teotihuacan, is precisely because Teotihuacan has been of little help. Teotihuacan as a culture and in its art seems to have been uninterested in communicating much about itself to the outside world, other than its gigantic architecture and cosmic layout. It is not just that we scholars are particularly dense when it comes to Teotihuacan—Teotihuacan was not an exhibitionistic civilization; perhaps it was even a secretive one. We will eventually have to square this feature of Teotihuacan with the evidence of its widespread presence in Classic Mesoamerica, because, while in some ways they may have been reaching out, in others they apparently wished to remain hidden.

On one relief the Goddess is represented entirely without a face, only with ornaments, including the nosebar and earplugs, reduced to geometric abstractions that are arranged so as to suggest a face (Fig. 18). In the painting of the Goddess at Tetitla (see Berlo, this volume, fig 2), it is not clear what is a mask and what is a face. One gets the sense of something being hidden, secret, kept back, not said. Hiding is also evident in architecture. *Adosadas,* small pyramid platforms, were placed at the foot of the great pyramids thus effectively "hiding" what would be the beginning of the stairway and either displacing it to the sides, or creating an alternative access on the *adosada* stairs until the actual pyramid stairs are reached, one level further in the back. Thus the actual pyramid stairways are set in deeper, like the mask in the censer. On the Pyramid of the Sun this was done in Miccaotli times, while on the Pyramid of the Moon, in Tlamimilolpa times. This suggests that the notion of hiding and distancing devices were being developed in the course of Teotihuacan history and were not necessarily there from the beginning.

Abstraction and the Rise of a Utopian State

Fig. 18 Stone relief, possibly an *almena* or roof ornament. Ht. approx. 20 in. Teotihuacan site museum.

The Temple of the Feathered Serpent is a special case in that its *adosada* built in the Tlamimilolpa period hides most of the earlier pyramid, so that most of the magnificently carved heads were invisible (Fig. 19). Although this extreme example was probably a political move and hid a temple perhaps associated with excessive centralization or even personal rule, the tradition of *adosadas* goes back to early times. No other culture in Mesoamerica placed *adosadas* in front of its pyramid stairways. The apartment compounds, too, with their high walls and few entrances suggest a preoccupation with privacy and with the marking of boundaries between groups. Their beautiful mural paintings, their spacious and attractive patios appear to be available by invitation only. It has been suggested by several scholars that Teotihuacan might have been a place of pilgrimage for Mesoamerica as a whole or that it disseminated certain religious ideas (R. Millon 1981: 228–231). I am struck by the fact that one strong aspect of Teotihuacan art was apparently concerned with denying access, with holding back, with privacy, and perhaps even with secrecy. Based on this, I have trouble seeing Teotihuacan as a proselytizing society.

This issue of communication is directly related to the question of writing. Why is it that, unlike the Maya, Teotihuacan has only a few glyphs in its art and no tradition of public inscriptions? It is not that a system of glyphic notation was lacking, because there are enough examples of glyphs to indicate that writing, perhaps nearly as developed as that of the Aztecs, did exist (Berlo 1989; Langley, 1986; see also Langley, this volume). I have no doubt that the major reason for this is that Maya and Monte Alban hieroglyphic inscriptions are associated with dynastic rulers and their self-glorification. In

Fig. 19 *Adosada* platform in front of the Temple of the Feathered Serpents.

contrast, this was taboo at Teotihuacan. Perhaps at Teotihuacan writing was common in perishable media, such as codices. Teotihuacan was not interested in publicly proclaiming its story and recording it for posterity on monuments or in non-perishable media. As has been indicated above, Teotihuacan was not interested in narrative or history in any case, whether of texts or images. Glyphs, when they occur, are usually the names of things, people, or dates, but names and dates are not combined. Some of the most complex series of glyphs are to be found on the plants from Techinantitla where glyphs that were most likely the names of the plants are embedded in the trunks (Pasztory 1988b). We are still uncertain about the language spoken at Teotihuacan—Mixe Zoquean, Totonac, Nahuatl, and even Maya have been suggested (Brown, n.d.). Perhaps they spoke more than one language, and as Kelley (1983) has suggested, found picture writing particularly congenial because the same symbols could be pronounced in different languages. Given the Teotihuacan insistence on collectivity and uniformity, one language still must have been the privileged one used in political and religious discourse. Perhaps one day we shall determine which it was.

What Teotihuacan is interested in, however, is oral expression—speech, song, prayer, cries. One of the most ubiquitous images is the well-known speech scroll, simple or fancy, that emerges from the mouths of humans and

Abstraction and the Rise of a Utopian State

animals alike (Fig. 20). Many Teotihuacan mouths are shown open, like the masks, which once had inlaid teeth, as if suggesting the potential of oral expression. Why did Teotihuacan make so much of the representation of oral expression in visual form, which is a rather hard thing to do? If their purpose had been the communication of a specific message, glyphs and texts in visual form would have been a far simpler solution. The preference for speech scrolls over glyphs may be another aspect of the commitment to a collective, non-individualistic, non-dynastic view of the world. The emphasis on speech and oral expression suggests a small place, where people can talk to one another, and not a megalopolis. (Perhaps one impetus for the development of Maya hieroglyphic writing was the need for distant centers to communicate with one another.) I feel that the integration of the population of Teotihuacan was such that talking *was* possible, that in effect, though having built an urban center, they continued to act as though they were living in a small town. This would be consistent with the continuation of village cults such as figurines. At Teotihuacan, writing exists, but it is speech that is glorified in art. This speech is entirely local in character; it is among members of the group who know what they are saying, and it is not clarified for an outsider. One can decipher Maya hieroglyphic writing, but one cannot decipher most speech scrolls (Pasztory 1988b: 185–193). The images suggest that Teotihuacan silence and secretiveness can give way to speech, but that this speech has local meaning.

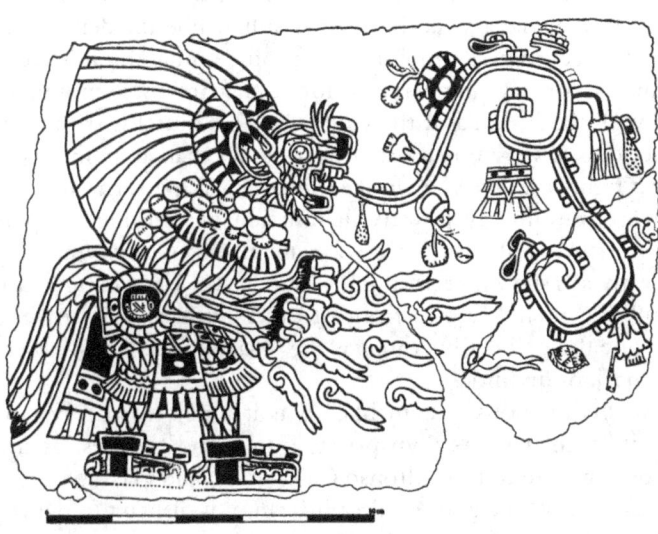

Fig. 20 Feline figure with elaborate speech scroll from the murals of Techinantitla (after Berrin 1988: fig. VI.15).

Esther Pasztory

On the basis of the analysis of some of the features of its art and architecture, I suggest that Teotihuacan as a culture was opposed to the dynastic cults, the naturalistic and anthropomorphic art styles, and the writing of the other great cultures in Mesoamerica, both earlier and contemporaneous. Instead, collective organization was writ large on an urban scale, and an art was developed that glorified an idealized collective persona and the structural relations demonstrating how many small parts made up the community. They were more interested in standardization and in mass production than in aesthetic refinement. Teotihuacan appears to have been the realization of the utopian vision of many small Preclassic communities that came together to form a city with the decision, however, to remain "preclassic" in some very important ways. In my view, Teotihuacan was primarily interested in itself, with its own internal affairs and its own social integration. Primary in this process was religion. Both the creation and maintenance of the Teotihuacan polity was based on religion, which took the place of the dynastic ruler cult in the cultures of the south.

THE NATURE OF TEOTIHUACAN RELIGION

The difference between the Teotihuacan and Maya relationship between the human and divine worlds can be illustrated by the comparison of Tikal stela 1 (Fig. 21) and the Temple of Agriculture mural (Fig. 22). The Maya ruler, Stormy Sky, is a large, heroic figure, while the deities are little creatures emerging from his ceremonial bar of office or climbing his back device. In effect, the Maya ruler is shown controlling the gods with power and confidence. On the Maya stela the ruler is still, while the deities scramble around. On the Teotihuacan mural small profile human figures are shown making offerings to large, impersonal forms that resemble mountains and are topped with the insignia of the Goddess. This mural is striking in that even the Goddess is shown in a set of two, rather than as an individualized figure. Elite figures are shown in Teotihuacan art performing scattering rituals that are presumably priestly in function or carrying weapons and dressed as warriors, but they are always members of anonymous groups and they are always shown performing service tasks. Human figures are not shown humbling themselves in front of other humans. The Aztecs were right about one thing: Teotihuacan was the "Place of the Gods." Men ruled behind the mask of divinities.

What was this religious system like? Was it a polytheistic system with separate gods, each with its own priests, idols, and temples, as in Aztec times? Despite the attempt by Alfonso Caso (1966) and Hasso von Winning (1987) to make lists of the gods of Teotihuacan, it is difficult to put together much of the pantheon of deities. It is impossible to come up with enough deities to be the patrons of the twenty *trecenas* of the ritual calendar. Many figures, such as the animal representations, appear to be allegorical and

Abstraction and the Rise of a Utopian State

metaphoric as George Kubler (1967) suggested, and not gods in the sense of spirits being worshiped. At Teotihuacan we know more about household rituals than about the state rituals. Most objects used were ritual vessels—the Storm god vessels were probably used to pour water, the Old Man and Goddess braziers were used to burn incense. None of these is an "idol" or necessarily a "worshiped image" in itself. What was done with the figurines is a mystery, except for the suggestions of use in curing or household altars. Generally, however, they too do not represent gods. The mural paintings are similarly problematic from the point of view of their function—most decorate the walls of apartment compounds. Although deities are a common subject, we do not know whether these rooms had sacred functions, like chapels. Perhaps the central patios and other areas of the apartment compounds had both sacred as well as residential functions. However, we still do not know whether the murals were merely a kind of background setting or decoration, or whether they functioned directly in any kind of religious activity.

What did they do in the state temples? Our information on this is almost nothing. Recent excavations have shown that there was one type of object restricted to the central shrines—large greenstone figures (Fig. 23). Such figures were found by Leopoldo Batres in 1905, collected by Cristos Dominik Bilimek for the Vienna Museum für Völkerkunde in the nineteenth century, and excavated in the 1980s by Rubén Cabrera Castro (Cabrera, Rodriguez, and Morelos 1982a, 1982b). Large greenstone blocks, from which other images might have been carved, have been found in the vicinity of the Calle de los Muertos Complex, presumably abandoned at the time of the fall of the city (Cabrera Castro, personal communication, 1984). Since about half of these large figures were naked, there is the possibility that once they wore cloth and feather garments like the deities in the murals. These figures may have been the precious central idols in the temples. As we now know them, however, they do not have enough iconographic traits to suggest any deity identification, only gender identification. We might conclude from this, that, as in the case of the ceramic censers, variability in the outfit of one figure might have been an important value. Another possibility of interpretation is that these greenstone figures were not deities but idealized ancestors of various social groups. Some of these large greenstone figures are Olmecoid in character and possibly some were ancient images venerated as heirlooms (Cabrera, Rodriguez, and Morelos 1982b: 115). Teotihuacan may have maintained a connection with some Olmec-related images, even if they bypassed the Olmec-style dynastic cult.

Walking down the Avenue at Teotihuacan, I was pondering again the presence of all the temples, large and small, that line it on both sides. If this had been Tenochtitlan, each temple would have been dedicated to a different god, from the goddess of salt to the god of the hunt. While these deities

Esther Pasztory

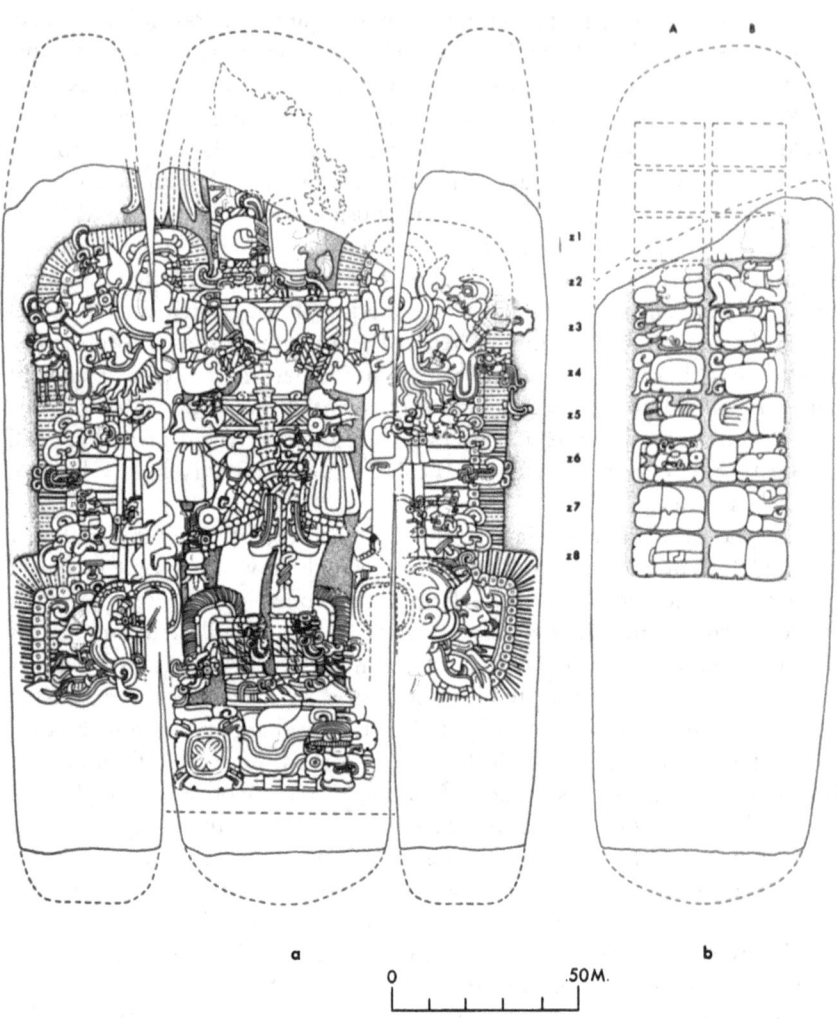

Fig. 21 Tikal stela 1, drawing (after Jones and Satterthwaite 1982: fig. 1).

Abstraction and the Rise of a Utopian State

Fig. 22 Temple of Agriculture Mural, Villagra copy. National Museum of Anthropology, storeroom.

Fig. 23 Greenstone figure. Ht. 46.5 cm, w. 20 cm. Museum für Völkerkunde, Vienna (after Becker-Donner 1965: pl. 11).

were worshiped particularly by certain groups—such as saltmakers and hunters—they were also keyed into the complex 260-day ritual cycle and the twenty monthly rituals each of which was dedicated to a deity. The richness of this system would be lost to us if we did not have the texts and the codices, but even if we consider merely Aztec stone sculpture, more deities are evident than in the art of Teotihuacan. At Teotihuacan, one gets the impression that essentially few gods were worshiped by everyone. These gods, however, could perhaps wear a different garb for different purposes. What seems to have been important was not the different gods, but the different groups of worshipers. If we examine religion not from the point of view of deities, but of the people worshiping them, then the material remains may be interpreted in other ways. The temples on the Avenue could have belonged to different social groups—lineages, territorial units—all of whose gods were basically the same. The ceramic censers suggest a similar commitment to the same deity, but by differentiated groups of people. I would not be surprised if Teotihuacan had some kind of structural arrangement between its temples and the social groups in the city somewhat like the complicated *ceque* system of the Inca in Cuzco, in which there was a shrine for every day of the year for which a given family was responsible.

WHY A GREAT GODDESS AND NOT A GREAT GOD?

Of the few gods that stand out at Teotihuacan, such as the Storm God, the Old Man of the stone braziers, a goggled war and sacrifice god (Pasztory 1974: 12–15), the most important is the Great Goddess. This importance is indicated by the fact that various animal figures and the Storm God are shown in a secondary position in relation to her. She is not shown in a secondary position to anyone; she appears to be a nature, water, fertility, and sustenance provider in a very broad sense. Despite my earlier identification of her as the equivalent of the Aztec fertility goddess Xochiquetzal, her characteristic image does not outlast the life of the city. An appropriate name for her would be the "Faceless Goddess," because in many representations she either lacks a face or her face is created by some kind of a mask (see Berlo, this volume, fig. 2). A nosebar hiding her mouth, a bird in her headdress, and a yellow and red zigzag band are her nearly standard attributes. She is an image of benevolence, for seeds, water, and jade treasures flow from her outstretched hands. (While her face is often not completely visible, her hands are, and often she is represented merely by isolated divine hands pouring gifts or holding symbols [A. Miller 1973: 146–150].) She does not talk; she gives. On some representations, watery scrolls emerge from her mouth. When the nosebar is removed, however, she shows rows of teeth that suggest something voracious, and her hands are sometimes exchanged for raptorial claws (Fig. 24). Warriors are also in her service, as the images of birds carrying her insignia and holding weapons indicate

Abstraction and the Rise of a Utopian State

Fig. 24 Emblematic representation of the Goddess with Clawed Hands. Techinantitla apartment compound. Ht. 66 cm, w. 107 cm. Staatliche Museen, Museum für Völkerkunde, Berlin (after Berrin 1988: fig. II 26).

(Pasztory 1988b: 168–181). Another name for her might be the "Ambivalent Goddess," because she seems to have creative as well as destructive aspects.

Why is this deity feminine? What has femininity to do with these qualities? For one thing, she is not feminine in any obvious way, such as having a sexual body. In fact, she is nearly asexual in appearance, and her femininity has been inferred from her and her attendants' costume and from symbols such as the spider in the Tepantitla mural prominently displayed above her head (Pasztory 1972). She has neither erotic nor motherly qualities. She is never shown nurturing children (although in one remarkable mural she is shown with a small, possibly baby net jaguar in her hands [Miller 1973: fig. 40]). Her relationship is entirely with the people of Teotihuacan, who give offerings to her, to whom she gives the gift of agriculture and riches, and at whom she bares her claws. She was probably a Great Mother whose children were the people of Teotihuacan.

It may be no accident that the heroes of the dynastic cult are male rulers, while the supreme deity of Teotihuacan is a goddess. The selection of a feminine figure perhaps assured a universal, nonpolitical, and nonpersonal image. Sherry Ortner (1974) has shown that women are universally seen as secondary to men by being closer to "nature" than to "culture." More precisely, women mediate between nature and culture, and in doing so often have an ambiguous role that may polarize symbolically into an evil witch/whore and a supremely benevolent madonna/mother. In this sense the benevolent concept of woman can actually transcend culture. In searching for a supreme symbol to whom everyone could rally, the cult of the female deity might have been an attractive choice. Perhaps the goddess lacks an individual face in the same way that we make the image of Justice (whom we personify as a woman) blindfolded; it might signify her invisible impartiality. Her femininity may also be comparable to our own practice of personifying various positive values with women, such as Justice, or Alma Mater. Columbia University's Alma Mater, for example, has a vacuous, nonindividualized expression because she represents a principle and not a being (Fig. 25). The patroness of the utopian vision of America, as the land of the free, is the colossal Statue of Liberty in New York harbor (Fig. 26). Most of our own public sculptures of men are individual great men, like Maya rulers, although, like Teotihuacan, generally we do not make monumental images of our presidents because our democratic ideology emerged in contrast to European monarchic traditions that did so honor its rulers. Feminine images seem to be called upon when principles of cohesion, integration, and unity are needed. Men appear to be too much associated with specificity, combativeness, individual action, and status to be able to play

Fig. 25 Alma Mater. Daniel Chester French, 1903. Bronze, Ht. 8 ft. Columbia University.

Abstraction and the Rise of a Utopian State

this cultural role as well as these womanly personifications. Teotihuacan embodied its values in a faceless, masked, or remote female image, above groups, factions, and politics. Her primary purpose was perhaps to be a symbol of integration for the city as a whole.

The choice of a major female deity for veneration is, at the same time, a turning away from a possible male choice and everything that implies. Like the avoidance of dynastic portraiture and historical inscriptions, the avoidance of a male supreme deity is in some ways a choice for the cosmic, the universal, the natural, in contrast to the historical, the particular, and the cultural. It is also worth noting that a universal female deity is a more remote and distant concept than a ruler who may be divine but still within a mortal body. Because the actual government of Teotihuacan was probably in the hands of men, the use of a feminine image tells us something about Teotihuacan's values and priorities.

We do not know the antiquity of the Great Goddess of Teotihuacan. Her image does not appear in art until the Tlamimilolpa period, and some of the early representations show her cryptically only by her headdress (Villagra

Fig. 26 Statue of Liberty. Auguste Bartholdi, 1886. Ht. 46 m (heel to top of head). New York Harbor.

Caleti 1971: 140, fig. 8). I suspect that her roots as a deity go back to the Preclassic period, and she may have been at Teotihuacan from the beginning, but was represented—if at all—only in perishable media, such as impersonator or deity costumes. It is also not out of the question that Teotihuacan might not have represented her in images in the first few centuries. There are enough indications that Teotihuacan had an iconoclastic streak in its make up, which might account for her facelessness or her representation only by a headdress. This is not uncommon in religions; a ban on the representation of the deity occurred both in Christianity and Buddhism in their early phases. In the Tlamimilolpa period the Great Goddess was finally represented in art more often, or, if the deity was new, she emerged at that time. In either case, the coincidence with the building of the apartment compounds suggests that at that time there might have been a need for a more powerful symbol of integration for the city as a whole. Images of her multiply in the final centuries of the life of the city. Towards the end of the history of Teotihuacan, when its collective structure may have been breaking down into personalized, rival factions, as illustrated by the murals with named personages, a huge image of her may have been begun. I agree with Hasso von Winning (1987, 2: 138–140) that the so-called Tlaloc of Coatlinchan was intended to be a colossal statue of the Great Goddess with the nosebar. It is tempting to infer that this image may have been carved as a symbolic attempt at fostering integration, and it may have been left unfinished due to the violent collapse of the temple center.

CONCLUSIONS

A semiotic analysis of some aspects of the art and architecture of Teotihuacan indicate four salient features: an opposition to the art and political structure of Southern Mesoamerica, a glorification of the Preclassic small town-village tradition of the Basin of Mexico, a preoccupation with the integration of a heterogeneous population through religion and symbolic imagery, and the development of a utopian ideology essential for the motivation of the building and the maintenance of the community over seven hundred years. Teotihuacan as a culture was opposed to the dynastic cult, individualism, naturalistic art style, and public inscriptions on monuments of the other great cultures in Mesoamerica both earlier and contemporaneous. Instead, Teotihuacan glorified the small town-village traditions of its origins as indicated by the continuation of the cult of figurines, Old God braziers, and Storm God vessels. Collective organization was writ large on an urban scale, and an abstract art style was developed that glorified an idealized collective persona as in the case of the masks. A major purpose of this art was to express visually the structural relations of the community and its many various parts, expressed most graphically in the composite censers. Hierarchy, variety, and order characterize this organization.

Abstraction and the Rise of a Utopian State

I see Teotihuacan being founded as a sacred city by individuals who began a powerful utopian religious ideology. This began in the Patlachique phase and found its fulfillment in the building of many three-temple complexes, including the Pyramids of the Sun and Moon in the Tzacualli phase. Although the nature of the deity or deities to whom they were dedicated are not known, the tenets of some of the ideology can be reconstructed from the art of the later periods. The two intertwining themes of Teotihuacan art at all times are earthly paradise and martial might. I suggest that the pyramid builders were convinced that they were creating a new utopian universe, in which a supreme deity (perhaps the Goddess) would provide a verdant paradise on earth. They were prepared to support this order with blood sacrifice and military activity.

One aspect of the ideology of this new Teotihuacan utopia appears to have been that it would not be run by and for divine kings and an aristocracy, but for the people as a whole as they were grouped in lineages or residential sectors. I imagine that these lineages or residential sectors were ranked and that the highest ranking provided the city with its priest-rulers who were expected to maintain a low personal profile, and in fact they did so for most of those seven hundred years. (One great exception may be a Miccaotli Period ruler [or faction] who built the Temple of the Feathered Serpent and whose burial, though not yet found, may be inside the pyramid, surrounded by scores of military dressed sacrifical victims that Rubén Cabrera Castro's recent excavations have brought to light [Sugiyama 1989]. Subsequently in the Tlamimilolpa Phase, Teotihuacan returned to its more collective rulership and covered that temple with the largest possible *adosada*.) With its grid plan, palatial dwellings, and participatory politics, Teotihuacan may have prided itself on having created a world based on rational organization, better attuned to the structure of the cosmos, than had its neighbors.

One of the most striking discoveries of this analysis was, for me, the view of a city preoccupied with itself and its own organization and surprisingly uninterested in the outside world. (Baudrillard [1988] levels a similar charge at modern America.) Why is it that the rulers of Tikal and Monte Alban claim Teotihuacan affiliation in their monuments, while Teotihuacan makes no such claims to any outsider in its art? Why is it that, despite the presence of Teotihuacan-related artificats in many parts of Mesoamerica, suggesting trade and even colonies, Teotihuacan is preoccupied with expressing concepts of privacy, silence, and non-communication at home? I suggest that Teotihuacan may have felt morally superior to its neighbors and guarded its traditions jealously. Perhaps sociopolitical integration was a hard task and had to be continuously worked on. Semiotic analysis breaks down at the point of reconstructing moral attitudes, but it seems likely to me that the religion of Teotihuacan had some lofty moral mission, for men are often

Esther Pasztory

more willing to build superhuman projects or die in battle for abstract principles, such as our concept of freedom, rather than for mere material benefits. Whatever this was at Teotihuacan, we cannot tell, because nosebars either hide their mouths or the speech scrolls issuing from them are blank.

BIBLIOGRAPHY

APOSTOLIDES, ALEX
 1987 Chalcatzingo's Painted Art. In *Ancient Chalcatzingo* (David C. Grove, ed.): 171–199. University of Texas Press, Austin.

BARBOUR, WARREN
 n.d. The Figurines and Figurine Chronology of Ancient Teotihuacan, Mexico. Ph.D. dissertation, Dept. of Anthropology, University of Rochester, 1976.

BARRON, STEPHANIE
 1980 The Russian Avant-Garde: A View from the West. In *The Avant Garde in Russia 1910–1930* (Stephanie Barron and Maurice Tuchman, eds.): 15. Los Angeles County Museum of Art.

BARTHES, ROLAND
 1982 *Empire of Signs*. Hill and Wang, New York.

BATRES, LEOPOLDO
 1906 *Teotihuacan*. Fidencio S. Soria, Mexico, D.F.

BAUDRILLARD, JEAN
 1988 *America*. Verso, London and New York.

BECKER-DONNER, ETTA
 1985 *Die Mexikanischen Sammlungen des Museum für Völkerkunde*. Museum für Völkerkunde, Vienna.

BERLO, JANET CATHERINE
 1982 Artistic Specialization at Teotihuacan: The Ceramic Incense Burner. In *Pre-Columbian Art History: Selected Readings* (Alana Cordy-Collins, ed.): 83–100. Peek Publications, Palo Alto.
 1983a The Warrior and the Butterfly: Central Mexican Ideologies of Sacred Warfare and Teotihuacan Iconography. In *Text and Image in Pre-Columbian Art History* (Janet C. Berlo, ed.). BAR International Series 180, Oxford.
 1983b Conceptual Categories for the Study of Texts and Images in Pre-Columbian Art. In *Text and Image in Pre-Columbian Art History* (Janet C. Berlo, ed.). BAR International Series 180, Oxford.
 1984 *Teotihuacan Art Abroad: Parts I and II*. BAR International Series 199, Oxford.
 1989 Early Writing in Central Mexico: *In Tlilli, In Tlapalli* before A.D. 1000. In *Mesoamerica after the Decline of Teotihuacan* (R. A. Diehl and J. C. Berlo, eds.): 19–47. Dumbarton Oaks, Washington D.C.

BERRIN, KATHLEEN
 1988 *Feathered Serpents and Flowering Trees: Reconstructing the Murals of Teotihuacan* (Kathleen Berrin, ed.). The Fine Arts Museums of San Francisco.

BROWN, DAVID
 n.d. The Linguistic Affiliation and Phoneticism of Teotihuacan Iconography. Ph.D. dissertation. Dept. of Art History, University of New Mexico, Albuquerque, New Mexico, 1988.

Cabrera Castro, Rubén, Ignacio Rodriguez, and Noel Morelos (eds.)
    1982a   *Teotihuacan 80–82, Primeros Resultados.* Instituto Nacional de Antropología e Historia. Mexico, D.F.
    1982b   Memoria del Proyecto Arqueológico Teotihuacan 80–82. *Colección Científica 132,* INAH. Mexico, D.F.

Caso, Alfonso
    1966   Dioses y signos teotihuacanos. In *Teotihuacan: Onceava Mesa Redonda* 1: 249–275. Sociedad Mexicana de Antropología.

Cowgill, George L.
    1983   Rulership and the Ciudadela: Political Inferences from Teotihuacan Architecture. In *Civilization in the Ancient Americas: Essays in Honor of Gordon R. Willey* (Richard M. Leventhal and Alan L. Kolata, eds.): 313–343. Cambridge, Mass.
    n.d.   Ideology and the Teotihuacan State. In *Ideology and the Cultural Evolution of Civilization* (Geoffrey N. Conrad and Arthur Demarest, eds.). School of American Research Seminar (in press).

Foster, Hal
    1985   *Recodings: Art, Spectacle, Cultural Politics.* Bay Press, Port Townsend, Wash.

Gamboa, Fernando
    1963   *Masterworks of Mexican Art from Pre-Columbian to the Present.* Los Angeles County Museum of Art exhibition, October 1963–January 1964. Los Angeles County Museum of Art, Los Angeles.

Gombrich, E. H.
    1960   *Art and Illusion.* Princeton University Press.

Grove, David (ed.)
    1987   *Ancient Chalcatzingo.* University of Texas Press, Austin.

Jones, Christopher, and Linton Satterthwaite
    1982   *The Monuments and Inscriptions of Tikal: The Carved Monuments of Tikal Report 33,* Part A. University of Pennsylvania, Philadelphia.

Kelley, David H.
    1983   The Maya Calendar Correlation Problem. In *Civilizations in the Ancient Americas: Essays in Honor of Gordon R. Willey* (Richard M. Leventhal and Alan L. Kolata, eds.): 157–208. Cambridge, Mass.

Kubler, George
    1967   *The Iconography of the Art of Teotihuacan.* Studies in Pre-Columbian Art and Archaeology 4. Dumbarton Oaks, Washington, D.C.

Langley, James C.
    1986   *Symbolic Notation of Teotihuacan.* BAR International Series 313, Oxford

Linné, Sigvald
    1934   *Archaeological Researchers at Teotihuacan, Mexico.* The Ethnological Museum of Sweden, n.s. 1. Stockholm.

Miller, Arthur G.
    1973   *The Mural Painting of Teotihuacan, Mexico.* Dumbarton Oaks, Washington, D.C.

Abstraction and the Rise of a Utopian State

MILLER, VIRGINIA E.
    1988   *The Role of Gender in Pre-Columbian Art and Architecture*. University Press of America, Lanham, Md.

MILLON, CLARA HALL
    1973   Painting, Writing, and Polity in Teotihuacan, Mexico. *American Antiquity* 38 (3): 294–314.
    1988   A Reexamination of the Teotihuacan Tassel Headdress Insignia, and Catalogue of the Wagner Murals Collection. In *Feathered Serpents and Flowering Trees: Reconstructing the Murals of Teotihuacan* (Kathleen Berrin, ed.): 114–134 and 195–228. The Fine Arts Museums of San Francisco.

MILLON, RENÉ
    1973   *The Teotihuacan Map, Urbanization at Teotihuacan, Mexico*. 1. University of Texas Press, Austin.
    1981   Teotihuacan: City, State and Civilization. In *Handbook of Middle American Indians, Supp. I: Archaeology* (Victoria R. Bricker and Jeremy A. Sabloff, eds.): 198–243. University of Texas, Austin.

MOORE, HENRIETTA (ED.)
    1988   *Femininism and Anthropology*. University of Minnesota Press, Minneapolis.

MORE, THOMAS
    1965   *Utopia* (1516). Penguin Books, London.

ORTNER, SHERRY B.
    1974   Is Female to Male as Nature is to Culture? In *Woman, Culture, and Society* (Michelle Z. Rosaldo and Louise Lamphere, eds.): 67–88. Stanford University Press, Stanford, Calif.

PASZTORY, ESTHER
    1972   The Gods of Teotihuacan: A Synthetic Approach in Teotihuacan Iconography. *Atti del XL Congresso Internazionale degli Americanisti* 1: 147–159. Rome.
    1974   *The Iconography of the Teotihuacan Tlaloc*. Studies in Pre-Columbian Art and Archaeology 15. Dumbarton Oaks, Washington, D.C.
    1976   *The Murals of Tepantitla, Teotihuacan*. Garland, New York.
    1988a   The Aztec Tlaloc: God of Antiquity. In *Smoke and Mist: Mesoamerican Studies in Memory of Thelma O. Sullivan* (J. Kathryn Josserand and Karen Dakin, eds.): 289–327. BAR International Series 402, Oxford.
    1988b   A Reinterpretation of Teotihuacan and Its Mural Painting Tradition, and Catalogue of the Wagner Murals Collection. In *Feathered Serpents and Flowering Trees: Reconstructing the Murals of Teotihuacan* (Kathleen Berrin, ed.): 45–77 and 135–193. The Fine Arts Museums of San Francisco.
    n.d.   An Image Is Worth a Thousand Words: Teotihuacan and the Meanings of Style in Classic Mesoamerica. In *Latin American Horizons* (Don Stephen Rice, ed.). Dumbarton Oaks, Washington D.C. (in press).

PLATO
    1945   *The Republic* (trans. with an intro. and notes by Francis MacDonald Cornford). Oxford.

SANDERS, WILLIAM J., JEFFREY R. PARSONS, AND ROBERT SANTLEY
    1979   *The Basin of Mexico: Ecological Processes in the Evolution of a Civilization.* Academic Press, New York.

SÉJOURNÉ, LAURETTE
    1959   *Un palacio en la cuidad de los dioses.* INAH, Mexico, D.F.

SELER, EDUARD
    1915   Die Teotiuacan-Kultur des Hochlands von Mexico. In *Gesammelte Abhandlungen zur Amerikanischen Sprach- und Altertumskunde* 5: 405–585. Behrend, Berlin.

SEMPOWSKI, MARTHA L.
    n.d.   Mortuary Practices at Teotihuacan, Mexico: Their Implications for Social Status. Ph.D. dissertation, Dept. of Anthropology, University of Rochester, 1983.

SHAW, J. F.
    1983   *Nicene and Post-Nicene Fathers of the Christian Church* (1886, reprint). William B. Eerdmans, Grand Rapids, Mich.

STOREY, REBECCA
    1985   An Estimate of Mortality in a Pre-Columbian Population. *American Anthropologist* 87 (3): 519–535.

SUGIYAMA, SABURO
    1989   Burials Dedicated to the Old Temple of Quetzalcoatl at Teotihuacan, Mexico. *American Antiquity* 54 (1): 85–106.

TAUBE, KARL A.
    1983   The Teotihuacan Spider-Woman. *Journal of Latin American Lore* 9 (2): 107–189

UMBERGER, EMILY
    1987   Antiques, Revivals, and References to the Past in Aztec Art. *RES* 13: 63–106.

VILLAGRA CALETI, AGUSTÍN
    1971   Mural Painting in Central Mexico. In *Handbook of Middle American Indians* 10 (Robert Wauchope, Gordon F. Ekholm, and Ignacio Bernal, eds.): 135–156. University of Texas Press, Austin.

VON WINNING, HASSO
    1987   *La iconografía de Teotihuacán: Los dioses y signos,* 2 vols. Universidad Nacional Autónoma de México, Mexico, D.F.

WESTHEIM, PAUL
    1965   *The Art of Ancient Mexico.* Doubleday, New York (1950).

WHEATLEY, PAUL
    1971   *Pivot of the Four Quarters.* Aldine, Chicago.

ZERVOS, CHRISTIAN
    1952   *Fernand Léger, oeuvres de 1905 à 1952.* Editions Cahiers d'Art, Paris.

The Economic Organization of the Teotihuacan Priesthood: Hypotheses and Considerations

LINDA MANZANILLA

INSTITUTO DE INVESTIGACIONES ANTROPOLÓGICAS,
UNIVERSIDAD NACIONAL AUTÓNOMA DE MÉXICO

INTRODUCTION

THE APPEARANCE OF URBAN SOCIETY and the process of state formation are subjects that are current in the archaeological literature of recent decades. After a period of fertile and contrasting theoretical formulations, there is perhaps a need to obtain more consistent data on certain aspects of these societies.

There are cases of pristine urban developments, such as the Teotihuacan example of the Basin of Mexico, where there are vast realms of culture (social organization, power spheres, etc.) with lack of crucial data. Thus alternative explanations should be suggested to be tested systematically against new and old information, keeping in mind the particular indicators that would incline the balance in one particular direction.

Some scholars interested in pre-Hispanic Mexico share the idea that tribute and market economy are institutions present throughout the Classic and Postclassic horizons of Mesoamerican history (Matos Moctezuma 1976: 12; Nalda 1982: 116). In this paper (controversial as it may be), nevertheless, I will propose a less stable development, where tribute and market are historical by-products of specific organizational bodies of the Postclassic horizon, preceded by other forms of surplus control and exchange. Undoubtedly there will be some disagreement with my position; yet, with scanty current data, there is a fertile ground to expose different models that can elucidate aspects of the Teotihuacan economy and look for futher data pertinent to answer such questions as: what kinds of goods distribution networks are present at Teotihuacan; who controls them; which sectors of the Teotihuacan society are involved in each circuit?

Elsewhere (Manzanilla 1983, 1985a, 1986, 1987) I have proposed the existence of two different organizational spheres: (a) The temple-centered sphere, which would be responsible for the development of pristine urban institutions, such as the organized centralization of economic surplus, the presence of full-time specialists (particularly in the manufacturing sector), the auspice of a long-distance exchange network undertaken by temple emissaries, the appearance of complex administrative systems, and all of these instances as by-products of a redistributional circuit administered by the priesthood; and (b) The palace-centered organization (viewing the palace as the seat of government), on the other hand, would account for the development of a state where tribute substitutes redistribution as the basic form of centralization of surplus production, conquest as a means of assuring the continuous flow of goods and land, and the emergence of markets as institutions closely articulated to the palace interests (as Pedro Carrasco [1982] proposed).

In a comparative analysis of the appearance of control institutions in Mesoamerica, the Andes, and the Near East, a parallelism emerges that can shed light on how these two spheres came into being, and how they were transformed through time. Yet, the comparison should not be made between the Sumerian and Aztec societies, as Robert Adams (1966) once proposed, because they are not homotaxial. The comparison should be made, rather, between the proto-Sumerian development and the Teotihuacan case.

In the study of the Teotihuacan society, few considerations have been made on how people were organized. In particular, we will be interested in how the Teotihuacan priesthood could have been involved directly in the supervision of productive and redistributive tasks. Before exposing my hypotheses, I would like to review briefly the proto-Sumerian development with respect to the appearance of centralizing institutions.

THE TEMPLE AND ITS REDISTRIBUTIVE NETWORK IN MESOPOTAMIA

In the fifth and fourth millennia B.C., Lowland Mesopotamia is the scene of the appearance of temple buildings in the largest settlements. These pristine monumental constructions have no parallel in secular architecture and are characterized by a tripartite plan, consisting of a central sanctuary, surrounded by lines of storage rooms. These are particularly notable in the site of Uruk-Warka (in Lowland Mesopotamia) during the Late Uruk-Jemdet Nasr Periods (ca. 3,200–2,900 B.C.) (Nissen 1972: 794) but can also be detected in the Mesopotamian borders, for example at Arslantepé, in Eastern Anatolia (Palmieri 1973). In this last site, a standardized ceramic production associated with the temple constructions—to account for the redistribution of food rations—was studied (Espinosa and Manzanilla 1985).

Yet, not only food was redistributed. For the temple of Khafajah, in Central Mesopotamia, Henry Frankfort (1951: 67) cites the storage of grain,

The Economic Organization of the Teotihuacan Priesthood

sesame, onions, dates, beer, wine, salted or dried fish, grease, wool, skins, rushes, wood, asphalt, marble, diorite, and tools.

For the Early Dynastic period (ca. 2,900–2,340 B.C.), there are tablets that enlist temple food rations consisting of bread and grain for different people (Wright 1969: 42): persons who were participating in communal work, priests and other officials, and artisans. Some of the stored grain was kept for future agricultural cycles; another part went to feed temple flocks; another was channeled to the temple's brewery, bakery, and kitchen; and yet another was used for long-distance exchange of raw materials which were nonexistent in Mesopotamia (Frankfort 1951: 68, 72, 74). The temple was, thus, the center of a redistributive circuit, that permitted the maintenance of the temple officials as well as full-time artisans (particularly potters developing for the first time fast-wheel techniques to deal with the mass-production required by the redistribution of food rations, but surely also metallurgists).

If we characterize an early urban society as one with complex division of labor—and thus, the existence of specialists devoted to activities other than the production of subsistence goods—with institutions that coordinate economic processes and have authority over common people, and generally with an urban center that provides specific services and goods to the surrounding region, serving as the living-working locus for the majority of the specialists (Manzanilla 1987: 271), then we would conclude that from Uruk times (ca. 3,500–3,100 B.C.) onwards we have this type of society in Mesopotamia.

If we then define an archaic state society as one with a classist organization, with clear indications of accumulation of wealth, a relatively precise demarcation of frontiers, conquest as a form of territorial appropriation, and tribute as the way of acquiring goods and labor force (Manzanilla 1987), then we would say that this organization would correspond in Mesopotamia to Akkadian times (ca. 2,340–2,159 B.C.).

The Early Dynastic period (ca. 2,900–2,340 B.C.) would be a transitional one, with the following characteristics:

1. Urban institutions are fully settled.
2. The palace (as the seat of government) appears as the temple's rival economic institution.
3. It also concentrates land, cattle, products, and raw materials.
4. The palace has adopted the temple's administrative organization, originally suited to deal with redistributional tasks, and has converted it into a closed circuit.

Returning to the temple sphere in Mesopotamia, I could say that the history of redistribution begins in the Neolithic horizon in the northern Mesopotamian plains, where we find settlements (such as Umm Dabaghiyah,

Hassuna, or Yarim Tepé, from the sixth and fifth millennia B.C.) where the central sector of the village is occupied by rows of small rooms that served as storehouses for meat and grain. Due to the fact that there were no control institutions—such as temples or palaces—yet detected in these communities, I have pointed out the possibility that a situation similar to present "lineage societies" occurred: the elders' council would have been the organism devoted to communal tasks such as the redistribution of the communal produce stored in the center of the village to all members that contributed to it, in a "circular redistributional circuit" (Manzanilla 1983: 7; 1987: 278).

When the temple appears as an institution that seems to inherit and expand the above-mentioned phenomenon, it converts it into an asymmetrical network, deviating some of the stored production to the maintenance of craftsmen and bureaucrats and to long-distance exchange (Manzanilla 1983, 1987). Thus, it was possible for Mesopotamian temple administrators to obtain all the raw materials (rocks, minerals, and metals) nonexistent in their territory but necessary for the production of the most essential tools, as well as for sumptuary goods.

Thus, in regions with homogeneous and relatively limited resources, such as the Mesopotamian Lowlands, or the Maya Lowlands, asymmetrical redistribution would serve as the circuit that allows the supply of nonexistent raw materials possible. Kent Flannery and Michael Coe (1972) have also proposed that in the Maya Lowlands, maize produced by peasants was channeled to the regional center, to be redistributed to those lineages supplying services: bureaucrats, artisans, lapidaries, stone-cutters, and so forth.

There are other areas with more diversified resources, where there are two options for Formative communities: (a) The "economic symbiosis" model (proposed by Sanders 1968: 100), where communities located in different altitudinal positions specialize productively and cooperate intercommunally, having a distribution center where all the surplus is exchanged—a model that could be applied to Formative Basin of Mexico and Oaxaca Valley; and (b) The "vertical archipelago" model of ecological complementarity, proposed by John Murra (1975, 1985a, 1985b) for the Andean Region, where each "ethnic group made an effort to control a maximum of floors and ecological niches" maintaining "permanent colonies situated in the periphery in order to control distant resources." The relations between center and periphery "were those that are called reciprocity and redistribution in economic anthropology" (Murra 1985b: 15–16).

RECIPROCITY AND REDISTRIBUTION IN THE ANDES

John Murra has stated that "when cultivation made its appearance, the calendrical cycle allowed the pooling and redistribution of distinct and geographically separate resources" (Murra 1987: 10). From Chavin times onwards (the second half of the second millennium B.C.), Luís Lumbreras (1987: 336–337) has detected new types of public constructions devoted not only to cult purposes, but to star observation, workshop production, and warehouse operations. Similar complexes are found along the Marañon Andes.

Thus, we find here the first hints of the "temple sphere" outlined before, where probably the priesthood was in charge of cult and redistributive tasks, maintaining craftsmen associated with ritual production.

In the "vertical archipelago" model, the type of exchange between the highland settlements and its low valley colonies would be reciprocal, and the rights would be claimed through kinship ties and would be "periodically reaffirmed ceremonially in the settlements of origin" (Murra 1985b: 16).

Ramiro Condarco Morales (in Murra 1985a: 6) thought that this type of complementarity generated interrelationships and solidarity that formed the basis of the total unification of the Central Andes by Tiwanaku or the Inca. John Murra (1985b: 11) adds that complementarity prevailed in times when there were no marketplaces but many state-operated warehouses and was an excellent means to handle "a multiple environment, vast populations, and hence high productivity"; the key aspect of highland economies being massive storage (Murra 1985: 4).

During Inca times, we have archaeological and ethnohistorical evidence with respect to storage facilities. These warehouses are vital when there are continuous frosts or droughts, but also served to maintain state personnel, the army, and state craftsmen (Murra 1975). The deposits were located either inside the settlements or on the mountain slopes (Earle and D'Altroy 1982).

Craig Morris (1978) and William Isbell (1978) have detected a difference in the number of warehouses with respect to the site hierarchy and also different products being stored in deposits having either circular or rectangular forms. At Huanuco Pampa—a provincial capital—Morris (1978) detected 497 warehouses constructed and administered by the state, which served to maintain the population of the settlement. He also excavated forty workshops and ten related constructions destined to textile production—a key element for reciprocal relations between the Inca (the state) and the people from the communities—and to *chicha* preparation and consumption. In two large plazas located near the public sector of Huanuco Pampa, tons of ceramic vessel fragments were found associated with these activities, and Morris observed that the ceramic production was standardized.

This example reminds me of our Mesopotamian example. Yet, the Andean case differs in the form that redistribution takes place: collective meals versus food rations (Manzanilla 1985a: n.d.). In either process, there is a need for a standardized ceramic production, and thus potters were one of the categories that the redistributional circuit sponsored.

Nevertheless, the Andean example should be seen as a case in which redistribution is a relict institution inside the "palace sphere," but that was so efficient in Andean conditions as to persist through time. Similar relict redistributional activities have been detected in the Aztec state by Pedro Carrasco (1982) and Johanna Broda (1976: 42–53), where one of the ritual functions of the Aztec *tlatoani* was the redistribution of weapons and insignia to nobles and warriors. The nobles also sponsored communal banquets and gift exchanges, occasions that served to redistribute goods ritually.

If we think, nevertheless, of a homotaxial example for Teotihuacan, we should invoke the Tiwanaku example (in Bolivia) where redistribution could have been not a relict institution but the axis of economic networks that would explain the colonies established in the coast and lowland valleys. Unfortunately for Tiwanaku there is even less fieldwork and concrete data than for Teotihuacan. It is the major urban center in the Bolivian plateau and the southern Central Andean Region during the first millennium A.D., yet only recently has there been systematic research at the site.

In recent extensive excavations at the main temple of Tiwanaku (the Pyramid of Akapana), I have detected not only cult constructions on its summit, but also multiroom complexes probably devoted to priestly domestic and storage functions (Manzanilla and Woodard 1990). These contexts belong to the Tiwanaku III and IV periods (ca. 300–900 A.D.). Even though these are only preliminary data, I propose that redistributive activities could have been carried out by the priesthood, involving not only local foodstuff but also goods coming from colonies on the coast and in the tropical sectors to the east of the high plateau (*Chione undatella* clam shells, tropical fruits [Sapotaceae or Sapindaceae], etc.).

THE TEOTIHUACAN CASE

The "economic symbiosis" model could well account for the situation in the Basin of Mexico prior to the emergence of Teotihuacan. From Middle Formative times, we have cases—such as Loma Torremote—where centralized storing activities in the hands of specific households took place (Reyna Robles 1977). In Late Formative times, sites with monumental ceremonial architecture, such as Cuicuilco and Tlapacoya, could have been the distribution centers specified by Sanders' model, and I would add that probably the priests were the group who organized centralized storage.

The priest was certainly a central figure in Teotihuacan society. The frequency of priests' representations, particularly in mural art, is high. René Millon (1967: 149–150), for example, states that priests played undoubtedly a very important role and that the integration of the city could have been possible through the pilgrimage-temple-market complex. He also states (R. Millon 1988: 109) that the political realm was sacralized, without a formal differentiation between religious and political spheres. Teotihuacan was a

The Economic Organization of the Teotihuacan Priesthood

religious center without equal in its time, a sacred city, the center of the cosmos, the place where time began (R. Millon 1988).

William Sanders (1967: 134) also argues that perhaps priestly institutions controlled alluvial and piedmont land and that religion was probably one of the most important integrative factors in Teotihuacan. I agree with the idea that the priest was surely the most important figure in the Teotihuacan hierarchy; if there had been secular groups who would have claimed a politically predominant position in society—in a way equivalent to the figure of a king, lord, or ruler—surely there would have been innumerable iconographic representations of them and a cult of the dynastic ruler, as Esther Pasztory (1978: 130) has detected for the Maya Lowlands and the Valley of Oaxaca during the Middle Classic period.

I would further propose that the Teotihuacan priesthood centralized the surplus production from communities of the central part of the Basin of Mexico, maintained full-time artisans—probably obsidian workers, some potters who were producing standardized and ritual ceramic types, and sumptuary goods craftsmen—and also had emissaries who established different types of relations with foreign Mesoamerican regions. This situation would not be very different from those reviewed formerly, except perhaps by the scale of the phenomenon, which would be closer to that of Tiwanaku than that of the proto-Sumerian centers.

I will try to review some of the specific data that could be cited for each of these premises.

The Centralization and Storage of Surplus Production

When we review the floral and faunal subsistence data recovered from Teotihuacan excavations, we find that many products could have come from sectors of the Basin of Mexico other than the Teotihuacan Valley. We could cite, for example, lacustrine resources (turtles, fish, and waterfowl) (Starbuck 1987); fresh water snails, and a small rabbit (*Romerolagus diazi*), probably from the Chichinautzin Sierra to the south of the Basin of Mexico (Valadez and Manzanilla 1988). Emily McClung de Tapia (1987: 58) shares the same idea with respect to paleobotanical macrofossils, stating that the Teotihuacanos imported basic products from a large sector of the Basin of Mexico.

Much of the subsistence base detected for the urban center of the Classic horizon was already present at Formative villages such as Cuanalan (Manzanilla 1985b). I propose, then, that this diversified subsistence base could have been recreated on a larger scale during the Classic horizon, through a regional network of redistributive activities involving groups from different parts of the Basin of Mexico, who were offering their surplus to the Teotihuacan gods (and priests). This type of circulation is not proposed as an exclusive one; direct exchange between producers would be a parallel circuit. Yet, in this paper, I would like to underline that the market would not have been an institution corresponding to the Teotihuacan "temple sphere," as we will propose further on.

The Temple of Agriculture's main mural painting (at the intersection of the Street of the Dead and the Moon's Plaza) could be one of the particular cases that could reinforce the existence of offering scenes, such as the ones depicted in Uruk period vases from Warka. Even though René Millon (1967: 152) considers that the painting discovered by Leopoldo Batres could be a marketplace, I would alternatively argue that it could be seen as the first part of the redistributive circuit, when people are depositing surplus production in the form of offerings to temple symbols.

The problem of centralized storage of food and raw materials is one that deserves particular attention. In Mesopotamia, the warehouses are integrated architecturally with the sanctuary. In the Andean Region and in Mesoamerica, they should be searched for in the immediate vicinity of the ritual structures. I would think that, for example, the low, standing row of rooms that closes the southern part of many three-temple complexes at Teotihuacan would be one possible place. Another would be certain sectors inside the apartment compounds specifically devoted to storage. Yet, in this case, the domestic scale of the storage phenomenon would prevail, masking the centralized public scale that we are searching for, except in the case that a specific apartment compound would not have been devoted to living, but to administrative and/or public purposes (the constructions along the Street of the Dead, for example).

At this stage, I would like to add that when we touch the administrative realm for Mesoamerica, we are dealing with archaeological contexts that have not been studied at all and the particular archaeological indicators that would be related to this type of activity have not been detected. Thus we often hear that a specific structure is said to be used for administrative purposes, without knowing why this particular function is ascribed to it. One of the only indicators that has been cited is the nonexistence of burials (Noel Morelos, in R. Millon 1988: 162).

In the Near East, the appearance of complex administrative activities was a by-product of the temple's redistributive network. They are represented by seals and their respective clay sealings, tablets, and *bullae*. What are their counterparts in Mesoamerican archaeology?

Returning to the problem of storage, one of the particular indicators that has been proposed is San Martin Orange *amphorae*. George Cowgill (1987) states that it is a type particularly common in Xolalpan times, specially in Tlajinga (where there were workshops devoted to its production), in Oztoyohualco (N6W3), and in a band 300 m to the west of the northern part of the Street of the Dead. For this last sector, I would propose that we could be dealing with centralized storage facilities. At Oztoyohualco, however, we could have a mixed count between domestic San Martin ceramics coming from the apartment compounds and probably some coming from the three-temple complexes.

We recently excavated an apartment compound at Oztoyohualco (N6W3: 15b), where there were particular rooms devoted to storage, and these were rooms where food preparation had taken place (Manzanilla and Barba 1990). We were excavating this compound with the purpose of studying what particular activities took place in each room by comparing palinological, paleobotanical, phytolithical, paleozoological, chemical, and archaeological data (Barba et al. 1987; Manzanilla 1988–89b; Valadez and Manzanilla 1988). Storage rooms were always represented by San Martin Orange pottery, high pollen counts, the presence of macrofossils of economically important and medicinal plants, and low pH and carbonate values. Jeffrey Altschul (n.d.) also proposed similar sectors in an intensive surface analysis of another compound at S3W3:L3 square, using the distribution of San Martin Orange pottery.

The degree to which centralized storage was incorporated to Aztec palace economy has been recently reviewed by José Rojas (1987). The *Huey tlatoani* had warehouses not only in Tenochtitlan, but also in each provincial capital (Rojas 1987: 31) (as was the case in the Inca and Akkadian examples). The historical sources also cite openings of the imperial storehouses to face catastrophes (p. 36), such as the ones under Motecuhzoma, Nezahualcóyotl, and Totoquihuatzin.

Redistribution of Food, Raw Materials, and Manufactures

With respect to the redistribution of food, a difference should be made between the regular maintenance of artisans and bureaucrats by the system and the occasional collective ritual meals. For the first case, I would propose that the production of standardized pottery would probably be an indicator. There is, however, little done in this field. If we used the Late Uruk example as suggestive, we should have to study bowls in this perspective. Yet, I would also suggest that the handled covers whose distribution is said to be related to high-status architecture, could be another example.

I would invoke here George Cowgill's (1967: 176–183) original idea that these "covers" served to consume food at a certain distance from where it was prepared, with the possibility that this activity required reheating. If the priests and bureaucrats ate often from these or related vessels, their exceptionally high proportions near the Street of the Dead would be explained.

Yet these covers were not distributed only in high-status residences. They have been found also in clear intermediate-status domestic contexts, at my excavation in Oztoyohualco, together with copa vases, censers, Thin Orange pottery, incised ceramics, and other types that have been used as indicators of high status. So there is a long way before us, in determining

Linda Manzanilla

particular repetitive behavior with respect to specific types, a task that can only be accomplished by the careful recording of activity areas and associations in extensive excavations and not any more by producing surface distributional maps.

Ideologically, the redistributional activities in the hands of the priest-administrator devoted to the agricultural fertility cult would be reinforced by the reception of oblations granted by groups coming from different sectors of the Basin of Mexico and by the offering of communal meals and warehouse openings, such as the ones detected in the two large plazas at Huanuco Pampa, Peru (Morris 1978). I would further suggest that the Great Compound of Teotihuacan, more than a market, would be the storage place for the different social sectors and probably also one of the main redistributional loci of the city. The regional interests that Rebecca Sload (1987) invokes for her Great Compound apartment constructions could be precisely the storage of products from specialized sectors—particularly manufactures—and their further pooling into the redistributive network.

It is not by chance that the Ciudadela stands just in front of this place, being that ceremonialism is a way of reinforcing ideologically the prodigality of the gods (and their priests). The binome Great Compound and Ciudadela would be perhaps a functional one, regarding redistribution of manufactured items and ritual meals, respectively, and the administration of all the network.

Redistribution in the hands of priests could also be reiterated visually through the multiple representations of ritual officials from whose hands come out "falling panels" with *mantenimientos:* seeds, sea shells, jadeite carvings, and so on (see C. Millon 1973; Miller 1973). Not only in mural paintings, but also in theater censers are there depictions of priests devoted to the Great Goddess' cult (Pasztory 1973) or the Butterfly God's cult, where food and manufactured items flow from their hands (Manzanilla and Carreón 1990).

The redistribution of exotic raw materials would be a restricted circulation circuit that we will mention when speaking of long-distance exchange.

The Auspices of Manufacturing Specialists

With respect to obsidian workers, obviously not all the workshops depended on the redistributional network. Following Michael Spence's (1987) classification, only precinct workshops located near major public structures, and probably regional workshops, were under the priests' control. In the first case, the distribution of precinct workshops would be around the Moon Pyramid, in the Great Compound, and to the northeast of the Ciudadela (Spence 1987: 434). Regional workshops were also located near major public structures or major streets of the city. These would also be

The Economic Organization of the Teotihuacan Priesthood

sponsored by the priesthood, to pool their products into the long-distance exchange network that they also controlled, as we will suggest further on.

Thus, Spence's (1987: 444) impression that the obsidian industry was "administered" and "highly centralized" would be explained by the fact that it was one of the main by-products of the redistributional circuit. And we should add that in his comparison between Classic and Postclassic obsidian industries, the last one is seen as much less centralized and in the hands of part-time specialists (Spence 1987), because it no longer was sponsored by the "temple sphere" and was no longer needed for middle-range exchange.

Certain potters would also be maintained by the system. One of the examples that could be cited is the large workshop of censers' molded parts found just to the north of the Ciudadela (Múnera Bermúdez n.d.). Other Matte Ware workshops (for three-prong burners, censers, miniatures, *candeleros*, etc., as well as finely decorated wares) could also belong to this group.

Long-Distance Networks and Colonies

The problem regarding the relationships between Teotihuacan and the rest of Mesoamerica is not a simple one to solve. A recent summary of current data and interpretations has been offered by René Millon (1988). I agree with most of them. Yet, I would like to add some considerations on how the flow of exotic goods from regions such as the Maya Lowlands could be seen as a highly controlled movement.

First of all I should say that my model stipulated that there should be no market at Teotihuacan in the way we should expect it at Tlatelolco in Mexica times, nor should there be *pochteca* merchants. I am proposing that the high-status raw materials that came from abroad (cacao, shells, feathers, hides, honey, incense, copal, jadeite, serpentine, hematite, cinnabar, malachite, etc.) were all of them products that entered a restricted circulation circuit. Many were used directly in ritual or for conspicuous consumption. So there could have been a direct involvement of the priesthood in their supply.

I am proposing that it was through temple emissaries that the flow was controlled. In particular, four possible colonies could be cited, where Teotihuacan emissaries were perhaps living together with local populations: Matacapan, Kaminaljuyu, and probably Alta Vista and Tingambato. This type of colony reminds us of the ones probably established by Tiwanaku in the coastal and lowland valleys in the Central-South Andean Region (Moquegua, in the Peruvian coast, for example).

The tassel headdress that Clara Millon (1973) proposes as a symbol of the Teotihuacan polity in foreign regions could be the basic characteristic of these emissaries. This same headdress is portrayed on priests' heads in different mural paintings. We should not be surprised that some of these persons are depicted with weapons in Maya contexts. Traveling so far from the Central Mexican Highlands would not have been an easy endeavor.

Let us speak of obsidian, for example. If Teotihuacan obsidian reached Tikal in such a small quantity (1%) and if it was surely not by marketplace exchange but rather by gift exchange among persons of high status (Sidrys 1977; Spence, in Millon 1988: 119), then we should think that one of the products that the Teotihuacan emissaries took with themselves was precisely obsidian in the form of prismatic cores and some bifacial products. Fine pottery would be another possibility.

A different circuit would be the one that involved products from the Oaxaca Valley and the Gulf Coast. The Oaxaca and Merchants' *Barrios* at Teotihuacan show goods that are not precisely high-status: pottery and some other manufactured items. René Millon (1988: 127) has recently asked himself whether these foreigners were really merchants. And even when addressing the subject of Teotihuacan merchants, he recognizes that there is nearly no information.

Barter between producers, foreign people bringing some allochtonous manufactured goods, redistributive networks to assure surplus concentration and craft patronage, long-distance elite exchange between temple emissaries—all are circuits that could have coexisted, involving different goods and social sectors.

RECONSIDERATIONS

In the evolutive framework that Elman Service (1971, 1975) proposed, redistribution would be one of the main characteristics of chiefdoms, so it would seem strange that I have been proposing this economic phenomenon as an indicator of early urban societies. Yet, I should underline that there are no extant ethnographic counterparts of these societies, so there is less probability that they should have been defined with sufficient accuracy as bands, tribes, chiefdoms, and states.

The advantages of redistribution at a local scale were: to have a stored stock to face future harvests and eventualities in the agricultural cycle; to constitute a deposit of diversified goods coming from sectors specialized productively; to serve as a feeding basis for specialists not devoted to the production of foodstuff; and to constitute a material stock for long-distance exchange (Manzanilla 1985a).

At a vaster scale, Isbell (1978: 306–307) would propose that in those areas where energetic perturbations were common, there were two alternatives: either to decrease the demographic or the organizational level of society, or to select in favor of progressively larger redistributive spheres. This latter alternative would have been chosen in the Central Andean region, and probably also in Classic Central Mexico. Morton Fried (1974: 30–31) adds

The Economic Organization of the Teotihuacan Priesthood

that the advantages of redistribution would also lie not only in security in the face of adversities in food production, but also in the diversification of diet.

In the social realm, the greater the surplus, the greater the degree of stratification, as Frank Hole (1974) stated. Thus, all the basic components of early urban life—surplus concentration, complex division of labor, long-distance exchange networks, and social stratification—could be explained through the analysis of the redistributive organization.

Some of the causes that René Millon (1988: 149) evokes for the end of Teotihuacan were the following: a mismanagement of the economy and polity, a rigid inflexibility towards change, an inefficient and incompetent bureaucracy, and the deterioration of exchange networks. Naturally, the complexity of the articulation between all the circuits and social sectors that we have cited, and the enormous scale that the phenomenon adopted, was such that any factor could have broken this fragile equilibrium, where ideology was the main reinforcement agent.

The changing conditions of the Epiclassic population readjustments, the emergence of palace institutions as economic rivals of the temple sphere, the beginnings of a political realm separated from the religious one—all opened a new perspective in Mesoamerican history: one dominated by the tributary state of the Postclassic period.

BIBLIOGRAPHY

ADAMS, ROBERT MCCORMICK
  1966   *The Evolution of Urban Society. Early Mesopotamia and Prehispanic Mexico.* Aldine, Chicago.
ALTSCHUL, JEFFREY H.
  1987   Social Districts of Teotihuacan. In *Teotihuacan: Nuevos datos, nuevas síntesis, nuevos problemas* (Emily McClung de Tapia and Evelyn Childs Rattray, eds.): 191–217. Instituto de Investigaciones Antropológicas, UNAM, Serie Antropológica 72. Mexico, D.F.
  n.d.   Spatial and Statistical Evidence for Social Groupings at Teotihuacan, Mexico. Ph.D. dissertation, Brandeis University, 1981.
BARBA, LUIS, BEATRIZ LUDLOW, LINDA MANZANILLA, AND RAÚL VALADEZ
  1987   La vida doméstica en Teotihuacan. Un estudio interdisciplinario. *Ciencia y desarrollo* (año XIII) 77, CONACYT: 21–32.
BRODA, JOHANNA
  1976   Los estamentos en el ceremonial mexica. In *Estratificación social en la Mesoamérica prehispánica* (Pedro Carrasco et al., eds.): 37–66. SEP-INAH, Mexico, D.F.
CARRASCO, PEDRO
  1982   La economía del México prehispánico. In *Economía política e ideología en el México prehispánico* (Pedro Carrasco and Johanna Broda, eds.): 13–76. Editorial Nueva Imagen, Mexico, D.F.
COWGILL, GEORGE L.
  1987   Métodos para el estudio de relaciones espaciales en los datos de la superficie de Teotihuacan. In *Teotihuacan: Nuevos datos, nuevas síntesis, nuevos problemas* (Emily McClung de Tapia and Evelyn C. Rattray, eds.): 161–189. Instituto de Investigaciones Antropológicas, UNAM, Mexico, D.F.
EARLE, T. K., AND T. N. D'ALTROY
  1982   Storage Facilities and State Finance in the Upper Mantaro Valley, Peru. In *Contexts for Prehistoric Exchange* (Jonathon E. Ericson and Timothy K. Earle, eds.): 265–290. Academic Press, New York.
ESPINOSA, GUILLERMO, AND LINDA MANZANILLA
  1985   Consideraciones en torno a la capacidad de los cuencos troncocónicos de Arslantepé, Turquía Oriental (Período VIA, Bronce Antiguo I). *Quaderni de 'La Ricerca Scientifica'* 112: 64–85. Rome.
FLANNERY, KENT V., AND MICHAEL D. COE
  1972   Social and Economic Systems in Formative Mesoamerica. In *New Perspectives in Archeology* (Sally R. Binford and Lewis R. Binford, eds.): 267–283. Aldine, Chicago.
FRANKFORT, HENRY
  1951   The Last Predynastic Period in Babylonia. In *The Cambridge Ancient History* 1 (2): 71–92. Cambridge University Press, Cambridge.

FRIED, MORTON H.
  1974 On the Evolution of Social Stratification and the State. In *The Rise and Fall of Civilizations: Modern Archaeological Approaches to Ancient Cultures* (C. C. Lamberg-Karlovsky and Jeremy A. Sabloff, eds.): 26–40. Cummings Publishing Co., Menlo Park, Calif.

HOLE, FRANK
  1974 Investigating the Origins of Mesopotamian Civilization. In *The Rise and Fall of Civilizations: Modern Archaeological Approaches to Ancient Cultures* (C. C. Lamberg-Karlovsky and Jeremy A. Sabloff, eds.): 269–281. Cummings Publishing Co., Menlo Park, Calif.

ISBELL, WILLIAM H.
  1978 Environmental Perturbations and the Origin of the Andean State. In *Social Archeology: Beyond Subsistence and Dating* (Charles Redman et al., eds.): 303–313. Academic Press, Studies in Archeology. New York.

LUMBRERAS, LUÍS GUILLERMO
  1987 Childe and the Urban Revolution: The Central Andean Experience. *Studies in the Neolithic and Urban Revolutions: The V. Gordon Childe Colloquium, Mexico 1986* (Linda Manzanilla, ed.): 327–344. BAR International Series 349, Oxford.

MANZANILLA, LINDA
  1983 La redistribución como proceso de centralización de la producción y circulación de bienes. Análisis de dos casos. *Boletín de Antropología Americana* 7: 5–18. Instituto Panamericano de Geografía e Historia, Mexico, D.F.
  1985a Templo y palacio: Proposiciones sobre el surgimiento de la sociedad urbana y el Estado. *Anales de Antropología* 22, IIA, UNAM, Mexico: 91–114.
  1985b El sitio de Cuanalan en el marco de las comunidades pre-urbanas del Valle de Teotihuacan. In *Mesoamérica y el centro de México. Una antología* (Jesús Monjarás-Ruiz, Rosa Brambila, and Emma Pérez Rocha, eds.): 133–178. INAH, Colección Biblioteca del INAH, Mexico, D.F.
  1986 *La constitución de la sociedad urbana en Mesopotamia: Un proceso en la historia*. Instituto de Investigaciones Antropológicas, Universidad Nacional Autónoma de México, Arqueología, Serie Antropológica 80, Mexico, D.F.
  1987 The Beginnings of Urban Society and the Formation of the State: Temple and Palace as Basic Indicators. In *Studies in the Neolithic and Urban Revolutions: The V. Gordon Childe Colloquium, Mexico, 1986* (Linda Manzanilla, ed.): 271–286. BAR International Series 349, Oxford.
  1988–89 The Study of Room Function in a Residential Compound at Teotihuacan, Mexico. *Origini* 14, *L'Interpretazione Funzionale dei Dati in Paletnologia. Giornate di Studio in Ricordo di Salvatore Maria Puglisi*: 175–186. Universitá La Sapienza, Rome.
  n.d. Apuntes para el estudio arqueológico del almacenamiento y el problema de la redistribución. *Cuadernos del Instituto Nacional de Antropo-*

logía, in honor of Alberto Rex González, Ministerio de Educación y Justicia, Buenos Aires (in press).

MANZANILLA, LINDA, AND LUIS BARBA
    1990   The Study of Activities in Classic Households: Two Case Studies from Coba and Teotihuacan. *Ancient Mesoamerica* 1 (1): 41–49.

MANZANILLA, LINDA, AND EMILIE CARREÓN
    1990   Un incensario teotihuacano en contexto doméstico. Restauración e interpretación. *Antropológicas* 4: 5–18. Instituto de Investigaciones Antropológicas, UNAM, Mexico, D.F.

MANZANILLA, LINDA, AND ERIC WOODARD
    1990   Restos humanos asociados a la Pirámide de Akapana (Tiwanaku, Bolivia). *Latin American Antiquity* 1 (2): 133–149.

MATOS MOCTEZUMA, EDUARDO
    1976   Proyecto Tula: Objetivos y método. In *Proyecto Tula. Segunda Parte:* 7–13. INAH, Mexico, D.F.

MCCLUNG DE TAPIA, EMILY
    1987   Patrones de subsistencia urbana en Teotihuacan. In *Teotihuacan: Nuevos datos, nuevas síntesis, nuevos problemas:* 57–74, Instituto de Investigaciones Antropológicas, Serie Antropológica 72. UNAM, Mexico, D.F.

MILLER, ARTHUR G.
    1973   *The Mural Painting of Teotihuacan.* Dumbarton Oaks, Washington, D.C.

MILLON, CLARA
    1973   Painting, Writing, and Polity in Teotihuacan, Mexico. *American Antiquity* 38 (3): 294–314.

MILLON, RENÉ
    1967   Teotihuacan. *Scientific American* 216 (6): 38–48.
    1988   The Last Years of Teotihuacan Dominance. In *The Collapse of Ancient States and Civilizations* (Norman Yoffee and George L. Cowgill, eds.): 102–164. The University of Arizona Press, Tucson.

MORRIS, CRAIG
    1978   The Archaeological Study of Andean Exchange Systems. In *Social Archeology. Beyond Subsistence and Dating* (Charles L. Redman et al., eds.): 315–327. Academic Press, Studies in Archeology, New York.

MÚNERA BERMÚDEZ, AND LUIS CARLOS
    n.d.   Un taller de cerámica ritual en la Ciudadela. M.A. thesis, Teotihuacan. Escuela Nacional de Antropología e Historia, Mexico, D.F., 1985.

MURRA, JOHN V.
    1975   *Formaciones económicas y políticas del mundo andino.* Instituto de Estudios Peruanos, Lima.
    1985a   "El Archipiélago Vertical" Revisited. In *Andean Ecology and Civilization: An Interdisciplinary Perspective on Andean Ecological Complementarity* (Shozo Masuda, Izumi Shimada, and Craig Morris, eds.): 3–13. Uni-

versity of Tokyo Press, Papers from the Wenner-Gren Foundation for Anthropological Research, Symposium 91, Tokyo.

1985b The Limits and Limitations of the "Vertical Archipelago" in the Andes. In *Andean Ecology and Civilization: An Interdisciplinary Perspective on Andean Ecological Complementarity* (S. Masuda, I. Shimada, and C. Morris, eds.): 15–20. University of Tokyo Press, Papers from the Wenner-Gren Foundation for Anthropological Research, Symposium 91, Tokyo.

NALDA, ENRIQUE

1982 México prehispánico: Origen y formación de las clases sociales. In *México, un pueblo en la historia* 1 (Enrique Semo, ed.): 49–177. Editorial Nueva Imagen, Universidad Autónoma de Puebla, Mexico, D.F.

NISSEN, HANS JÖRG

1972 The City Wall of Uruk. In *Man, Settlement, and Urbanism* (Peter J. Ucko, Ruth Tringham, and G. W. Dimbleby, eds.): 793–798. Duckworth, Hertfordshire.

PALMIERI, ALBA

1973 Scavi nell'area sud-occidentale di Arslantepé. *Origini* 7: 55–228. Istituto di Paletnologia, Rome.

PASZTORY, ESTHER

1972 The Gods of Teotihuacan: A Synthetic Approach in Teotihuacan Iconography. *Atti del XL Congresso Internazionale degli Americanisti* 1: 147–159. Rome.

1978 Artistic Traditions of the Middle Classic Period. In *Middle Classic Mesoamerica: A.D. 400–700* (Esther Pasztory, ed.): 108–142. Columbia University Press, New York.

POLANYI, KARL

1976 La economía como actividad institucionalizada. In *Comercio y mercado en los imperios antiguos* (Karl Polanyi et al., eds.): 289–315. Editorial Labor, Monografías Labor Universitaria, Barcelona.

REYNA ROBLES, ROSA MA.

1977 Desarrollo y evolución de la "unidad habitacional" en una aldea preclásica del Altiplano Central: Loma Torremote como un ejemplo. In *Los procesos de cambio (en Mesoamérica y áreas circunvecinas)* 1. XV Mesa Redonda: 377–383. Sociedad Mexicana de Antropología, Guanajuato.

ROJAS, JOSÉ LUIS DE

1987 El control del granero del imperio y la consolidación del estado mexica. In *Almacenamiento de productos agropecuarios en México* (Gail Mummert, ed.): 29–38. El Colegio de Michoacán, Zamora.

SANDERS, WILLIAM T.

1967 Life in a Classic Village. In *Teotihuacan: Onceava Mesa Redonda 1966*: 123–147. Sociedad Mexicana de Antropología, Mexico, D.F.

1968 Hydraulic Agriculture, Economic Symbiosis, and the Evolution of the State in Central Mexico. In *Anthropological Archeology in the Americas*

(Betty Meggers, ed.): 88–107. The Anthropological Society of Washington, Brooklyn.

SERVICE, ELMAN R.
 1971 *Primitive Social Organization: An Evolutionary Perspective*. Studies in Anthropology, Random House, New York.
 1975 *Origins of the State and Civilization: The Process of Cultural Evolution*. W. W. Norton, New York.

SIDRYS, RAYMOND
 1977 Mass-Distance Measures of the Maya Obsidian Trade. In *Exchange Systems in Prehistory* (Timothy K. Earle and Jonathon E. Ericson, eds.): 91–107. Academic Press, Studies in Archaeology, New York.

SLOAD, REBECCA
 1987 The Great Compound: A Forum for Regional Activities. In *Teotihuacan: Nuevos datos, nuevas síntesis, nuevos problemas* (E. McClung de Tapia and E. C. Rattray, eds.): 219–241. Instituto de Investigaciones Antropológicas, Serie Antropológica 72. UNAM, Mexico, D.F.

SPENCE, MICHAEL W.
 1987 The Scale and Structure of Obsidian Production in Teotihuacan. In *Teotihuacan: Nuevos datos, nuevas síntesis, nuevos problemas* (E. McClung de Tapia and E. C. Rattray, eds.): 429–450. Instituto de Investigaciones Antropológicas, Serie Antropológica 72. UNAM, Mexico, D.F.

STARBUCK, DAVID R.
 1987 Faunal Evidence for the Teotihuacan Subsistence Base. In *Teotihuacan Nuevos datos, nuevas síntesis, nuevos problemas* (E. McClung de Tapia and E. C. Rattray, eds.): 75–90. UNAM, Mexico, D.F.

VALADEZ, RAÚL, AND LINDA MANZANILLA
 1988 Restos faunísticos y áreas de actividad en una unidad habitacional de la antigua ciudad de Teotihuacan, *Revista Mexicana de Estudios Antropológicos* 34 (1): 147–168. Sociedad Mexicana de Antropología, México.

WRIGHT, HENRY T.
 1969 *The Administration of Rural Production in an Early Mesopotamian Town*. Museum of Anthropology, University of Michigan, Anthropological Papers 38, Ann Arbor.

Teotihuacan Studies: From 1950 to 1990 and Beyond

RENÉ MILLON

UNIVERSITY OF ROCHESTER

INTRODUCTION

WHAT WAS THERE ABOUT TEOTIHUACAN that makes it stand apart as so different from other cities of its time? It was large by Mesoamerican standards, but it was not extraordinarily large in global perspective. The city included at least two foreign *barrios;* the people in one of these neighborhoods maintained their ethnic identity for some 400 years. The city's principal deity was female. These are important characteristics and form part of the distinctiveness of Teotihuacan. But in themselves they would not be sufficient to set the city apart so clearly from its contemporaries and predecessors.

Teotihuacan already was a city of impressive size when it explosively expanded, more than doubling in area and population in a very short time. Most of the population of its region, the Basin of Mexico (Evans and Berlo, this volume, fig. 2), was persuaded or compelled to move permanently to Teotihuacan early in the first century A.D. This population concentration persisted for some seven centuries with only moderate resettlement of the Basin. Despite its potential wealth, the Basin remained under-utilized for these seven centuries compared with what had gone before and with what followed. Yet striking as this was, similar concentrations are said to have occurred early in the history of cities in Sumer and Egypt.

Late in the city's history, it appears that infant mortality was so high among those low on the social scale that the city's population could have been maintained only by attracting outsiders. But in this it was not alone. Similar conditions existed in non-industrialized cities in medieval and early modern Europe.

What then makes Teotihuacan's urban society so extraordinary, so intriguingly different? There is, first of all, what we can infer about its political history. Its early rulers appear strong and powerful, like their contemporaries in other parts of Mesoamerica. This phase culminates in the third century A.D. with hierarchy and domination bluntly and directly expressed in the mass sacrifice of 150–175 soldiers and twenty or more other persons

René Millon

in the dedication of the Temple of the Feathered Serpent in the Ciudadela, the city's political and religious center (Fig. 1). A strong reaction occurred after this mass immolation. A check on the exercise of arbitrary rule was institutionalized and maintained for the next 400–500 years, a state of affairs worthy of wonder today.

The scale of monumental architecture on the city's principal avenue, the "Street of the Dead,"[1] was without precedent anywhere in pre-Hispanic Mesoamerica. This monumentality—the sheer mass and height of its great pyramids, the multiplicity of its temples and public buildings, the scale of the avenue where all this was built—must have been intended to overwhelm and overawe not only outsiders but also the ordinary Teotihuacano. The architecture on the "Street of the Dead" and many aspects of the city's art proclaim power and hierarchy. Murals, ceramics, and figurines frequently portray personages of high status. Yet Teotihuacan art is almost totally free of any representations of domination or of explicit hierarchical relationships. Rulers are not publicly portrayed engaging in grand exploits. This absence of overt manifestations of domination contrasts sharply with the Maya and with ancient societies in Peru, Egypt, and Sumer.

Even heart sacrifice, a ritual of central importance, was usually represented in indirect ways. Human hearts are depicted in conventionalized fashion and are shown impaled on knives, but the actual act of human sacrifice is not portrayed. The same is true of sacrificial bloodletting in autosacrifice—spines used in sacrifice are shown with bloodied tips but are not shown in use.

Teotihuacan's residential architecture also was distinctive. Nothing remotely comparable in number and size occurs elsewhere in Mesoamerica. The basic residential unit was a compound, with rooms arranged to accommodate many households. Some were palatial; others were of shoddy construction. They varied greatly in size; a common intermediate size was close to 200 feet on a side. There were some 2,000 of these apartment compounds. These compounds, with their distinctive characteristics, were the basic units in the city's social and political structure.

Rulership at Teotihuacan for the last 400–500 years of its history appears to have been kept in check by a collective leadership. The apparent maintenance of this collective leadership for so many centuries is one of the most unusual and distinctive aspects of Teotihuacan society.

These are some of the ways Teotihuacan stands apart from its predecessors, contemporaries, and successors. The search for explanations of its distinctiveness and the exploration of its dimensions is bound to quicken and transform

[1] The "Street of the Dead" designation (Nahuatl *miccaotli*) was given to the city's principal avenue by the Aztecs, hundreds of years after the buildings bordering it had been burned and fallen into ruins.

Teotihuacan Studies

our knowledge, leading us to a new level of understanding. The transformation I foresee would be the fourth in Teotihuacan studies. The first came in the early 1920s based on the work of many investigators, including the synthesis of Eduard Seler (1915) and the pioneering multi-disciplinary study of Teotihuacan's past and present by Manuel Gamio and his associates (1922). The second synthesis dates to 1950 and centers on the work of Pedro Armillas (1950, 1951).[2] We are now enjoying the fruits of the third transformation in our knowledge, principally as a result of Mexican government research of the 1960s directed by Ignacio Bernal (1963), and the 1980s directed by Rubén Cabrera Castro (Cabrera, Rodriguez, and Morelos 1982a, 1982b), the Basin of Mexico research of William Sanders and his associates (Sanders 1981; Sanders, Parsons, and Santley 1979), the Rochester-Toronto-Brandeis research of the Teotihuacan Mapping Project (R. Millon 1973; Millon, Drewitt, and Cowgill 1973), and many fundamental studies of Teotihuacan iconography of outstanding significance, among which George Kubler's *Iconography of the Art of Teotihuacan* (1967) stands out as the most influential (see Evans and Berlo, this volume).

1950 AND 1990 COMPARED

The year 1950 was pivotal in Teotihuacan studies; Pedro Armillas published an extraordinarily influential article, his synthesis of what was then known about Teotihuacan. Also influential was a theoretical formulation I

---

[2] Armillas' synthesis was made possible in part by the landmark study by Kidder, Jennings, and Shook (1946) of Esperanza phase Kaminaljuyu in the Valley of Guatemala and its connections with Teotihuacan.

Fig. 1 (*overleaf*) Central Teotihuacan, an area of 3 mi² (7 km²). Entire city covered 8 mi² (20 km²) with an estimated seventh-century population of 125,000. Beyond the temples, public buildings, palaces, and other structures on and adjoining the city's main street, the "Street of the Dead," are the buildings occupied by most of the city's inhabitants. The Teotihuacan Mapping Project established that the basic residential structure was a one-story apartment compound; 2,000 were mapped in surface survey. Open rectangles on the map represent unexcavated apartment compounds. Yayahuala, Zacuala Palace, and Tetitla (left center) are completely excavated apartment compounds, with high windowless walls and rooms clustered about courtyards. Atetelco and the five La Ventilla compounds (left) and Teopancaxco, Xolalpan, Tepantitla, Tlacuilapaxco, and Techinantitla (right) represent partially excavated apartment compounds. The northern half of the "Street of the Dead" shown here is 1½ mi. long (2½ km). The Mall in Washington, D.C., is almost 2 mi. long (3 km). The "Street of the Dead" Complex (center), a large walled administrative and temple complex, covers an area of more than 30 acres (the Pentagon in Arlington, Virginia, covers 29 acres). The Ciudadela compound, bottom right, the city's political and religious center, covers 40 acres. The Great Compound, bottom left, was still larger. For views on how it was used, see Figs. 8a–c and text.

René Millon

Teotihuacan Studies

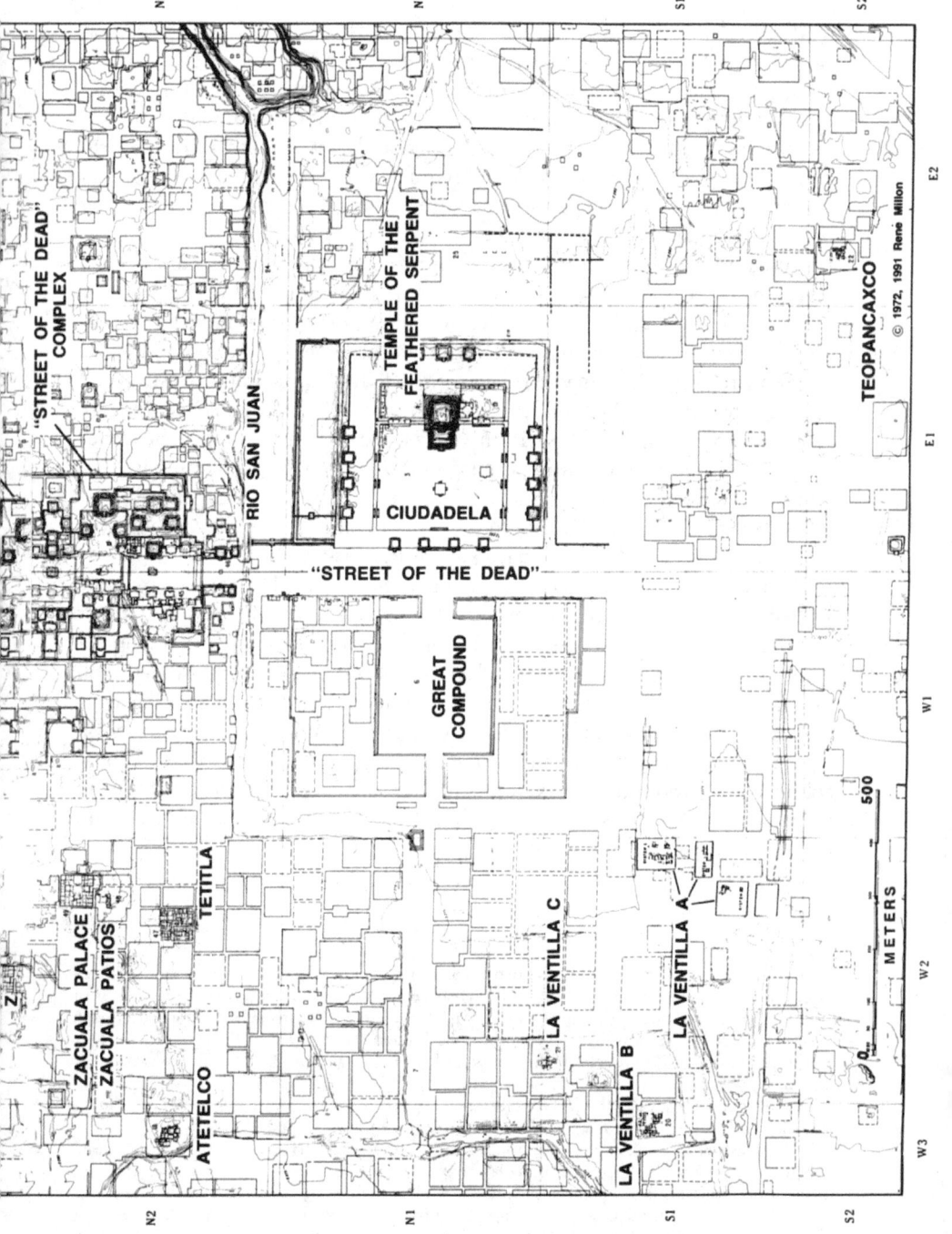

René Millon

heard him deliver at the Congress of Americanists in New York in 1949 on stages of cultural development in Mesoamerica (Armillas 1951). Ignacio Marquina's massive *Arquitectura Prehispánica* was published in 1951, with a long chapter on Teotihuacan. And it was in 1950 that Gordon Childe related his "urban revolution" concept for the first and only time to a New World civilization, that of the ancient Maya (Childe 1950).

Forty years ago it was possible to argue whether Teotihuacan was a city or a ceremonial center. But to Pedro Armillas the evidence was clear—Teotihuacan was a metropolis of pyramids, temples, palaces, and houses covering an area of at least 7½ km² (3 mi²) (Armillas 1950: 37). Today Teotihuacan is recognized by the overwhelming majority of investigators to have been a city by any definition. As we have seen, Teotihuacan at its height in the sixth century A.D. was one of the largest non-industrialized urban centers the world had seen. We now know that it covered an area of 8 mi², with an estimated population of 125,000. Its urban status, however defined, is no longer an issue because in the interim Teotihuacan has been subjected to detailed mapping as part of the Teotihuacan Mapping Project (Millon, Drewitt, and Cowgill 1973). This mapping gave the study of the urbanization process at Teotihuacan an enormous impetus.[3]

Most houses in Teotihuacan built prior to the third century A.D. were leveled in the reconstruction process that saw the building of apartment compounds throughout the city. To provide firm foundations for apartment compounds, the earth was cleared and the underlying indurated soil (*tepetate*) was leveled. This resulted in the destruction of most earlier construction. As a result, pre-apartment compound housing survives only on the city's peripheries[4] or as surviving remnants in the foundations of some apartment compounds (for example, in the Oaxaca *barrio* in site 7:N1W6). It is evident, nevertheless, that Teotihuacan had a population approaching 100,000 in the first century A.D.[5]

---

[3] I found it productive to view the urbanization process in a traditional, non-industrialized community like Teotihuacan as an active creative force in the transformation not only of Teotihuacan but of the region in which it was located. Here the insights of John Friedmann (1961) and Paul Wheatley (1971, 1972) must be singled out, as well as those of Robert McCormick Adams (1972, 1981, 1988), Jorge Hardoy (1968, 1973) and S. N. Eisenstadt and A. Shachar (1989).

[4] As in squares N4W6 (Millon, Drewitt, and Cowgill 1973: 25, sites 7E, 8, 9, 10) and N7W8 (Blucher n.d.: 191–202, 249–255; R. Millon 1973: fig. 13a).

[5] The density of Tzacualli phase ceramic and other artifactual surface residues at Teotihuacan, when compared with those of the Xolalpan phase (ca. A.D. 400–650) for which we have population estimates based on architecture (R. Millon 1973: 44–45), leave no doubt that the early city had a residential population closer to 100,000 than 50,000 (Cowgill 1974). The 1950 view of some that Teotihuacan was a ceremonial center with few permanent inhabitants is no longer tenable in 1990 for any part of its history.

Teotihuacan Studies

The Question of Dating

In addition to arguing that Teotihuacan was a city of impressive size, Armillas also was able to demonstrate its chronological placement in the early and middle centuries of the first millennium A.D. rather than much later, as it still had been possible to argue only a few years earlier. The key to establishing this was linking the time of maximum Teotihuacan "influence" in Mesoamerica to the Maya calendar through cross-dating. This was possible because Alfred Kidder and his associates found distinctive Teotihuacan ceramics of the Teotihuacan III phase (redesignated the Xolalpan phase by Armillas) juxtaposed with lowland Maya ceramics in tombs beneath or in front of the staircases of Esperanza phase Teotihuacan-style temples in the highland Guatemala center of Kaminaljuyu.[6] Because chronological phases in so many parts of Mesoamerica were roughly coeval with Teotihuacan's Xolalpan phase (Teotihuacan III), its chronological placement now established that all of them fell somewhere in the A.D. 400–600 time span. Mesoamerican chronology now had a backbone around which phases stratigraphically earlier or later could be organized (Armillas 1950: 63–64, 69–70). This was especially important because in 1950 radiocarbon dating had only just been discovered.

We know much more about Teotihuacan's chronology in 1990, thanks to radiocarbon dating and to many more stratigraphic excavations and ceramic analyses of them carried out since 1950, some of which are discussed below (Figs. 2, 3a, 3b).[7] Nevertheless, many important problems in Teotihuacan's chronology remain to be solved.

---

[6] The lowland Maya ceramics were assignable to what was called the Tzakol II–III phase in the ceramic sequence of the lowland Guatemala Peten Maya center of Uaxactun. Tzakol phase Maya pottery sherds had also been found at Teotihuacan. Through other associations that Tzakol phase was, in turn, related to dated inscriptions in the Maya Long Count. These made it possible to date the Tzakol phase to the period from A.D. 300 to 600. Linking Teotihuacan with the chronology of the Maya did much more than clarify the chronological position of Teotihuacan itself. Teotihuacan's "influence" at its height was far-flung, extending, as Armillas recounted it, from Copan in Honduras in the southeast to the Pacific coast state of Colima in Mexico in the northwest. When the Teotihuacan III (Xolalpan) phase was dated to the 5th and 6th centuries A.D., it was then possible to place as roughly equivalent in time the Monte Alban IIIA phase in the Valley of Oaxaca and relevant portions of the ceramic sequences of centers in Puebla, of such Gulf Coast centers as El Tajin, Cerro de las Mesas, and Tres Zapotes, and of centers in west Mexico from Guerrero to Colima.

[7] The major contributors to ceramic analysis were, initially, James Bennyhoff, Florencia Müller, and Laurette Séjourné, and subsequently, Evelyn Rattray, Robert Smith, Mary Hopkins, Charles Kolb, Paula Krotser, Louanna Lackey, William Sanders, and, for figurines, Warren Barbour. The Teotihuacan chronological chart was prepared in 1964 and modified in 1979. It was based both on radiocarbon dates (for example, for the Tzacualli phase, see Millon, Drewitt, and Bennyhoff 1965: 33) and cross-dating, especially with the lowland Maya, on which there is much more information in 1990 than in 1950. Two important Teotihuacan Mapping Project (TMP) excavations analyzed by Evelyn Rattray that played a critical role in establishing the ceramic stratigraphy of the city's last 400 years were carried out in apartment compounds famous for their murals—Tepantitla (TE23) (Fig. 2) and Tetitla (TE24) (Fig. 3a,b).

René Millon

Pushing back the heart of Teotihuacan's chronology to the middle years of the first millennium A.D. had the consequence of firmly disentangling Teotihuacan from the historic Toltecs of Tollan or Tula.[8] Toltec-related deposits at Teotihuacan were stratigraphically separated from Teotihuacan constructions by deposits of the Coyotlatelco phase. Pedro Armillas saw the latter accumulating over the ruins of a city burned and destroyed (Armillas 1950: 58–59, 69). He based this conclusion on his own excavations in the Viking Group and Tepantitla (Armillas 1944: 122–123, 131) and on the earlier observations on the "Street of the Dead" by Eduard Seler (1915: 408, 433).

In 1990 we know much more about what burned and what did not in the fires Armillas wrote about in 1950. Mapping the entire city made it possible to put the evidence of fire in context. The fires were concentrated in the city's center, on and near the "Street of the Dead" from the Ciudadela north to the Moon Pyramid. Many of the temples outside the city center show evidence of burning, but this was true of only a small percentage of apartment compounds. What could not have been clear in 1950 is that the concentration of fires on and adjoining the "Street of the Dead" formed part of a systematic process of ritual destruction carried out on a monumental scale with such rigor, such intensity, and such violence that its purpose must have been political—the annihilation of those who led Teotihuacan and the ideology with which they were identified. The result was the annihilation of Teotihuacan political dominance (R. Millon 1988a: 145–156). To prevent

---

The long stratigraphic sequence at Tetitla includes thirty-eight floors of earth, most of them kitchen floors that built up by slow accretion.

[8] This is not to say that there may not be echoes of Teotihuacan in Tollan legends. The archaeological identification of the ancient city of Tula, Hidalgo, 50 mi northwest of Teotihuacan, with the Tollan of the chronicles was established in 1940 when the earlier historical analyses of Wigberto Jiménez Moreno were confirmed in excavations at Tula by Jorge Acosta (Armillas 1950: 64–65).

Fig. 2 (*opposite*) Tepantitla. TMP stratigraphic trench (TE23) 10 m south of Portico 10, the Portico of the Jaguars, east of Portico 9, the feline deity patio (earlier misnamed the "Red Tlaloc" Patio) (Miller 1973: 93, plan IX; Pasztory 1976: 56, 230–242, 281, fig. 6). This was a domestic part of the compound through most of its 300-year history, with a succession of earth floors, some of which were kitchens. Sometime after Concrete Floor 1 was laid down, probably in the latter part of the Metepec phase (early eighth century), rubbish, much of it broken Metepec phase pottery, was allowed to accumulate on it (layer 7) until the fiery destruction that demolished the city center and other parts of the city, including Tepantitla (Armillas 1944: 122, n. 2). Subsequent deposition of material of the Coyotlatelco (Xometla) phase relates to a smaller urban community with different cultural traditions that arose on the ruins of the destroyed metropolis. TE23 was excavated by Hilda Castañeda.

Teotihuacan Studies

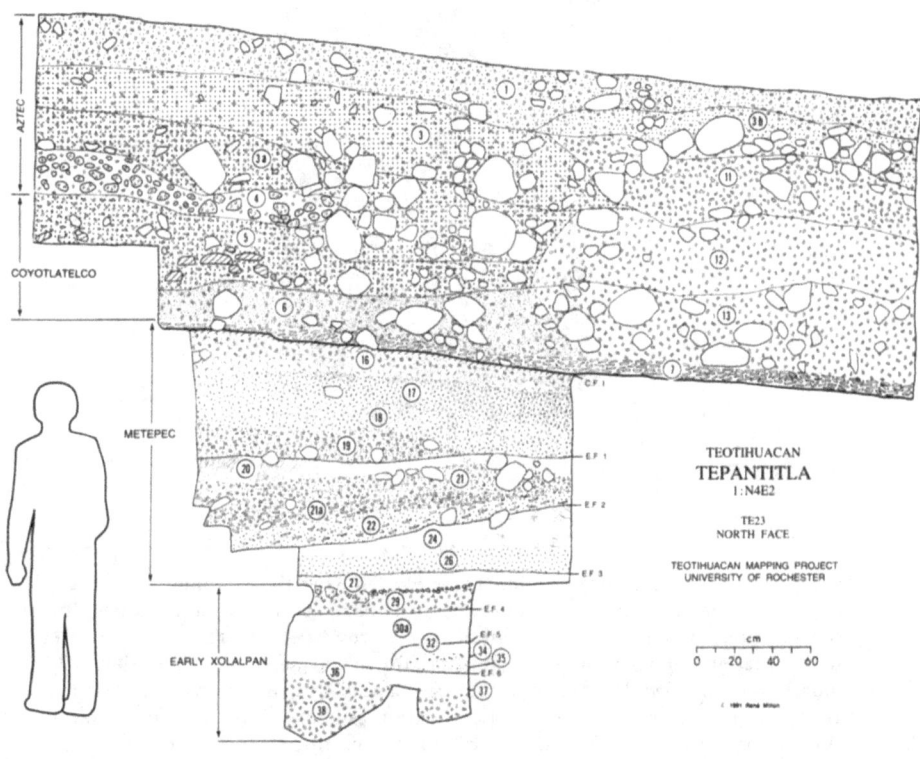

René Millon

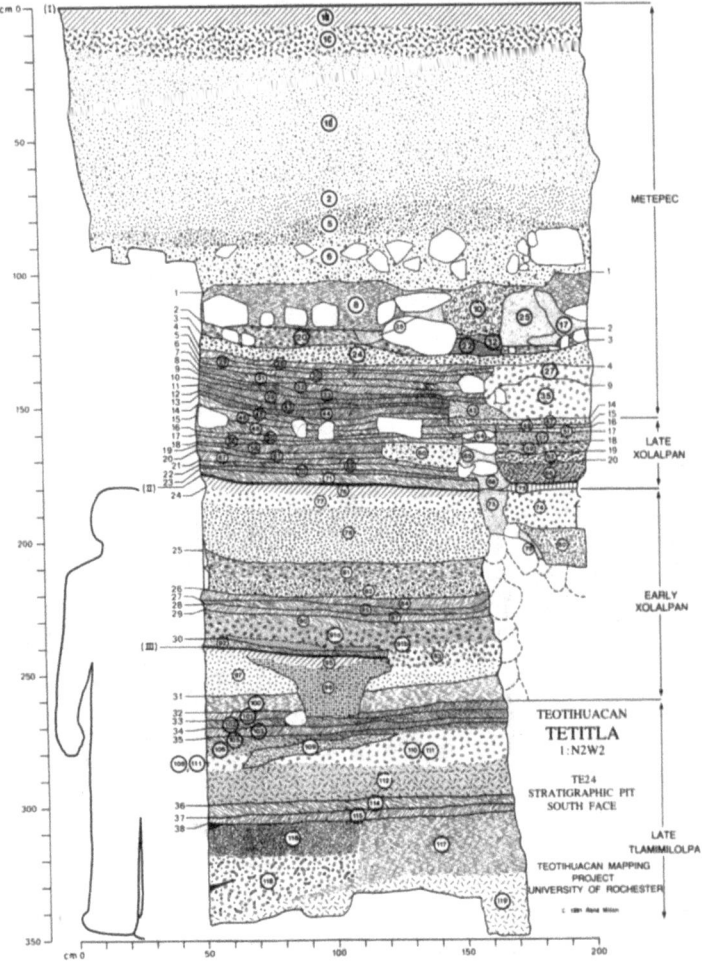

Fig. 3a   Tetitla. TMP stratigraphic pit (TE24) in Room 12A (Miller 1973: 119, plan XIII), an interior room in the southeast apartment of the compound's penultimate construction level. Room 12A is immediately west of Room 12, a room with eight representations of a kneeling net jaguar figure approaching a temple. One of these murals was removed by looters in the 1940s and is now in Dumbarton Oaks (Miller 1973: fig. 317, mural 8). The TE24 excavation establishes that this mural and its in situ companions, as well as other murals in this apartment date to the middle years of the Metepec phase (seventh to eighth centuries A.D.) (Appendix). The construction history revealed in this pit spans a period of 400 years and disclosed two earlier construction levels with floors of concrete and 38 floors of earth, more than half of which were kitchens (Fig. 3b). The first eight floors of earth preceded the first use of concrete in this part of the compound.

Teotihuacan Studies

CONCRETE FLOORS

(I) Concrete floor (II) Concrete floor (III) Concrete floor

EARTH FLOORS

1. EF Sandy clay
2. EF Clay, tepetate & stone
3. EF Clay & crushed tepetate
4. EF Clay
5. EF Compact sandy clay w/cascajo
6. EF Compact sandy clay w/cascajo & crushed tepetate
7. EF Clay & crushed tepetate
8. EF Clay & crushed tepetate
9. EF Clay, charcoal, soot & ash
10. EF Clay, charcoal, soot & ash
11. EF Clay, charcoal & soot
12. EF Clay, ash & soot
13. EF Clay & soot
14. EF Compact clay
15. EF Clay & ash
16. EF Clay & burned earth
17. EF Clay & crushed tepetate
18. EF Clay, crushed tepetate, ash & charcoal
19. EF Sandy clay & crushed tepetate
20. EF Clay & burned earth
21. EF Compact clay & burned earth
22. EF Compact clay & burned earth & ash
23. EF Compact clay, cascajo & crushed tepetate
24. "Floor" 24 (crushed tepetate)
25. EF Clay, cascajo, tepetate & stones
26. EF Compact clay, ash & charcoal
27. EF Clay, ash & charcoal
28. EF Clay, ash, charcoal & crushed tepetate
29. EF Clay, ash, charcoal & crushed tepetate
30. EF Compact clay, crushed tepetate & charcoal
31. EF Compact clay
32. EF Clay w/charcoal
33. EF Clay w/burned earth
34. EF Compact sandy clay, burned earth & tepetate
35. EF Compact clay, ash & charcoal
36. EF Compact clay
37. EF Compact clay & charcoal
38. EF Sandy clay & charcoal

TEOTIHUACAN
TETITLA
1:N2W2

TE24
STRATIGRAPHIC PIT
SOUTH FACE

LAYERS

(1b) Concrete
(1c) Crushed tepetate (w/inclusions of stone & tepetate)
(1d) Fill of stones, tepetate, cascajo & crushed tepetate
(2) Compact earth fill w/sparse inclusions
(5) Compact earth fill w/stone & cascajo
(6) Stone & earth fill
(8) Sandy clay
(10) Earth & rubble fill
(12) Compact yellowish earth (matrix of offering A)
(17) Prepared clay mortar (drain well)

(20) Clay, tepetate & stone
(22) Water deposited silt
(24) Earth & crushed tepetate
(25) Prepared clay mortar (lodo preparado)
(26) Clay
(27) Intrusive pit (loose soil)
(29) Compact sandy clay w/casacajo
(30) Compact sandy clay w/cascajo & crushed tepetate
(31) Clay & crushed tepetate
(32) Clay & crushed tepetate

(33) Clay, charcoal, soot & ash
(35) Intrusive pit (loose fill)
(39) Clay, charcoal, soot & ash
(42) Compact earth & charcoal
(43) Clay, charcoal & soot
(44) Clay, ash & soot
(45) Clay & soot
(46) Compact clay
(47) Earth fill w/stones
(48) Clay & ash
(49) Earth fill w/stones

(50) Clay & burned earth
(51) Compact earth fill
(56) Clay & crushed tepetate
(57) Compact sandy earth fill
(58) Clay, crushed tepetate, ash & charcoal
(59) Clay & stone fill
(60) Tepetate fill
(61) Sandy clay & crushed tepetate
(62) Burned earth fill
(64) Prepared clay mortar

(65) Prepared clay mortar
(66) Burned earth, charcoal, ash & tepetate fill
(67) Clay & burned earth
(68) Prepared clay mortar
(69) Compact clay & burned earth
(70) Compact clay, burned earth & ash
(71) Compact clay, cascajo & crusted tepetate
(73) Concrete base of drain
(74) Crushed tepetate
(75) Prepared clay mortar

(76) Concrete
(77) "Floor" 24 (crushed tepetate)
(78) Tepetate fill
(80) Fill of earth, cascajo, stones & charcoal
(81) Clay, cascajo, tepetate & stones
(82) Fill of earth, charcoal, tepetate & cascajo
(84) Compact clay, ash & charcoal
(85) Clay, ash & charcoal
(87) Clay, ash, charcoal & crushed tepetate
(89) Clay, ash, charcoal & crushed tepetate

(90) Clay, ash, charcoal & crushed tepetate
(91a) Fill of tepetate, cascajo & earth
(91b) Fill of tepetate, cascajo & earth
(92) Compact clay, crushed tepetate & charcoal
(93) Loose fill of earth & tepetate
(95) Concrete
(96) Cascajo & earth fill
(97) Compact earth fill
(100) Compact clay
(101) Clay w/charcoal

(102) Clay w/burned earth
(103) Compact sandy clay, burned earth & tepetate
(105) Compact clay, ash & charcoal
(106) Compact sandy earth fill
(108) Loose earth fill
(109) Fill of earth, charcoal & ash
(110) Loose earth fill
(111) Loose earth fill
(112) Loose sandy fill with tepetate
(114) Compact clay

(115) Compact clay & charcoal
(116) Firepit X Sandy clay & charcoal
(117) Sandy clay fill
(118) Fill of earth, stones, sherds & charcoal
(119) Tepetate

Fig. 3b Tetitla. Layer identifications for TMP stratigraphic pit (TE24). TE24 was excavated by Darlena K. Blucher and Evelyn Rattray.

René Millon

Teotihuacan's leadership from ascending again to a position of dominance, it must have been thought necessary to extirpate the institutions embodying Teotihuacan ideology. To accomplish this, it was necessary not only to demolish its sacred buildings but to desacralize what remained by ritual destruction through fire.

For various reasons set forth elsewhere (R. Millon 1988a: 156–158), I have argued that this fiery destruction was led by Teotihuacanos rather than by outsiders. Those responsible for the demolition carried it out so effectively that the city that subsequently arose around this ruined center, while large and populous, never approached the prominence of the Teotihuacan that had dominated central Mexico for so many centuries. No longer was it a major religious center; most of the buildings on the "Street of the Dead" were never rebuilt or used again. The break with the past was sharp and abrupt. As Richard Diehl (1989: 16) has observed, post-destruction Teotihuacan "apparently lacked an architectural tradition, large public construction efforts, monumental art, and even a definable art style." The sharpness of this break is particularly clear in residential architecture.[9] There must have been some period, however brief, when the city was largely abandoned, followed by a gradual return to a place that no longer was a community—where new community ties developed to form a new and very different urban tradition.[10]

The association in 1950 of the end of Teotihuacan with fiery destruction has stood the test of time, even though we now see the process as much more complex. In 1950 it was not known that a new city, much more modest in size, arose on both sides of the "Street of the Dead" a short time after its buildings had been destroyed. The size of the new city and its profound differences from its predecessor did not emerge until the results of the mapping of Teotihuacan had been analyzed.

Much less was known in 1950 about the beginnings of Teotihuacan than about its end. Pedro Armillas (1950: 70) dated the building of the Pyramids of the Sun and Moon to the second and third centuries A.D., only a century or so later than they would be dated today. But because the extent of the ceramic residues left by the inhabitants of early Teotihuacan was not known, the phase called Teotihuacan I by George Vaillant (1938) and

---

[9] For instance, at Tepantitla deep Aztec and Coyotlatelco deposits without architectural associations directly overlie Metepec phase sherds (layer 7) on the uppermost floor of a long architectural sequence in the southeast quadrant of the compound (see Fig. 2).

[10] In 1966, the Teotihuacan Mapping Project (TMP) adopted the name *Oxtoticpac* for this brief phase of near abandonment following its definition in cave deposits bordering the ancient city by personnel from Sanders' project. Ceramics and figurines associated with this phase are discussed and illustrated in Sanders (1986: 369–371) and Barbour (1987: 704–714; n.d.a). Evelyn Rattray (n.d.a) has been unable to isolate similar ceramic evidence from stratigraphic deposits in TMP excavations within the city. This may be partly due to its relative scarcity in the city because the Oxtoticpac phase was so brief (50 years or less) and dwelling areas attributable to it are likely to have been few (Millon 1967: 13–14).

Tzacualli by Armillas (1950: 67–68) was thought to have been prior to the construction of all known buildings at Teotihuacan. He saw the beginnings of urbanization as occurring with the construction of the Pyramids of the Sun and Moon as this phase ended.[11]

The mapping survey subsequently demonstrated that Tzacualli phase Teotihuacan was large and populous—estimated at 80,000 or more—and that the still earlier Patlachique phase community also was large (more than 3 mi^2) with an estimated population of 20,000–40,000 (Cowgill 1974, 1979: 55; R. Millon 1981: 220, 221).[12] Teotihuacan developed into a city in the Patlachique phase (ca. 150–1 B.C.) (see map, Sanders 1981: fig 6.13). The construction of the pyramids and other monumental structures was undertaken in the Tzacualli phase (ca. A.D. 1–150), following the concentration of most of the Basin of Mexico's population in the city at the beginning of the Tzacualli phase (Evans and Berlo, this volume, fig. 2). No one had any inkling of this in 1950. Its discovery could only have followed surveys of the entire Basin of Mexico which were not attempted until 1960 when they were begun by William Sanders and his associates (Sanders, Parsons, and Santley 1979).[13] These transformed our knowledge of settlements and land use over time and made it possible to deal with the settlement history of the Basin as a whole from period to period, from the earliest settlements to the Spanish Conquest.[14]

---

[11] Armillas differed with most earlier workers at Teotihuacan (R. Millon 1960: 2–3) in arguing that the Tzacualli phase ceramics found in the interior of the Sun Pyramid had been made by the founders of Teotihuacan culture and did not represent the cultural remnants of a people unrelated to the builders of the pyramid. Not long after, it became clear that Tzacualli phase ceramics covered an extensive area (8–9 mi^2) (R. Millon 1964, 1973: 52–54, figs. 13a, b; Cowgill 1974: 385–388) and Tzacualli phase constructions were uncovered far from the city center and its pyramids (e.g., Millon and Bennyhoff 1961; Blucher n.d.).

[12] In 1950 Armillas named the pre-Tzacualli phase *Chimalhuacan* based on the ceramic complex from a settlement that had bordered Lake Texcoco in the southeastern part of the Basin of Mexico. Though it had not been isolated at Teotihuacan, he believed this phase to be antecedent to the Tzacualli phase on stylistic grounds (Armillas 1950: 60, 67). Subsequent discoveries proved him right. Because the Chimalhuacan phase did not refer to Teotihuacan or any other settlement in the Valley of Teotihuacan, *Patlachique,* a local place-name was chosen to replace it. William Sanders suggested this name because he and his associates had located surface concentrations of the complex on the lower slopes of Cerro Patlachique in 1963 in the course of their Valley of Teotihuacan surface surveys (Millon, Drewitt, and Bennyhoff 1965: 32–33; Blucher n.d.; Sanders, Parsons, and Santley 1979).

[13] An integral part of the Basin of Mexico surface surveys and excavations of Sanders, Parsons, and Santley was tracing the development of agriculture, especially of irrigation and terracing and relating this to patterns of settlement and demography. This was an extension of the researches and interests of Armillas (1949; West and Armillas 1950). Among its many accomplishments, the Sanders project established the economic importance of irrigation in the Teotihuacan Valley during the rise of Teotihuacan.

[14] Armillas (1950: 60, 61) also discussed excavations at another center closely related to Teotihuacan in the Basin of Mexico—Azcapotzalco. He erroneously thought the ceramics of Azcapotzalco represented a Teotihuacan occupation (which he named Ahuitzotla-Amantla) (also called Teotihuacan IV) that was only sparsely represented at Teotihuacan itself because he thought Teotihuacan by this time had been destroyed by fire. But material of this phase proved

René Millon

By 1990 the "Street of the Dead" had been totally transformed in appearance from what it had been in 1950 when only a few structures between the Moon Pyramid and the Ciudadela had been excavated or partly excavated. This transformation was effected by the Mexican government excavations of the Instituto Nacional de Antropología e Historia (INAH)—the extensive, large-scale Proyecto Teotihuacan excavations of 1960–64, directed by Ignacio Bernal (1963), and the more intensive, more problem-oriented excavations of the Proyecto Arqueológico Teotihuacan of 1980–82, directed by Rubén Cabrera Castro (Cabrera, Rodriguez, and Morelos 1982a, 1982b).

It is difficult to overstate the effect produced by the 1960–64 excavations. Even though what was exposed were the skeletal remains of temple-platforms and other public buildings, the exposure of more than a mile and a quarter of this monumental construction qualitatively changed the appearance of the city center.[15] It forcibly drew attention to the multiplicity of temples and public buildings disposed on both sides of the avenue, to the scale of the conception of those who planned and built the "Street of the Dead," and to their clear intent to overwhelm the viewer.

Even though much of the 1960–64 work remains unpublished, the array of buildings excavated has brought the city center to life in ways that could not have been anticipated. To illustrate this one has only to compare the relative simplicity of Ignacio Marquina's reconstruction of the "Street of the Dead" made before the avenue was excavated (Gamio 1922, I(I): lám. 12) with the complexity revealed by excavation (Fig. 1). The 1960–64 excavations, together with those of 1980–82, have made it possible to draw conclusions, raise questions, and pose problems that could not have been intelligently formulated earlier. The gulf between 1950 and 1990 is truly enormous here.

In 1950 what was known of Teotihuacan residential architecture was based on a half dozen partly excavated residential complexes on the "Street of the Dead" and the same number beyond the city center. These were sufficiently diverse to mask their common characteristics and to work against recognition of how truly distinctive Teotihuacan's residential architecture was. It was not until the early 1960s when Laurette Séjourné completely excavated first Yayahuala, then Zacuala Palace[16] and Tetitla that it

---

to be much more abundant at Teotihuacan than Armillas realized. We designated it by a local name, *Metepec*. Armillas was not sure whether the Tlamimilolpa phase followed or preceded the Xolalpan phase. Sigvald Linné (1956), after reanalyzing Burial 1 at Tlamimilolpa, argued persuasively that the Tlamimilolpa phase was earlier (also R. Millon 1960: 5–7). Subsequent excavations established beyond question that the Tlamimilolpa phase preceded Xolalpan (Fig. 3).

[15] For a discussion of some of the issues involved in the conservation of architecture on the "Street of the Dead" and elsewhere in the city and of problems posed by attempts at architectural restoration at Teotihuacan, see Cabrera (1987).

[16] Laurette Séjourné (1959, 1966a) did not excavate Zacuala Palace completely when she first dug there.

became apparent that the city's basic residential unit was a permanent, often large, one-story apartment compound (Séjourné 1966a). They were compounds with high, windowless outer walls that presented a faceless exterior; floors were of distinctive concrete or earth; walls were of stone or adobe; surfaces were commonly covered with lime plaster; interiors consisted of groupings of rooms organized around patios with under-floor drainage systems. The Teotihuacan Mapping Project (TMP) crews were mapping the city at the same time, and it was the overall perspective provided by these surveys and the map made from them that led to the realization that there were some 2,000 apartment compounds in the city at its height ca. A.D. 600 (Evans and Berlo, this volume, fig. 3) (R. Millon 1970, 1976: 215–226; 1981: 203–210). Recognition of the role played by the apartment compound in the structure of Teotihuacan society and of its significance in Teotihuacan history fundamentally transformed our understanding of the city.[17] The mapping of the entire city also led to a recognition of the scope and complexity of urban planning.[18]

In 1950, when Pedro Armillas wrote of the spread of the "influence" of Teotihuacan, he singled out as evidence the presence in centers in many other parts of Mesoamerica of Teotihuacan's flat base, cylindrical tripods, and of vessels of Thin Orange ware that either were obtained in trade or, in the case of the tripods, were made locally in imitation of the Teotihuacan form (Armillas 1950: 69). Thin Orange ware was not made in the city but was disseminated from Teotihuacan and ceased to be made after the fires that destroyed the center of the city.[19] His purpose in pointing out the manifestations of this Teotihuacan influence was, as noted, to point to their importance in cross-dating a critically important ceramic phase at Teotihuacan

---

[17] The apartment compound replaced earlier residential construction of less permanent materials over a span of 100 to 200 years, beginning in the 3rd century A.D. during the Early Tlamimilolpa phase. I called this process "urban renewal" before we knew that it spanned so long a period of time (R. Millon 1973: 56).

[18] For example, the discovery of East and West Avenues, a subordinate axis to the "Street of the Dead"; the recognition that there was a mega-complex at the union of the two axes that was the geographic, political, religious, and economic center of the city (mapping disclosed that the Ciudadela had a mammoth counterpart on the other side of the "Street of the Dead"—the Great Compound) (see Fig. 1); the recognition that stream courses in the city were canalized; the discovery that the orientations of buildings and streets in the city were related to astronomical observations recorded in stone and concrete (Drewitt 1967, 1987, n.d.; R. Millon 1973: 18–20, 37–38, 42–44; Séjourné 1966a). There are useful insights on urban planning at Teotihuacan in Robertson (1963), Hardoy (1968, 1973), and Wheatley (1971).

[19] Evelyn Rattray (1990a, 1990b) recently confirmed Carmen Cook de Leonard's hypothesis that Thin Orange ware was made in the vicinity of San Juan Ixcaquistla in the Tepexi de Rodriguez region of southern Puebla (Cook de Leonard 1953, n.d.). Rattray excavated two workshops where Thin Orange was manufactured in the Rio Carnero drainage some five miles west of Ixcaquistla. But surface collections and excavations in the site in Ixcaquistla itself, where Cook de Leonard had excavated, uncovered no workshop debris.

with a specific time range in Maya ceramic chronology and thereby with the Maya Long Count. He did not consider in this article whether anything more than trade might have been involved.

Kaminaljuyu and, to a lesser extent, Matacapan (Valenzuela 1945) in southern Veracruz, provided the first inkling that more than trade was involved in the expansion of Teotihuacan "influence," principally because of the presence at both centers of temple platforms bearing the characteristic Teotihuacan *talud-tablero* design on their facades. What has been learned since has profoundly deepened what is known of Teotihuacan's connections with so many different parts of Mesoamerica. But, as is to be expected, major problems of interpretation remain. In 1990, we can say that the widespread "presence" of Teotihuacan in Mesoamerica appears to be concentrated in the fourth and fifth centuries A.D.

The closest relationship that can be documented was with Tikal, the greatest of the Maya cities.[20] In the latter part of the fourth century the Tikal hierarchy adopted from the Teotihuacanos a militaristic cult of war and sacrifice manifested earlier in Teotihuacan's Feathered Serpent Temple, and adapted it to their own ends.[21] Much could be said about Teotihuacan and other regions of Mesoamerica, but the focus of this volume is the city itself, not its external relationships. The contiguous area of the Teotihuacan state did not extend beyond a relatively small area in central Mexico covering some 10,000 mi^2 (an area a little larger than Massachusetts). Extensions of the Teotihuacan state beyond this core area seem to have occurred on several occasions, persisting for various periods of time. For a recent overview, see R. Millon (1988a: 114–136). Teotihuacan's relationship with other regions differed markedly from region to region and from one period to another. Great care must be taken not to overstate the nature of these relationships.

The shift in emphasis from culture, to culture and society, is another difference between the way Teotihuacan was regarded in 1950 and the way it is viewed in 1990. In 1990 Teotihuacan culture is still a major concern of many investigators, of course, but is almost always discussed implicitly if not explicitly in a social context, in the context of Teotihuacan's urban society. This is true both of iconographic studies and of subjects and problems derived from the perspective provided by maps of the city as a whole and by the collections made in surface survey for each of the structures and

---

[20] It appears that some Teotihuacanos of high status, accompanied by soldiers, were at Tikal beginning in the 4th century A.D. These contacts had been preceded by contacts sufficiently strong to have led to the construction of Teotihuacan-style *talud-tablero* temples (see note 64) in what was then Tikal's religious center, now known as Mundo Perdido, and in a neighborhood a short distance to the south. High level exchanges of prized materials seem likely to have taken place. How much mercantile exchange there was remains to be established (R. Millon 1988a: 115–121).

[21] Linda Schele and David Freidel (1990) present a Mayanist view of this process as it appears to them from the standpoint of Tikal.

Teotihuacan Studies

structurally related spaces on the map. In 1950, Teotihuacan social structure was discussed in general terms (for example, Armillas 1951: 24–28), but its basic social units were not a subject of inquiry. This changed in the 1950s and became an active area of inquiry after the city was mapped.[22]

Method and Theory: 1950 and 1990

One further contrast with 1950 has to be considered: the gulf in method and theory between 1950 and 1990. In the general intellectual climate of theorists such as Marx and Weber, the theoretical formulation most under discussion in 1950 was functional and developmental, a precursor of neo-evolutionism. It was an exciting time and Pedro Armillas played an important part. Karl Wittfogel's (1938) argument for the despotic potential inherent in the managerial requirements of large-scale irrigation agriculture was attracting interest. Julian Steward (1949) drew on it in his argument for regularities in the paths taken by early civilizations in the Old World and the New. Armillas (1951: 29, 30) noted that a variant of Wittfogel's theory might be applicable to conditions in parts of Mesoamerica, but that there was not enough evidence to resolve the question.[23] Gordon Willey's (1953) revolutionary late 1940s Virú Valley surface survey of settlement and irrigation in Peru was the forerunner of, and inspiration for, the TMP and Sanders' Basin of Mexico surveys. In art and architecture Janet Berlo (Evans and Berlo, this volume) has pointed out the methodological significance of Armillas' (1945) "stratigraphic approach to iconography"; analysts such as Miguel Covarrubias (1946), Pál Kelemen (1943), Ignacio Marquina (1951), Salvador Toscano (1944), Paul Westheim (1950), and Hasso von Winning (1947a, 1947b, 1948, 1949) were making an impact. This is a rough approximation of the background of Teotihuacan studies in 1950.

The forty years since 1950 have seen the development of neo-evolutionism, the rise in the 1960s of "new" or processual archaeology, and in the 1980s of post-processualism. All have contributed to research at Teotihuacan. The past forty years also have seen the development of a multitude of field and laboratory techniques and methods within archaeology and anthropology and in other disciplines in the physical and social sciences and the arts. Many of these have been used in Teotihuacan research. Radiocarbon dating has been mentioned. Some of the other techniques and

---

[22] The core unit of the apartment compound, as suggested by Susan Kellogg and Martha Sempowski (R. Millon 1981: 208–209), is likely to have been a cognatic descent unit with an agnatic bias; i.e., one in which descent was reckoned through both male and female lines but with a bias toward the male line. But see also Spence (1974). The cognatic descent unit would have been relatively flexible, permitting the individual to activate the most advantageous ties possible, not solely those in the male line, in determining post-marital residence and group affiliation.

[23] While Armillas does not cite them, the influence of Gordon Childe and Graham Clarke is evident in this 1951 article.

methods are of such importance that they must be specified here. There is, first of all, the revolution in formal approaches in archaeology in which George Cowgill has played such an important part (Cowgill 1986, 1989). At Teotihuacan, sampling techniques and collection criteria in surface survey and excavation, and statistical manipulation of large bodies of data in computers in the lab are but two of the formal applications to archaeology that have been used (Cowgill 1968, 1974, 1987; Cowgill, Altschul, and Sload 1984; Manzanilla and Barba 1990). A related contribution to method of great consequence was Cowgill's critical analysis of the use of population pressure as an "explanation" for social change and increases in social complexity (Cowgill 1975a, 1975b). Mary Hopkins (1987a, 1987b) used network statistics to analyze plans of Teotihuacan apartment compounds. Jorge Angulo Villaseñor (1987) undertook an architectural analysis of these compounds.

Aerial photography, photogrammetry, and remote sensing techniques have made fundamental contributions to our knowledge of the city through mapping and survey (Millon, Drewitt, and Cowgill 1973; Sanders et al. n.d.; Nichols 1987). The Tikal map (Carr and Hazard 1961) was one of the models for the Teotihuacan map. The proton magnetometer is being used to locate caves and tunnels in the area of the Pyramids of the Sun and Moon, in the "Old City," and in the area intervening (Manzanilla et al. 1989; Manzanilla 1990). Contextual analysis of activity areas, households, and large social units in residential compounds have been carried out in different parts of the city using some similar and some distinct techniques (Storey and Widmer 1989; Manzanilla and Barba 1990). Chemical analyses of alterations in plastered floors are being used to isolate activity areas in a compound in the "Old City" (Manzanilla and Barba 1990).

Paleobotanical and paleozoological analyses, long a staple of analysis (for example, Sears 1951) have been enormously enriched by the flotation of excavated deposits (Struever 1968; McClung de Tapia 1987, n.d.; Starbuck 1977, 1987, n.d.). Human bone now can be chemically analyzed for dietary evidence; bone from Feathered Serpent Temple sacrifices is now being analyzed for this purpose in Japan (George Cowgill, personal communication). Human bone from burials at Teotihuacan has been analyzed in innovative ways by Michael Spence (1974, n.d.) and Rebecca Storey (1985, 1986, 1987, n.d.a, 1992). Garman Harbottle (Sayre and Harbottle n.d.) has analyzed the provenience of pottery sherds from mapping project and related excavations using neutron activation. Jeffrey and Mary Parsons (1990) have created an "archaeological ethnography" of maguey utilization in central Mexico. Dermatoglyphics have been used by Warren Barbour (n.d.b) to analyze gender ratios among the makers of figurines and pottery at Teotihuacan. Gordon Wasson (1980) has analyzed Teotihuacan mural art for evidence of the use of hallucinogenic mushrooms in ritual.

Teotihuacan Studies

Observations relating to astronomical orientations at Teotihuacan have transformed our knowledge of these critically important questions since 1950. It is now clear that astronomical observations governed the orientation of the city. The investigators who established this include James Dow (1967), David Drucker (1977, n.d.a), Anthony Aveni (1980: 222-234; Aveni and Gibbs 1976) and Vincent Malmström (1978). I return to this later.

This does not exhaust the methods and techniques that have been or are being used in excavation and analysis, but it demonstrates how great is the gulf between 1950 and 1990. This is worth noting. We should not, however, exaggerate the degree to which the level of sophistication in 1990 has surpassed that in 1950. We should look at the achievements of the past forty years in a less self-congratulatory fashion and try to place them in perspective.[24]

The social context of archaeological research at Teotihuacan and the symbolic importance of Teotihuacan in Mexican society and culture must be acknowledged. Its proximity to Mexico City is one reason Teotihuacan is, or is reputed to be, the country's most visited archaeological site, contributing significantly to income from tourism in Mexico. The limited access highway from Mexico City inaugurated in 1964 made the site even more accessible. In 1950 Teotihuacan was commonly referred to simply as *"Las Pirámides"* — "The Pyramids." Although this designation still is used in 1990, the excavations and partial restorations since 1960 present the visitor today with a much more complex context for its great monuments. The nationalistic role now played by Teotihuacan and its urban society in Mexican political and cultural life (Lorenzo 1984: 100) is exemplified in the comic book series *Episodios Mexicanos* launched in 1981 by the Consejo Nacional de Fomento Educativo, an arm of the federal ministry of education. The subtitle of the series, which was to have eighty titles, makes the point: *"Un recorrido por la historia de México: Desde Teotihuacan hasta la Expropriación Petrolera."*[25]

The potential for the delineation of Teotihuacan in its historical context for Mexicans today remains to be realized (Lorenzo 1984: 99-100). These circumstances give added meaning and significance to archaeological researches at Teotihuacan by non-Mexicans and place special responsibilities

---

[24] The most effective way I know to do this is to recall what Robert Murphy said in a different context more than thirty years ago. A noted anthropologist had just returned from a stay in the Soviet Union and was reporting on the state of anthropology there to a meeting of students and faculty at Berkeley. He had just concluded by remarking that Russian anthropologists were at least twenty years behind American anthropologists when Murphy observed: "Yes—and it might take them at least two weeks to catch up."

[25] "A Journey through the History of Mexico: From Teotihuacan to the Oil Expropriation," the latter a reference to the landmark expropriation of foreign oil companies by President Lázaro Cárdenas in 1938, as part of the consolidation of the 1910 Mexican Revolution. See also José Luis Lorenzo (1980, 1984), Bruce Trigger (1989: 174, 180-181), and Esteban Krotz (1990). Mark Leone (1982: 754-757) discusses problems in the presentation of U.S. history in reconstructions at historic archaeology sites.

René Millon

on outsiders who engage in research there, including an obligation to reach as wide an audience of non-specialists as possible (Trigger 1990).

THE CONFERENCE PAPERS

Iconography in 1990

The six iconographic studies in this volume dramatically differ from the predominantly cultural concerns of iconographic studies up to 1950. It is necessary only to list some of the important iconographic analyses written before 1950 to demonstrate the contrast with 1990: Pedro Armillas (1945, 1947), Hermann Beyer (1920, 1921, 1922a, 1922b, 1922c, 1930), Alfonso Caso (1939, 1942), Sigvald Linné (1934, 1941, 1942), Antonio Peñafiel (1900), Eduard Seler (1915) and Hasso von Winning (1947a, 1947b, 1948, 1949). The chapters in this volume are more sophisticated than those known in 1950 not only because of advances in methods, techniques, and theory, but also because their cultural analyses have social contexts that enrich while greatly complicating them.

The questions raised by George Cowgill in this volume about two of the glyphs from the feathered serpent and flowering trees murals from Techinantitla are a measure of the gulf between 1950 and 1990. Techinantitla is a large apartment compound some 550 yards east of the Moon Pyramid (see Fig. 1). Excavations we carried out there in 1984 established Techinantitla and a neighboring compound as the source of most of the mural paintings stolen from Teotihuacan that have appeared in museums and private collections since 1960 (R. Millon 1988b). Evidence from these compounds argues that Techinantitla was the headquarters of a military *barrio* of long tradition and that it housed officers of the highest rank. George Cowgill (this volume) concludes that at least one, and perhaps two, of the glyphs in the serpent-flowering trees murals can be read as the names of plants important in sixteenth-century Aztec ritual. There is more here than continuity in plant names, Cowgill argues; the probability is that "there is also continuity in significant ritual symbolism."

This may be an indication that the other glyphs in the serpent-flowering trees murals name plants of ritual significance, one of Esther Pasztory's suggestions (1988a: 159–161). The central glyph of the nine repeated glyphs in the only complete set in these murals consists of three upturned maguey *pencas*. Because it is almost certain that spines from maguey *pencas* were used in blood-letting rituals, I have suggested that the serpent-flowering trees murals commemorated blood-letting (R. Millon 1988b: 106). This would not necessarily contradict the case made by Janet Berlo (1989: 20–23) that these glyphs represent toponyms nor some of the other interpretations discussed by Pasztory (1988a: 161).

As George Cowgill points out, his glyphic correspondences do not necessarily imply that a Nahua language was spoken at Teotihuacan. This raised the question of the language spoken by Teotihuacanos, or rather of the dominant language, because it seems probable that several languages were spoken in the city. In 1950, Armillas (1950: 41) reported the conclusion of Wigberto Jiménez Moreno that the language of the builders of Teotihuacan was Totonac. Jiménez Moreno (1974) later changed his mind and argued that a Nahua language was the dominant language. But, as Cowgill reports, linguistic evidence argues against the presence in central Mexico of languages closely related to Nahuatl while Teotihuacan was a dominant power. Once again in 1990, as in 1950, Totonac is the weakly favored candidate, although Nahua and languages such as Otomí are not ruled out. Although I cannot discuss this further here, I still find it hard to believe that a Nahua language was not being spoken at Teotihuacan by A.D. 500.

Teotihuacan is a Nahua word. Pedro Armillas (1950: 37) records three renderings of its meaning: *lugar de adoración, habitación de los dioses, lugar de apoteosis* (place of worship or the place where the gods were worshiped; abode of the gods or where the gods lived; and place of apotheosis or the place where men became gods). The latter is the interpretation of Fray Bernardino de Sahagún. There are other interpretations as well. The one I find most persuasive is the one Nahua scholar Thelma Sullivan (personal communication, 1972) concluded was its most likely meaning—"The Place of Those Who Have the Road (or Avenue) of the Gods."

In 1950 the preeminent deity at Teotihuacan was believed to be the rain god or the god of the waters as Armillas (1950: 52, 53) called him, usually identified by the name of his Aztec counterpart, Tlaloc (Caso 1942; Armillas 1945). He has since been disentangled from the Aztec deity and is now called the Storm God (Pasztory 1974; R. Millon 1988b: 100). In 1990, Teotihuacan's preeminent deity is recognized to be the Great Goddess as first established by Esther Pasztory (1973, 1976). Janet Berlo (this volume) recounts the steps leading to the relatively recent recognition of her preeminence. Her attributes are protean—she is a goddess of earthly waters, a patroness of warfare who requires sacrifices, mother of the gods, and the fertile mountain from which all things come. The recently discovered murals in the Techinantitla apartment compound emphasize the subordinate position of the Storm God to the goddess (R. Millon 1988b: 99–102).[26]

It seems probable that the goddess was the deity to whom the earliest Moon Pyramid was dedicated, given its ineluctable association with the

---

[26] Marvin Cohodas (1990: 158) may be correct in his observation that the inner room north of the Anteroom of the Gods is not likely to bear any representation of the goddess. But if he is, it will be for the wrong reason. His observation is based on the treatment of interior rooms of painted porticos but is not true for all. An inner room behind a portico at Tetitla bears representations of the Storm God on its walls (Miller 1973: plan XIII, Room 19; fig. 261). Moreover, porticos with inner rooms represent only one of several architectural contexts for interior murals (R. Millon 1988b: 109–110, n. 12, fig. IV.16).

majestic mountain behind it and the association of that mountain with the goddess (see Berlo, this volume, fig. 24). I will argue in the final section that the earliest Moon Pyramid probably was built earlier than the earliest Sun Pyramid. Even so the goddess may not have assumed her preeminent position until after the Sun Pyramid was built. An earlier Sun Pyramid only a few meters lower than the present one almost certainly had twin temples on its summit (Figs. 4, 5). The Great Goddess and the Storm God may then have occupied "separate but equal" temples. This would have been sometime around A.D. 100. It is possible that the rise to preeminence of the Great Goddess cult did not occur for another hundred years or so, that is, until ca. A.D. 250 or later, as part of a political reform, discussed below.

Looking at Teotihuacan abroad, Janet Berlo asks why the Great Goddess is preeminent in the Guatemalan piedmont and highlands whereas the Storm God is preeminent among the Peten Maya. Although both have associations with war and the military, James Langley (1986 and this volume) has demonstrated how pervasive these associations are with the Storm God. The differences Berlo points to between the two regions of Guatemala are explainable, it seems to me, by the fact that Teotihuacan did not exercise political control over any part of the Peten, while it does seem to have

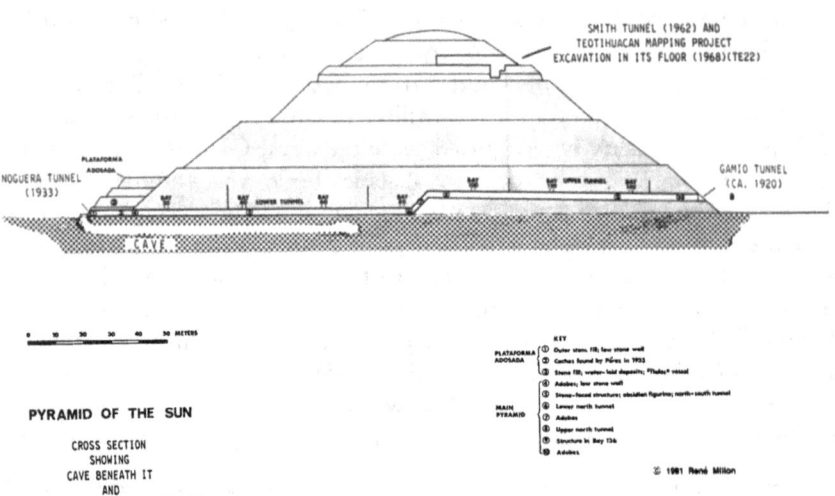

Fig. 4 Pyramid of the Sun, ht. 210 ft. Cross-section showing cave 20 ft. beneath it and archaeological tunnels at and near ground level (1933 and 1920, respectively) and near its summit (1962). The TMP excavation (TE22) in the floor of the 1962 tunnel exposed more than 2 m (7 ft.) of a great sloping wall (*talud*) of earth (Fig. 5).

Teotihuacan Studies

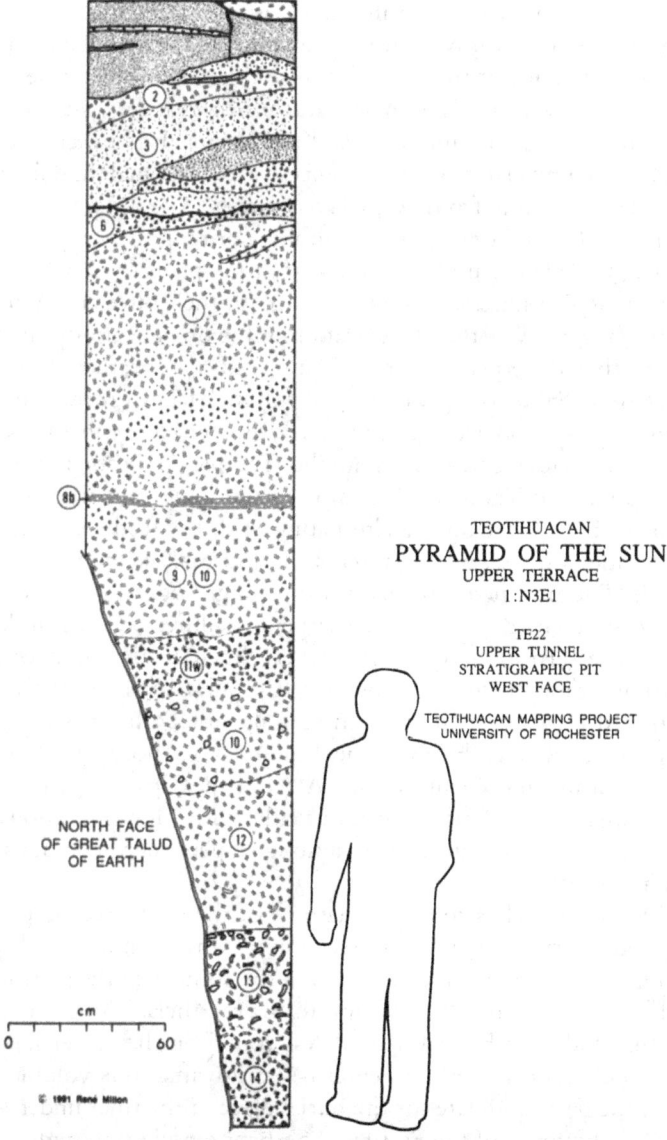

Fig. 5 Pyramid of the Sun. Great *talud* with mud plaster surface exposed in the 1968 TMP excavation (TE22) in the floor of the 1962 tunnel near the top of the pyramid (see Fig. 4). The *talud* was part of a structure on the summit of the first Sun Pyramid (not depicted on Fig. 4) which would have been more than 150 ft. high. All layers except the uppermost at top, right, resting against the *talud* and lying above it, date to the latter part of the Tzacualli phase (early to mid-second century A.D.). TE22 was excavated by Evelyn Rattray.

controlled parts of the highlands and the piedmont for a time. The goddess was preeminent where Teotihuacan was in control.

Berlo points out how unusual a preeminent female deity appears to be in the Mesoamerica of the time. Because this seems to be true of succeeding centuries as well, it is another characteristic that serves to set Teotihuacan apart from its contemporaries and successors. Having an ancestral female deity is not unusual in itself. But ancestral deities, male and female, often are regarded as remote from everyday activities. The difference at Teotihuacan is that the Great Goddess is ubiquitous, not remote.

In 1950 Pedro Armillas (1945, 1947) took pains to separate the Feathered Serpent at Teotihuacan from Quetzalcoatl, the Toltec and Aztec deity. One of his concerns was the identification of the other sculpture alternating with the feathered serpent on the Temple of the Feathered Serpent in the Ciudadela. Saburo Sugiyama (this volume) takes on this question and its implications in an iconographic analysis considered in the context of the spectacular new excavations in the Temple of Feathered Serpent. Both Sugiyama, and Taube (n.d.), came to the same conclusion independently; namely, that the sculpture alternating with the feathered serpent heads on the facade of the temple represents a headdress (see Sugiyama, this volume, fig. 2). The argument for this is compelling. Sugiyama believes that what is being represented is a feathered serpent headdress; Taube (n.d.) argues that it is a fire serpent or war serpent headdress. Sugiyama does not see "any morphological distinctions" between the putative fire or war serpent and the feathered serpent. If the two images do not both represent the feathered serpent, Sugiyama believes the headdress is more likely to represent a Teotihuacan antecedent to the Aztec god Cipactli (Lopez, Lopez, and Sugiyama 1991). Certainly it is difficult, with a few exceptions, to establish consistent, clear-cut differences among serpent representations in other media in the city.

Sugiyama finds strong associations of the Feathered Serpent deity with war and sacrifice, as well as associations with authority and, perhaps, rulership, especially when considered in the context of the sacrificial and other burials found there.[27] In addition to the sacrificial burials, a large and deep pit that had been heavily looted was found on the center line between the pyramid's staircase and its center (see Sugiyama, this volume, fig. 6). This pit is the best candidate for the burial place of the ruler under whose leadership the building of the Feathered Serpent temple-pyramid was undertaken as well as the construction of the Ciudadela compound itself. Sugiyama singles out two other sites that may have served as royal tombs. One of these may have been the burial place of the immediate successor of the ruler

---

[27] David Carrasco's (1982: 106) discussion of the Feathered Serpent in Mesoamerica as the "symbol of the sanctification of authority" and as the "paradigm of legitimate rule and order" is relevant here, as is his discussion of the Feathered Serpent and Teotihuacan (pp. 104–126).

who began the construction of the pyramid. Presumably the Temple of the Feathered Serpent was completed under his leadership. He may have been the last in a line of powerful, near absolute, if not autocratic rulers.

The Temple of the Feathered Serpent was built in the space of a very few years. Stratigraphic evidence relating it to the South Palace established that it had to have been completed in the very early years of the Tlamimilolpa Phase; that is, by ca. A.D. 225. A TMP excavation in the South Palace (TE25N) near its outer north wall uncovered a succession of concrete floors, all of which date to the Early Tlamimilolpa Phase (ca. A.D. 200–300) (Fig. 6). The foundation of the Feathered Serpent Temple was associated with or prior to the earliest of these (Sugiyama 1989: fig. 4).

Saburo Sugiyama makes a strong case that the Feathered Serpent deity's associations with the military and sacrifice are paramount in the Temple of the Feathered Serpent. James Langley (this volume) has demonstrated how strong and pervasive are these same associations with the Storm God. Janet Berlo demonstrates such associations with the Great Goddess, although they are not as direct, as pervasive, or as sweeping. The associations of military themes and sacrificial ritual with Teotihuacan's three principal deities are unmistakable and necessarily color our interpretations of Teotihuacan society, military organization, religion, and ideology (C. Millon 1973, 1988a, 1988c; Pasztory 1990).

The growing recognition of the prominence at Teotihuacan of martial themes and of the pervasiveness of bloodletting and heart sacrifice ritual provides one of the sharpest contrasts in iconographic interpretation between 1950 and 1990. Some of the overt evidence for the importance of war and sacrifice at Teotihuacan was known in 1950. Hasso von Winning (1948) had just published his study of what he called the Teotihuacan owl-and-weapon symbol. Human sacrifices had been reported from the corners of the terraces of the Sun Pyramid (Batres 1906: [40]) and from the four corners at the base of the Feathered Serpent Temple (Dosal 1925). Atetelco's murals with their themes of militarism and sacrifice had been uncovered; murals on upper walls were being reconstructed by Agustín Villagra (Armillas 1950: 53). The architectural and other evidence of a Teotihuacan presence at Kaminaljuyu in far-off highland Guatemala had been uncovered and published (Kidder, Jennings, and Shook 1946). Kidder had commented that Kaminaljuyu might have been conquered "by a small group of war-like adventurers" from Teotihuacan (p. 255). But all of this had yet to make substantial inroads on the prevailing view of Teotihuacan as a largely peaceful community. The possible role of sacrifice and human sacrifice in this setting was not stressed. This is what I was taught in 1949 and 1950. Armillas said little to contradict the prevailing view.

Contrast this with James Langley's chapter, which adds to and reinforces the conclusions of his landmark study of symbolic notation at Teotihuacan

René Millon

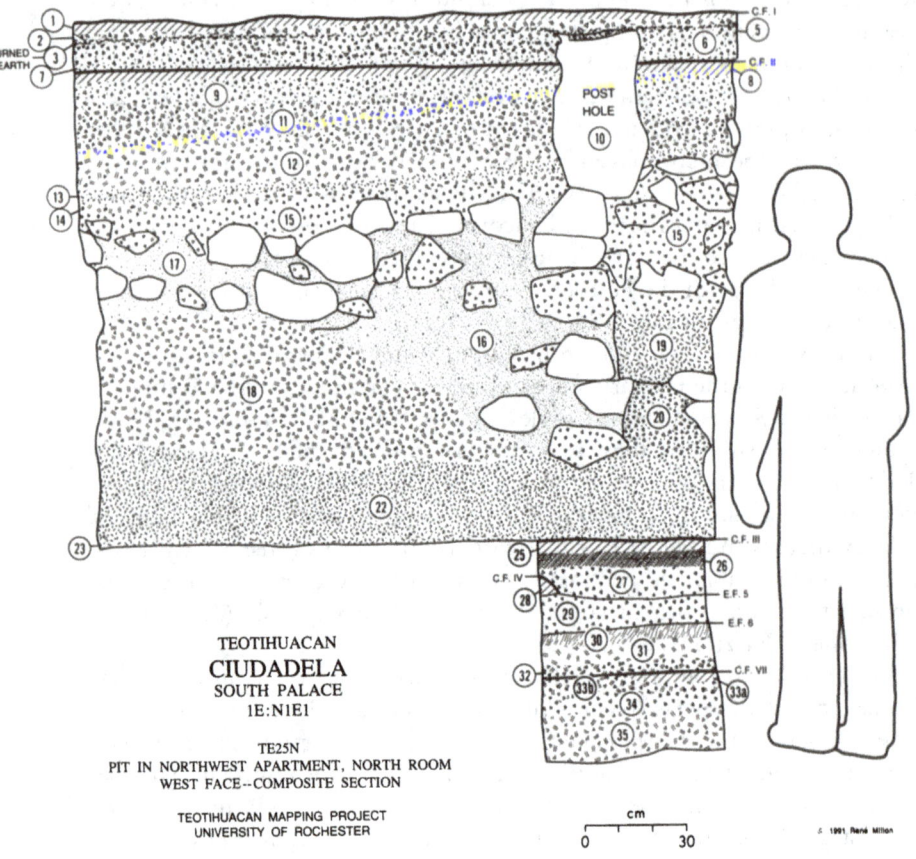

Fig. 6   Ciudadela, South Palace. TMP excavation (TE25N) in the north room of the northwest complex in the South Palace (Millon, Drewitt, and Cowgill 1973: 76, 1E:N1E1; Cabrera, Rodriguez, and Morelos 1982b: 158, Plaza E). TE25N established that the construction phases in the South Palace uncovered here, including all five concrete floors, date to the Early Tlamimilolpa phase (fourth century A.D.). One of the city's earliest murals was found deep in a Proyecto Arqueológico Teotihuacan 80–82 excavation in this room (Cabrera, this volume; Appendix). Its early date was established by the TE25N excavation which was carried out by Darlena K. Blucher.

(Langley 1986): that military power and sacrifice were the principal subjects of the Teotihuacan notational system. Merely to state this demonstrates the immense gulf between the concerns of 1950 investigators and those of 1990. Yet there is a sense in which Langley's conclusion was foreshadowed forty years ago when von Winning (1948) isolated an iconographic cluster that dealt with warfare. In the ensuing years we have come to realize the importance of the role the military played in Teotihuacan society and how sacrifice permeated it (Séjourné 1956, 1959; C. Millon 1973, 1988a, 1988b, 1988c, 1988d; Berlo 1983; von Winning 1987; Pasztory 1990).[28]

Karl Taube's masterly analysis of the iconography of mirrors at Teotihuacan amplifies the military evidence. Sugiyama mentioned that many of the bound sacrificed soldiers found at the Feathered Serpent Temple were accompanied by round mirrors so placed as to suggest that they had been worn on their backs. Taube suggests that although these mirrors may have served a protective function, they may also have served as symbols of war; their simultaneous and multiple associations with fire and water would invoke the burning water metaphor for war—*atl-tlachinolli* in Nahuatl.[29]

Martial associations, of course, are only a few of those invoked by mirrors. The association of greatest significance is that of mirrors with caves and passageways because of the central importance of the cave beneath the Sun Pyramid and because of the association of the Great Goddess with caves and passageways.[30] Karl Taube (this volume) argues that the symbolism of cave as passageway pervades the Feathered Serpent Temple, with the feathered serpent heads and the headdresses with which they alternate, represented as passing through "a great facade of feathered mirrors." This is a fascinating concept, for it links beliefs centered on the cave beneath the Sun Pyramid with the imagery of the central temple in the Ciudadela.

The last of the iconographic analyses is that of Esther Pasztory. Her chapter has such scope and raises so many questions and issues that it is considered separately. Two other contributions also require extended discussion, Rubén Cabrera Castro's chapter on recent mural discoveries and Linda Manzanilla's discussion of the political economy of Teotihuacan.

---

[28] In a discussion of "the reality and the rhetoric" of Teotihuacan military power, Esther Pasztory (1990) argues that priests, soldiers, and military images can be found in all residential compounds where murals have been found and concludes that no single compound or compounds can be singled out as being particularly associated with the military or any other special activity, that there need not have been any professional soldiers, and that military activities need not have been restricted to certain persons or areas and were widely dispersed. Her argument does not stand up. Mural painting was not a city-wide phenomenon. In fact, when looked at in the context of the city as a whole, few apartment compounds and other residential complexes in the city reveal evidence of mural paintings. Two-thirds (16 of 24) of the residential compounds and complexes not on the "Street of the Dead" that have been excavated entirely or in significant part had either very few and small murals or no murals at all. In only two compounds with an abundance of murals do martial and sacrificial themes predominate, Atetelco and Techinantitla. In this they clearly stand apart from other compounds and residential structures where martial figures occur but are not dominant.

[29] As James Langley notes, H. B. Nicholson pointed out in the discussion that the metaphor exists in Otomi and Mixtec and perhaps other languages and is not tied only to Nahuatl. In addition, an important part of the ritual carried out in the cave beneath the Sun Pyramid in the 1st and 2nd centuries A.D. involved the use of fire and water, and those who first penetrated the cave found carved stone mirror backs (R. Millon 1981: 231–235; Heyden 1975, 1981; Taube 1986).

[30] As Berlo indicates, when Taube refers to a spider goddess, his referent is the Great Goddess.

René Millon

Craft Workshops and Luxury Goods

The number and diversity of craft workshops and neighborhoods now known for a variety of media is another measure of the gulf between 1950 and 1990. In 1950 there was no basis for a study of craft production in the city. Margaret Turner contrasts craft production in temple workshops, in particular a Moon Pyramid workshop where iron pyrite mirrors[31] were made for restricted distribution, with a workshop presumably free of temple or state control on the city's outskirts where fine stone and shell were worked for city-wide distribution. Whether the distribution of these exotic materials was effected through marketplace exchange, as Turner suggests, or in a process of temple-centered redistribution, as Linda Manzanilla argues, is a problem to which I will return later.

The identification of a possible shell workshop specialized in the working of *Spondylus* in the "Old City," together with surface finds of *Spondylus* from a nearby cemetery area argues that what this putative workshop produced was consumed locally, within the "Old City" itself. Charles Kolb (1987: 67, 68) identifies what he describes as a *bodega* (storehouse) of *Spondylus* shells in the ancient Teotihuacan village at Maquixco Bajo (TC-8 [Sanders]), a short distance west of the western edge of the city. The context would not suggest that the *bodega* was a state storehouse.

Margaret Turner's evidence suggests that there may have been at least three levels at which craft workshops in exotic, precious, and semi-precious minerals and shells operated: (1) temple workshops, where the worker's product was controlled by the temple or state, with distribution restricted to those of high status; (2) workshops serving the city as a whole, where part of the worker's product exchanged in the marketplace may have been taxed but the remainder was not directly controlled by the state, with distribution directed at those of intermediate status; and (3) workshops serving a local clientele, probably free of intervention by the state in the distribution of its products. The lapidary workshop in the Tlajinga 33: S3W1 compound in the southwestern quadrant of the city, which existed early in the compound's history, may have fallen into this third category (Storey and Widmer 1989; Storey 1992). Workshop zones where obsidian was worked to produce basic everyday tools and weapons seem to manifest the same distinctions (Spence 1981).[32] Craft workers whose workshops served either local or city-wide clienteles probably were required to spend part of their time working in temple workshops. Martha Sempowski also is concerned with the procurement, manufacture, and distribution of exotic materials—"luxury" goods. The evidence from her analysis of burials argues that the

---

[31] Taube concentrates primarily on iron pyrite mirrors in his discussion of the importance and ubiquity of mirrors.

[32] I refer to workshop zones because of Hattula Moholy-Nagy's (1990: 276) suggestion that her criticism of individual workshop identifications would not apply to workshop zones.

Teotihuacan Studies

Teotihuacan "populace at large" had much freer access to exotic goods than did the population of Tikal, the greatest of the Maya cities. She does not contend that there was no differential access to such materials at Teotihuacan. She cites the presence of *Spondylus* shell in only "a few special burials" at La Ventilla B, an apartment compound occupied by people of modest status. The evidence from burials at a similar apartment compound (Tlajinga 33:S3W1) supports Sempowski's analysis (Storey 1992).

When the Teotihuacanos began to move north after A.D. 500, Sempowski suggests that it may have been in response to disruptions in traditional connections to the south and east. These disruptions, following the pullback of Teotihuacan's power and influence, do not seem to have markedly affected the movement of luxury goods, perhaps because exchange was facilitated by intermediary groups in coastal lowlands (e.g., Santley n.d.a). Merchants operating without state protection might also be part of the explanation.

There is an apparent decline in the supply of exotic luxury goods in the Metepec phase during the city's last century. Jade, shell, and mica were less available than they had been to people of intermediate status. The same is true of locally made luxury goods. There is not enough evidence, however, to judge whether the reason was a significant drop in the import of exotic materials, an increased demand by those in the society's upper levels, or perhaps because of newly enacted or more strictly enforced sumptuary laws. Possibly those at the top were channeling scarce resources for their own use, while the people in the middle range of Teotihuacan society were experiencing a deterioration in their standard of living.

Foreign Barrios

One of the most distinctive aspects of Teotihuacan society were its foreign *barrios,* of which there were at least two, the Oaxaca *barrio*—Tlailotlacan (see Evans and Berlo, this volume, fig. 3, 17) near the city's western edge and the "Merchants' *Barrio*" on its northeastern edge (see Evans and Berlo, this volume, fig. 3, 9). The latter may be a misnomer.[33] It appears from recent excavations in the *barrio* (Rattray n.d.b) that it was occupied by people from the Gulf Coast who built and lived in distinctive round structures. Evelyn Rattray found much pottery from the Gulf Coast and the Maya area in her excavations there (see also Rattray 1987, 1989). In 1950, the only suggestion of anything unusual about this part of the city came from Sigvald Linné's excavation of the Tlamimilolpa compound, immediately north of the "Merchants' *Barrio.*" Linné (1942) reported finding Tzakol Phase Maya polychrome pottery sherds in deep deposits near the western end of his excavation. It now seems likely that the vessels from which these

---

[33] I gave it that name because of concentrations of foreign pottery found on its surface, which were confirmed in two small TMP excavations (TE4, TE11).

René Millon

came were obtained from their foreign neighbors to the south. Michael Spence's excavations in Tlailotlacan, the Oaxaca *barrio*, adjoin the compound where, beginning in 1966, extensive excavations were carried out first by University of the Americas, then by TMP personnel (TE3, TE3A) (R. Millon 1973: 41, 42). Spence's emphasis is on the variety of ways the inhabitants of the Oaxaca *barrio*, who may have been middlemen in trade, expressed and maintained their distinctive ethnic identity during centuries of residence in a large urban center.

In seeking to explain the persistence of early Oaxacan forms for centuries, Spence cogently argues that the early Oaxaca-derived ceramics took on a "new symbolic load" to help the people of the *barrio* maintain their "beleaguered ethnic identity." He suggests that these early ceramic forms were deliberately frozen and used self-consciously to preserve a distinctive ethnic identity. His skeletal evidence suggests "some degree of endogamy," which would have been another means of maintaining cultural identity. Drawing on comparative evidence from enclaves in other parts of the world, he suggests that *barrio* contact with the Oaxacan homeland was "brief, rare, or restricted" to only a small number of its residents and that such sporadic ties would have fostered the growth of the "fragmented and anachronistic version" of Oaxacan culture represented in the Oaxaca *barrio*.

Spence's analysis has an obvious bearing on our understanding of what kind of a city Teotihuacan was. It was a city in which foreigners were allowed in some cases to form permanent ethnic enclaves in the city, of which the Oaxaca *barrio* is a clear example, and to maintain their cultural identities. We have no way of judging whether this was because of an enlightened state policy. But the evidence does argue for a degree of de facto toleration, if only by default. Of course, the privacy afforded by the large apartment compounds with their faceless, windowless exteriors would facilitate the maintenance of such distinctive practices. As an example, because it was a city custom to bury the dead beneath apartment compound floors, no special attention would have been called to exotic burial practices, as would have been the case had burial taken place outside the compound or *barrio*.

Recently Excavated Murals

Rubén Cabrera Castro's discussion of the murals from the "Street of the Dead" uncovered in the 1980–82 Proyecto Arqueológico Teotihuacan excavations in the Archaeological Zone is as useful for what was *not* found as for what was. His drawings of the murals and his discussion of their stratigraphic and architectural contexts are invaluable in themselves but also demonstrate once again a most important point—how few of Teotihuacan's walls actually bore murals, even in the central "Street of the Dead" area. Now when we encounter painted walls, we must ask why they were painted—why were these walls in this building at this particular time se-

Teotihuacan Studies

lected to bear mural paintings? An apartment compound like Atetelco stands out dramatically because of its murals. This gives added meaning to Cabrera's drawings and reconstructions of new murals from Atetelco recently excavated by Laurette Séjourné.

In the Ciudadela the simple red scroll mural with an incised outline on white plaster found by Saburo Sugiyama deep in the South Palace (1E:N1E1) is among the earliest murals uncovered; we know from a TMP excavation (TE25N) (Fig. 6) that the floors overlying it date to the Early Tlamimilolpa phase in the third century A.D. (Cowgill 1983: 326–328; see also TE25S, Fig. 7).[34]

Other early paintings in the Ciudadela are those found by Cabrera in Structure 1B' (1B':N1E1), the scrolls on the floor of Sub-Structure 4 and the distinctive geometric figure with black outlines on the *tableros* of Sub-Structure 2, a temple platform (Cabrera, this volume, Fig. 6), which may have calendrical, astronomical, or directional significance in Teotihuacan ritual and for which Cabrera points to parallels in later mural art, architecture, and ceramics.[35]

The new murals uncovered by Laurette Séjourné at Atetelco are of special interest because Atetelco was a military compound where heart sacrifice ritual featuring military figures was prominently portrayed (C. Millon 1988c: 212–216). The new murals were found in the northern part of Atetelco, east of the heart sacrifice murals of the White Patio. It is not clear if they form a part of the building level associated with the Painted Patio, the building level overlying the White Patio. One of the new murals portrays armed military personages facing left (in procession?) bearing weapons and accoutered as net jaguars (not illustrated). Judging from the way its head is drawn (Cabrera, this volume, fig. 15), another repeated figure appears to be a feathered coyote seated on a "vessel" (or throne or pedestal?) associated

---

[34] Also dating to this early period in the South Palace and presumably also in a sub-structure in the North Palace (1D:N1E1) are mural fragments painted directly on mud plaster surfaces. David Drucker (n.d.b: 297–298), in a 1972 TMP excavation (TE25S) found similar mural fragments on mud plaster in Early Tlamimilolpa Phase deposits deep in the Transverse Platform giving access to the South Palace (layer 24) (Fig. 7). An adobe bore what appeared to be three marine shells in yellow on a green background, reminiscent of the second layer of black outline wall paintings on mud plaster in the Temple of Agriculture (Villagra 1971: fig. 8) near the northern end of the "Street of the Dead" (see Fig. 1). Armillas said that he found mural fragments beneath floors in the Viking Group (see Fig. 1) in the "Street of the Dead" Complex in what are now recognized to have been Tlamimilolpa phase deposits that similarly were reminiscent of Temple of Agriculture murals (Hall n.d.: 48).

[35] In discussing these early paintings, Cabrera makes reference to Clara Millon's 1966 periodization of Teotihuacan mural art, which its author considers to be obsolete but which never has been corrected in print (C. Millon 1972; R. Millon 1967; 11). To remedy that, a tabulation of mural chronology that is stratigraphically based is appended (Appendix). Much of this stratigraphic evidence did not exist when the earlier periodization was made in 1966. The Appendix also serves to correct similar inaccuracies in the chart of periods of Teotihuacan mural art in von Winning's (1987, 1: 47) invaluable sourcebook.

René Millon

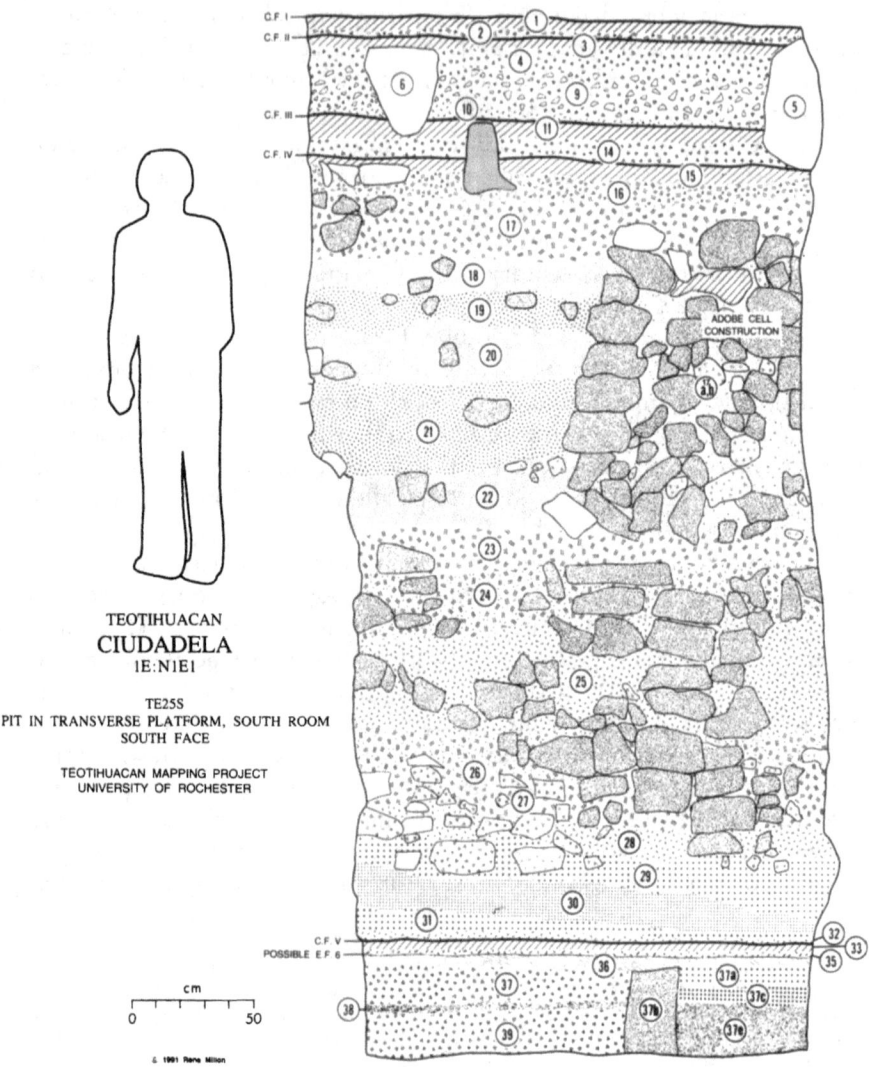

Fig. 7 Ciudadela, South Transverse Platform. TMP excavation (TE25S) in the South Room of the South Transverse Platform, separating the South Palace from the great plaza of the Ciudadela (see Fig. 1) (Millon, Drewitt, and Cowgill 1973: 76; Cabrera, Rodriguez, and Morelos 1982b: 12). Most of the construction here, from Concrete Floor IV down, dates to the Early Tlamimilolpa phase (fourth century A.D.). An adobe bearing early polychrome mural designs outlined in black was found in the fill of layer 24, together with other painted adobe fragments (Appendix). A long hiatus in construction intervened between Concrete Floor IV and the three concrete floors above it which date to the Metepec phase (seventh and eighth centuries A.D.). TE25S was excavated by David Drucker (n.d.b).

Teotihuacan Studies

with the Great Goddess, beneath which are stylized sacrificial knives and *biznaga* cacti, associated with auto-sacrifice, also found elsewhere at Atetelco.[36] These new murals amplify the martial and sacrificial emphases in the murals of Atetelco and demonstrate their continuity in two or more successive construction periods.

Art, Ideology, and Society

Esther Pasztory's chapter represents the first comprehensive attempt to theorize about the extent to which Teotihuacan art might have expressed critical aspects of its society and culture. Using semiotic analysis, her aim is to reconstruct Teotihuacan from an outsider's point of view, although she does not do this consistently. What sets apart her chapter from all but her most recent work is her recognition of how truly distinctive and unusual Teotihuacan society and its culture were and how much Teotihuacan differed from its predecessors, contemporaries, and successors.

Pasztory argues that there was a preoccupation in the city with problems of internal organization and that this preoccupation was "one of the purposes of the symbolic communication coded in its works of art." She characterizes the art style of Teotihuacan as "the most abstract" in Mesoamerican history and suggests it was "on some level an intentional cultural choice" in which Teotihuacanos were expressing a rejection of the naturalistic, "more organically structured traditions" of the Olmec, Maya, and others. I find this latter argument unconvincing.[37]

Pasztory uses the now-accepted differences that set apart Teotihuacan art in its middle and late centuries from other Mesoamerican art traditions to develop her argument that human representations in Teotihuacan art are depersonalized. Her argument refers primarily to fifth century A.D. (Xolalpan) and later Teotihuacan art because there are few surviving representations of humans in sculpture and painting before that time. She uses these depersonalized representations to develop a concept of a "collective persona," of which the Teotihuacan stone mask is a "prime object."[38] Besides being impersonal, Teotihuacan masks are standardized, which Pasztory interprets as an expression of an "ideal of collective uniformity" that, following her reasoning, would have referred to images of deities.[39] She sees the

---

[36] Clara Millon (personal communication) points out that Cabrera's fig. 15 would be the first representation of a feathered coyote as a prominent subject in Teotihuacan art.

[37] Pasztory does not, indeed could not, establish her assertion that intentional choice was involved, based as her argument is on analogies from European art history that are not pertinent and are inappropriate. The historical contexts are totally different; the critical evidence she cites comes from written sources. A critique (Klein 1990: 95) of similar passages in another work of Pasztory points out the inherent weakness of such an argument.

[38] Little is known about the archaeological contexts of these masks, and Pasztory suggests that they may have formed part of composite deity images in temples.

[39] In considering why the preeminent deity was female, Pasztory argues that a female would

same ideal embodied in the so-called "portrait" figurines with very similar mold-made heads on handmade bodies in varying positions.

Pasztory argues for the continuity into later times of popular ritual from the late first millennium B.C. Basin of Mexico populations as exemplified by the presence of small clay figurines, Old God braziers, and Storm God jars[40] throughout Teotihuacan's history and on their use in apartment compounds. She sees this as "remarkable" primarily because there was not a similar continuity in the use of figurines among the lowland Maya when dynastic ruler cults became ascendant there. The retention for centuries of the same class of objects for use in household ritual is not remarkable, is not unique, and should cause no surprise in a city as complex as Teotihuacan. Their presence need have no bearing on the absence of public dynastic art.[41]

Pasztory's argument that oral expression was emphasized is persuasive. This can be seen in the ubiquity and often inordinate size of sound scrolls. This seems to contradict her observation that the nose pendant symbolizes cutting off of speech or communication because it hides the mouth. But if we regard the nose pendant as analogous to the veil worn over the lower part of the face of Tuareg men, about which Robert Murphy (1964) wrote so brilliantly, the contradiction disappears and an interpretation consonant with Pasztory's emerges. The wearing of the nose pendant would be seen as a means of maintaining symbolic reserve, of separating while relating, of withdrawal or depersonalizing the self—all as a means of coping with ambivalences in social relationships in a heterogeneous urban society with a high potential for confrontation and conflict.[42]

Pasztory sees the concern with denying access and holding back, with privacy and perhaps secrecy, as an indication that Teotihuacan was not a

---

be "non-political." This is an appealing argument, but it does not follow. A major constituent of the final destruction of central Teotihuacan was the destruction of the state cult over which she presided, an eminently political act. Deities, whatever attributes they may have and whatever other functions they may serve, act as integrating forces and have political functions. Male as well as female deities can be cosmic and universal as well as remote and distant. This is not a question that can be answered in the abstract. Deities develop in particular historical and social contexts and cannot be "explained" apart from those contexts.

[40] Unlike figurines and Old God braziers, Storm God jars are not ubiquitous; the few found have been almost always in well-endowed burials (Sempowski n.d.).

[41] Another indication that no great social significance should be attached to their continuation from the first millennium B.C. is the fact that, after the end of Teotihuacan's dominance, figurines continued to be made in great numbers in all Basin of Mexico societies down to the time of the Spanish Conquest.

[42] The platforms attached (adosada) to Teotihuacan's principal pyramids—the Pyramids of the Sun and Moon and the Temple of the Feathered Serpent, Pasztory sees as another instance of a concern with keeping something hidden and secret—in these instances as serving to remove the pyramids themselves and their staircases from access, to make them more remote. If the adosada platforms had this effect, they also would have served an opposite purpose—to provide a highly visible platform for the performance of ritual. Even though the three pyramids differ greatly in height and mass, all three of their adosada platforms are about the same

proselytizing society. Keeping secrets from the uninitiated is hardly a bar to proselytization. Nevertheless, I do not believe that Teotihuacan religion can be characterized as proselytizing and, despite what Pasztory implies, have not argued that it was.[43] I have argued that Teotihuacan was a sacred place of enormous prestige, whose religion must have encompassed a belief system that transcended ethnic, linguistic, and regional ties. The physical focus of this belief system would have been the sacred cave beneath the Sun Pyramid seen as both the place where time began and the place of origin of humankind. This is discussed further in a later section.

Pasztory is right when she says that Teotihuacan was primarily interested in itself and its own internal affairs and social integration. But she is far off the mark when she says that Teotihuacan "as a culture and in its art seems to have been uninterested in communicating much about itself to the outside world, other than its gigantic architecture and cosmic layout." Teotihuacan's "gigantic architecture and cosmic layout" cannot be neatly isolated from its "culture and art." They are intimately and inextricably linked in countless ways.[44] Pasztory does not deny that its "gigantic architecture" communicated something to outsiders. When it did so it was communicating something fundamental about Teotihuacan culture, about Teotihuacan religion, about the core of beliefs that was the rationale for all this construction—what it was that this architecture commemorated and celebrated. This is why it is a mistake to try to separate the impact this majestic array of monumental architecture had on outsiders from the message it conveyed about the critical importance for all humankind of the rituals performed there.

The emphasis on speech and oral expression in Teotihuacan suggests to Pasztory a small community, where people could talk to one another, rather than a great city. Oral traditions in religion are important in many societies, large and small, from very simple to highly complex. The existence of such traditions does not mean that people acted like villagers. All it implies is a common oral vocabulary for a common religion.

By far the weakest and most unconvincing part of Pasztory's analysis is her argument for the existence of a utopian religious ideology. She sees the city as the "realization of the utopian vision of many small Preclassic communities"

---

height, from a little less than 40 to a little more than 50 ft. Ritual performances carried out on these platforms would have been highly visible to those below. By contrast, ritual performances carried out in or in front of the temples surmounting the Sun and Moon pyramids would have been remote and difficult to follow (see Fig. 4).

[43] Stephan Borhegyi (1971) does come close to arguing that Teotihuacan was a proselytizing society.

[44] Spiro Kostof (1985: 240–241) says it well in his concluding observations on Teotihuacan: "To mediate between cosmos and polity, to give shape to fear and exorcise it, to effect a reconciliation of knowledge and the unknowable—that was the charge of ancient architecture."

that was "founded as a sacred city by individuals who began a powerful utopian religious ideology . . . in the Patlachique phase" (ca. 150 B.C.). Her "utopian" cosmic vision involves a concept of rational order that was a radical break with past and contemporary traditions, a turning away from military aristocracies and powerful rulers to the creation of this "Mesoamerican social and religious experiment." She sees Teotihuacan's grid layout and city plan as a "material representation of some kind of rational social planning that may be characterized as utopian." The construct Pasztory creates is inherently improbable when applied to Teotihuacan and is at total variance with what can be inferred of the city's early history. Pasztory relates the "animus towards a personality cult" in Teotihuacan art and the vigorous negation of the "institution of the semi-divine ruler" to the rejection of southern Mesoamerican cultural traditions. She argues that "opposition to the art and political structures of Southern Mesoamerica" was one of "four salient features" of the art and architecture of Teotihuacan. She sees this as supportive of her utopian argument, but it undercuts it. In her formulation the presumed adoption of a utopian religious ideology would not be a reaction to local conditions in the Basin of Mexico perceived as intolerable, but rather an almost abstract rejection of beliefs and practices of distant outsiders, well removed from local problems, however well known they might have been to those in the upper levels of the newly created Patlachique Phase community. The likelihood of this occurring would be extremely remote, even if the utopian argument were plausible.[45] In the second century B.C. there were contending petty states in the Basin of Mexico, most of them temple-centered, with a modest-sized urban center in the southwest—Cuicuilco (see Evans and Berlo, this volume, fig. 2). There were no longer any Olmec-related societies in the southern Basin.

Apart from its inappositeness, an additional point must be made about Pasztory's utopian argument. She extends to everyday social relations her postulated ideological formulations concerning what ought to be, as though there were a one-to-one correspondence between the strictures of an ideology and what goes on in daily life.[46] What can be inferred about ideology

[45] Because much of the evidence Pasztory cites as supporting or as associated with her utopian argument follows the founding of the city by hundreds of years, dating to the 4th century A.D. and later, does the utopian argument make any more sense for that period than for the earlier period? It does not. As discussed in the final section, the reaction for which there is evidence in the 3rd century and the changes that followed it were not in any sense utopian. They are consonant with some of Pasztory's interpretations of Teotihuacan art but not with her utopian argument.

[46] Cecelia Klein (1990: 95) comments on this. Pasztory makes no distinction between what is propounded in ideology and what is social reality. One of the dimensions commonly found in a state ideology in a non-industrialized society is its consonance with the interests of those ruling the society—whatever else it does, it rationalizes and justifies the social order and the domination of the majority by those who rule them. It may do this by masking exploitive relations; by denying them; by setting forth an ideal of equity; by emphasizing, glorifying, and exaggerating status differences; or in countless other ways.

must be compared with what can be inferred about social conditions in the society in question. Pasztory does not do this. Her discussion of the apartment compound had asserted that "most of the population of the city lived in nearly 'palatial' dwellings." Ideology and social reality coincide in her presentation. But the published evidence from twenty-four excavated or partially excavated apartment compounds and residential complexes not on the "Street of the Dead" shows that only a handful could be characterized as palatial.[47] There is a great gulf between Zacuala Palace, a spacious stone-walled, lavishly adorned compound and the crowded tenement-like conditions in Tlamimilolpa, La Ventilla B, and Tlajinga 33:S3W1.[48]

Analyses of burial evidence from the Tlajinga compound by Rebecca Storey (1985, 1986, 1992, n.d.a, n.d.b) have disclosed appalling conditions of perinatal mortality and relatively short life spans for those who survived.[49] The view that I and others propounded until Storey's work and that is implicitly accepted by Pasztory—that Teotihuacan was a prosperous place for most of its population for most of its history (which never made much sense)—is no longer tenable. In its place is a much more complex urban dynamic. Thus, even if there had been an expressed ideal of a rational order that included placing everyone in the same kind of dwelling, reality dramatically departed from the ideal.

One of the "four salient features" that emerged from Pasztory's analysis of Teotihuacan art and architecture remains—the concern with integrating a heterogeneous population through religion and symbolic imagery. Crippling problems encumber two others—the presumed concern with glorifying pre-Teotihuacan small town-village traditions and the alleged utopian ideology. The fourth—opposition to the art and political structures of southern Mesoamerican societies—is better and more easily understood as a reaction in art and other primarily political and religious dimensions to conditions in Teotihuacan itself, as discussed in the final section.

---

[47] The quality of craftsmanship and of construction materials varied greatly. It is common to find rooms that are small and crowded together and shoddy, slap-dash construction. It seems probable that the great majority of compounds and complexes not on the "Street of the Dead" were in this category, even though slightly less than half of those excavated so far would be so classified. This is because the evidence from excavation is skewed in favor of more richly endowed compounds with mural paintings, since most of these came to the attention of Mexican officials and archaeologists as a result of looting.

[48] Tlajinga 33:S3W1 is largely of adobe brick construction (Storey and Widmer 1989).

[49] Pasztory mentions these analyses in relation to population movements into the city and the social composition of apartment compounds but does not otherwise consider their implications. Storey's data argue that relatively late in the city's history less than 40% of those ever born lived to be adults and that those who did had a relatively short life span. There are enough data from other compounds occupied by people of roughly similar socioeconomic status to argue that Storey's data probably apply to the lower strata in the city as a whole.

René Millon

The Teotihuacan Economy: Production and Distribution

In 1950 Teotihuacan economic organization was not a subject of inquiry except in the most general terms (Armillas 1951). In 1990, it is the subject of many inquiries from many points of departure.[50] Linda Manzanilla has taken on questions of fundamental importance to our understanding of Teotihuacan society that have a bearing on all the other chapters in this volume. Her basic concerns are production, distribution, and storage in the Teotihuacan economy. She draws on comparative evidence from ancient Sumer and the Central Andes.

She raises important questions about where produce and goods rendered to temples were stored and suggests that rooms that often close the southern side of three-temple complexes might have been used for this purpose.[51] Manzanilla also wonders why some buildings at Teotihuacan are described as administrative (e.g., the Great Compound, Fig. 8). Indeed, the reasons for some of the designations, however problematic they may be, have not been explained as fully as they might have been.[52] These are good questions. But there is a major problem with Manzanilla's analysis that stems from the nature of her model. She has elevated redistribution

[50] In addition to the brief analyses of Linda Manzanilla and myself in this volume, other recent analyses include Sanders, Parsons, and Santley (1979, esp. pp. 105–129, 221–358, maps 24, 25), Sanders (1981: 180–184, figs. 6-2, 6-16), Sanders and Santley (1983), Santley (1983, 1984, n.d.b), Charlton (1987), Hirth (1978), Kurtz (1987) and McClung de Tapia (1977, 1987). Other important studies, the majority of which deal with the economics of obsidian working and exchange, include Charlton (1978, 1984), Charlton and Spence (1982), Clark (1986), Kolb (1986, 1987), Moholy-Nagy (1990), Santley, Kerley, and Kneebone (1986) and Spence (1981, 1984, 1986, 1987).

[51] Manzanilla also focuses on San Martin Orange pottery, whose surface distribution, both within apartment compounds and in the city as a whole, has been examined by Altschul (n.d.) and Cowgill (1987: 165–171; Cowgill, Altschul, and Sload 1984: 166, 167), who comment on the ware's two major forms: amphorae for storage and craters used in food preparation. Manzanilla suggests that centralized storage facilities may exist in a north-south zone 300–500 m west of the "Street of the Dead," where a high proportion of San Martin Orange ware was found. But what she singles out is not a high proportion of amphorae but of all San Martin Orange ware, the vessels used in food preparation as well as for storage. Because this is a continuously built-up zone of prosperous apartment compounds, it seems more likely that the concentration reflects domestic activities, like those Manzanilla and her associates brilliantly demonstrated were recoverable from the floors of rooms in an "Old City" residential compound (Manzanilla and Barba 1990).

[52] Manzanilla looks at the apartment compounds on the north and south platforms of the Great Compound, which Sload (1987) had suggested were foci of many regional interests in the city, and suggests that they may have been used for the storage of products brought to this central location for redistribution. Here she might have singled out the eastern half of the north platform of the Great Compound for its high proportion of San Martin Orange ware (Cowgill 1987; Cowgill, Altschul, and Sload 1984), although again we do not know how much can be attributed to amphorae. Because there is no place in her model for marketplace exchange, Manzanilla suggests that the central plaza of the Great Compound also was used for storage and as a place where ritual meals were consumed. Evidence from surface survey and excavation do not support the former (Fig. 8a, b, c). But enough of the plaza has been left relatively untouched to make possible the excavation and detailed examination of its successive floors of earth and concrete for what else they may reveal about their use.

into the sole explanatory principle needed to understand it. To argue that all the evidence can be understood in terms of redistributive networks is to oversimplify the problem.

Manzanilla greatly overstates the role of redistribution in part because her theoretical model is so spare and Procrustean, with the only alternative the more complex economy of her palace-centered sphere. Her model also oversimplifies the evidence from Mesopotamia, where city formation and early urban communities no longer can be understood solely in terms of the temple community model. Her discussion of Andean societies, while overly simplified, highlights some of the differences between Mesoamerican and Andean societies that appear to stem partly from distinct historical traditions that led to characteristically different cultural resolutions to problems posed by similar ecological conditions.

It seems clear that the Teotihuacan polity was sacralized and that temples were involved in some economic activities. How then was the Teotihuacan economy likely to have been organized? Pedro Carrasco (1982) has argued that at the time of the Spanish Conquest labor service on state lands formed the primary source of revenue in agricultural produce in central Mexican states and in many other New World states. Given the pervasiveness of such institutions in pre-Hispanic times, they seem likely to have had considerable time depth (see also Angulo 1987: 311–312, 315). Accordingly, if we are going to hypothesize about how the Teotihuacan economy was organized, it seems to make more sense to postulate that central to it were not the rendering of produce and products to the temple for redistribution nor their appropriation by the state in taxation but rather labor service obligations to the state. These would be obligations for most of those designated to work a given number of days on temple lands or public lands (which would have meant the same thing then), for a smaller number of craft specialists to work a given number of days in temple or state workshops, and perhaps for all to work a given number of days on public works, however defined. The remainder of a person's working time in agriculture or craft activities likely would have been largely at the service of his or her corporate group in the apartment compound or other residential complex where he or she lived, and to the *barrio* to which the apartment compound belonged. If the apartment compound group held rights to the use of lands outside the city, such lands presumably would have been worked by group members during the days at their disposal. Although most of the Valley of Teotihuacan's best lands are likely to have been public lands (including the irrigated alluvial plain), large private landholdings controlled by persons of high status also may have existed, worked by people in dependency relationships to such landholders.

Why would the right to exact labor service obligations have been accepted by the populace? Because most of the city's population almost certainly

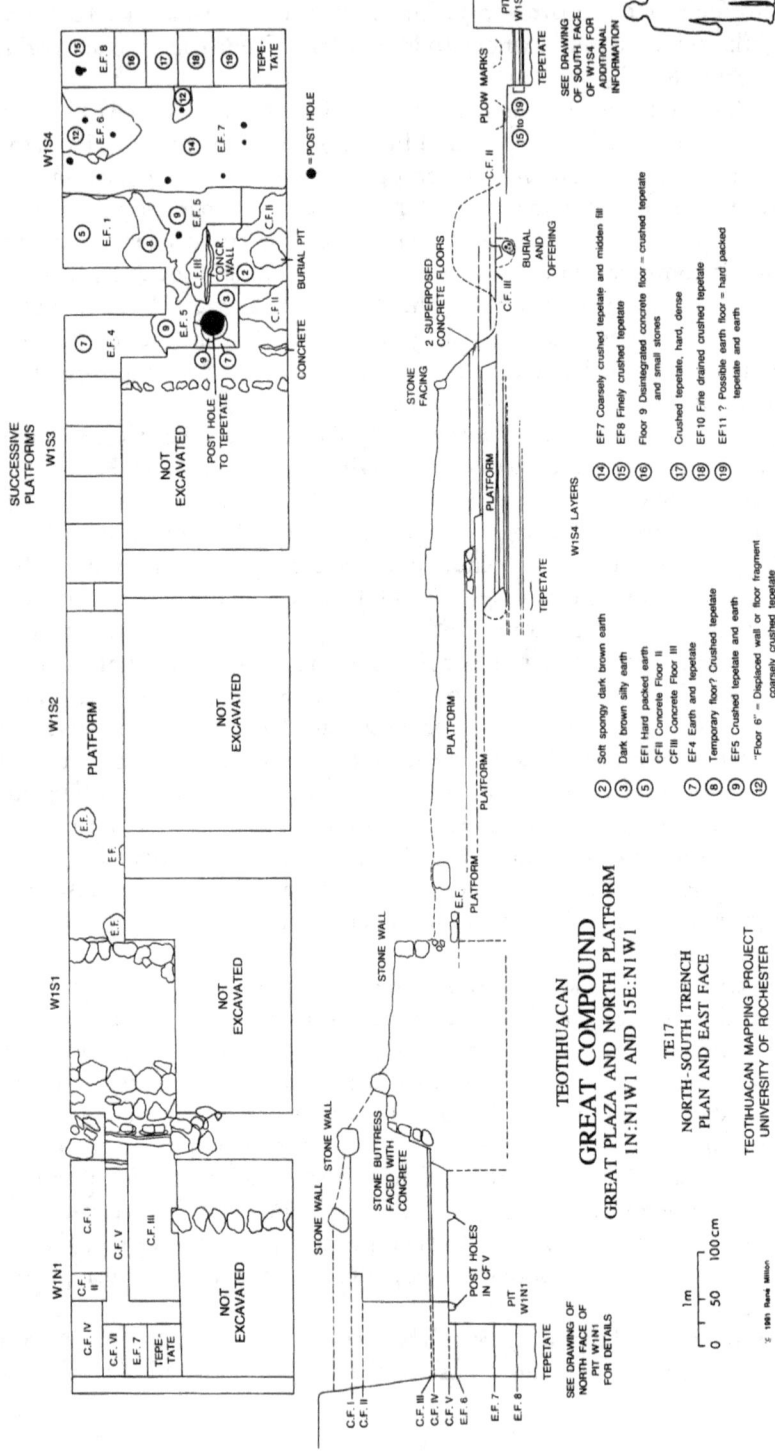

Teotihuacan Studies

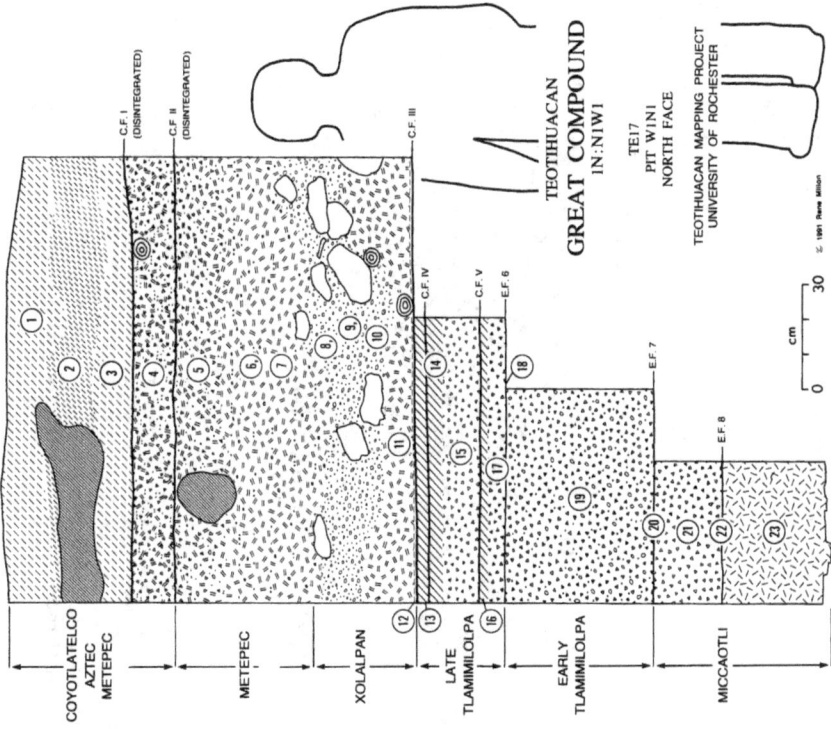

Fig. 8a (*above*) Great Compound, TMP stratigraphic trench (TE17). North Platform, left; terrace, center; great plaza, right; 185 m west of the "Street of the Dead," opposite the Ciudadela (Fig. 1). Figs. 8b and 8c present more detailed views of the stratigraphy on the North Platform and in the great plaza. TE17 was excavated by Matthew Wallrath.

Fig. 8b (*right*) Great Compound, North Platform. Together with its counterpart, the South Platform (see Fig. 1), the Great Compound's platforms were the probable loci of administrative activities. Whether compounds on these platforms housed administrators and bureaucrats directly responsible to the ruler and the ruling leadership, or leaders representing regional political and economic interests in the city, as suggested by Sload (1987), or both, or something else altogether, is not known. The first two interpretations would be consonant with the use of sections of these compounds for storage of goods, raw materials and foodstuffs, as suggested by Manzanilla (this volume). The construction history of the North Platform begins late in the second century A.D. in the Miccaotli phase with two pre-platform constructions—the leveling of the natural *tepetate* subsurface (layer 23) to form a floor of earth (EF8), that was covered shortly thereafter by a crushed tepetate floor underlying another earth floor (EF7). The first construction period of the North Platform itself dates to the third century (Early Tlamimilolpa phase) (EF6). The first concrete floors (CFs III, IV, and V) covering this part of the North Platform were built in the fourth century (Late Tlamimilolpa phase).

379

René Millon

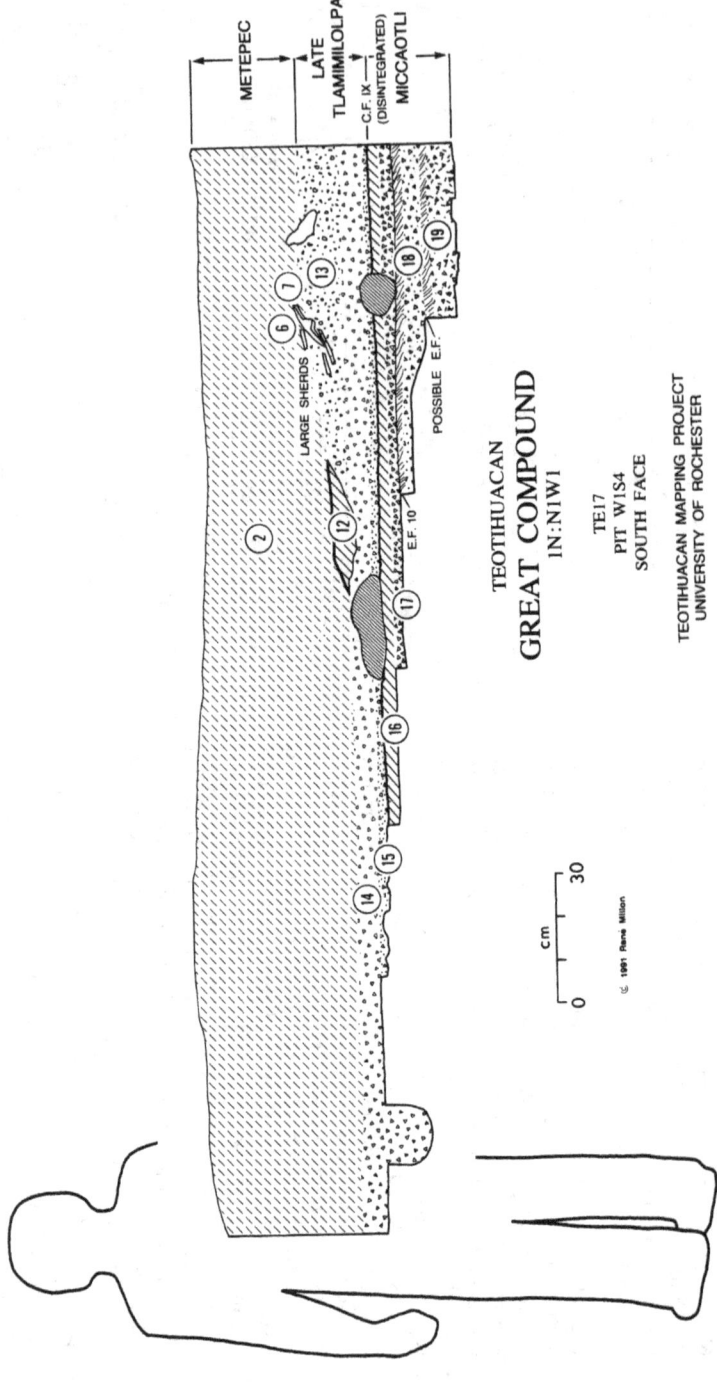

Fig. 8c Great Compound. Northern edge of great plaza which the author considers to have been the city's central marketplace. Manzanilla (this volume) argues that it was used for storage and the consumption of ritual meals.

would have perceived themselves as sharing the goals of its leaders, who would have been perceived as carrying on activities necessary for the city's well being and the maintenance of social order. Most people are likely to have accepted the exercise of authority by city leaders as legitimate—the authority involved in levying labor obligations, in organizing the labor so mobilized, and in directing the execution of the tasks required. This is not to say that a significant minority may not have resisted the exercise of authority by the leadership.[53]

The explosive growth of the city at or near the beginning of the first century A.D. would have catapulted the city into a position of leadership in the region. The sudden juxtaposition of populations from diverse ethnic groups, in which populations of provincial newcomers confronted longtime city dwellers and in which "old timers" had the upper hand economically and politically, could have provoked conflict so disruptive and destructive as to blow apart the newly constituted urban agglomeration as it came into being. We know that this did not happen. We know that the city prospered and provided the milieu for the growth of the later metropolis. This argues that the newly arrived populations must have found that there were advantages as well as disadvantages in having been uprooted. Among these advantages must have been economic opportunities.[54]

We have no information on how goods and services were exchanged in the first century A.D. The great area in the middle of the city that I argue served as its central marketplace from ca. A.D. 175–200 onward had not yet come into use, and we do not know how external exchange was then

[53] It would be a mistake to picture labor exactions as having been carried out by force against the will of most workers. This would have been true even for many, if not most, of those compelled to move into the city. In most non-industrialized stratified societies authority almost certainly was exercised not through force alone but through a combination of violence and consent (Godelier 1978, 1979, 1988: 156–164). For most of the populace for most of the time we can infer an acceptance of the legitimacy of rulership and of the right of those high in the hierarchy to require the expenditure of labor time in such activities as work on public lands and on public works. Those groups and individuals who might have tried to resist or evade such obligations would have been subject to the ultimate threat of enforcement by the military and if that failed, the relatively rare invocation of force to ensure that obligations to the state were not flagrantly shirked. This does not mean that sources of disruptive conflict would not have been a continuing danger to public order.

[54] These would have been primarily in crafts and services; opportunities are likely to have been limited in agriculture. The quantum leap in the size of the city would have generated enormous pressures associated with urban living at an unprecedented level of complexity. There must have been a wide range of problems where governmental responses were inadequate, inappropriate, or non-existent—problems with the housing of new populations, the furnishing and replenishing of household goods and utensils, the provisioning of households, the hauling of water, the removal of waste, the bearing of burdens. No doubt many of these needs were met on a neighborhood basis. But in a city of 80,000 or more there must have been many that were not met, with resulting opportunities. Old settlers would have moved in to exploit some of them, with newcomers, if involved, playing subordinate roles. But there probably were other opportunities that for one reason or another were not exploited by "old timers." Newcomers could have filled these interstices and prospered.

effected. Internal exchange could have taken place in formal or informal localized areas.

From the second century A.D. on, how would the product of work in the fields and workshops under the control of apartment compound leaders and *barrio* organizations have been exchanged? In Manzanilla's model some of the product would have been bartered, the remainder directed to the temple sphere for redistribution. Marketplace exchange would not exist until the temple-centered sphere had given way to a palace-centered sphere in a tributary state which, she argues, did not come into being in central Mexico while Teotihuacan was flourishing. These are the only alternatives she considers. But the pervasiveness of marketplace institutions in central Mexico was so great at the time of the Conquest that they must have had considerable time depth. In addition, marketplace exchange seems to have been the product of distinctively *Mesoamerican* cultural responses to ecological settings that under apparently similar conditions in the Central Andes did not lead to a prominent role for marketplace exchange. In some regions of the Central Andes a quite different solution was reached, based on *Andean* cultural biases (Murra 1975; Murra, Wachtel, and Revel 1986: 4–5). For these reasons it seems likely that marketplace institutions would have existed at Teotihuacan, even though the economy was not dominated by a palace-centered sphere. Following this interpretation, it would have been in such marketplaces that most of the lapidary materials described by Turner were exchanged, as well as other craft products, such as worked obsidian (Spence 1981).

Existing evidence bears only on aspects of Manzanilla's hypotheses and mine. Testing critical dimensions of either will not be easy, even though the problem is of such central importance. Still I think it reasonable to predict that means and methods will be developed to resolve some of the matters at issue before many years have passed.

ART, IDEOLOGY, AND POLITY: A PERSONAL VIEW

I turn now to my own views of art, ideology, and polity. Teotihuacan was even more remarkably distinctive than Pasztory indicates because the evidence suggests that it did not begin with the institutionalization of earlier "small town" traditions, but with powerful, audacious, and probably charismatic leaders, who exercised personal rule, established military traditions, and provided themselves with impressive tomb burials. It seems likely that it was in reaction to a growing absolutism that some of the characteristics of later Teotihuacan society, to which Pasztory referred, developed. But the form taken by the reaction was in no sense utopian.

The one explanation that makes more sense than any other of Teotihuacan architecture, religion, and ideology stems from Drucker's (n.d.a) and Malmström's (1978) argument that Teotihuacan has its distinctive east-of-north orientation, because it was oriented to the day that time began in the Mesoamerican calendrical system. The Conquest period creation myths associating Teotihuacan with the beginning of the cosmos probably reflected earlier myths. It is my contention that Teotihuacan was oriented to the *day* that time began because it was believed that Teotihuacan was *where* time began. This would make sense of the grid plan of the city, of the use of the cave to determine the location of the Pyramid of the Sun, and of the layout of monumental architecture on an avenue whose length and breadth were unprecedented in Mesoamerica before and since.

If Teotihuacan was oriented to the day that time began because of a belief that it was *where* time began, the grid plan of buildings with its distinctive orientation would have been an eternal celebration of this. The grid was imposed on the landscape, not as a utopian exercise, but because the repeated expression of the orientation commemorated an event of such profound significance and cosmic scope. The conviction that Teotihuacan was where the world came into being would have been at the core of a belief system giving the Teotihuacanos an unrivalled pride of place. So many other things fall into place when this assumption is made that it has to be given serious consideration and tested.

Visitors to Teotihuacan today ask the same questions time and again. Why is the Sun Pyramid where it is, off to one side? Why is it not at the head of the avenue? Why is the "Street of the Dead" oriented the way it is? Does its orientation have any special meaning or significance? Still other questions come up frequently. How did this overpowering concentration of monumental buildings ever come to be built? Was it the product of a single plan or a sequence of successively larger and more comprehensive plans? What was it that set all this in motion?

As Janet Berlo points out, the Great Goddess was associated with Cerro Gordo, the mountain that dominates the vista north of the "Street of the Dead" (see Berlo, this volume, fig. 24). I hypothesize that this association of sacred mountain and goddess goes back to the beginnings of Teotihuacan, and that this association preceded the layout of the earliest "Street of the Dead." This brings us to the cave. Caves were sacred places in Mesoamerica because they were believed to lead to the underworld and to be places of emergence—birthplaces, as Doris Heyden (1975, 1981) and Karl Taube (1986) have stressed. Teotihuacan was built over a series of caves.[55] Sometime in the first century B.C. one of these caves, whose entrance is on the centerline of the Sun Pyramid came to be thought of as the place where the present era began, where the present cycle of time was born. A sightline from the cave's entrance to the western horizon was related to astronomical and calendrical phenomena.

---

[55] Linda Manzanilla et al. (1989); Manzanilla (1990). See also Manzanilla's discussion of tunnels related to these caves (1990).

These phenomena were thought to be so significant that Teotihuacan's leaders commemorated them in monumental architecture early in the first century A.D. A powerful, probably charismatic ruler concentrated the Basin of Mexico's population in the city and directed the construction of an avenue relating the cave to the sacred mountain. This avenue extended north from the cave, perpendicular to the cave sightline, to end at Teotihuacan's first great pyramid—the earliest, innermost Moon Pyramid. At the same time temple platforms associated with the cave were built. Seventy-five to one hundred years later the avenue was extended south, and the first Sun Pyramid was built, centered on the cave entrance. Shortly afterward, in the late second and early third century A.D., the avenue was extended farther south; the Sun Pyramid we see today was built, then two immense enclosures to the south, the Ciudadela and the Great Compound (Figs. 1, 9). The

Fig. 9 The Ciudadela (upper left) and the Great Compound (upper right): the geographic, political, religious, and economic center of the city. The Yayahuala, Zacuala Palace, Zacuala Patios (partially excavated), and Tetitla apartment compounds, from right foreground to center right, respectively (see Fig. 1) (© 1965 by René Millon).

construction of this mile and a half of monumental architecture in two centuries almost certainly was directed by a succession of powerful rulers. It does not look like anything conceived in committee deliberations. Both pyramids probably house tombs. As we know, the tomb on the center line of the Temple of the Feathered Serpent was looted. After the mass sacrifice at the Feathered Serpent Temple, there was a reaction that effectively and permanently limited the power of rulers for the remaining 500 years of Teotihuacan's history.

Before the second century B.C. the Valley of Teotihuacan was a backwater in the Basin of Mexico. The development of a prosperous urban center was the outgrowth of several circumstances, not all of which can be discussed here. The potential productivity of the valley's alluvial plain under irrigation began to be exploited; craft activities, particularly the working of obsidian began to expand; the young city's leaders began to exploit its geopolitical importance as the potential gatekeeper controlling movement through the only unimpeded passage into the Basin of Mexico from populous, prosperous regions to the east. State lands and state enterprises were probably supported by labor-time exactions and obligations. The city's leaders were probably in contact by then, directly or indirectly, with Gulf Coast, Oaxaca, and highland Maya centers.[56] Early Teotihuacan grew and prospered and, in the first century B.C., was the larger of the two major cities in the Basin of Mexico—the other was Cuicuilco at the opposite, southwest end of the Basin (Sanders 1981: fig 6.13).

At some point in this early history one of the many caves underlying parts of the city came to be considered special. It was a long, relatively narrow cave—a lava tube, twenty feet below the surface, extending a hundred yards east-southeast and ending in a chamber with four lobes (see Figs. 4, 10— TMP plan, TE28) (R. Millon 1981: figs. 7-9, 7-10). The Teotihuacanos altered the form of the cave in various ways, made offerings of food and performed rituals in it involving fire, water, fish, and shell (TE28). Before long the cave must have assumed overriding cosmological significance, because a century or so later, when the Teotihuacanos built the Sun Pyramid, it was centered on the cave entrance and oriented to a sightline from the cave and its perpendicular. The belief system of the Teotihuacanos must have rested on the central role of the cave as *the* place of emergence in the creation of the present cycle or era of time. The world as they knew it was born in this cave. Many peoples develop cosmologies placing themselves at the center of their creation myths. What sets this apart is the scale and distinctive orientation of the avenue of monumental structures the Teotihuacanos built to commemorate it.

[56] For the way I use the concepts of *city* and *state*, see R. Millon (1981: 215–217).

René Millon

Teotihuacan Studies

Like many other ancient peoples, Mesoamericans were concerned with cardinal directions, with heavenly bodies and their apparent motions, and with the relations of these motions to cycles of time and counts of days. In my opinion the most persuasive explanation for Teotihuacan's distinctive orientation—15½° east of north—is that the Teotihuacanos related a sight-line to the western horizon from their sacred cave to astronomical observations and to specific days of the year and counts of days that also would have been regarded as significant by other Mesoamericans.

Thanks to David Drucker (1977, n.d.a) we can infer that late in the first century B.C. observers at the cave entrance found that on two days of the year—12 August and 29 April—the sun set at the same spot on the western horizon, 15½° north of west. The interval between 12 August and 29 April is 260 days; the interval between 29 April and 12 August is 105 days; 29 April is 52 days before the summer solstice; 12 August is 52 days after it; the summer solstice is the 105th day. These numbers would have been regarded as highly significant because at this time two calendars or day counts were in use in Mesoamerica—the 365-day year that we call the vague year and a 260-day count used everywhere in many aspects of ritual, especially divination. The two counts when permutated produced the famous 52-year calendar round. This is why the 260-day interval and the 105-day interval (52+1+52) would have appeared to be so significant. Also relevant is that in a zone of the Maya area that includes Izapa and other major centers, 29 April and 12 August were then the two zenith passage days of the sun—the two days of the year the sun passed directly overhead at noon (Malmström 1978).

Fig. 10 (*opposite*) Sun Pyramid cave. Plan of the cave beneath the Sun Pyramid (see cross-section, Fig. 4). Plan shows the natural width of the cave and the various ways it was modified by the Teotihuacanos in the Tzacualli phase and earlier to produce a passageway much more sinuous and serpentine than the natural cave. The cave must have been centrally important in Teotihuacan religion because its entrance determined the locus and center line of the Sun Pyramid. Every aspect of the modified cave manifests ritual. The western section of the cave, between its entrance and the transverse cave, was altered four times by narrowing and by the construction of low, slab-covered ceilings, so that those penetrating the cave would have to repeatedly alternate between standing and crouching and kneeling. In the second century A.D., the eastern section of the cave was sealed by a succession of 17–19 blockages of stone, most of which were faced with standard Teotihuacan mud concrete. These barriers were penetrated in Teotihuacan times, probably during the fourth century A.D. (Late Tlamimilolpa phase). TMP explorations and excavations in the floor of the cave (TE28) by Jeffrey H. Altschul disclosed evidence of Tzacualli phase rituals involving fire and water and offerings of shell and tiny fish spines and bones in association with three distinctive ceramic forms (a plate, a bowl, and a jar) found in quantity only in the cave. The cave was surveyed by Darlena K. Blucher to prepare this plan.

Around A.D. 1 the Pleiades star cluster set on or very close to the same 15½° north of west sightline at Teotihuacan. This phenomenon would have been seen as doubly significant cosmologically, because the Pleiades cluster makes its first yearly appearance in the spring in the *east* (heliacal rising) before dawn on the day of the first zenith passage of the sun at Teotihuacan, around 18 May, when the spring rains should be starting.

The setting sun on 12 August would also have commemorated the legendary date for the beginning of the present era—"the day that 'time' began" in the Maya calendar we call the Long Count (Malmström 1978).[57] It must have seemed fraught with cosmic significance that the sightline from Teotihuacan's sacred cave commemorated the *day* that time began since they believed that Teotihuacan was *where* time began.

Following this reasoning, the sightline from the cave entrance to the hills on the western horizon (15½° north of west) commemorated and celebrated: the beginning of the present era, the birth of the cosmos, the day that time began; the zenith passage of the sun at Teotihuacan and in part of the Maya area; and, by extension, the summer solstice, the 260-day sacred almanac, and the 52-year calendar round.[58] An indication of the importance of the sightline to the western horizon is a distinctive marker, the pecked cross, that recorded it in two locations in the city hundreds of years later.[59] The two markers form a right angle with the "Street of the Dead," accurate to within less than ¼°.

What transformed these early observations from the esoteric and parochial to wider significance was the decision by Teotihuacan's leaders to orient the city's new avenue and later the city's entire eight square miles to the sightline from the cave and its perpendicular, and in so doing to commemorate and celebrate Teotihuacan and its sacred cave forever as the birthplace of the present cycle of time.

Teotihuacan dominated the Basin of Mexico by the beginning of the first century A.D. This is when the city was transformed by two decisions that must have been made by its ruler and his advisors: (1) to embark on a huge program of public works—of monumental buildings and a great avenue oriented to commemorate permanently the city's unique cosmological significance; and (2) to require that the overwhelming majority of the popula-

---

[57] Depending on how it is calculated that beginning date is 11, 12, or 13 August in 3114 B.C. (R. Millon 1981: 239, 240; Schele and Freidel 1990: 81, 82).

[58] The observations and calculations for these relationships were made by James Dow (1967), David Drucker (1977, n.d.a), Vincent Malmström (1978), Anthony Aveni (1980: 222–228; Aveni and Gibbs 1976), John Carlson (1990: 90–94) and others. In my view no single observation or calculation is sufficient to make the case. But the combination of these observations and calculations when related to the cave *is* persuasive.

[59] One marker was on the floor of a public building on the east side of the "Street of the Dead" a short distance south of the cave and the Sun Pyramid (R. Millon 1973: fig. 57a). A hill in the distance is the site of the other marker, on the east edge of a built-up section of the city, 1½ mi. to the west (R. Millon 1973: fig. 57b).

tion living in the many communities in the Basin of Mexico move into the city itself. Some may have moved voluntarily; others must have been compelled to move. For various reasons, I think it likely that many of those forced to move were resettled in the "Old City" in the northwestern part of Teotihuacan.

The massive influx of populations from central and southern parts of the Basin must have posed particular problems for those who ruled the city. Many of those resettled must have been subject to regimes that were hostile to Teotihuacan and in competition with it (Spence 1984: 111; Sanders, Parsons, and Santley 1979: 103). Cuicuilco would have been the most prominent and powerful of these rival polities. The uprooting and resettling of thousands of people accustomed to life in the countryside or in smaller political centers would have posed such predictable problems of social control that the decision to carry it out could not have been undertaken lightly.

Resettlement in the city need not have been planned from the outset. But at some point in the process of gaining control over the entire Basin of Mexico, the city's leaders must have concluded that the problems for existing institutions of governing the populations in the rest of the Basin were sufficiently great that extraordinary measures would have to be taken to overcome them. The radical decision to persuade or compel outlying populations to move into the city must have been reached because the city's leaders thought it would pose fewer problems than trying to continue to rule through existing structures of domination.

The decision to concentrate the Basin's population in the city appears to have involved a simultaneous decision to commemorate the city's singular sacred history with a massive program of public works. One objective would have been to use Teotihuacan's emerging ideology to involve and motivate the existing and incoming populations. Ideology would have supported the moral order and the central beliefs, precepts, and rituals of Teotihuacan religion and would have focused on the importance of honoring with monumental construction what set Teotihuacan apart from all other settlements in its world—the belief that Teotihuacan's sacred cave was the source of the cosmos.

The influx of people greatly increased the labor force available for public construction. But the potential for conflict between old settlers and new arrivals would have been enormous. Pasztory correctly stresses the ethnic and probable linguistic diversity that would have existed. Controls instituted to maintain order among ethnically diverse newcomers would have reinforced the structure of domination already intensified by conquests and population displacements. To rationalize the reality of domination, to foster social cohesion, the city's emerging ideology would have had to stress the *unity* in this diversity, to promote the theme that Teotihuacan as the custodian of the place where the universe began had become a city united, favored, honored, and charged with the responsibility of keeping the cosmos in motion through the performance of common rituals on calendrically prescribed occasions in public and domestic settings from the city center to the household. This would have been a powerful source of integration and motivation in an increasingly stratified, ethnically divided society.

Shortly after the population concentration, a large temple platform was built over the cave's terminus, a smaller one was probably constructed east of the cave entrance, and a great avenue was laid out perpendicular to the sightline to celebrate the connection between cave and sacred mountain. The avenue extended north for half a mile where it culminated in a surrogate sacred mountain, the first great pyramid, probably dedicated to the Great Goddess. This was the first Moon Pyramid, much simpler than the final one (Salazar n.d.), framed by and mimicking the massive outlines of Cerro Gordo, believed to be the source of the city's ground water. Mesoamericans attached religious meaning to mountains as well as to caves, and earlier sacred architecture in the city probably had been related to Cerro Gordo.

The early transformation also included the building of many three-temple complexes on both sides of the avenue and to the northwest (Evans and Berlo, this volume, fig. 3; Fig. 1). The Moon Pyramid itself was the principal temple in a three-temple complex (see Fig. 1) as was the later Sun Pyramid. Three-temple complexes were functioning temples, but their number and location argue that they also played important administrative roles in the urban hierarchy or cross-cutting it. By ca. A.D. 50 the early plan was realized. We can hypothesize that whoever was the ruler when the twin decisions were made is likely to be buried beneath the earliest Moon Pyramid.

The next step in the ambitious transformation of the urban landscape came with the decision to extend the "Street of the Dead," with temples on both sides, half a mile south, to where there is now a small seasonal river, the Rio San Juan, and to build a great pyramid east of and centered on the entrance to the cave. This was the first Sun Pyramid. Six more three-temple complexes as well as other temples were built. The first Sun Pyramid is smaller than the one visible today. It was more than 600 ft. on a side at the base and more than 150 ft. high. (The later pyramid, the one the visitor sees today, is 210 ft. high and almost 700 ft. at the base.) The interior of the first Sun Pyramid is primarily of earth with outer retaining walls of adobe. The outer facing of the inner pyramid is not known (see Fig. 4). It most likely had two temples on its summit, one dedicated to the Great Goddess, the other probably to the Storm God.[60]

---

[60] Saburo Sugiyama (this volume) questions the existence of these twin temples. I argue that they existed because we found the steeply sloping outer surface or *talud* of a temple platform that would have been on the south side of the summit platform of the first Sun Pyramid. Its existence on the south side implies a counterpart on the north side. This *talud* was uncovered in a TMP excavation (TE22) (see Fig. 4) carried out by Evelyn Rattray in the floor of a Mexican

Teotihuacan Studies

The planners and architects of the Sun Pyramid must have intended to build a pyramid immensely larger than the Moon Pyramid, to mark forever the location of the sacred cave's entrance. Ceramic dating at the pyramid's base by Robert Smith (1987) and in our TMP excavation at the top (TE22) places the completion of the pyramid at ca. A.D. 125,[61] seventy-five years, more or less, after the completion of the first phase of construction on the "Street of the Dead," ca. A.D. 50. In 1959 we found evidence of a tomb in or below the lowest terrace of the pyramid (Millon, Drewitt, and Bennyhoff 1965: fig. 123). This may be where the ruler who started the construction of the first Sun Pyramid is buried.[62]

The seventy-five to one hundred years after the completion of the earliest Sun Pyramid saw an immense amount of construction and engineering. The "Street of the Dead" was extended about a mile farther south. It was a prosperous time, a time of economic expansion in agriculture, crafts, and exchange. Lands beyond the Basin of Mexico, especially to the east in the Apan region, were probably taken over. These conquests may be part of what was being celebrated in the dedication of the Feathered Serpent Temple. This expansion and the many public works carried out argue that the city continued to be headed by a powerful executive able to mobilize and direct these activities effectively. The evidence from the Feathered Serpent Temple suggests that this period culminated in ostentatious personal rule.

Three major enterprises were undertaken during the third phase of construction. First, they enlarged the Sun Pyramid to create the pyramid we see today. They faced it with stone, covered it with concrete, surfaced it with lime plaster, and decorated the platform they attached to its western face with carved stone and sculpture, now largely collapsed. Its staircase was centered on the entrance to the sacred cave. Second, they constructed an immense politicoreligious and economic-administrative complex in what was to become the new center of the city. There they built the first identifiable royal palaces together with a great temple of carved stone; they created an immense plaza probably used as a city-wide marketplace in the other, administrative half of the complex. Third, they diverted, redirected, and

---

government tunnel at the midpoint of the rear of the uppermost body of the pyramid we see today (R. Millon 1973: fig. 17b). Fig. 5 shows the north *talud* of the south temple platform.

[61] Smith's account of the excavation of the upper tunnel and his analysis of the ceramics from it cannot be taken at face value because of the stratigraphic evidence that is ignored (Smith 1987). It would take too long to demonstrate this here.

[62] The way I have separated construction on the "Street of the Dead" into two phases, with the earliest Moon Pyramid built earlier than the earliest Sun Pyramid remains to be verified in excavation. We have evidence that the first Sun Pyramid was completed ca. A.D. 125 and that the population concentration occurred in the first years of the 1st century A.D. The size of the Sun Pyramid and the initial construction of the "Street of the Dead" are more understandable if the earliest Moon Pyramid was built first. But the Moon Pyramid data are not precise (Salazar n.d.). An excavation in the Moon Pyramid's interior is needed to find out when in the 1st century A.D. the earliest Moon Pyramid was built and whether there is a tomb within it.

canalized the Rio San Juan so that it would follow the Teotihuacan grid and provide unobstructed level space in the new center (see Fig. 1). In the latter part of this period (from ca. A.D. 150 to 225) the earliest residential compounds of permanent materials were built in neighborhoods outside the center. These were built with the same cosmologically significant orientations as the public structures on the "Street of the Dead."

In the performance of the city's cosmically oriented rituals, the very orientation of the buildings where rituals were performed, from apartment compound to great pyramid, would have contributed to their efficacy and would have been an incentive to the maintenance of this orientation in new construction. Teotihuacan was a city of more than 100,000 for more than 500 years, and this orientation continued to be maintained in domestic settings for the rest of the city's history in its more than 2,000 apartment compounds and other residential complexes (see Fig. 1). The orientation was maintained even in foreign *barrios*, except for a section of one, where some structures were round rather than rectilinear.[63]

The special cosmic responsibility that Teotihuacanos bore could have fostered an arrogance that would have led them to expect outsiders to be attracted to their city and cultural traditions, while they felt no comparable attraction to cultural traditions in foreign places. A partial analogy is the way those in the upper levels of traditional Chinese society viewed foreigners and the world outside the Middle Kingdom.

Many peoples see themselves at the center of the cosmos. What set Teotihuacan apart is that its leaders were able to act on that belief after the population concentration and to mobilize and motivate that population to realize the grandiose architectural vision that memorialized the city's unique significance. What might have been no more than a localized cosmic delusion centered on a parochial cult was transformed by charismatic leaders into the unique message of a triumphant religion and ideology when it was realized in material form.

Even so, none of this could have happened had not Patlachique-phase Teotihuacan developed in the first century B.C. into the largest and most prosperous community in the Basin of Mexico, with Cuicuilco as its only significant rival. The transformation that followed must have been led by a charismatic leader possessed by a compelling belief in the central importance

---

[63] The importance of these recurring orientations cannot be overstressed. Apartment compounds enclosed in their faceless walls would have been isolated from each other, their inhabitants forced into close interaction; preoccupied with the interests of the corporate group; clinging to their traditional customs, beliefs, and cult practices; generating over time their own variants of Teotihuacan customs and beliefs. This would set them off from other compounds, as microdifferences developed, intensified in some by ethnic differences. Those faced with the problem of city-wide integration would have had to combat this. One way would have been through ritual and sacrifice rooted in cosmic concerns, which would have been enhanced and reinforced by the cosmically significant orientations of the settings in which they were carried out.

of his cosmic vision. This is the person I postulate is buried in the center of the Moon Pyramid. The ruler who had the audacity to plan and begin the building of the earliest Sun Pyramid may be buried in the tomb that appears to lie in its center.

Several generations later the architectural focus of the city was shifted to what was to become its geographic, religious, political, and economic center for the next 500 years, the intersection of north-south and east-west axes, the site of the Ciudadela and the Great Compound, each covering some 40 acres (see Fig. 1).

The Ciudadela was the locus of seventeen temples, including the city's third largest; two palaces, one public, one private; an administrative complex; and a plaza so large George Cowgill (1983: 322) has calculated it could have held 100,000 people. It was the city's political center in a sacred setting. The Ciudadela's temples and the facades of its great platforms bear the hallmark of Teotihuacan temple architecture, the *talud-tablero* form, a recessed tablet above a sloping basal apron (Fig. 11).[64] Both the Feathered Serpent Temple and the platform attached to the front of the Sun Pyramid built a little earlier, ca. A.D. 175, bore carved stone *talud-tablero* architecture.

The near simultaneous construction of both the Ciudadela and the Great Compound formed the core of a master plan to create a new central focus for the city, a mega-complex located in the only extensive level area on the full length of the main avenue, at the intersection of the "Street of the Dead" and a new east-west axis formed by East and West Avenues.[65]

The building of the Ciudadela marked a dramatic break with previous public architecture, which achieved its effects with height and mass, with verticality and sheer volume. In the Ciudadela the architect stressed the horizontal, a horizontality accentuated by the *talud-tablero* form.[66] The constructions around the Sun Pyramid do not form an architectural whole (see Fig. 1). In contrast, the Ciudadela compound is a complex and sophisticated architectural entity, dominated on the outside by its immense outer platforms rather than by its principal pyramid. Most of the space in the interior is occupied by a vast central plaza, an open space of almost 11 acres. The inner sanctum of the Ciudadela was distanced from the onlooker not by

---

[64] Because an early temple bearing *talud-tablero* construction was found in western Puebla where the form appears briefly and was forever abandoned in the first century A.D. (García Cook 1981, 1984), it has been argued that the *talud-tablero* forms on temples at Tikal in Manik 1 contexts (A.D. 250–300) are not derived from Teotihuacan (e.g., Laporte n.d.; Laporte and Fialko 1990: 46, 59, 65, 66). Those who argue this should pay close attention to the stratigraphic evidence both at Teotihuacan and in Puebla. It does not support their interpretation.

[65] The eastern half of the east-west axis was slightly skewed to the south—by $1\frac{1}{2}°$ (i.e., 17° south of east), as were the east-west orientations of many other later buildings and streets. For discussion of this, see Drewitt (1967, 1987), Chiu and Morrison (1980), and Peterson and Chiu (1987).

[66] Ricardo Robina pointed this out long ago in a public lecture in Mexico City I attended in 1956.

Fig. 11 The Temple of the Feathered Serpent, the central temple in the Ciudadela (see Fig. 1), the city's most spectacular carved stone monument, built in the early years of the Early Tlamimilolpa phase (early second century A.D.). Associated with its construction and dedication were more than a hundred sacrificed soldiers, twenty other individuals at its center, and a tomb, subsequently looted, probably of the ruler who promoted the construction of the Ciudadela and this temple.

overpowering height and mass, as in the Sun Pyramid, but by expanses of platforms, staircases, and open spaces. The result, though on a much smaller and more modest scale, parallels that created by Beijing's Forbidden City, as demonstrated by Nelson Wu (1963: figs. 135–138).

What does the construction of this magnificent complex tell us about what was happening in the city? For one thing, as George Cowgill (1983: 335) has said, it argues that its construction was "the physical realization of the vision of an extremely powerful ruler." What has been found since in and around the Feathered Serpent Temple by Cabrera, Cowgill, and Sugiyama dramatically strengthens Cowgill's suggestion. Much has been written about why the shift from the focus on the Sun Pyramid occurred. It seems to me to be the product of a desire by a ruler with grandiose visions to build a new residence that would be endowed with pivotal meaning in the Teotihuacan religious system. This seems likely to have been effected in two ways: (1) by linking the creation myth associated with the cave beneath the Sun Pyramid to the imagery on the Ciudadela's principal temple—the symbolism of the cave as passageway represented in the passage of feathered serpent heads through "a great facade of feathered mirrors" (Taube, this volume), and (2) by giving its sacred precinct and the sacred center of its principal temple—where twenty persons were sacrificed with rich offerings—a critical role in the creation myth, perhaps as the point from which a deity or deities had ascended to the heavens. The new seat of political authority had to be endowed with cosmic origins.

The Feathered Serpent Temple was a poor third to the Sun and Moon pyramids in height and mass—a little more than 50 ft. high and about 200 ft. on a side at the base—but it is strikingly different. The feathered serpent is the dominant image, alternating on the *tablero* with another sculpture which, as Sugiyama points out, is associated with war and sacrifice.

In creating a subordinate east-west axis and a new geographic center for the city, the builders of the Ciudadela must have been affirming another aspect of their legendary history. The Ciudadela was at the crossroads of the cosmos (as were the centers of many other cities in the Old World and the New). It served as the pivot around which the cosmos revolved (Wheatley 1971) and, most important of all for central Mexican ritual concerns, the place where ritual must be performed to ensure its survival.

The theme of war and sacrifice in the temple's iconography takes macabre form in the mass sacrifice of soldiers—a dramatic proclamation of the necessity of sacrifice to maintain cosmic motion. Human sacrifice does not begin at Teotihuacan with the dedication of the Feathered Serpent Temple nor did it end there. Twelve human sacrifices were reported by Leopoldo Batres (1906) from the Sun Pyramid, and there may have been others.[67] But as far as we know now, the mass immolation that occurred in and around the Feathered Serpent Temple was without precedent and was never repeated.

We do not know how much may have been new, how much may have been an adaptation of prior ritual, how much may have been stressing

---

[67] Leopoldo Batres (1906: 10, 11, 23, [40]). We found a human sacrifice at the south-east corner of the Sun Pyramid in a TMP excavation (TE16B), but it post-dated the construction of the enlargement of the final pyramid.

subordinate aspects of earlier ritual. But building a new city center seems to have involved a shift in emphasis to ritual performances associated with war and sacrifice, later adopted by the Maya of Tikal, that transformed the Ciudadela into the political as well as the religious center of the city.

Teotihuacan owed its dominant position in central Mexico and beyond in large part to its great ecological potential, its strong, expanding, and diversified economy, and its innovative and effective political system (Sanders 1981: fig 6.16). But an essential ingredient in the transformation of Teotihuacan from a regional power to a power of widespread consequence in Mesoamerica was the way religion was used instrumentally to make Teotihuacan and its ritual significant to peoples elsewhere in Mesoamerica.

Despite caveats by its excavators that we may never know its significance (Cabrera, Sugiyama, and Cowgill 1991; Cowgill, personal communication, 1991), the looted tomb on the center line of the Feathered Serpent Temple nonetheless seems likely to have been the site of the burial of the "extremely powerful ruler" under whose direction the Feathered Serpent Temple was planned and begun and who caused the Ciudadela itself to be built. Because the looting was so extensive, this may remain in doubt. Nevertheless, given what was found in the tomb and elsewhere in and around the temple, this seems the most reasonable interpretation of the evidence. The successor to the ruler who began the Feathered Serpent Temple, under whose leadership the pyramid was completed, may have been buried at the foot of the staircase of the temple and have had few, if any accompanying sacrifices (Cabrera, Sugiyama, and Cowgill 1991). The subsequent history of Teotihuacan argues that there was a strong reaction against the kind of personal rule that had developed and that this reaction persisted. It makes more sense of the evidence to see this reaction as a response to local conditions perceived as intolerable than as a rejection of the political structures of southern Mesoamerican societies, as Pasztory argues.

The evidence argues that it was in response to an increasingly burdensome domination of Teotihuacan society by a succession of increasingly powerful rulers that strong institutional and ideological curbs were placed on the exercise of despotic rule, curbs so efficacious that they continued effectively to inhibit such rule for half a millennium—an extraordinary achievement. In a non-industrialized, hierarchically ordered society, such an enduring reform could have been carried out only by the collective action of the upper echelon of its leaders.

This might have been done by using the perilously charged properties of sacredness to limit the power of the ruler rather than enhance it, as has occurred in states in other parts of the world (Africa, for example), and to sharply circumscribe the scope of his activities, especially in access to and control over resources, including people. This need not mean that the ruler could not have exercised effective executive authority, nor that Teotihuacan would not have had capable, strong rulers thereafter. It means that effective measures were institutionalized by the collective leadership to prevent rulers from transforming executive authority into arbitrary personal rule.[68] When was the reform abolishing personal rule established? Existing evidence argues that it was developed during the regime of the ruler who succeeded the "extremely powerful ruler" responsible for the construction of the Great Compound, the Ciudadela, the Feathered Serpent Temple with its mass dedicatory sacrifices, and the start of construction on the palace areas bordering the temple. The reform may have been carried out at his death, before his successor was able to accede, perhaps in his name or that of his successor. This is likely to have happened between A.D. 250 and 300.

The Great Compound and the Ciudadela were the last mega-constructions undertaken, the last in 200 years of mega-construction, the last in a century or more of near continuous construction. Thereafter, for the next 450 to 500 years new construction on the "Street of the Dead" was on a decidedly smaller scale, and existing mega-constructions underwent only relatively modest enlargement.[69] (The Ciudadela's South Palace was built and re-built at least four times in the third century, never thereafter, see Fig. 6.) Nor was the elaborate sculptural treatment of a temple facade ever again repeated. Given the cruciform layout of the city, the location of one or more great monumental complexes might have been anticipated on the southern half of the "Street of the Dead." None ever was built. The abrupt cessation of two centuries of mega-construction and of elaborate sculptural decoration in stone, as well as the cessation of repeated rebuildings of palace areas—this architectural evidence for the institutionalization of effective checks on the power of rulers receives little support from artistic evidence for another 100 to 150 years—that is, until the fifth century (Early Xolalpan phase), when human figures become widely represented in Teotihuacan art.

It was apparently early in the fifth century that part of the front face of the Feathered Serpent Temple was covered by the construction of a four-tiered temple platform that abutted it (George Cowgill, personal communication, 1991). This may have been intended to commemorate the extraordinary reforms that by that time would have successfully contained the exercise of arbitrary rule for some 150 years. The platform abutting the Temple of the Feathered Serpent is austere in comparison to the temple. It was decorated with polychrome murals. Faded remnants have symbols associated with the Great Goddess. Ideological support for the suppression of personal rule may

[68] Who would have comprised this collective leadership? High-ranking priests and the highest echelons of the military certainly would have belonged. If large landholders existed who were neither high-ranking priests nor military leaders, they also could have been included.

[69] George Cowgill (personal communication, 1991) suggests that the "Street of the Dead" Complex may be a partial exception both in architecture and carved stone, but even there building activity was not on the scale of earlier construction.

have been associated with her cult, and her rise to preeminence may have been associated with that reform. The relatively modest palace areas in the Ciudadela, largely unmodified for four centuries—the North Palace (residential) and the South Palace (used in state functions)—are understandable when associated with rulers whose power was circumscribed.[70] Both are consonant with the austere political climate that contrasts so sharply with the prior climate of excess.

The collective leadership would have sought ideological support for the suppression of personal rule. This is when Esther Pasztory's concept of the "collective persona" and of collective uniformity is likely to have been elaborated and institutionalized. But the community as a whole is not likely to have been the primary focus of the emphasis on collective ideals at the outset. Instead it is likely that the emphasis would have been on the primacy of collective leadership and that this would have been elevated to a general principle in ideology. The emphasis would have been on ideological support for the reformation of the political system, on the pragmatic use of ideology to support the collective leadership in carrying out political reform at the top in the context of the city's established and successful religious system. We do not know what oral means may have been used to inculcate an ideological emphasis on collective ideals to support the principle of collective leadership. Most of the little public art that has survived does not appear to bear on this. Stone masks would be an important exception if they were used in public contexts as Pasztory suggests.

Two of the three emphases Pasztory sees in the city's composite incense burners are hierarchy and order. If we accept this interpretation, this may be evidence that obedience to authority as well as subordination of the individual to the group were values emphasized in Teotihuacan ideology and may have been inculcated in ritual associated with these burners, providing a possible parallel with ancient Sumer (Jacobsen 1946: 202–207) and traditional China (Bodde 1957: 49–50).[71]

The concern of the collective leadership to ensure the success of their reforms and the continuing exercise of checks on the powers of rulers would have required effective means to achieve and maintain social and political cohesion. Three stand out.

---

[70] Cowgill (1983: 338) discusses the implications for rulership of the size and construction history of the Ciudadela palaces in the context of a hypothesis that "political management" was "largely shifted away from the Ciudadela" after A.D. 300 for 300–400 years.

[71] Care should be taken with the use of the term *corporate* above the level of the apartment compound and neighborhood. Such terms as *corporate ideology, corporate alliance,* and *corporate value system of the state* (e.g., Pasztory 1988b: 50, 53, 57, 67, 74, 75) convey the opposite of what we know of the Teotihuacan state and Teotihuacan ideology as they developed and persisted for half a millennium. Teotihuacan was the opposite of the "corporate state"; its ideology was diametrically opposed to a "corporate ideology," as those terms are commonly used, for they refer to systems and ideologies that glorify personal rule and the cult of the leader.

Teotihuacan Studies

First, the cosmic concerns so pervasively expressed in architecture and the artistic preoccupation with military themes and sacrifice make it probable that ritual performances centering on sacrifice required to maintain the cosmos in motion were seen as a special responsibility of Teotihuacanos and were probably a primary source of integration and cohesion. The supreme sacrifice would have been heart sacrifice on platforms in the city center visible to all at times specified in the city's ritual calendar.[72] These occasions would have been the most dramatic but not the only means by which cosmic motion was to be maintained. If all Teotihuacanos were responsible for the maintenance of cosmic order, the efficacy of human sacrifice in the city's center would have been enhanced by the performance of sacrificial ritual at the *barrio* and compound levels. There is evidence in Teotihuacan art in apartment compounds of animal sacrifice and auto-sacrifice, including mortification of the flesh with cactus and maguey spines (Cabrera, this volume, fig. 15).[73]

It seems likely that the composite censer dedicated to the Great Goddess would have played an important role in such ritual performances because military and sacrificial ritual associated with the goddess was exemplified in censers and their *adornos* (Berlo 1983). In addition to the emphasis seen by Pasztory on hierarchy, order, and diversity in these censers, the various plaques and *adornos* attached to them also specified, as James Langley (this volume) has argued, the calendric occasion and the nature of the ritual to be performed. This would have been "commemorative, dedicatory, or testimonial" including ritual designed to contribute directly to the efficacy of sacrifice in state ritual performed in the city center. The "strong martial overtones" in the state ritual associated with domestic censers, of which Langley writes, may be án indication that one of the purposes of sacrificial ritual in apartment compounds, in addition to reflecting the city's strong martial ethos, was to promote or celebrate success in taking prisoners for sacrifice in the city center. This does not mean that censers, along with other religious paraphernalia, were not equally devoted to ritual directed toward neighborhood, compound, household, and individual concerns.

Second, another source of cohesion can be seen in Pasztory's comments on the preoccupation of Teotihuacan art with symbolic imagery as a means

---

[72] Those sacrificed would have been primarily but probably not exclusively prisoners taken in war. For a different view see Pasztory (1990). See also the wide-ranging discussion of human sacrifice at Teotihuacan in Gomez-Chavez (1990). Some areas adjoining the Basin of Mexico appear never to have been brought under Teotihuacan control, while areas farther from the city were (R. Millon 1988a: fig. 5.3). One reason for this may have been the potential the former would have possessed for providing readily available prisoners for sacrifice. This may be why a large enclave in Tlaxcala and northwestern Puebla remained outside the political orbit of Teotihuacan. It is one of the reasons offered to explain why Tlaxcala never came under the domination of the Aztecs.

[73] Armillas (1950: lám. xiiia); Séjourné (1956: figs. 44, 53; 1959: 27, 29, fig. 9); Miller (1973: figs. 343, 356); C. Millon (1988b: fig. VI.24; 1988c: fig. VI.32b); Pasztory (1988a: 161).

of integrating a heterogeneous population and systematizing it by the collective leadership to rationalize their rule.

Third, another obvious agent for cohesion and integration is the apartment compound, instituted in the third century, that eventually provided permanent housing for most of the city's population.[74] The advantage to the state in having relatively large, structured populations in apartment compounds forming the basic building blocks of Teotihuacan society has been clear since their distinctive attributes were first set forth more than twenty years ago.

After the burial at the foot of the staircase of the Feathered Serpent Temple, Teotihuacan rulership appears to have been held sharply in check. No other potential tombs of rulers are known, and when the human form begins to be represented in painting and sculpture, no representations of rulers are known in public contexts, and no obvious representations are known from private contexts.[75] This is in sharp contrast to the ancient Maya and to ancient Egypt, Mesopotamia, and China. It may have been a pre-Hispanic central Mexican approximation of post-revolutionary Mexico's maxim—"No reelección" (No re-election)—from presidents on down.

Effective means were institutionalized by a collective leadership to prevent rulers from transforming executive authority into personal rule. The rejection of personal rule was so thorough and so lasting, and the checks on rulers so effective, that it placed its stamp on Teotihuacan's history for another 500 years, profoundly affecting its political system, its religion, and its art. Much of what we think we know of Teotihuacan and think of as characteristically Teotihuacan falls into this period of enduring reform. We need to find out much more about how the city's leaders managed this problem so successfully for so long. Their long-term success in checking the arbitrary exercise of executive power, while not unprecedented in political history, is of potential interest everywhere today, for this is a universal problem.[76]

---

[74] They were not constructed to a uniform plan, but the conclusion is inescapable that the people were persuaded to build and move into these compounds because the state assisted in their construction.

[75] Some of the throned figurines from late in Teotihuacan's history (for example, Pasztory 1988b: III.24; Séjourné 1966b: passim) might be representations of rulers.

[76] A restoration of personal rule may have taken place during the city's last century. A possible indication is the resumption of construction activity in the Ciudadela's palaces in the Metepec Phase after the passage of more than 350 years. (For successive Metepec Phase floors atop the public entrance to the South Palace, see Fig. 7; for the North Palace, see Drucker n.d.b: 109, 113–115, [323]; Cowgill 1983: 328). If that happened, at least one of the figures in the main Tassel Headdress procession in the Techinantitla apartment compound east of the Moon Pyramid (see Fig. 1)—the figure preceded by the serpent head on a mat symbol—might represent such a late ruler (C. Millon 1988a: fig. V.5c, e). (The principal title of the ruler may have been "Feathered Serpent.") A restoration of personal rule after so long a time might, in turn, have been a culminating factor precipitating the iconoclastic devastation visited on the heart of the city in the 8th century when the city as metropolis was destroyed.

Teotihuacan Studies

The foregoing is how Teotihuacan appears to me now with the evidence at our disposal.[77] Students of Teotihuacan forty years from now may not pay much attention to the speculations offered here. What surely will be of lasting importance to them, what they *will* turn to, are the richly illustrated analytic studies that grace this volume.

Acknowledgments The University of Rochester Teotihuacan Mapping Project excavations illustrated here in Figs. 2; 3a,b; 5–7; 8a,b,c; and 10 were supported by grants from the National Science Foundation.

I thank Joyce Marcus for sending me the first three issues of *Episodios Mexicanos* and so calling to my attention this Mexican government comic book series on the history of Mexico, which begins with Teotihuacan—*Un recorrido por la historia de México: Desde Teotihuacan hasta la Expropriación Petrolera. Episodios Mexicanos,* no. 1, 1981, *El misterio de la urna,* dramatized the importance when it was in use of the Monte Albán IIIA urn from Oaxaca found at Teotihuacan in the TE3 Teotihuacan Mapping Project excavation in 1967.

George Cowgill read the penultimate draft of this chapter and made many helpful suggestions and critical observations from which it benefited substantially. I am also indebted to James Langley for his many useful comments in the verbal and written interchanges we have had about matters and issues important to this chapter.

Janet Berlo's suggestions and criticisms were instrumental in changing this chapter into its present form. I thank her for her consideration and patience.

My indebtedness to Clara Millon throughout every step in the process of preparing this chapter is too great to be adequately expressed here.

---

[77] What I have postulated may turn out to have little to do with what really happened. Even so, as a great scientist is supposed to have said about his practice of taking on only large scientific questions, "It is much more exciting not to catch a big fish than not to catch a little fish."—Attributed to Albert Szent-Györgyi by Teru Hayashi (1988).

René Millon

VALLEY OF TEOTIHUACAN CHRONOLOGY
Table of Concordances

			Phase Names [1]		Phase Numbers [2]	
LATE HORIZON	A.D. 1500		Teacalco		Aztec IV	
	1400		Chimalpa		Aztec III	POST-
	1300					
	1200		Zocango		Aztec II	CLASSIC
SECOND INTER-MEDIATE PERIOD	1100		Mazapan		Mazapa	
	1000					PERIOD
	900		Xometla		Coyotlatelco	———— 900 A.D.
	800		Oxtoticpac		Proto-Coyotlatelco	
	700	T	METEPEC		Teotihuacán IV	CLASSIC
	600	E		Late	Teotihuacán IIIA	
MIDDLE HORIZON	500	O	XOLALPAN	Early	Teotihuacán III	
	400	T				PERIOD
	300	I	TLAMIMILOLPA	Late	Teotihuacán IIA-III	
	200	H		Early	Teotihuacán IIA	———— 300 A.D.
	100	U	MICCAOTLI		Teotihuacán II	TERMINAL
	A.D.	A	TZACUALLI	Late	Teotihuacán IA	PRE-CLASSIC
	B.C.	C		Early	Teotihuacán I	
	100	A	PATLACHIQUE	Chimalhuacán *		PERIOD
		N			Proto-Teotihuacán I	
FIRST INTER-MEDIATE PERIOD	200		Terminal Cuanalan; Tezoyuca	Cuicuilco *		LATE
	300		Late Cuanalan	Ticoman III *		PRE-CLASSIC
	400		Middle Cuanalan	Ticoman II *		PERIOD
	500		Early Cuanalan	Ticoman I *		
	600			Middle		MIDDLE
	700		Chiconauhtla	Zacatenco *		PRE-CLASSIC PERIOD
	B.C. 800					

[1] Phase names used by personnel of Teotihuacán Mapping Project (Millon and others) and by personnel of Valley of Teotihuacán Project (Sanders and others).

[2] Phase numbers used by personnel of the Proyecto Teotihuacán, of the Instituto Nacional de Antropología e Historia (see Acosta 1964: 58-59).

* Pre-classic phases elsewhere in the Valley of Mexico.

NOTE: The absolute chronology shown is that used by the Teotihuacán Mapping Project. Terminology for the Teotihuacán phases is based on the Armillas classification (1950) with modifications.

Chronological chart for Teotihuacan.

BIBLIOGRAPHY

ADAMS, ROBERT MCCORMICK
1972 Patterns of Urbanization in Early Southern Mesopotamia. In *Man, Settlement and Urbanism* (Peter J. Ucko, Ruth Tringham, and G. W. Dimbleby, eds.): 735–749. Gerald Duckworth, London.
1981 *Heartland of Cities: Surveys of Ancient Settlement and Land Use on the Central Floodplain of the Euphrates.* University of Chicago Press, Chicago.
1988 Contexts of Civilizational Collapse: A Mesopotamian View. In *The Collapse of Ancient States and Civilizations* (Norman Yoffee and George L. Cowgill, eds.): 20–43. University of Arizona Press, Tucson.

ALTSCHUL, JEFFREY H.
n.d. Spatial and Statistical Evidence for Social Groupings at Teotihuacan, Mexico. Ph.D. dissertation, Dept. of Anthropology, Brandeis University, 1981.

ANGULO VILLASEÑOR, JORGE
1987 Nuevas consideraciones sobre Tetitla y los llamados conjuntos departamentales. In *Teotihuacan: Nuevos datos, nuevas síntesis, nuevos problemas* (Emily McClung de Tapia and Evelyn Childs Rattray, eds.): 275–315. Instituto de Investigaciones Antropológicas, Serie Antropológica 72. Universidad Nacional Autónoma de México, Mexico, D.F.

ARMILLAS, PEDRO
1944 Exploraciones recientes en Teotihuacán, México. *Cuadernos Americanos* 16(4): 121–136. Mexico, D.F.
1945 Los dioses de Teotihuacán. *Anales del Instituto de Etnología Americana* 6: 35–61. Universidad Nacional de Cuyo, Mendoza.
1947 La Serpiente Emplumada, Quetzalcoatl y Tlaloc. *Cuadernos Americanos* 31(1): 161–178. Mexico, D.F.
1948 A Sequence of Cultural Development in Meso-America. In *A Reappraisal of Peruvian Archaeology* (Wendell C. Bennett, assembler). *Memoirs of the Society for American Archaeology* 4: 105–111.
1949 Notas sobre sistemas de cultivo en Mesoamérica: Cultivos de riego y humedad en la cuenca del Río de las Balsas. *Anales del Instituto Nacional de Antropología e Historia* 3: 85–113. Mexico, D.F.
1950 Teotihuacán, Tula y los Toltecas: Las culturas post-arcaicas y pre-aztecas del centro de México. Excavaciones y estudios, 1922–1950. *Runa* 3: 37–70. Buenos Aires.
1951 Tecnología, formaciones socio-económicas y religión en Mesoamérica. In *The Civilizations of Ancient America: Selected Papers of the XXIXth International Congress of Americanists* (Sol Tax, ed.): 19–30. University of Chicago Press, Chicago.

AVENI, ANTHONY F.
1980 *Skywatchers of Ancient Mexico.* University of Texas Press, Austin.

AVENI, ANTHONY F., AND SHARON L. GIBBS
1976 On the Orientation of Pre-Columbian Buildings in Central Mexico. *American Antiquity* 41(4): 510–517.

BARBOUR, WARREN
  1987 Ceramic Figurines from Oxtotipac. The Toltec Period Occupation of the Valley, Part 2: Surface Survey and Special Studies. In *The Teotihuacan Valley Project Final Report* (William T. Sanders, ed.) 4: 697–754. Occasional Papers in Anthropology 15. Pennsylvania State University, University Park.
  n.d.a The Figurines and Figurine Chronology of Ancient Teotihuacan, Mexico. Ph.D. dissertation, Dept. of Anthropology, University of Rochester, 1976.
  n.d.b Sex and Gender in Teotihuacan Figurine Manufacture: Preliminary Results. Paper presented at 42nd annual meeting of the Society for American Archaeology, New Orleans, 1977.

BATRES, LEOPOLDO
  1906 *Teotihuacán*. Fidencio S. Soria, Mexico, D.F.
  1908 *Exploraciones y consolidación de los monumentos arqueológicos de Teotihuacán*. Buznego y Léon, Mexico, D.F.

BERLO, JANET CATHERINE
  1983 The Warrior and the Butterfly: Central Mexican Ideologies of Sacred Warfare and Teotihuacan Iconography. In *Text and Image in Pre-Columbian Art: Essays on the interrelationship of the verbal and visual arts* (Janet Berlo, ed.): 79–117. Proceedings of the 44th International Congress of Americanists, Manchester, 1982. BAR International Series 180, Oxford.
  1989 Early Writing in Central Mexico: *In Tlilli, In Tlapalli* before A.D. 1000. In *Mesoamerica after the Decline of Teotihuacan A.D. 700–900* (Richard A. Diehl and Janet Catherine Berlo, eds.): 19–47. Dumbarton Oaks, Washington, D.C.

BERNAL, IGNACIO (ED.)
  1963 *Teotihuacan: Descubrimientos, reconstrucciones*. Instituto Nacional de Antropología e Historia, Mexico, D.F.

BERRIN, KATHLEEN (ED.)
  1988 *Feathered Serpents and Flowering Trees: Reconstructing the Murals of Teotihuacan*. Fine Arts Museums of San Francisco, San Francisco.

BEYER, HERMANN
  1920 La gigantesca diosa de Teotihuacán. *Revista de Revistas*, 17 de octubre de 1920. Reprinted in 1965 in *El México Antiguo* 10: 419–423. Mexico, D.F.
  1921 Una máscara prehispánica con mosaico de turquesa. *Revista de Revistas*, 23 October 1921. Reprinted in 1969 in *El México Antiguo* 11: 341–344. Mexico, D.F.
  1922a Estudio interpretativo de algunas grandes esculturas. In *La población del Valle de Teotihuacán* (Manuel Gamio and others) 1 (1): 168–174. Secretaría de Agricultura y Fomento, Mexico, D.F.
  1922b Relaciones entre la civilización teotihuacana y la azteca. In *La población del Valle de Teotihuacán* (Manuel Gamio and others) 1 (1): 273–293. Secretaría de Agricultura y Fomento, Mexico, D.F.

Teotihuacan Studies

    1922c   Sobre una plaqueta con una deidad teotihuacana. *Memorias y Revista de la Sociedad Científica "Antonio Alzate"* 40: 549–558. Reprinted in 1965 in *El México Antiguo* 10: 413–418. Mexico, D.F.

    1930   A Deity Common to Teotihuacan and Totonac Cultures. *23rd International Congress of Americanists:* 82–84. Reprinted in 1965 in Spanish in *El México Antiguo* 10: 365–368.

BLUCHER, DARLENA K.
    n.d.   Late Pre-Classic Cultures in the Valley of Mexico: Pre-Urban Teotihuacan. Ph.D. dissertation, Dept. of Anthropology, Brandeis University, 1971.

BODDE, DERK
    1957   *China's Cultural Tradition: What and Whither?* Holt, Rinehart and Winston, New York.

BORHEGYI, STEPHAN F.
    1971   Pre-Columbian Contacts—The Dryland Approach: The Impact and Influence of Teotihuacán Culture on the Pre-Columbian Civilizations of Mesoamerica. In *Man across the Sea: Problems of Pre-Columbian Contacts* (Carroll L. Riley, J. Charles Kelley, Campbell W. Pennington, and Robert L. Rands, eds.): 79–105. University of Texas Press, Austin.

CABRERA CASTRO, RUBÉN
    1987   Architectural Restoration at Teotihuacan: A Historical Analysis. In *In Situ Archaeological Conservation: Proceedings of Meetings April 6–13, 1986, Mexico* (Miguel Angel Corzo and Henry W. M. Hodges, eds.): 176–185. Instituto Nacional de Antropología e Historia de México and the Getty Conservation Institute, Century City, Calif.

CABRERA CASTRO, RUBÉN, IGNACIO RODRIGUEZ, AND NOEL MORELOS (EDS.)
    1982a   *Teotihuacan 80–82: Primeros Resultados.* Instituto Nacional de Antropología e Historia, Mexico, D.F.
    1982b   Memoria del Proyecto Arqueológico Teotihuacan 80–82. *Colección Científica 132.* Instituto Nacional de Antropología e Historia, Mexico, D.F.

CABRERA CASTRO, RUBÉN, SABURO SUGIYAMA, AND GEORGE L. COWGILL
    1991   The "Templo de Quetzalcoatl" Project at Teotihuacan: A Preliminary Report. *Ancient Mesoamerica* 2: 77–92.

CARLSON, JOHN B.
    1990   America's Ancient Skywatchers. *National Geographic* 177 (3): 76–107.

CARR, ROBERT F., AND JAMES E. HAZARD
    1961   Map of the Ruins of Tikal, El Peten, Guatemala. *Tikal Reports* 11. Museum Monographs, University Museum, University of Pennsylvania, Philadelphia.

CARRASCO, DAVID
    1982   *Quetzalcoatl and the Irony of Empire: Myths and Prophecies in the Aztec Tradition.* University of Chicago Press, Chicago.

CARRASCO, PEDRO
   1982   The Political Economy of the Aztec and Inca States. In *The Inca and Aztec States 1400–1800: Anthropology and History* (George A. Collier, Renato I. Rosaldo, and John D. Wirth, eds.): 23–40. Studies in Anthropology, Academic Press, New York.

CASO, ALFONSO
   1937   ¿Tenían los teotihuacanos conocimiento del Tonalpohualli? *El México Antiguo* 4: 131–143.
   1942   El paraíso terrenal en Teotihuacán. *Cuadernos Americanos* 6 (6): 127–136.

CHARLTON, THOMAS H.
   1978   Teotihuacan, Tepeapulco, and Obsidian Exploitation. *Science* 200: 1227–1236.
   1984   Production and Exchange: Variables in the Evolution of a Civilization. In *Trade and Exchange in Early Mesoamerica* (Kenneth G. Hirth, ed.): 17–42. University of New Mexico Press, Albuquerque.
   1987   Teotihuacan Non-Urban Settlements: Functional and Evolutionary Implications. In *Teotihuacan: Nuevos datos, nuevas síntesis, nuevos problemas* (Emily McClung de Tapia and Evelyn Childs Rattray, eds.): 473–488. Instituto de Investigaciones Antropológicas, Serie Antropológica 72. Universidad Nacional Autónoma de México, Mexico, D.F.

CHARLTON, THOMAS H., AND MICHAEL W. SPENCE
   1982   Obsidian Exploitation and Civilization in the Basin of Mexico. In *Mining and Mining Techniques in Ancient Mesoamerica* (Phil C. Weigand and Gretchen Wynne, eds.): *Anthropology* 6 (1, 2): 7–86. State University of New York, Stony Brook.

CHILDE, V. GORDON
   1950   The Urban Revolution. *Town Planning Review* 21: 3–17.

CHIU, BELLA C., AND PHILIP MORRISON
   1980   Astronomical Origin of the Offset Street Grid at Teotihuacan. *Archaeoastronomy* (Supplement to *Journal for the History of Astronomy*) 2: S55–64.

CLARK, JOHN E.
   1986   From Mountains to Mole Hills: A Critical Review of Teotihuacan's Obsidian Industry. In *Economic Aspects of Prehispanic Highland Mexico* (Barry L. Isaac, ed.): 23–74. Research in Economic Anthropology, Supp. 2, JAI Press, Greenwich, Conn.

COHODAS, MARVIN
   1990   Review of *Feathered Serpents and Flowering Trees* (Kathleen Berrin, ed.). *American Indian Culture and Research Journal* 14 (3): 156–160.

COOK DE LEONARD, CARMEN
   1953   Los popolocas de Puebla (Ensayo de una identificación etnodemográfica e histórico-arqueológica). In Huastecos, Totonacos y sus Vecinos (Ignacio Bernal and Eusebio Dávalos, eds.), *Revista Mexicana de Estudios Antropológicos* 13 (2, 3): 423–445.
   n.d.   El origen de la cerámica anaranjada delgada. M.A. thesis, Escuela Nacional de Antropología e Historia, Mexico, 1957.

Teotihuacan Studies

COVARRUBIAS, MIGUEL
    1946   El arte "olmeca" o de La Venta. *Cuadernos Americanos* 28 (4): 153–179.

COWGILL, GEORGE L.
- 1968   Computer Analyses of Archaeological Data from Teotihuacán, Mexico. In *New Perspectives in Archaeology* (Sally R. Binford and Lewis R. Binford, eds.): 143–150. Aldine, Chicago.
- 1974   Quantitative Studies of Urbanization at Teotihuacán. In *Mesoamerican Archaeology: New Approaches* (Norman Hammond, ed.): 363–396. Duckworth, London.
- 1975a   On Causes and Consequences of Ancient and Modern Population Changes. *American Anthropologist* 77: 505–525.
- 1975b   Population Pressure as a Non-Explanation. In *Population Studies in Archaeology and Biological Anthropology: A Symposium* (Alan C. Swedlund, ed.). Memoirs of the Society for American Archaeology 30: 127–131.
- 1979   Teotihuacan, Internal Militaristic Competition, and the Fall of the Classic Maya. In *Maya Archaeology and Ethnohistory* (Norman Hammond and Gordon R. Willey, eds.): 51–62. University of Texas Press, Austin.
- 1983   Rulership and the Ciudadela: Political Inferences from Teotihuacan Architecture. In *Civilization in the Ancient Americas* (Richard M. Leventhal and Alan L. Kolata, eds.): 313–343. University of New Mexico Press and Peabody Museum of Archaeology and Ethnology, Harvard University, Cambridge.
- 1986   Archaeological Applications of Mathematical and Formal Methods. In *American Archaeology Past and Future* (D. Meltzer, D. Fowler, and J. Sabloff, eds.): 369–393. Smithsonian Institution Press, Washington, D.C.
- 1987   Métodos para el estudio de relaciones espaciales en los datos de la superficie de Teotihuacan. In *Teotihuacan: Nuevos datos, nuevas síntesis, nuevos problemas* (Emily McClung de Tapia and Evelyn Childs Rattray, eds.): 161–189. Instituto de Investigaciones Antropológicas, Serie Antropológica 72. Universidad Nacional Autónoma de México, Mexico.
- 1989   Formal Approaches in Archaeology. *Archaeological thought in America* (C. C. Lamberg-Karlovsky, ed.): 74–88. Cambridge University Press, Cambridge.

COWGILL, GEORGE L., JEFFREY H. ALTSCHUL, AND REBECCA S. SLOAD
    1984   Spatial Analysis of Teotihuacan: A Mesoamerican Metropolis. In *Intrasite Spatial Analysis in Archaeology* (Harold J. Hietala, ed.): 154–195. Cambridge University Press, Cambridge.

DIEHL, RICHARD A.
    1989   A Shadow of Its Former Self: Teotihuacan during the Coyotlatelco Period. In *Mesoamerica after the Decline of Teotihuacan, A.D. 700–900* (Richard A. Diehl and Janet Catherine Berlo, eds.): 9–18. Dumbarton Oaks, Washington, D.C.

DOSAL, PEDRO
　　1925　Descubrimientos arqueológicos en el Templo de Quetzalcoatl. *Anales del Museo Nacional de Arqueología, Historia y Etnografía*, Época IV, 3: 216–219. Mexico, D.F.

DOW, JAMES W.
　　1967　Astronomical Observations at Teotihuacan. *American Antiquity* 32: 326–334.

DREWITT, BRUCE
　　1967　Planeación en la antigua ciudad de Teotihuacán. In *Teotihuacán: XI Mesa Redonda* 1: 79–94. Sociedad Mexicana de Antropología, Mexico, D.F.
　　1987　Measurement Units and Building Axes at Teotihuacan. In *Teotihuacan: Nuevos datos, nuevas síntesis, nuevos problemas* (Emily McClung de Tapia and Evelyn Childs Rattray, eds.): 389–398. Instituto de Investigaciones Antropológicas, Serie Antropológica 72. Universidad Nacional Autónoma de México, Mexico, D.F.
　　n.d.　Data Bearing on Urban Planning at Teotihuacán. Paper presented at the 68th annual meeting of the American Anthropological Association, New Orleans, 1969.

DRUCKER, R. DAVID
　　1977　A Solar Orientation for Teotihuacan. In *Los Procesos de Cambio (en Mesoamérica y áreas circunvecinas)*. XV *Mesa Redonda* 2: 277–284. Sociedad Mexicana de Antropología and Universidad de Guanajuato.
　　n.d.a　The Shortest Day of the Year at Teotihuacán and the Solution to the Problem of the Orientation of the Ancient City and the Location of Its Major Structures. Paper presented at joint meeting of Consejo Nacional de Ciencia y Tecnología and American Association for Advancement of Science, Mexico, 1973.
　　n.d.b　Renovating a Reconstruction: The Ciudadela at Teotihuacan, Mexico: Construction Sequence, Layout, and Possible Uses of the Structure. Ph.D. dissertation, Dept. of Anthropology, University of Rochester, 1974.

EISENSTADT, S. N., AND A. SHACHAR
　　1989　*Society, Culture and Urbanization*. Sage Publications, Newbury Park, Calif.

FRIEDMANN, JOHN
　　1961　Cities in Social Transformation. *Comparative Studies in Society and History* 4: 86–103.

GAMIO, MANUEL
　　1922　*La población del valle de Teotihuacan*. Secretaría de Agricultura y Fomento, Mexico, D.F.

GARCÍA COOK, ANGEL
　　1981　The Historical Importance of Tlaxcala in the Cultural Development of the Central Highlands. In *Supplement to the Handbook of Middle American Indians* 1 (Victoria R. Bricker and Jeremy A. Sabloff, eds.): 244–276. University of Texas Press, Austin.

1984 Dos elementos arquitectónicos "tempranos" en Tlalancaleca, Puebla. *Cuadernos de Arquitectura Mesoamericana* 2: 29–32. Facultad de Arquitectura, Universidad Nacional Autónoma de México, Mexico, D.F.

GODELIER, MAURICE
1978 Infrastructures, Societies, and History. *Current Anthropology* 19: 763–771.
1979 On Infrastructures, Societies, and History: Reply. *Current Anthropology* 20: 108–111.
1988 *The Mental and the Material: Thought Economy and Society* (Martin Thom, trans.). Verso, London.

GOMEZ-CHAVEZ, SERGIO
1990 La función social del sacrificio humano en Teotihuacan: Un intento para formalizar su estudio e interpretación. In *La Época Clásica: Nuevos hallazgos, nuevas ideas* (Amalia Cardos de Mendez, ed.): 147–159. Museo Nacional de Antropología, Instituto Nacional de Antropología e Historia, Mexico, D.F.

HALL [MILLON], CLARA
n.d. A Chronological Study of the Mural Art of Teotihuacan. Ph.D. dissertation, Dept. of Anthropology, University of California, Berkeley, 1962.

HARDOY, JORGE E.
1968 *Urban Planning in Pre-Columbian America*. Braziller, New York.
1973 *Pre-Columbian Cities* (Judith Thorne, trans.). Walker, New York.

HAYASHI, TERU
1988 Attribution to Albert Szent-Györgyi at symposium in honor of Szent-Györgyi at Marine Biological Laboratory at Woods Hole. Recorded in Random Samples (Gregory Byrne, ed.), *Science* 241: 1165.

HEYDEN, DORIS
1975 An Interpretation of the Cave Underneath the Pyramid of the Sun in Teotihuacan, Mexico. *American Antiquity* 40: 131–147.
1981 Caves, Gods, and Myths: World-View and Planning in Teotihuacan. In *Mesoamerican Sites and World Views* (Elizabeth P. Benson, ed.): 1–39. Dumbarton Oaks, Washington, D.C.

HIRTH, KENNETH G.
1978 Teotihuacan Regional Population Administration in Eastern Morelos. *World Archaeology* 9: 320–333.

HOPKINS, MARY R.
1987a An Explication of the Plans of Some Teotihuacan Apartment Compounds. In *Teotihuacan: Nuevos datos, nuevas síntesis, nuevos problemas* (Emily McClung de Tapia and Evelyn Childs Rattray, eds.): 369–388. Instituto de Investigaciones Antropológicas, Serie Antropológica 72. Universidad Nacional Autónoma de México, Mexico, D.F.
1987b Network Analysis of the Plans of Some Teotihuacan Apartment Compounds. *Environment and Planning B: Planning and Design* 14: 387–406.

JACOBSEN, THORKILD
    1946 Mesopotamia. In *The Intellectual Adventure of Ancient Man: An Essay on Speculative Thought in the Ancient Near East* (Henri Frankfort, H. A. Frankfort, John A. Wilson, Thorkild Jacobsen, and William A. Irwin): 123–219. University of Chicago Press, Chicago. Reprinted in 1977.

JIMÉNEZ MORENO, WIGBERTO
    1974 Los portadores de la cultura teotihuacana. *Historia Mexicana* 24 (1): 1–12. El Colegio de México, Mexico, D.F.

KELEMEN, PÁL
    1943 *Medieval American Art*, 2 vols. Macmillan, New York.

KIDDER, ALFRED V., JESSE JENNINGS, AND EDWIN M. SHOOK
    1946 *Excavations at Kaminaljuyu, Guatemala.* Carnegie Institution of Washington Pub. 561. Washington, D.C.

KLEIN, CECILIA F.
    1990 Review of *Feathered Serpents and Flowering Trees* (Kathleen Berrin, ed.). *African Arts* 23 (3): 93–96.

KOLB, CHARLES C.
    1986 Commercial Aspects of Classic Teotihuacan Period "Thin Orange" Wares. In *Economic Aspects of Prehispanic Highland Mexico* (Barry L. Isaac, ed.): 155–205. Research in Economic Anthropology, Supp. 2, JAI Press, Greenwich, Conn.
    1987 *Marine Shell Trade and Classic Teotihuacan, Mexico.* BAR International Series 364, Oxford.

KOSTOF, SPIRO
    1985 *A History of Architecture: Settings and Rituals.* Oxford University Press, New York.

KROTSER, PAULA H.
    1987 Levels of Specialization among Potters of Teotihuacan. In *Teotihuacan: Nuevos datos, nuevas síntesis, nuevos problemas* (Emily McClung de Tapia and Evelyn Childs Rattray, eds.): 417–427. Instituto de Investigaciones Antropológicas, Serie Antropológica 72. Universidad Nacional Autónoma de México, Mexico, D.F.

KROTZ, ESTEBAN
    1990 A Panoramic View of Recent Mexican Anthropology. *Current Anthropology* 32 (2): 183–188.

KUBLER, GEORGE
    1967 *The Iconography of the Art of Teotihuacan.* Studies in Pre-Columbian Art and Archaeology 4. Dumbarton Oaks, Washington, D.C.

KURTZ, DONALD V.
    1987 The Economics of Urbanization and State Formation at Teotihuacan. *Current Anthropology* 28 (3): 329–353.

LANGLEY, JAMES C.
    1986 *Symbolic Notation of Teotihuacan: Elements of Writing in a Mesoamerican Culture of the Classic Period.* BAR International Series 313, Oxford.

Teotihuacan Studies

LAPORTE MOLINA, JUAN PEDRO
n.d.   Alternativas del Clásico Temprano en la Relación Tikal-Teotihuacan: Grupo 6C-XVI, Tikal, Peten, Guatemala. Ph.D. dissertation, Universidad Nacional Autónoma de México, Mexico, 1989.

LAPORTE MOLINA, JUAN PEDRO, AND VILMA FIALKO
1990   New Perspectives on Old Problems: Dynastic References for the Early Classic at Tikal. In *Vision and Revision in Maya Studies* (Flora S. Clancy and Peter D. Harrison, eds.): 33–66. University of New Mexico Press, Albuquerque.

LEONE, MARK
1982   Some Opinions about Recovering Mind. *American Antiquity* 47 (4): 742–760.

LINNÉ, SIGVALD
1934   *Archaeological Researches at Teotihuacan, Mexico*. Ethnographical Museum of Sweden, n.s. Pub. 1. Stockholm.
1941   Teotihuacan Symbols. *Ethnos* 6 (3–4): 174–186. Stockholm.
1942   *Mexican Highland Cultures*. Ethnographical Museum of Sweden, n.s. Pub. 7. Stockholm.
1956   Radiocarbon Dates in Teotihuacan. *Ethnos* 21 (3–4): 180–193. Stockholm.

LÓPEZ AUSTIN, ALFREDO, LEONARDO LÓPEZ LUJAN, AND SABURO SUGIYAMA
1991   The Temple of Quetzalcoatl at Teotihuacan: Its Possible Ideological Significance. *Ancient Mesoamerica* 2: 93–105.

LORENZO, JOSÉ LUIS
1980   Notas sobre arqueología en México. *America Indigena* 40: 381–392.
1984   Mexico. In *Approaches to the Archaeological Heritage* (H. Cleere, ed.): 89–100. Cambridge University Press, Cambridge.

MALMSTRÖM, VINCENT H.
1978   A Reconstruction of the Chronology of Mesoamerican Calendrical Systems. *Journal for the History of Astronomy* 9 (2, 25): 105–116.

MANZANILLA, LINDA
1990   Sector Noroeste de Teotihuacan: Estudio de un conjunto residencial y rastreo de tuneles y cuevas. In *La Época Clásica: Nuevos hallazgos, nuevas ideas* (Amalia Cardos de Mendez, ed.): 81–88. Museo Nacional de Antropología, Instituto Nacional de Antropología e Historia, Mexico, D.F.

MANZANILLA, LINDA, AND LUÍS BARBA
1990   The Study of Activities in Classic Households: Two Case Studies from Coba and Teotihuacan. *Ancient Mesoamerica* 1 (1): 41–49.

MANZANILLA, LINDA, LUIS BARBA, RENÉ CHAVEZ, JORGE ARZATE, AND LETICIA FLORES
1989   El inframundo de Teotihuacan: Geofísica y arqueología. *Ciencia y Desarrollo* 15 (85): 21–35.

MARQUINA, IGNACIO
    1951   *Arquitectura prehispánica.* Memorias del Instituto Nacional de Antropología e Historia 1, Mexico, D.F.
MCCLUNG DE TAPIA, EMILY
    1977   Recientes estudios paleo-etnobótanicos en Teotihuacan, México. *Anales de Antropología* 14: 49–61. Instituto de Investigaciones Antropológicas, Universidad Nacional Autonóma de México, Mexico, D.F.
    1987   Patrones de subsistencia urbana en Teotihuacan. In *Teotihuacan: Nuevos datos, nuevas síntesis, nuevos problemas* (Emily McClung de Tapia and Evelyn Childs Rattray, eds.): 57–74. Instituto de Investigaciones Antropológicas, Serie Antropológica 72. Universidad Nacional Autónoma de México, Mexico, D.F.
    n.d.   Plants and Subsistence in the Teotihuacan Valley: A.D. 100–750. Ph.D. dissertation, Dept. of Anthropology, Brandeis University, 1979.
MILLER, ARTHUR G.
    1973   *The Mural Painting of Teotihuacan.* Dumbarton Oaks, Washington, D.C.
MILLON, CLARA
    1972   The History of Mural Art at Teotihuacan. In *Teotihuacan: XI Mesa Redonda* 2: 1–16. Sociedad Mexicana de Antropología, Mexico, D.F.
    1973   Painting, Writing, and Polity in Teotihuacan, Mexico. *American Antiquity* 38 (3): 294–314.
    1988a   A Reexamination of the Teotihuacan Tassel Headdress Insignia. In *Feathered Serpents and Flowering Trees: Reconstructing the Murals of Teotihuacan* (Kathleen Berrin, ed.): 114–134. Fine Arts Museums of San Francisco.
    1988b   Maguey Blood Letting Ritual. In *Feathered Serpents and Flowering Trees* (Kathleen Berrin, ed.): 194–205. Fine Arts Museums of San Francisco.
    1988c   Coyote with Sacrificial Knife. In *Feathered Serpents and Flowering Trees* (Kathleen Berrin, ed.): 206–217. Fine Arts Museums of San Francisco.
    1988d   Coyotes and Deer. In *Feathered Serpents and Flowering Trees* (Kathleen Berrin, ed.): 218–221. Fine Arts Museums of San Francisco.
MILLON, RENÉ
    1960   The Beginnings of Teotihuacan. *American Antiquity* 26: 1–10.
    1964   The Teotihuacan Mapping Project. *American Antiquity* 29: 345–352.
    1967   Cronología y periodificación: Datos estratigráficos sobre períodos cerámicos y sus relaciones con la pintura mural. In *Teotihuacan: XI Mesa Redonda* 1: 1–18. Sociedad Mexicana de Antropología, Mexico, D.F.
    1970   Teotihuacán: Completion of Map of Giant Ancient City in the Valley of Mexico. *Science* 170: 1077–1082.
    1973   *Urbanization at Teotihuacán, Mexico,* Vol. 1, pt. 1: *The Teotihuacan Map: Text.* University of Texas Press, Austin.
    1976   Social Relations in Ancient Teotihuacan. In *The Valley of Mexico: Studies in Pre-Hispanic Ecology and Society* (Eric R. Wolf, ed.): 205–248. University of New Mexico Press, Albuquerque.

1981 Teotihuacan: City, State and Civilization. In *Handbook of Middle American Indians,* Supp. 1 (Victoria R. Bricker and Jeremy A. Sabloff, eds.): 198–243. University of Texas Press, Austin.

1988a The Last Years of Teotihuacan Dominance. In *The Collapse of Ancient States and Civilizations* (Norman Yoffee and George L. Cowgill, eds.): 102–164. University of Arizona Press, Tucson.

1988b Where Do They All Come From? The Provenance of the Wagner Murals from Teotihuacan. In *Feathered Serpents and Flowering Trees: Reconstructing the Murals of Teotihuacan* (Kathleen Berrin, ed.): 78–113. Fine Arts Museums of San Francisco.

MILLON, RENÉ, AND JAMES A. BENNYHOFF

1961 A Long Architectural Sequence at Teotihuacán. *American Antiquity* 26 (4): 516–523.

MILLON, RENÉ, BRUCE DREWITT, AND JAMES A. BENNYHOFF

1965 *The Pyramid of the Sun at Teotihuacán: 1959 Investigations.* Transactions of the American Philosophical Society, n.s. 55 (6). Philadelphia.

MILLON, RENÉ, BRUCE DREWITT, AND GEORGE L. COWGILL

1973 *Urbanization at Teotihuacán, Mexico, Vol. I, pt. 2: The Teotihuacan Map: Maps.* University of Texas Press, Austin.

MOHOLY-NAGY, HATTULA

1990 The Misidentification of Mesoamerican Lithic Workshops. *Latin American Antiquity* 1 (3): 268–279.

MURPHY, ROBERT F.

1964 Social Distance and the Veil. *American Anthropologist* 66: 1257–1274.

MURRA, JOHN V.

1975 *Formaciones económicas y políticas del mundo andino.* Instituto de Estudios Peruanos, Lima.

MURRA, JOHN V., NATHAN WACHTEL, and JACQUES REVEL (EDS.)

1986 *Anthropological History of Andean Polities.* Cambridge University Press, Cambridge.

NICHOLS, DEBORAH L.

1987 Prehispanic Irrigation at Teotihuacan, New Evidence: The Tlajinga Canals. In *Teotihuacan: Nuevos datos, nuevas síntesis, nuevos problemas* (Emily McClung de Tapia and Evelyn C. Rattray, eds.): 133–160. Instituto de Investigaciones Antropológicas, Serie Antropológica 72. Universidad Nacional Autónoma de México, Mexico, D.F.

PARSONS, JEFFREY R., AND MARY H. PARSONS

1990 *Maguey Utilization in Highland Central Mexico: An Archaeological Ethnography.* Anthropological Papers of the Museum of Anthropology 82, University of Michigan, Ann Arbor.

PASZTORY, ESTHER

1973 The Gods of Teotihuacan: A Synthetic Approach in Teotihuacan Iconography. In *Atti de XL Congresso Internazionale degli Americanisti* 1: 147–159. Genoa.

1974 The Iconography of the Teotihuacan Tlaloc. Studies in Pre-Columbian Art and Archaeology 15. Dumbarton Oaks, Washington, D.C.
1976 The Murals of Tepantitla, Teotihuacan. Garland, New York.
1988a Feathered Serpents and Flowering Trees with Glyphs. In *Feathered Serpents and Flowering Trees* (Kathleen Berrin, ed.): 136–161. Fine Arts Museums of San Francisco.
1988b A Reinterpretation of Teotihuacan and Its Mural Painting Tradition. In *Feathered Serpents and Flowering Trees* (Kathleen Berrin, ed.): 45–77. Fine Arts Museums of San Francisco.
1990 El poder militar como realidad y retórica en Teotihuacan. In *La Época Clásica: Nuevos hallazgos, nuevas ideas* (Amalia Cardos de Mendez, ed.): 181–201. Museo Nacional de Antropología, Instituto Nacional de Antropología e Historia, Mexico, D.F.

PEÑAFIEL, ANTONIO
1900 *Teotihuacán: Estudio histórico y arqueológico*. Oficina Topográfica de la Secretaria de Fomento, Mexico, D.F.

PETERSON, CYNTHIA W., AND BELLA C. CHIU
1987 On the Astronomical Origin of the Offset Street Grid at Teotihuacan. *Archaeoastronomy* (Supplement to *Journal for the History of Astronomy*) 11: S13–18.

RATTRAY, EVELYN C.
1987 Los barrios foráneos de Teotihuacan. In *Teotihuacan: Nuevos datos, nuevas síntesis, nuevos problemas* (Emily McClung de Tapia and Evelyn Childs Rattray, eds.): 243–273. Instituto de Investigaciones Antropológicas, Serie Antropológica 72. Universidad Nacional Autónoma de México, Mexico, D.F.
1989 El barrio de los comerciantes y el conjunto Tlamimilolpa: Un estudio comparativo. *Arqueología* 5: 105–129. Dirección de Monumentos Prehispánicos, Instituto Nacional de Antropología e Historia, Mexico, D.F.
1990a Nuevos Hallazgos sobre los Orígenes de la Cerámica Anaranjado Delgado. In *La Época Clásica: Nuevos hallazgos, nuevas ideas* (Amalia Cardos de Mendez, ed.): 89–106. Museo Nacional de Antropología, Instituto Nacional de Antropología e Historia, Mexico, D.F.
1990b New Findings on the Origins of Thin Orange Ceramics. *Ancient Mesoamerica* 1 (2): 181–195. Cambridge University Press, New York.
n.d.a The Teotihuacan Ceramic Chronology. Unpublished manuscript, 1979.
n.d.b The Merchants' Barrio, Teotihuacan, Mexico: Preliminary Report to Instituto Nacional de Antropología e Historia and Instituto de Investigaciones Antropológicas, Universidad Nacional Autonóma de México, Mexico, 1987.

ROBERTSON, DONALD
1963 *Pre-Columbian Architecture*. Braziller, New York.

SALAZAR ORTEGON, PONCIANO
    n.d.   Trabajos en Zona I, "Plaza de la Luna," Temporadas IV y V, Años 1962–1964, Proyecto Teotihuacan, Instituto Nacional de Antropología e Historia, Mexico. Manuscript, ca. 1968.

SANDERS, WILLIAM T.
    1981   Ecological Adaptation in the Basin of Mexico: 23,000 B.C. to the Present. In *Handbook of Middle American Indians,* Supp. 1 (Victoria R. Bricker and Jeremy A. Sabloff, eds.): 147–197. University of Texas Press, Austin.
    1986   Ceramic Chronology. The Toltec Period Occupation of the Valley, Part 1—Excavations and Ceramics. In *The Teotihuacan Valley Project Final Report* (William T. Sanders, ed.) 4: 367–373. Occasional Papers in Anthropology 13. Pennsylvania State University, University Park.

SANDERS, WILLIAM T., DEBORAH NICHOLS, REBECCA STOREY, AND RANDOLPH WIDMER
    n.d.   A Reconstruction of a Classic Period Landscape in the Teotihuacan Valley. Final Report to the National Science Foundation, Department of Anthropology, Pennsylvania State University, University Park, 1982.

SANDERS, WILLIAM T., JEFFREY R. PARSONS, AND ROBERT S. SANTLEY
    1979   *The Basin of Mexico.* Academic Press, New York.

SANDERS, WILLIAM T., AND ROBERT S. SANTLEY
    1983   A Tale of Three Cities: Energetics and Urbanization in Prehispanic Central Mexico. In *Prehistoric Settlement Patterns: Essays in Honor of Gordon R. Willey* (E. Z. Vogt and Richard M. Leventhal, eds.): 243–291. University of New Mexico Press, Albuquerque.

SANTLEY, ROBERT S.
    1983   Obsidian Trade and Teotihuacan Influence in Mesoamerica. In *Highland-Lowland Interaction in Mesoamerica: Interdisciplinary Approaches* (Arthur G. Miller, ed.): 69–124. Dumbarton Oaks, Washington, D.C.
    1984   Obsidian Exchange, Economic Stratification, and the Evolution of Complex Society in the Basin of Mexico. In *Trade and Exchange in Early Mesoamerica* (Kenneth G. Hirth, ed.): 43–86. University of New Mexico Press, Albuquerque.
    n.d.a   Teotihuacan Influence at Matacapan: Alternative Models and Explanatory Frameworks. Paper presented at the 52nd annual meeting of the Society for American Archaeology, Toronto, 1987.
    n.d.b   The Political Economy of Ancient Teotihuacan. In *Pattern and Process in Ancient Mesoamerica* (Robert S. Santley and Richard A. Diehl, eds.) (forthcoming).

SANTLEY, ROBERT S., JANET M. KERLEY, AND RONALD R. KNEEBONE
    1986   Obsidian Working, Long-Distance Exchange, and the Politico-Economic Organization of Early States in Central Mexico. In *Economic Aspects of Prehispanic Highland Mexico* (Barry L. Isaac, ed.): 101–132. Research in Economic Anthropology, Supp. 2, JAI Press, Greenwich, Conn.

SAYRE, EDWARD V., AND GARMAN HARBOTTLE
n.d. The Analysis by Neutron Activation of Archaeological Ceramics Related to Teotihuacan: Local Wares and Trade Sherds. Unpublished manuscript, 1979.

SCHELE, LINDA, AND DAVID FREIDEL
1990 *A Forest of Kings: The Untold Story of the Ancient Maya*. William Morrow, New York.

SEARS, PAUL B.
1951 Pollen Profiles and Culture Horizons in the Basin of Mexico. In *The Civilizations of Ancient America: Selected Papers of the XXIXth International Congress of Americanists* (Sol Tax, ed.): 57–61. University of Chicago Press, Chicago.

SÉJOURNÉ, LAURETTE
1956 *Burning Water: Thought and Religion in Ancient Mexico*. Thames and Hudson, London.
1959 *Un palacio en la ciudad de los dioses: Exploraciones en Teotihuacán, 1955–58*. Instituto Nacional de Antropología e Historia, Mexico, D.F.
1966a *Arquitectura y pintura en Teotihuacán*. Siglo XXI Editores, Mexico, D.F.
1966b *El lenguaje de las formas en Teotihuacán*. Gabriel Mancera 65, Mexico.

SELER, EDUARD
1915 Die Teotiuacan-Kultur des Hochlandes von México. In *Gesammelte Abhandlungen zur Amerikanischen Sprach- und Altertumskunde* 5: 405–585. Behrend, Berlin. Reprinted in 1961 by Akademische Druck- und Verlagsanstalt, Graz, Austria.

SEMPOWSKI, MARTHA
n.d. Mortuary Practices at Teotihuacan, Mexico: Their Implications for Social Status. Ph.D. dissertation, Dept. of Anthropology, University of Rochester, 1983.

SLOAD, REBECCA
1987 The Great Compound: A Forum for Regional Activities. In *Teotihuacan: Nuevos datos, nuevas síntesis, nuevos problemas* (Emily McClung de Tapia and Evelyn Childs Rattray, eds.): 219–241. Instituto de Investigaciones Antropológicas, Serie Antropológica 72. Universidad Nacional Autonóma de México, Mexico, D.F.

SMITH, ROBERT ELIOT
1987 *A Ceramic Sequence From the Pyramid of the Sun, Teotihuacan, Mexico*. Papers of the Peabody Museum of Archaeology and Ethnology, 75. Harvard University, Cambridge.

SPENCE, MICHAEL W.
1974 Residential Practices and the Distribution of Skeletal Traits in Teotihuacán, Mexico. *Man*, n.s. 9 (3): 262–272.
1981 Obsidian Production and the State in Teotihuacan. *American Antiquity* 46 (4): 769–788.

1984 Craft Production and Polity in Early Teotihuacan. In *Trade and Exchange in Early Mesoamerica* (Kenneth G. Hirth, ed.): 87–114. University of New Mexico Press, Albuquerque.
1986 Locational Analysis of Craft Specialization Areas in Teotihuacan. In *Economic Aspects of Prehispanic Highland Mexico* (Barry L. Isaac, ed.): 75–100. Research in Economic Anthropology, Supp. 2, JAI Press, Greenwich, Conn.
1987 The Scale and Structure of Obsidian Production in Teotihuacan. In *Teotihuacan: Nuevos datos, nuevas síntesis, nuevos problemas* (Emily McClung de Tapia and Evelyn Childs Rattray, eds.): 429–450. Instituto de Investigaciones Antropológicas, Serie Antropológica 72. Universidad Nacional Autónoma de México, Mexico, D.F.
n.d. Skeletal Morphology and Social Organization in Teotihuacán, Mexico. Ph.D. dissertation, Dept. of Anthropology, Southern Illinois University, 1971.

STARBUCK, DAVID R.
1977 Animal Utilization and Urban Adaptations in the City of Teotihuacán, Mexico. *The Western Canadian Journal of Anthropology* 7: 151–162.
1987 Faunal Evidence for the Teotihuacan Subsistence Base. In *Teotihuacan: Nuevos datos, nuevas síntesis, nuevos problemas* (Emily McClung de Tapia and Evelyn Childs Rattray, eds.): 75–90. Instituto de Investigaciones Antropológicas, Serie Antropológica 72. Universidad Nacional Autónoma de México, Mexico, D.F.
n.d. Man-Animal Relationships in Pre-Columbian Central Mexico. Ph.D. dissertation, Dept. of Anthropology, Yale University, 1975.

STEWARD, JULIAN H.
1949 Cultural Causality and Law: A Trial Formulation of the Development of Early Civilizations. *American Anthropologist* 51 (1): 1–27.

STOREY, REBECCA
1985 An Estimate of Mortality in a Pre-Columbian Urban Population. *American Anthropologist* 87 (3): 519–535.
1986 Perinatal Mortality at Pre-Columbian Teotihuacan. *American Journal of Physical Anthropology* 69: 541–548.
1987 A First Look at the Paleodemography of the Ancient City of Teotihuacan. In *Teotihuacan: Nuevos datos, nuevas síntesis, nuevos problemas* (Emily McClung de Tapia and Evelyn Childs Rattray, eds.): 91–114. Instituto de Investigaciones Antropológicas, Serie Antropológica 72. Universidad Nacional Autónoma de México, Mexico, D.F.
1992 *Life and Death in the Ancient City of Teotihuacan: A Modern Paleodemographic Synthesis.* University of Alabama Press, Tuscaloosa.
n.d.a Preindustrial Urban Lifestyle and Health. In *Health and Life-Style Change* (R. Huss-Ashmore, ed.). MASCA Research Papers in Science and Archaeology (in press).
n.d.b Los enterramientos humanos de Tlajinga 33, Teotihuacan, Mexico. Paper presented at V Coloquio de Antropología Física Juan Comas, Mexico, 1989.

STOREY, REBECCA, AND RANDOLPH J. WIDMER
    1989   Household and Community Structure of a Teotihuacan Apartment Compound: S3W1:33 of the Tlajinga Barrio. In *Households and Communities: Proceedings of the 21st Annual Chacmool Conference* (Scott MacEachern, David J. W. Archer, and Richard D. Garvin, eds.): 407–415. Archaeological Association of the University of Calgary, Calgary.

STRUEVER, STUART
    1968   Flotation Techniques for the Recovery of Small-Scale Archaeological Remains. *American Antiquity* 33: 353–362.

SUGIYAMA, SABURO
    1989   Burials Dedicated to the Old Temple of Quetzalcoatl at Teotihuacan, Mexico. *American Antiqutiy* 54 (1): 85–106.

TAUBE, KARL A.
    1986   The Teotihuacan Cave of Origin. *Res* 12: 51–82.
    n.d.   The Temple of Quetzalcoatl and the Cult of Sacred War at Teotihuacan. *Res* (in press).

TOSCANO, SALVADOR
    1944   *Arte Precolombino de México y de la América Central.* Instituto de Investigaciones Estéticas, Universidad Nacional Autonóma de México, Mexico, D.F.

TRIGGER, BRUCE G.
    1989   *A History of Archaeological Thought.* Cambridge University Press, Cambridge.
    1990   The 1990s: North American Archaeology with a Human Face? *Antiquity* 64: 778–787.

VAILLANT, GEORGE C.
    1938   A Correlation of Archaeological and Historical Sequences in the Valley of Mexico. *American Anthropologist* n.s. 40: 535–573.

VALENZUELA, JUAN
    1945   Las exploraciones efectuadas en Los Tuxtlas, Veracruz. *Anales del Museo Nacional de Arqueología, Historia y Etnología* 3: 83–107. Mexico, D.F.

VILLAGRA CALETI, AGUSTÍN
    1971   Mural Painting in Central Mexico. In *Handbook of Middle American Indians* 10 (Robert Wauchope, Gordon F. Ekholm, and Ignacio Bernal, eds.): 135–156. University of Texas Press, Austin.

VON WINNING, HASSO
    1947a   A Symbol for Dripping Water in the Teotihuacan Culture. *El México Antiguo* 6 (9–12): 333–341.
    1947b   Representations of Temple Buildings as Decorative Patterns on Teotihuacan Pottery and Figurines. *Notes on Middle American Archaeology and Ethnology* 83: 170–177. Carnegie Institution of Washington, Washington, D.C.
    1948   The Teotihuacan Owl and Weapon Symbol and Its Association with "Serpent Head X" at Kaminaljuyu. *American Antiquity* 14: 129–132.

1949 Shell Designs on Teotihuacan Pottery. *El México Antiguo* 7: 126–153.
1987 *La iconografía de Teotihuacan: Los dioses y los signos*, 2 vols. Universidad Nacional Autonóma de México, Mexico, D.F.

WASSON, R. GORDON
1980 *The Wondrous Mushroom: Mycolatry in Mesoamerica.* McGraw-Hill, New York.

WEST, ROBERT C., AND PEDRO ARMILLAS
1950 Las chinampas de México. *Cuadernos Americanos* 50 (2): 165–182.

WESTHEIM, PAUL
1950 *Arte antiguo de México* (Eng. trans. 1965, New York). Fondo de Cultura Económica, Mexico, D.F.

WHEATLEY, PAUL
1971 *The Pivot of the Four Quarters: A Preliminary Enquiry into the Origins and Character of the Ancient Chinese City.* Aldine, Chicago.
1972 The Concept of Urbanism. In *Man, Settlement and Urbanism* (Peter J. Ucko, Ruth Tringham, and G. W. Dimbleby, eds.): 601–637. Gerald Duckworth, London.

WILLEY, GORDON R.
1953 *Prehistoric Settlement Patterns in the Virú Valley, Peru.* Bureau of American Ethnology Bulletin 155, Smithsonian Institution, Washington, D.C.

WITTFOGEL, KARL A.
1938 Die Theorie der orientalischen Gesellschaft. *Zeitschrift für Sozialforschung* 7: 90–122 (Eng. trans.: The Theory of Oriental Society). In *Readings in Anthropology*, 2nd ed., 1963 (Morton Fried, ed.) 2: 179–188. Crowell, New York.

WU, NELSON I.
1963 *Chinese and Indian Architecture: The City of Man, the Mountain of God, and the Realm of the Immortals.* Braziller, New York.

APPENDIX : Teotihuacan Murals Datable Stratigraphically

MURAL	DESCRIPTION	LOCATION	SOURCES
Scroll	Simple white scroll with red background. Outline of scroll scribed in white plaster. Similar to scroll in Seler (1915: abb. 6) except that it turns to the right	Ciudadela, South Palace, Northwest Apartment, North Room. *Talud* in early, possibly pre-Palace construction (Fig. 1)	Proyecto Arqueológico Teotihuacan 1980–82. Cabrera, this vol.; Saburo Sugiyama, personal communication, 1983; Cabrera, Rodriguez, and Morelos (19826:166, plan. 2, dibujos I, 3)
Fragments on mud plaster	Mural fragments on mud plaster. No discernible designs but colors outlined in black	Ciudadela, South Palace, North Palace. Early substructures (Fig. 1)	Proyecto Arqueológico Teotihuacan 1980–82. Cabrera, this vol.
Shells	Painted adobe, row of three yellow shells on green background. Black outlines. Other painted adobe fragments with fine black outlines	Ciudadela, South Transverse Platform. Stratigraphic pit in South Room, layer 24 (Fig. 7)	TMP TE25S, 1972 Drucker (n.d.b)
Bird	Bird spewing liquid on stylized plant, black outlines	Palace of Quetzalpapalotl, Substructure 2, Temple of the Plumed Shells. Murals on *tableros* of platform supporting the temple	Proyecto Teotihuacan 1960–64, Zone 2 Miller (1973: figs. 52–57, plan III, inset A)
Birds	Birds on vertical border. Fine black outlines	Mythological Animals murals room, earlier wall, "Street of the Dead" (Fig. 1)	Proyecto Teotihuacan 1960–64, Zone 4 Miller (1973: figs. 97–99, plan V-A, no. 2)

CERAMIC PHASE	OTHER MURALS POSSIBLY CLOSE TO THE SAME AGE
Early Tlamimilolpa (*very early in phase*): Early construction beneath North Room. All construction layers in this room dated to the Early Tlamimilolpa Phase (Fig. 6) (analysis by Evelyn Rattray, hereafter ER)	
No later than Early Tlamimilolpa: South Palace fragments were found in early construction beneath South Palace where all subsequent construction dates to the Early Tlamimilolpa Phase (Fig. 6) (analysis by ER)	
Early Tlamimilolpa: (analysis by ER)	Temple of Agriculture, Central Panel, first two layers with black outlines (Villagra 1971: fig. 8)
Early Tlamimilolpa: (analysis by Florencia Müller and James A. Bennyhoff, hereafter FM and JAB)	
Late Tlamimilolpa: (analysis by FM and JAB)	

MURAL	DESCRIPTION	LOCATION	SOURCES
Mythological Animals	Murals of animals, some of which are composite creatures. Fine black outlines	Mythological Animals murals room, "Street of the Dead" (Fig. 1)	Proyecto Teotihuacan 1960–64, Zone 4 Miller (1973: figs. 89–96, plan V-A, no. 1)
All the murals in the exposed level of Zacuala Palace	Eight major murals, most repeated many times, all with red outlines	Zacuala Palace apartment compound (Fig. 1)	Séjourné 1959; Miller (1973: figs. 198–212, plan XI)
"Enthroned" Pumas	Portico with pumas on *taludes*, astride *metates*, symbolic hearts falling from their mouths, upper wall tassel headdress figures and associated borders	Tetitla apartment compound (Fig. 1). Antepenultimate construction level, probably construction level 3	Séjourné (1966a: figs. 15, 152, lám. XLIX, CXII); Miller (1973: figs. 286–289, plan XIII, portico 13)

Teotihuacan Studies: Appendix

CERAMIC PHASE	OTHER MURALS POSSIBLY CLOSE TO THE SAME AGE
Late Tlamimilolpa: (analysis by FM and JAB) Simple murals probably dating to the Tlamimilolpa phase were found in 1964 by Juan Vidarte in the La Ventilla B apartment compound (Fig. 1). One of these on an altar is illustrated by Séjourné (1966a: fig. 87c)	Temple of Agriculture (Fig. 1), Offering Scene. Fragments of this mural, bearing fine black outlines, were rediscovered ca. 1970 by Miller (1973: 173, 174; figs. 68–78; R. Millon 1976: 242). Sun Disk murals with black outlines near Sun Pyramid, zone 5A. Miller (1973: figs. 139–141, plan VI, platform 4) Ciudadela, Structure 1B':N1E1, Substructure 2, geometric figure outlined in black on *tableros*. Cabrera, this vol.
Early Xolalpan: Based on dating of Burial 27, a dedicatory burial at the compound entrance (analysis by ER). These are the first murals listed that were not on or adjoining the "Street of the Dead," apart from the simple murals found in La Ventilla B, referred to above	Puma Mural, "Street of the Dead," Proyecto Teotihuacan 1960–64, Zone 3 Miller (1973: figs. 86, 87, plan IVB); R. Millon (1973: figs. 10a, b). This mural shares a stylistic idiosyncrasy with Tetitla's "Enthroned" Pumas, below. The puma in this mural is outlined in red. The background "waves" are outlined in black (examined in situ in 1976 by Darlena Blucher and the author). No other murals in this and subsequent phases have black outlines
Early Xolalpan: Based on associating Concrete Floor II in the TMP TE24 pit in Room 12A (Figs. 3a, b) with the Puma mural building level in the southeastern part of Tetitla (analysis by ER)	Other murals from the same construction level in Tetitla (Séjourné 1966a: [8], niv. 3), probably including Miller (1973: porticos 1–3, Corridor 21, Room 22, Portico 24, Rooms 18 & 18A; Portico 19, Room 19; Porticos 20 & 20A, Patio 5, Room 7; Portico 26, Room 27, Corridor 25; Porticos 25 & 25A, Portico 14; figs. 229–239, 241–285, 291–293)

MURAL	DESCRIPTION	LOCATION	SOURCES
Miniature altar; *tablero* bearing mouth with bared teeth; other associated murals	Miniature altar bearing scrolls and eyes on its *tableros*; mouth with bared teeth in center of *tablero*, flanked by vegetation, eyes and other motifs; rattlesnake tail; banks of eyes	Zacuala Patios (Fig. 1), penultimate construction level	Séjourné (1959: figs. 31–34); Miller (1973: fig. 227); Sempowski (n.d.: 623)
Murals in the Quetzalpapalotl Palace and its antechambers	Stepped frets in patio of palace; eyes and "waves" in antechamber	Quetzalpapalotl Palace (Fig. 1)	Proyecto Teotihuacan 1960–64, Zone 2 Miller (1973: figs. 4–11, plan II)
Small puma; coiled serpent	Cartouche with puma on its haunches holding small animal; rectilinear coiled serpent with stepped frets	Palace of the Sun (Fig. 1), upper construction level	Proyecto Teotihuacan 1960–64, Zone 5A Miller (1973: figs. 101–106, plan VI, rooms 1 and 5). R. Millon (1973: fig. 20b) shows the serpent head facing upward. This is how it was recorded by TMP personnel when it was excavated and how it appeared in situ in the 1965 Proyecto Teotihuacan mural catalogue. Miller (1973: figs. 102, 103) shows the head held horizontally
Red circles; kneeling feline figure	Pale red circles on red background; kneeling feline figure with temple adjoining road with footprints	Tetitla (Fig. 1), penultimate construction level, southeast apartment, Rooms 12 and 12A	Armillas (1950: 55, lám. XIVa, b); Villagra (1971: figs. 13–15); Miller (1973: figs. 317–321, 328, plan XIII, Rooms 12 and 12A)

Teotihuacan Studies: Appendix

CERAMIC PHASE	OTHER MURALS POSSIBLY CLOSE TO THE SAME AGE
No later than Late Xolalpan: Based on ER analysis of Burial 7, which penetrated the floor of this construction level and dates to Late Xolalpan	
Metepec: Based on analysis of ceramics under the floor in the southwestern part of the structure by JAB; dated to Late Xolalpan by FM	
Metepec: Based on TMP TE14 in Room 5, which dated the floor in this room and two earlier concrete floors to the Metepec phase (analysis by ER). The serpent mural was in the adjoining room to the west (Room 1)	
Metepec: Based on TMP TE 24 (Fig. 3a, b) in Room 12A whose walls bear the pale red circle mural	Other Tetitla murals from the same apartment in this construction level date to the Metepec phase. These include the Jade Goddess murals in Portico 11, the murals featuring hands in Room 11, and the "Pinturas Realistas" from Corridor 12, largely unpublished (Miller 1973: figs. 301–306, plan XIII; C. Millon 1973: fig. 4; Pasztory 1976: fig. 67)

MURAL	DESCRIPTION	LOCATION	SOURCES
Fragmentary remnants	Fragmentary remnant on upper wall above floor scar which appears above the murals of hands in Room 11, Tetitla; mural fragment on upper wall above floor scar on north side of north wall of Corridor 12	Tetitla (Fig. 1), uppermost construction level, southeast apartment. These mural remnants represent what remains of the murals from the final construction level at Tetitla. The floor scars associated with these murals were verified in the field by the author and other TMP personnel	Millon (1973: fig. 46b; Miller 1973: plan XIII, Room 11, Corridor 12); Séjourné (1966a: [2], niv. 2). The Séjourné plan shows the north side of the north wall of the southeast apartment as it was in the penultimate construction level; Miller's plan combines the structurally exposed parts of the penultimate and antepenultimate construction levels
Feline	A depiction of a feline was found on one of the *taludes* of a portico on the northeastern margin of the excavated area of Tepantitla	Tepantitla (Fig. 1), lower construction level than Tlalocan patio and associated rooms	Pasztory (1976: 49; figs. 14, 15); Miller (1973: plan IX, portico 10)
Sacrificial knives and hearts; serpent head; serpent tongue; six other murals	Sacrificial knives and hearts on *tablero* border; serpent head; serpent tongue; strange (composite?) animals; quincross cartouche; stars; eyed drops	Zacuala Patios (Fig. 1), uppermost construction level. Murals facing patio and in corridors in northeast and northwest on plan in Séjourné (1959: fig 21)	Séjourné (1959: figs. 21–30); Miller (1973: figs. 214–224, plan XII); Sempowski (n.d.: 624)

Teotihuacan Studies: Appendix

CERAMIC PHASE	OTHER MURALS POSSIBLY CLOSE TO THE SAME AGE
Metepec: The final construction level at Tetitla probably dates to the latter part of the Metepec phase since the construction level that preceded it also dates to the Metepec phase	
Metepec: An *olla* is inset into the floor of the room behind Portico 10. Its rim was identified as Metepec by JAB	
Metepec: Based on ER dating of Burial 8, which penetrated the floor of the construction level below this	

MURAL	DESCRIPTION	LOCATION	SOURCES
Shell and wave motif, serpent, and other murals	Shell and wave motif; serpent and dart butts(?); circles on dark background; trapeze and triangle sign	Yayahuala apartment compound (Fig. 1), exposed construction level	Séjourné (1966a: figs. 132–134); Miller (1973: fig. 197, plan X, Portico 1, Room 5)
Procession with central glyph; figure with weapons	Procession of richly attired figures on east wall and south wall with central glyph on south wall; figure with *atlatl* (spear thrower) and three blunted darts	Teopancaxco (Fig. 1)	Gamio (1922:1:1: 156–157, lám. 34, 35, 75–77); Seler (1915: abb. 8, taf. X–XII); Marquina (1951: lám. 28); Villagra (1971: fig. 6). North is at right in plan in Gamio and Marquina
Storm Gods	Three manifestations of the Storm God—on a *talud*, a lower wall, and an upper wall	Techinantitla (Fig. 1), Anteroom of the Gods	R. Millon (1988b: figs. IV.16 [new murals], IV.18, IV.19, IV.21a, b, c)
Maguey Ritual; Great Goddess	Maguey bloodletting ritual, figure before upturned maguey *pencas*; Great Goddess manifestation with bared teeth and clawed hands	Tlacuilapaxco (Fig. 1)	R. Millon (1988b: fig. IV.11, IV.14e); C. Millon (1988b); Pasztory (1988b: fig. III.26); R. Millon (1973: fig. 48b)

Teotihuacan Studies: Appendix

CERAMIC PHASE	OTHER MURALS POSSIBLY CLOSE TO THE SAME AGE
Metepec: Based on TMP TE26 in southeast apartment in Yayahuala, which dates this construction level at Yayahuala to the Metepec phase (analysis by ER)	
Metepec: Based on TMP TE20 in room adjoining room with murals on northeast, south side of main patio. Upper layers date to Metepec phase (analysis by ER, Paula Krotser, and author)	
Metepec: Based on Metepec phase ceramic refuse on the floor in front of these murals (analysis by author). Pre-Metepec dating unlikely but cannot be ruled out	The Tassel Headdress and Serpent/Trees murals, and the many other murals from Techinantitla (Berrin 1988) appear also to be late, dating probably to the late Xolalpan and Metepec phases (A.D. 600–750) based on survey and excavation in Techinantitla under the direction of the author
Late Xolalpan to Metepec: Surface survey and excavation in Tlacuilapaxco directed by the author (R. Millon 1988b) suggests a Metepec date for these murals but stratigraphic evidence is insufficient to establish this. Could date to Late Xolalpan	

Index

Page references to illustrations are in *italics*.

Acoculco, 80
Acolhuacan, 239
Adornos: incensario, 259–274, *260, 262,*
    301, 302; on mirrors, 184; quatrefoil,
    261, 262–263, *262;* representing eyes,
    182
Adosada, 302–303, *304,* 372n
Alta Vista, 331
Angulo Vallaseñor, Jorge, 356
Apartment compounds, 285–288, *286,*
    287, 340; burials at, 29–30, 286–287;
    conditions in, 375; construction of,
    299, 344, 392; and Great Goddess
    symbolism, 314; reflecting relation-
    ship of individual to society, 299; re-
    flecting secretive culture, 303; role in
    uniting multiethnic population, 399,
    400. *See also barrios;* La Ventilla;
    Oztoyohualco; Palacio; Techinantitla;
    Tetitla; Yayahuala; Zacuala; Zacuala
    Palace; Zacuala Patios
Architecture: altar complex, 61, *62;*
    Ciudadela marking break in style,
    393–395; compared to Monte Alban,
    67; compared to Zapotec, 67–68; re-
    flecting secretive culture, 302–303; re-
    lation to population's ethnic diver-
    sity, 296–297; and sacred associa-
    tions, 8–9, *10–11,* 13, 66, 67, 119–
    120, *120,* 357, 383–384, *385,* 387–
    388, 390, 392, 395; *talud-tablero,* 15,
    67, *116, 117, 117,* 118–119, *119,* 120–
    122, *121,* 122–123, *122, 123,* 205, 255,
    361, 393, *394;* temple, 393; at
    Tlailotlacan, 61, *62;* Tlamimilolpa to
    Metepec, 67–68; and utopian vision,
    315; variations in, over time, 302. *See*
    also names of individual structures

Arm (motif), 239
Armillas, Pedro, 16, 17, 341, 345, 346,
    350, 355, 362
Art: abstract and depersonalized nature
    of, 15, 288–295, *289, 293,* 371–372;
    changes in, after end of despotic rule,
    400; compared to Monte Alban, 299;
    compared to Olmec, 288–289, *290;*
    floor painting, 115, *116;* fostering egali-
    tarianism, 15; fostering veneration of
    natural forces, 15; preoccupation with
    structural relations, 299–302; reflect-
    ing secretive nature of culture, 302–
    303; reflecting utopian vision, 292,
    293–295, *294;* role in uniting multieth-
    nic population, 399. *See also* Murals
Atetelco, 369; murals, *114,* 125, *125, 126*
Authority: associated with feathered ser-
    pent, 215–222, *216;* associated with
    headdresses, 216, *217,* 261; associated
    with jaguar, 216, *217;* associated with
    mat, 215, *216;* associated with shells,
    216, *217*
Aveni, Anthony, 357
Aztec: association of mirrors with sun,
    193–194, *194;* belief system, 151–154;
    Calendar Stone, 193–194, *195;* cul-
    ture, 282–283; greenstone goddess,
    186, *188, 189;* iconography, 129–130,
    231–232, 240, 242–243, 275; Storm
    God imagery, 257, *257, 258,* 259. *See*
    also Chalchihuitlicue; Chantico;
    Cipactli; Coatlicue; Coyolxauhqui;
    Huitzilopochtli; Itzpapalotl; Tenan;
    Teteoinnan; Tlaloc; Xochiquetzal

Bands, interlaced (motif): depicted on
    incensario, 267, *267,* 268, *269*

Index

Barbour, Warren, 356
Barrios: merchants', 367–368; workshops, 92–95, 107. *See also* Tlailotlacan
Barthes, Roland, 283–284, 285
Basin of Mexico, 4–5; geography and climate of, 2, 6; history of, 6–7
Baskets (motif), 239
Bat (motif), 75, 78
Batres, Leopoldo, 16
Beads: associated with Great Goddess, 137, 140; burial offerings, 60, 64, 66, 80, 210, 222, 223, 224; drilling of, 99–100, *101*
Becan, Campeche: mirrors, 179, *180*
Belief system, 306–310; compared to Aztec, 151–154; compared to Maya, 306, 360; humans depicted in service to divine, 306; and influx of population to Teotihuacan, 389–390; role of water, 6; Teotihuacan as place where time began, 383–384, 385, 387; uniting diverse population, 389, 392–393, 399; veneration of natural world, 12, 15, 119–120, *120*, 387–388. *See also* Architecture, and sacred associations; Cerro Gordo; Feathered Serpent; Great Goddess; Storm God
Bernal, Ignacio, 352
Bigotera (motif): associated with Storm God, 248, 249, *249, 250, 251,* 255
Bird: associated with javelins, 240; associated with warfare, 213, 266; associated with zoomorphic headdress, 262; depicted in mural, 125; depicted on *incensario*, 265
Bird and weapon (motif), 255
Bird foot (motif), *190,* 191
Bird headdress: associated with Great Goddess, 136, 140, 142, 144, *145, 282,* 310
Bird jaguar, 193, *194*
Bones: burial offerings, 60, 65, 209, 222
Bowls: burial offerings, 65, 66; found with mirrors, 177; Thin Orange, 141–142, *141*
Burial offerings, 33–53; beads, 210; bowls, 65, 66; earplugs, 210; at Feathered Serpent Temple-Pyramid, 212, 222, 223, 224; greenstone objects, 210; Metepec phase, 66–67, *67;* Miccaotli phase, 66; obsidian, 210; shell, 209, 210; Storm God vessels, 297, *298;* at Tlailotlacan, 60–67, *63, 67,* 80; Xolalpan phase, 63–65, *64. See also* Burials

Burials, 27–58; at apartment compounds, 29–30, 286–287; compared to Zapotec, 78; cremation, 31, 33; diverse practices in ethnic enclaves, 60–67; factors determining, 30; at Feathered Serpent Temple-Pyramid, 209–213, *211, 212,* 220–221, 391, 396; and imported luxury goods, 46–51; of infants, 30, 60, 63–65, *72;* at La Ventilla B, *32,* 367; Metepec phase, 66; method of analysis, 33–35; mirrors used in, 174–175, *174,* 178; painting of skeletal remains, 31; positions, 31, *32,* 65; at Pyramid of the Moon, 390, 393; at Pyramid of the Sun, 29, 391, 393; of soldiers, 210, *211, 212,* 213; Tlamimilolpa phase, 61–62, *63;* wrapping of bodies, 31; Xolalpan phase, 66. *See also* Burial offerings; Human sacrifice
Butterfly: associated with feathered eyes, 263; associated with flames, 184, 186; associated with Great Goddess, 147; associated with *incensarios*, 259; associated with warfare, 266; associated with zoomorphic headdress, 262; depicted on *adorno*, 252, *254;* depicted on *incensarios*, 189, *190,* 264, *264, 265,* 266, 267, *267;* depicted on mirrors, 184; depicted on vessel, 265
Butterfly Goddess, 136–137, *136, 137*
Butterfly headgear: associated with Great Goddess, 141, 143, *145;* worn by Toltec warriors, 154

Cabrera Castro, Rubén, 209, 210, 352
Cacaxtla: Great Goddess imagery found at, 154; mural, 256
Calle de los Muertos Complex: Great Goddess sculpture, 281, *282;* greenstone blocks, 307
Candelero, 66
Cantares mexicanos: and Teotihuacan imagery, 231, 237–238, 240, 243
Caracol: stela, 195, *196*
Caso, Alfonso, 17
Cat (motif): associated with

Index

zoomorphic headdress, 262; depicted in mural, 121–122, *121*, *305*
Caves: associated with Great Goddess, 365; associated with mirrors, 194–197, *195*, *196*, *197*, *365*; beneath Pyramid of the Sun, 9, 158; beneath Teotihuacan, 383–384, 385, *386*; pervasive symbolism of, in Feathered Serpent Temple-Pyramid, 365; as sacred passageways, 365, 383–384; *See also* Architecture, and sacred associations
Censers. *See Incensarios*
Ceramics: coarse domestic wares, *63*, 68–71, *69*, *70*, *71*; fine wares, 72, *72*; granular ware, 98–99; micaceous ware, 73; zoomorphic bowls, 73, *73*
Cerro Gordo, 8, *12*, *148*; associated with Great Goddess, 8, 147, 383; represented by Pyramid of the Moon, 15, 390; represented by Pyramid of the Sun, 15. *See also* Architecture, and sacred associations
Chalcatzingo: monument may depict Great Goddess, 149–150, *150*; cave paintings, 289, *290*
Chalchihuitlicue, 147
Chalchuiutl, 50
Chantico, 133, *133*, 186
Chert, 97, 106
Chevron (motif): on mirror, 189; associated with sacrifice, 215; associated with warfare, 215; associated with water, *188*, 189
Chichen Itza: back mirrors, 172, 177. *See also* Temple of the Chac Mool
Childe, Gordon, 344
Cipactli, 362
Circle (motif): depicted in mural, 118, 119, *119*; symbol of liquid, 252, 253, 254; symbol of preciousness, 252, *254*; associated with Storm God, 249, *250*, *251*, 252, 253, *253*, 255, 258
Circular nets (motif): associated with Great Goddess, 138, *140*
Ciudadela, *364*, 384, *384*; ceramic workshop, *214*; construction of, 393; control of *incensario* manufacture, 260; and increase in human sacrifice, 395, 396; marking break in public architecture, 393–395; murals, 113–115, *114*, *116*, 117–120, *117*, *118*, *119*, *120*; relationship of ceremony to economy, 330. *See also* North Palace; South Palace
Classic period: and mirrors, 198; Great Goddess, main deity during, 132
Claws (motif): associated with Great Goddess, 137, 140, 142, *143*, 310, *311*
Cloud (motif), 62, 64
Clubs (motif), 124, *124*
Coatlicue, 151–153
"Coatlinchan Idol," depiction of Great Goddess, 138, *139*
Codex Borgia, 186, *187*, *188*
Codex Cospi, *196*, 197
Codex Féyérváry-Mayer, 119, *120*
Comb and bar (motif): associated with feathered headdress, 262; associated with warfare, 266; depicted on *incensario*, 266, *266*, 267, *267*, 268, 269
Copas: burial offering, 65
Cosmology. *See* Belief system
Cotton (motif): associated with mirror, 189, *190*, 191
Coyolxauhqui, 151–153, *152*
Coyote (motif): associated with Great Goddess, 369, 371; associated with warfare, 210, 213; depicted in mural, 125
Coyotlatelco, 241
Crocodile (motif), 262
Cuicuilco, 6, 7, 389
Curl Nose, 47, 48

Dartbutts (motif): associated with headdresses, 261, *262*; associated with warfare, 263, 266; depicted on *incensario adornos*, 262–263, *262*
Dow, James, 357
Drucker, David, 357, 369n
Drum-major headdress, *217*

Earflares, 184
Early Classic period: intense contact with Kaminaljuyu, 170; Teotihuacan, powerful force during, vii–viii
Earplugs: associated with Great Goddess, 142, *142*; associated with Storm God, 248, *249*; burial offerings, 210
Earspools: associated with Great Goddess, *142*; associated with mirrors, 182, *183*; burial offerings, 223, 224

Index

Economy, 7, 321–333; compared to Mesopotamian civilizations, 322–324; labor service, 377, 381; manufacturing specialists, 330–331; obsidian industry, 330, 331, 332; palace-centered model, 322; production and distribution, 27, 329–330, 376–382; role of Ciudadela, 330; role of Great Compound, 330; role of priests, 321–322, 326–327, 330; role of Tlailotlacan, 79–80; storage of surplus production, 327–329; temple-centered model, 321–322, 324–325; Teotihuacan colonies, 331–332. *See also* Luxury goods; Trade; Workshops

Elongated eye (motif), 266, *266*

El Tajin, 52, 115

El Tesoro, 80

Escuintla, 178

Eyes: represented by minerals, 181; represented by mirrors, 181–182, *182*. *See also* Elongated eye; Feathered eyes; Reptile eye; Rhomboid eye

Face (motif): represented by mirrors, 182–183, *183*

Fangs (motif): associated with feathered headdress, 262; associated with Storm God, 248, 249, *249*, 251, *250*, 253, 256

Feathered disk (motif), 262

Feathered eyes (motif): associated with butterflies, 263; associated with headdresses, 261, 262, *262*; depicted on *incensario adornos*, 262–263, *262*

Feathered headdress: associated motifs, 261, 262, *262*; associated with Storm God, 216–219, *218*; mirrors used in, 178, *179*; sign cluster indicating, 261, 263

Feathered serpent: associated with authority, 215–222, *216*; associated with nose pendant, 206, *207*; associated with sacrifice, 213, *214*, 215, *215*, 220, 363; associated with warfare, 213, 220, 363; compared to Quetzalcoatl, 362; depicted in murals, *207*, 208, 209, *209*, 233, *234*, *235*; headdress, 206, *207*, 208, *208*, 213, *214*, 362; iconography, 205–225. *See also* Feathered Serpent Temple-Pyramid

Feathered Serpent Temple-Pyramid: 12, *13*, 18, 205–213, *394*; architecture, 303, *304*; burials, 14, 209–213, *211*, *212*, 220–221, 391, 396; cave symbolism throughout, 365; construction of, 225, 363; curbs on despotic rule following sacrifice at, 391, 396, 400; evidence of hierarchical sociopolitical system, 339–340; feathered serpent reliefs, 206–209, *207*, 220–221, 222–224, 225, 363, 365, 385, 395–396; Kaminaljuyu pyramids modeled after, 220; looting of, *211*, 220–221, 222–223, 224, 225, 362, 385; manifestation of feathered serpent deity, 220; marking an exception to utopian ideology, 315; platform commemorating Great Goddess, 397–398; royal tomb, 220–221, 224–225, 362–363, 396. *See also* Feathered serpent; Human sacrifice

Feathers (motif): associated with Great Goddess, 140; associated with shields, 192, *193*; depicted on back mirrors, 171, 175, 176; depicted on *manta*, 271, 272; depicted in murals, 121, *121*, 123, *124*; luxury goods, 27, 48

Fertility: associated with Great Goddess, 134, 151

Figurines, 74–75, *74*; burial offerings, 60, 66, 223; and variability vs. uniformity, 295, *296*, 297

Fire: associated with Great Goddess, 142, *282*; represented by mirrors, *145*, 184, 186, *187*

Fire serpents: depicted on Aztec Calendar Stone, *195*; depicted on back mirror, 172, *193*, *194*; depicted in Codex Borgia, 186, *187*; depicted at Temple of Quetzalcoatl, 197, *197*

Firewood (motif), 273

Floreros, *37*, 39, 66

Flowering trees (motif): depicted in murals, 233–236, *234*, *235*, 358

Flowers: associated with Great Goddess, 137; associated with shields, 192, *193*; metaphors for people, 233; red bone (motif), 231, *235*, 236–237; red pack-basket (motif), *235*, 238–240; represented by mirrors, 184, *185*

Frog (motif), 75, 78

Index

Gaia, 158, 159
Gamio, Manuel, 16
Goggles (motif): associated with Storm God, 131, *218*, 249, *250*, 256
Great Compound, *378–380*, 384, *384*; construction of, 393; place of exchange for lapidary items, 108; storage facility, 330
Great Goddess, 129–168, *282*, 302–303, *303*, 310–314, *311*; associated with Cerro Gordo, 8, 147, 383; associated with curbs on despotic rule, 397–398; associated with death, 134; associated with Feathered Serpent Temple-Pyramid, 397–398; associated with fertility, 134, 151; associated with Pyramid of the Moon, 147, 359–360, 390; associated with Pyramid of the Sun, 147; associated with sacrifice, 151, 363; associated with warfare, 144, *146*, 147, 151; and Chalcatzingo monument, 149–150, *150*; compared to Aztec deities, 147; compared to Christian Virgin of Mexico, 159; compared to Gaia, 158, 159; compared to Itzpapalotl, 136, 147; compared to Tenan, 147; compared to Teteoinnan, 147; decline in imagery, 154–155, 159; depicted in murals, 130–134, *130*, *132*, *133*, *134*, 137, 140, *141*, *311*; depicted in stone sculpture, 137–138, *139*, 142, 143, *144*, *146*, *282*; depicted on *incensarios*, 301; depicted on mirror backs, 143, *145*; depicted on vessel, 144, *146*; depicted with Storm Gods, 137; emergence of, 132, 281, 313–314; equivalent figure in Kogi belief system, 148–149; feminine vs. masculine gods, 310–314; forming (with Tlaloc) fundamental mythic pair, 150–151; fragmentation of during Postclassic period, 154–155; imagery at Cacaxtla, 154; imagery at Tlaxcala, 154; imagery at Tula, 154, *155*; imagery at Xochicalco, 154, *156*; precursor to Xochiquetzal, 133, 136; recognition of, 359; representation of thought to depict Chantico, Tlaloc, 130–132, *131*, *132*, 133, *133*; superior to Storm God, 359; symbol of integration, 314

Great Goddess, associated motifs: agriculture, 311; bared teeth, 134, *135*, 138, 140, 142, *143*, 154, *156*, 310; caves, 365; circular nets, 138, *140*; claws, 137, 140, 142, *143*, 310, *311*; earplugs, 142, *142*; earspools, *142*; feathered coyote, 369, 371; feathers, 140; fire, 142, *282*; hands, 134, *135*, 136, 138, *139*, 140, 141, 142, 154, *156*, *282*; headdress/headgear, 134, *135*, 136, 138, 140, 141, 142, *143*, 144, *145*, 154, *282*, 310; *incensarios*, 399; jade beads, 140; masks, 140; mirrors, 134, *135*, 136, 143, *145*; morning glory, 138, 148; nosebar, 131, *131*, 133, 138, 142, *142*, 310; noseplugs, 140; *quechquemitl*, 138, *139*, 140, 142, *143*, 154, *155*; red, 140, 141, 310; sawtooth border, 140; scepter, 141; 7 reptile eye, 142, 154, *156*; shields, 136; spiders, 136, 311; water, *130*, 133, 141, 142, *282*, 143, *145*, 151; wings, 141; yellow, 140, 310; zigzag band, 310
Greenstone: burial offerings, 66, 210, 223, 224; figures, used in state temples, 307, *309*
Guacimo, back mirror, *188*, 189
Guerrero: trade with, 49, 106

Half-star (motif): associated with zoomorphic headdress, 262
Hands (motif): associated with Great Goddess, 134, *135*, 136, 138, *139*, 140, 141, 142, *282*; depicted in Xochicalco stone sculpture, 154, *156*
Harbottle, Garman, 356
Headband with triple knot: associated with Storm God, 248, *249*, 256
Headdress: associated with authority, 216, *217*, *261*; figurine, 73, *73*. *See also* Bird headdress; Drum-major headdress; Feathered headdress; Feathered serpent, headdress; Great Goddess, headdress/headgear; Tasseled headdress; Zoomorphic headdress
Heart (motif), *190*, 191
Hopkins, Mary, 356
Huichol: mirror lore, 183, 186, 191, 192, 194–195, *196*
Huitzilopochtli, 151–154
Human sacrifice: at Atetelco, 369; and

construction of Ciudadela, 396; curbs on despotic rule following, 385, 396, 400; at Feathered Serpent Temple-Pyramid, 339–340, 363, 365, 385; growing recognition of importance, 363–365; at Pyramid of the Sun, 363; role in maintaining cosmos, 399; and serpent-flowering trees murals, 358; at Temple of Quetzalcoatl, 29

Iconography: compared to Aztec, 129–130; compared to Maya, 14; compared to Toltec, 129–130; compared to Zapotec, 14; and politicoreligious ideology, 13–15; sign clusters, 247–276. *See also* Motifs
Incensarios, 74, 299–302, *300, 301, 302*; burial offerings, 65, 66; depicting butterflies, 189, *190*, 259, 264, *264*, *265*, *266*, *267*; depicting Butterfly Goddess, 136; depicting comb and bar, 266, *266*; depicting elongated eye, 266, *266*; depicting mirrors, 176, 186, 189, *190*; depicting rhomboid eye, 266, *266*; and headdress complex, 261–263; and relationship of individual to society, 301–302; ritual use of, 259–261, 399; sign clusters associated with, 259–274, *264*, *265*, *266*, *267*, *269*; Tetitla, 184; workshop, 259–260. *See also* Mantas
Infants: burials, 30, 60, 63–65, *72*; mortality, 297
Instituto Nacional de Antropología e Historia, 18, 209, 352
Itzpapalotl, 136, 147

Jadeite: absence from *barrio* workshops, 102; absence from Metepec phase burials, 46; beads, 64, 66, 177; burial offerings, 33, 36, 39, 46–51, 60, 64, 66; imported from Guerrero and Puebla, 106; lapidary sawing, 96–97, *97*; luxury goods, 27, 49, 95, 103; mask, 89, *91*; pendants, 177; trade, 48, 51; use on back mirrors, 175, 176–177, *176*
Jaguar (motif): associated with authority, 216, *217*; associated with Storm God, 252, *253*; associated with warfare, 213; net, depicted in mural, 369
Javelins (motif), 240

Kaminaljuyu: mirrors, *171*, 172, 174, *174*, 175, *175*, 176, 177, 178, 184, 189, 198; pyramids modeled on Teotihuacan's, 220; source of precious materials, 106; Teotihuacan presence at, 48, 107, 331, 354, 363; trade with, 50, 170
Kan cross (motif): associated with Storm God, 248, 249, *249*, 252, 256, 257, *258*
Kidder, Alfred, 345
Kogi, 148–149
Kubler, George, 17

Ladle, 65
Languages: spoken at Teotihuacan, 7, 17, 231–232, 240–242, 359. *See also* Nahuatl; Totonac
Lapidary: *barrio* workshops, 102–103; imported material, 105–106; production controlled by state, 103, 105–109; techniques, 95–103, *96, 97, 98–99, 98, 101, 102*; technological style, 89–112; tools, 96; workshops, 366. *See also* Chert; Jadeite; Mica; Pyrite; Quartzite; Serpentine; Shell; Slate; *Tecali*
Late Classic period: decline of Teotihuacan, 19–20
La Ventilla B: burial offerings, 36, *37*, 39, *43*, 45, 46, 47; burials, *32*, 367; tenement-like conditions in, 375
Lightning bolt (motif), 216, *218*
Linné, Sigvald, 16
Looting: of Feathered Serpent Temple-Pyramid, *211*, 220–221, 222–223, 224, 225, 362, 385; of Techinantitla, 232–233; of Tetitla, 232
Luxury goods: distribution of, 366–367; frequency of, in burial offerings, *45*; locally produced, 51–52; public access to, compared to Mayan, 47, 52; public access to, during Metepec phase, 367; public access to, during Tlamimilolpa and Xolalpan phases, 52; trade in, 46–52. *See also* Economy; Trade

Maguey spines (motif), 239, 358
Maize (motif), 218–219, *219*
Malmström, Vincent, 357

Index

Mantas: associated with Storm God, 272, *274;* sign clusters, 270–274, *271.* See also *Incensarios*
Marquina, Ignacio, 344, 352
Masks: associated with Great Goddess, 140; burial offerings, 65; *incensario* type characterized by, 259–274, *260, 262;* jadeite, 89, *91;* lapidary manufacture, 103; reflection of "collective persona," 294–295, *294, 296,* 299, 301, *301;* represented on *incensario,* 299, *301;* serpentine, 89, *90;* standardized, 109
Mat (motif), 215, *216*
Matacapan: Teotihuacan presence at, 48, 331, 354; Tlailotlacan enclave at, 81–82; trade with, 50–51
Maya: access to luxury goods, 47; belief system, 306, 360; mirror iconography, 189, *190,* 193, 195, *196;* mirrors, 180, *180;* no Great Goddess figure, 149; serpent iconography, 220; shields, 192, *193;* Storm God iconography, 255–256, *256.* See also Cacaxtla; Caracol; Chichen Itza; Curl Nose; Nebaj; Piedras Negras; Stormy Sky; Tikal; Uaxacatun; Yaxchilan; Yaxha; Zaculeu
Mesoamerica, *3;* belief systems, 7–8; cultural homogeneity of, 2; gender shift in powerful deities, 155, 157–158, 159–160
Metepec phase: burials, 35, *35,* 39, *43, 44,* 45–46, *45,* 52, 66–67, *67;* decline in supply of luxury goods, 51, 367; extensive construction, 51; internal problems, 51; production of Thin Orange ware, 51–52
Methodology: ethnographic analogy, 16; feminist, 155, 157; linguistic model, 17; New Archaeology, 157–158; scholarly, 355–358; semiotic analysis, 283–284, *285;* stratigraphic, 16, 17; and technological advances, 356
Mezcala, lapidary techniques, 98–99
Mica: burial offerings, 33, 36, 39, 46–51, 64, 65, 66; decline in use during Metepec phase, 46, 51; imported from Puebla and Oaxaca, 106; used to represent eyes, 181

Miccaotli phase: burial offerings, 66; excavations, 61
Miller, Arthur, 18
Mirrors: associated with earspools, 182, *183;* associated with Great Goddess, 134, *135,* 136, 143, *145;* associated with *incensarios,* 186; associated with warfare, *173,* 365; back, 172–177, *173, 174, 175, 176, 183, 185, 194,* 197–198, 210; breast, 177–178, *178;* depicted on *incensario,* 189, *190;* feather-rimmed, 170, *171, 172;* at Feathered Serpent Temple-Pyramid, 210; in headdresses, 178–179, *179,* 184, *185;* Huichol lore regarding, 183; iconography of, 169–198; Kaminaljuyu, 172, 174, *174,* 184; large, 179–180, *180;* production of, 366; pyrite-backed slate, 103, *104,* 108; representing eyes, 171, 181–182, *182;* representing face, 182–183, *183;* representing fire, *145,* 184, 186, *187;* representing flowers, 184, *185;* representing jaguar face, *140,* 183; representing shields, 191–192, *193;* representing sun, 192–194; representing supernatural passageway/cave, 194–197, *195, 196, 197,* 365; representing water, 186, *188,* 189, *190;* representing webs, 189–191, *190, 193;* slate backs, 143, *145;* Tikal, 172, *173;* Tula, 172, *183;* used in burials, 174–175, *174,* 178, 365; workshops, 103, 108
Mixtec, 191
Monte Alban: architecture, 67; art, 299; bowls, 61, 62, 64–65; ceramics, 69, 71, 72, 73, 74, 75, 76, 79; mirrors, 180, 191; stelas, 208, *208*
Monte Alban II–IIIA Transition phase: arrival of Zapotecs, 76
Morning glories (motif): associated with Great Goddess, 138, 148; depicted in mural, *130, 132,* 133
Motifs: continuity with Aztec, 231–232, 240; reflection of disinterest in history/narrative, 304; reflection of multilingual culture, 304, 305; relation to language, 78; and Teotihuacan "writing," 232–233. See also names of individual motifs
Murals, 13, 14, 113–126; Atetelco, *114,*

437

Index

125, *125, 126;* Cacaxtla, *256;* Ciudadela, 113–115, *114, 116,* 117–120, *117, 118, 119, 120;* and "embedded texts," 14; Palace of the Jaguars, 134, *135;* Plaza of the Superposed Altars, *114,* 115–117, *116, 117;* Pyramid of the Moon, 120; scarcity of, 368–369; South Palace, 369, *370;* Techinantitla, 137, *218, 219,* 233–236, *234, 235, 239, 240, 242, 305, 311,* 358, 359; Temple of Agriculture, 133, *134, 309;* Tepantitla, 130–131, *130,* 134, 136, *207,* 208; Tetitla, 120, 131, *131, 133, 133,* 134, *135,* 136, 232; West Plaza Group, *114,* 120–126, *121, 122, 123, 124;* Xelha, 137, *137;* Zacuala, 209, *209;* Zacuala Palace, 239

Nahuatl, 17; belief system, 12; *Cantares mexicanos* texts composed in, 237–238; *Psalmodía christiana* chants composed in, 236–237; Teotihuacan language, 240–242
Nebaj, 186, 189
Noguera, Eduardo, 16
North Palace, vessel, *215*
Nose pendant (motif), 206, *207*
Nosebar (motif), 131, *131,* 133, 138, 142, *142,* 310
Noseplugs (motif), 140

Oaxaca, 49, 80, 106
Obsidian: burial offerings, 33, 36, 39, 60, 64, 65, 210, 222, 223, 224; decline of use in Metepec phase burials, 46; knife, associated with zoomorphic headdress, 262; lapidary tools, 96, 97; trade, 27, 80; used to represent eyes, 181; workshops, 80, 103
Old Man braziers, 297, *298*
Ollas, 65, 71, 80
Olmec: art, 288–289, *290;* mirrors iconography, 192; mask, 89, *91*
Oztoyohualco: centralized storage facilities, 328–329; shell workshop, 106, 108

Pacal, 216, *217*
Pachuca, 80
Palace of the Jaguars, 134, *135*
Palacio, *41*

Palenque, 216, *217*
Panofsky, Erwin, 17
Parsons, Jeffrey and Mary, 356
Patlachique period, 295
Peñafiel, Antonio, 16
Pendants, 177; burial offerings, 222, 223, 224; nose, 223, 224, 267, *267, 268, 269, 270*
Piedras Negras: stela, *194*
Plants: metaphors for people, 233
Plaza of the Superposed Altars: mural, *114,* 115–117, *116, 117*
Postclassic period: fragmentation of Great Goddess imagery, 154–155, 159
Priesthood, economic organization of, 321–333
Primeros Memoriales, 257, *257, 258*
Proyecto Arqueológico Teotihuacan, 18, 143, 352, 368
Psalmodía christiana: and red bone-flower image, *235,* 236–237; Teotihuacan imagery, 231, 236–240; Tepantitla mural images, 236–237, 238, 243
Puebla, 106
Pyramid of the Feathered Serpent. *See* Feathered Serpent Temple-Pyramid
Pyramid of the Moon, 12, *148;* architecture related to ethnic diversity, 296–297; associated with Cerro Gordo, 9, 15, 390; associated with Great Goddess, 147, 359–360, 390; construction of, 384; murals, 120; and production of mirrors, 366; royal tomb, 390, 393; workshops near, 103, 108
Pyramid of the Sun, 12, *148,* 360, *360, 361;* architecture related to ethnic diversity, 296–297; associated with Cerro Gordo, 9, 15; associated with Great Goddess, 147, 360, 362; burials, 29; construction of, 390–391; human sacrifice at, 363; royal tomb, 391, 393; sacred nature of caves beneath, 158, 365, 383–384, *385, 386*
Pyrite: burial offerings, 60; mirrors, 103, *104,* 108, 169–198; used to represent eyes, 181

Quartzite: bead, *101;* imported from Guadaloupe range, 106; lapidary saw blades, 97

Index

Quatrefoil (motif): depicted on *incensarios*, 262–263, *262*, 268, *269*

Quechquemitl (motif): associated with Great Goddess, 138, *139*, 140, 142, *143*; depicted in Tula sculpture, 154, *155*; depicted at Temple of Quetzalcoatl, 197, *197*

Quetzalpapalotl Palace, stone sculpture, *254*

Quirigua, 177

Rectangle (motif), 119, *119*

Red (motif): associated with Great Goddess, 137, 140, 141, 310, *311*; in murals, 122–123, *122*

Reptile eye (motif): associated with calendar, 272; associated with feathered headdress, 262; associated with Great Goddess, 142; associated with mirrors, 178, *185*; depicted on *incensario*, 267, *267*; depicted on *manta*, 270, *271*, 272; depicted in Xochicalco stone sculpture, 154, *156*

Rhomboid eye (motif): associated with warfare, 266; depicted on *incensario*, 266, *266*; depicted in mural, 118, *119*

Rio de San Juan, 9, 12

Roller stamp: burial offering, 60

Sacrifice, human: associated with feathered serpent, 213, *214*, 215, *215*, 220, 363; associated with Great Goddess, 151, 363; associated with Storm God, 363; at Feathered Serpent Temple-Pyramid, 209–210, *212*, 220, 221, 223–224, *225*; principal subject in Teotihuacan symbolism, 274

Sahagún, Fray Bernardino de, 236, 237, 238, 257

San Jose, Belize: back mirrors found at, 177

Sawtooth border (motif), 137, 140, *311*

Scepters (motif), 141

Scrolls (motif), 115, *116*, 121, *121*, 122–123, *122*, *123*, 267, *267*

Séjourné, Laurette, 352–353, 369

Seler, Eduard, 16

Serpent Mouth Mask Deity: Zapotec motif, 78

Serpentine: fracturing technique, 95–96; lapidary material, 95, 103; mask, 89, *90*, *294*; tau, *93*; trade, 106

Serpents: emerging from mirrors, 195, *196*, 197, *197*; surrounding mirrors, *194*. See also Feathered serpent; Fire serpents; Quetzalcoatl; Serpent Mouth Mask; Xiuhtecuhtli

Shell: absence in *barrio* workshops, 102; associated with authority, 216, *217*; burial offerings, 33, 36, 39, 46–51, 60, 64, 65, 66, 80, 209, 210, 222, 223, 224; conch, 252, *254*; controlled distribution, 108; decline of use in Metepec phase, 46, 51; depicted in mural, 125; luxury goods, 27, 48, 95; trade, 49, 106; use in mortuary ritual, 106, 107; workshops, *96*, 106, 108, 366. See also Lapidary

Shields: associated with feathers, 192, *193*; associated with flowers, 192, *193*; associated with Great Goddess, 136; associated with spider web, 191–192, *193*; associated with Storm God, 250, 251; depicted in murals, 123–124, *124*; depicted in *Primeros Memoriales*, 257, *257*, *258*; represented by mirrors, 191–192, *193*

Slate: burial offerings, 36, 222, 223; fracturing technique, 95, 96; lapidary material, 95; mirrors, 103, *104*, 108; pendant, 100, *101*; plaque, *105*. See also Lapidary

Sociopolitical organization: absolutist, 339–340, 382; egalitarian, 14, 15, 294–295, 305, 306, 313, 315, 340, 440; ethnic diversity, 295–297, 304, 305, 389, 392–393; nonproselytizing, 373; relationship of individual to society, 299, 301–302; role of art, 15, 292, 293–295, *294*, 400; secretive society, 302–303, 372–373; significance of Great Goddess, 313–314; utopian foundation, 288–292, 293–295, *294*, 306, 315, 373–375; variant standards of living for residents, 375. See also Apartment compounds; Belief system; Economy

South Palace, *364*; mural, 369, *370*

Speech, emphasis on, 302–305, 372; scroll (motif), 304–305, *305*

Spence, Michael, 356

439

Index

Spider goddess, 134, 136, *171*, 191–192, *193;* associated with Great Goddess, 311; associated with warfare, 192, *193*
Spiders (motif): associated with Great Goddess, 136; associated with headdress, *190;* associated with mirror, 189, *190,* 191
Spools: on back mirrors, *171, 175–176, 175, 194;* on breast mirrors, 177, *178*
Squash (motif), 218–219, *219*
Star (motif), 62
Steward, Julian, 355
Stone. *See* Lapidary
Storey, Rebecca, 356
Storm God: associated with Bigotera, 248, 249, *249,* 250, *251,* 255; associated with circles, 249, *250, 251,* 252, 253, *253,* 255, *258;* associated with earplugs, 248, *249;* associated with feathered headdress, 216–219, *218;* associated with food, 218–219, *219;* associated with goggles, 249, *250,* 256; associated with headband, 248, *249,* 256; associated with jaguar, 248, 249, *249, 251,* 252, *253,* 256; associated with Kan cross, 248, 249, *249,* 252, 256, *257, 258;* associated with *manta* sign cluster, 272, *274;* associated with sacrifice, 363; associated with serpent, 249, *250;* associated with shield, *250, 251;* associated with tassel headdress, 252–253, *255;* associated with warfare, 252–253, *255,* 256–257, *256, 257, 258,* 363; Aztec and Teotihuacan insignia compared, 257, *257, 258, 259;* Aztec imagery compared, 257, *257, 258, 259;* compared to Tlaloc, 359; depicted on vessels, *40, 249;* depicted with Great Goddess, 137; insignia, 248–259, *249, 250, 251, 252, 253, 254, 255, 256, 257, 258;* Maya and Teotihuacan insignia compared, 255–256, *256;* subordinate to Great Goddess, 359; vessels, 297, *298*
Stormy Sky, 47, 306
Street of the Dead, 8–9, *10–11, 12;* burning of, 346, 350; construction during Metepec phase, 51; and destruction of monuments, 19; monuments evidence of sociopolitical system, 440; sacred nature of location, 8–9, 390;

Storm God imagery absent, 150–151. *See also* West Plaza Group
Sun, represented by mirrors, 192–194
Swords (motif), 124, *124*

Tassel headdress, 252, *254;* associated with Storm God, 252–253, *255;* associated with warfare, 216, 252–253, *255;* depicted on cylindrical tripod, *40;* sign cluster indicating, 262; symbol of authority, 216; used by Teotihuacan emissaries, 331–332
Tau (T-forms), *93,* 109
Tecali, 97, *98,* 106
Techinantitla: looting of, 232–233; murals, 137, *218, 219,* 233–236; *234, 235, 239, 240, 242, 305, 311,* 358, 359
Teeth, bared (motif): associated with Great Goddess, 134, *135,* 137, 138, 140, 142, *143,* 310; depicted in Xochicalco stone sculpture, 154, *156*
Temple of Agriculture: murals, 133, *134, 309,* 328; storage of surplus production, 328
Temple of the Chac Mool, 177, *194*
Temple of the Feathered Serpent. *See* Feathered Serpent Temple-Pyramid
Temple of Quetzalcoatl, 60; back mirrors, 174; depiction of feathered serpents with mirrors, 197, *197;* human sacrifice at, 29; murals, 117–118
Temples, 376, *378–380. See also* names of individual temples
Templo Mayor, 186, *188, 189*
Tenan, 147
Teotihuacan, *11, 342–343;* burning of, 346, 350; chronology, 345–355, 402; colonies, 331–332; decline of, 19–20, 45, 49, 242, 333, 367; distribution of population, 285; growth of, 295, 354, 381, 385, 388–390; history of study of, 341–358; importance of, in modern Mexican culture, 357; influence of, 1, 47–48, 385; multilingual, 231–232, 240–242, 295–297, 359; settling of, 6–7, 339
Teotihuacan Archaeological Project, 113
Teotihuacan Mapping Project, 18, 60, 89, 341, 344, 353
Tepantitla, *347;* images in *Psalmodía chris-*

440

Index

tiana, 236–237, 238, 243; murals, 130–131, *130,* 134, 136, *207, 208*
Teteoinnan, 147
Tetitla, *348, 349, 384;* burial offerings, 39, *41, 43,* 45, 46; *incensario,* 184; looting of, 232; murals, 120, 131, *131, 133, 133,* 134, *135,* 136, 191–192, 232
Tezcacuitlapilli. See Mirrors, back
Tezcatlipoca, 186, 192; depicted in Codex Borgia, 186, *188*
Thin Orange ware: bowl, 141–142, *141;* burial offerings, 36, 39, *41,* 60, 62, 64, 66; ceramic fragment, *216;* control of trade by Tlailotlacan, 80; production during Metepec phase, 51–52; distinctive Teotihuacan trade item, 353; luxury good, 27
Tikal: stelas, 172, *173, 194,* 306, *308;* Storm God insignia, 255; trade with, 50, 106, 354
Tingambato, 331
Tlailotlacan, 59–88, *62;* burial practices, 60–67; compared to other ethnic enclaves, 81; economic role of, 79–80; and Monte Alban, 81, 82; Oaxacan ethnic identity, 76–79, 368; obsidian workshops, 80
Tlajinga: conditions in, 375
Tlaloc: associated with eye goggles, 131; compared to Storm God, 359; icons wrongly labeled as depicting, 130–132, *131, 132;* ringed eyes representing mirrors, 181; vessels, 39, 41, 46, 223; *See also* Storm God
Tlamimilolpa, 36, 39, 375
Tlamimilolpa phase: architecture, 61, *62;* burial offerings, 31, *32,* 35, *35,* 36–38, *37, 38,* 61–62, *63;* construction of apartment compounds, 299, 313–314; construction of Feathered Serpent Temple-Pyramid, 363; emergence of Great Goddess imagery, 281, 313–314; public access to luxury goods, 47, 52
Tlaxcala, 154
Toltec: iconography, 129–130, 193, *194*
Tongue (motif), 249, *250*
Totonac: association of mirrors with sun, 192–193; Teotihuacan language, 241, 242, 359
Trade, 331–332; decline of, during Metepec phase, 51; following decline of Teotihuacan, 367; of luxury goods, 27, 46–52; and professional merchants, 50; rival centers, 52; role of cylindrical tripods, 353; role of Thin Orange ware, 353; role of Tlailotlacan, 80; with Kaminaljuyu, 50, 170; with Matacapan, 50–51; with Oaxaca, 49, 80; with Pachuca, 80; with Tikal, 50. *See also* Economy; Luxury goods
Trapeze and ray (motif): associated with feathered headdress, 262; associated with military headdresses, 272, *274*
Trapezoid (motif): depicted on *adorno, 273;* depicted on *manta,* 271, 272
Trefoil (motif): associated with cotton, 268, *269;* depicted on *incensario,* 268, *269*
Triangle (motif): associated with calendar, 272; depicted on *manta,* 271, 272; depicted in mural, 124, *124*
Trilobe (motif): associated with feathered headdress, 262
Tripod jars, 65, 66
Tripods, cylindrical, *146,* 353; absence of, in Metepec phase burials, 46, 52; burial offerings, 36, *37,* 39, *40, 43*
Tubes (ritual artifacts), 75–76
Tula: Great Goddess imagery found at, 154, *155;* mirrors, 172, 183, *183*
Turquoise: absence from *barrio* workshops, 99; burial offerings, 64
Tzacualli phase: construction of pyramids and monuments, 351; growth of city, 295; Tlailotlacan excavations, 61

University of the Americas, 60
Urns, 75, *75*

Vaillant, George, 16
Vases: burial offerings, 65, 66, *67;* "Tlaloc," 39, 41, 46
Vaticanus B, 186
Vessels, *215;* burial offerings, 33, 60–61, *136;* Storm God, 297, *298;* Thin Orange, 66. *See also* Bowls; Vases; Tripods
Volutes (motif): depicted in murals,

Index

115, *116*, 117, *118*, 122–123, *122, 123;* in *talud* design, *117*

Warfare: associated with bird, 213, 255, 266; associated with butterfly, 266; associated with comb and bar, 266; associated with coyote, 210, 213; associated with dartbutts, 263, 266; associated with elongated eye, 266; associated with feathered serpent, 213, 220, 363; associated with Great Goddess, 144, *146*, 151, 363; associated with jaguar, 213; associated with mirrors, *173*, 365; associated with rhomboid eye, 266; associated with Storm God, 252–253, *255*, 256–257, *256, 257, 258*, 363; associated with tassel headdress, 216, *252–253, 255;* principal subject in Teotihuacan symbolism, 274
Wasson, Gordon, 356
Water: associated with Great Goddess, 141, 142, 143, *145*, 151, *282;* iconography of, 12–13; represented by chevrons, *188*, 189; represented by mirrors, 186, *188*, 189, *190;* role in belief system, 6. *See also* Rio de San Juan
Waterlily (motif), 189, *190*
Watery bands (motif), *130*, 133
Web, represented by mirror, 189–191, *190*, 193
West Plaza Group: murals, *114*, 120–126, *121, 122, 123, 124*
Willey, Gordon, 355
Wings (motif), 141
Winning, Hasso von, 17
Wittfogel, Karl, 355
Workshops, 366–367; *barrio*, 92–95, 102–103, 107; ceramic, *214; incensario*, 259–260; lapidary, 93–95, *94*, 366; obsidian, 80, 103, 366–367; slate mirrors, 103; shell, 106, 366
Writing system, lack of, 302–306

Xelha: mural, 137, *137*
Xiuhcoatl. *See* Fire serpent
Xiuhtecuhtli: depicted in Codex Borgia, 186, *187*
Xixiuhoca. *See* Fire serpent
Xochicalco, 154, *156;* rival trade center, 52; stela, 267, *267*
Xochiquetzal, 137; Great Goddess as precursor to, 133, 136
Xolalpan phase: burial offerings, 35, *35*, 39, 40–43, *40, 41, 42, 45;* burials, 60–61, 63–65, *64*, 66; construction of apartment compounds, 299; public access to luxury goods, 47, 52
Xolotl, viii

Yaxchilan: back mirror, *194;* stela, 176, 193, *194*
Yaxha: stela, *255*
Yayahuala, *287, 384;* burial offerings, 39
Yellow: associated with Chantico, 133; associated with Great Goddess, 137, 140, 310, *311*

Zacatecas: trade, 50, 105–106
Zacuala, *286;* feathered serpent mural, 209, *209*
Zacuala Palace, *384;* burial offerings, 39; murals, 239
Zacuala Patios, *384;* burial offerings, 39, *40*, 45, 46
Zaculeu: back mirrors, 174, *175; incensarios* associated with mirrors, 186
Zapotec: architecture, 67–68; ceramics, 68–76; iconography, 14; motifs and rituals of, 78; presence at Teotihuacan, 59–88, 76–79
Zigzag band (motif), 310
Zoomorphic headdress, 262